THE MACMILLAN & SILK CUT YACHTSMAN'S HANDBOOK

Editors
Commander R.L. Hewitt LVO RN MIMechE, MRINA, FRIN
Rear Admiral I.J. Lees-Spalding CB

Consultant Editors
K.E. Best
B. D'Oliveira OBE, MRIN
Dr D.M. Justins MB, BS, FFARCS
M.W. Richey MBE, Hon MRIN
Dr D.H. Sadler OBE, Hon MRIN
J. Teale

MACMILLAN

GALLEY: 1 MGM AUG 24 SAT 7.40
FILE: MM10 P:0 CODE CRE1 Credits

First published 1984 by Macmillan London Limited
4 Little Essex Street London WC2R 3LF
and Basingstoke

Associated companies in Auckland, Dallas, Delhi, Dublin, Hong Kong, Johannesburg, Lagos, Manzini,
Melbourne, Nairobi, New York, Singapore, Tokyo, Washington and Zaria

Reprinted with revisions 1985, 1986

This book is sold subject to the standard conditions of the Net Book Agreement.

ISBN 0 333 36544 5

Macmillan Consultant Editor: Klaus Boehm

Important Note
Whilst every care has been taken in compiling the information contained in
this book, the Publishers, Editors and Sponsors accept no responsibility for
any errors or omissions, or for any accidents or mishaps which may arise from
its use.

Correspondence
Letters on editorial matters should be addressed to:
  The Editors, *The Macmillan & Silk Cut Yachtsman's Handbook*
  Macmillan London Limited
  Houndmills, Basingstoke, Hampshire RG21 2XS

Filmset in Baskerville by Filmtype Services Limited, Scarborough, North Yorkshire.

Printed and bound in Hong Kong

Designed by Dick Vine

Artwork by Geoff Adams, Peter Barry, Chris Evans, Hilary Evans,
Bernard Fallon, Ray Harvey MRINA BSc CEng, Dick Vine, E.N. Wilson

THE
MACMILLAN
&
SILK CUT
YACHTSMAN'S
HANDBOOK

Contents

Although this new *Yachtsman's Handbook*, which will not be republished each year, is primarily intended as a companion volume to *The Macmillan & Silk Cut Nautical Almanac* (revised and reprinted annually), the book contains a very great deal of information on all aspects of owning, operating and maintaining a modern yacht, and can be used independently of the *Almanac* if so desired.

However, Chapters 2–9 of this *Yachtsman's Handbook* and of the *Almanac* deal with related subjects. Standing information and instructional details are included in this *Handbook*, while data that is subject to regular or occasional change will be published each year in the *Almanac*. Any important changes to the material in the *Handbook* which occur between reprintings will be notified in the *Almanac* or its supplements. Taken in combination, therefore, these two books provide the most comprehensive and economical set of references available to the yachtsman on navigation and other matters concerned with running a yacht.

Who wrote it

To write this *Handbook*, Macmillan and Silk Cut have found a team of editors and consultant editors who combine excellent knowledge of their various subjects with a wealth of practical experience of yachts and boats of all kinds.

The editors

Dick Hewitt has sailed since the age of seven. During 32 years in the Navy he took up ocean racing, helmed the Dragon *Bluebottle* in 1953/54 for HM The Queen and The Duke of Edinburgh with some distinction, regularly navigated the 12-metre yachts *Flica II* and *Sovereign* during the early 1960s, and competed in three Admiral's Cup series. But he says the yachting he enjoyed most was two years in HM Yacht *Britannia*, during which she went through the Panama Canal five times and Suez once.

As captain of the Navy sailing team he won races in boats as different as National Fireflies and Seaview Mermaids.

He has served on the RYA Council, and on various committees, and has written a number of publications for the RYA which, in April 1980, honoured him with an award for his special services to yachting.

He was editor of the magazine *Motor Boat and Yachting* from 1972 to 1979, when he left to start work on the preparation of *The Macmillan & Silk Cut Nautical Almanac* which first appeared for 1981. He is a member of the Royal Yacht Squadron, Royal London Yacht Club, Royal Ocean Racing Club, Royal Southern Yacht Club, Royal Navy Sailing Assocation, Hamble River Sailing Club, Island Sailing Club, and the Cruising Assocation.

Tim Lees-Spalding joined the Navy from Blundells in 1938, aged 18. His early sailing experiences were from Teignmouth in South Devon, but later included sailing on the River Nile – where the helmsman stepped out of the boat onto a rock which swam away, proving to be a crocodile.

His sailing adventures in the Navy extended from the West Indies to the South China Sea, and he was once arrested by Tito's men for straying too close to Brioni in the Adriatic. Overland his journeys have included a trip home from Japan via Siberia, the Daily Express London–Sydney Marathon Car Rally, and taking a Land Rover across the Sahara Desert and through the jungles of the Congo.

For some years he was Administrator of the London International Film School. He is a member of the Royal Naval Sailing Association and of the Cruising Association. With Dick Hewitt, he is editor of *The Macmillan & Silk Cut Nautical Almanac*.

Other contributors

Keith Best (meteorological consultant) is the Senior Met. Officer at the Southampton Weather Centre – a job which brings him into frequent contact with the particular needs of yachtsmen in determining what the weather is going to do. Many will be familiar with the RYA publication *The Yachtsman's Weather Map*, which he helped to produce. Keith owns a Caprice, based in Langstone Harbour, and has sailed small cruisers in the Solent area for many years.

Basil D'Oliveira (navigational aids) is a retired Wing Commander, who now works in the Civil Aviation Authority. His specialised interest is in electronic navigation aids, with particular emphasis on the use of calculators as an aid to navigation, a subject he has covered in *Yachting World, Motor Boat and Yachting* and *Yachting Monthly*. His sailing activities have included cruising in the Pacific, New Zealand and the Caribbean, as well as Mediterranean and home waters. Recently he was part-owner for five years of a Nicholson 35, in which he made two cruises to the Mediterranean. His main contributions to the *Handbook* are advice on radio navigation aids, aids, and the sections which deal with the use of calculators for both coastal and astro navigation.

Douglas Justins, who contributed the section on first aid afloat, is an anaesthetist at a London hospital, who sailed the Sydney–Dover leg of the *Financial Times* Clipper Race and is a regular crew in RORC races.

Michael Richey was for many years the Director of the Royal Institute of Navigation which, in 1979, as an exceptional measure, conferred on him its gold medal in recognition of his outstanding contribution to the Institute's objects of advancing the science and practice of navigation and of promoting knowledge in navigation and its associated sciences. He is also Secretary General of the International Association of Institutes of Navigation. He has navigated in a great many ocean races, on both sides of the Atlantic, over the last 30 years and has competed in most of the classic events. He has also crossed the Atlantic alone several times in his junk-rigged Folkboat *Jester* and three times taken her solo to the Azores and back.

Donald Sadler (who has compiled the special sight reduction tables) is a former President of the Royal Institute of Navigation. For over 30 years he served as Superintendent of HM Nautical Almanac Office, in charge of the production of *The Astronomical Ephemeris, The Nautical Almanac, The Air Almanac* and many other navigational tables. He is the leading authority on such matters, and few people have made such a significant contribution to the development of astronomical tables.

John Teale has been an independent yacht and commercial craft designer for the past 20 years or so. Before that he was in the design or drawing offices of such concerns as John I. Thornycroft, Brooke Marine, Watercraft and the RNLI and also worked for the east coast yacht designer, J. Francis Jones. For two spells he was on the editorial staff of the magazine *Motor Boat and Yachting*, once under Dick Hewitt.

He has lived and worked in South Africa, Sweden and Ireland but now resides in Somerleyton, Suffolk where he also bases his boat. This is the 24th craft he has owned and of these he actually built 13 (the biggest being 26ft (7.9m) in length). The present boat is a 25ft (7.6m) steel motor sailer and, perhaps coincidentally, most of his work is now in steel with a fair sprinkling of timber plus the occasional aluminium alloy vessel.

Chapter 1

Introduction

Contents

1.1 About this Handbook

1.1.1 Introduction

Ever since *The Macmillan & Silk Cut Nautical Almanac* was first published in 1981, a number of users have suggested that the *Almanac* could with benefit be divided into two books – an almanac containing all the navigational data which is subject to change, and a permanent handbook giving more lasting information. This, in effect, is what has now been done.

The new *Macmillan & Silk Cut Yachtsman's Handbook* covers the many subjects of a more permanent nature that are concerned with owning and using a boat. It is intended to be used as a reference book alongside *The Macmillan & Silk Cut Nautical Almanac*, which will continue to be published each year, and which will contain navigational information (such as tide tables and ephemeris) which changes completely, together with other data which is liable to alter and which must be kept up to date to ensure safe navigation.

It will be seen that Chapters 2–9 of the *Handbook* and the *Almanac* deal with related subjects, and these chapters are cross-indexed between the two books where this is helpful to the user. Most of the 'how to do it' information which previously appeared in the *Almanac* has been transferred to this *Handbook*, and the opportunity has been taken to improve and amplify these subjects.

Chapters 10–16 of this *Handbook* largely comprise new material, related to using and looking after a boat. So, supplemented by the *Almanac* for navigational details liable to change, the *Handbook* provides the yachtsman with all the information he needs in order to own, operate and care for his boat in a sensible and responsible manner.

The aim throughout has been to present

information at least to the standard and depth of knowledge that would be expected of a candidate for the Royal Yachting Association/Department of Trade Yachtmaster (Offshore) Certificate.

1.1.2 Who wrote it

In general this *Handbook* has been compiled by the same team as have been responsible for *The Macmillan & Silk Cut Nautical Almanac*, with the addition of John Teale who has written Chapters 10, 12 and 14. Basil D'Oliveira has advised on the use of electronic calculators and navigation aids, Michael Richey has written about Astro-Navigation (Chapter 5), Keith Best has helped with the Weather in Chapter 7, and Dr Douglas Justins has expanded his original piece on First Aid Afloat in Chapter 8. Dr Donald Sadler has designed and compiled the sight reduction table.

Most of the contributors are practical and experienced yachtsmen, who have owned boats. Between them they combine expert knowledge on all aspects of using and running a yacht.

1.1.3 How to use it

The subject matter of the following chapters is related in the *Handbook* and the *Almanac*:

Chapter 2	General Information
3	Coastal Navigation
4	Radio Navigational Aids
5	Astro-Navigation
6	Communications
7	Weather
8	Safety
9	Tides

For ease of reference, each chapter is divided into numbered sections, prefaced by the number of the chapter. Thus the sections in Chapter 7 (for example) are numbered 7.1, 7.2, 7.3 and so on. Within each section, the key paragraphs are numbered, as for example 7.3.1, 7.3.2, 7.3.3 and so on. Diagrams carry the chapter number, followed by a consecutive number in brackets. There is a comprehensive index at the back of the *Handbook*.

1.1.4 Acknowledgments

The Editors wish to record their thanks to the many individuals and official bodies who have assisted by providing essential information and much advice in the preparation of this *Handbook*. They include the Hydrographic Department of the Ministry of Defence (Navy), HM Stationery Office, HM Customs, the Meteorological Office, HM Coastguard, British Telecom, the Department of Trade, and the Royal National Lifeboat Institution.

Extracts from the *International Code of Signals, 1969* and from *Meteorological Office Leaflets Met 0.1* and *Met 0.3* are published with the permission of the Controller of HM Stationery Office. Material from the *Handbook for Radio Operators* is included by permission of British Telecom. *International Regulations for Preventing Collisions at Sea, 1972* are reproduced by permission of the International Maritime Organisation.

Technical information on ropes has kindly been supplied by Bridon Fibres and Plastics Limited, the makers of Marina yacht ropes. The illustrations of bends, hitches and splices are taken from their *Marina Manual of Yacht Ropes*, available at most chandlers.

The colour cloud scenes are published with acknowledgment to R. K. Pilsbury/BP Educational Service. The photographs are by R. K. Pilsbury ISO, FRPS, FRMetS.

Acknowledgment is made to the RYA Seamanship Foundation for assistance with illustrating the IALA buoyage system, and to *Yachting World* for their help in illustrating navigation lights.

1.2 Getting Afloat

1.2.1 Responsibilities of yachtsmen

Being in charge of any boat at sea, even as mate of the watch while the skipper snatches a couple of hours' sleep, places serious responsibility on the individual concerned. For the skipper that responsibility is total, since he is solely accountable for the safety of the yacht and her crew – even while he is asleep.

Apart from being able to handle the boat under sail and/or power in all conditions (which may include winds of gale force), the skipper must be completely familiar with every aspect of the boat and her equipment, and be able to cope with whatever emergencies may arise – such as fire, man overboard, engine failure or dismasting. He needs to understand the rule of the road and be able to interpret it in a seamanlike way. He must be competent to navigate safely from place to place and be able to read the weather. Very importantly, the skipper has a duty to select and train his crew so that they can play their full part in managing the boat and so that they are neither a danger to themselves or to others on board.

All these requirements, and many others, are described in the pages which follow. They are based on considerable theoretical knowledge and practical experience, without which it would be rash for any skipper to put to sea. One of the attractions of yachting is the freedom which it offers – the sense of getting away from all the restrictions which seem to govern life ashore. But as well as being a pleasure, going to sea is something of an adventure, and it does involve complying with certain regulations, safeguarding the welfare of your crew, and even taking responsibility for the lives of people in other vessels or manning the rescue services.

In Britain we are lucky that the authorities are anxious to place the minimum restraints on the use of small pleasure craft. Yachts over 45ft (13.7m) in overall length are required by law to carry certain safety equipment, but there are no such legal requirements for smaller craft. Nor are there (as yet) compulsory standards of competence for those who skipper or handle yachts. Such regulations would be difficult and expensive to enforce, but they do exist in other countries and it should not be imagined that our authorities would be deterred from imposing tedious rules and expensive licences if the situation should so require. The best safeguard against such an eventuality is that all who go afloat for pleasure should have sufficient knowledge and practical experience to be able to cope with any problem that can reasonably be foreseen, and that their boats should be built, equipped and maintained to a proper standard.

1.2.2 Training schemes

For anybody who wants to learn to sail, or to improve his or her ability in any particular aspect of boat handling, there are a variety of training schemes which are administered by the Royal Yachting Association. From the basic handling of a dinghy or a sailboard these cater for all levels of competence – up to courses in navigation which can lead to the award of RYA/DoT Yachtmaster certificates. In all, courses are run by some 600 teaching establishments distributed throughout the country and include training in powered craft.

Details of the cruising courses which are recognised by the Royal Yachting Association are given in RYA booklets G15 (Sail) and G18 (Motor Cruising), available from the RYA, Shaftesbury Road, Gillingham, Dorset, SP8 4PQ. The courses provide a mixture of shore-based instruction and practical training afloat, which must be consolidated by experience gained in actual passages at sea before a certificate is awarded. There are five grades of course – Competent Crew, Day Skipper/Watch Leader, Coastal Skipper, Yachtmaster Offshore and Yachtmaster Ocean. The current scheme of training is summarised in Fig. 1(1).

The addresses and details of principal schools which run practical cruising courses are available from the Royal Yachting Association, see 2.8.1.

Many institutes and clubs run evening courses on a weekly basis during the winter months. These may cover such subjects as navigation, meteorology, basic seamanship, signalling, safety, and engine maintenance. In every case those who attend are extending their knowledge. They may be raw beginners, anxious to become useful crews in cruising boats, or competent and experienced crews who want to buy their own boats. Others may be skippers with limited experience who wish to improve their standards for cruising further afield. Although the majority of these courses cater for those who cruise under sail, a parallel scheme exists for motor yachtsmen.

1.2.3 Association of Sea Training Organisations

The Association of Sea Training Organisations (ASTO) comprises those organisations (such as the Sail Training Association and the Ocean Youth Club) which operate sea training vessels or encourage sea training. By different methods they all aim to provide an opportunity for young people to go to sea in a sailing vessel, thereby not only experiencing a unique adventure but also developing their initiative, sense of responsibility, discipline and team work.

A bursary scheme can help defray the cost of a cruise for those who cannot afford it. Some of the vessels have vacancies for adults and many of them welcome suitably experienced yachtsmen who can help take charge. From time to time ASTO vessels take part in the Tall Ship races together with sail training vessels from other countries.

Details can be obtained from the Association of Sail Training Organisations, c/o Royal Yachting Association, Victoria Way, Woking, Surrey, GU21 1EQ.

1.2.4 RYA Seamanship Foundation

The Seamanship Foundation is registered under the Charities Act 1960 and is established to foster good seamanship. It encourages and assists with training yachtsmen by producing a range of instructional aids, from sophisticated audio visual programmes to simple posters. The Foundation also provides lectures and demonstrations on the use of distress flares, liferafts, fire fighting and other safety equipment.

The Foundation also gives opportunities for sail training to those otherwise unable to afford it, by either providing boats or by subsidising training courses. Over a hundred dinghies have been bought for use by youth clubs, Scouts and schools.

The Foundation is particularly concerned in organising courses and providing boats or equipment to enable the disabled to learn to sail and afterwards participate on equal terms with the able-bodied. Every year the Foundation organises a course on cruising yachts for thirty-six visually handicapped students, and in addition, encourages and assists sailing clubs to run their own course.

Not many young people have the opportunity to skipper a cruising yacht, and thereby develop the qualities needed at an early age. So in 1982 the Young Skippers' Scheme was started whereby, for a modest fee, people aged 17–23 have the opportunity to be totally responsible for a yacht and her crew. Several Sonatas have been bought, to cruise together under the overall control of a group leader with some offshore sailing experience. Some of the crew of each boat must also be competent helmsmen. Applications for this scheme should be made to the Director, at the address below.

The Foundation is supported entirely by subscription from the public and its ability to continue its work depends directly on the support which it receives. All enquiries should be

SAIL

Grade	Shorebased	Practical Course	Seatime	Examination
RYA Competent Crew	Combined course for both grades, seamanship and navigation.	5 days. Mainly seamanship and sailing.	5 days 100 miles 4 night hours	None. Completion certificates awarded on satisfactory completion of courses.
RYA Day Skipper/ Watch Leader		5 days. Seamanship, sailing and navigation.	10 days 200 miles 8 night hours	None. Completion certificates awarded on satisfactory completion of courses.
RYA/DoT Coastal Skipper	Combined course for both grades, navigation and meteorology.	5 day course on practical skippering	20 days 400 miles 12 night hours	Oral for holders of shorebased and practical course completion certs. Practical for others.
RYA/DoT Yachtmaster Offshore		None	50 days 2,500 miles 5 passages over 60 miles, 2 as skipper and 2 overnight passages.	Practical examination
RYA/DoT Yachtmaster Ocean	Astro navigation and world-wide meteorology.	None	Ocean passage	Open only to Yachtmasters Offshore. Assessment of sights taken at sea + written exam if shorebased proficiency certificate not held.

POWER

Grade	Shorebased	Practical Course	Seatime	Examination
Introduction to Motor Cruising	Introductory shorebased course			None. Course completion certificates awarded on satisfactory completion of courses.
RYA Competent Crew (Motor)	Combined course for both grades, seamanship and navigation.	2 days. Seamanship and boat handling.	5 days 100 miles	None. Completion certificates awarded on satisfactory completion of courses.
RYA Day Skipper (Motor)		5 days. Seamanship, boat handling and navigation.	10 days 200 miles 4 night hours	None. Completion certificates awarded on satisfactory completion of courses.
National Motor Cruising Certificate – Awarded to holders of course completion certificates, shorebased and practical, for Day Skipper.				
RYA/DoT Coastal Skipper (Motor)	Combined course for both grades, navigation and meteorology.	5 day course on practical skippering	20 days 400 miles 12 night hours	Oral for holders of shorebased and practical course completion certs. Practical for others.
RYA/DoT Yachtmaster Offshore (Motor)		None	50 days 2,500 miles 5 passages over 60 miles, 2 as skipper and 2 overnight passages.	Practical examination
RYA/DoT Yachtmaster Ocean (Motor)	Astro navigation and world-wide meteorology.	None	Ocean passage	Open only to Yachtmasters Offshore. Assessment of sights taken at sea + written exam if shorebased proficiency certificate not held

Fig. 1(1) Royal Yachting Association schemes for cruising courses and qualifications (1983).

addressed to: The Director, RYA Seamanship Foundation, Victoria Way, Woking, Surrey GU21 1EQ.

1.3 How to buy a boat

1.3.1 Choosing a boat

There are so many boats of different types and sizes on the market, plus of course a large number of second-hand boats at any time, that the choice can be quite bewildering even for the relatively experienced yachtsman. Do not hesitate to seek advice on this important step. A bad decision here may, in every sense of the word, prove to be a disaster, which at best may put you and your family off boats for ever. In order to arrive at the right solution you need to ask yourself a lot of questions, and it is important that the answers are well-considered and truthful.

First, why do you want a boat at all? In this context you need to decide where the boat is to be kept, how often she is to be used, where she is going to operate, and who is likely to be on board. Will the boat take the place of holiday trips, or only be used for occasional weekends during the summer?

If you can satisfy yourself, and perhaps your wife, that a boat is justified, exactly how much money can you afford for the project? Remember that, quite apart from the first cost, to run and maintain a boat of any size is going to incur the expenditure of several hundred pounds a year for items such as insurance, moorings, fuel, maintenance and repairs. If he has sufficient time available a handyman may be able to save money on the last two items, but the others are inescapable. An allowance should also be made for depreciation in the value of the boat year by year, and for the capital locked up in her. If money has to be borrowed for the purchase (see 1.3.8) the cost of servicing the loan must be considered. When buying a new boat remember that quite a large sum will be needed for vital equipment which is not included in the price – navigational items, safety equipment, a tender, galley gear and other domestic items are likely to fall into this category. This is one possible reason for buying a second-hand boat, where most of such items will probably be included. Taking all these figures into account gives some idea of the cost, and hence the size, of boat that can be afforded.

Then it is time to return to such questions as where the boat is to be kept. Will she be on a mooring, and how sheltered will it be? Will she need to dry out – either when on the mooring or in her intended cruising area? Remember that the smallest cruising boats (but only the smallest) can be kept ashore on a trailer, and towed to different locations. Is it intended to sail locally, or

to undertake coastal cruises, or perhaps sail further offshore? What sort of crew will normally be available, and how strong are they in physique and in experience? Is the boat to be sail or power, or a combination of the two?

By now a general idea of the type and size of boat should be developing, and it will be time to start considering which of the many cruising boats available might fit the specification. Study the appropriate magazines to see what is on offer, and visit one of the major boat shows to size up the market.

It is, however, necessary to consider some more detailed requirements which might include hull form and material, accommodation layout, rig, type of engine and deck plan. Unless you are an experienced yachtsman it may be advisable to seek advice on some of these points, although mention is made of them in the chapters which follow.

Before starting to search in earnest, draw up a detailed specification, based on the answers to the questions above, and decide on the priority of the various items. Make sure that the requirements are not mutually exclusive, or your hunt will be a waste of time and money. Travel is expensive, so try to cover boats in your locality before journeying to the other end of the country.

You may discover that your dream boat does not exist in production form, and there may be good reasons for this. But if you wish to persist the only solution would be to have a boat specifically designed and built for your purpose – an expensive undertaking in all probability, but one likely to produce the best answer for unusual requirements.

Another possible approach is to take a stock hull (a large variety of glassfibre mouldings are readily available, for example) and have it completed to your own specifications. If you have the necessary skills and plenty of spare time, you may be able to undertake some of this work yourself, with a consequent saving in cost.

There are two ways that an individual owner may be able to afford a more expensive boat – joint ownership and time sharing. The former is well established, even if it does provide practical difficulties. It is essential that partners have a common approach to how the boat is operated and maintained, and problems are likely to arise when one or the other wishes to sell his share. Time sharing is relatively new, and one wonders how it (and the boats concerned) will stand the test of time.

If you find it difficult to justify owning a boat because of the limited use she might have, do not overlook the possibility of chartering which is described in 1.7.

1.3.2 Buying a boat – general

New boats are sold either by their builders or by distributors acting on their behalf. The larger firms advertise prominently, and exhibit their products at the major boat shows, but there are many smaller yards which produce good boats and have lower overheads. In boat building, big is not necessarily beautiful. Second-hand boats are sold either privately by the owner (sometimes in a boat auction), or through a yacht broker. Standard forms of agreement for these transactions are jointly sponsored by the Ship and Boat Builders' National Federation (see 2.8.3) and the Royal Yachting Association (see 2.8.1). In order to try to eliminate any problems it is always advisable to use one of these agreements, and it is helpful to have some understanding of modern consumer legislation. This is well set out in *Consumer Protection for Boat Users* by A. A. Painter (Nautical Books).

For practical purposes items (including a finished boat) which a yachtsman buys are defined as 'goods'. The law requires that such goods must correspond to the description they are given, be of merchantable quality (capable of performing as described, subject to the price paid), and be fit for the purpose intended. The last provision means that where the purchaser depends on advice from the seller, an item which he buys should meet his requirements: hence it is always best to get the opinion of the seller, so that if the item fails in service the purchaser has redress.

In brief, a retailer is responsible for what he sells, and this applies just as much to a complete boat as to a single shackle. Be warned that if you buy a foreign boat (or an item of gear) direct from an overseas supplier, you may have no claim under British law if some problem should arise.

Another fundamental point when buying a boat is to ensure that she legally belongs to the person who is selling her, and that she is 'free of all encumbrances' as the saying goes. There may be money owing on the boat, perhaps on a hire purchase agreement, or a boat yard may claim a lien for work that has not been paid for. Worse still, the boat may have been stolen. If the boat is registered (see 1.5) it is not too difficult to establish title, and to find out if there is any outstanding mortgage on the boat. In any event it is wise to ask the present owner to produce whatever evidence he has of title – whether it be a Building Certificate, a Bill of Sale, or merely a copy of the invoice from the previous owner.

1.3.3. **Buying a new boat**

A standard form of agreement for the construction of new craft is obtainable from the Ship and Boat Builders' National Federation or from the Royal Yachting Association. In a boat which is being built to order instalment payments should be agreed, typically as follows: 20 per cent on signing the agreement; 30 per cent on the hull being available at the builders; 30 per cent on the completion of interior joinery work, installation of the engine, or stepping of the mast; 20 per cent on completion of the acceptance trial to the satisfaction of the customer.

It should be noted that where VAT is payable it forms part of the price, and the figures written into the contract should include VAT at the rate applicable at the date of the agreement. The form also sets out the expected dates for an acceptance trial, and for delivery. It may also include an Agreed Damages Clause, as a time-penalty against late delivery.

For stock production boats the above system of stage payments is usually modified to provide for a deposit of (say) 10 per cent on order, and the balance on delivery.

A purchaser should insist on a proper sea trial for any boat, whether she is new or second-hand. Ideally such a trial should demonstrate not only that the boat is in working order but she and all the equipment therein perform in accordance with the designed specification. This however takes a lot of time, and can only be achieved with expensive instrumentation. So yacht owners have to be content with a purely functional trial. This, however, should demonstrate all aspects of the boat and her equipment. It should, for example, be shown that the engine runs satisfactorily for a reasonable time, without overheating and without undue noise or vibration, and that it propels the boat at the designed speed while operating within its designed rpm. Ahead and astern operation of the gearbox should be demonstrated. Engine instrumentation should be checked, together with any alarms that may be fitted (for example to indicate high circulating water temperature). Similar trials should be conducted for all other items of equipment – anchor windlass, steering gear, navigational instruments, autopilot, bilge pumps, refrigerator, galley stove, lighting systems etc.

The purchaser may refuse to accept the boat until any faults exposed by the acceptance trial have been rectified. When this has been done the buyer must sign the acceptance form and make the final payment, whereupon ownership of the boat is transferred to the purchaser – who should arrange insurance cover from that moment (see 1.3.9).

Should any fault subsequently develop with the boat, the buyer still has redress under the Sale of Goods Act, or under more recent consumer legislation. Any such dispute may be argued in the courts, but the Ship and Boat Builders' National Federation also sponsor a scheme of arbitration for settling disagreements between yards and their customers. Both parties must be agreeable to this procedure, and this may be written into the original contract. Notes on arbitration are available on application to the SBBNF, Boating Industry House, Vale Road, Oatlands, Weybridge, Surrey, KT13 9NS.

The possible bankruptcy of a boat builder has always been of concern to clients, but the problem has been somewhat reduced by the inclusion of a special clause in the agreement referred to above, which establishes that material or equipment obtained by the builder specifically for a certain contract becomes the property of the purchaser of the boat on settlement of the first instalment payment. The purchaser should ensure that valuable items, such as an engine, received by the yard are clearly identified as being appropriated for his yacht.

1.3.4 Buying a second-hand boat

Second-hand boats are mostly sold through yacht brokers, or are advertised and sold privately. A few are sold at marine auctions, where it should be noted that a boat is sold as she lies, so that it is very important to find out all about her before bidding.

Unless the condition of a yacht has been misrepresented, a buyer has no redress against a private individual who sells him a boat which proves to be unsatisfactory. There is only protection for the purchaser in this respect if he buys the boat from somebody who is selling it in connection with his trade or business. So, although there may be good bargains to be had, buying a second-hand boat can be chancy for an inexperienced yachtsman unless he is prepared to seek professional advice. Use the services of a qualified surveyor – see 1.3.7.

When buying direct from an individual it is most advisable to have a written agreement, which should cover the following points. The intending purchaser, having paid a deposit of 10 per cent of the agreed price, is free to arrange a survey of the boat at his own expense within a period of 14 days. On completion of the survey the purchaser may withdraw from the agreement, in which case he must restore the boat to her original condition before his deposit is refunded. If the purchaser wishes to proceed, any defects found on survey must be discussed between the two parties, so that the seller either agrees to make them good or to reduce the price accordingly, taking into consideration the age and value of the boat. If agreement cannot be reached, the contract is void. The agreement should include statements to the effect that the boat is being sold free of all encumbrances or lien (i.e. that nobody else has any claim on the boat), and that there are no known defects other than those which have been shown to the purchaser.

If a yacht is registered under the Merchant Shipping Act, 1894, certain additional formalities have to be completed. These involve a Bill of Sale and a Declaration of Transfer, which have to be forwarded with the Certificate of Registry and the appropriate fee to the Registrar of Ships at the port of registry. For a yacht on the Small Ships Register, registration is automatically terminated on change of ownership, and the certificate should be surrendered by the previous owner. The new owner must make a fresh application. More information about registration appears in 1.5.1, 1.5.2 and 1.5.3.

1.3.5 Yacht brokers

Yacht brokers provide an important service for buying and selling boats. Those who belong to the Association of Brokers and Yacht Agents, or to the Yacht Brokers, Designers and Surveyors Association or to the National Yacht Harbours Association operate under a *Code of Practice for the Sale of Used Boats*, obtainable from the Ship and Boat Builders' National Federation (see 2.8.3). They use a standard form of agreement, which sets out the following terms. The agreed purchase price is stated, and 10 per cent of this is paid on signing the agreement, allowing the purchaser to have the yacht hauled out and surveyed at his own expense. This survey should normally be completed within 14 days, although this period may be extended by agreement. Within a stated time of completion of the survey, if any material defects or deficiencies have been found, the purchaser may either reject the yacht (giving notice of the defects or deficiencies discovered), or ask the seller either to make good such shortcomings or to reduce the price accordingly.

If the sale proceeds, the agreement states the yacht is considered to have been accepted by the purchaser and the balance of the agreed price to be due if:

(1) A period of 14 days elapses, and no survey has been made, or
(2) after an agreed time after the survey the purchaser has not acted, or
(3) the seller remedies any specified defects to the satisfaction of the surveyor, or
(4) an agreed reduction in price is made.

The form also includes other provisions concerning the obligations of the two parties, default by the purchaser, the transfer of risk, and arbitration procedure in the event of any dispute.

If you are buying a boat of any size, or if you are not experienced in such matters, it is most advisable to deal through a yacht broker. He can advise on the suitability of a boat for your particular purpose, and can track down those which are likely to suit your requirements. He can help with the arrangements for slipping and survey (very useful if you happen to live elsewhere), with insurance (see 1.3.9), and with a mortgage, if required (see 1.3.8). He can check details such as the inventory of the boat, and ensure that documentation is properly completed so that title is fully transferred. Further information can be obtained from the Association of Brokers and Yacht Agents, Haven Brokerage, Lymington Yacht Haven, Kings Saltern Road, Lymington, Hampshire, SO4 9XY, (Tel: Lymington (0590) 73212).

It should be explained that if the seller is a private individual (not selling the boat in the course of trade or business), and if that fact is known to the buyer, there is no question of warranty on the sale of a second-hand yacht, because the purchaser is quite at liberty to inspect the craft and to satisfy himself as to her condition – either in person or by employing a surveyor. It must be emphasised that a surveyor should always be used, except perhaps in the case of a very small and cheap boat where the buyer has enough experience to detect any serious faults. The work of surveyors is discussed in 1.3.7. On the matter of defects, a broker is legally liable to divulge known defects to a purchaser when acting in a sale.

The services of a yacht broker naturally cost money, and the fees are paid by the seller of the boat, as an agreed commission based on the selling price. The current scale is shown below, and VAT is payable at the ruling rate.

Selling price	Commission
Up to £1000	10% of selling price
Up to £5000	8% of selling price
£5000–25,000	8% of first £5000 plus 6% of balance
Over £25,000	6% of selling price

Buying and selling yachts can be a complicated business, particularly when the boat, the seller and the buyer are well separated geographically. It often involves two brokers, and the provision of access etc by the yard or yacht harbour where the boat is lying. Consequently the Code of Practice referred to above makes provision for a fair split of the total commission between those concerned. (Further notes on the work of yacht brokers in the sale of yachts appear in 1.4.3.)

1.3.6 Part-exchange of yachts

In recent years the practice of trading in a second-hand yacht against the purchase of a new one has greatly increased, and several yacht builders and distributors now offer this facility. Some firms only accept their own make of boat in such transactions, while others will take any boat that is in sufficiently good condition for re-sale, but may limit the value of the second-hand boat compared to the cost of the new one. Some builders and dealers operate their own brokerage firms to dispose of boats taken in part-exchange, while others sell them through normal brokerage channels.

Inevitably the price offered for part-exchange is less than could be obtained by private sale or through a yacht broker, and sometimes it is well below that figure. But to offset this there are certain advantages – no commission to be paid, none of the costs such as advertising that are incurred in a private sale, plus the benefit of being able to make an immediate transaction which may enable advantage to be taken of a special discount on the price of the new boat.

It should, however, be emphasised that there are no general rules which govern such transactions, along the lines of those operated by the Association of Brokers and Yacht Agents for brokerage sales, so anybody buying a boat on part-exchange should look into the deal very carefully.

1.3.7 Surveyors

As already stated in 1.3.4, it is foolish to buy a second-hand boat without recourse to a proper survey, with the boat out of the water. To get a proper survey you need a proper surveyor, and it is a sad fact that a small minority of surveyors lack the knowledge and experience required. It is best to employ a person who is a member of the Yacht Brokers, Designers and Surveyors Association (YBDSA), and who has professional qualifications. The YBDSA will provide details of their surveyors in your area, on application to their office at The Wheelhouse, 5 Station Road, Liphook, Hampshire, GU30 7DW (Tel: Liphook 722322).

The purpose of a full survey is to determine the condition of the entire yacht – hull, rig, machinery, gear and all the equipment which pertains to her operation. A competent surveyor should report on every aspect of the boat's structure, depending on the materials concerned. He should comment on whether the condition of the various items is attributable to fair wear and tear, or whether other factors such as poor design, inferior materials, bad workmanship or lack of maintenance are involved. His examination should include all items such as fastenings, chain plates, shafting, steering gear and rudder fittings. It may be that the engine itself will need to be dealt with as a separate item, although the surveyor should certainly be able to assess the general installation.

It is a good idea to have a preliminary inspection of the yacht with the surveyor. He should then be able to judge, from his experience, which parts of the boat may require more careful scrutiny or where expensive dismantling may perhaps be avoided. Then give the surveyor his instructions in writing, as this forms the contract with him.

Apart from condition surveys, as described above, surveyors also assess accident damage for insurance purposes, or undertake the supervision of repairs or modifications.

1.3.8 Marine finance

Many people buying boats need at least some measure of financial help and borrowing money is expensive at the best of times, so it pays to shop around and get the best rates and the most favourable repayment terms. It is also necessary to consider whether registration is needed, whether a survey will be required (and to what extent), what security may be asked for, and what the effect of future changes of interest rate will be. Tax relief on interest charges is not allowable unless your inspector can be convinced that the boat is your sole or principal residence.

Small boats and marine equipment can be

financed by personal loans which are available from various institutions including banks and the major finance houses. Some marine traders offer similar facilities which, although possibly more expensive, may provide protection against sub-standard goods.

Larger and more expensive craft can be purchased on a marine mortgage, where the required loan is secured against a mortgage on the boat. The precise details vary. The cost of the loan (i.e. the interest to be charged) may be added to the sum financed at the outset, and the total then repaid in equal instalments. But nowadays it is more common for institutions to offer contracts where the interest varies with the money market, usually related to the Finance House Base Rate. This can be done either by altering the amount of the instalments from time to time, or by keeping the instalments the same and altering the number of payments (i.e. the time over which repayment is made). Normally the borrower is expected to put down 20 per cent of the purchase price, but sometimes more. The repayment period is typically five years, with a maximum term of ten years for some special schemes.

Only a statutory mortgage provides the necessary legal security for a sea-going vessel, and this requires the yacht to be registered (see 1.5.1). Some institutions will however provide loans against a non-statutory mortgage (not applicable under Scottish law) for which registration is not required, but the terms are somewhat restrictive.

A survey is not normally required for a new boat, but is needed for a second-hand one. The yacht must be insured against all normal risks, as described in 1.3.9.

Marine mortgages can be arranged to provide for stage payments for a boat under construction, and also to finance major refits or improvements.

1.3.9 Yacht insurance

Any owner should insure his boat for her full value. Nothing is ever certain at sea, and however careful a skipper may be there is always a risk that a boat can become a total loss or be seriously damaged. Yacht policies are normally based on the standard Lloyd's marine policy, modified by what are called the Institute Yacht Clauses, but some underwriters have worded their own policies: these may be easier to understand, but are not necessarily better in other respects. In any case it is important to read the proposal form very carefully, and to fill in the answers to the various questions accurately and truthfully – or the insurers may deny liability.

The policy normally covers the boat for a certain period in commission each year. Should it be required to extend this period, be sure to inform the company beforehand. Similarly cover is arranged for a certain cruising area (as for example, in order of risk, non-tidal waters of the United Kingdom, coastal cruising within a certain radius of the home port, or full sea-going cruising within what are described as home trade limits between Brest and the Elbe). Make certain that the declared limits are kept, or make special arrangements when necessary. European inland waters, for example, are not normally included.

The policy contains numerous warranties, either implied or expressed. These can be identified by reading the various clauses carefully, and they usually include the following important points:

(1) The owner must maintain the boat and all items of her equipment in a proper seaworthy condition, and must exercise due care in safeguarding them.
(2) Insurance does not cover charter or hire of the boat, unless this is specially arranged.
(3) In the event of any incident which may give rise to a claim, prompt notice must be given to the underwriters. Tenders may be required for repairs to be undertaken.
(4) A reduction may be made to a claim for fair wear and tear in respect of items such as outboard motors, sails and running rigging.
(5) Items of equipment are only covered for theft where forcible entry or removal can be shown. Outboards must be securely locked to the boat. Tenders must be clearly marked with the name of the parent vessel. No claim is allowable for dropping an outboard overboard.
(6) No claim is allowable for sails which are blown out, unless due to damage to spars or caused by the yacht being stranded or in collision. Nor when racing, unless caused by the boat being stranded, sunk, on fire or in collision. Racing risks may however be covered as a separate item with extra premium.
(7) Damage to or loss of engine or other mechanical or electrical items is only covered if caused by the yacht being flooded, sunk, stranded, burned or in collision; or while being moved to or from the yacht; or by theft of the entire boat; or by theft following forcible entry; or by fire in a store ashore; or by malicious acts.
(8) Personal effects are not covered, unless specially arranged.
(9) Boats with a speed of 17 knots or more are subject to 'Speedboat Clauses' which specify certain conditions and require additional premiums.
(10) Clauses dealing with Third Party Liability deserve special attention. Cover for at least £500,000 is recommended. Normally cover includes somebody using the boat with the consent of the owner, but this should be confirmed. Note that if a young person (say) took the boat away without permission, liability would not be accepted.
(11) As for motor insurance, if the insured bears

the first £50 (say) of any claim, a small reduction in premium may be agreed.

(12) When trailing by road, a boat may be covered for accidental loss or damage, but the policy excludes all third party liabilities or offences against the current road traffic legislation.

(13) In the event of no claim being made under the policy, a no-claim bonus will be granted. This is typically a premium reduction of 5 per cent after one year, 7½ per cent after two years, 10 per cent after three years and 15 per cent after four years.

In marine insurance matters it is important to have some understanding of the limitation of liability, which was introduced to protect the owner of a vessel from the negligence of the vessel's master or crew (but not from his own negligence). Limitation of liability has to be obtained by a limiting decree from the courts, which can be expensive, and it overrides the normal insurance policy by restricting the amount of damages payable depending on the registered tonnage of the vessel limiting liability. A higher limit is set for personal injury than for damage to property.

If, for example, two boats collide and the owner of the boat which is at fault limits liability, the innocent owner may not recover the cost of whatever repairs are needed. This is one very good reason for a boat to be fully insured, whatever the experience and competence of the skipper and crew, rather than to be covered only for third party risks.

Where an innocent owner's insurers assume liability for part of a claim (because the guilty owner's insurers limit liability), the innocent owner stands to lose his no-claim bonus, although some insurers recognise the injustice of this.

Due to the expense of obtaining a limiting decree, the parties often agree that the owner claiming limited liability shall pay rather more than the strict legal limit (but less than the limit plus the cost of the decree). Hence the innocent owner, or his insurers, can recover rather more than the limit imposed by the tonnage rule.

Marine insurance is a specialised business. Either deal with a broker who is experienced in yacht insurance or write off to a number of established companies who advertise in the yachting press, and ask for their proposal forms. When these are received it will be apparent that some companies give wider cover than others. Complete those forms which seem the most satisfactory for your purpose, and then compare the quotations. It should be recognised, however, that firms with the lowest premiums are not necessarily the best when it comes to settling claims.

Useful information is given in RYA booklet G10, *You and the Law*, which covers problems which may be met by clubs as well as by individual yachtsmen.

1.4 Selling a boat

1.4.1 General points on selling

At this stage of the book it may seem premature to consider selling, but most yachtsmen change their boat at least once – generally because they wish to trade up to something larger – and so it is appropriate to discuss it at this point, while dealing with the transfer of ownership in general terms. There are basically two ways of selling a boat – privately or through a yacht broker. There is a third method, by means of a boat auction, but this is comparatively rare and follows a similar procedure to any other kind of auction sale.

It is vital to decide the right price for the boat. This implies a good knowledge of the market and is where a yacht broker can advise. It is also important to present the boat in the best possible condition – clean and tidy, and with all outstanding defects attended to as far as possible.

1.4.2 Selling privately

On the face of it, selling a boat privately should give the maximum return. This, however, assumes that the owner can correctly judge what the asking price should be. This ought to be the most that can be obtained within whatever time limit is set for the sale, but few yachtsmen can have sufficient insight to the second-hand market unless they have a boat which is of a type that is numerically large and is regularly traded.

Most probably some advertising costs will be incurred, and these can soon build up at about 50p per word for classified advertisements in most yachting journals. To include a small photograph of the boat is likely to cost about £30 a time. When drafting an advertisement it is perfectly fair to emphasise the particular merits of the boat, but important not to misrepresent her condition. In order to answer enquiries (which may conveniently be arranged through a box number), it is useful to have a printed sheet which gives full particulars of the boat, where she is lying, and arrangements for inspection. One or two good photographs should be included.

The seller will have to attend at the boat whenever potential buyers wish to inspect her. Apart from travelling costs, this can involve a good deal of waiting around – particularly for those who never show up. It can also be expected that some viewers will arrive without the slightest intention of buying the boat.

Be sure that the boat is scrupulously clean, inside and out, and that all repairs have been made good before she is put on the market. If there are known defects or important examinations outstanding it is best to declare them honestly, rather than to have them exposed by the buyer or his surveyor.

Naturally it creates a better impression if the boat can be inspected conveniently and in good surroundings, rather than in a mud berth a couple of miles from the nearest road.

Once an individual shows real interest in buying the boat, it is likely that negotiations will start on the price. It is necessary to be prepared for this, and to decide the lowest figure to accept. Much will depend on how long the boat has been on the market, what other offers have been received and the urgency of the sale.

When a price has been agreed the sale can proceed in the way described in 1.3.4. As stated there, it is most advisable to have a written agreement. It is most important to make sure that the entire payment has been received before the boat is surrendered.

1.4.3 Selling through a yacht broker

Although it costs money, selling through a yacht broker eliminates most of the work and problems that are involved with a private sale, and because a broker has access to a wide market it may enable a higher price to be obtained or a quicker sale to be achieved. It is advisable to instruct a broker who is a member of the Yacht Brokers, Designers and Surveyors Association, or whose firm is affiliated to the Association of Brokers and Yacht Agents. These two associations, together with the National Yacht Harbours Association, operate under a *Code of Practice for the Sale of Used Boats*. This is fundamentally a trade agreement, but it ensures good business standards and is of benefit to clients because of the protection it affords.

When instructing a broker to sell a boat, the owner will be asked to complete a form which requires full particulars of the boat and of her material condition. It is important that the statements are accurate. At the same time it should be agreed with the broker whether or not he is to be the sole agent (see below) and whether the owner may at the same time try to obtain a private sale (not very popular with brokers). Arrangements should also be made with the broker about viewers inspecting the boat, to ensure that they are accompanied by a responsible person.

A broker acts as a go-between for buyers and sellers of yachts all over the world. If a broker is appointed as sole agent he will pass full details of the boat to other selected brokers, who will receive half of the eventual commission if they produce a sale. Central listing facilities, as offered by Central Yacht Brokerage Services Limited or by Computayacht, allow the interchange of information about boats for sale between all participating brokerage firms, so that the net is spread as wide as possible.

Very importantly, a broker is able to advise on the correct price at which a boat should be offered – a price that is likely to attract some response, but which will be fair to the seller. It is in the interest of the broker to obtain the best figure possible, because his commission is based on the selling price (see 1.3.5).

Any advertising material produced by the broker must be accurate because, being in business, he is liable under the Trade Descriptions Act. He will advertise the boat in whichever journal(s) he considers most appropriate, and will handle all enquiries and inspections. When a potential buyer appears the broker will prepare a Sale Agreement on a standard form of contract. If the sale proceeds after survey, he can advise the owner regarding any defects that may have been found, in order to negotiate a fair price. The general procedure is outlined in 1.3.4. Finally the broker prepares the Bill of Sale, and ensures that title is not transferred until the purchase money has been received.

1.5 Documentation of yachts

1.5.1 Registration – general

The law which covers the registration of yachts is contained in the Merchant Shipping Act, 1894, as amended by the Merchant Shipping Act, 1983. Until 1983 it was a legal requirement that any ship or vessel not propelled by oars should be registered unless she was less than 15 Register tons and was used only on the rivers or coasts of the United Kingdom (or of a British possession where the owner lived). In fact the law was never enforced so far as yachts were concerned, although it was very desirable that any boat which cruised abroad was registered and thereby acquired the status of a British ship. Registration under the Merchant Shipping Act, 1894, also helped identify the yacht and was useful in the event of any problem arising in a foreign port. Registration was also necessary before applying for a warrant to wear a special ensign (see 6.7.2), facilitated obtaining a marine mortgage, and was relevant in applying for limitation of liability in any claim for damage (see 1.3.9).

Yachts which were not registered and whose owners wished to cruise abroad could be issued with an International Certificate for Pleasure Navigation, and many owners took advantage of this for occasional cruises to foreign countries.

Matters, however, came to a head when the French insisted that, as from 1 January 1984, British yachts arriving in French waters must be registered – or in other words that the British authorities should be required to enforce the British law on the subject. Full registration, under the 1894 Act as described in 1.5.2, is a relatively tedious and expensive business for a small yacht, which has to follow the same procedure as a supertanker. The time had come to produce a simpler and cheaper way of registering yachts, and this is why the Small

Ships Register, described in 1.5.3, came into being.

It should be emphasised that the previous, full registration procedure is still in force, and is in fact required for recording marine mortgages and for establishing title (ownership).

1.5.2 Registration (Merchant Shipping Act, 1894)

Full registration, under the Merchant Shipping Act, 1894, is the job of the Registrar of Ships at one of many Registry ports around the British Isles. He is a Customs and Excise official, and his office is usually in the Custom House. The procedure follows a set pattern, which is briefly as follows. It is fully described in Notice No. 382, obtainable from any Registrar of British Ships.

First decide on the name, which must not duplicate an existing one on the Register. Write to the chosen Registrar for application forms for the approval of the name (by the Registrar General of Shipping and Seamen, Llantrisant Road, Llandaff, Cardiff) and for registration of the yacht. At least three names should be submitted: note that the prefix 'the' is not allowed, nor is the name of a listed port, but a boat may be named after a harbour which is not a port of registration.

When the name has been approved, the Registrar will write, stating what fees and documents he requires, which are very briefly as follows. An application form to register at the port concerned, the optional appointment of an agent, and a statement of yacht club membership. A Builder's Certificate, which is a form showing details of the initial construction of the boat, and Bills of Sale covering all previous owners (if any). An appropriate declaration of ownership depending on whether the boat is owned by an individual, or is part or joint owned, or owned by a Body Corporate. The appropriate fee for registration. A measurement survey by an approved surveyor.

At this point it should be noted that it is no use proceeding with the survey unless the previous documents can be produced; the Registrar requires absolutely clear proof about the ownership and identity of the vessel.

The boat must be owned by a British subject or Body Corporate. Ownership is by tradition as to 64 shares, and so it is expressed in documents. Part Owners can each have any number of shares from 1/64 to 63/64. Joint Owners have 64/64 jointly. If one Part Owner dies the shares pass to his or her estate. Joint Ownership follows the rules for property of any kind at law. A Body Corporate must act within its Articles of Association, and has to authorise under seal the individual to sign documents in respect of the vessel.

The measurement survey required for registration of yachts of less than 45ft (13.7m) in length may be undertaken by Lloyds surveyors, surveyors of the Yacht Brokers, Designers and Surveyors Association, or by measurers of the Royal Yachting Association. When the measurements have been taken the Registrar informs the owner of the Register Tonnage which has to be carved into the main beam of the vessel, together with the Official number allocated. Special provisions are made for the 'carving' of glassfibre boats.

Normally the boat must have her name and port of registry marked on the stern, in letters at least 4in (10cm) high, either black on white or white on black. These must be in permanent form, either cut or etched in to the surface, or by raised letters welded on. Members of certain clubs may be exempt from having the port of registry inscribed, in which case it is customary to put the club's initials under the name.

The procedure above, if followed carefully, should result in a Certificate of Registry being issued within a few weeks, but difficulties sometimes arise – usually on the question of title, particularly with older boats.

When buying a registered boat it is wise to see if the seller has registered his ownership, and this can be done by inspecting the Register at the port of Registry, for a small fee. Alternatively the Registrar will forward relevant particulars of registry. In either case it is possible to see if there is any outstanding mortgage on the boat.

When the boat is already registered, and therefore named, it is easier to transfer registration on change of ownership if the name remains with the vessel. This should be part of the deal, but sometimes the seller wishes to retain the name, for his next boat. Then another name has to be given, either before or after change of ownership. Either way costs money and may take a couple of months or so.

If important changes are made to a registered vessel, such as fitting a new or different engine, she must be re-surveyed. The Registrar should be informed if the owner changes his address or sells the boat, or if she is lost or broken up.

1.5.3 Small Ships Register (Merchant Shipping Act, 1983)

The Merchant Shipping Act, 1983, set up a Small Ships Register for vessels less than 79ft (24m) in length. Instead of being measured under the tonnage regulations of the 1894 Act, such vessels are measured by overall length.

The new regulations apply to small vessels which are wholly owned by individuals each of whom is a United Kingdom or Commonwealth citizen ordinarily resident in the United Kingdom. Ships owned by companies, fishing vessels and submersible vessels are not eligible, and must continue to register under the arrangements described in 1.5.2.

Registration, which costs £10, is normally for a period of five years, and is renewable for a further period or further periods of five years.

Application should be made, enclosing a stamped addressed envelope, to the Royal Yachting Association, Victoria Way, Woking, Surrey, GU21 1EQ.

The new Small Ships Register procedure will satisfy existing requirements for privileged ensigns and for embarking duty free stores, but it provides no facility for establishing title (ownership) or for recording marine mortgages.

1.5.4 International Certificate for Pleasure Navigation

Prior to 1 January 1984, an unregistered yacht proceeding aboard could hold an International Certificate for Pleasure Navigation, obtainable from the Royal Yachting Association.

With the introduction of the Small Ships Register (see 1.5.3) this certificate now has no relevance in respect of yachts owned by United Kingdom or Commonwealth citizens who are resident in the United Kingdom. It is however still issued for yachts owned by other persons (e.g. United Kingdom or Commonwealth citizens resident outside the United Kingdom, or foreign persons who are resident in the United Kingdom).

1.5.5 Helmsman's (Overseas) Certificate of Competence

Unless a skipper or owner has one of the appropriate RYA Certificates for the type of boat which he is taking abroad (i.e. Sportsboat, Motor Cruising, Day Skipper or the RYA/DoT Coastal Skipper or Yachtmaster Offshore), it may be necessary in certain countries to produce some kind of certificate of competence. This can be provided by the RYA to United Kingdom residents on receipt of the appropriate application form, which has to be endorsed by the secretary or flag officer of an RYA club or the principal of an RYA recognised teaching establishment, to the effect that the person is competent to handle the boat specified. It is valid for two years, and is free to Full Personal members of the RYA.

1.5.6 Lloyd's Register of Shipping

The registration of yachts, as described in 1.5.1 has no connection with classification under the Rules of Lloyd's Register of Shipping. Lloyd's Register of Shipping provides an advisory and consultancy service to owners, builders, moulders and designers. It publishes rules for the construction of yachts in wood, steel or glassfibre or those built to the international rating rule. Experienced surveyors approve drawings, supervise moulding, inspect fitting out, check the machinery and certify the completed yacht. Yachts built under such supervision can be classed ✠100A1. The Maltese cross shows that the boat was built under survey; the 100A implies that the materials used and the workmanship

conformed to good practice. The ultimate digit 1 indicates that the yacht carries adequate anchors, cables and warps. To keep in class a yacht must be inspected by the Society's surveyors every two years.

As an alternative to full classification Lloyd's Register Building Certificate (LRBC) is provided to newly built yachts which have been constructed of any approved material in accordance with the Society's rules, and under the supervision of its surveyors, without the requirement for periodical survey. The stages leading to the award of the LRBC are as follows.

(1) Hull Moulding Release Note. This is issued to the moulder/builder and shows the basic items of construction, from moulded hull to finished yacht, which will be inspected by the Society's surveyors.
(2) Hull Construction Certificate. This is issued when all the items specified in (1) above have been examined and found satisfactory.
(3) Machinery Installation Certificate. Issued when the machinery and electrical installation has been installed under the supervision of the Society's surveyor.

On receipt of the Hull Construction and Machinery Installation Certificates from the builder, an owner may apply for a Lloyd's Register Building Certificate to The Secretary, Lloyd's Register of Shipping, Yacht and Small Craft Department, 69 Oxford Street, Southampton, SO1 1DL. Tel: Southampton (0703) 20353.

Lloyd's also undertake condition surveys of yachts which have been moulded or built in accordance with the Society's yacht rules and under supervision for owners or purchasers.

1.6 Looking after a boat

1.6.1 An organised approach

Having once taken the important step of buying a boat, a whole lot of new problems arise about how to look after her. Proper maintenance of a boat is important for two reasons. First, unless she is kept in good order even a new boat will soon tend to become unreliable in various respects, and a boat which is not reliable is unseaworthy and a possible danger. Second, unless a boat is well maintained she will start to depreciate in value much more quickly than one which is well looked after. Repairs of any kind are expensive, so it is much more sensible to try to forestall any failures.

In the chapters which follow, advice is given on various aspects of running and looking after a boat, but it is important for any owner to get himself well organised from the outset, so no excuse is offered for introducing the subject at this stage.

Organisation is perhaps the key word, because the successful operation of a modern yacht does require administrative ability, a methodical approach towards her material preparation, and systematic maintenance. A boat is a substantial capital investment, and one which can deteriorate all too quickly unless properly serviced and maintained. A systematic approach to all this work is essential, particularly where the owner does not live near the boat and is therefore unable to carry out routine upkeep during the week. Come the weekend and such chores as inspecting the rigging aloft are liable to be neglected in the rush to cast off the mooring and get away to sea.

In general a well organised boat – where the gear is reliable, and everything functions as it should – is also a much happier affair for her owner and her crew than one where things are left to chance. She is also likely to be a great deal safer.

So why not get organised? For a start an owner should find it useful to complete the page of Boat Details provided, so that a record is kept of at least some of the more important facts that should be known. For a particularly comprehensive record of a boat and her equipment, reference is suggested to *Ready for Sea* (Adlard Coles Ltd).

Perhaps some yachtsmen may consider that any such form of documentation is making rather a business of what is essentially a sporting activity. But experience has shown that a systematic approach to all the work and routine checks which are required to get a boat into good order and to keep her in that state is well worth the initial effort which is involved. Even in a fairly simple yacht there are a number of things which have to be memorised unless they are put down on paper, and some of us are not always too good at remembering details in the heat of the moment.

In an age when an increasing number of boats are berthed in marinas, and often spend a substantial proportion of their lives secured alongside, it is hoped that this *Handbook* will encourage owners and skippers to make worthwhile cruises to other ports and harbours. Boats are for going places, and the satisfaction of successfully completing a well planned passage and of arriving in some strange harbour – yet fully aware of the possible dangers it presents as well as the facilities which it offers – must be experienced to be believed.

Many people find the joys of cruising infectious, and for a lucky few it becomes a way of life. But most of us lack either the time or the money, if not both, to be able to make long and adventurous passages across the oceans. However, any coastal cruise can be something of a challenge, and there is plenty to be learned especially if you are new to the game – so please read on.

1.7 Chartering

1.7.1 Chartering – general
While discussing yacht ownership, it is natural to consider chartering, which has become big business in recent years. On one side of the coin a yachtsman can help to pay some of his running costs or the instalments on his marine mortgage by chartering his boat. On the other side, chartering allows a person who does not own a boat, for whatever reason, to get afloat and enjoy a holiday not necessarily in home waters but perhaps in more reliably sunny climes. In either case it is important to have a proper written agreement (or charter party) which covers every conceivable eventuality.

With reference to chartering it is necessary to understand certain terms:

Bareboat charter. This means that the yacht is supplied, but no crew or skipper. Bareboat charters are usually applicable to yachts up to about 40ft (12m). The owner or the charter company will need some evidence as to the competence of the charterer, or they may insist on providing a skipper (at extra cost) for the first few days until they are satisfied that the boat is in good hands. Less experienced charterers should either arrange for a skipper in advance, or consider one of the growing number of flotilla cruises which are now available (see 1.7.6).

Crewed charter. This implies that the yacht is supplied complete with skipper and crew, the number of which depends on the size and luxury of the yacht concerned. A crewed charter yacht of, say, 50ft (15m) might be crewed by a husband and wife team who live on board. Larger yachts come with larger crews (and possibly a larger bill for feeding them).

Headboat. A headboat is a yacht or similar craft which carries a number of passengers, not necessarily of the same party, at so much a head – more like a floating hotel or a miniature cruise ship.

1.7.2 An owner chartering his boat
If sensibly managed, a yachtsman can recover at least some of the expense of running his yacht by chartering her (bareboat) for a few weeks each year. Should he have the time available, perhaps as a retired person, he can of course alternatively offer skippered charters. For the sort of person who uses his boat very regularly, and possibly keeps her in commission throughout the year, chartering is not such an attractive proposition as for the yachtsman who finds it difficult to make full use of his boat.

The main problem for the private owner with bareboat chartering is to find responsible people who will take good care of his yacht, and commercially he is in direct competition with charter companies and their fleets of boats. At best it must be anticipated that there will be

Boat details

Owner's name .... Address ....

.... Tel. No. ....

Name .... Official No. .... Port of Registry ....

Displacement .... Thames tonnage .... Register tonnage ....

LOA .... LWL .... Beam .... Draught ....

Sail area .... (actual) .... (measured) Mast height above WL ....

Sail No. .... Rating .... Date of issue .... TMF ....

Designer .... Builder .... When built ....

Classification .... Date and place of last survey ....

Insurance company .... Policy No. .... Renewal date ....

Engine make/type/serial No. (s) ....

H.P. .... at .... rpm. Fuel cons. .... at .... rpm

Fuel capacity .... Fresh water .... Lub. oil type/grade ....

Gearbox .... Lub. oil type .... Capacities ....

Propeller diam. .... Pitch ....

Battery capacity .... Date new ....

Radio call sign .... Ship Licence No. .... Renewal due ....

Compass last swung .... Liferaft serviced .... Serial No. ....

Flares renewed .... Other safety equipment checked ....

Serial Nos.

Outboard .... Radio ....

....

Boat last slipped .... Antifouling used .... Coats ....

Anchor cable markings ....

CG Form 66 held by .... Shore contact ....

Tel. Nos.

Harbour Master .... Boatyard .... Sailmaker ....

Yacht Club .... Customs .... Coastguard ....

Weather ....

....

Other information

....

much more wear and tear on the boat and her gear (so increasing maintenance costs), and some charterers may not leave the boat as clean and tidy as the owner might wish. If the yacht is based at her normal home port it may perhaps be possible for the owner to advertise and book the charters, to meet the charterers when they arrive and show them the boat, to check over the boat and her inventory on completion of the charter, and then to clean and service the boat before the next party arrives. But this is quite a tall order, and it is more than likely that somebody else will have to do some of these tasks. If time is short between charters there may well be problems with spares that are suddenly needed, since the private owner cannot afford the sort of spares back-up that is expected in a well-run charter company. If the yacht is based abroad, say in the Mediterranean, it will definitely be necessary to employ a reliable agent to look after the boat, so this will syphon off some of the profit.

It is essential to have a proper form of agreement (charter party) covering such items as the date, time and place for taking over and handing back the boat; booking deposit; balance of the charter money (payable before the charter starts); arrangements for cancellation; a security deposit for loss or damage (returnable on completion of the charter); any insurance excess which the charterer may have to bear; cruising limits, where applicable; payment for items such as fuel, harbour dues, food, laundry etc; what penalty may be imposed for late return of the boat; and, should a crew be carried, who pays for their food.

Before chartering your boat – even to a friend for the weekend – it is essential to inform your insurance company.

One organisation through which private owners can charter their boat (either bareboat, or with the owner acting as skipper) is The Charter Club, 17/23 Southampton Row, London, WC1B 5BR. Tel:(01) 404 0235.

1.7.3 Bareboat chartering

Many people nowadays find it preferable to charter a yacht for two or three weeks rather than face the continuing responsibility of looking after a boat for 12 months a year. Because so many British harbours have become increasingly congested and unattractive, and since air fares are now cheaper in real terms, those who charter are often sensibly inclined to do so in areas like the Mediterranean or Caribbean, where the weather is more reliable. One of the attractions of chartering is the ability to explore different places. There are however quite a few charter boats available around the British Isles, with some of them in nicer areas such as the west coast of Scotland.

Whatever company or private owner you charter from, be sure to have the sort of written agreement described in 1.7.2. Find out as much

as possible about the firm or the individual concerned, preferably from people who have had first-hand experience of the boats or boat. Check carefully what equipment is provided – you should be sent a comprehensive list. Pay particular regard to navigational items and to safety equipment. What is the age of the boat, and is she the best type for your purpose? Does the accommodation really match your requirements? Look closely at insurance to see what excess is included, and check the third party cover, which should be for at least £500,000. What sort of service is provided in the event of some problem developing with the boat during the charter period (probably none, if you are chartering from a private individual). If the boat becomes unusable, what refund will be offered?

1.7.4 Bareboat chartering in Britain

Chartering in home waters is naturally cheaper, because travel costs are much reduced. Also, if required, it is feasible to change the composition of the crew during the charter. Several of the more responsible British charter firms belong to the Yacht Charter Association, which demands certain minimum standards for equipment, spares and service from its member companies. Details can be obtained from the Secretary, Yacht Charter Association, Lymington Yacht Haven, Kings Saltern Road, Lymington, Hampshire, SO4 9XY. Tel: Lymington (0590) 72472.

For a wide range of other charter opportunities, see the advertisement pages of current yachting journals.

1.7.5 Bareboat chartering abroad

Opportunities are steadily increasing for people who want to charter boats in other parts of the world. There are established operations in the Mediterranean and in the Caribbean, where the British Virgin Islands are popular and well provided with responsible charter operators. Other areas include the Bahamas and the Great Barrier Reef in Australia.

In most cases the yachts are fitted with radiotelephones, allowing them to keep in touch with base, and invaluable should any problem arise with the boat. The company is likely to have a fast motor boat, which can reach any yacht which has trouble with gear or engine (for example) in a matter of a few hours. With the larger companies the spares back-up is usually very impressive, with makes and types of equipment rationalised amongst their fleet, which may number 50 boats.

Similar considerations apply in respect of choosing the boat and company as in 1.7.3. If going to the Caribbean (say), travel becomes a major factor – certainly in cost. Any responsible charter company, or their agent in this country, will not only advise on route and timings but do the necessary booking. Get in early, so as to take full advantage of whatever cheap fares are available. Also remember that when taking travelling into account, a three week holiday is more economical per week than a fortnight's holiday, particularly since a few charter companies make reductions for the third week of a charter.

Most companies will arrange for provisioning the boat in advance, to a scale agreed by the charterers. It is often wise to take advantage of such a scheme, since there may be no convenient shops on arrival. 'Split provisioning' provides enough food if three or four main meals are taken ashore each week.

The inventory is normally very comprehensive and the firm should provide a detailed list. Although items such as snorkel gear are included, binoculars are usually not provided. It may be advisable to take your own pilot guide to the area concerned. The firm will almost certainly give a 'chart briefing' ashore, in which will be described the better anchorages and shore facilities, where to get items such as ice, and any areas which are 'off limits'. In some localities sailing is forbidden after dark, due to the absence of shore lights and the danger of reefs.

1.7.6 Flotilla sailing

Flotilla sailing gives a good opportunity for less experienced sailors to start cruising, with advice from the flotilla 'leader' always readily available. Probably the boats are fitted with VHF radiotelephones, so that help is readily on call.

Most flotilla operations are in relatively small yachts, sleeping four or six persons, and often ideal for a family holiday. The leader knows the area – the best anchorages, the more attractive harbours, and the places ashore where food and drink are good and cheap. He can also help, where necessary, with matters such as Customs formalities.

It is likely that such a holiday will be offered as a complete 'package', including air travel and transfers. Greece is the most popular area.

Companies which offer flotilla sailing holidays include: *Bahamas Flotilla Cruising*, 213 Sandbanks Road, Lilliput, Poole, Dorset, BH14 8EY; tel: Poole (0202) 677272. *Club Mirage*, Charfleet, Canvey Island, Essex, SS7 OPU; tel: Canvey Island (0268) 696555. *Flotilla Sailing Club Ltd*, 2 St John's Terrace, Harrow Road, London, W10 4RB; tel: (01) 969 5423. *Island Sailing Ltd*, Northney Marina, Hayling Island, Hampshire;

tel: Hayling Island (0705) 466331. *Sail America*, 372 Prince Avenue, Westcliff-on-Sea, Essex; tel: Southend-on-Sea (0702) 335536. *Seascape Sailing Holidays Ltd*, 32 Cranbourn Street, London, WC2; tel: (01) 836 4932. *Seven Seas Sailing Club*, (Dept B5), 10 Storey's Gate, London, SW1P 3AY; tel: (01) 222 2733. *Yacht Cruising Association*, Old Stone House, Judge's Terrace, East Grinstead, Sussex, RH19 1AQ; tel: East Grinstead (0342) 311366.

1.7.7 Larger charter yachts

A fully-crewed charter yacht can provide an unequalled holiday, and at a cost per person which compares quite favourably with a cruise in a luxury passenger ship. But in a charter yacht you have complete freedom about the itinerary and about every aspect of life on board. And of course there's that added bonus – you choose your fellow passengers!

The range of yachts available is enormous – from 40ft (12m) sailing yachts with perhaps a skipper and cook/stewardess, to 200ft (60m) motor yachts which can accommodate 20 guests and as many crew.

Certain standard terms are used in describing charter rates:

Western Mediterranean Terms include the hire of the yacht with her crew, and insurance of the yacht. Operating expenses such as food and fuel are borne by the charterer.

Greek Terms include the hire of the yacht and crew, and insurance of the yacht, and also the crews' food, fuel for five hours cruising per day, harbour dues, water and ship's laundry.

Caribbean Terms include hire and insurance of the yacht, the crews' salaries and food, all maintenance, fuel, laundry, harbour dues and three meals per day for the charterer's guests.

Operating expenses such as fuel and food for the crew vary considerably, depending on the area, while the charterer's food bill also depends on the sort of cuisine expected. Charter agents will give advice on these sorts of expenses, and also whether quoted charter rates may be subject to local taxes.

Two leading charter agents in this country are Halsey Marine Limited, 22 Boston Place, Dorset Square, London, NW1 6HZ, tel: (01) 724 1303, and Camper & Nicholsons Yacht Agency, 16 Regency Street, London, SW1P 4DD, tel: (01) 821 1641/3.

Chapter 2

General Information

Contents

2.1 Rule of the Road

Any skipper should have a sound working knowledge of the 'Collision Regulations', as they are often called, so that at sea or in a busy harbour he can apply them almost instinctively. It is also necessary to be able to recognize the lights, shapes and other signals which are prescribed for different types of vessels under various conditions.

The 1972 regulations, which came into force in 1977, are printed in full below, and include various amendments which came into force on 1 June 1983. Also included are diagrams and explanatory notes which do not form part of the official regulations.

International Regulations for Preventing Collisions at Sea, 1972

Published by the International Maritime Organization (IMO) and reprinted with permission.

Part A – General

Rule 1 *Application*
(a) These Rules shall apply to all vessels upon the high seas and in all waters connected therewith navigable by seagoing vessels.
(b) Nothing in these Rules shall interfere with the operations of special rules made by an appropriate authority for roadsteads, harbours, rivers, lakes or inland waterways connected with the high seas and navigable by seagoing vessels. Such special rules shall conform as closely as possible to these Rules.
(c) Nothing in these Rules shall interfere with the operation of any special rules made by the Government of any State with respect to additional station or signal lights, shapes or whistle signals for ships of war and vessels proceeding under convoy, or with respect to additional station or signal lights or shapes for fishing vessels engaged in fishing as a fleet. These additional station or signal lights, shapes or whistle signals, shall, so far as possible, be such that they cannot be mistaken for any light, shape or signal authorized elsewhere under these Rules.
(d) Traffic separation schemes may be adopted by the Organization for the purpose of these Rules.
(e) Whenever the Government concerned shall have determined that a vessel of special construction or purpose cannot comply fully with the provisions of any of these Rules with respect to the number, position, range or arc of visibility of lights or shapes, as well as to the disposition and characteristics of sound-signalling appliances without interfering with the special function of the vessel, such vessel shall comply with such other provisions in regard to the number, position, range or arc of visibility of lights or shapes, as well as to the disposition and characteristics of sound-signalling appliances, as her Government

shall have determined to be the closest possible compliance with these Rules in respect of that vessel.

Notes
1. Rule 1(a) – Harbour and similar authorities may make special rules for their own waters, but they should conform as closely as possible to these Rules.
2. Rule 1(c) – Details of such lights and signals are shown in the Annual Summary of Admiralty Notices to Mariners.
3. Rule 1(d) – See Rule 10.
4. Rule 1(e) – Submarines, for example, carry their steaming lights low down, and in other warships the disposition of the masts brings the steaming lights closer together than would otherwise be required, which can make it difficult to judge their aspect.

Rule 2 *Responsibility*
(a) Nothing in these Rules shall exonerate any vessel, or the owner, master or crew thereof, from the consequences of any neglect to comply with these Rules or of the neglect of any precaution which may be required by the ordinary practice of seamen, or by the special circumstances of the case.
(b) In construing and complying with these Rules due regard shall be had to all dangers of navigation and collision and to any special circumstances, including the limitations of the vessels involved, which may make a departure from these Rules necessary to avoid immediate danger.

Notes
1. What Rule 2 implies is that rules alone are not enough – it is the seamanlike actions (taking into consideration all the relevant factors) of those who have to interpret and apply them that avoid collisions.
2. The Rules do not give any vessel 'right of way' over another completely regardless of special circumstances which may apply; factors to consider might be the presence of other vessels under way or at anchor, shallow water, poor visibility, traffic separation schemes, fishing fleets etc. – or the handling characteristics of the vessels concerned in the prevailing conditions.
3. Rule 2(b) specifically states that a departure from these Rules may be necessary in certain circumstances, and that to avoid immediate danger a vessel is not merely justified in doing this, but is expected to do so.

Rule 3 *General Definitions*
For the purpose of these Rules, except where the context otherwise requires:

(a) The word 'vessel' includes every description of water craft, including non-displacement craft and seaplanes, used or capable of being used as a means of transportation on water.

(b) The term 'power-driven vessel' means any vessel propelled by machinery.

(c) The term 'sailing vessel' means any vessel under sail provided that propelling machinery, if fitted, is not being used.

(d) The term 'vessel engaged in fishing' means any vessel fishing with nets, lines, trawls, or other fishing apparatus which restrict manoeuvrability, but does not include a vessel fishing with trolling lines or other fishing apparatus which do not restrict manoeuvrability.

(e) The word 'seaplane' includes any aircraft designed to manoeuvre on the water.

(f) The term 'vessel not under command' means a vessel which through some exceptional circumstances is unable to manoeuvre as required by these Rules and is therefore unable to keep out of the way of another vessel.

(g) The term 'vessel restricted in her ability to manoeuvre' means a vessel which from the nature of her work is restricted in her ability to manoeuvre as required by these Rules and is therefore unable to keep out of the way of another vessel. The term 'vessels restricted in their ability to manoeuvre' shall include but not be limited to:

   (i) a vessel engaged in laying, servicing or picking up a navigation mark, submarine cable or pipeline;

   (ii) a vessel engaged in dredging, surveying or underwater operations;

   (iii) a vessel engaged in replenishment or transferring persons, provisions or cargo while underway;

   (iv) a vessel engaged in the launching or recovery of aircraft;

   (v) a vessel engaged in mineclearance operations;

   (vi) a vessel engaged in a towing operation such as severely restricts the towing vessel and her tow in their ability to deviate from their course.

(h) The term 'vessel constrained by her draught' means a power-driven vessel which because of her draught in relation to the available depth of water is severely restricted in her ability to deviate from the course she is following.

(i) The word 'underway' means that a vessel is not at anchor, or made fast to the shore, or aground.

(j) The words 'length' and 'breadth' of a vessel mean her length overall and greatest breadth.

(k) Vessels shall be deemed to be in sight of one another only when one can be observed visually from the other.

(l) The term 'restricted visibility' means any condition in which visibility is restricted by fog, mist, falling snow, heavy rainstorms, sandstorms or any other similar causes.

Part B – Steering and Sailing Rules

SECTION I – CONDUCT OF VESSELS IN ANY CONDITION OF VISIBILITY

Rule 4 *Application*
Rules in this Section apply in any condition of visibility.

Rule 5 *Look-out*
Every vessel shall at all times maintain a proper look-out by sight and hearing as well as by all available means appropriate in the prevailing circumstances and conditions so as to make a full appraisal of the situation and of the risk of collision.

Notes
1. A most important rule for all seamen, including yachtsmen. In sailing yachts, particular care is needed to cover arcs which may be blinded by sails or by the heel of the boat. In yachts with a wheelhouse certain arcs may be wooded by the boat's structure.
2. During darkness care must be taken to preserve night vision, by having only dim and well screened lights for the compass and the chart-table – and throughout the accommodation.
3. A lookout must use his ears as well as his eyes, particularly in restricted visibility, when one crew member should if possible be stationed forward.

Rule 6 *Safe Speed*
Every vessel shall at all times proceed at a safe speed so that she can take proper and effective action to avoid collision and be stopped within a distance appropriate to the prevailing circumstances and conditions.

In determining a safe speed the following factors shall be among those taken into account:
(a) By all vessels:

   (i) the state of visibility;

   (ii) the traffic density including concentrations of fishing vessels or any other vessels;

   (iii) the manoeuvrability of the vessel with special reference to stopping distance and turning ability in the prevailing conditions;

   (iv) at night the presence of background light such as from shore lights or from back scatter of her own lights;

   (v) the state of wind, sea and current, and the proximity of navigational hazards;

(vi) the draught in relation to the available depth of water.

(b) Additionally, by vessels with operational radar;

   (i) the characteristics, efficiency and limitations of the radar equipment;

   (ii) any constraints imposed by the radar range scale in use;

   (iii) the effect on radar detection of the sea state, weather and other sources of interference;

   (iv) the possibility that small vessels, ice and other floating objects may not be detected by radar at an adequate range;

   (v) the number, location and movement of vessels detected by radar;

   (vi) the more exact assessment of the visibility that may be possible when radar is used to determine the range of vessels or other objects in the vicinity.

Notes

1. Large ships going fast cannot stop quickly. The faster two vessels are approaching each other, the less time there is for either to appreciate the situation and take the necessary action to avoid a collision – and the greater the impact should such action fail.

2. For motor yachts the same considerations apply as for larger ships, particularly of course at night or in bad visibility. So far as sailing yachts are concerned, sheer speed is not so much a problem as the way the boat is sailed. For example a boat under spinnaker and with her main boom guyed forward sacrifices considerable manoeuvrability in the quest for greater speed; even if she is only doing eight knots through the water, such action would contravene Rule 6 in poor visibility or amongst a lot of other vessels.

3. Radar is not infallible. Experience is needed to adjust the set correctly for the prevailing conditions, and to interpret what is seen on the screen.

Rule 7 *Risk of Collision*

(a) Every vessel shall use all available means appropriate to the prevailing circumstances and conditions to determine if risk of collision exists. If there is any doubt such risk shall be deemed to exist.

(b) Proper use shall be made of radar equipment if fitted and operational, including long-range scanning to obtain early warning of risk of collision and radar plotting or equivalent systematic observation of detected objects.

(c) Assumptions shall not be made on the basis of scanty information, especially scanty radar information.

(d) In determining if risk of collision exists the following considerations shall be among those taken into account:

   (i) such risk shall be deemed to exist if the compass bearing of an approaching vessel does not appreciably change;

   (ii) such risk may sometimes exist even when an appreciable bearing change is evident, particularly when approaching a very large vessel or a tow or when approaching a vessel at close range.

Notes

1. So far as yachts are concerned the invariable rule should be to take a compass bearing, and record it, of any approaching or crossing vessel; then take a series of bearings at suitable intervals. Unless the actual bearing (not the relative bearing) changes appreciably, there is risk of collision.

2. Particular care should be taken in respect of Rule 7(d)(ii). Taking bearings of the bow of a supertanker might show that a yacht would miss that end, but she might hit the other.

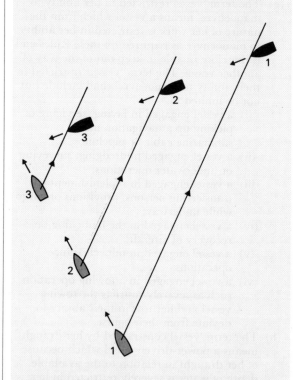

Fig. 2(1) Rule 7. The bearing of Black from Blue (and of Blue from Black) is steady. Blue should have taken action long before position 2 by altering course to starboard by at least 45°. to pass under Black's stern.

Rule 8 *Action to avoid Collision*

(a) Any action taken to avoid collision shall, if the circumstances of the case admit, be positive, made in ample time and with due regard to the observance of good seamanship.

(b) Any alteration of course and/or speed to avoid collision shall, if the circumstances of the case admit, be large enough to be readily apparent to another vessel observing visually or by radar; a succession of small alterations of course and/or speed should be avoided.

(c) If there is sufficient sea room, alteration of course alone may be the most effective action to avoid a close-quarters situation provided that it is made in good time, is substantial and does not result in another close-quarters situation.

(d) Action taken to avoid collision with another vessel shall be such as to result in passing at a safe distance. The effectiveness of the action shall be carefully checked until the other vessel is finally past and clear.

(e) If necessary to avoid collision or allow more time to assess the situation, a vessel shall slacken her speed or take all way off by stopping or reversing her means of propulsion.

Notes

1. This Rule emphasises the importance of taking early and positive action to avoid collision, and of watching the situation until the other vessel is well clear. Large and distinct alterations of course and/or speed are much more evident to the other skipper than a succession of small ones. This is particularly so at night when, by altering course to show a different light, a vessel can make her intentions completely clear.
2. While keeping clear of one vessel it is important to keep a good watch on others in the vicinity.
3. If necessary slow down, stop, or even go astern. Apart from minimising the effect of any collision, this gives more time to assess the situation. Such action can seldom be wrong when in poor visibility another vessel is detected forward of the beam.

Rule 9 *Narrow Channels*

(a) A vessel proceeding along the course of a narrow channel or fairway shall keep as near to the outer limit of the channel or fairway which lies on her starboard side as is safe and practicable.

(b) A vessel of less than 20 metres in length or a sailing vessel shall not impede the passage of a vessel which can safely navigate only within a narrow channel or fairway.

(c) A vessel engaged in fishing shall not impede the passage of any other vessel navigating within a narrow channel or fairway.

(d) A vessel shall not cross a narrow channel or fairway if such crossing impedes the passage of a vessel which can safely navigate only within such channel or fairway. The latter

vessel may use the sound signal prescribed in Rule 34(d) if in doubt as to the intention of the crossing vessel.

(e) (i) In a narrow channel or fairway when overtaking can take place only if the vessel to be overtaken has to take action to permit safe passing, the vessel intending to overtake shall indicate her intention by sounding the appropriate signal prescribed in Rule 34(c)(i). The vessel to be overtaken shall, if in agreement, sound the appropriate signal prescribed in Rule 34(c)(ii) and take steps to permit safe passing. If in doubt she may sound the signals prescribed in Rule 34(d).

(ii) This Rule does not relieve the overtaking vessel of her obligation under Rule 13.

(f) A vessel nearing a bend or an area of a narrow channel or fairway where other vessels may be obscured by an intervening obstruction shall navigate with particular alertness and caution and shall sound the appropriate signal prescribed in Rule 34(e).

(g) Any vessel shall, if the circumstances of the case admit, avoid anchoring in a narrow channel.

Notes

1. A 'narrow channel' is not defined, and depends upon the relative sizes of the vessels and the waters concerned.
2. Sailing yachts are required to keep to the starboard side of a fairway, as far as practicable, just as much as power-driven vessels, and are equally bound by Rules 9(b) and 9(d).
3. All yachts must avoid impeding a vessel which can safely navigate only within a narrow channel or fairway, which means that they should keep sufficiently clear so that risk of collision does not develop.

Rule 10 *Traffic Separation Schemes*

(a) This Rules applies to traffic separation schemes adopted by the Organization.

(b) A vessel using a traffic separation scheme shall:

(i) proceed in the appropriate traffic lane in the general direction of traffic flow for that lane;

(ii) so far as practicable keep clear of a traffic separation line or separation zone;

(iii) normally join or leave a traffic lane at the termination of the lane, but when joining or leaving from either side shall do so at as small an angle to the general direction of traffic flow as practicable.

(c) A vessel shall so far as practicable avoid crossing traffic lanes, but if obliged to do so shall cross as nearly as practicable at right angles to the general direction of traffic flow.

(d) Inshore traffic zones shall not normally be used by through traffic which can safely use the appropriate traffic lane within the adjacent traffic scheme. However, vessels of less than 20 metres in length and sailing vessels may under all circumstances use inshore traffic zones.

(e) A vessel other than a crossing vessel or a vessel joining or leaving a lane shall not normally enter a separation zone or cross a separation line except:
  (i) in cases of emergency to avoid immediate danger;
  (ii) to engage in fishing within a separation zone.

(f) A vessel navigating in areas near the terminations of traffic separation schemes shall do so with particular caution.

(g) A vessel shall so far as practicable avoid anchoring in a traffic separation scheme or in areas near its terminations.

(h) A vessel not using a traffic separation scheme shall avoid it by as wide a margin as is practicable.

(i) A vessel engaged in fishing shall not impede the passage of any vessel following a traffic lane.

(j) A vessel of less than 20 metres in length or a sailing vessel shall not impede the safe passage of a power-driven vessel following a traffic lane.

(k) A vessel restricted in her ability to manoeuvre when engaged in an operation for the maintenance of safety of navigation in a traffic separation scheme is exempted from complying with this Rule to the extent necessary to carry out the operation.

(l) A vessel restricted in her ability to manoeuvre when engaged in an operation for the laying, servicing or picking up of a submarine cable, within a traffic separation scheme, is exempted from complying with this Rule to the extent necessary to carry out the operation.

Note
Comments on Traffic Separation Schemes and the interpretation of Rule 10 are given in Section 2.2.19.

SECTION II – CONDUCT OF VESSELS IN SIGHT OF ONE ANOTHER

Rule 11 *Application*
Rules in this Section apply to vessels in sight of one another.

Rule 12 *Sailing Vessels*
(a) When two sailing vessels are approaching one another, so as to involve risk of collision, one of them shall keep out of the way of the other as follows:

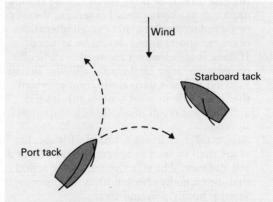

Fig. 2(2) Rule 12(a)(i). When two sailing boats are on opposite tacks the one on port tack (on the left above) must keep clear.

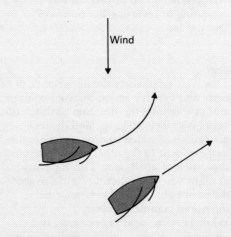

Fig. 2(3) Rule 12(a)(ii). When two sailing boats are on the same tack, the windward one (on the left above) must keep clear.

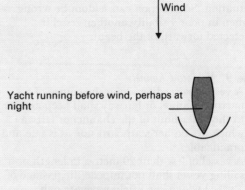

Fig. 2(4) Rule 12(a)(iii). If a port tack sailing yacht cannot decide whether an approaching vessel under sail to windward is on port or starboard tack, she shall keep clear.

(i) when each has the wind on a different side, the vessel which has the wind on the port side shall keep out of the way of the other;

(ii) when both have the wind on the same side, the vessel which is to windward shall keep out of the way of the vessel which is to leeward;

(iii) if a vessel with the wind on the port side sees a vessel to windward and cannot determine with certainty whether the other vessel has the wind on the port or on the starboard side, she shall keep out of the way of the other.

(b) For purposes of this Rule the windward side shall be deemed to be the side opposite to that on which the mainsail is carried or, in the case of a square-rigged vessel, the side opposite to that on which the largest fore-and-aft sail is carried.

Notes

1. The implications of this rule are shown in figs. 2(2), 2(3) and 2(4). Rules 8, 13, 16 and 17(a), (b) and (d) also refer. Rule 12 does not apply if either of the two vessels under sail is also motoring.

2. One sailing vessel overtaking another – from a direction more than $22\frac{1}{2}°$ abaft the beam – must keep clear, regardless of the wind direction, under Rule 13 which over-rides all other Rules in Part B, Sections I and II.

3. Rule 12(a)(iii) applies particularly at night.

Rule 13 *Overtaking*

(a) Notwithstanding anything contained in the Rules of Part B, Sections I and II any vessel overtaking any other shall keep out of the way of the vessel being overtaken.

(b) A vessel shall be deemed to be overtaking when coming up with another vessel from a direction more than $22\frac{1}{2}°$ abaft her beam, that is, in such a position with reference to the vessel she is overtaking, that at night she would be able to see only the sternlight of that vessel but neither of her sidelights.

(c) When a vessel is in any doubt as to whether she is overtaking another, she shall assume that this is the case and act accordingly.

(d) Any subsequent alteration of the bearing between the two vessels shall not make the overtaking vessel a crossing vessel within the meaning of these Rules or relieve her of the duty of keeping clear of the overtaken vessel until she is finally past and clear.

Notes

1. Although the overtaking vessel always has the obligation to keep clear, the one overtaken also has a duty not to hamper her.

2. Before altering course always look astern to make sure another vessel is not coming up on either quarter.

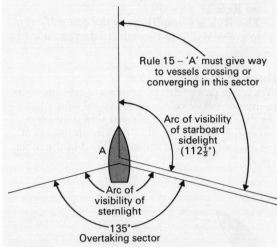

Fig. 2(5) Rule 13. Any vessel coming up with and overtaking A in this sector (ie when her sternlight is visible but neither of her sidelights) must keep out of her way.

Rule 14 *Head-on Situation*

(a) When two power-driven vessels are meeting on reciprocal or nearly reciprocal courses so as to involve risk of collision each shall alter her course to starboard so that each shall pass on the port side of the other.

(b) Such a situation shall be deemed to exist when a vessel sees the other ahead or nearly ahead and by night she could see the masthead lights of the other in a line or nearly in a line and/or both sidelights and by day she observes the corresponding aspect of the other vessel.

(c) When a vessel is in any doubt as to whether such a situation exists she shall assume that it does exist and act accordingly.

Notes

1. This Rule applies only to power-driven vessels, and places equal responsibility on two vessels

Fig. 2(6) Rule 4. When two power driven vessels are approaching on reciprocal or nearly reciprocal courses, each shall alter to starboard so that they pass port to port.

meeting on nearly reciprocal courses, both to alter course to starboard. See Fig. 2(6).

2. A substantial alteration may be required, accompanied by the appropriate sound signal, see Rule 34.

3. This Rule is summed up by the adage 'Green to green, red to red – perfect safety, go ahead'.

Rule 15 *Crossing Situation*

When two power-driven vessels are crossing so as to involve risk of collision, the vessel which has the other on her own starboard side shall keep out of the way and shall, if the circumstances of the case admit, avoid crossing ahead of the other vessel.

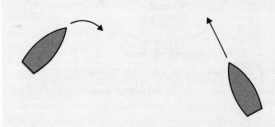

Fig. 2(7) Rule 15. When two power driven vessels are crossing so as to involve risk of collision, the one which has the other on her starboard side shall keep clear, and should if possible avoid crossing ahead of the other.

Notes

1. 'If to starboard red appear, 'tis your duty to keep clear'. This applies even if the vessel which has the other on her starboard side is under way but stopped, unless she is not under command.

2. Normally the correct action for the giving-way vessel is to alter course to starboard. Very exceptionally (if for example there is shallow water to starboard) an alteration to port may be justified – in which case a substantial alteration may be needed to avoid crossing ahead of the other vessel.

3. Rule 15 does not apply if one of the vessels is in the categories described in Rule 18(a)(i), (ii) or (iii).

Rule 16 *Action by Give-way Vessel*

Every vessel which is directed to keep out of the way of another vessel shall, so far as possible, take early and substantial action to keep well clear.

Rule 17 *Action by Stand-on Vessel*

(a) (i) Where one of two vessels is to keep out of the way the other shall keep her course and speed.

(ii) The latter vessel may however take action to avoid collision by her manoeuvre alone, as soon as it becomes apparent to her that the vessel required to keep out of the way is not taking appropriate action in compliance with these Rules.

(b) When, from any cause, the vessel required to keep her course and speed finds herself so close that collision cannot be avoided by the action of the give-way vessel alone, she shall take such action as will best aid to avoid collision.

(c) A power-driven vessel which takes action in a crossing situation in accordance with sub-paragraph (a)(ii) of this Rule to avoid collision with another power-driven vessel shall, if the circumstances of the case admit, not alter course to port for a vessel on her own port side.

(d) This Rule does not relieve the give-way vessel of her obligation to keep out of the way.

Notes

1. The stand-on vessel is only required to hold her course and speed under Rule 17(a)(i) in a two-vessel situation, and not at long range before risk of collision develops – this is the opportunity for a yacht to avoid confronting a larger vessel, particularly since a yacht will usually see a large ship before the ship sees her.

2. Once risk of collision develops, the stand-on vessel is required to hold her course and speed. But when it becomes apparent that the other is not taking action she may take avoiding action herself. This must not conflict with possible belated action by the give-way vessel, and hence in accordance with Rule 17(c) she should normally alter course substantially to starboard.

3. In the case of a manoeuvrable yacht the best action may often be to turn completely away from an oncoming ship.

4. Rule 17(b) makes it compulsory for the stand-on vessel to take the best possible avoiding action in the circumstances.

Rule 18 *Responsibilities between Vessels*

Except where Rules 9, 10 and 13 otherwise require:

(a) A power-driven vessel underway shall keep out of the way of:

(i) a vessel not under command;

(ii) a vessel restricted in her ability to manoeuvre;

(iii) a vessel engaged in fishing;

(iv) a sailing vessel.

(b) A sailing vessel underway shall keep out of the way of:

(i) a vessel not under command;

(ii) a vessel restricted in her ability to manoeuvre;

(iii) a vessel engaged in fishing.

(c) A vessel engaged in fishing when underway

shall so far as possible, keep out of the way of:
  (i) a vessel not under command;
  (ii) a vessel restricted in her ability to manoeuvre.
(d) (i) Any vessel other than a vessel not under command or a vessel restricted in her ability to manoeuvre shall, if the circumstances of the case admit, avoid impeding the safe passage of a vessel constrained by her draught, exhibiting the signals in Rule 28.
  (ii) A vessel constrained by her draught shall navigate with particular caution having full regard to her special condition.
(e) A seaplane on the water shall, in general, keep well clear of all vessels and avoid impeding their navigation. In circumstances, however, where risk of collision exists, she shall comply with the Rules of this Part.

Notes
1. Rule 18 may not apply in narrow channels or traffic schemes, and does not apply in overtaking situations.
2. Although a power-driven vessel is required to keep clear of sailing vessels, sailing yachts which are possibly making frequent alterations of course should keep clear of larger ships.
3. In the event of a power-driven vessel failing to take early action to keep out of the way, a sailing yacht can usually avoid collision by conforming with Rule 17(a)(ii).
4. A sailing yacht is required to keep clear of a power-driven vessel under the provisions of Rules 9(b), 10(j), 13 and 18(b), and she is also required to avoid impeding a vessel constrained by her draught.

SECTION III – CONDUCT OF VESSELS IN RESTRICTED VISIBILITY

Rule 19 *Conduct of Vessels in Restricted Visibility*
(a) This Rule applies to vessels not in sight of one another when navigating in or near an area of restricted visibility.
(b) Every vessel shall proceed at a safe speed adapted to the prevailing circumstances and conditions of restricted visibility. A power-driven vessel shall have her engines ready for immediate manoeuvre.
(c) Every vessel shall have due regard to the prevailing circumstances and conditions of restricted visibility when complying with the Rules of Section 1 of this Part.
(d) A vessel which detects by radar alone the presence of another vessel shall determine if a close-quarters situation is developing and/or risk of collision exists. If so, she shall take avoiding action in ample time, provided that

when such action consists of an alteration of course, so far as possible the following shall be avoided:
  (i) an alteration of course to port for a vessel forward of the beam, other than for a vessel being overtaken;
  (ii) an alteration of course towards a vessel abeam or abaft the beam.
(e) Except where it has been determined that a risk of collision does not exist, every vessel which hears apparently forward of her beam the fog signal of another vessel, or which cannot avoid a close-quarters situation with another vessel forward of her beam, shall reduce her speed to the minimum at which she can be kept on her course. She shall if necessary take all her way off and in any event navigate with extreme caution until danger of collision is over.

Notes
1. When vessels can see each other they are subject to the Rules in Section II.
2. Safe speed is covered by Rule 6, and look-outs in Rule 5. Other safety factors for a yacht are an efficient radar reflector (properly mounted in the 'catch rain' position); keeping clear of shipping lanes and narrow channels (preferably keeping in water which is too shallow for larger ships); and being ready for immediate and drastic alterations of course – by not setting sails like spinnakers. In really thick fog the best action is to anchor in relatively shallow water, and comply with Rule 35(g) or (i).

Part C – Lights and shapes

Rule 20 *Application*
(a) Rules in this Part shall be complied with in all weathers.
(b) The Rules concerning lights shall be complied with from sunset to sunrise, and during such times no other lights shall be exhibited, except such lights as cannot be mistaken for the lights specified in these Rules or do not impair their visibility or distinctive character, or interfere with the keeping of a proper look-out.
(c) The lights prescribed by these Rules shall, if carried, also be exhibited from sunrise to sunset in restricted visibility and may be exhibited in all other circumstances when it is deemed necessary.
(d) The rules concerning shapes shall be complied with by day.
(e) The lights and shapes specified in these Rules shall comply with the provisions of Annex I to these Regulations.

Rule 21 *Definitions*

(a) 'Masthead light' means a white light placed over the fore and aft centreline of the vessel showing an unbroken light over an arc of the horizon of 225° and so fixed as to show the light from right ahead to $22\frac{1}{2}°$ abaft the beam on either side of the vessel.

(b) 'Sidelights' means a green light on the starboard side and a red light on the port side each showing an unbroken light over an arc of the horizon of $112\frac{1}{2}°$ and so fixed as to show the light from right ahead to $22\frac{1}{2}°$ abaft the beam on its respective side. In a vessel of less than 20 metres in length the sidelights may be combined in one lantern carried on the fore and aft centreline of the vessel.

(c) 'Sternlight' means a white light placed as nearly as practicable at the stern showing an unbroken light over an arc of the horizon of 135° and so fixed as to show the light $67\frac{1}{2}°$ from right aft on each side of the vessel.

(d) 'Towing light' means a yellow light having the same characteristics as the 'sternlight' defined in paragraph (c) of this Rule.

(e) 'All-round light' means a light showing an unbroken light over an arc of the horizon of 360°.

(f) 'Flashing light' means a light flashing at regular intervals at a frequency of 120 flashes or more per minute.

Notes

1. Although in Rule 21(a) the term masthead light is used, the light does not necessarily have to be on a mast. It should however be above and clear of all other lights and obstructions.

2. With respect to Rule 21(c), a power-driven vessel of less than 12 metres may, under rule 23(c) as revised, have her sternlight combined with the masthead light to form an all-round white light with improved visibility astern.

Rule 22 *Visibility of Lights*

The lights prescribed in these Rules shall have an intensity as specified in Section 8 of Annex I to these Regulations so as to be visible at the following minimum ranges:

(a) In vessels of 50 metres or more in length:
- a masthead light, 6 miles;
- a sidelight, 3 miles;
- a sternlight, 3 miles;
- a towing light, 3 miles;
- a white, red, green or yellow all-round light, 3 miles;

(b) In vessels of 12 metres or more in length but less than 50 metres in length:
- a masthead light, 5 miles; except that
- where the length of the vessel is less than 20 metres, 3 miles;
- a sidelight, 2 miles;

- a sternlight, 2 miles;
- a towing light, 2 miles;
- a white, red, green or yellow all-round light, 2 miles;

(c) In vessels of less than 12 metres in length:
- a masthead light, 2 miles;
- a sidelight, 1 mile;
- a sternlight, 2 miles;
- a towing light, 2 miles;
- a white, red, green or yellow all-round light, 2 miles.

(d) In inconspicuous, partly submerged vessels or objects being towed: – a white all-round light, 3 miles.

Rule 23 *Power-driven Vessels underway*

(a) A power-driven vessel underway shall exhibit:
  (i) a masthead light forward;
  (ii) a second masthead light abaft of and higher than the forward one; except that a vessel of less than 50 metres in length shall not be obliged to exhibit such light but may do so;
  (iii) sidelights;
  (iv) a sternlight.

(b) An air-cushion vessel when operating in the non-displacement mode shall, in addition to the lights prescribed in paragraph (a) of this Rule, exhibit an all-round flashing yellow light.

(c) (i) A power-driven vessel of less than 12 metres in length may in lieu of the lights prescribed in paragraph (a) of this Rule exhibit an all-round white light and sidelights;
  (ii) a power-driven vessel of less than 7 metres in length whose maximum speed does not exceed 7 knots may in lieu of the lights prescribed in paragraph (a) of this Rule exhibit an all-round white light and shall, if practicable, also exhibit sidelights;
  (iii) the masthead light or all-round white light on a power-driven vessel of less than 12 metres in length may be displaced from the fore and aft centreline of the vessel if centreline fitting is not practicable, provided that the sidelights are combined in one lantern which shall be carried on the fore and aft centreline of the vessel or located as nearly as practicable in the same fore and aft line as the masthead light or the all-round white light.

Notes

1. The specifications for lights in Annex I are much more precise than used to be the case.
2. The lights to be displayed by various classes of vessels are illustrated on pages 55–58.
3. Under Rule 23(c) – as revised from 1 June

1983 – a yacht of less than 12 metres under power may show sidelights (or a combined lantern) and a single all-round white light (which combines the previous requirement for a separate masthead light and sternlight). The white light must be at least 1 metre above the sidelights (or combined lantern).

Rule 24 *Towing and Pushing*
(a) A power driven vessel when towing shall exhibit:
  (i) instead of the light prescribed in Rule 23(a)(i) or (a)(ii), two masthead lights in a vertical line. When the length of the tow, measuring from the stern of the towing vessel to the after end of the tow exceeds 200 metres, three such lights in a vertical line;
  (ii) sidelights;
  (iii) a sternlight;
  (iv) a towing light in a vertical line above the sternlight;
  (v) when the length of the tow exceeds 200 metres, a diamond shape where it can best be seen.
(b) When a pushing vessel and a vessel being pushed ahead are rigidly connected in a composite unit they shall be regarded as a power-driven vessel and exhibit the lights prescribed in Rule 23.
(c) A power-driven vessel when pushing ahead or towing alongside, except in the case of a composite unit, shall exhibit:
  (i) instead of the light prescribed in Rule 23(a)(i) or (a)(ii), two masthead lights in a vertical line;
  (ii) sidelights;
  (iii) a sternlight.
(d) A power-driven vessel to which paragraphs (a) or (c) of this Rule apply shall also comply with Rule 23(a)(ii).
(e) A vessel or object being towed, other than those mentioned in paragraph (g) of this Rule, shall exhibit:
  (i) sidelights;
  (ii) a sternlight;
  (iii) when the length of the tow exceeds 200 metres, a diamond shape where it can best be seen.
(f) Provided that any number of vessels being towed alongside or pushed in a group shall be lighted as one vessel:
  (i) a vessel being pushed ahead, not being part of a composite unit, shall exhibit at the forward end, sidelights;
  (ii) a vessel being towed alongside shall exhibit a sternlight and at the forward end, sidelights.
(g) An inconspicuous, partly submerged vessel or object, or combination of such vessels or objects being towed, shall exhibit:
  (i) if it is less than 25 metres in breadth,

one all-round white light at or near the forward end and one at or near the after end except that dracones need not exhibit a light at or near the forward end;
  (ii) if it is 25 metres or more in breadth, two additional all-round white lights at or near the extremities of its breadth;
  (iii) if it exceeds 100 metres in length, additional all-round white lights between the lights prescribed in sub-paragraphs (i) and (ii) so that the distance between the lights shall not exceed 100 metres;
  (iv) a diamond shape at or near the aftermost extremity of the last vessel or object being towed and if the length of the tow exceeds 200 metres an additional diamond shape where it can best be seen and located as far forward as is practicable.
(h) Where from any sufficient cause it is impracticable for a vessel or object being towed to exhibit the lights or shapes prescribed in paragraph (e) or (g) of this Rule, all possible measures shall be taken to light the vessel or object towed or at least to indicate the presence of such vessel or object.
(i) Where from any sufficient cause it is impracticable for a vessel not normally engaged in towing operations to display the lights prescribed in paragraph (a) or (c) of this Rule, such vessel shall not be required to exhibit those lights when engaged in towing another vessel in distress or otherwise in need of assistance. All possible measures shall be taken to indicate the nature of the relationship between the towing vessel and the vessel being towed as authorized by Rule 36, in particular by illuminating the towline.

Rule 25 *Sailing Vessels underway and Vessels under Oars*
(a) A sailing vessel underway shall exhibit:
  (i) sidelights;
  (ii) a sternlight.
(b) In a sailing vessel of less than 20 metres in length the lights prescribed in paragraph (a) of this Rule may be combined in one lantern carried at or near the top of the mast where it can best be seen.
(c) A sailing vessel underway may, in addition to the lights prescribed in paragraph (a) of this Rule, exhibit at or near the top of the mast, where they can best be seen, two all-round lights in a vertical line, the upper being red and the lower green, but these lights shall not be exhibited in conjunction with the combined lantern permitted by paragraph (b) of this Rule.
(d) (i) A sailing vessel of less than 7 metres in length shall, if practicable, exhibit the lights prescribed in paragraph (a) or (b)

of this Rule, but if she does not, she shall have ready at hand an electric torch or lighted lantern showing a white light which shall be exhibited in sufficient time to prevent collision.

(ii) A vessel under oars may exhibit the lights prescribed in this Rule for sailing vessels, but if she does not, she shall have ready at hand an electric torch or lighted lantern showing a white light which shall be exhibited in sufficient time to prevent collision.

(e) A vessel proceeding under sail when also being propelled by machinery shall exhibit forward where it can best be seen a conical shape, apex downwards.

Notes

1. Rule 25(b) – as revised from 1 June 1983 – extends the size of sailing vessel which may show a tricolour light at or near the masthead from 12 metres to 20 metres.
2. Rule 25(b) is a useful provision, so as to show efficient lights with the minimum battery drain. Yachts with auxiliary engines must however be fitted with additional sidelights (lower down) and a sternlight and masthead light for use when under power. See also Note 3 to Rule 23.

Rule 26 *Fishing Vessels*

(a) A vessel engaged in fishing, whether underway or at anchor, shall exhibit only the lights and shapes prescribed in this Rule.

(b) A vessel when engaged in trawling, by which is meant the dragging through the water of a dredge net or other apparatus used as a fishing appliance, shall exhibit:

(i) two all-round lights in a vertical line, the upper being green and the lower white, or a shape consisting of two cones with their apexes together in a vertical line one above the other; a vessel of less than 20 metres in length may instead of this shape exhibit a basket;

(ii) a masthead light abaft of and higher than the all-round green light; a vessel of less than 50 metres in length shall not be obliged to exhibit such a light but may do so;

(iii) when making way through the water, in addition to the lights prescribed in this paragraph, sidelights and a sternlight.

(c) A vessel engaged in fishing, other than trawling, shall exhibit:

(i) two all-round lights in a vertical line, the upper being red and the lower white, or a shape consisting of two cones with apexes together in a vertical line one above the other; a vessel of less than 20 metres in length may instead of this

shape exhibit a basket;

(ii) when there is outlying gear extending more than 150 metres horizontally from the vessel, an all-round white light or a cone apex upwards in the direction of the gear;

(iii) when making way through the water, in addition to the lights prescribed in this paragraph, sidelights and a sternlight.

(d) A vessel engaged in fishing in close proximity to other vessels engaged in fishing may exhibit the additional signals described in Annex II to these Regulations.

(e) A vessel when not engaged in fishing shall not exhibit the lights or shapes prescribed in this Rule, but only those prescribed for a vessel of her length.

Notes

1. All vessels engaged in fishing show sidelights and sternlight when making way through the water, but not when stopped.
2. A fishing vessel may, in accordance with Rule 36, direct the beam of a searchlight in the direction of a danger.

Rule 27 *Vessels not under Command or Restricted in their Ability to Manoeuvre*

(a) A vessel not under command shall exhibit:

(i) two all-round red lights in a vertical line where they can best be seen;

(ii) two balls or similar shapes in a vertical line where they can best be seen;

(iii) when making way through the water, in addition to the lights prescribed in this paragraph, sidelights and a sternlight.

(b) A vessel restricted in her ability to manoeuvre, except a vessel engaged in mineclearance operations, shall exhibit:

(i) three all-round lights in a vertical line where they can best be seen. The highest and lowest of these lights shall be red and the middle light shall be white;

(ii) three shapes in a vertical line where they can best be seen. The highest and lowest of these shapes shall be balls and the middle one a diamond;

(iii) when making way through the water, a masthead light or lights, sidelights and a sternlight, in addition to the lights prescribed in sub-paragraph (i);

(iv) when at anchor, in addition to the lights or shapes prescribed in sub-paragraphs (i) and (ii), the light, lights or shape prescribed in Rule 30.

(c) A power-driven vessel engaged in a towing operation such as severely restricts the towing vessel and her tow in their ability to deviate from their course shall, in addition to the lights or shapes prescribed in Rule 24(a),

exhibit the lights or shapes prescribed in sub-paragraphs (b)(i) and (ii) of this Rule.
(d) A vessel engaged in dredging or underwater operations, when restricted in her ability to manoeuvre, shall exhibit the lights and shapes prescribed in sub-paragraphs (b)(i), (ii) and (iii) of this Rule and shall, in addition, when an obstruction exists, exhibit:
  (i) two all-round red lights or two balls in a vertical line to indicate the side on which the obstruction exists;
  (ii) two all-round green lights or two diamonds in a vertical line to indicate the side on which another vessel may pass;
  (iii) when at anchor, the lights or shapes prescribed in this paragraph instead of the lights or shape prescribed in Rule 30.
(e) Whenever the size of a vessel engaged in diving operations makes it impracticable to exhibit all lights and shapes prescribed in paragraph (d) of this Rule, the following shall be exhibited:
  (i) three all-round lights in a vertical line where they can best be seen. The highest and lowest of these lights shall be red and the middle light shall be white;
  (ii) a rigid replica of the International Code flag 'A' not less than 1 metre in height. Measures shall be taken to ensure its all-round visibility.
(f) A vessel engaged in mineclearance operations shall in addition to the lights prescribed for a power-driven vessel in Rule 23 or to the lights or shape prescribed for a vessel at anchor in Rule 30 as appropriate, exhibit three all-round green lights or three balls. One of these lights or shapes shall be exhibited near the foremast head and one at each end of the fore yard. These lights or shapes indicate that it is dangerous for another vessel to approach within 1000 metres of the mineclearance vessel.
(g) Vessels of less than 12 metres in length, except those engaged in diving operations, shall not be required to exhibit the lights and shapes prescribed in this Rule.
(h) The signals prescribed in this Rule are not signals of vessels in distress and requiring assistance. Such signals are contained in Annex IV to these Regulations.

Rule 28 *Vessels constrained by their Draught*
A vessel constrained by her draught may, in addition to the lights prescribed for power-driven vessels in Rule 23, exhibit where they can best be seen three all-round red lights in a vertical line, or a cylinder.

Rule 29 *Pilot Vessels*
(a) A vessel engaged on pilotage duty shall exhibit:

  (i) at or near the masthead, two all-round lights in a vertical line, the upper being white and the lower red;
  (ii) when underway, in addition, sidelights and a sternlight;
  (iii) when at anchor, in addition to the lights prescribed in sub-paragraph (i), the light, lights or shape prescribed in Rule 30 for vessels at anchor.
(b) A pilot vessel when not engaged on pilotage duty shall exhibit the lights or shapes prescribed for a similar vessel of her length.

Rule 30 *Anchored Vessels and Vessels aground*
(a) A vessel at anchor shall exhibit where it can best be seen:
  (i) in the fore part, an all-round white light or one ball;
  (ii) at or near the stern and at a lower level than the light prescribed in sub-paragraph (i), an all-round white light.
(b) A vessel of less than 50 metres in length may exhibit an all-round white light where it can best be seen instead of the lights prescribed in paragraph (a) of this Rule.
(c) A vessel at anchor may, and a vessel of 100 metres and more in length shall, also use the available working or equivalent lights to illuminate her decks.
(d) A vessel aground shall exhibit the lights prescribed in paragraph (a) or (b) of this Rule and in addition, where they can best be seen:
  (i) two all-round red lights in a vertical line;
  (ii) three balls in a vertical line.
(e) A vessel of less than 7 metres in length, when at anchor not in or near a narrow channel, fairway or anchorage, or where other vessels normally navigate, shall not be required to exhibit the lights or shape prescribed in paragraphs (a) and (b) of this Rule.
(f) A vessel of less than 12 metres in length, when aground, shall not be required to exhibit the lights or shapes prescribed in sub-paragraphs (d)(i) and (ii) of this Rule.

Note
As written this Rule places obligations on the great majority of yachtsmen to display anchor balls or anchor lights, the only exception (in certain circumstances) being for a boat of less than 7 metres in length (Rule 30(e)).

Rule 31 *Seaplanes*
Where it is impracticable for a seaplane to exhibit lights and shapes of the characteristics or in the positions prescribed in the Rules of this Part she shall exhibit lights and shapes as closely similar in characteristics and position as is possible.

Part D – Sound and light signals

Rule 32 *Definitions*
(a) The word 'whistle' means any sound signalling appliance capable of producing the prescribed blasts and which complies with the specifications in Annex III to these Regulations.
(b) The term 'short blast' means a blast of about one second's duration.
(c) The term 'prolonged blast' means a blast of from four to six second's duration.

Rule 33 *Equipment for Sound Signals*
(a) A vessel of 12 metres or more in length shall be provided with a whistle and a bell and a vessel of 100 metres or more in length shall, in addition, be provided with a gong, the tone and sound of which cannot be confused with that of the bell. The whistle, bell and gong shall comply with the specifications in Annex III to these Regulations. The bell or gong or both may be replaced by other equipment having the same respective sound characteristics, provided that manual sounding of the prescribed signals shall always be possible.
(b) A vessel of less than 12 metres in length shall not be obliged to carry the sound signalling appliances prescribed in paragraph (a) of this Rule but if she does not, she shall be provided with some other means of making an efficient sound signal.

Notes
1. Rule 33(b) permits vessels less than 12 metres in length to carry alternative sound signals, but they must be efficient.
2. The effectiveness of a sound signal should be judged against its audibility from the bridge of a large ship, with conflicting noise from other sources. Some sound signals carried in yachts do not measure up to this standard.

Rule 34 *Manoeuvring and Warning Signals*
(a) When vessels are in sight of one another, a power-driven vessel underway, when manoeuvring as authorized or required by these Rules, shall indicate that manoeuvre by the following signals on her whistle:
    – one short blast to mean 'I am altering my course to starboard';
    – two short blasts to mean 'I am altering my course to port';
    – three short blasts to mean 'I am operating astern propulsion'.
(b) Any vessel may supplement the whistle signals prescribed in paragraph (a) of this Rule by light signals, repeated as appropriate, whilst the manoeuvre is being carried out:
    (i) these light signals shall have the following significance:
    – one flash to mean 'I am altering my course to starboard';
    – two flashes to mean 'I am altering my course to port';
    – three flashes to mean 'I am operating astern propulsion'.
    (ii) the duration of each flash shall be about one second, the interval between flashes shall be about one second, and the interval between successive signals shall be not less than ten seconds;
    (iii) the light used for this signal shall, if fitted, be an all-round white light, visible at a minimum range of 5 miles, and shall comply with the provision of Annex I to these Regulations.
(c) When in sight of one another in a narrow channel or fairway:
    (i) a vessel intending to overtake another shall in compliance with Rule 9(e)(i) indicate her intention by the following signals on her whistle:
    – two prolonged blasts followed by one short blast to mean 'I intend to overtake you on your starboard side';
    – two prolonged blasts followed by two short blasts to mean 'I intend to overtake you on your port side';
    (ii) the vessel about to be overtaken when acting in accordance with Rule 9(e)(i) shall indicate her agreement by the following signal on her whistle:
    – one prolonged, one short, one prolonged and one short blast, in that order.
(d) When vessels in sight of one another are approaching each other and from any cause either vessel fails to understand the intentions or actions of the other, or is in doubt whether sufficient action is being taken by the other to avoid collision, the vessel in doubt shall immediately indicate such doubt by giving at least five short and rapid blasts on the whistle. Such signal may be supplemented by a light signal of at least five short and rapid flashes.
(e) A vessel nearing a bend or an area of a channel or fairway where other vessels may be obscured by an intervening obstruction shall sound one prolonged blast. Such signal shall be answered with a prolonged blast by any approaching vessel that may be within hearing around the bend or behind the intervening obstruction.
(f) If whistles are fitted on a vessel at a distance apart of more than 100 metres, one whistle only shall be used for giving manoeuvring and warning signals.

Note
1. Under Rule 34(a), three short blasts means 'I am operating astern propulsion', but this does not necessarily mean that the vessel is going astern – particularly with a large ship which may take some time to lose her way, even with the engines running astern.

Rule 35 *Sound Signals in restricted Visibility*
In or near an area of restricted visibility, whether by day or night, the signals prescribed in this Rule shall be used as follows:
(a) A power-driven vessel making way through the water shall sound at intervals of not more than 2 minutes one prolonged blast.
(b) A power-driven vessel underway but stopped and making no way through the water shall sound at intervals of not more than 2 minutes two prolonged blasts in succession with an interval of about 2 seconds between them.
(c) A vessel not under command, a vessel restricted in her ability to manoeuvre, a vessel constrained by her draught, a sailing vessel, a vessel engaged in fishing and a vessel engaged in towing or pushing another vessel shall, instead of the signals prescribed in paragraphs (a) or (b) of this Rule, sound at intervals of not more than 2 minutes three blasts in succession, namely one prolonged followed by two short blasts.
(d) A vessel engaged in fishing, when at anchor, and a vessel restricted in her ability to manoeuvre when carrying out her work at anchor, shall instead of the signals prescribed in paragraph (g) of this Rule sound the signal prescribed in paragraph (c) of this Rule.
(e) A vessel towed or if more than one vessel is towed the last vessel of the tow, if manned, shall at intervals of not more than 2 minutes sound four blasts in succession, namely one prolonged followed by three short blasts. When practicable, this signal shall be made immediately after the signal made by the towing vessel.
(f) When a pushing vessel and a vessel being pushed ahead are rigidly connected in a composite unit they shall be regarded as a power-driven vessel and shall give the signals prescribed in paragraphs (a) or (b) of this Rule.
(g) A vessel at anchor shall at intervals of not more than one minute ring the bell rapidly for about 5 seconds. In a vessel of 100 metres or more in length the bell shall be sounded in the forepart of the vessel and immediately after the ringing of the bell the gong shall be sounded rapidly for about 5 seconds in the after part of the vessel. A vessel at anchor may in addition sound three blasts in succession, namely one short, one prolonged and one short blast, to give warning of her position and of the possibility of collision to an approaching vessel.
(h) A vessel aground shall give the bell signal and if required the gong signal prescribed in paragraph (g) of this Rule and shall, in addition, give three separate and distinct strokes of the bell immediately before and after the rapid ringing of the bell. A vessel aground may in addition sound an appropriate whistle signal.
   (i) A vessel of less than 12 metres in length shall not be obliged to give the above-mentioned signals but, if she does not, shall make some other efficient sound signal at intervals of not more than 2 minutes.
   (ii) A pilot vessel when engaged on pilotage duty may in addition to the signals prescribed in paragraphs (a), (b) or (g) of this Rule sound an identity signal consisting of four short blasts.

Notes
1. A sailing vessel under way sounds one prolonged blast, followed by two short ('D').
2. Sound signals are made when a vessel is near (not necessarily in) an area of restricted visibility.
3. The maximum interval between all whistle or foghorn signals is two minutes; they should be sounded more frequently if other craft are near.

Rule 36 *Signals to attract Attention*
If necessary to attract the attention of another vessel any vessel may make light or sound signals that cannot be mistaken for any signal authorized elsewhere in these Rules, or may direct the beam of her searchlight in the direction of the danger, in such a way as not to embarrass any vessel. Any light to attract the attention of another vessel shall be such that it cannot be mistaken for any aid to navigation. For the purpose of this Rule the use of high intensity intermittent or revolving lights, such as strobe lights, shall be avoided.

Notes
1. Although a powerful torch shone on the sails, or in the general direction of an approaching vessel, may call attention to a yacht's presence, the most effective means is by a white hand flare.
2. Do not use any signal which may be mistaken for one elsewhere in the Rules, particularly distress signals. (See Rule 37 and Annex IV).
3. Strobe lights, which can be confused with a North cardinal buoy, must not be used.

Rule 37 *Distress Signals*

When a vessel is in distress and requires assistance she shall use or exhibit the signals described in Annex IV to these Regulations.

Notes

1. Some of the authorised distress signals are more suitable for yachts than others, and these are indicated in the notes to Annex IV. Distress signals for yachts are covered in more detail in 8.3.10.
2. A distress signal must only be used when a vessel is in serious and immediate danger, and when help is urgently required.

Part E – Exemptions

Rule 38 *Exemptions*

Any vessel (or class of vessels) provided that she complies with the requirements of the International Regulations for Preventing Collisions at Sea, 1960, the keel of which is laid or which is at a corresponding stage of construction before the entry into force of these Regulations may be exempted from compliance therewith as follows:

(a) The installation of lights with ranges prescribed in Rule 22, until four years after the date of entry into force of these Regulations.

(b) The installation of lights with colour specifications as prescribed in Section 7 of Annex I to these Regulations, until four years after the date of entry into force of these Regulations.

(c) The repositioning of lights as a result of conversion from Imperial to metric units and rounding off measurement figures, permanent exemption.

(d) (i) The repositioning of masthead lights on vessels of less than 150 metres in length, resulting from the prescriptions of Section 3(a) of Annex I to these Regulations, permanent exemption.

   (ii) The repositioning of masthead lights on vessels of 150 metres or more in length, resulting from the prescriptions of Section 3(a) of Annex I to these Regulations, until nine years after the date of entry into force of these Regulations.

(e) The repositioning of masthead lights resulting from the prescriptions of Section 2(b) of Annex I to these Regulations, until nine years after the date of entry into force of these Regulations.

(f) The repositioning of sidelights resulting from the prescriptions of Sections 2(g) and 3(b) of Annex I to these Regulations, until nine

years after the date of entry into force of these Regulations.

(g) The requirements for sound signal appliances prescribed in Annex III to these Regulations, until nine years after the date of entry into force of these Regulations.

(h) The repositioning of all-round lights resulting from the prescription of Section 9(b) of Annex I to these Regulations, permanent exemption.

Notes

1. This Rule allows time for changes to be made to lights and sound signalling apparatus, so that they comply to the Rules.
2. The new regulations came into force on 15 July 1977. Hence (a) and (b) above have expired.

Annex I

POSITIONING AND TECHNICAL DETAILS OF LIGHTS AND SHAPES

1. **Definition**

The term 'height above the hull' means height above the uppermost continuous deck. This height shall be measured from the position vertically beneath the location of the light.

2. **Vertical positioning and spacing of lights**

(a) On a power-driven vessel of 20 metres or more in length the masthead lights shall be placed as follows:

   (i) the forward masthead light, or if only one masthead light is carried, then that light, at a height above the hull of not less than 6 metres and, if the breadth of the vessel exceeds 6 metres, then at a height above the hull not less than such breadth, so however that the light need not be placed at a greater height above the hull than 12 metres;

   (ii) when two masthead lights are carried the after one shall be at least 4.5 metres vertically higher than the forward one.

(b) The vertical separation of masthead lights of power-driven vessels shall be such that in all normal conditions of trim the after light will be seen over and separate from the forward light at a distance of 1000 metres from the stem when viewed from sea level.

(c) The masthead light of a power-driven vessel of 12 metres but less than 20 metres in length shall be placed at a height above the gunwale of not less than 2.5 metres.

(d) A power-driven vessel of less than 12 metres in length may carry the uppermost light at a height of less than 2.5 metres above the gunwale. When however a masthead light is carried in addition to sidelights and a sternlight, then such masthead light shall be carried at least 1 metre higher than the sidelights.

(e) One of the two or three masthead lights prescribed for a power-driven vessel when engaged in towing or pushing another vessel shall be placed in the same position as either the forward masthead light or the after masthead light; provided that, if carried on the aftermast, the lowest after masthead light shall be at least 4.5 metres vertically higher than the forward masthead light.

(f) (i) The masthead light or lights prescribed in Rule 23(a) shall be so placed as to be above and clear of all other lights and obstructions except as described in sub-paragraph (ii).

   (ii) When it is impracticable to carry the all-round lights prescribed by Rule 27(b)(i) or Rule 28 below the masthead lights, they may be carried above the after masthead light(s) or vertically in between the forward masthead light(s) and after masthead light(s), provided that in the latter case the requirement of Section 3(c) of this Annex shall be complied with.

(g) The sidelights of a power-driven vessel shall be placed at a height above the hull not greater than three-quarters of that of the forward masthead light. They shall not be so low as to be interfered with by deck lights.

(h) The sidelights, if in a combined lantern and carried on a power-driven vessel of less than 20 metres in length, shall be placed not less than 1 metre below the masthead light.

(i) When the Rules prescribe two or three lights to be carried in a vertical line, they shall be spaced as follows:

   (i) on a vessel of 20 metres in length or more such lights shall be spaced not less than 2 metres apart, and the lowest of these lights shall, except where a towing light is required, be placed at a height of not less than 4 metres above the hull;

   (ii) on a vessel of less than 20 metres in length such lights shall be spaced not less than 1 metre apart and the lowest of these lights shall, except where a towing light is required, be placed at a height of not less than 2 metres above the hull;

   (iii) when three lights are carried they shall be equally spaced.

(j) The lower of the two all-round lights prescribed for a vessel when engaged in fishing shall be at a height above the sidelights not less than twice the distance between the two vertical lights.

(k) The forward anchor light prescribed in Rule 30(a)(i), when two are carried, shall not be less than 4.5 metres above the after one. On a vessel of 50 metres or more in length this forward anchor light shall be placed at a height of not less than 6 metres above the hull.

3. Horizontal positioning and spacing of lights

(a) When two masthead lights are prescribed for a power-driven vessel, the horizontal distance between them shall not be less than one half of the length of the vessel but need not be more than 100 metres. The forward light shall be placed not more than one quarter of the length of the vessel from the stem.

(b) On a power-driven vessel of 20 metres or more in length the sidelights shall not be placed in front of the forward masthead lights. They shall be placed at or near the side of the vessel.

(c) When the lights prescribed in Rule 27(b)(i) or Rule 28 are placed vertically between the forward masthead light(s) and the after masthead light(s) these all-round lights shall be placed at a horizontal distance of not less than 2 metres from the fore and aft centreline of the vessel in the athwartship direction.

4. Details of location of direction-indicating lights for fishing vessels, dredgers and vessels engaged in underwater operations

(a) The light indicating the direction of the outlying gear from a vessel engaged in fishing as prescribed in Rule 26(c)(ii) shall be placed at a horizontal distance of not less than 2 metres and not more than 6 metres away from the two all-round red and white lights. This light shall be placed not higher than the all-round white light prescribed in Rule 26(c)(i) and not lower than the sidelights.

(b) The lights and shapes on a vessel engaged in dredging or underwater operations to indicate the obstructed side and/or the side on which it is safe to pass, as prescribed in Rule 27(d)(i) and (ii), shall be placed at the maximum practical horizontal distance, but in no case less than 2 metres from the lights or shapes prescribed in Rule 27(b)(i) and (ii). In no case shall the upper of these lights or shapes be at a greater height than the lower of the three lights or shapes prescribed in Rule 27(b)(i) and (ii).

5. Screens for sidelights

The sidelights of vessels of 20 metres or more in length shall be fitted with inboard screens painted matt black, and meeting the requirements of Section 9 of this Annex. On vessels of less than 20 metres in length, the sidelights, if necessary to meet the requirements of Section 9 of this Annex, shall be fitted with inboard matt black screens. With a combined lantern, using a single vertical filament and a very narrow division between the green and red sections, external screens need not be fitted.

6. Shapes
(a) Shapes shall be black and of the following sizes:
  (i) a ball shall have a diameter of not less than 0.6 metre;
  (ii) a cone shall have a base diameter of not less than 0.6 metre and a height equal to its diameter;
  (iii) a cylinder shall have a diameter of at least 0.6 metre and a height of twice its diameter;
  (iv) a diamond shape shall consist of two cones as defined in (ii) above having a common base.
(b) The vertical distance between shapes shall be at least 1.5 metres.
(c) In a vessel of less than 20 metres in length shapes of lesser dimensions but commensurate with the size of the vessel may be used and the distance apart may be correspondingly reduced.

7. Colour specification of lights
The chromaticity of all navigation lights shall conform to the following standards, which lie within the boundaries of the area of the diagram specified for each colour by the International Commission on Illumination (CIE).

  The boundaries of the area for each colour are given by indicating the corner co-ordinates, which are as follows:
  (i) *White*
      x 0.525 0.525 0.452 0.310 0.310 0.443
      y 0.382 0.440 0.440 0.348 0.283 0.382
  (ii) *Green*
      x 0.028 0.009 0.300 0.203
      y 0.385 0.723 0.511 0.356
  (iii) *Red*
      x 0.680 0.660 0.735 0.721
      y 0.320 0.320 0.265 0.259
  (iv) *Yellow*
      x 0.612 0.618 0.575 0.575
      y 0.382 0.382 0.425 0.406

8. Intensity of lights
(a) The minimum luminous intensity of lights shall be calculated by using the formula:

$$I = 3.43 \times 10^6 \times T \times D^2 \times K^{-D}$$

where I is luminous intensity in candelas under service conditions,
      T is threshold factor 2×10^{-7} lux,
      D is range of visibility (luminous range) of the light in nautical miles,
      K is atmospheric transmissivity.
      For prescribed lights the value of K shall be 0.8, corresponding to a meteorological visibility of approximately 13 nautical miles.

(b) A selection of figures derived from the formula is given in the following table:

Range of visibility (luminous range) of light in nautical miles	Luminous intensity of light in candelas for K = 0.8
D	I
1	0.9
2	4.3
3	12
4	27
5	52
6	94

Note: The maximum luminous intensity of navigation lights should be limited to avoid undue glare. This shall not be achieved by a variable control of the luminous intensity.

9. Horizontal sectors
(a) (i) In the forward direction, sidelights as fitted on the vessel shall show the minimum required intensities. The intensities shall decrease to reach practical cut-off between 1° and 3° outside the prescribed sectors.
    (ii) For sternlights and masthead lights and at 22½° abaft the beam for sidelights, the minimum required intensities shall be maintained over the arc of the horizon up to 5° within the limits of the sectors prescribed in Rule 21. From 5° within the prescribed sectors the intensity may decrease by 50 per cent up to the prescribed limits; it shall decrease steadily to reach practical cut-off at not more than 5° outside the prescribed sectors.
(b) All-round lights shall be so located as not to be obscured by masts, topmasts or structures within angular sectors of more than 6°, except anchor lights prescribed in Rule 30, which need not be placed at an impracticable height above the hull.

10. Vertical sectors
(a) The vertical sectors of electric lights as fitted, with the exception of lights on sailing vessels shall ensure that:
    (i) at least the required minimum intensity is maintained at all angles from 5° above to 5° below the horizontal;
    (ii) at least 60 per cent of the required minimum intensity is maintained from 7½° above to 7½° below the horizontal.
(b) In the case of sailing vessels the vertical sectors of electric lights as fitted shall ensure that:
    (i) at least the required minimum intensity is maintained at all angles from 5° above to 5° below the horizontal;
    (ii) at least 50 per cent of the required minimum intensity is maintained from 25° above to 25° below the horizontal.

(c) In the case of lights other than electric these specifications shall be met as closely as possible.

11. Intensity of non-electric lights

Non-electric lights shall so far as practicable comply with the minimum intensities, as specified in the Table given in Section 8 of this Annex.

12. Manoeuvring light

Notwithstanding the provisions of paragraph 2(f) of this Annex the manoeuvring light described in Rule 34(b) shall be placed in the same fore and aft vertical plane as the masthead light or lights and, where practicable, at a minimum height of 2 metres vertically above the forward masthead light, provided that it shall be carried not less than 2 metres vertically above or below the after masthead light. On a vessel where only one masthead light is carried the manoeuvring light, if fitted, shall be carried where it can best be seen, not less than 2 metres vertically apart from the masthead light.

13. Approval

The construction of lights and shapes and the installation of lights on board the vessel shall be to the satisfaction of the appropriate authority of the State whose flag the vessel is entitled to fly.

Annex II

ADDITIONAL SIGNALS FOR FISHING VESSELS FISHING IN CLOSE PROXIMITY

1. General

The lights mentioned herein shall, if exhibited in pursuance of Rule 26(d), be placed where they can best be seen. They shall be at least 0.9 metre apart but at a lower level than lights prescribed in Rule 26(b)(i) and (c)(i). The lights shall be visible all round the horizon at a distance of at least 1 mile but at a lesser distance than the lights prescribed by these Rules for fishing vessels.

2. Signals for trawlers

(a) Vessels when engaged in trawling, whether using demersal or pelagic gear, may exhibit:
  (i) when shooting their nets:
    two white lights in a vertical line;
  (ii) when hauling their nets:
    one white light over one red light in a vertical line;
  (iii) when the net has come fast upon an obstruction:
    two red lights in a vertical line.
(b) Each vessel engaged in pair trawling may exhibit:
  (i) by night, a searchlight directed forward and in the direction of the other vessel of the pair;
  (ii) when shooting or hauling their nets or when their nets have come fast upon an obstruction, the lights prescribed in 2(a) above.

3. Signals for purse seiners

Vessels engaged in fishing with purse seine gear may exhibit two yellow lights in a vertical line. These lights shall flash alternately every second and with equal light and occultation duration. These lights may be exhibited only when the vessel is hampered by its fishing gear.

Annex III

TECHNICAL DETAILS OF SOUND SIGNAL APPLIANCES

1. Whistles

(a) *Frequencies and range of audibility*
The fundamental frequency of the signal shall lie within the range 70–700Hz.
  The range of audibility of the signal from a whistle shall be determined by those frequencies, which may include the fundamental and/or one or more higher frequencies, which lie within the range 180–700Hz (± 1 per cent) and which provide the sound pressure levels specified in paragraph 1(c) below.

(b) *Limits of fundamental frequencies*
To ensure a wide variety of whistle characteristics, the fundamental frequency of a whistle shall be between the following limits:
  (i) 70–200Hz, for a vessel 200 metres or more in length;
  (ii) 130–350Hz, for a vessel 75 metres but less than 200 metres in length;
  (iii) 250–700Hz, for a vessel less than 75 metres in length.

(c) *Sound signal intensity and range of audibility*
A whistle fitted in a vessel shall provide, in the direction of maximum intensity of the whistle and at a distance of 1 metre from it, a sound pressure level in at least one 1/3rd-octave band within the range of frequencies 180–700Hz (± 1 per cent) of not less than the appropriate figure given in the table below.

Length of vessel in metres	⅓rd-octave band level at 1 metre in dB referred to 2×10^{-5} N/m²	Audibility range in nautical miles
200 or more	143	2
75 but less than 200	138	1.5
20 but less than 75	130	1
Less than 20	120	0.5

The range of audibility in the table above is for information and is approximately the range at which a whistle may be heard on its forward axis with 90 per cent probability in conditions of still air on board a vessel having average background noise level at the listening posts (taken to be 68dB in the octave band centred on 250Hz and 63dB in the octave band centred on 500Hz).

In practice the range at which a whistle may be heard is extremely variable and depends critically on weather conditions; the values given can be regarded as typical but under conditions of strong wind or high ambient noise level at the listening post the range may be much reduced.

(d) *Directional properties*
The sound pressure level of a directional whistle shall be not more than 4dB below the prescribed sound pressure level on the axis at any direction in the horizontal plane within ±45° of the axis. The sound pressure level at any other direction in the horizontal plane shall be not more than 10dB below the prescribed sound pressure level on the axis, so that the range in any direction will be at least half the range on the forward axis. The sound pressure level shall be measured in that 1/3rd-octave band which determines the audibility range.

(e) *Positioning of whistles*
When a directional whistle is to be used as the only whistle on a vessel, it shall be installed with its maximum intensity directed straight ahead.

A whistle shall be placed as high as practicable on a vessel, in order to reduce interception of the emitted sound by obstructions and also to minimize hearing damage risk to personnel. The sound pressure level of the vessel's own signal at listening posts shall not exceed 110dB (A) and so far as practicable should not exceed 100dB (A).

(f) *Fitting of more than one whistle*
If whistles are fitted at a distance apart of more than 100 metres, it shall be so arranged that they are not sounded simultaneously.

(g) *Combined whistle systems*
If due to the presence of obstructions the sound field of a single whistle or of one of the whistles referred to in paragraph 1(f) above is likely to have a zone of greatly reduced signal level, it is recommended that a combined whistle system be fitted so as to overcome this reduction. For the purposes of the Rules a combined whistle system is to be regarded as a single whistle. The whistles of a combined system shall be located at a distance apart of not more than 100 metres and arranged to be sounded simultaneously.

The frequency of any one whistle shall differ from those of the others by at least 10Hz.

2. Bell or gong
(a) *Intensity of signal*
A bell or gong, or other device having similar sound characteristics shall produce a sound pressure level of not less than 110dB at a distance of 1 metre from it.

(b) *Construction*
Bells and gongs shall be made of corrosion-resistant material and designed to give a clear tone. The diameter of the mouth of the bell shall be not less than 300mm for vessels of 20 metres or more in length, and shall be not less than 200mm for vessels of 12 metres or more but of less than 20 metres in length. Where practicable, a powerdriven bell striker is recommended to ensure constant force but manual operation shall be possible. The mass of the striker shall be not less than 3 per cent of the mass of the bell.

3. Approval
The construction of sound signal appliances, their performance and their installation on board the vessel shall be to the satisfaction of the appropriate authority of the State whose flag the vessel is entitled to fly.

Annex IV

DISTRESS SIGNALS

1. The following signals, used or exhibited either together or separately, indicate distress and need of assistance:
   (a) a gun or other explosive signal fired at intervals of about a minute;
   (b) a continuous sounding with any fog-signalling apparatus;
   (c) rockets or shells, throwing red stars fired one at a time at short intervals;
   (d) a signal made by radiotelegraphy or by any other signalling method consisting of the group ··· ─── ··· (SOS) in the Morse code;
   (e) a signal sent by radiotelephony consisting of the spoken word 'Mayday';
   (f) the International Code Signal of distress indicated by N.C.;
   (g) a signal consisting of a square flag having above or below it a ball or anything resembling a ball;
   (h) flames on the vessel (as from a burning tar barrel, oil barrel, etc.);
   (i) a rocket parachute flare or a hand flare showing a red light;
   (j) a smoke signal giving off orange-coloured smoke;
   (k) slowly and repeatedly raising and lowering arms outstretched to each side;

(l)   the radiotelegraph alarm signal;

(m) the radiotelephone alarm signal;

(n)   signals transmitted by emergency position-indicating radio beacons.

2. The use or exhibition of any of the foregoing signals except for the purpose of indicating distress and need of assistance and the use of other signals which may be confused with any of the above signals is prohibited.

3. Attention is drawn to the relevant sections of the International Code of Signals, the Merchant Ship Search and Rescue Manual and the following signals:

(a)   a piece of orange-coloured canvas with either a black square and circle or other appropriate symbol (for identification from the air);

(b)   a dye marker.

Notes

1. A distress signal must only be made when a vessel is in serious and immediate danger, and help is urgently required.

2. Of those listed above, the following are the ones more suited to yachts and small craft, and their use is more fully described under 'Safety' in 8.3.10, (b), (d), (e), (f), (g), (i), (j) and (k).

3. With reference to 1.(l) above, the radiotelegraph alarm signal is a series of twelve four-second dashes with intervals of one second.

4. With reference to 1.(m) above, the radiotelephone alarm signal is two audio tones transmitted alternately at a frequency of 2200Hz and 1300Hz for a duration of 30 seconds to one minute.

5. With reference to 1.(n) above, the signal is either as in 4. above, or a series of single tones at a frequency of 1300Hz.

2.2 Limits and Dangers

Although we talk about the 'freedom of the sea', yachtsmen should recognise that limits and restrictions are imposed by international agreements or by national decrees. These brief notes do not give full legal coverage of these matters: subjects such as international waters and fishing limits are complicated and liable to international dispute.

2.2.1 Territorial waters

Countries may exercise sovereignty over the territorial sea along their coasts, but the width varies as does the method of measurement. In general (as in the United Kingdom) the baseline is the low water line along the coasts of the mainland and islands. Deep bays may be closed by a line up to 24 miles (38km) in length across the entrance, or at a point where the bay narrows to that distance. Coasts which are deeply indented or with a fringe of islands, such as the west coast of Scotland, may have a system of straight baselines.

Waters on the landward side of these baselines are internal waters, over which the country concerned has sovereignty. In the territorial sea foreign vessels have the right of innocent passage but must obey laws and regulations of the state concerned. Innocent passage does not allow anchoring except where necessary for ordinary navigation or due to force majeure or distress.

The table in fig. 2(8) shows the breadth of sea claimed by various countries as territorial waters and as fishing limits (see below).

2.2.2 Fishing limits

Most states control fishing for 200 miles (322km) from the baselines referred to in 2.2.1. The UK (like other European countries) exercises fisheries jurisdiction to 200 miles (322km) from the territorial sea baselines, or to a median line with other countries where that line is less than 200 miles (322km).

The UK also claims a 6 mile (10km) exclusive fishing zone round its coasts, and a further 6-mile zone where only certain countries are allowed to fish in particular areas.

Country	Claimed widths (miles)	
	Territorial waters	Fishing jurisdiction
Albania[1]	15	15
Algeria, Egypt[1], Italy[1], Monaco, Poland, Tunisia, Yugoslavia[1]	12	12
Belgium, Denmark[1], West Germany[1], Irish Republic[1], Netherlands, UK[1]	3	200
Finland[1]	4	12
France[1], Iceland[1], Morocco, Portugal[1], Spain[1], Sweden[1], USSR[1]	12	200
Greece, Israel, Lebanon	6	6
Libya	12	20
Malta	12	25
Norway[1]	4	200
Turkey[1]	6	12

Note: [1]Uses straight baseline systems along either all or part of the coast

Fig. 2(8) Claimed distances for territorial waters and fisheries jurisdiction.

2.2.3 Fishing vessels

Yachtsmen should remember that, whether under sail or power, a yacht must keep clear of a vessel trawling or fishing. Such vessels should show the shapes or lights as in Rule 26 of the Collision Regulations (see 2.1). Fishing boats are often very insistent as to their rights and it is best to give them a wide berth.

Particular concentrations of fishing vessels round the coasts of Britain are likely to be met as outlined below. Keep a good look-out, and remember that drift nets may extend a mile or more – usually to windward of the fishing boat.

(1) *England – South Coast*. Single and pair trawlers may be met between the Scillies and Start Point, generally within 12 miles (19km) of the coast from September to March. Hand line boats fish in this area throughout the year. Pots and nets are placed in areas all along the south coast, sometimes 15 miles (24km) offshore. Oyster dredgers operate in the Western Solent.

(2) *England – East Coast*. Fixed fishing gear is often met up to 12 miles (19km) offshore, from north Norfolk to the Scottish border.

(3) *England – North-East Coast*. Concentrations of vessels fishing for sprats may be met from October to March, up to 75 miles (120km) offshore between 53° 00′ N and 55° 30′ N. Small fishing boats with salmon drift nets may be concentrated from April to August up to 6 miles (10km) offshore between Whitby and Holy Island.

(4) *England – North West Coast*. Concentrations of fishing boats, mostly single and pair trawlers, may be met during August and September within 12 miles (19km) of land between Chicken Rock and Douglas. Concentrations of trawlers may be met up to 25 miles (40km) west of Morecambe light-buoy in April/May and from mid-August to October.

(5) *Scotland*. Concentrations of vessels fishing for mackerel and herring may be met June–December in the Minches and Firth of Clyde, and outside the Hebrides.

2.2.4 Surveying ships

While surveying, these display the signals prescribed in Rule 27(b) of the Collision Regulations, and may also show International Code group 'IR' ('I am engaged in submarine survey work. Keep clear of me and go slow'). During this work a survey ship may proceed across shipping lanes, and may tow instruments up to 900ft (300m) astern.

Vessels undertake seismic surveys while exploring for oil or gas; they may tow a detector cable up to 2 miles (3.2km) astern and initiate harmless explosions.

2.2.5 Measured distances

Around the coast are measured distances, shown on charts and in Sailing Directions, where vessels run speed trials and calibrate logs, etc. Such vessels fly the International Code flags 'SM', and should be given a wide berth – including the turning area each end of the run.

2.2.6 Hovercraft

Hovercraft may be met in coastal waters, or further offshore. Since they can be blown sideways by the wind, their aspect may not indicate their true direction of travel. At night or in poor visibility they show a quick-flashing yellow light. Their noise may make sound signals inaudible.

2.2.7 Dracones

Dracones are flexible oil barges, which float very low in the water and are difficult to see. By day the towing vessel shows a black diamond shape, and the dracone (or last dracone, if more than one) tows a float with a similar shape. By night the towing vessel shows the lights prescribed by the Collision Regulations, and may illuminate the tow by searchlight. The dracone (or last dracone) tows a float with a white all-round light.

2.2.8 Incinerator vessels

Vessels burning chemical waste may be met in areas designated on charts and in Sailing Directions. These vessels have limited manoeuvrability, and show the signals prescribed in Rule 27(b) of the Collision Regulations. Avoid the noxious fumes by passing to windward.

2.2.9 Navigational aids

Take care when passing navigational buoys, Lanbys, light-vessels, etc. Larger ships are asked to be vigilant due to the damage they can cause to such aids, possibly with serious consequences for other vessels. In the case of yachts, however, it is more likely to be the yacht which will be damaged by any collision. Nevertheless, any contact should be reported at once (e.g. via HM Coastguard or the nearest coast radio station) in case damage has been done to the navigational aid. It is an offence to make fast to any navigational buoy, Lanby, light-vessel, etc.

2.2.10 Warships on exercises

Yachtsmen should realise the possible danger in approaching a formation of warships, or other vessels in convoy, too closely. Warships operating aircraft may have to steer as dictated by the wind, when they will show the lights or shapes as in Rule 27(b) of the Collision Regulations. Aircraft carriers may have masthead lights displaced to one side of the vessel, normally to starboard, while their sidelights may be each side of the hull or each side of the island. At night they may use red or white flight deck lighting. Due to their configuration, some other warships cannot comply fully with the requirements for navigation lights.

Warships replenishing at sea are connected to auxiliary vessels by jackstays and hoses, and are restricted in manoeuvrability and speed. They display the appropriate signals in Rule 27(b), and other vessels must keep well clear.

2.2.11 Practice and exercise areas

Areas for firing or bombing exercises, and for other defence exercises, occur round the United

Kingdom, and in many other parts of the world. Those in Home Waters are shown on six small scale Admiralty charts of the PEXA series. In general, details of these areas are not shown on charts or in navigational publications, except for such range beacons, lights or buoys which may help navigation. Practice areas are marked by yellow buoys with two red stripes intersecting at the top, and the letters 'DZ' in black on the sides.

An annual *Notice to Mariners* describes the sorts of practices carried out. Warning signals, if given, are usually red flags by day, and fixed or flashing red lights by night. Range authorities are responsible for ensuring that the area is clear, and that there is no danger to vessels in the vicinity. If a yacht finds herself in an area where practices or exercises are in progress she should, if possible, maintain her course and speed; but if she is not able to do this for navigational reasons, she should clear the area as quickly as possible.

2.2.12 Submarines

Submarines may be encountered anywhere at sea, not just in designated Submarine Exercise Areas. The masthead lights and sidelights of submarines are placed well forward, and low above the water; similarly the stern light, which may be obscured by spray or wash. Some submarines carry an additional yellow quick-flashing light above the after masthead light.

International Code group 'NE2' flown by a surface ship indicates that submarines are in the vicinity. A submarine below periscope depth occasionally streams red and yellow or red and white floats on the surface astern of her. The following pyrotechnics and smoke signals may be used by submerged submarines:

Smoke	Signifies
White smoke candle (with or without flame or dye). Yellow smoke candles. Green flares launched about 50ft (15m) into the air, burning for about 10 secs.	Indicates position in response to request from ship or aircraft.
Red flares or smoke (may be accompanied by other smoke candles).	Keep clear, am carrying out emergency surfacing procedure. Do not stop propellers. Clear the area. Stand by to give help.
Alternate red flare/ white smoke.	Submarine in distress. Take action as above. Keep clear.
Two white or yellow smoke candles released singly about 3 minutes apart.	Keep clear. Am preparing to surface. Do not stop propellers. Clear the immediate vicinity.

A submarine unable to surface will show her position by:
(1) Releasing an indicator buoy (with a whip aerial) on the end of a long wire, which must not be broken. See below.
(2) Firing yellow, red or white smoke candles. Some are fitted with a dye marker and a message carrier.
(3) Pumping out fuel, lubricating oil.
(4) Blowing out air.

A submarine indicator buoy is orange, cylindrical, and marked by a serial number and the words 'Finder inform Navy, Coastguard or Police. Do not secure to or touch'. A light flashes once a second, for about 60 hours. An automatic distress signal 'SOS – SUBSUNK' is transmitted on 4340kHz for about 36 hours.

A submarine indicator buoy should not be confused with a sonobuoy, dropped by aircraft to detect submarines. A British sonobuoy is a thinner and longer cylinder, and although it has a whip aerial it does not have a light or the marking described above.

2.2.13 Mine countermeasures – exercises

Minelaying and mine countermeasures exercises are normally confined to certain areas, published in *Notices to Mariners* each year. Harmless practice mines which lie on the bottom and eject red, green or white flares may be used.

The lights shown by mine clearance vessels are in Rule 27(f) of the Collision Regulations. Minehunters show the lights prescribed for a vessel restricted in her ability to manoeuvre, and usually work with small craft from which divers may be operating. Such craft exhibit Flag 'A' of the International Code. The mine hunter shows Flag 'A' by day when divers are operating, or signals the letter 'A' by flashing light at night if approached by other vessels. Yachts should keep well clear of such operations, which may extend 3300ft (1000m) from the minehunter.

Minesweeping and minehunting operations require the laying of small buoys, usually fitted with a radar reflector, which may have numeral or alphabetical flags attached. At night such buoys are illuminated with green, white or red flashing lights, which are visible for about 1 mile (1.6km).

2.2.14 Minefields

Most of the minefields laid during World War II have been swept, but in a few areas mines can still be a hazard – as may uncharted wrecks or shoals therein which have not been surveyed. Any drifting mine that is seen is likely to be a lost exercise mine, but it should be reported. Do not try to recover it or take it in tow.

2.2.15 Wrecks

Under the Protection of Wrecks Act, 1973, some wrecks are protected due to their historical or archaeological significance. It is prohibited to anchor in these areas, or to dive, or to tamper with any part of the wreck. Certain dangerous wrecks are also designated prohibited areas under the same Act. These sites are shown on charts and in Sailing Directions, and are listed in a *Notice to Mariners,* published annually.

2.2.16 Offshore oil and gas fields

Where preliminary surveys show the possibility of oil or gas in commercial quantities, a drilling rig is used to drill test wells. These rigs are large structures, marked by lights and fog signals, and there may be lighters and other support vessels moored nearby, with mooring wires extending a mile from the rig itself. These rigs are moved from place to place and hence their positions are not charted, although they may be promulgated in *Temporary Notices to Mariners* or broadcast in Navigational Warnings from coast radio stations. Three main types of drilling rig are used:

(1) Jack-up rigs are towed into position, the steel legs are lowered to the sea bed, and the drilling platform is then jacked-up above sea level. They are used in shallower waters.

(2) Semi-submersible rigs float on submerged caissons, and some are self-propelled. They are used in depths up to about 1000ft (300m).

(3) Drillships are used in deeper waters, where mooring is impossible, and are kept precisely in position by electronic station-keeping gear which actuates a number of propellers round the vessels. By these means drillships can be used in depths of 8000 ft (2500m) or more.

Several exploration wells may be drilled to establish the extent of a field. Those wells not required are sealed, while others are capped with pipes etc. projecting above the sea bed, and are marked on charts as 'Well' or 'Wellhead'.

When oil or gas is to be extracted from a field, a production platform is installed. These massive structures are shown on charts and in Sailing Directions, and are marked by lights and usually by fog signals. They may have mooring points for tankers, or mooring buoys and other dangers a mile or more away.

Permanent platforms are marked by lights flashing Morse 'U' every 15 seconds, while fog signals sound Morse 'U' every 30 seconds. Corners of the platform not marked by the main light are marked by red lights flashing Morse 'U'.

Under international law safety zones of up to 1690ft (500m) are established round drilling rigs, production platforms and single point moorings (SPM). Yachts must not enter these zones except to save life, or on account of stress of weather or if in distress.

2.2.17 Submarine cables

Cables, sometimes carrying high voltage, are laid in coastal waters and are shown on charts. Damage to such cables can be very costly, and yachts should avoid anchoring near them. If a yacht fouls a cable, every effort should be made to clear it by normal means, but great care must be taken not to damage the cable. If necessary the anchor warp or cable should be buoyed and slipped, but in no circumstances should the cable be cut or damaged.

2.2.18 Overhead power cables

In various estuaries and rivers high-voltage overhead cables present a serious danger to craft passing underneath. Depending on the voltage concerned, a safety margin should be allowed for the possible discharge of electric current to the mast of a yacht.

The elevation of cables (and similar obstructions) is shown on charts as the height above Mean High Water Springs (MHWS). Spurious radar echoes can be received, and can easily be misinterpreted, when passing under power cables.

2.2.19 Traffic separation schemes

Under Rule 10 of the *International Regulations for Preventing Collisions at Sea (1972)* it is a legal requirement to observe traffic separation schemes which have been adopted by the International Maritime Organization (IMO).

Separation schemes are essential for the safety of larger ships, and while they may at times be inconvenient for yachtsmen they must be accepted as another element of passage planning, and should be avoided where possible.

Separation schemes are marked on Admiralty charts but are liable to detailed amendment and should be kept up to date from *Notices to Mariners.* Those schemes currently in force around the British Isles are summarised in *The Macmillan & Silk Cut Nautical Almanac.*

Rule 10 is stated in full in 2.1 (*International Regulations for Preventing Collisions at Sea*). It should be clearly understood that the whole of Rule 10 is applicable to yachts.

Contrary to the impression gained by some people, traffic separation schemes and Rule 10 do not modify the Collision Regulations when two vessels meet or converge. If for example a vessel is proceeding under power down a traffic

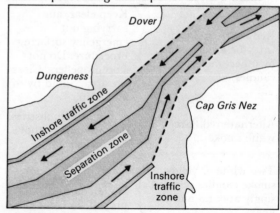

Fig. 2(9) Traffic separation scheme – Dover Strait.

lane, and another vessel which is crossing that lane appears on a collision course on her starboard bow, then the vessel in the lane is obliged to keep clear – just as if she had been in mid-ocean. The crossing vessel however, if less than 65ft (20m) in length or a sailing vessel, would in this case have infringed para (j) of Rule 10. In this context the words 'shall not impede' may be taken to mean 'shall navigate in such a way as to avoid the development of risk of collision'. If however a situation develops so as to involve risk of collision, then the relevant steering and sailing Rules must be complied with.

A sailing yacht beating to windward must keep to the correct lane, so that she is proceeding 'in the general direction of traffic flow'. Even so she must not 'impede' the safe passage of a power-driven vessel following the lane. She must certainly not beat to windward in the wrong lane – against the traffic flow.

If there is much traffic it would be more prudent to motor to windward along the correct lane, rather than tack backwards and forwards with the risk of impeding some vessel. Alternatively it may be better still to use the inshore traffic zone, to which there is no objection provided that the yacht keeps well clear of the boundary of the adjacent lane.

Should it be necessary to cross a traffic lane, do so heading at as near right angles as possible regardless of tidal stream – thereby reducing the time crossing to the minimum and also presenting a clear aspect to lane users – who again must not be impeded. In a sailing yacht, if the wind falls light and speed drops much below three knots, the engine should be used if one is fitted.

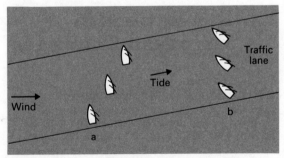

Fig. 2(10) When crossing a traffic lane, and considering the effects of wind and tide, (a) is the correct course – steering at right angles to the traffic lane, crossing as quickly as possible, and presenting a clear aspect to other lane users.

It is accepted that, due to leeway and/or tidal stream, when maintaining a *heading* at right angles to the traffic flow a yacht's *track* (as seen for example on a shore radar set) may not be at right angles to the traffic flow, but no official action will result from any identification made if it is evident that the yacht made every effort to steer the required course.

In order to comply with traffic separation schemes, accurate navigation is important, so that a yacht knows exactly where she is in relation to traffic lanes, etc.

Note that 'YG' in the *International Code* means 'You appear not to be complying with the traffic separation scheme'. There are heavy financial penalties for breaking the rules.

2.3 HM Customs

2.3.1 General information

Yachts arriving in or departing from the UK from or to places abroad must conform to the regulations contained in Customs Notice No. 8 (March 1984) which is summarised below. Copies of this notice, the forms mentioned, and further information may be obtained from any Customs and Excise office or from HM Customs and Excise, Dorset House, Stamford Street, London SE1 9PS (Tel: 01-928 0533). Yachts moving between the Isle of Man and the United Kingdom are not subject to the requirements of Customs Notice No. 8.

Yachtsmen are warned that a boat may be searched at any time; everything obtained abroad must be declared; nothing must be landed or transferred to another vessel until permission is given or the reporting formalities completed; all animals or birds must be securely confined below and out of contact with any other animals, and not landed except when licensed by an officer representing the Ministry of Agriculture, Fisheries and Food; the penalties for smuggling are severe and may include forfeiture of the boat.

2.3.2 Notice of departure

Each intended departure from the UK must be notified to HM Customs on Part I of Form C1328, copies of which are available at Customs offices (see 2.3.10) and from most yacht clubs, etc. The form is in three parts. When completed Part I must be posted or delivered to the Customs office nearest the place of departure, so as to arrive before departure. It is valid for up to 48 hours after the stated time of departure. Should the voyage be abandoned, Parts II and III should be posted or delivered to the same office marked 'voyage abandoned'. Failure to give notice of departure may result in delay and inconvenience on return, and may lead to prosecution.

2.3.3 Stores

In general there is no restriction on reasonable quantities of food, fuel and other stores on which all duties and VAT have been paid. Duty free stores are normally restricted to vessels of 40 tons net register or more, but may be allowed for smaller yachts proceeding south of Brest or north of the Eider – details can be obtained from any

Customs office. No other goods may be shipped unless all customs and export procedures are met.

2.3.4 Immigration

The skipper must ensure that the presence of any non-patrials (people not having the right to live in the UK) is reported to the immigration authorities – usually represented by the Customs officer. To take advantage of the quick report procedure (see 2.3.7), for yachts proceeding to places outside the Channel Islands, Republic of Ireland or Isle of Man, all persons on board must carry a valid passport.

2.3.5 Arrivals

On arrival from abroad (including the Channel Islands and the Republic of Ireland) yachts are subject to Customs control, and the skipper must make a written report on Form C1328. The skipper is also responsible for conforming to public and animal health and immigration requirements. Health regulations are stated in Form Port 38, Appendix A to Customs Notice No. 8, whereby any death, illness, infectious disease, animal, bird, etc. on board must be reported. The signal 'QQ', or by night a red light over a white light, means 'I require health clearance'. See 6.4.2.

On entering UK waters from abroad a yellow flag ('Q' in the International Code) must be flown, and be illuminated at night, until formalities are completed. Within two hours of arrival notify a Customs officer in person or as follows. Where Freefone applies notification must be by phone. Elsewhere first ring the nearest office. Where an answering machine operates notify names of yacht and yourself, time and date of arrival, where lying, whether eligible for full or short report (below), whether animals or birds on board. If no reply ring nearest alternative office. If contact cannot be made as above, deposit completed Part II of Form C1328 in Customs office letter box.

2.3.6 Full report

The full report procedure is applicable if duty and/or VAT is payable on the vessel; or if the vessel has goods on which duty and/or VAT is payable; or has had repairs/modifications done abroad; or has on board any animal or bird, or goods which are prohibited or restricted; or non-patrials or patrial without a passport (except from Channel Isles or Ireland); or the vessel left the UK more than one year previously; or was not cleared outwards on Part I of Form C1328; or has any death or notifiable illness on board. Under the above circumstances the skipper must make a full report by completing Parts II and III of Form C1328 and awaiting the arrival of a Customs Officer.

2.3.7 Quick report

When none of the conditions in the previous

paragraph apply, and animal and health clearance is not required, the skipper is to complete Parts II and III of Form C1328. If the yacht is not visited by a Customs officer within two hours of notifying arrival, deliver Part II to the Customs office concerned (or post it) and retain Part III for reference. All patrials (and non-patrials arriving from the Republic of Ireland and the Channel Islands) may then proceed ashore.

2.3.8 Arrival after 2300

If arriving between 2300 and 0600 and you do not wish to leave the yacht then, providing that there are no animals or birds on board, notification of arrival and making a full or quick report may be delayed until 0800.

2.3.9 Light dues

Yachts of 20 tons and above are liable to an annual payment for light dues, and Customs officers may enquire about such payments. The tonnage limit is determined by register tonnage for a registered vessel, or by Thames measurement if unregistered.

2.3.10 HM Customs – telephone numbers

The telephone number of the appropriate Customs office (HM Customs in the United Kingdom, and the equivalent overseas) is shown for each port entry in Chapter 10 of *The Macmillan & Silk Cut Nautical Almanac*, published annually.

2.4 Regulations in European Countries

2.4.1 General

Before cruising to any foreign country it is necessary to be aware of the various formalities required, which are likely to include the items listed below. Brief notes on countries in Europe are given below. More detailed information can be obtained from the RYA booklets C1, C2 and C3 (*Planning for Going Foreign*) or from the London tourist office of the country concerned.

(1) It is essential to conform to British Customs requirements, as stated in 2.3.

(2) The yacht must either be registered (a definite requirement for France) or carry the International Certificate for Pleasure Navigation (see 1.5.4).

(3) The yacht should in any case be insured, but some countries insist on Third Party cover.

(4) A few countries insist on the skipper holding a Certificate of Competence (see 1.5.5), in particular for inland waterways.

(5) Take passports for all the crew, plus any special vaccination certificates that may exceptionally be needed. It is necessary to comply with health and immigration regulations – reporting any infectious disease, for example.

(6) Customs formalities vary in different countries, and it is the skipper's responsibility to find out what they are and to conform. In most countries it is obligatory to fly Flag 'Q' on arrival, particularly if carrying more dutiable stores than the normal 'tourist' allowance, and if in doubt this is the safest procedure. Possibly the Customs officer will visit the yacht, but more probably the skipper will need to go to the Customs office on arrival, and produce documents such as the certificate of registry and the passports of the crew. It is useful to carry duplicated lists showing the names of the persons on board and their passport numbers.

In general Customs authorities in EEC countries allow yachts to carry small quantities of dutiable alcohol and tobacco (to the scale allowed for tourists), but larger amounts are liable to be sealed under bond. It is possible to embark duty free stores in some countries, but care must be taken to comply with the regulations. For example, in France, if subsequently visiting another French port, any duty free stores previously embarked must be declared.

In some countries it is a requirement to clear Customs outwards, on final departure.

(7) A British-owned yacht should wear the Red Ensign (or a special ensign, if eligible – see 6.7.2) in foreign waters, and also a courtesy ensign for the country concerned. Flag 'Q' must be carried in order to comply with Customs formalities.

(8) Some countries (e.g. France, Greece) have strict rules about foreign yachts being used for any form of commercial activity, such as charter. In France it is even illegal to lend a yacht to somebody else.

(9) It is necessary to conform to any local regulations concerning radiotelephone transmissions in foreign harbours.

(10) Some countries, very sensibly, have regulations about putting any form of waste over the side, and require gash to be deposited only in special dumps ashore.

(11) So far as logistics are concerned, it is necessary to consider matters such as galley fuel, since Continental gas cylinders are different from those generally used in Britain see 14.1.13.

2.4.2 Belgium

Fly flag 'Q' at port of entry. The yacht may be boarded by Customs officers (in khaki) and/or Immigration officers (in blue uniform). There are special formalities and charges for yachts staying more than two months.

Belgian National Tourist Office, 38 Dover Street, London, W1X 3RB. Tel: (01) 499 5379.

2.4.3 Denmark

Dutiable stores in excess of the normal EEC tourist allowance must be declared, and will be put under seal.

Danish Tourist Board, Sceptre House, 169/173 Regent Street, London, W1. Tel: (01) 734 2637.

2.4.4 Federal Republic of Germany

Clear Customs at Borkum, Norderney, Norddeich, Wilhelmshaven, Bremerhaven or Cuxhaven. It is not necessary to fly flag 'Q' coming from EEC or from Scandinavia; go ashore and report to Customs (Zoll). If only intending to transit Kiel Canal (for which special rules apply, obtainable at locks) it is not necessary to clear Customs, but fly Third Substitute. A Certificate of Competence is recommended for the inland waterways.

German National Tourist Office, 61 Conduit Street, London, W1. Tel: (01) 734 2600.

2.4.5 Finland

There is strict control over routes to harbours for Customs inspection and passport control, and many areas are prohibited to yachts. Government vessels may stop and search yachts ('L' in International Code), and actively enforce the various regulations. Any excess alcohol or tobacco over normal 'tourist' allowance must be declared on entry. Wines and spirits can only be bought from Government liquor stores.

Finnish Tourist Board UK Office, 66 Haymarket, London, SW1. Tel: (01) 839 4048.

2.4.6 France

British yachts visiting France must be registered. A private owner taking his yacht to France qualifies for six months *Importation en Franchise Temporaire* (IFT), with no duty payable. But if he stays on board longer in French waters, the yacht becomes liable to TVA (French VAT) and to an annual tax called *Droit de Passeport*. To qualify for IFT the yacht should normally be skippered by the owner: while in France she must not be chartered, or even lent. Crew members must not contribute to running expenses. Special regulations apply to yachts chartered from outside France, and to yacht deliveries.

It is not necessary to fly flag 'Q', or to clear Customs on entry, if the purpose of the visit is legitimate and no goods are carried which should be declared.

If duty free goods are to be embarked, it is necessary to obtain a *Passeport du Navire Etrangé*.

If subsequently visiting any other French port, it is essential to declare such stores.

French Government Tourist Office, 178 Piccadilly, London, W1V 0AL. Tel: (01) 491 7622.

2.4.7 Greece

On arrival it is necessary to fly flag 'Q', and to clear at one of the designated harbours where there are Customs and Immigration officers. It is necessary to wear a Greek courtesy ensign. For a fee, the yacht is issued with a Transit Log, which is completed with various details of the boat and her crew. The Transit Log must be produced as required by harbour authorities, and returned when clearing outwards at the end of the visit. Foreign yachts must not be chartered in Greek waters.

National Tourist Organisation of Greece, 195/197 Regent Street, London, W1R 8DL. Tel: (01) 734 5997.

2.4.8 Irish Republic

Yachts from abroad (whether or not with dutiable stores) must fly flag 'Q' by day or show a red light over a white light by night, and report to local Customs (or Civic Guard, where no Customs officer is stationed). Further details from the Revenue Commissioners, Dublin Castle, Dublin 2. No passports are required by UK citizens.

Yachts imported temporarily for pleasure purposes only by visitors whose only or principal place of residence is outside Ireland may be imported free of value added tax for a period of 12 months from the date of importation.

Bord Failte Eireann (Irish Tourist Board), Ireland House, 150 New Bond Street, London, W1Y 0AQ. Tel: (01) 493 3201.

2.4.9 Italy

On arrival it is necessary to obtain a *Costituto* from local Customs. This requires ship's papers, passports of the crew together with a nominal list giving dates of birth, and sometimes a certificate of insurance. The *Costituto* has to be shown at subsequent ports, and surrendered on final departure. Foreign yachts are taxed while in Italian waters, at a daily rate based on tonnage. Foreign yachts must not be chartered.

Italian State Tourist Office, 201 Regent Street, London, W1R 8AY. Tel: (01) 439 2311.

2.4.10 Netherlands

On arrival, report to Customs with documentation and passports to obtain entry certificate, to be retained on board. Fly flag 'Q' if dutiable goods are carried. Yachts should carry the Vaarreglement (collision regulations, etc.), and also (where applicable) the special regulations which apply to the Rivers Rhine, Lek and Waal.

Netherlands Tourist Office, 143 New Bond Street, London, W1. Tel: (01) 499 9367.

2.4.11 Norway

On arrival, report to the Customs (Toll) at one of the larger harbours. Excess liquor and tobacco will be sealed in a suitable locker. In Norway wines and spirits are only available from state liquor shops, and it is an offence to sell or give liquor to a local. It is important to clear Customs outwards on departure.

Norwegian National Tourist Office, 20 Pall Mall, London, SW1Y 5NE. Tel: (01) 839 6255.

2.4.12 Portugal

On arrival, report to Customs and Immigration offices with documentation of the yacht and passports of the crew.

Portuguese National Tourist Office, 1 New Bond Street, London, W1. Tel: (01) 493 3873.

2.4.13 Spain

Fly flag 'Q' on arrival. It is probable that the yacht will be boarded by an official: if not, seek out the Customs office. British yachts visiting Spain must be registered. A licence is required to charter the yacht while she is in Spanish waters.

Spanish National Tourist Office, 57/58 St James's Street, London, SW1. Tel: (01) 499 0901.

2.4.14. Sweden

Entry must be made through one of the main harbours which have Customs and passport control. On leaving it is necessary to go through passport control, but not Customs unless carrying stores or goods which must be declared. Alcohol and tobacco in excess of the normal tourist allowance may be sealed up on board, or even put ashore. There are strict import restrictions on various items, including live animals. There are some prohibited (military) areas.

Swedish Travel Bureau, c/o Norwegian State Railways, 21 Cockspur Street, London, SW1. Tel: (01) 930 6666.

2.4.15 Turkey

On arrival it is necessary to visit the offices of the Health Authority, Police, Port Captain and Customs – in that order. The same officials must be visited before departure.

Turkish Tourist Office, 49 Conduit Street, London, W1R 0EP. Tel: (01) 734 8681.

2.4.16 Yugoslavia

It is necessary to enter at one of the nominated ports. Fly flag 'Q', and courtesy ensign. If the yacht is not boarded, the skipper should go to the Harbour Office. Full documentation, including a Certificate of Competence, is required. A Permit of Navigation, which has to be stamped by the Harbour master and by the Customs officer, will be issued for a fee. This Permit may be asked for at subsequent harbours visited: it lists certain prohibited areas.

Yugoslav National Tourist Office, 143 Regent Street, London, W1R 8AE. Tel: (01) 734 5243.

2.5 Yacht tonnage measurement

The principal types of tonnage, as applied to yachts are as follows. Despite the use of the word 'ton', only two of them (displacement and deadweight) refer in any way to the weight of the boat, and deadweight tonnage is seldom if ever used in respect of yachts.

2.5.1 Displacement

This is the actual weight of the yacht, or more correctly the weight of the water displaced by her which is of course the same thing. Displacement varies depending on how the boat is loaded – whether she is fully stored and full of fuel and water for example.

An approximate formula for displacement (in tons) is:

$$\frac{L \times B \times D \times C_b}{35}$$

where L = waterline length in feet, B = waterline beam in feet and D = draught amidships in feet, and C_b is the Block Coefficient.

The Block Coefficient is the ratio of the immersed volume of the hull to the volume of the cube formed by the waterline length, the maximum beam and the draught (excluding the keel). It is typically about 0.45 for a boat of moderate displacement, but less for modern light displacement types.

In metric units displacement in tonnes is:

$$L \times B \times D \times C_b \times 1.025$$

where the measurements are expressed in metres.

Displacement can be calculated much more accurately from the lines of the boat, by taking the areas of the different sections and applying Simpson's First Rule. This is a method of obtaining the approximate area under a curve, where there are an odd number of ordinates, equally spaced, of known quantities. The area equals the sum of the first and last ordinates, plus twice the sum of the remaining odd ordinates, plus four times the sum of the even ordinates, the whole being multiplied by one-third the distance between the ordinates.

2.5.2 Thames Measurement (TM)

This is an approximation of the internal capacity of the yacht. The formula (unique to this country) was evolved by the Royal Thames Yacht Club in 1854, and amended in 1962.

$$\text{Tonnage (TM)} = \frac{(L - B) \times B^2}{188}$$

where L = the length from the forward side of the stem at deck level to the aft side of the stern-post at deck level. (Where the stern-post does not extend to deck level, the measurement is taken to the prolongation of the aft side of the stern-post,

or the centre line of the rudder stock at deck level. If there is no stern-post or fixed rudder stock, or if the rudder stock is wholly abaft the transom, the measurement shall be taken to the aft side of the transom at deck level).
B = maximum beam, excluding rubbing strakes, chain plates or other protrusions.

The measurements are taken in feet and decimals of a foot, and the resulting tonnage is expressed to the nearest ton. The rule does not apply to yachts with more than one hull.

2.5.3 Net and Gross Tonnages

These terms apply to the official registered tonnage of yachts which appear on the registry. Since 1 June 1975 new regulations have applied to the calculation of tonnage for British registered yachts under 13.7m (45ft) in length, so that only one tonnage is now computed and this is known as registered tonnage. This tonnage may be measured by surveyors of Lloyd's Register of Shipping (Lloyds Register of Shipping, Yacht and Small Craft Department, 69 Oxford Street, Southampton, SO1 1DL), or of the Yacht Brokers, Designers and Surveyors Association (The Wheelhouse, 5 Station Road, Liphook, Surrey), or by official measurers of the Royal Yachting Association, Victoria Way, Woking, Surrey. Tonnage measurements of yachts over 13.7m (45ft) in length must be done by surveyors of the Department of Trade.

2.5.4 Lloyd's Register Tonnage (LT)

This is used for estimating hull survey fees for yachts classed at Lloyd's, according to the formula:

$$LT = \frac{LOA \times B \times D \times 0.45}{100}$$

where LOA = maximum length (feet), B = maximum beam (feet), excluding protrusions, and D = moulded depth (distance from top of floors to upper deck beams, amidships) in feet.

If the measurements are expressed in metres, the formula is:

$$LT = \frac{LOA \times B \times D \times 15.9}{100}$$

2.5.5 Deadweight tonnage

This is the number of tons of cargo, bunkers and stores that a ship will carry, or in other words it is the difference in displacement when the vessel is light and fully loaded.

2.5.6 One Ton Cup, etc.

Most offshore yacht racing is conducted under the handicap provisions of the International Offshore Rule, with systems of time allowance to permit yachts of different ratings and potential speeds to race together. In recent years however a number of 'level rating' classes have emerged, in which the competitors race boat for boat with no handicap. Since the first such major event was raced for an old trophy called the One Ton Cup, these level rating classes have all adopted similar names, as follows:

For boats with maximum rating of

One Ton	30.5ft	Half Ton	22.0ft
Three-Quarter		Quarter Ton	18.5ft
Ton	24.5ft	Mini Ton	16.5ft

It will therefore be seen that the description 'One Ton' in this context refers only to the rating measurement of the boat, and has nothing to do with her weight or displacement.

2.6 Units and conversions

2.6.1 British units of weights and measures

Lengths

12 inches	=	1 foot
3 feet	=	1 yard
6 feet	=	1 fathom
1 shackle	=	15 fathoms
1 cable	=	1/10 nautical mile (approx 200 yards)
1 nautical mile	=	approx 6080 feet
1 statute mile	=	1760 yards (5280 feet)

Weights (Avoirdupois)

16 drams	=	1 ounce
16 ounces	=	1 pound
14 pounds	=	1 stone
28 pounds	=	1 quarter
4 quarters	=	1 hundredweight
20 hundred-weights	=	1 ton (2240 lb)

Volume

4 gills	=	1 pint
2 pints	=	1 quart
4 quarts	=	1 gallon
2 gallons	=	1 peck
4 pecks	=	1 bushel
8 bushels	=	1 quarter
5 quarters	=	1 load
36 bushels	=	1 caldron

Area

144 sq in	=	1 sq ft
9 sq ft	=	1 sq yd
$30\frac{1}{4}$ sq yds	=	1 sq pole
40 sq poles	=	1 rood
4 roods	=	1 acre (4840 sq yds)
640 acres	=	1 sq mile

Weight and volume of water

One Imperial gallon = 277.274 cu in, or 0.16 cu ft, or 10lb, or 4.546 litres

One US gallon	=	231 cu in, or 0.133 cu ft, or 8.33lb, or 0.83 Imp gallons, or 3.8 litres
One cu ft of water	=	6.232 Imp gallons, or 28.375 litres, or 0.284 cu metres, or 62.39lb
One cu ft of salt water weighs		64lb (or 1/35th ton)

Pressures

A column of water 1ft high	=	Pressure of 0.434lb/sq in
A column of water 1m high	=	Pressure of 1.43lb/sq in
A column of water 2.31ft high	=	Pressure of 1lb/sq in

At 30in mercury (34ft water) atmospheric pressure is 1 atmosphere (14.7lb/sq in)

| Pressure in atmospheres | = | 0.068 × pressure in lb/sq in |

2.6.2 Système International (SI units)

The SI version of the metric system is based on seven units denoting physical quantities. They are:

Quantity	Unit	Symbol
Length	metre	m
Mass	kilogram	kg
Time	second	s
Electric current	ampere	A
Thermodynamic temperature	kelvin	K
Luminous intensity	candela	cd
Amount of substance (only used in physical chemistry)	mole	mol

Note that the kilogram, unit of mass, is the only one with a multiple prefix.
1 kilogram = 1000 grams. Prefixes denoting different sizes of this mass unit are attached to the word 'gram', e.g. milligram = 1/1000 gram.

There are 15 derived units formed from base and/or supplementary units. They are:

Quantity	Name of SI derived unit	Symbol
Force	newton	N
Energy	joule	J
Frequency	hertz	Hz
Pressure and stress	pascal	Pa
Power	watt	W
Quantity of electricity	coulomb	C
Electric potential	volt	V
Electric capacitance	farad	F
Electric resistance	ohm	Ω
Electric conductance	siemens	S
Magnetic flux	weber	Wb
Flux density	tesla	T
Inductance	henry	H
Luminous flux	lumen	lm
Illuminance	lux	lx

Prefixes

The following prefixes are used to designate multiples:

			Prefix	**Symbol**
One thousand million	1 000 000 000	10^9	giga	G
One million	1 000 000	10^6	mega	M
One thousand	1 000	10^3	kilo	k
One hundred	100	10^2	hecto	h
Ten	10	10^1	deca	da
One tenth	0.1	10^{-1}	deci	d
One hundredth	0.01	10^{-2}	centi	c
One thousandth	0.001	10^{-3}	milli	m
One millionth	0.000 001	10^{-6}	micro	μ
One thousand millionth	0.000 000 001	10^{-9}	nano	n
One million millionth	0.000 000 000 001	10^{-12}	pico	p

2.6.3 Conversion factors and tables

To convert	Multiply by	To convert	Multiply by
Areas			
sq in to sq mm	645.16	sq mm to sq in	0.00155
sq in to sq cm	6.4516	sq cm to sq in	0.155
sq ft to sq m	0.0929	sq m to sq ft	10.76
sq yd to sq m	0.8361	sq m to sq yd	1.196
acres to sq m	4046.86	sq m to acres	0.000247
acres to sq yd	4840.0	sq yd to acres	0.0002
Consumption			
lb/hp/hr to gram/hp/hr	447.4	gram/hp/hr to lb/hp/hr	0.0022
Distances			
in to mm	25.40	mm to in	0.0394
in to cm	2.54	cm to in	0.394
ft to m	0.3048	m to ft	3.2808
yd to m	0.914	m to yd	1.094
fathoms to m	1.8288	m to fathoms	0.5468
statute miles to km	1.609	km to statute miles	0.6215
naut miles to statute	1.1515	statute miles to naut	0.8684
naut miles to m	1852	m to naut miles	0.00054
Force			
lbf to N	4.4482	N to lbf	0.2248
kgf to N	9.8066	N to kgf	0.101972
Mass			
oz to grams	28.35	grams to oz	0.0353
lb to kg	0.4536	kg to lb	2.205
tons to tonnes (1000kg)	1.016	tonnes to tons (2240lbs)	0.9842
tons to short (US) tons	1.12	short (US) tons to tons	0.893
Powers			
horsepower to kW	0.7457	kW to hp	1.341
hp to metric hp	1.014	metric hp to hp	0.9862
metric hp to kW	0.735	kW to metric hp	1.359
Pressures			
lb/sq in to kg/sq cm	0.0703	kg/sq cm to lb/sq in	14.22
lb/sq ft to kg/sq m	4.88	kg/sq m to lb/sq ft	0.205
lb/sq in to ft of water	2.31	ft of water to lb/sq in	0.433
lb/sq in to atmospheres	0.0680	atmospheres to lb/sq in	14.7

To convert	Multiply by	To convert	Multiply by
Speeds			
ft/sec to m/sec	0.3048	m/sec to ft/sec	3.281
ft/sec to knots	0.592	knots to ft/sec	1.689
ft/sec to miles/hr	0.682	miles/hr to ft/sec	1.467
ft/min to m/sec	0.0051	m/sec to ft/min	196.8
knots to miles/hr	1.1515	miles/hr to knots	0.868
miles/hr to km/hr	1.6093	km/hr to miles/hr	0.6214
knots to km/hr	1.8520	km/hr to knots	0.5400
Torque			
lbf ft to Nm	1.3558	Nm to lbf ft	0.7376
kgf m to Nm	9.8066	Nm to kgf m	0.1020
lbf ft to kgf m	0.1383	kgf m to lbf ft	7.2330
Volumes			
cu in to cu cm	16.387	cu cm to cu in	0.061
cu ft to cu m	0.0283	cu m to cu ft	35.31
cu ft to galls	6.25	galls to cu ft	0.16
cu ft to litres	28.33	litres to cu ft	0.035
pints to litres	0.568	litres to pints	1.76
galls to litres	4.546	litres to galls	0.22
Imp galls to US galls	1.2	US galls to Imp galls	0.833
US barrels to cu m	0.16	cu m to US barrels	6.29

Feet to metres, metres to feet

Explanation: The central columns of figures in bold type can be referred in either direction. To the left to convert metres into feet, or to the right to convert feet into metres. For example, five lines down: 5 feet = 1.52 metres, and 5 metres = 16.40 feet.

Feet		Metres	Feet		Metres	Feet		Metres	Feet		Metres
3.28	**1**	0.30	45.93	**14**	4.27	88.58	**27**	8.23	131.23	**40**	12.19
6.56	**2**	0.61	49.21	**15**	4.57	91.86	**28**	8.53	134.51	**41**	12.50
9.84	**3**	0.91	52.49	**16**	4.88	95.14	**29**	8.84	137.80	**42**	12.80
13.12	**4**	1.22	55.77	**17**	5.18	98.43	**30**	9.14	141.08	**43**	13.11
16.40	**5**	1.52	59.06	**18**	5.49	101.71	**31**	9.45	144.36	**44**	13.41
19.69	**6**	1.83	62.34	**19**	5.79	104.99	**32**	9.75	147.64	**45**	13.72
22.97	**7**	2.13	65.62	**20**	6.10	108.27	**33**	10.06	150.92	**46**	14.02
26.25	**8**	2.44	68.90	**21**	6.40	111.55	**34**	10.36	154.20	**47**	14.33
29.53	**9**	2.74	72.18	**22**	6.71	114.83	**35**	10.67	157.48	**48**	14.63
32.81	**10**	3.05	75.46	**23**	7.01	118.11	**36**	10.97	160.76	**49**	14.94
36.09	**11**	3.55	78.74	**24**	7.32	121.39	**37**	11.28	164.04	**50**	15.24
39.37	**12**	3.66	82.02	**25**	7.62	124.67	**38**	11.58			
42.65	**13**	3.96	85.30	**26**	7.92	127.95	**39**	11.89			

Inches to millimetres

inches	0	1/16	1/8	3/16	1/4	5/16	3/8	7/16	1/2	9/16	5/8	11/16	3/4	13/16	7/8	15/16
0		1.6	3.2	4.8	6.4	7.9	9.5	11.1	12.7	14.3	15.9	17.5	19.1	20.6	22.2	23.8
1	25.4	27.0	28.6	30.2	31.7	33.3	34.9	36.5	38.1	39.7	41.2	42.9	44.4	46.0	47.6	49.2
2	50.8	52.4	54.0	55.6	57.1	58.7	60.3	61.9	63.5	65.1	66.7	68.3	69.8	71.4	73.0	74.6
3	76.2	77.8	79.4	81.0	82.5	84.1	85.7	87.3	88.9	90.5	92.1	93.6	95.2	96.8	98.4	100.0
4	101.6	103.2	104.8	106.4	108.0	109.5	111.1	112.7	114.3	115.9	117.5	119.1	120.7	122.2	123.8	125.4
5	127.0	128.6	130.2	131.8	133.4	134.9	136.5	138.1	139.7	141.3	142.9	144.5	146.1	147.6	149.2	150.8
6	152.4	154.0	155.6	157.2	158.8	160.3	161.9	163.5	165.1	166.7	168.3	169.9	171.5	173.0	174.6	176.2
7	177.8	179.4	181.0	182.6	184.2	185.7	187.3	188.9	190.5	192.1	193.7	195.3	196.9	198.4	200.0	201.6
8	203.2	204.8	206.4	208.0	209.6	211.1	212.7	214.3	215.9	217.5	219.1	220.7	222.3	223.8	225.4	227.0
9	228.6	230.2	231.8	233.4	235.0	236.5	238.1	239.7	241.3	242.9	244.5	246.1	247.6	249.2	250.8	252.4
10	254.0	255.6	257.2	258.8	260.4	261.9	263.5	265.1	266.7	268.3	269.9	271.5	273.1	274.6	276.2	277.8
11	279.4	281.0	282.6	284.2	285.7	287.3	288.9	290.5	292.1	293.7	295.3	296.9	298.4	300.0	301.6	303.2
12	304.8															

Feet and inches to millimetres

inches	0	1	2	3	4	5	6	7	8	9	10	11
feet												
1	305	330	356	381	406	432	457	483	508	533	559	584
2	610	635	660	686	711	737	762	787	813	838	864	889
3	914	940	965	991	1016	1041	1067	1092	1118	1143	1168	1194
4	1219	1245	1270	1295	1321	1346	1372	1397	1422	1448	1473	1499
5	1524	1549	1575	1600	1626	1651	1676	1702	1727	1753	1778	1803
6	1829	1854	1880	1905	1930	1956	1981	2007	2032	2057	2083	2108
7	2134	2159	2184	2210	2235	2261	2286	2311	2337	2362	2388	2413
8	2438	2464	2490	2515	2540	2565	2591	2616	2642	2667	2692	2718
9	2743	2769	2794	2819	2845	2870	2896	2921	2946	2972	2997	3023
10	3048	3073	3100	3124	3150	3175	3200	3226	3251	3277	3302	3327

Fathoms and feet to metres

The following table is useful for converting feet (or fathoms and feet) into metres, or vice versa:

Feet		6	12	18	24	30	36	42	48	54	60
Fathoms		1	2	3	4	5	6	7	8	9	10
Feet		1.8	3.6	5.5	7.3	9.1	10.9	12.8	14.6	16.4	18.3
1	0.3	2.1	3.9	5.8	7.6	9.4	11.3	13.1	14.9	16.7	18.6
2	0.6	2.4	4.2	6.1	7.9	9.7	11.6	13.4	15.2	17.0	18.9
3	0.9	2.7	4.5	6.4	8.2	10.0	11.9	13.7	15.5	17.3	19.2
4	1.2	3.0	4.9	6.7	8.5	10.3	12.2	14.0	15.8	17.7	19.5
5	1.5	3.3	5.2	7.0	8.8	10.6	12.5	14.3	16.1	18.0	19.8

Temperature – Fahrenheit to Celsius (Centigrade)

°F	°C	°F	°C	°F	°C
212	100	100	37.7	45	7.2
200	93.3	95	35.0	40	4.4
190	87.7	90	32.2	35	1.7
180	82.2	85	29.4	32	0.0
170	76.6	80	26.7	30	− 1.1
160	71.1	75	23.9	25	− 3.9
150	65.5	70	21.1	20	− 6.7
140	60.0	65	18.3	15	− 9.4
130	54.4	60	15.6	10	− 12.2
120	48.8	55	12.8	5	− 15.0
110	43.3	50	10.0	0	− 17.7

Note: A more complete conversion scale is shown under Weather, Fig. 7(18).

To convert degrees Centigrade to Fahrenheit, multiply by 1.8 and add 32.

Example: $10°C \times 1.8 = 18 + 32 = 50°F$

To convert Fahrenheit to Centigrade, subtract 32 and divide by 1.8.

Example: $50°F − 32 = 18 \div 1.8 = 10°C$

2.7 Glossaries

2.7.1 Glossary of nautical terms

It is hardly surprising that those who go to sea have built up their own vocabulary of nautical terms, because many of the things which are expressed in nautical language have no equivalent ashore. In a boat it is often necessary to give precise instructions quickly, so communication can be very important. It is therefore essential for a sailor to understand and use at least certain of the more common terms. Here is a selection.

Aback A sail is aback when trimmed so that the wind is on the forward side of it

Abaft Behind; further aft than

Abeam On the beam; at right angles to the fore-and-aft line of the vessel

Aboard In or on the vessel; on board

About (to go) To change tack

A-Bracket Fitting shaped as an inverted A supporting the end of the propeller shaft

Adrift Loose; broken away; late

Afloat Waterborne

Aft Towards the stern

Ahead In front of; the direction of the bows

Amidships Midway between bow and stern, of the rudder or helm when it is centred (fore-and-aft)

Astern Behind; the direction of the stern

Athwart Across

Avast Stop (e.g. 'Avast heaving' – stop heaving)

Awash Level with the surface of the water

Aweigh When the anchor has broken out of sea bed

Back Of the wind – when it changes direction anti-clockwise. To back a sail is to haul it to windward, so that the wind fills it on the other side

Backstay A stay holding mast from after side

Bailer A small receptable for removing water from a boat (bailing)

Ballast Weight placed low down in a vessel to improve stability

Bar A shallow area (shoal) across the mouth of a harbour or river

Batten down To secure hatches, openings etc. before proceeding to sea

Battens Flexible strips of wood or plastic slipped into pockets in the leech of a sail to retain its shape

Beacon A mark to assist navigation

Beam The width of a boat; the timber on which deck is laid

Bearing The direction of one object from another, usually referring to the compass

Bear away To steer the boat away from the direction of the wind

Bear off To push away (e.g. the jetty or another boat)

Beating Sailing to windward, by tacking with the wind first on one side and then on the other

Beaufort scale A numerical measure of wind strength

Becket A loop or eye

Before Towards the bow

Belay To secure a rope, or make it fast. (Colloquially, to countermand an order)

Bend A form of knot

Berth Space for sleeping, or for a vessel to dock

Bight The middle of a rope (not the ends)

Bilge The curve of the underwater part of a boat, nearest the keel

Binnacle The casing that holds a compass

Bitts A pair of vertical posts for securing mooring lines or anchor warps

Bitter end Inboard end of anchor cable

Block A plastic, metal, or wooden shell holding one or more sheaves through which ropes are led

Bluff Steep-to, perpendicular

Boathook A stout stave with a hook at one end, used for bringing a boat alongside or for picking up a buoy

Bollard A vertical post on ship or shore, for securing mooring lines

Bolt rope A rope sewn to the luff or foot of a sail

Boom A spar used to extend the foot of a sail

Boom vang A rope used to hold a boom forward and downward

Bosun's chair A seat which can be attached to a halyard for sending a man aloft

Boot-topping Painted areas along the waterline

Bowline A knot that forms a fixed loop

Bow The front end of a vessel

Bowse To tighten (e.g. a rope, or lashing)

Bowsprit Spar projecting forward from the stem

Bring up To come to anchor

Broach To swing broadside on to the sea

Bulkheads Vertical partitions or divisions within a vessel

Bulwarks Solid rails around the deck edge

Bunk A bed

Buoy A float used as a navigational mark, or to take a mooring line

Burgee A triangular flag denoting membership of a club, flown at the masthead

By the head A vessel trimmed bow down

By the lee When running downwind, if the wind blows from side on which the boom is lying, possibly causing a gybe

By the stern A vessel trimmed stern down

Cable Anchor chain; or, as a measure of distance, $\frac{1}{10}$ of a nautical mile, i.e. about 200 yards

Cardinal mark Indicating navigable water on the named side of the mark

Careen To heel a vessel over to work on her bottom

Carry away, To To break or part

Carry way To continue to move through the water

Carvel A method of construction which gives a smooth finish, with planks edge to edge

Cast off, To To let go

Catamaran A vessel with two parallel hulls, joined by beams

Caulk, To To make a watertight joint in seams between planks

Cavitation Vibration and loss of power, caused by aeration of propeller working surfaces

Centre of buoyancy Centre of the immersed volume of a vessel

Centreboard A plate which can be lowered from a housing in the bottom of the hull, to increase lateral resistance (i.e. reduce leeway)

Chain plates Strong points on the hull each side of the mast, for attachment of shrouds

Chart Datum The level to which soundings and drying heights on a chart are related

Check (Of a rope) to ease out slowly; slowly to stop a vessel's movement

Chine The angle between the bottom and topsides in some designs of craft

Claw off Sailing close to the wind, to get off a lee shore

Cleat A fitting with projecting horns, for securing a rope

Clevis pin A small cylindrical pin, used in standing rigging

Clew The lower, aft corner of a sail, where the foot meets the leech

Clinker Method of wooden construction, where the edge of one plank overlaps the one below it

Close-hauled Sailing as close to the wind as possible

Clutter Unwanted reflections (e.g. from waves or rain) on a radar screen

Coachroof A raised structure to improve headroom below deck

Companion Ladder or stairway

Compass Navigational instrument which indicates a northerly point

Con, To To give orders to the helmsman

Contour A line on the chart joining points of equal elevation or equal depth

Counter The overhanging portion of the stern

Course The direction in which a boat is heading

Cradle Supporting frame for a boat out of the water

Cringle A loop, usually consisting of a metal eye roped to a sail

Crown (of an anchor) where the arms join the shank

Crutch Metal fitting that drops into gunwale of a boat to take an oar

Davits Cranes for hoisting boats and tenders

Dead reckoning Calculating position from course steered and distance run

Deck The floor of a vessel

Deck head Underside of the deck

Deviation Compass error caused by magnetism of the vessel

Dip, To To lower and re-hoist the ensign as a salute

Displacement The weight of a vessel (equal to the weight of water she displaces)

Dog watches The two-hour watches from 1600–1800 and 1800–2000

Downhaul A rope pulling downwards, usually on the tack of a sail

Down helm An order to the helmsman to put the tiller 'down', i.e. away from the wind

Dowse To extinguish a light or lower a sail; also to spray with water

Draught The depth of a vessel beneath the water, to the lowest part of the hull

Drogue A form of sea anchor; used for boats, liferafts and lifebuoys

Ebb The falling tide

Echo sounder Electronic instrument to measure the depth of water

Ensign A vessel's national flag. The British maritime flags are the red, white or blue ensigns (never the Union Flag)

Fairlead An opening or fitting for leading a (mooring) rope

Fairway A navigable channel

Fathom A measurement of depth, equals six feet

Fender Used to prevent damage to the ship's side when lying alongside another vessel or a jetty

Fend off, To To push off

Fetch To reach a desired destination: the distance which the wind has blown over open water

Fiddle A lip around horizontal surfaces to stop objects falling/sliding off

Fix A position found from accurate bearings, or observations of heavenly bodies

Flare Outward spread of the topsides near the bow of a boat; pyrotechnic signal used to call attention

Flashing Flashing navigation light, with period of light less than period of darkness

Flood The rising ride

Foot The bottom edge of a sail

Fore and aft The boat's major, or longitudinal axis

Foreguy Rope leading forward from boom end, to hold boom forward

Forestay Stay which runs from stem to mast

Foretriangle Triangle formed by forestay, mast and deck

Forward Towards the bow

Foul Opposite of 'clear', e.g. 'foul anchor', 'foul bottom'

Fractional rig A rig where the forestay does not extend to the masthead (i.e. not a masthead rig)

Frap To bind together

Freeboard The height of the deck above the waterline

Freshen A strengthening of the wind

Furl To lower and gather in a sail

Gaff Spar at head of a fore and aft sail (not Bermuda rig)

Gale Wind of force 8 or 9 on the Beaufort scale (37–47 knots)

Galley The kitchen

Gimbals Two pivoted concentric rings that hold items such as compass or lamps level at sea

Go about To tack, and bring the wind on the other side of the sails

Gooseneck Fitting which holds the boom to the mast

Goosewinged Running before the wind, with the foresail set on one side and the mainsail on the other

Ground tackle Anchor gear

Gunwale The upper edge along the side of a boat

Guy A rope used to control a derrick or spar. In a sailing yacht usually refers to the spinnaker guy, which adjusts the trim of the spinnaker pole

Gybe Altering from one tack to the other by putting the boat's stern through the wind (as distinct from tacking)

Halyard Rope for hoisting a sail or flag

Handsomely Gently, or slowly

Hank Fitting for attaching the luff of a sail to a stay

Hard A place for beaching boats

Hard a-port, hard a-starboard Helm order to use maximum helm in the required direction

Hatchway A deck opening with a cover (hatch)

Haul To pull, or to change bearing

Hawse pipe Through which the anchor cable runs in larger vessels

Hawser A heavy rope for mooring or towing

Head The top corner of a sail

Header A wind shift which brings the wind further ahead

Heading The direction in which a boat is pointing

Heads Marine lavatory

Headsail A sail set forward of the mast

Head sea A sea from ahead

Heave-To To stop, or reduce speed with vessel head to wind

Heaving line A light line with a weighted end for establishing contact with another vessel or shore

Heel The inclination of a vessel

Helm The tiller or wheel

Hitch, To To make a rope fast to an object (not another rope)

Holding ground The type of bottom for the anchor

Holiday Area left unpainted by mistake

Hour glass A spinnaker twisted in the middle, so that the wind fills the top and bottom parts

House Flag A rectangular, personal flag of owner

Hull The structure of a boat, to deck level

Inboard Towards the middle of a vessel

Inshore Towards the shore

Irons A sailing boat is in irons when stationary, head to wind, unable to pay off on either tack

Isophase A navigation light which flashes with equal periods of light and darkness

Jib Triangular sail, set forward of the mast

Jury Makeshift

Kedge A light or secondary anchor

Keel The lower fore and aft structure of a vessel

Kicking strap Tackle used to hold down boom, and reduce twist in sail

King spoke The spoke of steering wheel upright when rudder is centred

Knot One nautical mile per hour (speed)

Landfall First sight of land, approaching from seaward

Lashing Securing with rope

Lateral mark Navigation buoy marking port or starboard side of a well defined channel

Latitude Angular measurement of position north or south of equator

Launch, To To slip into the water

Lay The twist in the strands of a rope; or to go (e.g. along a course)

Lazy Extra or spare

Lead line Marked line with a lead weight, for measuring depth of water

Leading marks/lights Marks or lights which when brought into line indicate channel or best water

Leech The trailing (aft) edge of a sail

Lee helm The tendency of a boat to fall off the wind, due to improper balance

Leeward The side of a boat further from the wind (opposite to 'windward')

Leeshore Shore onto which the wind is blowing

Leeway The sideways movement of a boat, blown by the wind (to leeward)

Lifeline Line rigged to stop crew going overboard

Lift A wind shift allowing a boat to point higher (opposite to 'header'). Also a rope which supports a spar (e.g. spinnaker pole)

List Angle of heel

Log Instrument for measuring distance run through the water

Log book Record of vessels movements, positions, etc.

Longitude Angular measurement east or west of Greenwich meridian

Loom The inboard end of an oar; (of a light), reflection in the sky

Lubber's line Fixed mark on compass bowl, showing ship's head

Luff The leading edge of a sail. To luff – to sail closer to the wind

Mainsail Sail set on aft side of the main (principal) mast. Usually the largest working sail, and referred to as the main

Mainsheet Rope and tackle controlling mainsail

Make To reach port: of tides, when range is increasing

Make fast To secure a rope to an object

Make water To leak

Man To provide the crew for certain functions, e.g. man the pumps

Marline spike Pointed steel tool, used for splicing

Marry To bring two ropes together

Meridian A north-south line through any point

Messenger A light line, used for example to make preliminary contact between two vessels prior to hauling over a larger hawser, e.g. for towing

Midships Helm order to centre the rudder

Miss stays To fail to tack through the wind

Mizzen The aft mast in a yawl or ketch

Moor To anchor with two anchors, or secure alongside

Neaps When the tide does not rise or fall very much

Nothing to port (or starboard) Not to steer any further to port (or starboard)

Null When a direction finding radio receiver gives the weakest signal from a station, indicating its bearing

Occulting A navigation light, with the period of light greater than the period of darkness

Off the wind Not close-hauled

Offing Distance to seaward

Overboard Over the side (into the water)

Overhaul (Of a tackle), to draw the blocks apart

Painter The rope secured to the bows of a dinghy or tender, by which it is secured or towed

Pay off To allow the ship's head to swing away from the direction of the wind

Pay out To ease out a chain or rope

Pitch poled When a boat is rotated, stern over bow, in a very large sea

Pooped When a vessel is overtaken by a sea which breaks over the stern (poop)

Lights for Motor Yachts

Requirements depend on the length of the boat. The white masthead light shows over an arc $112\frac{1}{2}°$ on either bow; sidelights (red to port, green to starboard) each show from ahead to $22\frac{1}{2}°$ abaft the beam; the white sternlight shows $67\frac{1}{2}°$ either side.

1. 12–20 metres overall. A combined lantern may be used for sidelights in boats under 20m, but individual sidelights are preferable. Visibility: masthead light – 3 miles; sidelights and sternlight – 2 miles.

2. Under 12 metres overall. Masthead light must be at least one metre above sidelights (or combined lantern, as shown). Visibility: masthead light and sternlight (which may be combined in one all-round light) – 2 miles; sidelights – 1 mile

3 and 4. Boats under 7m overall length, and with a maximum speed of 7 knots, need only carry a white all round light visible for two miles. If practicable they should also carry sidelights.

Lights for Sailing Yachts

Vessels under sail (only) carry sidelights and sternlight, but no white masthead light. In boats under 20m the sidelights and sternlight may be combined in one lantern at the masthead, with the red and green sidelights visible 2 miles, and the white sternlight 2 miles. An all-round red light over an all-round green light may also be shown at or near the masthead, but not in conjunction with the combined tricolour lantern described above.

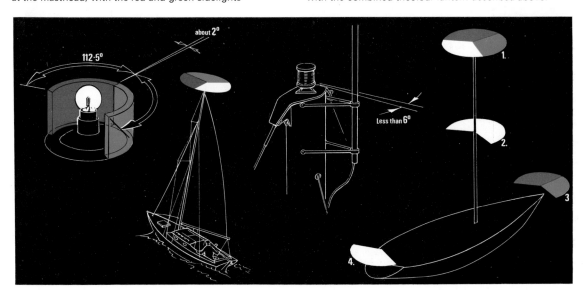

For yachts under 12m, sidelights must be visible 1 mile. To show over the correct arcs a combined lantern must be well engineered. A 25 watt bulb should be fitted to allow for voltage drop in the wiring. A combined lantern must not be shrouded by any other fitting over an arc of more than 6°.

Four separate lanterns meet all requirements for a sailing yacht under 12m. Lantern 1 is used under sail, with minimum battery drain, and lanterns 3 and 4 together provide a stand-by should 1 fail. Lanterns 2, 3 and 4 together are shown when under power. 1, 2 and 4 can be combined in a dual-switched lantern at the masthead.

A power-driven vessel over 50m must carry a second masthead light aft, and higher than the forward one.

If under 50m, a vessel under power need show only one masthead light. If under 12m, the masthead light may be combined with sternlight.

A sailing boat, when motoring (even with sails set), is a power-driven vessel and must conform accordingly.

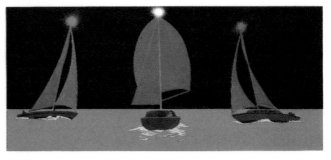

Sidelights of sailing yachts, when mounted low down as on the pulpit, may be obscured in a seaway.

The optional arrangement of a combined masthead lantern for sailing boat under 20m gives better visibility, as well as conserving the battery.

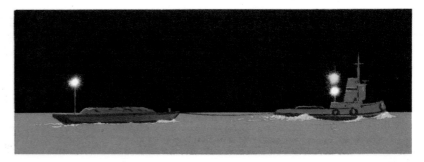

A small boat under oars need only show a white light, in time to prevent collision.

A tug and her tow. The tug shows a yellow towing light above her sternlight, and also shows a second masthead light forward. If the length of tow exceeds 200m the tug shows three masthead lights forward, arranged vertically, and both tug and tow show a diamond shape by day.

The tug (left) and tow from ahead. From this aspect the second masthead light of the tug could be confused with the aft masthead light of a ship more than 50m in length.

A vessel trawling, which should be given a wide berth. By day all vessels engaged in fishing show two cones, arranged vertically, point to point: or, if less than 20m, they exhibit a basket.

A vessel fishing (not trawling) and not making way (or she would show sidelights and sternlight). Gear extending more than 150m is shown by the all-round white light in that direction.

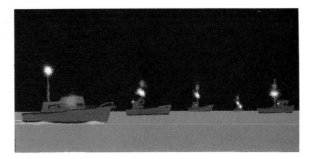

Fishing vessels often work together in a fleet, and it is best to take substantial avoiding action accordingly.

Vessels engaged in pair trawling may exhibit a searchlight directed forward and in the direction of the other vessel of the pair.

A vessel with restricted ability to manoeuvre. Masthead light and sidelights indicate she is making way through the water.

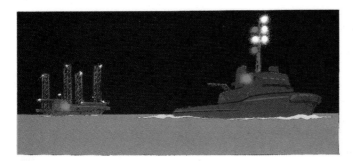

A tug (right) and tow, with restricted ability to manoeuvre. The three masthead lights of the tug indicate that the tow is more than 200m.

A dredger shows two vertical red lights (balls by day) on her foul side, and two vertical green lights (diamonds by day) on her clear side.

A vessel constrained by her draught shows three red lights vertically (or by day a cylinder) where best seen.

A vessel engaged in pilotage duties, at anchor.

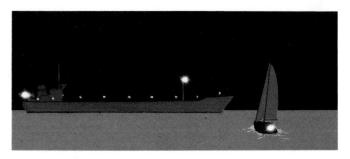

Vessels over 100m in length are required to show their deck lights when at anchor, and these may obscure other lights which are less bright.

Great care is often needed to differentiate between navigation lights of nearby vessels and lights ashore.

A vessel not under command shows two balls (or by night, two red lights) in a vertical line.

By day a vessel aground shows three balls in a vertical line, by night she shows her normal anchor light(s) plus two red lights vertically.

A minesweeper, with gear streamed, shows (in addition to the lights for a power-driven vessel) three green lights, or by day three balls, one at the foremast head and one at each yardarm.

Small vessels engaged in diving operations are required to exhibit a rigid replica of International Code flag 'A', not less than 1 metre in height. Such craft should be given a wide berth.

IALA Buoyage (Region A)

Lateral marks

Used generally to mark the sides of well defined navigable channels.

Port Hand marks

Light:
Colour – red
Rhythm – any

Navigable channel

Direction of buoyage

Starboard Hand marks

Light:
Colour – green
Rhythm – any

Cardinal marks

Used to indicate the direction from the mark in which the best navigable water lies, or to draw attention to a bend, junction or fork in a channel, or to mark the end of a shoal.

Lights: Always white

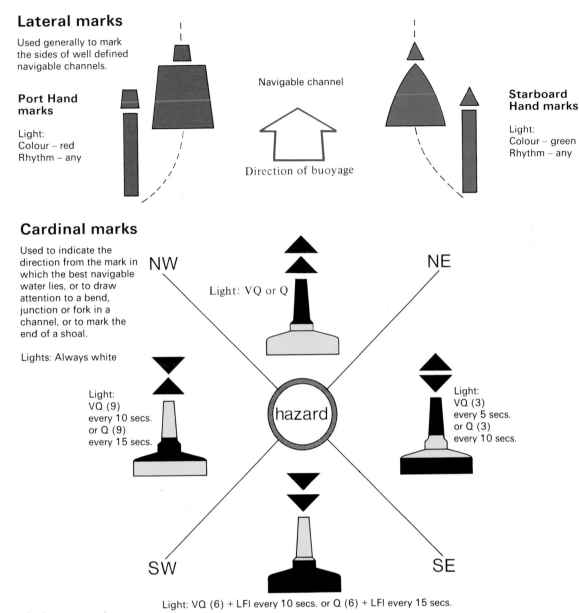

NW

NE

Light: VQ or Q

Light:
VQ (9)
every 10 secs.
or Q (9)
every 15 secs.

hazard

Light:
VQ (3)
every 5 secs.
or Q (3)
every 10 secs.

SW

SE

Light: VQ (6) + LFl every 10 secs. or Q (6) + LFl every 15 secs.

Other marks

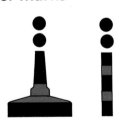

Isolated danger marks

Use: To mark a small isolated danger with navigable water all round.
Light: Colour – white
Rhythm – group flashing (2)

Safe water marks

Use: Mid-channel or landfall.
Light: Colour – white
Rhythm – Isophase, occulting or 1 long flash every 10 seconds.

Special marks

Any shape permissible.
Use: No navigational significance
Light: Colour – yellow
Rhythm – different from other white lights used on buoys.

Coastal navigation – Admiralty Metric Chart Symbols

A selection of the more common symbols from Admiralty Publication 5011

Reproduced by kind permission of H.M. Stationery Office and the Hydrographer of the Navy.

THE COASTLINE	ARTIFICIAL FEATURES	RADIO AND RADAR
Coast imperfectly known or shoreline unsurveyed.	Sea wall	RC Non-directional Radiobeacon
Steep coast	Breakwater	RD RD 269°30′ Directional Radiobeacon
Cliffy coast	Submerged jetty	RW Rotating Pattern Radiobeacon
Sandy shore	Patent slip	RG Radio Direction Finding Station
Low Water Line	Lock	**Radio Mast** Radio mast or tower **Radio Tr** Radio tower or scanner **Radar Tr** **Radar Sc** Landmarks for visual fixing only
Foreshore, Mud	Hulk	**TV Mast** **TV Tr** Television mast or tower
Foreshore, Sand	Steps	R Coast Radio Station providing QTG service
Foreshore, Boulders, Stones, Gravel and Shingle	Telegraph or telephone line, with vertical clearance (above HW) H 20m	Ra Coast Radar Station
Foreshore, Rock	Sewer, Outfall pipe Sewer Outfall pipe	Racon Radar Responder Beacon
Foreshore, Sand and Mud Sand Mud	Bridge (9m)	Radar Reflector
Limiting danger line	Fixed bridge with vertical clearance (above HW) H 17m	**Ra** (conspic) Radar conspicuous object.
Breakers along a shore	Ferry	Aero RC Aeronautical radiobeacon.
Half-tide channel (on intertidal ground)	Training wall Training Wall (covers)	Consol Bn Consol beacon.

Coastal navigation – Admiralty Metric Chart Symbols

A selection of the more common symbols from Admiralty Publication 5011

Reproduced by kind permission of H.M. Stationery Office and the Hydrographer of the Navy.

DANGERS	DANGERS	LIMITS
Rock which does not cover (with elevation above MHWS or MHHW, or where there is no tide, above MSL).	Wreck over which the depth has been obtained by sounding, but not by wire sweep.	**Leading Bns 089°53′** **Bn** **Bn** *Leading Line*
Rock which covers and uncovers (with elevation above chart datum).	Wreck over which the exact depth is unknown but thought to be more than 28 metres, or a wreck over which the depth is thought to be 28 metres or less, but which is not considered dangerous to surface vessels capable of navigating in the vicinity.	*Limit of sector*
Rock awash at the level of chart datum.		*Traffic separation scheme: one-way traffic lanes (separated by zone).*
Submerged rock with 2 metres or less water over it at chart datum, or rock ledge on which depths are known to be 2 metres or less, or a rock or rock ledge over which the exact depth is unknown but which is considered to be dangerous to surface navigation.	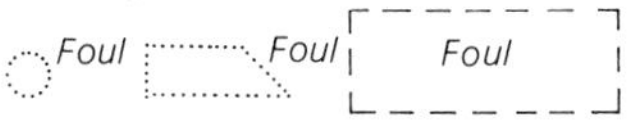 *Foul* *Foul* *Foul* The remains of a wreck, or other foul area no longer dangerous to surface navigation, but to be avoided by vessels anchoring, trawling, etc.	*Submarine cable (telegraph & telephone).* *Power* *Submarine cable (power).*
Shoal sounding on isolated rock.	Overfalls and tide-rips	*Limits of national fishing zones.*
Submerged rock not dangerous to surface navigation.	Eddies	 ✶ ✶ *Small Craft Anchorage.* *Anchorage Area.*
Submerged danger with depth cleared by wire drag.		*Type of anchorage is usually indicated by legend, e.g. Small Craft Anchorage, Naval Anchorage, Quarantine Anchorage, etc.*
Large scale charts Wreck showing any portion of hull or superstructure at the level of chart datum.	Kelp	*Recommended track for deep draught vessels (track not defined by fixed mark(s)).*
(Masts) (Mast 3 m) (Funnel) (Mast dries 2.1 m) *Large scale charts* Wreck of which the masts only are visible.	Breakers	*Where the minimum safe depth along the recommended track (or section thereof) is guaranteed by the competent harbour regional or national authority, the depth is indicated thus:*
Wreck over which the exact depth of water is unknown but is thought to be 28 metres or less, and which is considered dangerous to surface navigation.	Limiting danger line	>−DW−27m−> --> −DW−25m−> DW 27m DW 25m

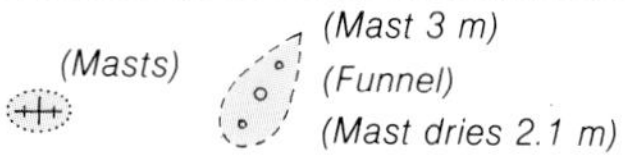

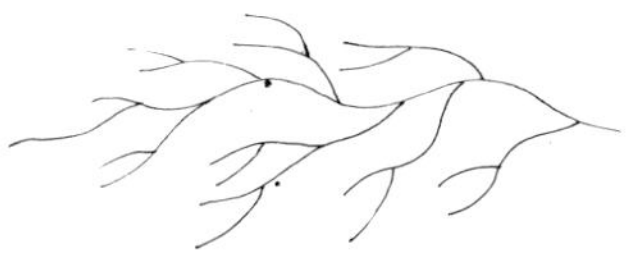

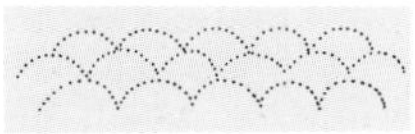

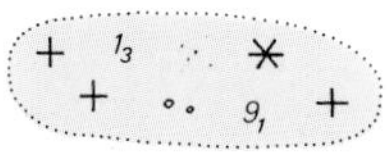

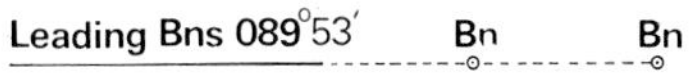

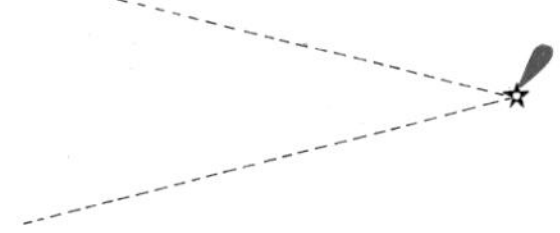

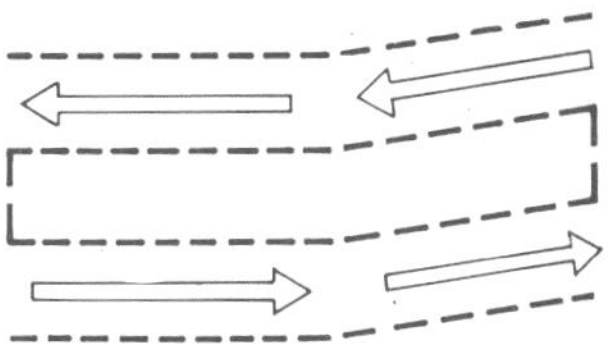

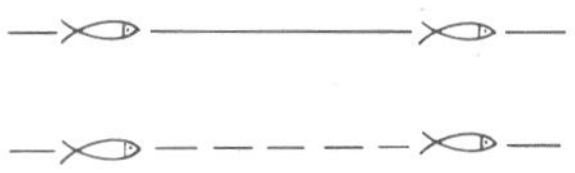

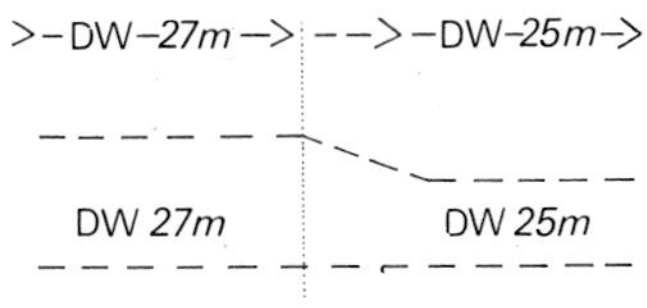

61

International Port Traffic Signals

No	Lights		Main message
1	 ⬤ ⬤ ⬤	Flashing	Serious emergency – all vessels to stop or divert according to instructions
2	⬤ ⬤ ⬤	Fixed or Slow Occulting	Vessels shall not proceed (*Note*: Some ports may use an exemption signal, as in 2a below)
3	⬤ ⬤ ⬤		Vessels may proceed. One way traffic
4	⬤ ⬤ ◯		Vessels may proceed. Two way traffic
5	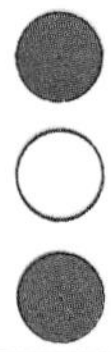 ⬤ ◯ ⬤		A vessel may proceed only when she has received specific orders to do so (*Note*: Some ports may use an exemption signal, as in 5a below)
	Exemption signals and messages		
2a	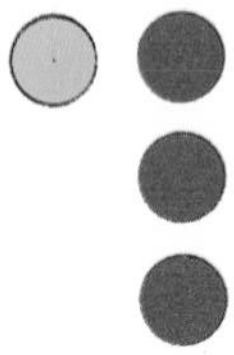 ◯ ⬤ ⬤ ⬤	Fixed or Slow Occulting	Vessels shall not proceed, except that vessels which navigate outside the main channel need not comply with the main message
5a	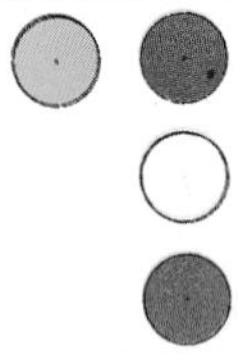 ◯ ⬤ ◯ ⬤		A vessel may proceed only when she has received specific orders to do so, except that vessels which navigate outside the main channel need not comply with the main message
	Auxiliary signals and messages		
	White and/or yellow lights, displayed to the right of the main lights		Local meanings, as promulgated in local port orders

This new system is gradually being introduced, but its general adoption is likely to take many years.

Notes on use:

(1)   The main movement message given by a port traffic signal shall always comprise three lights, disposed vertically. No additional light shall be added to the column carrying the main message. (The fact that the main message always consists of three vertical lights allows the mariner to recognise it as a traffic signal, and not lights of navigational significance). The signals may also be used to control traffic at locks and bridges.

(2)   Red lights indicate 'Do not proceed'.

(3)   Green lights indicate 'Proceed, subject to the conditions stipulated'.
    (For examples, see opposite).
   Note that, to avoid confusion, red and green lights are never displayed together.

(4)   A single yellow light, displayed to the left of the column carrying main messages Nos 2 or 5, at the level of the upper light, may be used to indicate that 'Vessels which can safely navigate outside the main channel need not comply with the main message'. This signal is of obvious significance to yachtsmen.

(5)   Signals which are auxiliary to the main message may be devised by local authorities. Such auxiliary signals should employ only white and/or yellow lights, and should be displayed to the right of the column carrying the main message. Ports with complex entrances and much traffic may need many auxiliary signals, which will have to be documented; but smaller harbours with less traffic may only need one or two of the basic signals, such as 'Vessels shall not proceed' and 'Vessels may proceed, two way traffic'.

   Some signals may be omni-directional – exhibited to all vessels simultaneously: others must be directional, and be shown either to vessels entering or to vessels leaving harbour.

   Signal No 5 is based on the assumption that some other means of communication such as VHF radio, signal lamp, loud hailer, or auxiliary signal will be used to inform a vessel that she may specifically proceed.

   The 'Serious Emergency' signal must be flashing, at least 60 flashes per minute. All other signals must be either fixed or slow occulting (the latter useful when background glare is a problem). A mixture of fixed and occulting lights must not be used.

Port (side) The left hand side of a vessel looking forward

Port tack When a sailing vessel has the wind blowing from her port side, and her main boom is to starboard

Quarter Midway between the beam and right aft

Race A local area of disturbed water

Racon A beacon which responds to a radar set's transmission, and shows up on the display

Radar Electronic instrument that shows the positions of other objects (ships, shore, buoys, etc.)

Radiobeacon A radio transmitter of known frequency, position, and signal from which a navigator with a suitable receiver can obtain a position line

Range (of cable), to flake down lengths of cable on deck, before anchoring: (of tide), the difference in height between successive high and low waters

Reach A point of sailing with the wind roughly on the beam

Reef To reduce the area of a sail; a ridge of rocks

Reeve To pass the end of a rope through a block etc.

Rhumb line A course which cuts all meridians at the same angle (a straight line on a Mercator's chart)

Riding light Anchor light

Rigging Ropes which support the masts, or control the sails

Rowlock A gap in the gunwale, into which an oar fits for rowing; also by common usage refers to a metal crutch, swivelling in the gunwale, for same purpose

Rubbing strake A piece of wood (usually) secured along the hull, that takes the wear alongside a jetty

Rudder Vertical plate, hinged on forward side, for steering

Run To sail before the wind: distance covered at sea

Samson post Post for securing anchor or tow line

Scantlings The dimensions of a vessel's timbers (constructional details)

Scuppers Holes in bulwarks to allow water to drain from deck

Scuttles Round openings in vessel's side

Seacock A valve on a pipe connected to the sea

Sheer The rising line of a vessel's side, towards bow and stern; to move a vessel relative to her anchor (e.g. by applying helm in a tideway)

Sheet Rope used to control a sail's angle to the wind

Ship To take on board

Shoal Shallow area of water

Shrouds Athwartships or lateral supports to mast

Skeg A fin extending aft of keel, and possibly supporting the rudder

Slack water When the tidal stream is stationary

Slip Slope for launching boats: to let something go

Sloop The most common rig for a sailing boat with one headsail and mainsail

Snatch block A block which can be hinged open to take the bight of a rope

Snub To check a line from running out round a winch cleat etc.

Sound To ascertain the depth

Spinnaker A triangular, full-bellied sail set when reaching or running before the wind

Spreaders Struts each side of the mast, giving a wider angle for the support of the shrouds. (Also called crosstrees)

Spring Mooring rope led from forward aft, or from aft forward

Spring tide When the range of the tide is greatest (opposite of 'neaps')

Stanchion Vertical support for lifelines running round deck edge

Standing part The fixed (not running) part of a rope

Starboard The right hand side of a vessel looking forward

Starboard tack When a sailing vessel has the wind blowing from her starboard side, and her main boom is to port

Stay Fore and aft support for mast

Steady Order to helmsman to maintain the course he is steering

Steerage way When a vessel is moving fast enough through the water to respond (answer) to her helm

Stem The foremost part of the hull

Stiff Not easily heeled over

Stop To secure a furled sail; to make up a spinnaker with cotton or elastic bands, so that it can be broken out (spread) after hoisting

Surge To allow a rope to be eased out under control round a winch or bollard

Swage A metal terminal pressed on to a wire rope

Swing (compass) Procedure for finding compass deviation

Tabernacle Deck fitting for the bottom of a mast that can be lowered

Tabling Reinforcement sewn to edge of a sail

Tack The forward lower corner of a sail; to work a boat to windward by sailing alternately on port/starboard tacks

Tackle Ropes and blocks, to give increased hauling power

Take a turn To pass a rope around an object such as a cleat

Tang Fitting on mast for attachment of shroud or stay

Telltale Wool, yard or ribbon as wind indicator

Thwart Seat running across (athwart) an open boat

Tidal stream The horizontal movement of the sea, caused by the tide

Tide The periodic rise and fall in the level of the sea, caused by the action of the moon and sun

Tiller Bar connected to the rudder for operating same

Toggle Metal fittings in rigging, to allow free movement while retaining tension

Topping lift Lift (rope) rigged to end of main boom or spinnaker pole, to support it

Topsides Surfaces on the hull above water

Track A channel mounted to deck or spar, which takes a traveller (e.g. sail slide)

Transom The flat stern of some designs of vessel

Transducer A sensor (e.g. for depth or water speed) for passing data to a navigational instrument

Trick A period at the wheel

Trim To alter the set of sails; the fore-and-aft attitude of a boat in the water

Turn up To make a rope fast

Under way When a vessel is not anchored or secured to the land or shore in any way

Up and down When the anchor cable is vertical

Veer To pay out anchor cable; (of the wind) when it changes direction clockwise

Wake Disturbed water astern of a vessel as she moves ahead

Warp Rope used for mooring or anchoring, or moving a vessel

Wash The waves caused by a vessel's progress through the water

Watches Periods of duty for members of the crew

Weather (or windward) The side of a vessel nearer the wind (opposite to 'leeward')

Weather helm The tendency of a boat to come up into the wind, due to improper balance

Weigh To raise the anchor

Wetted surface The area of the boat under water

Wind rode When a vessel is lying to the wind (rather than the tide)

Yard A spar on a mast for spreading a sail

Yaw To steer an unsteady course

2.7.2 Four language glossary

English	French	German	Dutch
Types of boat			
Cruiser	Bateau de croisière	Kreuzeryacht	Toerjacht
Cutter	Cotre	Kutter	Kotter
Dinghy	Canot, dinghy	Dingi, Beiboot	Bijboot
Ferry	Bac, ferry	Fähre	Veerboot
Fishing boat	Bateau de pêche	Fischereifahrzeug	Vissersboot
Ketch	Ketch	Ketsch	Kits
Launch	Vedette	Barkasse	Barkas
Life-boat	Bateau de sauvetage	Rettungsboot	Reddingboot
Merchant vessel	Navire de commerce	Handelsschiff	Koopvaardijschip
Motor cruiser	Croiseur à moteur	Motorkreuzer	Motorkruiser
Motor sailer	Bateau mixte	Motorsegler	Motorzeiljacht
Ocean racer	Bateau de course-croisière	Hochseerennyacht	Zeewedstrijdjacht
Pilot boat	Bateau pilote	Lotsenversetzboot	Loodskotter
Schooner	Goélette	Schoner	Schoener
Sloop	Sloop	Slup	Sloep
Tanker	Bateau citerne	Tanker, Tankschiff	Tanker, tankschip
Tug	Remorqueur	Schlepper	Sleepboot
Yacht	Yacht	Yacht	Jacht
Yawl	Yawl	Yawl	Yawl
Rigging, Sails			
Backstay	Pataras	Achterstag, Backstag	Achterstag
Batten pocket	Étui ou gaine de latte	Lattentasche	Zeillatzak
Boom	Bôme	Baum	Giek
Bowsprit	Beaupré	Bugspriet	Boegspriet
Chain plate	Cadène	Rüsteisen, Püttings	Putting
Clew	Point d'écoute	Schothorn	Schoothoorn
Crosstrees	Barres de flèche	Saling	Dwarszaling
Foot	Bordure	Unterliek	Voetlijk
Forestay	Étai avant	Vorstag, Fockstag	Voorstag, fokkestag
Genoa	Génois	Genua	Genua
Halyard	Drisse	Fall	Val
Head	Point de drisse	Kopf	Top
Jib	Foc	Fock	Fok
Leech	Chute	Achterliek	Achterlijk
Luff	Envergure	Vorliek	Voorlijk

English	French	German	Dutch
Mainsail	Grand'voile	Grossegel	Grootzeil
Mast	Mât	Mast	Mast
Mizzen	Artimon	Besan	Bezaan
Mizzen staysail	Voile d'étai d'artimon	Besanstagsegel	Bezaanstagzeil
Reef point	Garcette	Refföse	Knuttel
Shackle	Manille	Schäkel	Sluiting
Sheet	Écoute	Schot	Schoot
Shroud	Hauban	Want	Want
Spinnaker	Spinnaker	Spinnaker	Spinnaker
Staysail	Trinquette	Stagsegel	Fok
Tack	Point d'amure	Hals	Hals

Materials etc.

English	French	German	Dutch
Aluminium alloy	Aluminium	Aluminium	Aluminium
Bolt	Boulon	Bolzen	Bout
Bronze	Bronze	Bronze	Brons
Glass fibre	Fibre de verre	Glasharz	Fiberglas
Gunmetal	Bronze de canon	Rotguss	Geshutsbrons
Lead	Plomb	Blei	Lood
Marine plywood	Bois contre plaqué marin	Schiffsbausperrholz	Scheepstriplex
Nut	Écrou	Schraubenmutter	Moer
Nylon	Nylon	Nylon	Nylon
Rivet	Rivet	Niet	Klinknagel
Screw	Vis	Schraube	Schroef
Stainless steel	Acier inoxydable	Rostfreier Stahl	Roestvrij staal
Steel	Acier	Stahl	Staal
Terylene	Tergal	Polyester, Dacron	Dacron
Washer	Rondelle	Unterlegscheibe	Ring
Weld	Souder	Schweissen	Lassen
Wood	Bois	Holz	Hout

Parts of a boat

English	French	German	Dutch
Bilges	Cale	Bilge	Kim
Bulkhead	Cloison	Schott	Schot
Cabin	Cabine	Kajüte	Kajuit
Cockpit	Cockpit	Plicht, Cockpit	Kuip
Deck	Pont	Deck	Dek
Foc'sle	Poste avant	Vorschiff	Vooronder
Galley	Cuisine	Kombüse	Kombuis
Gunwale	Plat-bord	Dollbord	Dolboord
Hatch	Écoutille	Luk	Luik
Keel	Quille	Kiel	Kiel
Lifeline	Filière	Rettungsleine, Reling	Zeereling
Pulpit	Balcon avant	Bugkanzel	Preekstoel
Rudder	Gouvernail	Ruder	Roer
Stanchion	Chandelier	Stütze	Steun
Steering wheel	Roue de gouvernail	Steuerrad	Stuurrad
Stem	Étrave	Vorsteven	Voorsteven
Stern	Poupe	Heck	Achtersteven
Tiller	Barre	Pinne	Helmstok
Wheelhouse	Timonerie	Ruderhaus	Stuurhuis

Engine etc.

English	French	German	Dutch
Alternator	Alternateur	Wechselstrom-generator	Wisselstroom-dynamo
Atomiser, injector	Injecteur	Einspritzdüse	Inspuiter
Battery	Batterie	Batterie	Accu
Clutch	Embrayage	Kupplung	Koppeling
Diesel fuel pump	Pompe d'injection	Einspritzpumpe	Brandstofinspuitpomp
Distilled water	Eau distillée	Destilliertes Wasser	Gedestilleerd water

English	French	German	Dutch
Drive belt	Courroie de transmission	Treibriemen	Drijfriem
Fuel filter	Filtre à combustible	Treibstoffilter	Brandstoffilter
Fresh water	Eau douce, potable	Trinkwasser	Drinkwater
Gearbox	Boître de vitesse	Getriebe	Versnellingsbak
Generator	Dynamo	Lichtmaschine	Dynamo
Grease	Graisse	Fett	Vet
Hose	Tuyau	Schlauch	Slang
Hydraulic fluid	Liquide hydraulique	Hydraulisches Öl	Hydraulischeolie
Ignition coil	Bobine d'allumage	Zündspule	Onsteking-bobine
Oil	Huile	Schmieröl	Olie
Propeller	Hélice	Schraube	Schroef
Starter motor	Démarreur	Anlasser	Startmotor
Water pump	Pompe à eau	Wasserpumpe	Waterpomp

Navigation

English	French	German	Dutch
Abeam	Par le travers	Querab	Dwars
Ahead	En avant	Voraus	Voorwaarts
Anchorage	Mouillage	Ankerplatz	Ankerplaats
Astern	En arrière	Rückwärts, achtern	Achteruit
Bay	Baie	Bucht	Baai
Beacon	Balise	Bake	Baken
Binoculars	Jumelles	Fernglas	Kijker
Buoy	Bouée	Tonne, Boje	Ton, boei
Channel	Chenal	Fahrwasser	Vaarwater
Chart	Carte marine	Seekarte	Zeekaart
Compass	Compas	Kompass	Kompas
Course	Cap, route	Kurs	Koers
Degree	Degré	Grad	Graad
Depth	Profondeur	Tiefe	Diepte
Deviation	Déviation	Deviation, Ablenkung	Deviatie
Dividers	Pointes sèches	Kartenzirkel	Passer
East	Est	Ost	Oost
Echo sounder	Écho sondeur	Echolot	Echolood
Estuary	Estuaire	Flussmündung	Mond
Hand bearing compass	Compas de relèvement	Handpeilkompass	Handpeilkompas
Headland	Promontoire	Vorgebirge	Voorgebergte
Island	Île	Insel	Eiland
Latitude	Latitude	Breite	Breedte
Leading line	Alignement	Leitlinie	Geleidelijn
Longitude	Longitude	Länge	Lengte
Mud	Vase	Schlick, Schlamm	Modder
North	Nord	Nord	Noord
Overfalls	Remous	Stromkabbelung	Stroomrafeling
Parallel rulers	Règles parallèles	Parallellineal	Parallellineaal
Patent log	Loch enregistreur	Patentlog	Patent log
Port	Bâbord	Backbord	Bakboord
Radio direction finder	Radiogoniomètre	Funkpeiler	Radio peiltoestel
Radio receiver	Poste récepteur	Rundfunkempfänger	Radio-ontvangtoestel
Reef	Récif	Riff	Rif
Rocks	Rochers	Klippen, Felsen	Rotsen
Shoal	Haut fond	Untiefe	Droogte
South	Sud	Süd	Zuid
Starboard	Tribord	Steuerbord	Stuurboord
Variation	Déclinaison	Missweisung	Variatie
West	Ouest	West	West

Tides

English	French	German	Dutch
Chart datum	Zéro des cartes	Kartennull	Reductievlak:kaartpeil
Depth	Profondeur	Tiefe	Diepte
Ebb	Marée descendante	Ebbe	Eb

English	*French*	*German*	*Dutch*
Flood	Marée montante	Flut	Vloed
High water	Pleine mer	Hochwasser (HW)	Hoogwater (HW)
Low water	Basse mer	Niedrigwasser (NW)	Laagwater (LW)
Neap (tides)	Morte eau	Nipptide	Doodtij
Range	Amplitude	Tidenhub	Verval
Rate	Vitesse	Geschwindigkeit	Snelheid
Set	Porter	Setzen	Zetten
Spring (tides)	Vive eau, grande marée	Springtide	Springtij
Tidal stream	Courant	Gezeitenstrom	Getijstroom

Numbers etc.

One	un	eins	een
Two	deux	zwei	twee
Three	trois	drei	drie
Four	quatre	vier	vier
Five	cinq	fünf	vijf
Six	six	sechs	zes
Seven	sept	sieben	zeven
Eight	huit	acht	acht
Nine	neuf	neun	negen
Ten	dix	zehn	tien
Six hours	Six heures	Sechs Stunden, -Uhr	Zes uren
Twelve hours	Douze heures	Zwölf Stunden	Twaalf uren
Eighteen hours	Dix-huit heures	Achtzehn Stunden	Achttien uren
Twenty four hours	Vingt quatre heures	Vier und zwanzig Stunden	Vier en twintig uren
Thirty six hours	Trente six heures	Sechs und dreissig Stunden	Zes en dertig uren
Forty eight hours	Quarante huit heures	Acht und vierzig Stunden	Acht en veertig uren
Today	Aujourd'hui	Heute	Vandaag
Tomorrow	Demain	Morgen	Morgen

Radio

Call sign	Indicatif	Rufzeichen	Roepsein
Frequency	Fréquence	Frequenz	Frequentie
Operating time	Heures d'éission	Sendezeit	Seintijd
Radio beacon	Radiophare	Funkfeuer	Radiobaken
Radio station	Station d'émission	Rundfunksender	Radioomroepstation
Radio telephone	Radio téléphone	Sprechfunk-Gerät	Radiotelefoon

Note: A four-language glossary of weather terms is given in Chapter 7 (Weather).

2.8 Yachting and marine organisations

2.8.1 Royal Yachting Association (RYA)

The Royal Yachting Association was founded in 1875 as the Yacht Racing Association. Originally it only administered yacht racing, as its title then implied, but after the Second World War it adopted wider terms of reference and was transformed into the Royal Yachting Association in 1953.

Now it co-ordinates all aspects of pleasure boating, and is the national authority for the sport in the United Kingdom. The RYA still, of course, administers yacht racing in this country, and represents its interests within the International Yacht Racing Union, but the scope of its activities is greatly increased. For example it is involved with Government departments, Local Authorities, and various other bodies and committees whenever and wherever yachting interests are involved. It advises the Government on many aspects of the construction, operation, equipment and safety of boats of all kinds. It keeps a close eye on Parliamentary Bills, Harbour

Revision Orders, Byelaws, planning applications, and a mass of legislation which might affect the yachtsman.

One of the main aims of the RYA in recent years has been to develop all aspect of training, with its voluntary scheme of proficiency certificates at every level of competence – both for sail and for power. At the higher levels this scheme is recognised by the Government in the RYA/DoT Yachtmaster Certificates, details of which are contained in RYA booklets G15 (for sailing yachtsmen) and G18 (for motor yachtsmen).

The RYA publishes a number of booklets, giving detailed information on a wide range of subjects at very reasonable prices. A selection of these is available free every year to Full Personal Members, who also enjoy other benefits through their membership of the RYA.

Although the RYA employs a staff of about 40 persons, much of the work and the more important decisions come from the many yachtsmen who serve on the various committees – more than 30 of them, covering every kind of activity afloat.

Further details of the facilities available, and of membership, can be obtained by writing to the Royal Yachting Association, Victoria Way, Woking, Surrey, GU21 1EQ. Tel: Woking (04862) 5022.

2.8.2 RYA Seamanship Foundation

The Seamanship Foundation is registered under the Charities Act 1960 and is established to foster good seamanship. It encourages and assists with training yachtsmen by producing a range of instructional aids, from sophisticated audio visual programmes to simple posters. The Foundation also provides lectures and demonstrations on the use of distress flares, liferafts, fire fighting and other safety equipment.

The Foundation also gives opportunities for sail training to those otherwise unable to afford it, by either providing boats or by subsidising training courses. Over sixty dinghies have been bought for use by youth clubs, Scouts and schools.

The Foundation is particularly concerned in organising courses and providing boats or equipment to enable the disabled to learn to sail and afterwards participate on equal terms with the able-bodied. Every year the Foundation organises a course on cruising yachts for twenty-four visually handicapped students, and in addition, encourages and assists sailing clubs to run their own courses.

The Foundation is supported entirely by subscription from the public and its ability to assist the deprived and handicapped depends directly on the support which is received. All enquiries should be addressed to: The Director, RYA Seamanship Foundation, Victoria Way, Woking, Surrey GU21 1EQ.

2.8.3 Ship and Boat Builders National Federation (SBBNF)

The SBBNF is the trade organisation of the boating industry in this country. It was originally formed in 1913, and has changed its name more than once over the years, but its office is now at Boating Industry House, Vale Road, Oatlands Village, Weybridge, Surrey. Tel: Weybridge (0932) 54511. There are ten federated associations of boatbuilding employers divided into regional areas. Group associations include the Association of Brokers and Yacht Agents, the Marine Trades Association, and the Marine Engine and Equipment Manufacturers Association.

Also affiliated to the SBBNF are the National Yacht Harbour Association (the marina operators in other words); the Yacht, Brokers, Designers and Surveyors Association; the National Federation of Sailing Schools; and the Yacht Charter Association.

In all the Federation represents about 1000 members engaged in the small craft industry – boat building and repairing, engine manufacturing, sail making, retailing marine equipment of all kinds, yacht agents, the supply of gear and services, in fact every aspect of the boating trade.

Through National Boat Shows Ltd the SBBNF organises the London International Boat Show, and it also sponsors certain regional boat shows, and organises stands at overseas exhibitions and trade missions to selected countries.

2.8.4 Trinity House

The Corporation of Trinity House has three main functions: (a) It is the Lighthouse Authority for England and Wales, the Channel Islands and Gibraltar. (b) It is the principal Pilotage Authority in the United Kingdom. (c) It is a Charitable Organisation for the relief of mariners and their dependants.

A Charter of 1514 gave Trinity House powers to regulate pilotage. By the 17th century the activities of the Corporation included erecting beacons, laying buoys and granting certificates to pilots.

Trinity House is controlled by a Board of ten members with long experience in either the Merchant or Royal Navies, assisted by administrative, engineering and technical staff. It maintains 92 lighthouses, 21 light vessels on station and nearly 700 buoys, two thirds of which are lit. It also inspects many marks which are maintained by local and Harbour Authorities. Trinity House is responsible for dealing with wrecks around the coasts of England and Wales.

Much development work has been done on new forms of lights, fog signals and beacons – often automatically operated. On the international scene Trinity House plays an important role in the International Association of Lighthouse Authorities (IALA).

Trinity House is the Pilotage Authority for London and 40 other districts in England and Wales, including Southampton. The service, like the Lighthouse Service, is entirely self-supporting and receives no government funds. There are about 670 Trinity House pilots. To qualify a pilot must be British, physically fit, possess a Foreign-going Master Mariner's certificate and have had five years' watchkeeping experience and be under 35.

Trinity House pioneered the scheme, now generally adopted elsewhere, of replacing cruising pilot cutters with fast shore-based launches for the transfer of pilots to and from ships.

The Trinity House Small Craft Liaison Committee was established in 1975 so that yachtsmen and fishermen (for example) should be able to state their opinions and requirements regarding navigation and safety at sea. It includes representatives of the Royal Yachting Association, Department of Trade, the General Council of British Shipping, the Fisheries Organisation Society, and the National Federation of Sea Anglers.

The Royal Yachting Association co-ordinates requests from yachtsmen for alterations or additions to aids to navigation, and correspondence on such matters should be addressed to the Cruising Secretary, Royal Yachting Association, Victoria Way, Woking, Surrey.

In Scotland and Ireland, lights are maintained by the Northern Lighthouse Board and the Commissioners of Irish Lights respectively. Their addresses are as follows:

Northern Lighthouse Board, 84 George Street, Edinburgh, EH2 3DA.

Commissioners of Irish Lights, 16 Lower Pembroke Street, Box 73, Dublin 2.

2.8.5 Some useful addresses

Amateur Yacht Research Society, Hermitage, Newbury, Berkshire, RG16 9RQ. Tel: Hermitage (0635) 200668.

Association of Brokers and Yacht Agents, Haven Brokerage, Lymington Yacht Haven, Kings Saltern Road, Lymington, Hants. Tel: Lymington (0590) 73212.

British Level Rating Association, Secretary, 18/19 Bath Road, Cowes, I.O.W. Tel: Cowes (0983) 295744.

British Sub-Aqua Club, 70 Brompton Road, London, SW3 1HE. Tel: (01) 584 7163.

British Waterways Board, Melbury House, Melbury Terrace, London, NW1 6JX. Tel: (01) 262 6711.

Clyde Cruising Club, S. V. *Carrick*, Clyde Street, Glasgow, G1 4LN. Tel: (041) 552 2183.

Cowes Combined Clubs, Secretary, 18/19 Bath Road, Cowes, I.O.W. Tel: Cowes (0983) 295744.

Cruising Association, Ivory House, St Katharine's Dock, World Trade Centre, London, E1 9AT. Tel: (01) 481 0881.

HM Coastguard, Department of Transport, Sunley House, 80–84 High Holborn, London, WC1V 6LP. Tel: (01) 405 6911.

HM Customs and Excise, Dorset House, Stamford Street, London SE1 9PS. Tel: (01) 028 0533.

International Maritime Organization, 4 Albert Embankment, London, SE1. Tel: (01) 735 7611.

Inland Waterways Association, 114 Regents Park Road, London NW1 8UQ. Tel: (01) 586 2556.

Junior Offshore Group, 59 Queen's Road, Cowes, I.O.W. Tel: Cowes (0983) 291572.

Little Ship Club, Bell Wharf Lane, London, EC4R 3TB. Tel: (01) 236 7729.

Lloyd's Register of Shipping, Yacht and Small Craft Department, 69 Oxford Street, Southampton, Hants, SO1 1DL. Tel: Southampton (0703) 20353.

Maritime Trust, 16 Ebury Street, London, SW1H 0LH. Tel: (01) 730 0096.

Meteorological Office, London Road, Bracknell, Berkshire, RG12 2SZ. Tel: Bracknell (0344) 42042.

Royal Cruising Club, 42 Half Moon Street, London, W1. Tel: (01) 499 2103.

Royal Institute of Navigation, 1 Kensington Gore, London, SW7 2AT. Tel: (01) 589 5021.

Royal National Lifeboat Institution, West Quay Road, Poole, Dorset, BH15 1HZ. Tel: Poole (02013) 71133.

Royal Naval Sailing Association, c/o Royal Naval Club, Pembroke Road, Portsmouth, Hants, PO1 2NT. Tel: Portsmouth (0705) 23524.

Royal Ocean Racing Club, 20 St James Place, London, SW1A 1NN. Tel: (01) 493 5252.

Royal Thames Yacht Club, 60 Knightsbridge, London SW1X 7FF. Tel: (01) 235 2121.

Royal Yachting Association, Victoria Way, Woking, Surrey, GU21 1EQ. Tel: Woking (048 62) 5022.

Ship and Boat Builders National Federation, Boating Industry House, Vale Road, Oatlands, Weybridge, Surrey. Tel: Weybridge (0932) 54511.

Solent Cruising and Racing Association, 18/19 Bath Road, Cowes, I.O.W. Tel: Cowes (0983) 295744.

Sports Council, 70 Brompton Road, London, SW3 1HE. Tel: (01) 589 3411.

Trinity House, Corporation of, Trinity House, Tower Hill, London, EC3N 4DH. Tel: (01) 480 6601.

United Kingdom Offshore Boating Association, Secretary, 57 Glycema Road, London, SW11 5TP. Tel: (01) 223 8100.

Yacht Brokers, Designers and Surveyors Association, The Wheelhouse, 5 Station Road, Liphook, Surrey, GU30 7DW. Tel: Liphook (0428) 722322.

Chapter 3
Coastal Navigation

Contents

3.1 Terms and definitions

3.1.1 Latitude and longitude

The positions of vessels or objects on a nautical chart are referred to by their latitude and longitude. The latitude of a point is its angular distance north or south of the equator, measured from 0-90°N or S. The longitude is its angular distance east or west of the prime (Greenwich) meridian, measured from 0-180°E or W.

In angular measurement there are 360 degrees in a circle, and 60 minutes of arc to a degree. For greater accuracy there are 60 seconds to a minute, but latitude and longitude are more often shown in degrees, minutes and tenths of a minute – e.g. latitude 51°07′.6N. The scales are given along the border of an ordinary chart – latitude up and down each side, and longitude along the top and bottom.

Fig. 3(1) illustrates how the latitude and longitude of point A are referred to the equator

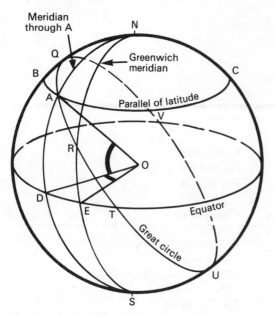

Fig. 3(1) Parallels of latitude, meridians and great circles.

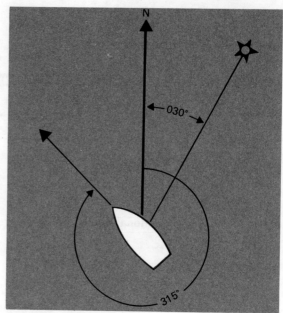

Fig. 3(2) A true bearing and a true course, related to true north.

and the Greenwich meridian respectively. Angle AOD is the latitude (north of the equator) and angle DOE is the longitude (west of Greenwich). BAC is the parallel of latitude through A, and NADS is the meridian through A.

3.1.2 Great circles

A great circle is the intersection of the surface of a sphere with a plane passing through its centre. The earth may be treated as a sphere, and in Fig. 3(1) it will be evident that all meridians are great circles (also passing through the poles). The equator is the only parallel of latitude which is a great circle. The circle indicated in the diagram by QARTUV is also a great circle.

The shortest distance between any two points on the surface of the earth lies along the great circle through them. Over long distances great circle sailing is sometimes used, either by means of special (gnomonic) charts, or by computing the courses and distances by formula, tables or calculator.

3.1.3 Courses and bearings

In order to proceed from place to place the navigator must have an indication of direction. Also if he knows the directions (bearings) of certain fixed objects marked on the chart he can establish his position. Courses and bearings are most simply measured in relation to true north, as given by the meridian passing through the place concerned – a line pointing straight up towards the top of a Mercator chart.

Courses and bearings are measured clockwise from north, and are always expressed in three figures. A true bearing of 090° is due east for example, and 180° is due south. In Fig. 3(2) the lighthouse bears 030° from the yacht, which is steering 315° (north west).

Course – rhumb line

The true course of a boat is the angle between true north and the direction in which she is heading, measured clockwise. As she sails along on a steady course she cuts all the meridians at the same angle. Such a line is called a rhumb line. If drawn on a globe it will normally appear as a spiral towards one of the poles, but as we will see (3.2.1) it is conveniently represented on a Mercator's chart by a straight line.

So a yacht, steering a steady course from one place to another, proceeds along a rhumb line. This is not quite the same as the line she would follow for the shortest distance between the two places, which would be the great circle joining them, but for practical navigation over comparatively short distances the difference is insignificant.

3.1.4 Standard navigational terms

Experienced skippers and navigators may well wish to preserve the terms which they have used to describe various features in navigation and chartwork. But certain standard terms as listed below are now used in shorebased courses. In any boat where more than one individual is involved in navigation, it is important to establish precisely the meanings of some terms in order to avoid confusion.

Track – the path followed or to be followed between one position and another. This path may be that over the ground (ground track) or through the water (water track).

*Track angle** – the direction of a track.

Track made good – the mean ground track actually achieved over a given period.

Heading – the horizontal direction of the ship's

---

* The word *angle* will be omitted in normal use unless there is a possibility of confusion.

head at a given moment. (This term does not necessarily require movement of the vessel.)

Course (Co) – the intended heading.

Course to steer – the course related to the compass used by the helmsman.

Set – the direction towards which a current and/or tidal stream flows.

Drift – the distance covered in a given time due solely to the movement of a current and/or tidal stream.

*Drift angle** – the angular difference between the ground track and the water track.

Leeway – the effect of wind moving a vessel bodily to leeward.

*Leeway angle** – the angular difference between the water track and the ship's heading.

Dead reckoning – the process of maintaining or predicting an approximate record of progress by projecting course and distance from a known position.

DR position (DR) – (1) the general term for a position obtained by dead reckoning; (2) specifically a position obtained using true course and distance run, the latter derived from the log or engine revolutions as considered more appropriate.

Estimated position (EP) – a best possible approximation of a present or future position. It is based on course and distance since the last known position with an estimation made for leeway, set and drift, or by extrapolation from earlier fixes.

3.1.5 Variation

In yachts and boats, courses and bearings are actually measured by a magnetic compass, which tries to point to the magnetic north, and not true north, which is different. The angular amount by which magnetic north is displaced from true north is called the variation. If variation is west, the magnetic north is to the west of true north; if variation is east it is to the east.

Variation alters from place to place on the earth's surface and, to a lesser extent, with the passage of time. Currently around the British Isles it ranges from about 6°W in the Dover Strait to about 11°W in the west of Scotland. The variation in a certain area is shown on the chart, e.g. 'Variation 8°46′W (1975) decreasing about 5′ annually'.

To correct a magnetic bearing or course to a true one, subtract westerly variation or add easterly. When converting from true to magnetic the opposite applies – add westerly variation or subtract easterly. Since in home waters variation is westerly, we will only consider this in the examples below. When in doubt it is helpful to draw a little diagram, like the ones shown.

In Fig. 3(3) a magnetic bearing of 081°(M) with a variation of 8°W results in a true bearing of 073°.

In Fig. 3(4) a true course of 030° and a variation of 7°W gives a magnetic course of 037°.

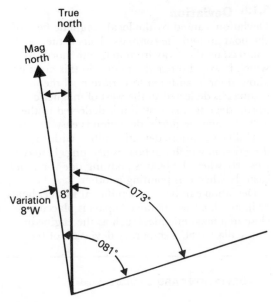

Fig. 3(3)

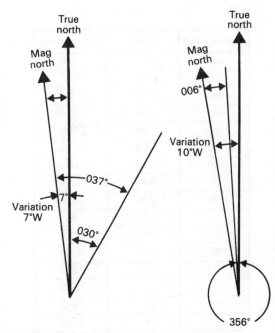

Fig. 3(4)   **Fig. 3(5)**

Figs 3(3)–3(5) The relation between true and magnetic courses and bearings, by applying westerly variation.

In order to distinguish this from a true course it is written 037°(M).

In Fig. 3(5) a true course of 356° with a variation of 10°W gives a magnetic course of 356 + 10 = 366° or 006°(M).

In certain isolated places there exist areas of Local Magnetic Anomaly. These are indicated on Admiralty charts by a wavy line, with figures such as ±15° in the centre – indicating that within the enclosed area the magnetic variation may deviate from the normal by the value shown.

3.1.6 Deviation

Deviation, caused by the local magnetic field of the boat around the compass, deflects the compass needle away from magnetic north to which it would otherwise point. So this must be allowed for in addition to variation. If the compass is deflected to the west of magnetic north, deviation is west: if it is deflected to the east of magnetic north, deviation is east.

Unlike variation, deviation alters with the direction in which the boat is heading. It may be westerly when the boat is pointing one way, and easterly when it is pointing another.

Deviation can be very significant in steel boats, or in any boat where the compass is placed too close to a magnetic mass such as the engine or iron ballast keel. Temporary deviation of the compass can be caused by inadvertently placing any magnetic object, such as a beer can, too close to it. In sailing boats which spend long periods on one tack or the other heeling error can also be a problem – see section 3.1.10.

In most boats deviation can largely be eliminated by a skilful compass adjuster, who places small corrector magnets near the compass so that they cancel out the local magnetic field. When the adjustment is complete, and as much of the deviation as possible has been removed, the boat is finally 'swung' on various headings (usually every 15°) to find out what deviation still remains, and a deviation card is drawn up as shown in Fig. 3(6). The procedures for checking, adjusting and swinging the compass are described in sections 3.1.7 to 3.1.11 below.

Deviation is applied in just the same way as variation. A useful mnemonic is the word CADET, meaning 'Compass to True, Add East'. The two end letters stand for 'Compass to True', and the three centre ones tell you to 'ADd East'. That is, when converting from compass to true add easterly variation or deviation (and subtract westerly).

Variation and deviation are added together to give the total compass error to be applied on any occasion. For example, if variation is 7°W and the deviation on the course being steered is 3°E, the total compass error is 4°W. In this instance a compass course of 168° – which is written in the form 168°(C) – would be a true course of 164°.

3.1.7 Compass checks

Every opportunity should be taken to check the accuracy of the steering compass. A quick comparison can always be made with a hand bearing compass, held on the fore and aft line well away from any metal object. This should show up any serious deviation on a particular course.

A more accurate method is to take a bearing of a known transit (two objects in line) and compare it with the bearing from the chart, remembering to allow for variation – where the bearing of a transit is shown on the chart (e.g. 'Lights in line') it is the true bearing from seaward. It is good practice to check the compass against all available transits, for example leading marks when entering or leaving harbour.

The sun, or any other heavenly body, can be used in conjunction with navigational tables which give the azimuth angle (Z) at the time and place concerned. The azimuth angle is the true bearing of a heavenly body, measured (in the northern hemisphere) eastward or westward from true north. From the azimuth angle is derived the azimuth (Zn), which is the true bearing of the heavenly body in 360° nomenclature, measured from true north.

The relationship between Z and Zn depends upon the Local Hour Angle (LHA) of the heavenly body, which is the angle measured

	DEVIATION CARD Steering compass	

Yacht _____

Date _____

Magnetic course	Deviation	Compass course
000	2W	002
015	2W	017
030	3W	033
045	3W	048
060	4W	064
075	3W	078
090	3W	093
105	3W	108
120	2W	122
135	1W	136
150	1W	151
165	1W	166
180	0	180
195	0	195
210	0	210
225	0	225
240	1E	239
255	2E	253
270	2E	268
285	3E	282
300	2E	298
315	1E	314
330	0	330
345	1W	346
360	2W	002

Fig. 3(6) Typical deviation card, showing actual magnetic course being steered compared to compass course.

TABLE 3(1) True bearing of sun at sunrise and sunset.

LAT	DECLINATION												LAT
	0°	1°	2°	3°	4°	5°	6°	7°	8°	9°	10°	11°	
	°	°	°	°	°	°	°	°	°	°	°	°	
30°	90	88.8	87.7	86.5	85.4	84.2	83.1	81.9	80.7	79.6	78.4	77.3	30°
31°	90	88.8	87.7	86.5	85.3	84.2	83.0	81.9	80.6	79.5	78.3	77.1	31°
32°	90	88.8	87.6	86.5	85.3	84.1	82.9	81.7	80.5	79.4	78.2	77.0	32°
33°	90	88.8	87.6	86.4	85.2	84.0	82.8	81.6	80.4	79.2	78.0	76.8	33°
34°	90	88.8	87.6	86.4	85.2	84.0	82.7	81.5	80.3	79.1	77.9	76.7	34°

Fig. 3(7) Extract from Table 3(1) in *The Macmillan & Silk Cut Nautical Almanac*.

westwards at the pole between the observer's meridian and the meridian of the heavenly body. In northern latitudes if LHA is greater than 180°, Zn = Z. If LHA is less than 180°, Zn = 360° – Z.

In order to achieve sufficient accuracy for checking a compass an azimuth mirror is needed, and the altitude of the heavenly body should not be more than about 35°.

3.1.8 Bearing of sun, rising or setting

At sea the compass may conveniently be checked against the azimuth of the sun when rising or setting – the only astronomical observation which needs no instrument. It is only necessary to know the approximate latitude of the boat, and the declination of the sun or other heavenly body, in order to enter Table 3(1) of *The Macmillan & Silk Cut Nautical Almanac* – a portion of which is reproduced above – and extract the required figure.

For example, in latitude 33° and with declination 9°, the tabulated figure is 79.2 (say 79°) which must be applied as follows.

The tabulated figure obtained is the true bearing – measured from north if the declination is north, or from south if the declination is south; towards the east if rising, or towards the west if setting. The following examples show how to derive the true bearing in different circumstances.

DR Lat	Declin- ation	Sun	Tabulated bearing	True bearing
33°	9°N	Rising	79°	N79°E or 079°
33°	9°N	Setting	79°	N79°W or 281°
33°	9°S	Rising	79°	S79°E or 101°
33°	9°S	Setting	79°	S79°W or 259°

Having obtained the true bearing from the table, it is then necessary to apply the local magnetic variation and compare the resulting figure with the bearing from the compass in order to determine the deviation on the course being steered.

Due to refraction, which is about 34' when observing bodies on the horizon, the bearing of the sun should be taken when its lower limb is a little over half a diameter above the horizon.

Very few yachts' compasses are fitted with azimuth rings, and steering compasses are often wooded over large sectors so that it is impossible to take bearings with them. This difficulty can be overcome by steering the boat directly towards, or away from, the rising or setting sun, and lining it up with the mast, forestay etc. Or it may be possible to line up the sun directly on the beam, using some athwartships part of the boat's structure. In all cases it is important to remember that the deviation determined only applies to the course being steered at the time of the observation.

3.1.9 Compass adjusting

The steering (or master) compass is the key navigational instrument in any yacht, and its accuracy is most important. No compass should be relied on unless it has at least been checked by 'swinging', to determine the deviation on various headings. The procedure is outlined below.

If a compass swing shows that the deviation is not more than a degree or two on any heading, no further action is required. But very often larger deviations will be disclosed on certain courses, and when these are plotted against their respective headings a curve such as is shown in Fig. 3(8) will be found.

This deviation curve is the sum of five different coefficients, called A, B, C, D and E. Of these A and E can normally be neglected in small vessels,

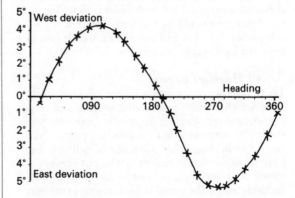

Fig. 3(8) Deviation curve, determined by swinging the compass.

and no means are provided to correct for them. The causes of coefficient D are items such as steel decks, not usually present in yachts, so that normally the yachtsman is only concerned with coefficients B and C.

Coefficient B causes deviations on east-west headings, and coefficient C causes deviations on north-south headings. Luckily the effects of both B and C can be greatly reduced or eliminated by placing suitable magnets near the compass, so as to counteract the local distortion of the earth's magnetic field.

Unlike poles of magnets attract each other, while like poles repel each other. For compass adjusting a north-seeking pole (such as the north end of a compass needle) is marked as a red pole, and a south-seeking pole is marked as a blue pole. Hence the north magnetic pole is a blue pole, and the south magnetic pole is a red pole.

Coefficient B, which causes the trouble on east-west courses, can be corrected by using fore and aft magnets which fairly obviously have no effect on the direction of the compass needle when the boat is heading north or south (because they only strengthen or weaken the earth's magnetic field). If the magnet is placed red (north) end forward, it corrects easterly deviation on easterly courses and westerly deviation on westerly courses. Conversely, if the magnet is placed blue (south) end forward, it corrects westerly deviation on easterly courses and easterly deviation on westerly courses.

Similarly, coefficient C, which gives rise to deviation on north-south courses, can be corrected by adding athwartships magnets – which have no effect on the compass when the boat is heading east or west. A magnet with its red (north) end to starboard corrects easterly deviation on northerly headings, and westerly deviation on southerly headings. A magnet with its blue (south) end to starboard corrects westerly deviation on northerly headings, and easterly deviation on southerly headings.

The effect of either fore and aft or athwartships magnets can be increased or reduced by varying the strength of the magnet or its distance from the compass card. Older compasses had wooden corrector boxes, drilled with holes into which small magnets could be inserted. Modern compasses have built-in correctors, which can be adjusted by a screw action.

3.1.10 Heeling error
There is, however, another source of compass error which should be attended to first, and that is heeling error. Vertical magnetic forces do not affect the compass when the boat is upright, but can cause heeling error when she is inclined. This is more important in sailing boats, but even in a motor boat heeling error can make the compass unstable when the vessel rolls. Heeling error can only be removed when there is suitable provision for placing vertical magnets underneath the

compass. The adjustment is carried out using an instrument called a dip needle, which is a horizontal magnet balanced on a knife edge. This is set up ashore, away from any magnetic influence, so that it is levelled with the north end pointing north (south in the southern hemisphere) by adjusting a balance weight. The dip needle is then put exactly in the position occupied by the compass, with the boat on an east/west heading and the needle pointing north. If it does not lie horizontally it can be adjusted by vertical correctors – red end up if the north end is dipped down, blue end up if the north end is raised.

Correction for heeling error must be done before any other corrections are made. By the same token, if any alteration is made to the vertical magnets used for heeling error correction, it is important to carry out a compass swing to check the deviation on all courses.

3.1.11 Compass swinging
The compass should be swung on specific occasions, or whenever there is reasonable doubt about its accuracy. Many yachts are not swung often enough, since with the passage of time the compensating magnets lose their magnetism. It should be done when the boat is new (or when a new compass is fitted), at the start of each season, if additional equipment (including electrical items) is fitted anywhere near the compass, and on any major change in latitude – say more than 10°.

A compass can be swung by taking bearings, from a known position, of an object about five miles or more away, using a pelorus or bearing plate. This consists of an azimuth ring graduated from 0°–360°, with a sighting arm for viewing the distant object. The pelorus is lined up with its zero mark in the fore and aft line of the boat, so that the relative bearing of the object can be read for various headings, and compared with the bearing from the chart. The principle is illustrated in Fig. 3(9) and in the accompanying table.

If a pelorus is not available it is possible to use a sextant, held horizontally, to take the bearings. First it is necessary to place two reference marks, accurately located on the centreline of the boat – say with one on the aft side of the mast and the other at the aft end of the coachroof, and the observer near the stern.

Professional compass adjusters may use the sun rather than a distant terrestial object, working from prepared azimuth tables. Unless conditions are very smooth, it is necessary for a yacht to be moored between three or four points, so that she can be warped round and held steady while the bearings are taken. Alternatively she can be kept under way, in the immediate vicinity of a buoy or beacon whose position is known. It is important however that the boat should not be close to large magnetic objects, and also to ensure that

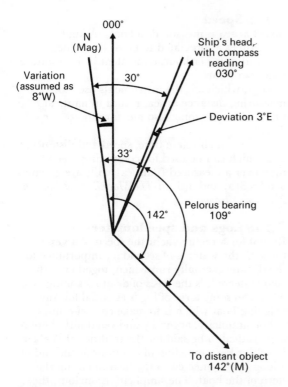

Fig. 3(9) The principle of compass swinging. How the relative bearing of a distant object, related to the known bearing from a certain position, gives the deviation on a particular heading, in this case 030°.

Ship's head (compass)	Pelorus bearing	Bearing of object by compass	Known bearing (Mag)	Deviation
000	140	140	142	2°E
030	109	139	142	3°E
060	081	141	142	1°E
090	052	142	142	0
120	023	143	142	1°W
etc				

there are no tools or spare corrector magnets anywhere near the compass.

The procedure is then briefly as follows. With the boat heading due east, fore and aft magnets are placed so as to remove the deviation. The procedure is then repeated with the boat heading due north, using athwartships magnets. The effect of these magnets is then examined with the boat heading due west and due south. If there is no appreciable deviation (say, less than 2°) no further correction is necessary, but if there is then remove half of it by placing the appropriate magnets. Then check again on east and north headings.

Having completed the adjustment so that the deviation on the four cardinal points is minimal, and hopefully only 1° or so in each case, the boat is then swung through 360° to measure the remaining deviation at steps of, say, 30° and these are the readings which form the deviation card.

Remember to impress upon all on board the importance of keeping magnetic objects well away from the compass at all times. Things like camera light meters, metal spectacle cases and beer cans can have a considerable influence on even the best adjusted compass.

3.1.12 Hand bearing compass

A good hand bearing compass is essential for coastal navigation, and at sea for taking bearings of an approaching vessel to see whether the latter is on a collision course. It can also be used for a quick check of the yacht's steering compass, and in emergency it can be taken aboard the liferaft or tender.

Such a compass needs to be accurate, with a scale that is easy to read, and sufficiently damped for the card to settle quickly. Illumination must be provided for use at night, and this is now almost universally achieved with Betalights.

The traditional type of Sestrel compass is an excellent instrument, with which very accurate bearings can be taken, but it is relatively bulky and the prism somewhat vulnerable to damage. Other designs, such as the well-known Mini compass from Offshore Instruments, are more compact, and by using modern optical systems the compass can be held close to the eye, to eliminate parallax, with both the object and the figures on the card readily visible. Other makes include Silva and Suunto, and such compasses can be hung on a lanyard round the neck, and stuffed inside one's oilskin jacket, so that they are always available when required – a great advantage.

Latest developments, which are not necessarily endorsed, include electronic compasses which take a reading when a trigger is pressed, and present the figures as a digital readout. It may be found that this type of compass is not easy to use under certain conditions, as for example when taking the bearing of an infrequently flashing light in bad weather.

For general daytime use it is difficult to fault the Offshore Binox – a pair of binoculars which includes a compass (plus a rangefinder recticule if required). The optical qualities of the Binox are excellent, and the compass is extremely deadbeat. It is light and compact, but expensive.

3.1.13 Relative bearings

Relative bearings are sometimes used at sea to indicate the direction of an object or another vessel in relation to the fore and aft line of one's own boat. Relative bearings to port are designated 'Red', and those to starboard 'Green', each being numbered from 000° (dead ahead) to 180° (dead astern). So a relative bearing of 'Green 080' indicates a direction 10° ahead of the starboard beam. 'Red 135' indicates a bearing on the port quarter.

The general concept of bearings relative to the ship's head is also used in connection with some types of radio direction finding equipment, described in Chapter 4.

3.1.14 Distances

Distances at sea are almost as important as
directions. They are measured in nautical miles,
often abbreviated to nm or M, which are longer
than statute or land miles. The nautical mile is
the length of a minute of latitude at the place
concerned, and because the earth is not a perfect
sphere it varies slightly in length from 6046ft
(1843m) at the equator to 6108ft (1862m) at the
poles. However this is not a problem because the
Mercator chart has a built-in scale of distances in
the form of the latitude scale, which is marked
down the margin either side.

Fig. 3(10) shows how a distance between two
points on the chart is transferred to the latitude
scale with dividers, in order to determine how far
they are apart in nautical miles.

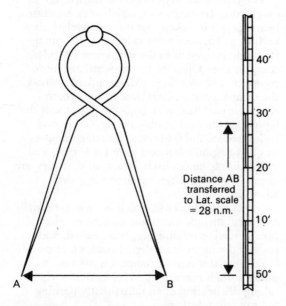

Fig. 3(10) Showing how dividers are used to transfer a
certain distance AB on the chart to the latitude scale for
measurement.

Instruments such as logs and radar sets which
measure distances are calibrated on a mean
figure of 6076ft (1852m), now universally
adopted as the International Nautical Mile.

A cable is one-tenth of a nautical mile, or for
practical purposes 200yd (183m). This unit is
often met in sailing directions, and may be
abbreviated to ca.

3.1.15 Speed

Speed at sea is measured in knots. A knot
(sometimes abbreviated to kn or kt) is one
nautical mile per hour, equivalent to 1.15 statute
miles per hour.

Logs, which are the instruments used for
measuring distance at sea, record in nautical
miles, although some also measure speed – see
3.1.16.

Tables which relate time, speed and distance,
and which can be used for computing speed from
time over a measured (nautical) mile are given as
Tables 3(5) and 3(6) in *The Macmillan & Silk Cut
Nautical Almanac*.

3.1.16 Logs and speedometers

Except for a racing yacht the speed of a vessel
through the water is of secondary importance to
the distance actually run which, together with
course steered, is the basis of dead reckoning (see
3.3.4). So some form of log is essential for any
seagoing boat which is to make coastal cruises.

For simplicity, accuracy and reliability there is
a great deal to be said for the traditional Walker
Excelsior log, consisting of a rotator at the end of
a long line connected to the instrument on the
stern of the boat. The simplicity is obvious, the
accuracy is due to the fact that the rotator is
operating well astern of the hull, and reliability is
ensured because, apart from routine cleaning and
lubrication, maintenance is minimal.
Furthermore, the whole can be stowed away in
its box when not needed. It is, however, wise to
carry a spare line and rotator.

When streaming a log, first hook it onto the
indicator and then (retaining the rotator
inboard) stream the bight of the line before
letting the rotator go. Otherwise the rotator will
twist the line into knots while it is being
streamed. Similarly, when recovering it, unhook
the end of the line from the indicator and pay it
out astern as the rotator is taken in – allowing the
line to untwist as it is eventually pulled inboard
from the rotator end.

The Excelsior log makes 1166 revolutions per
nautical mile, and it is easy to convert revolutions
per minute (or the time to make 50 revolutions,
for example) into the boat's speed. This can be
done using the scale given in Fig. 3(11).

Modern technology has produced several other
types of log – more expensive and not necessarily
any more accurate, but more convenient to use.

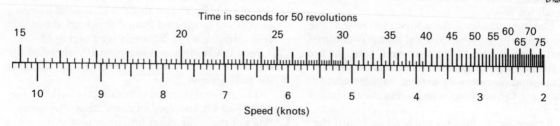

Time in seconds for 50 revolutions

Fig. 3(11) Speed table for Walker's Excelsior IV Log (1166 revolutions per nautical mile).

Some have a small impeller or paddlewheel mounted outside the hull; the rotating part incorporates a small magnet so that the magnetic impulse is passed to a unit inside the boat, which can count the number of pulses and hence record distance run and speed.

Some logs operate without any moving parts, so avoiding the problems of fouling by weed etc. An electro-magnetic log works on the principle that if a conductor moves in a magnetic field an electric current is induced in it, and the faster the movement the greater the current. The magnetic field is produced by an electromagnet inside the hull fitting, and the potential difference is sensed by two electrodes mounted flush with the outside of the hull.

Doppler logs measure the apparent shift in frequency between a transmitted signal and the signal reflected back from the water or (in shallower depths) from the bottom. When picking up the bottom signal the log measures distance and speed over the ground, rather than through the water.

If it is to be relied on, any log should be calibrated by running the boat over a measured distance. The procedure is described in 3.3.15.

Most electronic logs incorporate some form of adjustment for calibration, and few have theoretical operating errors of less than $\pm 1\frac{1}{2}$ per cent. In practice the error is likely to be greater than this and may vary with speed. So log readings must be used with caution when (for example) approaching dangers in poor visibility.

3.1.17 Depths
The depth of water is always of concern to yachtsmen, and since modern echo sounders are reliable and cheap they are a most useful aid to navigation. But to gain full benefit from them it is necessary to understand exactly what they measure.

Further information and definitions of terms used in connection with the tides are given in Chapter 9.

Once a yachtsman is aware of the significance of the soundings marked on a chart and how the height of the tide is expressed above chart datum, the echo sounder (or lead line) becomes a useful navigation aid, apart from telling him when he is about to run aground.

It is best if the echo sounder is adjusted to give the actual distance of the sea bed below sea level, and this should be checked with a lead line from time to time. Then, knowing the height of the tide at any moment (from tide tables) and the reading of the echo sounder, it is possible to calculate what depth should be shown on the chart.

Similarly the echo sounder can be used, perhaps in poor visibility, for 'contour navigation' – following a certain depth contour, maybe along the edge (but just clear) of the main shipping channel.

When anchoring it is important to know the height of the tide at that time so that, in conjunction with the depth of water shown by the echo sounder (or lead line), it is possible to calculate what will be the greatest and least depths of water at that place. The greatest depth will dictate how much scope should be given to the anchor cable, while the least depth will of course govern whether or not the boat will be safely afloat at low water.

3.1.18 Echo sounders
An echo sounder is the most useful item of electronic equipment for a boat of any type, and there is a large range of models available. Properly used as described above, an echo sounder is a navigational aid – not just a means of preventing involuntary grounding.

All echo sounders work on a similar principle, although there are different ways of presenting the information. An electronic pulse, usually at 150 or 200kHz, is transmitted downwards from the transducer, fitted in the bottom of the boat. The signal received back from the sea bottom is amplified and then made into a readable display. For small boats the most common is the flashing display with a rotating arm, at the end of which there is a light source. The light flashes at zero when the pulse is emitted, and it flashes again when the amplified signal is received back. For practical purposes the speed of sound in water is constant at about 4900ft/sec (1490m/sec), although it is slightly affected by differences in temperature and salinity. Since the arm rotates at a constant speed, the time taken for the pulse to go to the bottom and back is represented by the angular displacement between the two flashes.

The receiver will also record echoes that are returned from intermediate objects, between the transducer and the sea bed – fish, weed etc. Also, with experience, the echo from a hard bottom, such as rock, can be distinguished from soft mud.

Other types of display incorporate either a needle on a dial (i.e. a meter display) or a digital readout. Either may include a special microprocessor which tries to sort out the extraneous signals from fish etc which otherwise may cause the display to fluctuate wildly.

Most modern echo sounders are sufficiently powerful to allow the transducer to be installed inside a glassfibre hull. Apart from eliminating the need for a hole through the bottom, this also solves any problem of fouling on the face of the transducer. It does however reduce the sensitivity at maximum depths.

Some echo sounders have shallow-water alarms which can be useful, particularly if cruising short handed. In addition, some models have a deep-water alarm, or anchor watch features.

The most versatile type of echo sounder has a visual record display whereby the flash (similar to that of a rotating flashing display) marks a moving sheet of paper and thus provides a recorded picture of the echoes from the sea bed and from the water above it. Some such sounders combine this graphical display with a flashing light display which can be used in isolation (to save paper).

Yet another method of presentation is by cathode ray tube – and in colour so that different types of echoes (surface contamination, plankton layers, shoals of fish, and type of bottom) can be readily distinguished. Naturally, such sophisticated equipment is expensive and its use is normally confined to fish finding and similar uses.

3.1.19 Lead line
Even when a yacht is fitted with an echo sounder it is desirable to carry a hand lead and line. Apart from being required in the event of any failure of the electronic instrument, it is also useful on occasions at anchor, to tell whether the anchor is dragging.

Traditionally, lead lines have been marked in fathoms, as follows. (One fathom is six feet).

2 fathoms – Two strips of leather
3 fathoms – Three strips of leather
5 fathoms – A piece of white duck
7 fathoms – A piece of red bunting
10 fathoms – A piece of leather with a hole in it
13 fathoms – A piece of blue serge
15 fathoms – A piece of white duck
17 fathoms – A piece of red bunting
20 fathoms – Two knots.

With the change to metric units it is now more convenient for a lead line to be calibrated in metres, and the following markings are appropriate:

1 and 11 metres – One strip of leather
2 and 12 metres – Two strips of leather
3 and 13 metres – Blue bunting
4 and 14 metres – Green and white bunting
5 and 15 metres – White bunting
6 and 16 metres – Green bunting
7 and 17 metres – Red bunting
8 and 18 metres – Blue and white bunting
9 and 19 metres – Red and white bunting
10 metres   – Leather with a hole in it
20 metres   – Leather with a hole in it and two strips of leather

A 20 metre or 10 fathom lead line is adequate for most yachting purposes, particularly when mainly used as a stand-by for the echo sounder.

3.1.20 Tidal streams
Almost as important to yachtsmen as the depth of water caused by the rise and fall of the tide are tidal streams – the horizontal movement of water, usually changing direction every six hours or so. Explanations of tidal streams are given in Chapter 9(9.10). Details of tidal streams around the coasts of Britain and Western Europe are given in *The Macmillan & Silk Cut Nautical Almanac*.

3.1.21 Meteorological conditions
Tidal heights are computed and predicted for average meteorological conditions, and can be quite seriously affected by unusual weather and, to a lesser extent, by changes in barometric pressure. Details are given in Chapter 9(9.8).

3.2 Charts

3.2.1 Mercator's projection
An adequate chart of an area is the first requirement for any form of navigation. Without it the sailor has no idea of the relative positions or distances of one feature from another, or of what goes on beneath the surface of the sea.

A chart, like a map, must be a compromise because it has to represent the curved shape of the globe on a flat piece of paper. Details of the coastline, for example, have to be distorted somewhat to get them on a flat surface.

Most charts are drawn on Mercator's projection with the meridians shown as equally spaced parallel lines running up and down the chart – whereas in reality they converge towards the poles. The parallels of latitude, which in reality are equally spaced, are drawn on the chart further and further apart towards the poles.

Thus on a Mercator's chart land masses are greatly distorted in high latitudes, but this is not important around the British Isles.

A Mercator's chart has the following characteristics:
(1) A rhumb line, which cuts all the meridians at the same angle, is a straight line on the chart.
(2) The scale of distance is given by the latitude scale – at the latitude concerned.
(3) Angles on the earth's surface are equal to corresponding angles on the chart.
(4) Meridians are parallel straight lines, equally spaced, and the scale of longitude is constant for all latitudes.
(5) A great circle, which is the shortest distance between two points, appears as a curve. This is not a serious disadvantage unless long passages are contemplated.

3.2.2 Gnomonic charts
Some charts are based on a gnomonic (pronounced nom-on-ic) projection. Apart from harbour plans this projection is also used for polar charts and for great circle sailing. A gnomonic chart is a projection of the earth's surface from the centre on to a tangent plane, so that all great circles appear as straight lines. Large scale gnomonic charts, as used for harbour plans, are used in just the same way as a Mercator's chart.

3.2.3 Scale
The amount of detail shown on a chart depends upon its scale. Large scale charts (typically

1:50,000) are used for harbours and approaches, while small scale charts (1:1,000,000 for example) may be used for coastlines. The scale is the relationship between a distance shown on the chart and the actual distance on land or sea. i.e. 1:50,000 means that one foot on the chart represents 50,000ft on land/sea. So large scale charts cover small areas and have small numbers in their scale, while small scales charts cover big areas and have big numbers.

The scale is shown near the title to the chart. It is most important to use the largest scale chart available, particularly for inshore pilotage, because a lot of inshore details are deliberately omitted from small scale charts.

A good idea of the scale of a chart can be obtained by looking at the latitude scale, remembering that one minute is one nautical mile. It will be noticed that on Admiralty charts the design of the latitude scale varies with the scale of the chart. Care is needed in reading latitude and longitude scales. Read off the correct number of degrees first (taking the lower of the two figures on either side of the position), and then the number of minutes.

3.2.4 Chart corrections

It is a false economy to carry too few charts, or charts which are out of date. Admiralty charts show the date of publication and also the date of the last correction at the bottom.

Corrections to charts and to other navigational publications from the Hydrographic Department (such as the *Admiralty List of Lights and Fog Signals* and the *Admiralty List of Radio Signals*) are issued in the weekly *Admiralty Notices to Mariners*, which can be obtained from chart agents or are available for consultation at Mercantile Marine Offices and Customs Offices.

A *Small Craft Edition of Admiralty Notices to Mariners* is published periodically for those who navigate small craft in the waters round the British Isles. It summarises the corrections which are of direct interest to yachtsmen.

3.2.5 Yachtsman's charts

Commercial charts are available which are specifically intended for use in small craft. They either have comparatively small sheets or they can be folded like a map, making them handy to use in a small space. Stanford's charts for example cover the principal coastal areas of the country, and the more important yachting harbours. They also give pilotage notes and other information useful to yachtsmen. They are available from chandlers or from the publishers: Barnacle Marine Limited, The Warehouse, 1 Crowhurst Road, Colchester, Essex, CO3 3JN.

Imray, Laurie, Norie and Wilson (Imray's) produce three series of charts for yachtsmen. Their 'Y' series cover harbours or short lengths of coast, while the 'C' series are smaller scale for coastal cruising. The 'BB' series are even smaller

scale, but are suitable for passage making. They are available from yacht suppliers or from the publishers at Wych House, The Broadway, St Ives, Huntingdon, Cambridgeshire.

3.2.6 Admiralty charts

The full *Catalogue of Admiralty Charts and other Hydrographic Publications* (NP 131) lists some 6000 charts – sufficient to take a boat to almost every part of the world – as well as many other Admiralty publications. It also lists the location of Admiralty chart agents, which is repeated in *Admiralty Notice to Mariners* No. 2 each year.

A limited edition of the chart catalogue (NP 109) covering the British Isles and north-west Europe is published in January each year.

When ordered, charts should be referred to by their number as well as their title.

Apart from purely navigational charts the Hydrographic Department issues a variety of other charts and diagrams, of which the following may be of interest to yachtsmen:
(1) Latticed charts for electronic navigation systems such as Decca, Loran, Omega and Consol.
(2) Astronomical charts – azimuth diagrams and star charts, for navigational purposes.
(3) Routeing charts for ocean passages. The data includes routes and distances between ports, ocean currents, wind roses, ice limits, air and sea temperature, barometric pressure, and the incidence of fog and gales.
(4) Ships' boats' charts. Issued as a survival kit for ships' boats but useful for a liferaft on ocean passages.
(5) Instructional charts – cheap, uncorrected charts for navigational classes.
(6) Plotting charts.
(7) Uncorrected fathom charts of the Scilly Isles and Irish loughs.

3.2.7 Admiralty charts symbols and abbreviations

To make proper use of a chart it is essential to know at least the more common symbols and abbreviations which are used in order to make the best use of the space available. They are described in detail in Admiralty Chart 5011, which is in booklet form.

The information below refers to metric charts except where otherwise stated. There are still a number of older charts in use; in general the symbols and abbreviations on these are fairly similar but there is one notable exception – as already stated, depths on metric charts are given in metres whereas on older charts they are shown either as fathoms and feet or (for inshore charts) as feet. Always check which units apply.

An obvious function of a chart is to show the outlines of the coast and of off-lying islands. On metric Admiralty charts these features are made distinct by the land being tinted buff, and drying areas (between high water and low water) being

Coastal Features

G	Gulf
B	Bay
L	Loch, Lough, Lake
Cr	Creek
Str	Strait
Sd	Sound
Pass	Passage
Chan	Channel
Apprs	Approaches
Entce	Entrance
R	River
Est	Estuary
Mth	Mouth
Rds	Roads, Roadstead
Anch	Anchorage
Hr	Harbour
Hn	Haven
P	Port
I	Island
It	Islet
C	Cape
Promy	Promontory
Pt	Point
Mt	Mountain, Mount
Lndg	Landing place
Rk	Rock

Units

m	Metre(s)
dm	Decimetre(s)
cm	Centimetre(s)
mm	Millimetre(s)
km	Kilometre(s)
ft	Foot, feet
M	Sea Mile(s)
kn	knot(s)
Lat	Latitude
Long	Longitude
Ht	Height
No	Number

Adjectives etc

Gt Grt	Great
Lit	Little
Mid	Middle
Anct	Ancient
S St	Saint
conspic	Conspicuous
destd	Destroyed
projd	Projected
dist	Distant
abt	About
illum	Illuminated
Aero	Aeronautical
Hr	Higher
Lr	Lower
experl	Experimental
discontd	Discontinued
prohib	Prohibited
explos	Explosive

priv	Private
promt	Prominent
submd	Submerged
approx	Approximate
NM	Notices to Mariners
(P)	Preliminary(NM)
(T)	Temporary(NM)
SD	Sailing Directions
LL	List of Lights

Buildings etc

Cas	Castle
Ho	House
Va	Villa
Fm	Farm
Ch	Church, Chapel
Cath	Cathedral
Cemy	Cemetery
Ft	Fort
Baty	Battery
St	Street
Ave	Avenue
Tel	Telegraph
PO	Post Office
Hospl	Hospital
Mont	Monument, Memorial
Cup	Cupola
Ru	Ruin
Tr	Tower
Chy	Chimney
Sch	School
Bldg	Building
Tel	Telephone
Col	Column, Obelisk
Stn	Station
CG	Coastguard
LB	Lifeboat
Sig Stn	Signal Station
Sem	Semaphore
Storm Sig	Storm signal station
FS	Flagstaff
Sig	Signal
Obsy	Observatory
Off	Office
NB	Notice Board

Dangers

Bk	Bank
Sh	Shoal
Rf	Reef
Le	Ledge
Obstn	Obstruction
Wk	Wreck
dr	Drives
cov	Covers
uncov	Uncovers
PA	Position approximate
PD	Position doubtful
ED	Existence doubtful
posn	Position

unexamd	Unexamined
Repd	Reported

Quality of the Bottom

Gd	Ground
S	Sand
M	Mud
Oz	Ooze
Ml	Marl
Cy	Clay
G	Gravel
Sn	Shingle
P	Pebbles
St	Stones
R	Rock
Bo	Boulders
Ck	Chalk
Qz	Quartz
Sh	Shells
Oy	Oysters
Ms	Mussels
Wd	Weed
f	Fine
c	Coarse
so	Soft
h	Hard
sf	Stiff
sm	Small
l	Large
sy	Sticky
bk	Broken
ga	Glacial

Tides and Currents

HW/LW	High Water/Low Water
MTL	Mean Tide Level
MSL	Mean Sea Level
Sp/Np	Spring Tides/Neap Tides
MHWS	Mean High Water Springs
MHWN	Mean High Water Neaps
MLWS	Mean Low Water Springs
MLWN	Mean Low Water Neaps
HAT	Highest Astronomical Tide
LAT	Lowest Astronomical Tide
Vel	Velocity
Kn	Knots
Dir	Direction
OD	Ordnance Datum

Compass

Mag	Magnetic
Var	Variation
Annly	Annually

Fig. 3(12) Abbreviations used on Admiralty metric charts.

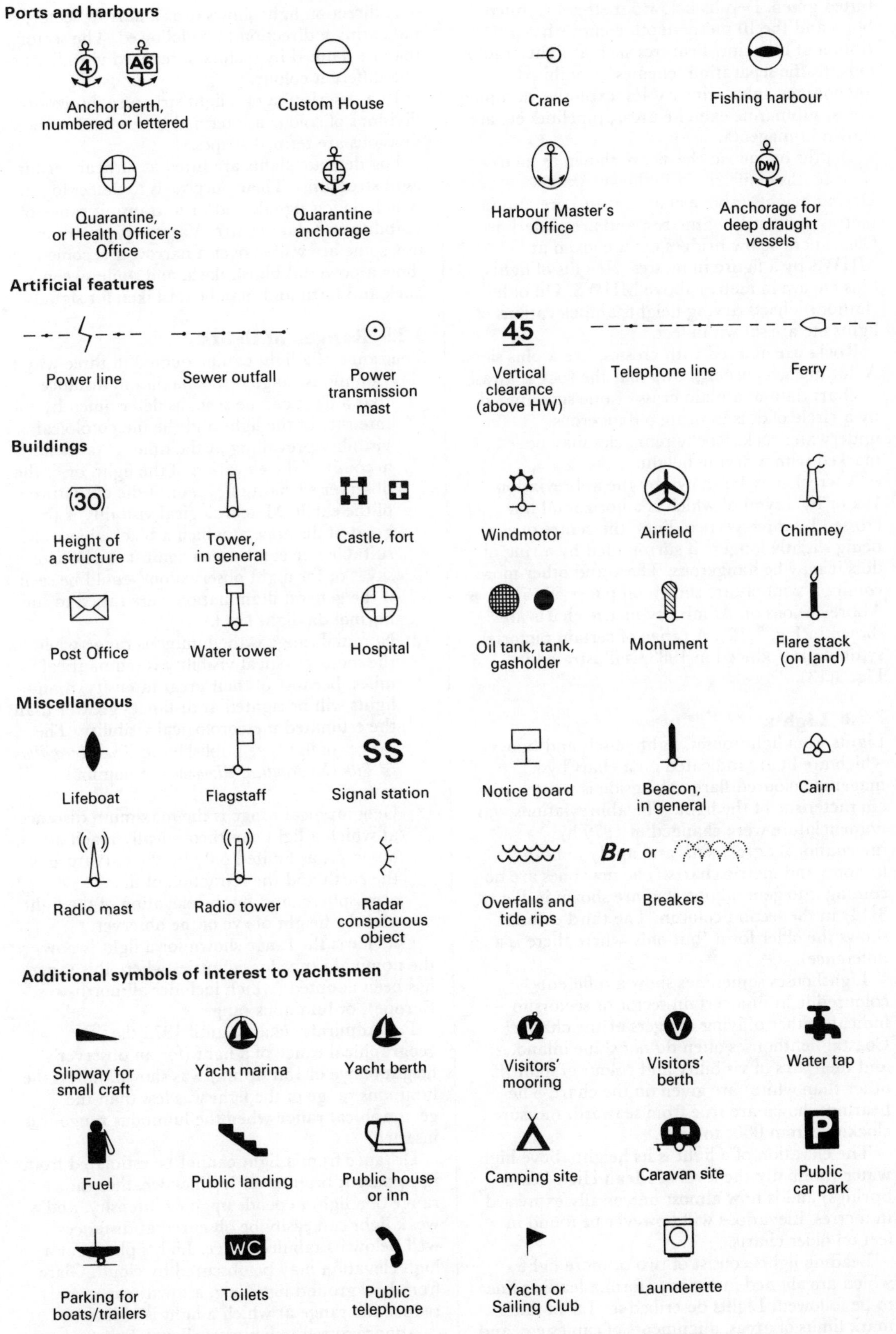

Ports and harbours

Anchor berth, numbered or lettered	Custom House	Crane	Fishing harbour
Quarantine, or Health Officer's Office	Quarantine anchorage	Harbour Master's Office	Anchorage for deep draught vessels

Artificial features

Power line	Sewer outfall	Power transmission mast	Vertical clearance (above HW)	Telephone line	Ferry

Buildings

Height of a structure	Tower, in general	Castle, fort	Windmotor	Airfield	Chimney
Post Office	Water tower	Hospital	Oil tank, tank, gasholder	Monument	Flare stack (on land)

Miscellaneous

Lifeboat	Flagstaff	Signal station	Notice board	Beacon, in general	Cairn
Radio mast	Radio tower	Radar conspicuous object	Overfalls and tide rips	Breakers	

Additional symbols of interest to yachtsmen

Slipway for small craft	Yacht marina	Yacht berth	Visitors' mooring	Visitors' berth	Water tap
Fuel	Public landing	Public house or inn	Camping site	Caravan site	Public car park
Parking for boats/trailers	Toilets	Public telephone	Yacht or Sailing Club	Launderette	

Fig. 3(13) Pictorial symbols on Admiralty charts.

tinted green. Depths below 5 metres are tinted blue, and the 10 metre depth contour has a ribbon of blue tint. Features such as lights, radio aids, traffic separation schemes, prohibited anchorages, submarine cables, explosive dumping areas, submarine exercise areas, pipelines etc are shown in magenta.

Depths on metric charts are shown as metres (and tenths of metres in shallower waters). Drying heights (above chart datum) are also in metres and tenths of metres, and are underlined. Clearances below bridges etc are given at MHWS by a figure in metres. Heights of lights, hills etc are in metres above MHWS. On older (fathom) charts drying heights and elevations of lights etc are shown in feet.

Rocks are marked with crosses, like a plus sign. A dot in each corner shows that the rock is awash at chart datum; a plain cross or one surrounded by a circle of dots indicate a dangerous underwater rock. Rocky pinnacles may be marked with a drying height.

A wreck may be shown by the abbreviation Wk or by a symbol which is a horizontal line crossed by three vertical lines, the centre one being slightly longer. If surrounded by a ring of dots it may be dangerous. These and other more common symbols are shown on pages 60–61. Abbreviations on Admiralty metric charts are shown in Fig. 3(12). A range of certain pictorial symbols, introduced in 1983, is illustrated in Fig. 3(13).

3.2.8 **Lights**
Lights from lighthouses, light vessels and buoys which are lit are indicated on a chart by a magenta coloured flare. Alongside is written the characteristic of the light. The abbreviations and nomenclature were changed in 1979 by international agreement, and apply to both fathoms and metric charts. The new ones are now coming into general use, and are shown in Fig. 3(14) in the second column. The third column shows the older form (but only where there is a difference).

Lighthouses sometimes show a different coloured light in a certain sector or sectors to indicate either offlying dangers or the channel. Coastal lighthouses often do not shine inland, and their arcs of visibility and colour of light (if other than white) are given on the chart. The bearings shown are true from seaward, measured clockwise from 000° to 359°.

The elevation of a light is its height above high water (normally the level of Mean High Water Springs) and is now almost universally expressed in metres. Elevations will however be found in feet on older charts.

Leading lights consist of two or more lights which are aligned in order to form a leading line to be followed. Lights described as 'Lts in line' mark limits of areas, alignments of cables etc, and do not mark a direction to be followed.

A direction light shows over a narrow sector, indicating a direction to be followed. The sector may be flanked by sectors of reduced visibility or of a different colour.

In a description of a light structure, horizontal divisions of colour are termed bands, and vertical divisions are termed stripes.

Fog detector lights are fitted at or near certain light structures. Their purpose is to detect fog, to switch on fog signals and/or to transmit range of visibility to a data centre. Various types are in use: some are visible over a narrow arc, some show a powerful bluish flash, and some sweep back and forth and may be mistaken for signals.

3.2.9 **Ranges of lights**
The range of a light can be quoted in three ways:
(1) Luminous range is the maximum distance that a light can be seen, as determined by the intensity of the light and the meteoroloical visibility prevailing at the time. It takes no account of the elevation of the light, or of the observer's height of eye, or of the curvature of the earth. Meteorological visibility is the greatest distance at which a black object of suitable size can be seen against the horizon sky – or for night observations, could be seen if the general illumination were raised to the normal daylight level.
(2) Nominal range is the luminous range when the meteorological visibility is ten nautical miles. Because of their great intensity, many lights will be sighted at distances greater than the estimated meteorological visibility. The ranges of lights as published in *The Macmillan & Silk Cut Nautical Almanac* are nominal ranges.
(3) Geographical range is the maximum distance at which a light can theoretically reach an observer, as limited only by the curvature of the earth and the refraction of the atmosphere, and by the elevation of the light and the height of eye of the observer.

On charts the range shown for a light is now the nominal range for countries where this range has been adopted (which includes all north-west Europe), or luminous range.

For Admiralty charts, until 1972 the geographical range of a light (for an observer's height of eye of 15ft or 5m) was shown, unless the luminous range of the light was less than the geographical range when the luminous range was inserted.

Distance from a light cannot be estimated from its apparent brightness. In thick weather the range of a light depends upon its intensity, and a weak light can easily be obscured at distances well below its tabuled range. Lights placed at a high elevation may be obscured by cloud. Glare from background light (e.g. a town) can greatly reduce the range at which a light is visible.

Abnormal refraction may allow a light to be seen further, and the loom of a light can often be

CLASS OF LIGHT		International abbreviations	Older form (where different)	Illustration Period shown
Fixed *(steady light)*		F		
Occulting *(total duration of light more than dark)*				
Single-occulting		Oc	Occ	
Group-occulting	*e.g.*	Oc(2)	Gp Occ(2)	
Composite group-occulting	*e.g.*	Oc(2+3)	Gp Occ(2+3)	
Isophase *(light and dark equal)*		Iso		
Flashing *(total duration of light less than dark)*				
Single-flashing		Fl		
Long-flashing (flash 2s or longer)		L Fl		
Group-flashing	*e.g.*	Fl(3)	Gp Fl(3)	
Composite group-flashing	*e.g.*	Fl(2+1)	Gp Fl(2+1)	
Quick *(50 to 79—usually either 50 or 60—flashes per minute)*				
Continuous quick		Q	Qk Fl	
Group quick	*e.g.*	Q(3)	Qk Fl(3)	
Interrupted quick		IQ	Int Qk Fl	
Very Quick *(80 to 159—usually either 100 or 120—flashes per minute)*				
Continuous very quick		VQ	V Qk Fl	
Group very quick	*e.g.*	VQ(3)	V Qk Fl(3)	
Interrupted very quick		IVQ	Int V Qk Fl	
Ultra Quick *(160 or more—usually 240 to 300—flashes per minute)*				
Continuous ultra quick		UQ		
Interrupted ultra quick		IUQ		
Morse Code	*e.g.*	Mo(K)		
Fixed and Flashing		F Fl		
Alternating	*e.g.*	Al.WR	Alt.WR	

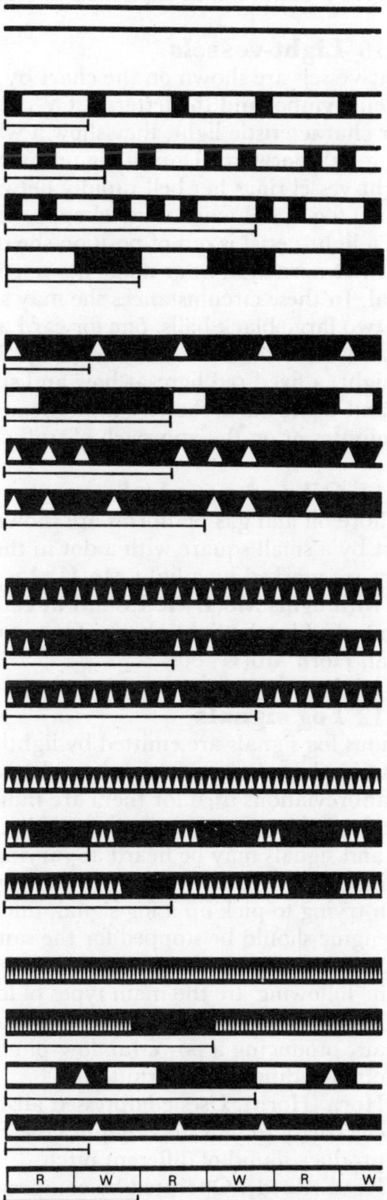

COLOUR	International abbreviations	Older form (where different)	RANGE in sea miles		International abbreviations	Older form
White	W *(may be omitted)*		*Single range*	*e.g.*	15M	
Red	R					
Green	G		*2 ranges*	*e.g.*	14/12M	14,12M
Yellow	Y					
Orange	Y	Or	*3 or more ranges*	*e.g.*	22-18M	22,20,18M
Blue	Bu	Bl				
Violet	Vi					

ELEVATION is given in metres (m) or feet (ft)	**PERIOD** in seconds *e.g.*	5s	5sec

Reproduced by kind permission of H.M. Stationery Office and the Hydrographer of the Navy

Fig. 3(14) Light characters (Fathoms and Metric Charts).

detected well beyond its geographical range.

The distance at which a light dips (or rises) over the horizon, combined with a bearing of it, can give a useful fix, as explained in 3.3.13.

3.2.10 Light-vessels

Light-vessels are shown on the chart by a self-evident symbol and the letters 'Lt V'. Apart from their characteristic light, they show a white riding light forward. During fog or low visibility a light-vessel rings her bell rapidly between her normal fog signal when a vessel approaches.

If a light-vessel is out of position she does not show her normal light or make her normal fog signal. In these circumstances she may show by day two large black balls, one forward and one aft, and the International Code group 'LO'; or by night, a fixed red light at bow and stern, and red and white flares shown simultaneously every 15 minutes or on the approach of traffic.

3.2.11 Oil and gas platforms

Offshore oil and gas platforms are shown on the chart by a small square with a dot in the centre. They are marked by a light Mo(U) 15s 15M, and with lights Mo(U) R 15s 3M at each corner not marked by the light above. They sound a fog signal, Horn Mo(U) 30s.

3.2.12 Fog signals

Various fog signals are emitted by lighthouses, light-vessels and some navigational buoys, and the abbreviations used for them are indicated in brackets below. Sound is very unpredictable in fog, and signals may be heard at varying distances. Under sail it may help to heave-to when trying to pick up a fog signal; under power, the engine should be stopped for the same purpose.

The following are the main types of fog signals:
(1) Diaphone (Dia). Operated by compressed air, producing a powerful, low-pitched sound often ending with a grunt.
(2) Horn (Horn). Uses compressed air or electricity to vibrate a diaphragm. Some produce sound of different pitch.
(3) Reed (Reed). Operated by compressed air, producing a weak, high-pitched sound.
(4) Siren (Siren) Operated by compressed air. Various types produce sounds of different intensities.
(5) Nautophone (Nauto). Electronically operated, producing a high note, from a vibrated diaphragm.
(6) Tyfon (Tyfon). Produces a medium note, like a ship's siren.
(7) Gun (Gun). This type of fog signal is obsolescent. The sound may be accompanied by a bright flash.
(8) Explosive (Explos). Produce reports like the sound of a gun.
(9) Bell, Gong and Whistle (Bell, Gong, Whis). May be operated by hand, by machinery, or by wave motion.

Fog signals in Morse code have the letters 'Mo' shown, followed by the letter or letters of the signal.

3.3 Chartwork

3.3.1 Courses

Headings and courses may be expressed as True, Magnetic or Compass – which are notated as (T), (M) or (C) respectively. The same applies to bearings. The symbol (T) is usually omitted, as for example in *Admiralty Sailing Directions* and in most yachtsman's pilot guides which state in the explanatory notes that all courses and bearings are true.

Attention is called to the standard navigational terms which are stated in 3.1.4.

The course to steer (or the course ordered) is different from the ground track from one point to another, when it is necessary to make allowance for set and drift due to a current and/or tidal stream. For example, in Fig. 3(15) the intended track of the boat is from A to B. Because the tidal stream is setting north, as indicated by the arrow in the diagram, it is necessary for the navigator to lay off a course in a direction such as AC, in order to achieve the required track AB. How the course AC is determined is explained in 3.3.3.

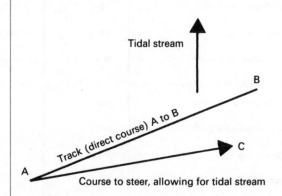

Fig. 3(15) The course to steer in order to get from place to place is often different from the direct course in order to allow for tidal stream and/or leeway.

It is often important for the navigator to know the mean heading which the helmsman has actually achieved over a certain period (usually every half-hour). This may not be the same as the course to steer, or course ordered, because the helmsman will not always be able to maintain this for a variety of reasons.

Leeway is the angle between a boat's heading and the actual direction she is moving through the water (water track). The amount of leeway a boat will make depends upon various factors – her hull design, the amount of windage of sails and/or hull, the strength and direction of the wind relative to the boat, and her speed through the water. About five degrees may be a typical figure for the average cruising yacht when beating to windward. There is less leeway on a reach, and of course no sideways movement of the boat in the water when she is running dead before the wind.

Yachtsmen should be aware of the possible existence of surface drift which (distinct from tidal stream or ocean current) is caused by the wind blowing in a certain direction for any length of time, and which may persist for a while after the wind has changed direction.

3.3.2 Instruments and equipment

In order to perform the basic tasks of navigation it is necessary to have a reasonable chart table on which to work, and suitable instruments. A flat, smooth surface is needed on which to spread a chart. If space is very limited some form of portable board will suffice, but it is difficult to do justice to the job at sea unless one can work on a fixed surface. Good illumination is important, but the light must be screened so that it does not worry the helmsman. Over the chart table there should be a small shelf or bookcase for publications such as sailing directions. A list of these covering the waters round the British Isles and Europe is given in 15.5.3.

Some form of log is essential, for entering navigational records, and these requirements are discussed in 15.5.1.

Most navigators also like to have a notebook in which they can calculate such things as compass courses, tidal heights etc, where the information is accessible should it be needed later. This little book may also be used for planning a passage, and for noting down all sorts of information extracted from various sources.

A handy stowage is needed for the different instruments – plenty of soft pencils (2B), a good soft rubber, a pair of dividers, and a parallel ruler or some form of protractor for measuring and transferring courses and bearings on the chart.

Parallel rulers come in two types – the roller variety which is really more suitable for larger vessels, and the hinged type with two parallel strips of perspex connected by metal arms each end. Many yachtsmen however prefer one of the various protractors which are available, such as the Hurst plotter or a Douglas protractor, which are easier to use than parallel rulers in a small boat.

The Hurst plotter has a square perspex grid (which can be aligned with a convenient meridian or parallel of latitude) as a base, a circular perspex disc graduated from 0 to 360° and adjustable for variation, and a rotating arm which can be aligned with the required course or bearing against the plotter's own compass rose. This device is simple and quick to use, and makes the conversion of bearings and courses from true to magnetic and vice versa unnecessary.

A Douglas protractor is a perspex square,

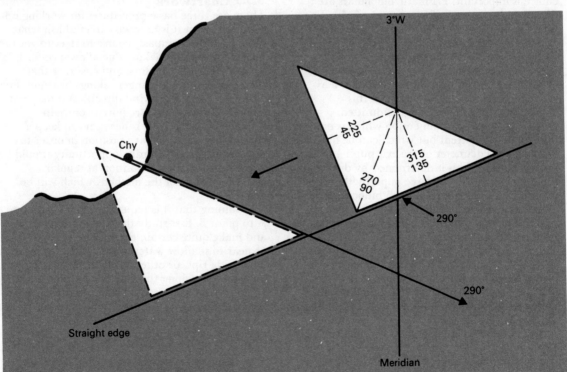

Fig. 3(16) Parallel rulers are not easy to manipulate in small boats, and some form of protractor is more convenient. Alternatively navigational set squares, as illustrated, provide a simple and cheap solution.

graduated round the edge from 0 to 360° in both directions, and with a small hole in the centre. The surface of the square is engraved with a grid, parallel to the sides, similar to the Hurst plotter. To establish the course from A to B the centre hole is placed over the line AB, the square is lined up with the nearest meridian or parallel of latitude with the north point at the top, and the course is then read off the edge of the square on the outer (clockwise) set of figures. A similar procedure is followed to determine the direction or bearing of an object.

Some navigators like to use navigational set squares, which are isosceles, right-angled triangles in perspex, graduated in degrees from the centre of the hypotenuse – from 0 to 180° on the outer scale, and from 180 to 360° on the inner. If for example the chimney in Fig. 3(16) bears 290°, one set square is aligned with the centre of its hypotenuse and its 290° mark on the nearest meridian, and then slid along the other square (or any suitable straight edge) until the hypotenuse cuts the chimney. The line of bearing is then drawn along the hypotenuse.

A good pair of dividers, preferably of the crossover type which can be operated in one hand, are essential for chartwork, and a pencil compass can be useful for some problems.

Any cruising yacht needs at least one pair of efficient binoculars. A good arrangement is to have one pair for the skipper/navigator, and a spare pair for general ship's use. The correct choice is important. Prismatic binoculars are described by two sets of figures, thus 7x50. The first figure or figures refer to the magnification, 10 for example meaning that an object viewed will appear ten times larger and ten times nearer than if viewed with the naked eye. The second set of figures is the diameter of the objective lens (furthest from the eye) in mm, and this determines the amount of light admitted.

Another important dimension which is not immediately apparent but which can be quickly derived is the diameter of the exit pupil – the lens nearest the eye. This is determined by dividing the diameter of the objective pupil by the magnification. Hence for a 7x35 binocular the diameter of the exit pupil is 5mm. A large exit pupil passes more light to the eye and gives a brighter image. About 7mm is a desirable figure. This is particularly important in poor light, and is assisted by special coatings on the lenses and prisms of good quality binoculars.

For marine use it is unwise to buy binoculars with a magnification of more than 7 or 8, since at sea it is impossible to hold them sufficiently steady to get a good image. Exceptionally 9 x or 10 x can be used in large yachts which provide a steady platform. For general use 7x50 is recommended. In a yacht binoculars need to be sturdy and waterproof. Those which have individual focusing for each eyepiece are more resistant to water than those with central focusing. Some kind of rubber coating helps to protect binoculars from the knocks which they are bound to receive in the cockpit of a yacht.

Other items of navigational equipment which are needed are listed below:
(1) Steering compass, adjusted and swung, with up to date deviation card. (See sections 3.1.6 to 3.1.11). The compass must be properly sited for the helmsman, and illuminated at night.
(2) Hand bearing compass, for taking bearings of shore objects, lights, or other vessels for collision avoidance. (See section 3.1.12).
(3) Distance reading log, to record distance through the water. (See section 3.1.16).
(4) Echo sounder, or lead line. (See section 3.1.18).
(5) Reliable clock or watch. An alarm clock can be useful to catch the tide or to hear the shipping forecast.
(6) Radio receiver. The very minimum requirement is to be able to hear the shipping forecasts on 200kHz(1500m). (See section 6.5).
(7) Stop watch. For identifying the characteristics of lights.
(8) Sailing directions or pilotage guides for appropriate cruising areas (see 15.5.3).
(9) Barometer, or barograph.
(10) Chart magnifier.
(11) *The Macmillan & Silk Cut Nautical Almanac.*

3.3.3 Chartwork

There are three basic procedures for working on the chart. First it is necessary to establish what should be the (compass) course to steer to get the boat from A to B, making due allowance for tidal streams and other factors, and ensuring that there are no hidden dangers along the route. For various reasons (e.g. wind direction) it may not be possible to steer the required course in practice, so secondly it is necessary to keep a running plot of the boat's position in order to monitor progress. Thirdly, opportunity should be taken to fix the boat's position at regular intervals by one of the methods which will be described.

Assuming that it is required to sail from point A to point B, first study the route on the chart and make quite certain that it does not pass over or near to shallow water, obstructions, prohibited areas, tide rips, or other hazards. Place the parallel ruler along the line AB, transfer it to the compass rose, and read off the true course. Suppose this is 073°. If variation is (say) 8°W this gives a magnetic course of 081°(M). Refer to the deviation card as in Fig. 3(6), and see what the deviation is on this heading. If it is for example 3°W then the compass course from A to B is 084°(C).

It is however more than likely that it will be necessary to make some allowance for tidal stream. In the example in Fig. 3(17) assume that

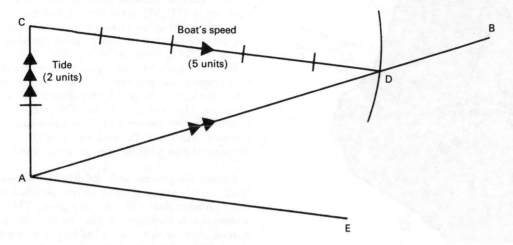

Fig. 3(17) How to determine the course to steer to allow for tidal stream.

the tidal stream is setting north at 2 knots, and that the boat's speed is 5 knots. From A construct AC pointing in the direction in which the tide is running (north), and two convenient units in length. From C, using a pair of compasses or dividers measure a length equal to five units (boat's speed) so that it meets AB at D. Draw AE parallel to CD. This is the course to steer (or course ordered). The boat starts from A, steering a course in the direction AE, but the tide carries it steadily north so that the ground track of the boat is along the line ADB.

The above assumes that the rate of the tidal stream remains constant at two knots, and that the speed of the boat is steady at five knots. On an actual passage either or both of these figures may change – the tidal stream may even reverse direction. In this case the passage must be divided up into a suitable number of parts, and the necessary course to steer calculated for each part, if it is desired to follow the track AB.

3.3.4 Plotting – Dead Reckoning (DR)
Referring to Fig. 3(18) if on sailing from point A the log reading is zero, after two hours on a course of (say) 080° it is possible to plot a rough position on the chart. If the log reading is ten miles, then assuming that the course of 080° has been maintained and neglecting any other effects of wind or tide, the boat will have moved to B. B is called the Dead Reckoning position, or DR for short, and it is marked on the chart with a cross and the time alongside it.

Estimated Position (EP)
Still referring to Fig. 3(18), if while the boat is sailing from A to B the tidal stream is setting due south at a steady two knots, it will carry the boat four miles south during the two hours. The effect of the tidal stream is shown by the tidal vector BC in the diagram, and the boat will end up at C and not at B. C is called the Estimated Position

(or EP) and is marked by a small triangle with a spot in the middle, and the time alongside.

The Estimated Position may be further refined by making an allowance for leeway (see 3.3.1).

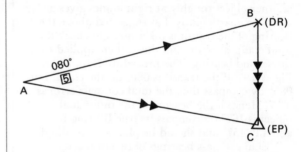

Fig. 3(18) Plotting – Dead Reckoning, indicated by a cross, and Estimated Position indicated by a triangle. By convention course has a single arrow, tidal stream three arrows, and the resultant track two arrows.

3.3.5 Position fixing
Periodically (how often depends upon circumstances) it is necessary to check the boat's position, or take a fix. This is done by establishing two or more position lines; where they cross gives the position of the boat at the time of the observations. At times however even a single reliable position line can be very useful, as for example to establish whether the boat is on her required track.

The most positive way of getting a position line is by means of a transit – when two known objects are in line with each other. Simply join the two objects on the chart, extend the line seaward, and the boat is somewhere along it. It is good practice to take a compass bearing of the transit and to check it against the bearing from the chart, in order to make sure that the objects have been correctly identified. Where the bearings of transits or leading marks are shown on the chart or in sailing directions, they are true

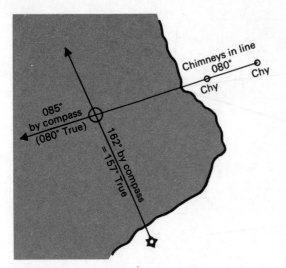

Fig. 3(19) A transit of two known objects, and a bearing of a third object, giving a cut approaching 90°, should result in a reliable fix.

bearings from seaward so it is necessary to apply variation. Taking the bearing is also a useful check on the compass.

A transit of two objects and a bearing of another object roughly at right angles gives a useful fix, particularly if as suggested above the bearing of the transit is taken so as to check the total compass error, and this is then applied to the second bearing. The procedure is shown in Fig. 3(19). If the transit is 080° on the chart, but 085° by compass then the total compass error is 5°W. Hence if the bearing of the individual object is 162° by compass its true bearing is actually 157° and should be plotted accordingly.

Visual compass bearings of two or more objects, carefully taken, can give a reasonable fix but it is desirable to take at least three. This is what is involved in plotting one of these bearings – that of the church in Fig. 3(20) – on the chart.

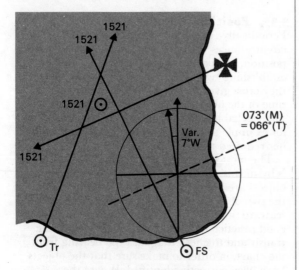

Fig. 3(20) When taking bearings to get a fix, if possible always use at least three objects. The size of the resulting cocked hat indicates the reliability of the position.

Assume that the reading from the hand bearing compass is 073°(M). As indicated, this is a magnetic bearing, so variation must be applied to get the true bearing. If the variation (from the chart) is 7°W the true bearing is 066°.

Place the parallel ruler against the centre of the compass rose and the 066° mark on the outer (true) scale, as indicated by the dotted line on the diagram. Then transfer the parallel ruler carefully to the church and draw a line to seaward. Mark it at the end with a single arrowhead and with the time of observation (1521).

Repeat the process with the other two objects. If all three bearings are completely accurate the three position lines will meet in a point. This seldom if ever happens, and in practice they form a small triangle called a cocked hat. The size of the cocked hat is a good indication of the accuracy of the fix. If a large cocked hat is obtained one or more of the bearings must be wrong or incorrectly plotted. This is why it is important to take at least three bearings; if only two objects are observed there is no check on reliability. It is also important that the objects should be selected so that the position lines from them give a good cut – at a sufficient angle. Ideally when three bearings are taken the position lines should meet at angles of about 60°. Be suspicious of fixes from position lines which cross at less than 30°.

If a cocked hat of a reasonably small size has been obtained, the fix is taken as its centre and is marked with a small circle and the time alongside, as in Fig. 3(20). If however there are dangers nearby then the fix is taken as the corner of the cocked hat nearest the danger so that the worst situation is assumed.

3.3.6 Running fix

If only one object or one light can be positively identified on a stretch of coast, it is still possible to get at least an approximate idea of the boat's position by a running fix as shown in Fig. 3(21). An initial bearing of a light L shows that the boat is somewhere along the line LA. When this bearing is taken the time and log reading are carefully noted (this should be the practice with any observation). The boat sails on her way, and a little later when the bearing of L has changed by at least 45° a second bearing is taken. Again the time and log reading are noted.

It is then necessary to work out how far the boat has travelled over the ground between the two bearings. This is calculated from the log readings (distance through the water, AB) and from the effect of the tidal stream during this period (BC). So AC represents the movement of the boat between the two bearings. The first position line is transferred by this amount as shown (transferred position lines are conventionally marked by double arrows each end), and crosses with the second position line at

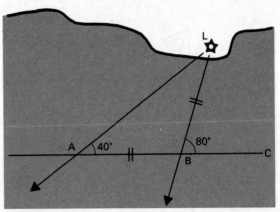

Fig. 3(22) Doubling the angle on the bow is a special type of running fix, and should be used with caution in tidal waters.

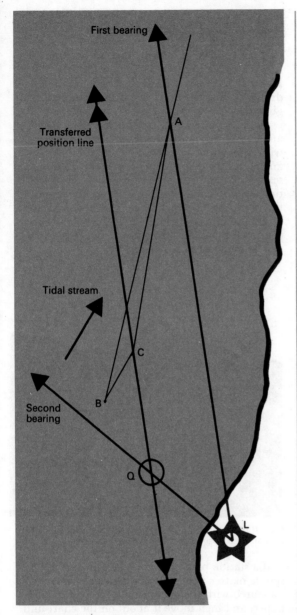

Fig. 3(21) The accuracy of a running fix, from consecutive beatings of one object, depends upon a correct assessment of the effects of tidal stream and leeway.

Q, which is the boat's position when the second bearing was taken.

3.3.7 Doubling the angle on the bow

This is a special example of a running fix, which is easy to calculate. Assume in Fig. 3(22) that the boat is sailing along the line AC. At A a relative bearing is taken of object L which is (say) 40° on the bow at a certain time and log reading. When this bearing has doubled, to 80°, the time and log reading are again noted, at B. It will be seen that ABL is an isosceles triangle and that AB (the distance sailed between the two bearings) equals BL (the distance of the boat from L). Although this is a quick and useful method of getting an

approximate position, it is not very accurate and should not be trusted in waters where there is any appreciable tidal stream.

3.3.8 Four point bearing, and other special angles

If, when doubling the angle on the bow as described above, the first relative bearing is 45° and the second is therefore 90°, then the distance run between the two bearings equals the distance which the object is abeam (when the second bearing is taken). This is called a four point bearing fix because under the old method of compass marking a point is $11\frac{1}{4}°$ and four points are 45°.

There are other special pairs of angles of an object on the bow which, if accurately taken and used when there is no tidal stream to consider, result in the distance run over the ground between the bearings being equal to the distance which the boat will pass abeam of the object. These pairs of angles on the bow are 22° and 34°; 25° and 41°; 32° and 59°; 35° and 67°; and 37° and 72°.

It is emphasised that all running fixes should be used with caution. It is important to be sure of the distance the boat has moved over the ground between the bearings, and to be certain that a steady and accurate course has been maintained.

3.3.9 Horizontal sextant angles

Horizontal sextant angles provide an accurate but often neglected method of fixing a boat's position. The method consists of taking the angles between fixed objects with the sextant held horizontally, instead of vertically, when obtaining the altitude of a heavenly body. Since an accuracy of half a degree is quite sufficient, even the cheapest plastic sextant is perfectly suitable.

To obtain a fix by horizontal sextant angles three objects must be visible, and as will be seen their relative positions are important. The method is based on the fact that the angle subtended by a chord at the centre of a circle is

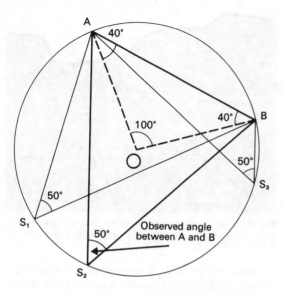

Fig. 3(23) The principle of a position circle, by taking the horizontal sextant angle between two known objects, A and B. If that angle is 50°, as shown, then the centre of the position circle AS₁S₂S₃B is such that the angle AOB is 100°, and hence OAB and ABO are both 40°.

double the angle at the circumference. Knowing the angle subtended by two objects gives a position circle, as shown in Fig. 3(23), where the angles AS_1B, AS_2B and AS_3B are all equal.

The position circle can be constructed in various ways. It can be done by plotting, as shown in Fig. 3(23). If, for example, the angle AS_2B is 50°, construct lines at A and B which are each $(90 - 50) = 40°$ to AB. Where they meet at O is the centre of the position circle ABS_2.

Should the angle ASB be greater than 90°, subtract 90° from it and construct AO and BO

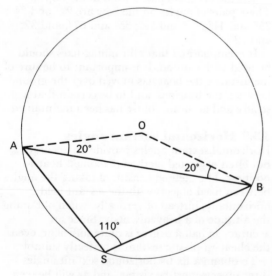

Fig. 3(24) If the observed sextant angle is more than 90°, as shown here, subtract 90 from the figure and construct the two radii OA and OB on the opposite side of the line joining the two objects.

on the opposite (landward) side of the line AB, as indicated in Fig. 3(24). Here for example ASB is 110°, so OAB and OBA are both 20°.

If the procedure for drawing one position circle is repeated for another angle between two objects B and C, then a second position circle can be drawn cutting the first. The point of intersection gives the fix required.

Another method of using horizontal sextant angles is with a station pointer – an instrument with three arms which can be set at selected angles, in this case the angles taken with the sextant. By adjusting the station pointer so that the bevelled side of each of its arms lies against the three objects which have been observed, the position of the boat is shown at the hole in the centre of the pivot, through which a pencil mark can be made as at S in Fig. 3(25).

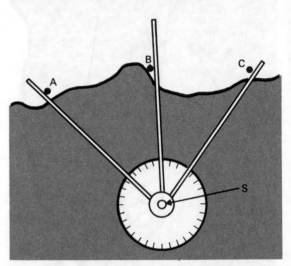

Fig. 3(25) A station pointer provides the simplest method of plotting a position from horizontal sextant angles.

If a station pointer is not available it is a simple matter to construct the two angles measured with the sextant on a piece of tracing paper, and then move it about on the chart until the three lines pass over the objects concerned. A Douglas protractor may also be utilised.

It is also possible to construct the position of the boat geometrically, as in Fig. 3(26). If P, Q and R are the objects which have been observed join PQ and QR. Assume that the angles measured of PQ and QR are x and y. From Q construct two lines QT and QU at angles of (90–x) to PQ and (90–y) to QR as shown. From P and R construct perpendiculars which cut QT and QU at V and W. Join VW. Drop a perpendicular QS onto VW, and S is the fix.

If a sextant angle is more than 90°, subtract 90 from it and construct the required angle on the opposite (landward) side of PQ or QR.

The advantages of horizontal sextant angles are that accuracy is not affected by compass errors, log readings or tidal streams. The angles can, with a bit of practice, be measured very

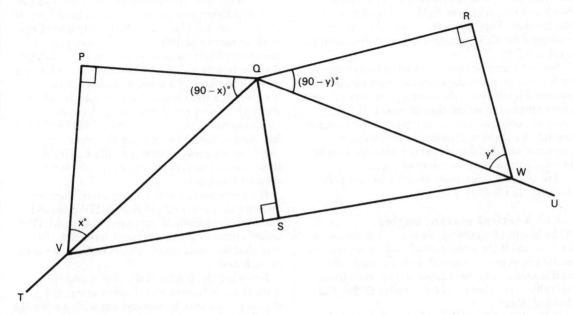

Fig. 3(26) From horizontal sextant angles the position of the boat can be determined geometrically, as it is shown in the diagram above.

accurately and there is no deviation or variation to bother about. Even if no sextant is carried the same method can be used with compass bearings, if only the differences between the bearings are considered and no reliance is placed on individual bearings; this too eliminates any errors due to deviation or variation.

It must be noted however that there are certain limitations on the choice of objects for fixing by horizontal sextant angles. First they should be chosen so that they subtend angles of at least 30°. Also:

(1) The three objects should be on or near a straight line, or
(2) The centre object must be on the boat's side of the line joining the two outer objects, or
(3) The boat must obviously be inside a triangle formed by the three objects.

A satisfactory position will not be obtained when the centre object is beyond the line joining the other two. No fix can be obtained if a circle passes through or near to the three objects and the boat.

3.3.10 Line of soundings

Apart from bearings of shore objects it is often useful to read the echo sounder and record the distance of what is usually the nearest point of land. Most seagoing boats are now fitted with an echo sounder, but the following procedure can be used with a lead and line if necessary.

For navigational purposes soundings must be corrected by the height of the tide at the time and place concerned, so that they can be compared with the figures on the chart. Even a single sounding can be helpful on occasions, but it is better to have a line of soundings taken at

regular intervals. Having been reduced to datum, by subtracting the height of the tide, mark the soundings at the proper intervals of distance (tidal stream may have to be allowed for here) on the edge of a piece of paper (or better still a piece of tracing paper) and then move it about the chart with its edge parallel to the track of the boat, until it matches the soundings on the chart.

Such a position line should obviously be used with caution, but in thick weather for example it can be very helpful, particularly if the sea bed has distinctive contours.

3.3.11 Bearing and distance

The bearing and distance of a known object which is marked on the chart will give a fix. If radar is available it is a simple matter to get the range of anything which presents a good radar target. Radar gives more accurate ranges than bearings, so it is good practice to take a radar range and a visual bearing with the hand bearing compass, but be careful that the same object is observed in each case.

An alternative to radar for finding the distance of an object is a rangefinder, but reasonably-priced instruments are not very accurate at ranges of over a mile or so. There are however some small distance reading meters on the market.

If the height of an object is known, and if the angle which it subtends vertically can be measured (as with a sextant), its range can be calculated or extracted from tables. The procedure is described in section 3.3.12. Combined with the bearing of the object, this will give a good fix.

The range of a light of known height can be

calculated or extracted from tables, for different heights of eye, when the light rises or dips over the horizon. This often gives a useful fix when making a landfall, and the method is described in section 3.3.13.

Should accurate ranges of two or more objects be known, by radar for example, a fix can be obtained by drawing the appropriate arcs on the chart and seeing where they intersect. If the ranges of only two objects are taken it is of course possible for them to intersect in two feasible positions, and for this reason it is sensible to take at least approximate bearings of each.

The use and limitations of radar in yachts is discussed in Chapter 4.

3.3.12 Vertical sextant angles

If the height of an object, such as a lighthouse, is known, and if the vertical angle which it presents to the observer is measured with a sextant, then its distance can be calculated or extracted from the tables provided in *The Macmillan & Silk Cut Nautical Almanac*.

A bearing of the object taken at the same time will provide an accurate fix of the boat's position.

Heights of prominent objects are shown on the chart or are given in sailing directions. On metric charts these are shown in metres (m). In the case of lights do not be confused by their range, shown in miles (M). Heights are above Mean High Water Springs (MHWS) and in the case of lights are to the centre of the lantern.

In practice it is not usual to allow for the height of the tide or for the height of eye, since by neglecting them the object is made to appear a little closer than it actually is, which gives a safety margin if it is assumed that any danger is inshore of the yacht (but not if it is to seaward). The sextant angle should however be corrected for index error.

The sextant angle to be measured is from the top of the object (the centre of the lantern in the case of a lighthouse) to the sea at its base – not to the horizon, see Fig. 3(27). From a height of eye of three metres or 10ft (which is about the maximum likely to be used in a small yacht) the horizon is only visible to a distance of 3.6 nautical miles. Therefore at a greater distance than this the base of a light tower, for example, is below the horizon and not visible to an observer. Consequently a measured sextant angle will be less than it should be, making the object appear to be further away than it actually is. Under these conditions vertical sextant angles must be used with caution.

If a more precise range is required, then the distance that sea level is below MHWS should be added to the height of the object (above MHWS) before entering the tables (see Chapter 9). Be sure that the same units (metres or feet) are used in each case.

Knowing the height of the object and the sextant angle (corrected for index error) the distance can easily be worked out with a scientific calculator from the formula shown in 3.3.16.

Table 3(2) in the Almanac is used as follows. Enter with the height of the object, either in metres or feet, in the column down the side of the page and then read across until the required sextant angle (corrected for index error) is met. Take out the distance of the object (in nautical miles) at the head of the column, interpolating as necessary.

Make certain that the table is entered with the correct units, either metres or feet as the case may be.

Example

Referring to Fig. 3(28), the vertical sextant angle of an object with an elevation of 79ft (24m) is 1°04′ (after correction for index error). How far away is it?

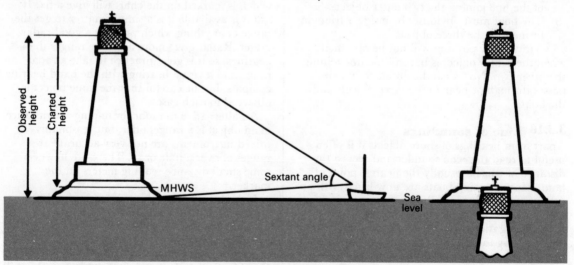

Fig. 3(27) A vertical sextant angle, combined with a bearing, of an object of known height gives a reliable fix. In order to get a really accurate range, the distance sea level is below the level of Mean High Water Springs should be added to the charted height of the object before entering the table.

TABLE 3(2) Distance off by Vertical Sextant Angle

Height of object ft m		0.1	0.2	0.3	0.4	0.5	0.6	0.7	0.8	0.9	1.0	1.1	1.2	1.3	1.4	1.5	Height of object m ft	
		° ′	° ′	° ′	° ′	° ′	° ′	° ′	° ′	° ′	° ′	° ′	° ′	° ′	° ′	° ′		
33	10	3 05	1 33	1 02	0 46	0 37	0 31	0 27	0 23	0 21	0 19	0 17	0 15	0 14	0 13	0 12	10	33
39	12	3 42	1 51	1 14	0 56	0 45	0 37	0 32	0 28	0 25	0 22	0 20	0 19	0 17	0 16	0 15	12	39
46	14	4 19	2 10	1 27	1 05	0 52	0 43	0 37	0 32	0 29	0 26	0 24	0 22	0 20	0 19	0 17	14	46
53	16	4 56	2 28	1 39	1 14	0 59	0 49	0 42	0 37	0 33	0 30	0 27	0 25	0 23	0 21	0 20	16	53
59	18	5 33	2 47	1 51	1 24	1 07	0 56	0 48	0 42	0 37	0 33	0 30	0 28	0 26	0 24	0 22	18	59
66	20	6 10	3 05	2 04	1 33	1 14	1 02	0 53	0 46	0 41	0 37	0 34	0 31	0 29	0 27	0 25	20	66
72	22	6 46	3 24	2 16	1 42	1 22	1 08	0 58	0 51	0 45	0 41	0 37	0 34	0 31	0 29	0 27	22	72
79	24	7 23	3 42	2 28	1 51	1 29	1 14	1 04	0 56	0 49	0 45	0 40	0 37	0 34	0 32	0 30	24	79
85	26	7 59	4 01	2 41	2 01	1 36	1 20	1 09	1 00	0 54	0 48	0 44	0 40	0 37	0 34	0 32	26	85
92	28	8 36	4 19	2 53	2 10	1 44	1 27	1 14	1 05	0 58	0 52	0 47	0 43	0 40	0 37	0 35	28	92
		⌐ 28	3 05	2 19	1 51	1 33	1 20	1 10	1 02	0 56	0 51	0 46	0 43	0 40	0 37		30	⌐
			2 28	1 58	1 39	1 25	1 14	1 06	0 59	0 54	0 49	0 46	0 42	0 40			
				2 06	1 45	1 30	1 19	1 10	1 03	0 57	0 53	0 49	0 4⌐				
					⌐ 51	1 35	1 24	1 14	1 07	1 01	0 56	0 ⌐					

Fig. 3(28) Portion of table of distance off by vertical sextant angle.

By inspection, for an object with height 79ft (24m) and an angle of 1°04′, the distance is 0.7 nautical miles.

If in this case the sea level was known to be 6½ft (2m) below the level of MHWS, the table would be entered with a height of 85ft (26m). By interpolation, it can be seen that an angle of 1°04′ would then give a distance of approximately 0.75 nautical miles.

Should it be required to keep a certain distance away from an object of known height, it is easy to extract the appropriate 'danger angle' from the table, and then ensure that this is not exceeded.

3.3.13 Distance of the horizon

It is useful to be able to extract from tables (or to calculate from formulae) the distance of the sea horizon for a certain height of eye. The actual distance may be affected by abnormal refraction. The appropriate table and formula for use with a calculator are given in *The Macmillan & Silk Cut Nautical Almanac*. An extract from Table 3(3) is shown in Fig. 3(29). It can be used, for example, for determining the distance of a light when it is on the horizon – see Fig. 3(30).

The distance OL is the sum of the distance of the horizon from the observer at O and the

TABLE 3(3) Distance of horizon for various heights of eye

Height of eye		Horizon distance	Height of eye		Horizon distance	Height of eye		Horizon distance
metres	feet	n. miles	metres	feet	n. miles	metres	feet	n. miles
1	3.3	2.1	21	68.9	9.5	41	134.5	13.3
2	6.6	2.9	22	72.2	9.8	42	137.8	13.5
3	9.8	3.6	23	75.5	10.0	43	141.1	13.7
4	13.1	4.1	24	78.7	10.2	44	144.4	13.8
5	16.4	4.7	25	82.0	10.4	45	147.6	14.0
6	19.7	5.1	26	85.3	10.6	46	150.9	14.1
7	23.0	5.5	27	88.6	10.8	47	154.2	14.⌐
	26.2	5.9	28	91.9	11.0	48	157.⌐	
	⌐ ⌐	⌐ ⌐	29	95.1				

Fig. 3(29) Portion of table of distance of horizon for various heights of eye.

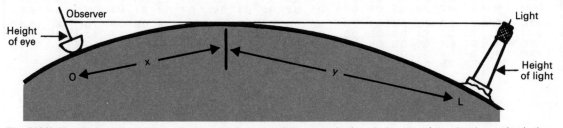

Fig. 3(30) The distance at which an observer can just see a light on the horizon is the sum of x and y above; that is the distance from the observer's eye to the horizon plus the distance from the light to the horizon.

TABLE 3 (4)   Lights — distance off when rising or dipping (n. miles)

Height of light		Height of eye									
metres	feet	metres	1	2	3	4	5	6	7	8	9	10
		feet	3	7	10	13	16	20	23	26	30	33
10	33		8.7	9.5	10.2	10.8	11.3	11.7	12.1	12.5	12.8	13.2
12	39		9.3	10.1	10.8	11.4	11.9	12.3	12.7	13.1	13.4	13.8
14	46		9.9	10.7	11.4	12.0	12.5	12.9	13.3	13.7	14.0	14.4
16	53		10.4	11.2	11.9	12.5	13.0	13.4	13.8	14.2	14.5	14.9
18	59		10.9	11.7	12.4	13.0	13.5	13.9	14.3	14.7	15.0	15.4
20	66		11.4	12.2	12.9	13.5	14.0	14.4	14.8	15.2	15.5	15.9
			11.9	12.7	13.4	14.0	14.5	14.9	15.3	15.7	16.0	16.4
			12.3	13.1	13.8	14.4	14.9	15.3	15.7	16.1	16.4	17.0
				14.2	14.8	15.3	15.7					
					15.2	15.7						

Fig. 3(31) Portion of table showing the distance off of lights when rising or dipping, for various heights of light and eye.

distance of the horizon from L. If the height of eye is 10ft (3m), and the height of the light is 72ft(22m), the distance OL is (3.6 + 9.8) = 13.4 nautical miles.

For convenience Table 3(4) in *The Macmillan & Silk Cut Nautical Almanac* combines selected heights of eye with selected heights of lights, to give the range at which a light may be seen to dip below or rise above the horizon. A portion of this table is shown in Fig. 3(31).

The heights of all major lights are shown on the chart. Remember that it is the small m which gives the height in metres, while the large M is the range of the light in nautical miles.

3.3.14 Time, speed and distance

When navigating by dead reckoning it is important to understand the relation between time, speed and distance. To assist, Table 3(5) in *The Macmillan & Silk Cut Nautical Almanac* relates these three quantities – for speeds from 2.5 to 20 knots, and for times up to one hour at one minute intervals. The tabulated figures are nautical

miles. A portion of this table is shown in Fig. 3(32).

Example

To determine how far the boat has sailed at 6.5 knots in 8 minutes– select the column headed 6.5 knots and read down to the 8 minute line at the side of the table. Answer–0.9 nautical miles. Conversely the table can be used to find out how long it will take to cover a known distance at a certain speed, or what speed is required to go a certain distance in a given time.

3.3.15 Measured mile table

Particularly in motor yachts it is important to know the boat's speed in relation to engine rpm. This is best done by running the boat over one of the measured distances which exist around the coast and are marked on large scale charts. Check the actual lenght of the measured distance from the chart. A few are not exactly a sea mile.

In order to offset the effects of tide, and possibly of wind, it is important to make at least

TABLE 3 (5)   Time, Speed and Distance Table

Time		Speed in knots														Time	
Decimal of hr.	Mins	2.5	3	3.5	4	4.5	5	5.5	6	6.5	7	7.5	8	8.5	9	9.5	10	Mins	Decimal of hr.
.0167	1				0.1	0.1	0.1	0.1	0.1	0.1	0.1	0.1	0.1	0.1	0.2	0.2	0.2	1	.0167
.0333	2	0.1	0.1	0.1	0.1	0.1	0.2	0.2	0.2	0.2	0.2	0.2	0.3	0.3	0.3	0.3	0.3	2	.0333
.0500	3	0.1	0.1	0.2	0.2	0.2	0.2	0.3	0.3	0.3	0.3	0.4	0.4	0.4	0.4	0.5	0.5	3	.0500
.0667	4	0.1	0.2	0.2	0.3	0.3	0.3	0.4	0.4	0.4	0.5	0.5	0.5	0.6	0.6	0.6	0.7	4	.0667
.0833	5	0.2	0.2	0.3	0.3	0.4	0.4	0.5	0.5	0.5	0.6	0.6	0.7	0.7	0.7	0.8	0.8	5	.0833
.1000	6	0.2	0.3	0.3	0.4	0.4	0.5	0.5	0.6	0.6	0.7	0.7	0.8	0.8	0.9	0.9	1.0	6	.1000
.1167	7	0.3	0.4	0.4	0.5	0.5	0.6	0.6	0.7	0.8	0.8	0.9	0.9	1.0	1.1	1.1	1.2	7	.1167
.1333	8	0.3	0.4	0.5	0.5	0.6	0.7	0.7	0.8	0.9	0.9	1.0	1.1	1.1	1.2	1.3	1.3	8	.1333
.1500	9	0.4	0.4	0.5	0.6	0.7	0.7	0.8	0.9	1.0	1.0	1.1	1.2	1.3	1.3	1.4	1.5		
.1667	10	0.4	0.5	0.6	0.7	0.8	0.8	0.9	1.0	1.1	1.2	1.3	1.3	1.4	1.5	1.6	1.7		
		0.5	0.5	0.6	0.7	0.8	0.9	1.0	1.1	1.2	1.3	1.4	1.5	1.6	1.6	1.7			
				0.7	0.8	0.9	1.0	1.1	1.2	1.3	1.4	1.5	1.6	1.7	1.8				
					1.0	1.1	1.2	1.3	1.4	1.5	1.6	1.7	1.8						
						1.2	1.3	1.4	1.5	1.6	1.7	1.9							
							1.5	1.6	1.8	1.9									

Fig. 3(32) Portion of time, speed and distance table.

TABLE 3(6)	Measured Mile Table — Knots related to time over one nautical mile										
Secs	**1 min**	**2 min**	**3 min**	**4 min**	**5 min**	**6 min**	**7 min**	**8 min**	**9 min**	**10 min**	**11 min**
0	60.00	30.00	20.00	15.00	12.00	10.00	8.57	7.50	6.67	6.00	5.45
1	59.02	29.75	19.89	14.94	11.96	9.97	8.55	7.48	6.66	5.99	5.45
2	58.06	29.51	19.78	14.88	11.92	9.94	8.53	7.47	6.64	5.98	5.44
3	57.14	29.27	19.67	14.81	11.88	9.92	8.51	7.45	6.63	5.97	5.43
4	56.25	29.03	19.57	14.75	11.84	9.89	8.49	7.44	6.62	5.96	5.42
5	55.38	28.80	19.46	14.69	11.80	9.86	8.47	7.42	6.61	5.95	5.41
6	54.55	28.57	19.35	14.63	11.76	9.84	8.45	7.41	6.59	5.94	5.41
7	53.73	28.35	19.25	14.57	11.73	9.81	8.43	7.39	6.58	5.93	5
8	52.94	28.12	19.15	14.52	11.69	9.78	8.41	7.38	6.57	5.92	
9			19.05	14.46	11.65	9.76	8.39	7.36	6.56		
					11.61	9.73	8.37				

Fig. 3(33) Portion of measured mile table – knots related to time over one nautical mile.

one run in each direction. Calculate the speed from the results obtained.

For accurate figures two or three runs should be made in each direction, and the speed calculated from the mean of means, as follows.

If six successive runs are done in alternate directions, take the speed of each run. Multiply consecutive speeds by 1, 5, 10, 10, 5, 1 and divide the total by 32.

If four runs are done in alternate directions, again take the speed of each run. Multiply the consecutive speeds by 1, 2, 2, 1 and divide the total by 6.

When doing measured mile runs it is important to keep a steady course, on the heading which is marked on the chart (perpendicular to the transit marks each end). Otherwise the distance steamed is greater than indicated.

Most measured distances are along a shoreline, which is sometimes shallow. Make certain that there is sufficient depth of water on your intended course, and remember that inaccurate results will be obtained in shallow water – particularly at higher speeds. Use the greatest depth which is practicable.

Table 3(6) in *The Macmillan & Silk Cut Nautical Almanac* gives speeds in knots for times over a nautical mile at one second intervals from one minute (60 knots) to 12 minutes (5 knots). A portion of this table is shown in Fig. 3(33).

During measured distance runs it is appropriate to take note of the following factors for subsequent reference:

Direction and strength of wind relative to course(s)
State of hull bottom (clean, foul etc)
Loading of boat (fuel, water, crew)
Engine rpm
Turbocharger boost pressure (if applicable)
Readings of log (if fitted) for calibration.
Sea water temperature
Ambient air temperature

Examples

(a) Runs in alternate directions give times of:

$$
\begin{array}{l}
6 \text{ min } 01 \text{ sec} = 9.97 \text{ knots} \\
\text{and } 6 \text{ min } 07 \text{ sec} = \underline{9.81 \text{ knots}} \\
\phantom{\text{and } 6 \text{ min } 07 \text{ sec} = } 19.78
\end{array}
$$

Hence mean speed ($\div 2$) = 9.89 knots

(b) Four runs are made in alternate directions, giving times of 7 min 02 sec, 7 min 08 sec, 7 min 00 sec and 7 min 06. These times are respectively 8.53, 8.41, 8.57 and 8.45 knots. To determine the speed from mean of means:

$$
\begin{array}{l}
1 \times 8.53 = 8.53 \\
2 \times 8.41 = 16.82 \\
2 \times 8.57 = 17.14 \\
1 \times 8.45 = \underline{8.45} \\
 50.94
\end{array}
$$

Divide by 6 = 8.49 knots

3.3.16 Navigation by electronic calculator

The formulae below help to solve problems when using scientific calculators. Any calculator used for navigation should be able to work in degrees, minutes and seconds of arc (DDMMSS) as well as Degrees and Decimals (D.d); have the powerful feature of polar to rectangular coordinate conversion, by which a sine and cosine can be calculated simultaneously, or an arc tangent resolved into its proper quadrant without having to apply rules, and sum the results; and be able to evaluate trigonometrical functions for all angles (not just those in the range 0° to 90°).

It must have adequate memory storage and recall facilities. Suggested minimum requirements for memory stores are :– coastal navigation, 4; celestial navigation, 6; and advanced navigation or yacht racing aplications, 26. Highly desirable features are statistical functions and accumulations ($\Sigma +$, $\Sigma -$, etc); the ability to add and subtract directly in hours or degrees, minutes and seconds; and a continuous memory facility, which means the ability to retain programmes and/or navigational data when switched 'off'.

For both coastal or celestial navigation, a programmable calculator is highly desirable to reduce potential errors resulting from numerous key operations, as they only require users to key in the required navigational data. There is the choice of two calculator languages – algebraic or reverse polish notation (RPN). The RPN system is unquestionably more suited to solving complex navigational problems. Which system to use is a matter of personal preference.

The most important factors are to thoroughly understand the operation, capability and limitations of the chosen calculator. Regular practice and familiarity with a particular type of calculator should allow any user to devise the best working procedures.

Speed, time and distance

$$\text{Speed} = \frac{\text{Distance} \times 60}{\text{Time (in mins)}}$$

$$\text{Time (in mins)} = \frac{\text{Distance} \times 60}{\text{Speed}}$$

$$\text{Distance} = \frac{\text{Speed} \times \text{Time (in mins)}}{60}$$

Distances and speed

Distance of horizon
(in nautical miles)
$$= 1.144 \times \sqrt{\text{Ht of eye (in feet)}}$$
or
$$= 2.072 \times \sqrt{\text{Ht of eye (in metres)}}$$

Distance a light is visible
(in nautical miles)
$$= 1.144 \times (\sqrt{h_o} + \sqrt{\text{Ht of eye}}) \text{ (in feet)}$$
or
$$= 2.072 \times (\sqrt{h_o} + \sqrt{\text{Ht of eye}}) \text{ (in metres)}$$

where: h_o is the height of object in feet or metres according to formula used.

Distance from mountains etc beyond horizon
(in nautical miles)
$$= \sqrt{3.71(h_o - HE) + (a - 1.76 \times \sqrt{HE})^2}$$
$$- (a - 1.76 \times \sqrt{HE}) \text{ for heights in metres}$$
or
$$\sqrt{1.13(h_o - HE) + (a - 0.972 \times \sqrt{HE})^2}$$
$$- (a - 0.972 \times \sqrt{HE}) \text{ for heights in feet}$$

where: h_o is the height of the mountain or object, HE is height of eye, and a is the sextant angle (in mins).

Distance to the radar horizon (in nautical miles)
$$= 2.21 \times \sqrt{\text{Ht of scanner (in metres)}}$$
or
$$= 1.22 \times \sqrt{\text{Ht of scanner (in feet)}}$$

$$\text{Boat speed over 1nm} = \frac{3600}{\text{time in seconds}}$$

Horizontal sextant angle

$$\text{Radius of position circle} = \frac{D}{2 \times \sin A}$$

where: D is distance between the objects in nautical miles, and A is the angle between them in degrees.

Vertical sextant angles

Distance off
(in nautical miles)
$$= \frac{\text{Height of object (above MHWS in feet)}}{6076 \times \tan \text{(sextant angle)}}$$
or
$$= \frac{\text{Height of object (above MHWS) in metres}}{1852 \times \tan \text{(sextant angle)}}$$

Note: In the above formulae, sextant angle in degrees and minutes must be corrected for index error.

An approximate distance off, adequate for most purposes, is given by the formulae;

Distance off
(in nautical miles)
$$= \frac{\text{Height of object (in feet)} \times 0.565}{\text{Sextant angle (in minutes)}}$$
or
$$= \frac{\text{Height of object (in metres)} \times 1.854}{\text{Sextant angle (in minutes)}}$$

Coastal Navigation

Where R is the distance run between two relative bearings of an object, the first A degrees, and the second B degrees,

$$\text{Distance (D) of object at second bearing} = \frac{R \times \sin A}{\sin (B - A)}$$

$$\text{To predict distance object will be off when abeam} = D \times \sin B$$

Conversion angle (half convergency)

Radio bearings follow great circle paths and therefore become curved lines when plotted on a Mercator chart. The angle between a great circle and rhumb line bearing is called 'conversion angle' or 'half convergency'. Near the equator, conversion angle is negligible, and as latitude increases, the error is larger.

If using a radiobeacon more than about 60nm away, a correction may be required before plotting on a Mercator chart. A great circle always lies on the polar side of the rhumb line, and conversion angle is ALWAYS applied towards the equator, and may be calculated from:–

Conversion angle (half convergency)
$$= \tfrac{1}{2} \text{ d.long} \times \sin \text{mid latitude}$$
or for small differences in latitude:
tan conversion angle
$$= \sin \text{mid latitude} \times \tan \frac{\text{d. long}}{2}$$

Latitude of receiver	Radiobeacon lies to	Correction
N	East	+
N	West	−
S	East	−
S	West	+

For further information see 4.3.3.

Course to Steer and Speed Made Good

Several different methods are available for calculating the Course to Steer Co(°T) and speed Made Good (SMG) given the required Track, Tr(°T), yacht's speed and the Set and Drift. The best methods are to calculate the Course to Steer and SMG in one operation.

The primary equations for this are:—

$$Co(°T) = Tr(°T) - \sin^{-1}(Drift \div yacht's\ speed) \times \sin(Set - Track)$$

and

$$SMG = Speed \times \cos(Co(°T) - Track) + Drift \times \cos(Set - Track)$$

Note: The Drift MUST always be less than the yacht's speed.

The relevant key sequences for a TI.57 are given below for solving the two most common navigation problems encountered which involve the triangle of velocity. Other calculators might require slightly different key operation (perhaps no second functions), but the principle applies to all algebraic calculators.

To find Course and Speed Made Good (CMG & SMG)

Example: Course steered 135°T Yacht's speed 6.5kts Set/Drift 075°/1.5kts

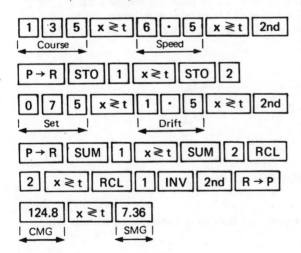

Note: If the course in display is negative (−), add +360°.

To find Course to Steer and Speed Made Good (Co.T & SMG)

Example: (using TI.57)

Track req'd. 042°T Yacht's speed 7.5kts Set/Drift 135°/1.2kts

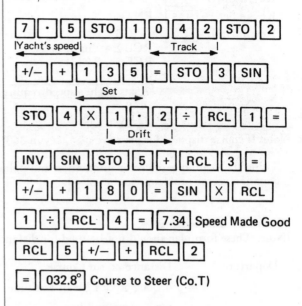

Note: If course in display is negative (−), add +360° to give the proper Co.T.

The same problems can be solved on an RPN calculator with far fewer key operations. The relevant key sequences to find the Course to Steer and SMG are as follows:

Key in Set	135	ENTER
Key in Track	042	STO 0 − sin
Key in Drift	1.2	×
Key in Yacht's speed	7.5	÷ sin⁻¹ RCL 0
		x ⇄ y −
		= 32.81 Co(T)
Key in Yacht's speed	7.5	→ R Σ +
Key in Set	135	ENTER
Key in Drift	1.2	→ R Σ + RCL
		11 RCL 13 → P
		= 7.34kts SMG

Note: If Course in display is negative (−), key in 360° + to give proper Co(T). In the case illustrated STORES 11 & 13 contain the vector summation.

With any calculations involving solutions to triangle of velocity problems, it is often easiest to use the Polar-Rectangular conversion facility in conjunction with vector addition capability (Σ+, Σ−, etc). Each type of calculator enters the x and y into specific memory stores so, to recall accumulated data, it is essential to identify which stores are used.

To find the Course to Steer and Yacht's speed

Using an RPN calculator: Given Track required 042°T, SMG required 7.3kts and the Set and Drift 135/1.2kts.

Key in Track $\boxed{042}$ ENTER

Key in SMG $\boxed{7.3}$ $\rightarrow R \Sigma +$

Key in Set $\boxed{135}$ ENTER

Key in Drift $\boxed{1.2}$ $\rightarrow R \Sigma +$

    RCL $\Sigma +$ (in this case

    RCL 13, RCL 11)

    $\rightarrow P\ =$

    $\boxed{\text{7.5kts yacht's speed required}}$

    $x \rightleftarrows y =$

    $\boxed{\text{32.8 Co(T)}}$

Note: If course displayed is negative $(-)$, key in $360°+$ to give proper Course (T).

Using the technique of vector summation and polar-rectangular capability, a variety of different navigation vector problems can be solved.

Short distance sailing

(Note: These formulae should not be used for distances over 600nm).

Departure	=	Distance × sin Course
	=	d.Long × Cos Mean Latitude
	=	tan Course × d.Lat
d.Lat	=	Distance × cos Course
d.Long	=	Departure ÷ Cos Mean Latitude
Distance	=	Departure ÷ sin Course
	=	d.Lat × sec Course
Sin Course	=	Departure ÷ Distance
Cos Course	=	d.Lat ÷ Distance
Tan Course	=	Departure ÷ d.Lat

Long distance sailing

Basic rhumb line sailing formulae are based on the Sphere, but can be modified for use with a Spheroid, commonly called Mercator sailing, for which tables of Meridional parts are published in nautical tables. Mercator sailing techniques should be used for the calculation of rhumb line tracks and distances over 600nm.

The basic formula for use with the Sphere are:—

$$\tan \text{Track} = \cfrac{\pi (\text{Long}_1 \sim \text{Long}_2)}{180° \left[\text{In tan} \left(45° + \dfrac{\text{Lat}_2}{2}\right) \sim \text{In tan} \left(45° + \dfrac{\text{Lat}_1}{2}\right) \right]}$$

$$\text{Distance} = 60 \times \frac{\text{Lat}_2 - \text{Lat}_1}{\cos \text{Track}}$$

When the track is 090° or 270°, the formula below should be substituted:

$$\text{Distance} = 60 (\text{Long}_2 \sim \text{Long}_1) \times \cos \text{Lat}$$

Note: The above formula for tan Track uses natural logarithms instead of common logarithms and this is shown by the abbreviation 'In'.

Mercator sailings are usually calculated on the Spheroid using the following basic formulae:

$$\tan \text{Track} = \frac{\text{d.Long (in mins)}}{\text{difference in meridional parts (dmp)}}$$

$$\text{Distance (nm)} = \frac{\text{d.Lat in mins}}{\cos \text{Track}}$$

d.Lat $\qquad$ = Distance × cos Track

$$\text{departure (nm)} = \frac{\text{d.Lat} \times \text{d.Long (in mins)}}{\text{dmp}}$$

Before starting, it is necessary to calculate the meridional parts (MP) for the Latitude of departure and destination in order to find the difference (dmp). Remember, that when the latitudes of departure and destination are of contrary name, the SUM of the two MP's is used for dmp.

For the International Spheroid (eccentricity (e) 0.08199189), the value of meridional parts (MP) for any given latitude can be calculated from the formula:

$$MP = 7915.704456 \times \log \tan \left(45° + \frac{\text{Lat}}{2}\right) - \sin \text{Lat} \times (23.110771 + 0.052051 \times \sin^2 \text{Lat}).$$

If the results are checked against, say, Nories tables, a slight difference will be noted between the figures. The reason for this is that Nories tables are based on the Clarke spheroid of 1880, which uses an eccentricity factor of 0.0824834.

Great circle sailing

Great circle sailing is used when it is desired to take advantage of the shortest distance between two points along the great circle, rather than the longer rhumb line distance. For practical purposes, the Earth is assumed to be a sphere. If higher accuracy is required, then great circle formulae based on the Spheroid should be used. The shortest great circle distance on the Spheroid is called a 'geodesic'.

$$\text{Initial Track} = \tan^{-1} \left[\frac{\sin \text{d.Long}}{(\cos \text{Lat}_1 \times \tan \text{Lat}_2) - (\sin \text{Lat}_1 \times \cos \text{d.Long})}\right]$$

Note: If the name of Lat_2 (destination) is contrary to that of Lat_1 (departure), then Lat_2 is treated as a negative $(-)$. The Track angle is calculated from the pole towards east or west.

Distance (nm) = $60 \times \cos^{-1}$ [(sin Lat_1 × sin Lat_2) + (cos Lat_1 × cos Lat_2 × cos d.Long)]

Worked example: Great circle

From: FALMOUTH 50° 09′N (50.150°)   05° 03′W (05.050°)
To: ANTIGUA   17° 00′N (17.000°)   61° 46′W (61.766°)

d.Lat   33° 09′S (33.150°)   d.Long   56° 43′W (56.716°)

$$\text{Initial Track} = \tan^{-1} \left[\frac{\sin 56.716°}{(\cos 50.150° \times \tan 17.000°) - (\sin 50.150° \times \cos 56.716°)}\right]$$

$$= \tan^{-1} \left[\frac{0.83596}{(0.64078 \times 0.30573) - (0.76772 \times 0.54879)}\right]$$

$$= \tan^{-1} \left[\frac{0.83596}{(0.19591) - (0.42132)}\right]$$

$$= \tan^{-1} \frac{0.83596}{-0.22541}$$

$$= \tan^{-1} -3.70862$$

$$= S - 74.90955° W$$

$$= 254.9° \text{ (T)}$$

Distance (nm) = $60 \times \cos^{-1}$ [(sin 50.150° × sin 17.000°) + (cos 50.150° × cos 17.000°

$$\times \cos 56.716°)]$$

$$= 60 \times \cos^{-1} [(0.76772 \times 0.29237) + (0.64078 \times 0.95630 \times 0.54879)]$$

$$= 60 \times \cos^{-1} [(0.22446) + (0.33629)]$$

$$= 55.89242 \times 60$$

$$= 3353.54 \text{ nm.}$$

3.3.17 **DR computers**

With the increasing use of microprocessors in the field of navigational instruments, several new and exciting aids have become available to yachtsmen, and more will follow. Despite the position fixing systems which are now available (described in Chapter 4), many yachts rely largely on DR positions. This is just one of the many functions of the Brookes & Gatehouse Hercules System 190, which can take inputs from compass and log, and continually provide information on distance and course made good from a certain point. The computer at the heart of the B&G data system accepts inputs from various sensors, and can produce navigational and performance information on a number of analogue indicators or multi-function digital displays, sited where required in the boat.

The days when navigators tediously plotted dozens of small velocity triangles are not perhaps quite over for the average yachtsman, but they may well be in the not too distant future. Microprocessors can do it more quickly and more accurately, and without getting seasick. Although of particular interest to racing yachtsmen, such a system has several applications for cruising boats, whether power or sail. We are likely to see a steady extension in the use and versatility of such equipment even in quite small yachts, and hopefully a steady reduction in price.

3.4 **Pilotage**

3.4.1 **Pilotage—general**

Pilotage is the navigation of a vessel using geographical features, buoys and other marks (or their lights) in conjuction with the chart, compass, echo sounder and radar (if fitted). It involves the navigator knowing his approximate position at any moment, and following a pre-determined track so that he can correctly identify objects appearing ahead, or maybe a transit astern for example.

Pilotage is often most difficult when there are a large number of confusing objects available—like the lights of a large sea port when first approached from seaward. But if the position of the boat is known or can be established at any time, it is a comparatively simple matter to take a bearing of an object or a light which appears in order to identify it from the chart. Alternatively it may happen that the object will be in transit with one that has been positively identified.

It is sometimes possible to work ahead by plotting what the bearings of certain future marks will be when the boat reaches a certain position. Then a quick check with the hand bearing compass should tell you which is which.

Pilotage is obviously much easier (and safer) if one person steers the boat and follows the courses ordered, and the navigator is completely free to concentrate on his job. In a difficult situation it pays to use two people for pilotage – one up top taking the bearings, and passing them to the other who is at the chart table. This is particularly helpful in darkness, because it preserves the night vision of the person in the cockpit.

For inshore pilotage always use fixed marks or beacons in preference to buoys, which may not be precisely on station.

3.4.2 **Leading marks and clearing lines**

Most charts show examples of leading marks – objects placed at a harbour entrance or in a narrow channel, so that by keeping them in line the best water is followed. Where they are lit pairs of leading marks sometimes have the same characteristics, to help identify them. Leading marks are described in the 'Pilot' and are shown on the chart thus 'Ldg Lts 047°'. This is the true bearing of the transit from seaward.

Another common use of transits is as clearing lines to keep a boat clear of hidden dangers. When using any form of transit always take a bearing of it, and check this against the chart or sailing directions, to see if the correct objects are being observed. Not all clearing lines are necessarily shown by transits. In some cases the bearing of a conspicuous object may be given.

3.4.3 **IALA Buoyage System (Region A)**

International buoyage is now harmonized into a single IALA Maritime Buoyage System which, applied to Regions A and B, differs only in the use of red and green lateral marks. In Region A (which includes all Europe and the Mediterranean) lateral marks are red on the port hand, and in Region B they are red on the starboard hand, related to the direction of buoyage. Shapes of lateral marks are the same for both regions.

Region A uses five types of marks, in any combination, as follows (see page 59):-
(1) *Lateral marks* used in conjunction with a conventional direction of buoyage, and indicating the port and starboard sides of a channel to be followed.
(2) *Cardinal marks* used in conjunction with a compass to show where dangers exist or where the mariner may find navigable water.
(3) *Isolated danger marks* to show isolated dangers of limited size that have navigable water all around them.
(4) *Safe water marks* to show that there is navigable water all round that position.
(5) *Special marks* not primarily for navigation, but indicating an area or feature referred to in nautical documents.

The significance of an individual mark depends upon its colour, shape or topmark by day, and the colour or rhythm of any light displayed at night.

Fig. 3(34) Direction of buoyage around the United Kingdom. In rivers and estuaries the direction of buoyage is normally from seawards inwards.

Lateral marks (Region A)

Lateral marks are used in conjunction with a direction of a buoyage shown by a special arrow on the chart; in and around the British Isles its general direction is from SW to NE in open waters –see Fig.3 (34)– but from seaward when approaching a harbour, river or estuary. Where port or starboard lateral marks do not rely on can or conical buoy shapes for identification they carry, where practicable, the appropriate topmarks. Any numbering or lettering follows the direction of buoyage.

| | Preferred channel | |
	To starboard	To port
Colour	Red, with one broad green horizontal band	Green with one broad red horizontal band
Shape (buoys)	Cylindrical (can), pillar or spar	Conical, pillar or spar
Topmark (if any)	Single red can	Single green cone, point up
Light (when fitted)	Red	Green
Rhythm	Composite group flashing Fl(2 + 1)R	Composite group flashing Fl(2 + 1)G

Fig. 3(35) Preferred channel marks, Region A.

Port hand marks:

Colour	Red
Shape (buoys)	Can or spar
Topmark (if any)	Single red can
Light (when fitted)	Red, any rhythm

Starboard hand marks:

Colour	Green (see note)
Shape (buoys)	Conical or spar
Topmark (if any)	Single green cone point up (see note)
Light (when fitted)	Green, any rhythm

Note: In exceptional cases black may be used instead of green.

At the point where a channel divides, when proceeding in the direction of buoyage, the preferred channel may be indicated by a modified port or starboard lateral mark as shown in Fig.3 (35) (for Region A).

Cardinal marks

Cardinal marks are named after the quadrant in which the mark is placed, in relation to the danger or point indicated. The four quadrants (North, East, South and West) are bounded by the true bearings NW–NE, NE–SE, SE–SW and SW–NW, taken from the point of interest. The name of a cardinal mark indicates that it should be passed on the named side. For example, a North cardinal mark (situated in the quadrant between NW and NE from the point of interest) should be passed to the northward. Similarly you should keep to the east of an East cardinal mark, and so on.

A cardinal mark may indicate the safe side on which to pass a danger, or that the deepest water is on the named side of the mark, or it may draw attention to a feature in a channel such as a bend, junction or fork, or the end of a shoal.

Cardinal marks are pillar or spar shaped, painted black and yellow, and always carry black double cone topmarks one cone above the other. Their lights are white, either very quick flashing (VQ or VQkFl), 120 to 100 flashes per minute, or quick flashing (Q or QkFl), 60 or 50 flashes per minute. A long flash (as used in the light for a South cardinal mark) is a flash of not less than two seconds duration.

North cardinal mark

Topmark	— Two black cones, points up
Colour	— Black above yellow
Shape	— Pillar or spar
Light (when fitted)	— White, VQ or Q.

East cardinal mark

Topmark	— Two black cones, base to base
Colour	— Black, with single horizontal yellow band
Shape	— Pillar or spar
Light (when fitted)	— White, VQ (3) every 5 sec or Q (3) every 10 sec.

South cardinal mark

Topmark	— Two black cones, points down
Colour	— Yellow above black
Shape	— Pillar or spar
Light (when fitted)	— White, VQ (6) plus long flash every 10 sec or Q (6) plus long flash every 15 sec.

West cardinal mark

Topmark	— Two black cones, point to point
Colour	— Yellow, with single horizontal black band
Shape	— Pillar or spar
Light (when fitted)	— White, VQ (9) every 10 sec or Q (9) every 15 sec.

To help identify cardinal marks, the double cones of north and south cardinal marks point north (up) and south(down) respectively. West cones for cardinal marks are point to point, or waisted. East cones have their points apart or extended. So far as the lights are concerned, the number of flashes increases in a clockwise direction–three at three o'clock (east), six at six o'clock (south),and nine at nine o' clock (west).

Isolated danger marks

Isolated danger marks are moored on or above, or erected on, an isolated danger such as a rock or a wreck which has navigable water all around it.

Topmark	— Two black spheres, one above the other
Colour	— Black, with one or more broad horizontal red bands
Shape (buoys)	— Pillar or spar
Light (when fitted)	— White, Fl(2).

Safe water marks

Safe water marks indicate that there is navigable water all round the mark, and are used for mid-channel or landfall marks.

Topmark (if any)	— Single red sphere
Colour	— Red and white vertical stripes
Shape	— Spherical, pillar with spherical topmark, or spar
Light (when fitted)	— White, isophase, occulting, or long flash every 10 secs.

Special marks

Special marks are not primarily intended to assist navigation, but indicate a special area or feature – such as spoil grounds, military exercise areas, water ski areas, cable or pipe line marks, Ocean Data Acquisition Systems (ODAS), or traffic separation marks where the use of conventional channel marking may cause confusion.

Topmark (if any)	— Single yellow 'X' shape
Colour	— Yellow
Shape	— Optional but not conflicting with navigational marks
Light (when fitted)	— Yellow, with a characteristic different from cardinal, isolated danger, or safe water marks.

New dangers may include naturally occurring obstructions such as a sandbank that has appeared or moved, or man made dangers such as wrecks. New dangers are marked in accordance with the rules above; in the event of a specially grave danger one of the marks may be duplicated. If lit the mark will have the appropriate cardinal or lateral characteristic.

3.4.4 **Practical passage making**

Apart from using the correct navigational techniques, there are elements of preparation and planning for any passage – even for short coastal trips. These matters are discussed in Chapter 15 (15.5).

3.5 **Bibliography**

Practical Yacht Navigator by Kenneth Wilkes (Nautical Books).

Navigation for Yachtsmen by Mary Blewitt (Stanford Maritime).

Coastwise Navigation by G. G. Watkins (Stanford Maritime).

Basic Coastal Navigation by Conrad Dixon (Adlard Coles Ltd).

Start to Navigate By Conrad Dixon (Adlard Coles Ltd).

Navigation by Pocket Calculator by Conrad Dixon (Adlard Coles Ltd).

Weekend Navigator by Bruce Fraser (Adlard Coles Ltd).

Coastal Navigation by Gerry Smith (Adlard Coles Ltd).

Little Ship Navigation by M. J. Rantzen (Barrie & Jenkins).

Chapter 4

Radio navigational aids

Contents

4.1 Aids to navigation

4.1.1 Developments

From the outset it should be emphasised that the growing number and bewildering variety of navigational aids and position fixing systems which are available to yachtsmen should in all cases be considered *as* aids, and not as replacing more traditional or fundamental methods of navigation and pilotage. There may be times, perhaps most awkward times, when an electronic device for one reason or another is not available, or (even worse) when it gives misleading results. Hence, whatever sophisticated equipment is fitted in a small boat, it is essential that the navigator can use and retain the basic navigation skills which have already been outlined in the previous chapter.

It is only about 35 years since the first direction finding radio receivers intended specifically for small boats became available to yachtsmen. Since then there have been considerable developments with various types of navigational aids, particularly during the early 1980s. The silicon chip and microprocessors have revolutionised marine electronics, which had fallen some way astern of the technology employed in space and aviation systems. Doubtless in the coming years we will see even more sensational developments for yachts and small craft. Hopefully we can expect smaller, more accurate, more versatile and more reliable equipment coming on the market, and at prices which will be increasingly competitive in real terms.

4.1.2 Navigational aids and position fixing systems

The present choice of navigational aids for the individual yachtsman depends on the usage of the boat concerned and the particular waters in which she operates – apart from the depth of the owner's pocket. For a world-girdling yacht, an instrument which can provide a fix anywhere on the earth's surface, to an accuracy of half-a-mile or less, might be worth a couple of thousand pounds. For the average coastal cruising boat, operating occasionally across the North Sea or the English Channel, it could be a waste of money.

The following is a summary of the radio navigational aids and position fixing systems available:

(1) Marine (and aeronautical) radiobeacons
(2) Radio Direction-finding stations
(3) Consol
(4) Decca
(5) Loran-C
(6) Omega
(7) Satellite navigation
(8) Radar, including radar beacons
(9) VHF Radio Lighthouses
(10) VHF Direction-finding
(11) HM Coastguard (Emergency Only) VHF DF

Each of the above has advantages and disadvantages when it comes to considering such matters as cost, accuracy, space occupied (including that for the aerial or antenna), power supply, simplicity of operation, reliability, and the way in which the information is presented.

It should be noted that in some cases, one set on board a yacht can cover two (or more) of the above. For example, a suitable MF receiver will cover (1), (2) and (3). A VHF radiotelephone will cope with (9) and (11). At a more sophisticated (and expensive) level, there are sets which combine satellite navigation and Omega, or satellite navigation and Loran-C.

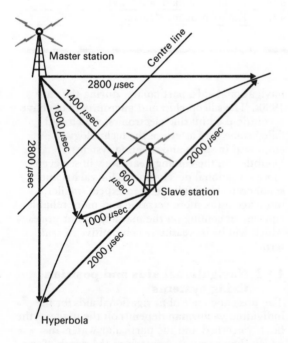

Fig. 4(1) The principle of a hyperbolic position line. For each point on the curve the difference in time between receipts of synchronised signals from the master station and slave station is 800 μsec.

Hyperbolic navigation systems

Since three of the systems listed above (Decca, Loran-C and Omega) all work on this same basic principle, it is useful to understand the theory of hyperbolic position lines. A hyperbola is formed by points whose distances from two fixed points always differ by a constant amount. The systems depend on the measurement of the difference in time taken by radio waves travelling from two fixed stations on shore to the vessel. Since the speed of radio waves is constant, from the time difference can be derived the actual difference in range of the two fixed stations, and hence the appropriate hyperbola which forms a position line – see Fig. 4(1). A similar measurement from another pair of fixed stations gives a second position line, and hence a fix.

In practice, three fixed stations in a triangular pattern are typically set up round a master station to form a 'chain'. The two pairs giving the best cut can be selected for a fix. As an alternative to the direct measurement of the time difference, the phase difference can be compared between continuous-wave signals from two fixed stations. Since a hyperbola consists of two parts which are symmetrical about the axis of the fixed stations, means have to be provided for determining which half forms the position line.

Hyperbolic systems display figures which correspond to lines on a latticed chart, from which is derived the position, and this gives the most accurate results. However, many instruments now give a direct read-out of latitude and longitude – not quite so precise, but very convenient.

Waypoint

With the advent of modern position fixing systems came the term 'waypoint'. A waypoint is a specified position which can be a departure point, a selected position along the intended route (perhaps where it is proposed to alter course), or a destination. Before starting a passage, waypoints can be entered as latitude and longitude, or often also as bearing and distance from some position or from another waypoint. On demand the set will then display such information as course and distance to the next waypoint (either by great circle or rhumb line) and estimated time of arrival (ETA). Typically ten waypoints might be provided, but some sets have many more.

Accuracy

It is important for the navigator to appreciate the accuracy that can be expected from any navigational system in the prevailing conditions. Although technical specifications may include terms such as Root Mean Square (RMS) error, the commonsense definition of accuracy (absolute accuracy) is the distance between the boat's actual position and the position obtained from the aid or system being used. However, one other term that may be met is repeatable accuracy. This defines the ability of the set to return to a position by repeating readings previously obtained for that position – useful for relocating fishing marks, wrecks or landfall buoys for example.

Do not be misled by the fact that a digital read-out may give figures to two or more decimal places. High resolution of a display does not necessarily imply high accuracy.

4.2 Marine and aero radiobeacons

4.2.1 Marine radiobeacons

This system of direction finding is a relatively simple method whereby yachtsmen can establish at least an approximate position from non-directional radiobeacons, using a receiving set which has an aerial with directional qualities. It is useful in poor visibility or when navigating out of sight of land, but the effective range of the system is limited and few beacons give bearings of reasonable accuracy at distances of more than 50 miles. The majority of beacons around the coast of Britain have effective ranges of even less than this.

A simple but adequate DF set can be bought for under £100 and is likely to be a small hand-held instrument powered by internal batteries. More sophisticated equipment, with better bearing discrimination at longer range, can cost a great deal more – as can the automatic DF set which, once tuned into a beacon frequency, automatically displays the required bearing.

Coastal radiobeacons of this type are non-directional, but they transmit on certain frequencies and at fixed intervals. The navigator tunes to the listed frequency, identifies the required beacon by its call sign in Morse, and rotates the aerial of the set so that it registers the minimum signal, or null. (The minimum signal is chosen because it is easier to identify that the maximum.) The position of the aerial then indicates the direction of the beacon.

Marine radiobeacons around the British Isles operate on frequencies between 285 and 315kHz (about 1050–950 metres on the Long Wave). Often up to 6 beacons which cover a certain area work on the same frequency, transmitting in succession. (See 4.2.3.) Each individual transmission last one minute and consists of the beacon's identification signal in Morse (usually two letters) lasting about 22 seconds, a long continuous dash of 25 seconds (when the null is obtained), a final identification signal which lasts about 8 seconds, and a short silence of at least 5 seconds before the next beacon starts to transmit.

On Admiralty charts marine radiobeacons are shown by a magenta circle with the letters 'RC'

alongside. On some old charts they may be shown as 'R°.B^n'.

4.2.2 DF receiving sets

Most simple DF sets have ferrite rod aerials, which give a minimum signal when they are pointing in line with the direction of the station. Often they incorporate a small compass, so that the magnetic bearing of the beacon can be read at the same moment as the operator identifies the null in his earphones (which are much better than a loudspeaker for this purpose). Such compasses are just as liable to error as any other magnetic compass, and they must not be used close to magnetic objects.

With other sets the receiver itself is fixed and the aerial rotates against a graduated scale which gives the relative bearing (that is relative to the ship's head). The course on the steering compass must then be noted at the same moment that the null point and the relative bearing are obtained. This requires co-operation between the operator and the helmsman. Against this disadvantage there is the benefit of having the aerial in a certain place, so that the set can be properly calibrated for any error – rather like a compass is swung for deviation. This type of set also allows the aerial to be fitted on deck, connected to the set by a long spindle, so that it is well away from magnetic influences. An extension of this principle is to use a cross-loop aerial above the wheelhouse or even at the masthead, connected to the receiver through a goniometer – an electronic device which produces a similar electro-magnetic field at the receiver to the one experienced at the aerial.

An Automatic Direction Finding (ADF) set is tuned to the required frequency, which may be crystal controlled, and will then lock on to any transmission automatically, and indicate the bearing of the beacon on an azimuth scale, a digital display, or a cathode ray tube. If there is a sequence of beacons on the same frequency it will point to each one in turn. Such sets usually have cross-loop aerials, and a sensing device to remove ambiguity about the direction of the beacon. (When a bearing is taken with an ordinary set the null point does not differentiate between a bearing and its reciprocal.) Aerials of this type can be positioned high up, even at the masthead, where they are well removed from undesirable magnetic influences within the boat. ADF sets have another advantage, in that whatever type of unit is fitted for sensing the Earth's horizontal magnetic field can be sited separately, in the part of the boat which is most magnetically neutral.

Developments in microprocessors and in silicon chip technology are leading to rapid improvements in all types of DF sets, and the precise timing offered by quartz crystal clocks allows beacons to be identified by their time sequence, as well as by their morse code signal, in many modern sets. The timing should however only be considered as an *aid* to identification: beacons must always be identified positively by their callsign, in order to prevent confusion with other beacons operating on similar frequencies, but received as a result of freak propagation.

4.2.3 Grouping and sequence of beacons

For convenience, two or more radiobeacons often share a common frequency, their transmissions being arranged on a strict time schedule so that they do not overlap. A common arrangement is for 6 beacons to share 1 frequency on a 6 minute cycle, each transmitting for 1 minute in a fixed sequence. In all cases the cycle of the group starts at the hour; thus the first beacon to transmit (Sequence Number 1) comes on the air at the hour, and subsequently at 06, 12, 18, 24 etc. minutes past. The beacon which is Sequence Number 6 transmits at 05, 11, 17, 23 etc. minutes past the hour. The table below shows the relation between sequence numbers and the start of transmission times, in minutes past the hour.

Sequence Number	1	2	3	4	5	6
	00	01	02	03	04	05
	06	07	08	09	10	11
Starts to	12	13	14	15	16	17
transmit at	18	19	20	21	22	23
these	24	25	26	27	28	29
minutes past	30	31	32	33	34	35
each hour	36	37	38	39	40	41
	42	43	44	45	46	47
	48	49	50	51	52	53
	54	55	56	57	58	59

4.2.4 Directional Radiobeacons (RD)

In a very few places, all of them overseas, a directional signal is transmitted, to assist vessels making harbour, the signal varying depending on the boat's position relative to the required bearing line. Automatic gain control should be switched off when using such devices: if the set has a direction finding aerial it should be tuned to the position of maximum reception.

On Admiralty charts the bearing is shown as a pecked line, with the legend RD. Allowance should be made for the width of the beam when the bearing line passes close to dangers. In small craft, for collision avoidance, it may often be wise to keep slightly to starboard of the indicating bearing.

It may sometimes be found, when a directional transmission is calibrated, that the observed beam deviates from the promulgated bearing along part of its length. Major deviations of this kind are given in the *Admiralty List of Radio Signals Vol 2*, where known. On Admiralty charts the bearing line is normally limited to the portion(s) in which the observed beam substantially coincides with the nominal or intended bearing line.

The Boulogne beacon which used to work on this principle is now discontinued.

4.2.5 Beacons incorporating distance finding

Occasionally yachtsmen may encounter radiobeacons which incorporate radio and sound signals which are synchronised for distance finding. The two signals are usually synchronised at an easily identifiable point in the cycle of each – say at the beginning or end of a long dash and a long blast of the fog signal. A stopwatch must be used, and the difference between the two times in seconds, multiplied by the factor of 0.18, gives the distance off in nautical miles.

Other systems involve the transmission by the beacon of a number of measuring signals, started when the fog signal is sounded. The number of measuring signals received before the fog signal is heard on board the boat is an indication of the distance, the time scale of the beacon being included in information on that station. An interval of 5.5 seconds between measuring signals is equivalent to a unit distance of one nautical mile.

A third form of synchronisation involves transmissions by the beacon of a count of units on RT; then it is only necessary to note the figure heard when the fog signal timing point is heard.

4.2.6 Aero radiobeacons

Aero radiobeacons are established for use by aircraft, but a few which are situated on or very near the coast can be useful to yachtsmen. Only selected aero radiobeacons are shown on charts, where they are marked by a small magenta circle and the letters Aero RC. It is necessary to plot the positions of other beacons which are listed, from their latitude and longitude as given.

Aero radiobeacons transmit continuously, which can be a considerable advantage, but care should be taken with their use because the land effect may be unpredictable.

Aero radiobeacons operate on a wider range of frequencies than marine ones – from 250kHz to 600kHz (500–1200m).

4.2.7 Types of emission (modes)

There are several different types of emission used in maritime radiobeacons and in radiotelephone services, and some understanding of their characteristics and designations is helpful in order to get good results from equipment on board a boat.

New designations for radio signal emissions came into force on 1 January 1982. In the following explanation the new designations are given, with the old designations shown in brackets since these are still used in certain publications.

Intelligence is impressed upon a radio emission by modulation. A continuous emission of constant amplitude (or strength) and of constant frequency carries no information, and the simplest way of impressing intelligence upon it is to switch it on and off (or key it), to make Morse

Code characters for example. This type of modulation is now designated as A1A (previously A1) and is used for the identification signal of older radiobeacons and in radiotelegraphy.

The amplitude of the radio emission can be fluctuated however at a rate and to a degree corresponding with a sound wave to produce speech, music or a plain musical tone. The latter may be keyed as necessary. These emissions are referred to as 'amplitude modulation' (AM), of which there are various types depending on whether the original (carrier) radio wave is transmitted with the so-called 'sidebands' generated in the process of modulation, or whether it is wholly or partially suppressed. One of the sidebands may also be suppressed to make better use of the transmitter's power and of the radio-frequency spectrum. The resulting 'single-sideband' (SSB) emission is the standard for maritime medium frequency (MF) radio, enabling the number of MF channels to be doubled.

The designation A2A (previously A2) refers to amplitude modulation, the type of transmission being telegraphy by the keying of an amplitude-modulating audio frequency (or audio frequencies), or by keying the modulated emission. It is commonly used for the identification signals of radiobeacons. A2* is similar to A2, but denotes an AM telegraphy emission in which the carrier is continuously present, and is now also classified as A2A.

A second way of impressing intelligence on a radio wave is to fluctuate the frequency, with the amplitude staying constant. This is called 'frequency modulation', and is used in VHF radiotelephones. It does not suffer so much as AM from outside interference, and it is simple and relatively cheap; but it occupies more spectrum width per channel and for this reason is not suitable for the HF and MF bands.

When using a radiobeacon it is important to know what type of radio emission is used in order to receive the transmissions correctly. A1A (A1) indicates that the transmissions are unmodulated, which generally requires a receiver with a built-in oscillator to produce an audible signal. This is usually referred to as a Beat Frequency Oscillator (BFO), which must be switched ON to receive A1A(A1) or NON A1A (AOA1) transmissions, and to identify them.

Nearly all British aeronautical radiobeacons are NON A2A (AOA2) – an unmodulated transmission with telegraphy identification by the keying of an amplitude modulating audio frequency, the carrier emission being continuous during the identification period. With a NON A2A (AOA2) beacon, to receive the DF tone any separate BFO control should be ON, and to receive the identification signal it should be OFF.

An increasing problem for yachtsmen has been the identification of A2* beacons, where the carrier is continuously present, the tone-modulated wave alone being keyed to give identification; because modern DF receivers are very selective, they pick up the signal of the continuous carrier, and the Morse signal is weak or inaudible. There are three possible solutions, first by reducing the selectivity of the set by switching to the DF or 'Radio' mode and, if possible, by switching the BFO to OFF: second by re-tuning the receiver to a frequency about 1kHz above the listed frequency of the beacon, until the Morse signal is heard more clearly (although this may widen the null): third, by using an accurate clock to help identify the beacon by its known sequence of operation.

Where a separate control is provided for BFO it should be adjusted as follows:

Emission		BFO setting	
New style	Old style	For DF use	For ident.
A1A	A1	ON	ON
NON A1A	AOA1	ON	ON
NON A2A	AOA2	ON	OFF[2]
A2A	{ A2	ON or OFF[1]	OFF[2]
	A2*	ON or OFF[1]	OFF[2]
A3E	A3	ON or OFF[1]	OFF[2]

Note:
(1) For best performance consult the maker's handbook.
(2) If BFO cannot be switched off, it may be difficult to hear morse identification.

With any set where the user is expected to listen for a null signal, the BFO should be switched on during the DF period while the bearing is being taken.

4.2.8 Radiobeacons – operating procedure

The detailed procedure depends upon the type of set, but normally includes the following.

(1) First it is necessary to select the beacons to be used, depending on their range and the angle of cut they will give for a good fix. As with taking bearings of land objects, it is desirable to use at least three beacons so that the resulting cocked hat gives an indication of the reliability of the fix. If three beacons are used it is best if the position lines they give cut at angles of about 60°. Extract from the list the frequency and call sign of each beacon, and the time at which it transmits. Some modern DF sets incorporate a quartz crystal clock, which is helpful in finding the required beacon quickly.

(2) Turn on the set, and the Beat Frequency Oscillator (BFO), if there is a separate control for this. BFO makes the signal clearer for directional purposes and produces a more precise null. It should be used in accordance with the table in 4.2.7 above.

(3) Tune the receiver to the required frequency. Often this is done by an ordinary tuning dial,

but some new sets have a keyboard rather like a simple calculator on which the required figures are keyed to give precise results. The aerial may incorporate a separate tuning control. Earphones are better than a loudspeaker for direction finding, and they don't disturb other members of the crew, particularly at night.

(4) When the required beacon has been identified from its call sign and the long dash commences, swing the aerial backwards and forwards over a diminishing arc to determine the null. In some sets a visual null (signal strength) meter assists with this.

(5) With sets fitted with an integral compass mounted on the aerial the magnetic bearing of the beacon can be read directly. Write it down against the name or the call sign of the beacon in the navigator's notebook. Before it is plotted on the chart it will need to be corrected for variation and also for Quadrantal Error (if this is known – see 4.2.10 below). If a compass is not fitted to the set the relative bearing is read and at the same moment the helmsman must read the steering compass. Write them both down – never trust to memory in these matters.

(6) The procedure is then repeated with the other beacons, and the time of the fix and the log reading should be noted before the bearings are plotted on the chart. This is done in exactly the same way as visual bearings are plotted. The likely accuracy of the fix can be judged by the size of the cocked hat.

4.2.9 **Errors in radio bearings**
Bearings from radiobeacons are subject to errors, which fall into two categories.

Signal errors
(1) The accuracy of a radio bearing decreases considerably with the distance from the beacon. Any bearing taken towards the maximum range of a beacon (particularly at night) should be treated with caution Fig. 4(2).

(2) Night effect (or sky-wave effect) can cause errors from one hour before sunset to one hour after sunrise, specially near sunset and sunrise. The error increases with distance from the beacon, but is less serious if within about 25 miles.

(3) If the beacon's radio beam passes along the coast or over high ground it may be bent by land effect (or coastal refraction) and thus give an incorrect bearing Fig. 4(2).

(4) Synchronised transmissions of two beacons are a possible source of error.

Errors on board
(1) Quadrantal Error is caused by the magnetic effect of objects in and around the boat,

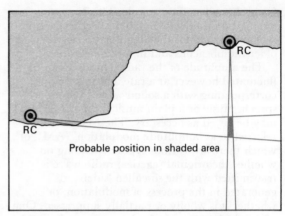

Fig. 4(2) Beams from a radiobeacon (on left) which come along the coast or over intervening land are refracted and less reliable. Due to refraction, the navigator will think that he is slightly further inshore than the shaded area. The diagram also shows how accuracy decreases with distance from the beacon.

which reradiate the signal being received so that its true direction is distorted. This effect on the radio waves on their way to the receiving aerial is usually greatest on each bow and quarter, and least when the beacon is on the beam or ahead/astern of the boat. With a fixed installation the set can be calibrated for Quadrantal Error in much the same way that a compass is swung. Visual and radio bearings of a convenient beacon are taken at the same time, and are compared on various headings. Beacons which provide a special calibration service are shown in 4.2.10.

(2) Compass error can be an important factor with a hand-held instrument unless it is used in a certain place which is known to be free from any magnet influences.

(3) Unless the set has a sensing device it is possible to take the reciprocal of the required bearing, when the beacon is on a light vessel or a lighthouse in the open sea for example.

(4) The error which may be caused by the operator depends upon his experience with the set concerned, and also on the prevailing weather conditions. Accurate radio bearings are not easy to get when the boat is moving around a great deal.

Radio bearings from a small yacht may therefore be a useful guide when taken by an experienced operator, using a set which has been properly installed and calibrated, as described in 4.2.10. But they can suffer from serious errors, and should not be relied on exclusively unless three or four position lines result in an acceptable cocked hat. Practice and experience help to get good bearings, but the results should always be compared with position lines from other sources (if available) so that they can be properly assessed. It is important to become familiar with the morse code signals of beacons which are likely to be used.

4.2.10 Calibration

Before it can be trusted (and there is no sense in having navigational equipment which cannot be trusted) a DF set must be calibrated in very much the same way that a compass is swung to establish its deviation.

The easiest way to calibrate a DF set is to get within visual range of a radiobeacon, and then take simultaneous radio and visual bearings of it with the boat on different headings. Unless a pelorus (or bearing plate) is available, and the visual bearings of the beacon can thus be related to the steering compass (which should previously have been corrected and swung), the visual bearings of the beacon will have to be taken with a reliable hand bearing compass, kept well clear of magnetic objects.

The two sets of bearings should be taken, say, every 15°, and it is helpful if the beacon concerned is one which transmits continuously – or the process can take rather a long time. As an alternative method radio bearings (only) of the beacon are taken from the boat when she is in a known position, so that the actual bearing of the beacon is known. In either case the object is to plot the Quadrantal Error for, say, every 15° of relative bearing.

The following stations in the British Isles provide a calibration service for DF sets. In each case the service is available from 1 hour after sunrise to 1 hour before sunset, and the range of the station is 5 n miles.

Humber Lt V, MB, 312.6kHz; Souter Light, PT, 312.6kHz; Point Lynas Light, PS, 310.3kHz; and Scarweather Lt V, RW, 312.6kHz.

Other stations provide a service on request, and a charge is made accordingly.

4.2.11 Details of Radiobeacons

A list of marine and aero radiobeacons, for the geographical area covered, is published each year in *The Macmillan & Silk Cut Nautical Almanac*. The information given includes:
(1) A reference number for each beacon, which can be used to assist identification on charts provided.
(2) Name of beacon, and whether it is grouped with other beacons (see 4.2.3).
(3) Latitude and longitude.
(4) The Morse Code identification signal (Ident), with the Morse symbols.
(5) The frequency of the transmission, in kilohertz (kHz).
(6) The mode of emission (see 4.2.7).
(7) The range, in miles, at which the field strength produced by the ground wave of the transmission falls to a minimum acceptable value. In some areas, where there are numerous radiobeacons, it is necessary to reduce power output at night, so day and night range are quoted. Elsewhere the ranges shown should be obtained in the absence of skywave effect. MF beacons should not be relied on at ranges of more than about 50 n miles in the presence of night effect, particularly near sunset and sunrise.
(8) Sequence number, for grouped stations – see 4.2.3. The service is normally continuously available, unless otherwise stated.

4.2.12 VHF Radio Lighthouse

This is a beacon which transmits a rotating directional signal that can be received by a VHF set capable of receiving frequency modulated signals. The signals are modulated with an audio tone varying between a maximum and a null. The 'null radial' rotates at a uniform speed of 4° per second, and the bearing of the beacon is determined by measuring the time that the null radial takes to reach the observer from a known starting point. To measure the time interval, the tone is broken into a number of half-second beats, each beat being the equivalent of 2° of bearing. The observer simply counts the number of beats from the start of each transmission, until the tone disappears, and then refers to a table which is published in *The Macmillan & Silk Cut Nautical Almanac* to determine the bearing.

The signal composition is as follows:

Pause	0.1s
Morse ident.	3.2s
Pause	1.0s
Digital data	0.3s
Pause	1.0s
70 Nav. beats	35.0s
Pause	1.0s
Morse ident.	3.2s
Pause	1.0s
Digital data	0.1s
Pause	12.1s
Static gap	2.0s
	———
	60.0s

The digital data is of no navigational significance, and is transmitted for the use of test equipment.

Beat numbers 10, 20, 30, 40, 50 and 60 are marked by a change in audio tone frequency.

All the VHF Radio Lighthouses currently in service transmit on VHF Ch 88 (162.025MHz). The mode of emission used is designated as FXX, in which the main carrier is frequency modulated.

In the event of a transmitting equipment fault, a warbling tone will be transmitted, rendering the preceding beats invalid.

In the absence of a table, the bearing can be found from the formula:

$$\text{Bearing} = A + 2(N - 7)$$

where N is the number of beats counted, and A is the start bearing for 7 beats.

Alternatively, the time (T) in seconds can be taken with a stopwatch between beat 7 and the null. Then:

$$\text{Bearing} = A + 4T$$

The overall bearing accuracy is estimated as ± 2° (root mean square error) or better.

It is emphasised that the stations are experimental, and transmissions may be altered or discontinued without warning.

4.2.13 QTG service from Coast Radio Stations

Certain Coast Radio Stations will, on request, transmit signals from which a yacht can obtain a DF bearing. The procedure to request this service, for which a charge is made, is as follows:

The yacht contacts the Coast Station, identifies herself, and sends 'QTG ...... (times) ...... (kHz)', meaning 'will you send two dashes of ten seconds each, followed by your call sign, repeated ...... times, on ...... kHz'.

The Coast Station replies 'QTG ...... (times) ...... kHz', followed by the signals requested.

Details of Coast Radio Stations, for the area covered, are given in Chapter 6 of *The Macmillan & Silk Cut Nautical Almanac*. The frequency used for a QTG request may be a special one reserved for the purpose, or any of the station's working frequencies. A request should specify 410kHz (if listed for that station) or a working frequency close to that on which the boat's DF is calibrated.

Stations providing QTG service are shown on Admiralty charts by the abbreviation R (or the obsolescent R°.) against a small circle indicating the position of the transmitter.

4.3 Radio direction finding

4.3.1 Principle of operation

Radio direction finding stations (which are few in number) are shown on charts by the letters RG, or by the obsolescent description of R.°DF. They are equipped with apparatus enabling them to ascertain the direction of signals transmitted from a vessel. A charge is usually made for the service.

The procedure is that the vessel calls the station concerned, and is requested to transmit a series of long dashes followed by her call sign. These are processed by the station (or sometimes stations) and the result, either as bearing or if more than one station is involved as a fix, is transmitted to the vessel.

4.3.2 Radio direction finding stations

In Western Europe the only radio direction finding stations are situated in the Federal Republic of Germany (Norddeich, Elbe-Weser and St Peter-Ording). There are also stations in Scandinavia. Details are given in the *Admiralty List of Radio Signals*, Vol. 2. There are no stations in the British Isles, other than the VHF DF stations which are described in 4.3.4.

4.3.3 Half Convergency

A radio wave moves along a great cirle, which is represented on a Mercator's chart by a curved line (except in the event of it being exactly north/south, when it coincides with a meridian). So the bearing of a distant radio station from a vessel is the angle between the circle through the station and the vessel, and the meridian through the vessel.

Meridians as depicted on a Mercator's chart are parallel straight lines, but in reality on the surface of the globe they converge towards the poles. The difference in the angles formed by the intersection of a great circle with two meridians is called convergency, and it depends on the differences of latitude and longitude between the two points of intersection. An approximate formula for convergency is:

Conv. (in mins) = diff Long (mins) × sin mid Lat

If the difference in longitude between the vessel and the radio station is more than about 3°, the true bearing of the radio signal should be converted into a mercatorial bearing by adding or subtracting half the convergency, before it is plotted on the chart (see also 3.3.16).

It must be remembered that in north latitudes the straight line bearing as plotted on a Mercator's chart is always to the south of the great circle bearing. It may help to draw a simple sketch as in Fig. 4(3) in order to determine whether half convergency should be added or subtracted, but in north latitudes the following rules apply:

For bearings of a radio station taken from a boat –

If the boat is:	Half convergency must be:
east of the station	subtracted
west of the station	added

For bearings of a boat provided by a direction finding station –

If the boat is:	Half convergency must be:
east of the station	added
west of the station	subtracted

Fig. 4(3) The diagram shows how half convergency is applied in N hemisphere to D/F bearings from a beacon or transmitter, i.e. + if the yacht is to the west, and − if to the east.

The converse applies in southern latitudes.

A table for half convergency is provided in *The Macmillan & Silk Cut Nautical Almanac*. It is entered with difference in longitude between the station and the boat (along the top), and mid-latitude between the station and the boat (down the side). The tabulated figures are half convergency, in degrees, and for practical purposes they can be used for distances up to 1000 n miles.

4.3.4 VHF emergency direction finding service

Direction finding can be applied to VHF radio transmissions in much the same way as to MF transmissions. A VHF direction finding set can in fact be fitted in a yacht, but the equipment is expensive and a rather bulky aerial unit consisting of four dipoles needs to be located at or near the masthead (a position for which other radio equipment makes conflicting demands). It is therefore more feasible to locate VHF DF sets ashore, and several stations have now been set up by HM Coastguard.

These VHF DF stations are intended *for emergency use only*, and should not be considered as a normal navigation aid. However in practice the term 'emergency' seems to be interpreted quite liberally. Except for those in Guernsey and Jersey the stations are controlled by a Coastguard MRCC or MRSC (see 8.4.2).

On a request, by VHF radiotelephone, from a yacht in distress or difficulty, the station transmits the bearing of the yacht *from the DF site*, which is marked by the symbol RG on Admiralty charts.

Watch is kept on Ch 16. A yacht should transmit on Ch 16 (for distress calls only) or on Ch 67 (Ch 82 for Jersey) for the station to obtain the bearing. The yacht's bearing *from the station* is transmitted on Ch 16 (distress calls only) or on Ch 67 (Ch 82 for Jersey). The stations providing this service are listed in *The Macmillan & Silk Cut Nautical Almanac*.

4.4 Consol

4.4.1 Principle of operation

Consol is a long-range navigational aid, primarily for aircraft, but can be useful for ocean navigation. The only equipment required to use it is a radio receiver, together with either a special Consol chart of the area or Consol tables in order to convert the signal received into a position line. The system is obsolescent.

A Consol station consists of an MF radio transmitter with a special directional aerial system. Three aerials in a line are evenly spaced at a distance of about three times the wavelength of the transmitter. Maximum accuracy of the signal is obtained on the perpendicular bisector of the base line of the aerials, and falls off as the extension of the base line is approached. Effective coverage is therefore limited to two sectors of about 120°.

The radiated pattern consists of alternate sectors, about 15° wide, of alternate dot and dash signals. This pattern rotates so that the equi-signal between the dots and dashes moves through a sector's width during the keying cycle of 30 seconds. Thus the equi-signal is heard once in each keying cycle, and the angular position in that sector is determined from the number of dots or dashes heard before the equi-signal.

Between the keying cycles the station transmits a continuous note, for accurate tuning of the receiver, and its call sign. The signals can be received by any normal set, preferably with a Beat Frequency Oscillator (BFO). A signal strength meter is sometimes useful when the dots/dashes merge into the equi-signal.

In good conditions bearings can be obtained at ranges up to 1000 miles by day, and slight more at night, but Consol should not be relied upon for coastal navigation or when making a landfall.

4.4.2 Consol – operating procedures

In order to use Consol it is necessary either to have the appropriate overprinted Consol chart (see the *Admiralty Chart Catalogue*, NP 131), or the bearing tables given in *Admiralty List of Radio Signals*, Vol. 5.

The receiver is tuned to the required station and a series of dots and dashes is heard lasting 30 seconds, followed by the station's call sign. During the 30-second period a total of 60 characters are transmitted, although not quite this number may be heard because it is not possible to identify them all individually when the dots change to dashes (or the dashes to dots) at the equi-signal. Consequently the actual count of dots and dashes is taken, and the total subtracted from 60 to establish the number lost in the equi-signal. Half the missing number are taken as dots, and half as dashes.

Examples:

(1)	Count taken	– 14 dots, 42 dashes
	Total count -	– 56
	Missing	– 4 (60 – 56)
	True count	– 16 dots, 44 dashes
(2)	Count taken	– equi-signal, 56 dots
	Total count	– 56
	Missing	– 4 (60 – 56)
	True count	– 2 dashes, 58 dots

The signal is named dot or dash, depending on which is heard before the equi-signal. Hence in the two examples above the first has a count of 16 dots, and the second has a count of 2 dashes. Repeat the count several times before referring to the table or the Consol chart.

There will be ambiguity unless the bearing of the Consol station is known to within ± 10°. The DR position can be checked from a DF bearing of the continuous signal of the Consol station. If, as is likely, the station is quite far away, it is necessary to apply half convergency, as described in 4.3.3.

For good results a receiver with narrow band characteristics is needed; it should not have an automatic gain control, which may obscure or even displace the equi-signal. A vertical or open aerial is recommended. If a DF aerial is used it should be rotated to the position of maximum reception while counting the Consol signal. If it is necessary to move the aerial away from this position, perhaps to suppress interference from some other station, it should not be rotated more than 45° from the maximum position, or an error may be introduced in the count, particularly at ranges of less than 300 n miles at night. The Consol system is not usable within 25 miles of the station.

Consol charts are over-printed with a coloured lattice, either dot or dash and the number of the count. Consol tables give the true bearing of the boat from the station, and also incorporate supplementary tables for half convergency.

Details of the Consol stations in operation are given in *The Macmillan & Silk Cut Nautical Almanac*. Currently (1985) there is only one in Western Europe – at Stavanger in Norway.

4.5 Position fixing systems

4.5.1 Decca

The Decca Navigator System is a very accurate, short to medium range position fixing system for coastal waters and for landfall navigation. It was introduced towards the end of World War II, but since then it has undergone considerable extension and refinement. Very good coverage is provided of coastal waters (to a range of about 350 n miles by day, and 250 n miles by night) in the whole of North West Europe, as shown in Fig. 4(4), and in certain other parts of the world such as South Africa, the Persian Gulf, India, Pakistan, Japan and Eastern Canada.

The Decca Navigator is extensively used by commercial shipping of all types, and the system is financed and operated by Decca. It is extremely accurate for coastal work and can give positions within 100 yards, or even less in good conditions and close to Decca stations. The latter consist of master and slave transmitters which send out continuous signals, picked up on board ship by a special receiver (Decca Navigator) which displays readings from the three stations on red, green and purple dials. These readings are transferred to red, green and purple hyperbolic lattices, overprinted on an Admiralty chart, giving a fix.

Until 1982 it was not possible to buy a set

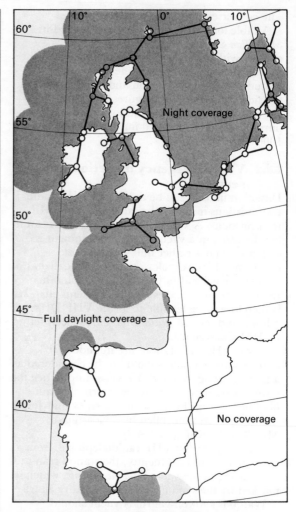

Fig. 4(4) Decca chain coverage – NW Europe.

which would give access to the system. The Decca Navigator has to be hired, part of the rental paying for the maintenance of the Decca stations. But in 1982 Racal-Decca introduced the Decca Yacht Navigator, in response to a receiver called the AP Navigator which Phillips had launched in Europe and which made use of Decca transmissions. This has resulted in continuing legal battles.

However, in 1983 certain agreements were reached between Racal-Decca and Phillips, and subsequently the Decca Yacht Navigator was withdrawn and was replaced on the British market by the AP Navigator, styled as the Decca Yacht Navigator II. This set is available only to the owners of pleasure craft, and in effect is subject to a long-term lease because the cost of about £1500 covers the use of the set under a special licence, while the set itself remains the property of Racal-Decca.

Unlike the commercial Decca Navigator, the original Decca Yacht Navigator (now withdrawn) and the AP Navigator (now the Decca Yacht Navigator II) give a direct read-out of latitude and longitude, which is more convenient but not quite so accurate as plotting the raw Decca data on a Decca chart. However, the original Decca Yacht Navigator does have the capability of using the Decca co-ordinates and a lattice chart when there is a receiver alarm signal or periodically as a cross check on the latitude/longitude read-outs, a decided advantage. Even so, the Decca Yacht Navigator II probably provides the best choice of position fixing equipment for yachtsmen in and around North-west Europe. Accuracy is very good, but depends on range from the transmitters and on their relative positions, signal path (whether over land or water, for example), time of day, and season of the year. The set gives a continuous update of computed position, without the need for any dead reckoning inputs. Nine waypoints are provided.

4.5.2 Loran-C
Loran-C is a low frequency position fixing system, which uses pulsed transmissions at 100kHz, and is controlled by the US Coast Guard. During World War II the United States pioneered a LOng RAnge radio Navigation system, now designated Loran-A. By the end of the war, 70 transmitting stations were sending Loran-A pulses to receivers on board 75,000 ships and aircraft, both military and commercial. This system was subsequently expanded, but is now being replaced by Loran-C, which is more accurate and less costly to operate.

Up to about 1000 n miles the signals are received as ground wave, along the shortest path from transmitter to receiver. The Loran-C pulses are also propagated as sky waves, the incidence of which varies between day and night and from place to place. The sky wave gives greater range, but much less accuracy.

Now (1984) there are 14 Loran-C chains in operation, covering an area of about 16 million square miles, including the entire seaboard of the United States and much of the northern hemisphere. Unfortunately, while there is ground wave coverage around Norway and in northern parts of the British Isles, there is only sky wave coverage for southern coasts of England or for the adjacent coasts of Europe. There is, however, a Mediterranean chain (an area not covered by Decca), as shown in Fig. 4(5).

Loran-C works by measuring the difference in the time of arrival of pulse signals from a master transmitting station and two or more slave stations. These measurements are made initially by matching the pulse envelopes (coarse difference) and then by matching the phase of the 100kHz carrier (fine difference). These differences are very accurately measured and recorded, and are then transferred to a special Loran chart overprinted with hyperbolic curves for the stations concerned. Selecting the correct hyperbola, or interpolating as required, gives a position line. The procedure is repeated with a

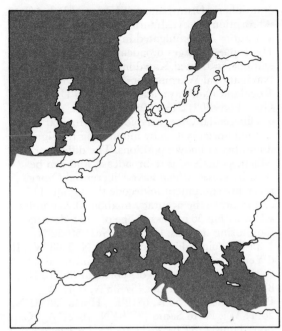

Fig. 4(5) Loran-C groundwave coverage in Europe. The other sea areas shown have skywave coverage which is much less accurate.

different slave station to get a fix. Some Loran-C sets are able to interpret the time differences which have been calculated in order to provide a direct display of latitude and longitude, and such sets can be entered with waypoints to provide course to steer, distance, ETA, etc. The data is presented continuously.

The accuracy of the system, for ground wave signals, varies from about 100 yards at a range of 200 miles to about 250 yards at 500 n miles, although better results can often be achieved. Errors are significantly reduced in the repeatable mode.

4.5.3 Omega
The Omega system is still being developed and is not yet fully operational (1983), but it already gives almost world-wide coverage. It is a long range aid, operating on Very Low Frequency (10–14kHz) radio waves from eight stations in Norway, Liberia, Hawaii, North Dakota, La Réunion, Argentina, Australia and Japan.

The extensive global coverage makes the system very attractive, although the accuracy is not so good as either Decca or Loran-C, about 1–2 n miles by day and 2–4 n miles by night.

Omega stations transmit on four frequencies, but the cheaper receivers only operate on 10.2kHz and these must be set with the correct lane number at a known position, and must subsequently track continuously.

Before they are plotted on a lattice chart, Omega readings must be corrected for such phase variations as are predictable, which are given in Propagation Prediction Correction Tables. Other, unpredictable, variations are Sudden

Ionospheric Disturbances (SIDs) and Polar Cap Absorption (PCA). Information on these variations is promulgated in Hydrolant and Hydropac messages broadcast by United States stations, in United Kingdom Long-range Radio Navigational Warnings, in broadcasts from Rogaland (Norway), and by dialling US Coast Guard on (202) 245–0298.

Differential Omega avoids the principal errors in the Omega system by monitoring the signal at a number of known positions. The difference which is obtained is re-broadcast, and can be used by vessels which have Differential Omega receiving equipment to decode the signal. This can improve the accuracy to about 0.25 n miles when within 50 n miles of one of the following monitoring stations: Cap Gris Nez (50°52′N, 1°35′E); Pointe de Créach (48°28′N, 5°08′W); Ile d'Yeu (46°43′N, 2°23′W); Cabo Finisterre (42°53′N, 9°16′W); Lagos, Portugal (37°10′N, 8°37′W); Cabo de Palos (37°38′N, 0°41′W); Porquerolles (42°59′N, 6°12′E); Horta (38°31′N, 28°41′W); Porto Santo (33°04′N, 16°21′W); Cap Bon, Tunisia (37°04′N, 11°03′E); La Isleta (28°10′N, 15°25′W); Port Bouët, Ivory Coast (5°15′N, 3°58′W); Tête de Galantry (46°46′N, 56°09′W).

4.5.4 Satellite navigation

The interest of yachtsmen in satellite navigation was stimulated by the appearance at the 1980 London Boat Show of the Walker Sat-Nav 801, selling for about £1500 – considerably below the price of any satellite receiver previously available.

There is nothing very new about satellite navigation, which has been available since 1967 from the US Navy's Navigation Satellite System (NNSS). The system comprises five operational Navsat, or Transit, satellites which circle the earth in polar orbits at a height of about 600 miles (1000km), as shown in Fig. 4(6). The rotation of the earth brings a user beneath each orbit in turn, and while a satellite is above the horizon a receiver can compute its own position from data transmitted to it from the satellite. Each satellite circles the earth once every 100 minutes, and the time between suitable passes varies with latitude, averaging about 1½ hours in the British Isles. The fact that the instrument does not give a continuous update of position (like Decca, for example) is undoubtedly a serious drawback to satnav. Between satellite passes the more expensive receivers can automatically present the DR position, computed from inputs from the vessel's log and compass, but with the average yacht's receiver, speed and course have to be fed in manually – alright on an ocean passage perhaps, but inconvenient (and often inaccurate) in coastal waters. However, on the credit side, satnav can be used worldwide, regardless of weather conditions; it is simple to use, requires no special charts or tables, and is very accurate – normally within ¼ mile at sea and

Fig. 4(6) The orbits of NNSS Transit satellites, forming a cage inside which the earth rotates. There are five operational satellites (as shown) and other non-operational or spare satellites (not shown). Due to launching errors the satellites are not evenly spaced around the world. Further (Nova) satellites of a new design are being launched.

considerably better when the yacht is stationary.

While a satellite is in orbit its transmissions are monitored by ground stations which track it very precisely, and thereby predict its exact orbit in the immediate future. These details are transmitted to the satellite and are stored in its memory. Every two minutes, precisely, the satellite transmits details of its orbit and other data on two carrier frequencies of 150MHz and 400MHz. The receiver's calculation of the fix is based on the Doppler effect on the frequency, as the slant distance between the satellite and receiver decreases and increases due to their relative movement. The whole process takes about 15 minutes. Two frequencies are used in order to refine the calculations, and yacht receivers which work on only one channel are not quite so accurate.

Other errors are caused by the lack of a consistent horizontal datum all over the world, and by inaccurate surveys in certain areas. It is also very important that the correct course and speed of the vessel is fed into the receiver, and it is best to keep these constant during a satellite pass. It is also necessary that the receiver has been switched on for the requisite time before the satellite pass, so that it is generating a stable reference frequency, against which it can measure the Doppler shift.

The yachtsman now has a wide choice of satellite receivers, with sets available from Racal-Decca, Brookes & Gatehouse, Mars Marine Systems, Sperry, Demek, Raytheon, Magnavox, Navidyne and Furuno, in addition to Walker. An important improvement for sailing yachts has been a reduction in current consumption of sets when standing by, and keeping DR up to date between satellite passes. Most sets have the capacity for several waypoints, which can be used as described in 4.1.2, as well as self-test facilities, and the ability to recall recent fixes.

Navstar

The next major development in satellite navigation will come with the introduction of the Navstar Global Positioning System (GPS) being developed by the US Department of Defense, and due to come into operation in the late 1980s. This will consist of 18 satellites deployed in 12-hour circular orbits at a height of about 12,400 miles (20,000km), and inclined at 55° to the equator. The pattern will be such that four satellites will always be visible at elevations greater than about 9.5°, and five satellites will almost always be above the horizon. In conjunction with control and monitor stations, these satellites will give a position on demand at any time, anywhere in the world, and to a high degree of accuracy.

However, whereas the accuracy available for military purposes in what is called the Precise Positioning Service (PPS) is likely to be about 60ft (18m), the accuracy for civil or commercial use (e.g. for yachtsmen) will be degraded to about 330ft (100m) for the Standard Positioning Service (SPS). For harbour, surveying and fishing navigation differential GPS techniques will improve accuracy to about 33ft (10m) near the reference station, down to about 50ft (15m) when the user is 150 n miles away.

User charges, as originally proposed, are no longer likely. Navstar will require different receivers to the present, first generation of satellite receivers used in yachts, but should be even more useful.

4.6 Radar

4.6.1 Radar in yachts

Radar is being increasingly used by yachtsmen, both as an aid to navigation and for collision avoidance. But in order to make proper use of its considerable advantages, and to enjoy its benefits in safety, it is essential to understand a little about how it functions, and to know how it should be operated. It is important to read the instruction book carefully, so that the various controls are well understood, and to practice using and adjusting the set to give optimum performance in different conditions. Finally, it is necessary to learn how to interpret what is actually seen on the display.

4.6.2 How radar works

Radar (short for RAdio Direction And Range) uses radio waves at super high frequency, concentrated in a series of powerful but very short pulses, each pulse lasting less than a microsecond (a millionth of a second). The number of pulses transmitted per second (the pulse repetition frequency, or pulse repetition rate) is usually between 800 and 3000. The wavelength is very short, 3cm (X-band) in yacht radars, but 10cm (S-band) in larger commercial sets. The pulses, generated by a device called a magnetron, are transmitted in a narrow beam by a rotating aerial, which also receives any echo reflected back from a target within range. The aerial rotates at a steady speed, usually about 30rpm, and the whole assembly is called the scanner. In yachts, aerials are normally of the slotted waveguide type, the pulses and returning echoes passing through accurately machined slots.

Radio waves travel extremely quickly (162,000 n miles per second, or about 1000ft a microsecond), so it only takes a very short time for a pulse to reach a target and be partially reflected back – 62 microseconds for example for an object 5 miles away, or only 1 microsecond for an object 500ft away. This is why each pulse must be very short, so that it is cut off before any echo returns – increasingly important as the range of the target is reduced. Most radar sets automatically reduce the pulse length when shorter ranges are selected on the range scale.

The range of an object is determined by the time interval between the outgoing pulse and the returning echo, and this has to be measured very accurately. This is done by a stream of electrons in a cathode ray tube (CRT), the larger end of which is the Plan Position Indicator (PPI) of the boat's radar display, normally sited in the wheelhouse. The centre of the PPI represents 'own ship', and a rotating trace on the display is synchronised with the rotation of the aerial. The electrons energise a chemical coating on the inside of the CRT, to give spots of light which persist for a short time after the flow of electrons has ceased. A returning echo received by the scanner is amplified by the receiver and passed to the CRT, so that the flow of electrons is intensified, and a bright spot or echo shows on the PPI. The distance of this spot from the centre of the PPI (own ship) represents the range of the target. Each outgoing pulse from the scanner is transmitted on a slightly different bearing, and, since the rotation of the scanner and the trace on the display are synchronised, the direction of the target is indicated on a scale graduated round the circumference of the PPI.

A radar beam is typically 2°–3° in width horizontally, and about 25° wide in the vertical plane to allow for the vessel's movement at sea. Echoes are returned from an object so long as it is within the beam: the echo of a ship, for example, therefore appears rather wider than it actually is, and it may be impossible to distinguish (say) a gap in a harbour wall. Put in more technical language – a radar set does not discriminate so well in bearing as it does in range. Also some of the transmitted beam escapes into 'side lobes', which can give spurious echoes.

The effective range of radar is only approximately line of sight, and most yacht radars have a maximum range of 16–24 n miles, although greater ranges are possible with more powerful sets. Under conditions of abnormal propagation radar range may be greatly increased (by super-refraction) or it may be reduced (by sub-refraction). Freak conditions called ducting may on occasions allow targets hundreds of miles away to be detected, or conversely prevent the identification of objects at short range.

It is important to remember that radar will not detect a low-lying coastline which is over the radar horizon, but may show up a range of hills several miles inland, as in Fig. 4(7). In this connection it is useful to calculate the distance of the radar horizon in nautical miles from the formula: distance $= 1.22\sqrt{h}$ where h is the height of the scanner in feet, or $2.2\sqrt{h}$ where the height is in metres.

From the above it is evident that the scanner should be mounted as high as possible, although topweight is an obvious consideration since the average unit for a yacht weighs about 55lb (25kg), though some are less. With a ketch rig the scanner can be conveniently mounted on the mizzen mast, but it should not be sited at or about the level of the spreaders on the mainmast. In some cases it is essential to use a radome to prevent the rotating aerial fouling sails or rigging. The scanner must not be sited where people are liable to be in the direct line of harmful emissions of radiation.

The display units needs to be in a sheltered position, at a safe distance from the steering compass (usually about 30in or 0.76m), and mounted so that it can be viewed from the chart table and/or steering position. Most yacht radars will accept 12/24/36 volts DC, or AC power supplies with a suitable rectifier. Consumptions vary from about 50 watts to over 300 watts for the more powerful sets.

Controls are mounted alongside the PPI, and typically consist of the following, although details vary from make to make:

(1) On/off switch, also controlling the brilliance of the display. Before switching the set on it is necessary to make certain settings to the controls for the warming-up period (usually a minute or two) or damage may occur to the CRT. Then adjust the brilliance so that the rotating trace is faintly visible.

(2) The gain control adjusts the amplification in the receiver, and the brightness of the echoes. Too much gain results in unwanted interference, with speckles over the screen. Too little gain results in weaker echoes not appearing.

(3) The range selector controls the scale, so that the full radius of the display can be made to represent (say) 0.5, 1.5, 3.0, 6.0, 12.0 or 24.0 n miles. With the 6-mile range scale selected, an object at the circumference of the display is 6 miles distant. If the 12-miles scale is then selected, the same object will reappear at half the radius from the centre (own ship). Range rings, which can be varied in brightness, are projected onto the display to help assess the ranges of echoes. A more sophisticated arrangement is a variable range marker (VRM), whereby the operator can measure a range, which is then displayed on a digital read-out.

(4) The bearing cursor is a transparent engraved screen over the face of the PPI, which can be rotated so that the bearing of an echo is read at the circumference. Equally spaced parallel lines each side of the main, diametric line form what is called the parallel index, which can be used for navigational problems and for collision avoidance. Some sets have an Electronic Bearing Marker (EBM) – an electronic cursor which can be placed over an echo to obtain a digital read-out of bearing. At this point is must be noted that yacht radars invariably have a relative motion or 'ship's head up' display. Own ship is at the centre, and any object at the top of the display (at 12 o'clock) is dead ahead. So all bearings, whether from a bearing cursor or EBM, are relative (to ship's head). Thus an echo at 3 o'clock on the display must be on the starboard beam; if own ship alters course 90° to starboard, that echo will then reappear at 12 o'clock, or dead ahead.

(5) Sea clutter control is used to reduce unwanted reflections from the sea around the yacht, in order that echoes from objects such as buoys and small craft are not obscured. This is achieved by reducing the gain out to a certain distance from the yacht. If too much sea clutter is applied, no echoes will be received at short range.

(6) Rain clutter control can reduce the echoes from precipitation, which would otherwise obscure the display, or parts of it, but may not be effective for heavy rain. It can be useful in good weather to help improve definition at short ranges, particularly when looking for small objects like buoys.

(7) Heading marker control is used to line up the heading marker (a line representing ship's

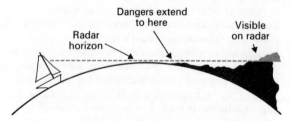

Fig. 4(7) High land, perhaps some distance from the coast, may be the first thing detected on radar when approaching from seaward. Lower ground may be hidden from view, over the radar horizon.

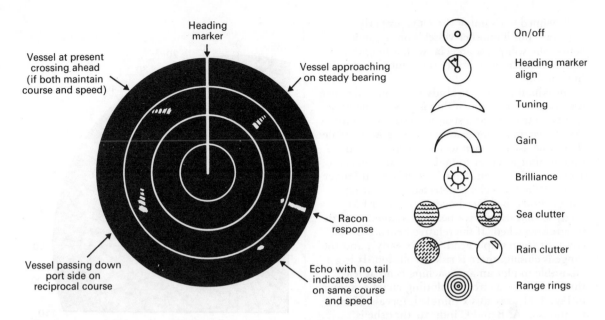

Heading marker

Vessel at present crossing ahead (if both maintain course and speed)

Vessel approaching on steady bearing

Racon response

Vessel passing down port side on reciprocal course

Echo with no tail indicates vessel on same course and speed

On/off

Heading marker align

Tuning

Gain

Brilliance

Sea clutter

Rain clutter

Range rings

Fig. 4(8) The 'tails' shown by echoes on the radar display can help to indicate movement, relative to own ship.

Fig. 4(9) Symbols for controls of radar set.

head) when the set is first switched on, so that it points straight upwards, at 12 o'clock. Some sets have means of suppressing the heading marker, so that it does not conceal an echo directly ahead.

It should be realised that some objects provide better radar targets than others. Radar beams are reflected in much the same way as rays of light on a mirror, and curved or sloping surfaces (such as low shorelines, chimneys or lighthouses) do not give such a good response as abrupt faces (like steep cliffs, breakwaters or buildings). Objects which are conspicuous by radar are marked on Admiralty charts. A ship beam-on will give a better echo than one with an aspect of 45°. Yachts, boats or buoys without radar reflectors do not show up at all well, but most major navigational buoys are now fitted with reflectors.

Due to the angular width of the radar beam, a target near the edge of the PPI will appear wider than an identical target at short range, as shown in Fig. 4(10). Experience will show that, apart from large targets which are nearby, there is little relation between the size of an echo on the screen and the actual size of the target it represents.

Overhead power cables reflect a radar echo at right angles to them, which may be identified as a ship on a collision course, on a constant bearing.

The most positive and identifiable response comes from one of the many radar beacons, or Racons, which are described in 4.6.5.

4.6.3 Radar for collision avoidance
At the outset it must be remembered that radar range is more accurate than bearings obtained from the PPI, and that the latter are relative to

ship's head. Although true motion displays (where static objects remain stationary on the display, and vessels move relative to them) are found in commercial ships, yacht radars invariably have a relative or ship's head up display, with the boat at the centre, apparently stationary. The shore, buoys and ships at anchor move past as the boat follows her course, which is always towards the top of the display no matter in what direction she is actually heading. If the boat alters course, then all the echoes on the display rotate accordingly.

If the target is moving in the same direction at the same speed, and is therefore stationary relative to own ship, its echo should be sharp and

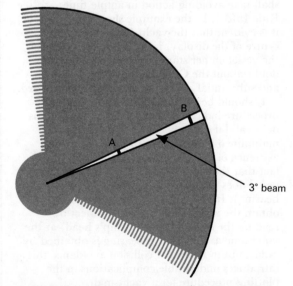

B

A

3° beam

Fig. 4(10) Targets A and B are in fact the same size, but on the radar display B appears to be twice the size of A, because it is further away and due to the spread of the radar beam.

well defined – assuming the set is properly adjusted. But if another vessel is on an opposite course she will paint an echo with a long tail, which indicates which way she is moving relative to own ship.

Initially it is easier to study collision avoidance if it is assumed that own ship is proceeding on a steady course and at a steady speed. For collision avoidance, in fog for example, a long range scale should be used in open water, but reduced from time to time in order to make sure that no echo appears which might have been missed at longer range. When an echo is detected the bearing cursor should be placed over it (or the EBM used) so that its relative bearing is noted, and its progress watched. If the relative bearing is constant (own ship's head being steady), and the range is closing, there is risk of collision. It is advisable to plot an approaching echo at least three times, on a circular plotting chart as shown in Fig. 4(11), say at six minute intervals. Her positions at A, B and C indicate that she is holding a steady course and speed, and when projected to D give the closest point of approach (CPA).

The actual course and speed of the other vessel can then be determined from the plot. If the vector AE represents the distance which own ship moves while the echo moves from A to B, then EB gives the course and speed of the target. This course is relative to own ship.

Only at this stage can a proper appreciation be made of the problem, and a decision made as to which vessel is required to keep clear under the Collision Regulations. In restricted visibility these require that 'a vessel which detects by radar alone the presence of another vessel shall determine if a close-quarters situation is developing and/or risk of collision exists. If so, she shall take avoiding action in ample time ...' (see Rule 19(d)). In the example shown in Fig. 4(11) it is evident that the yacht (own ship, in the centre of the display) is bound to keep clear of the vessel on her starboard bow, and if in any doubt about the CPA she should make an early and substantial alteration of course to starboard.

It should be emphasised that the plotting procedure indicated above and in Fig. 4(11) is only valid if a steady course and speed is maintained by own ship. In particular, the existence of risk of collision is established by the fact that the *actual* bearing of an approaching vessel does not alter significantly (not the *relative* bearing). It is of course perfectly feasible to obtain the actual bearing of any object by reading the compass course (ship's head) at the same time as the relative bearing is obtained by radar, but in respect of collision avoidance this introduces undesirable complications in the plotting procedure for a yachtsman.

In restricted waters there is usually not enough time for the procedure described in Fig. 4(11), and often not room for vessels to make significant

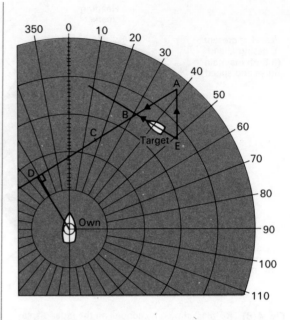

Fig. 4(11) To make proper use of a radar set for collision avoidance it is necessary to plot echoes as shown here, in order to determine their closest point of approach and their actual course and speed. Only then is it possible to make a correct decision about what should be done under the Collision Regulations.

alterations of course while following a channel. Under these circumstances the proper use of radar for collision avoidance is limited, and the set becomes more an additional and very valuable look-out. In poor visibility yachts should in any case keep out of shipping channels, or skirt along the very edge of them.

4.6.4 Radar as a navigation aid

Properly used, radar can be a useful aid to navigation, but it is necessary to be aware of its limitations. It cannot see behind other objects, or round corners, or over the horizon; also it may not pick up small targets or differentiate between two targets which are close together.

The chart should be carefully studied when making a landfall by radar, to decide what objects may appear first. High cliffs make a good target, but approaching a low coastline the first thing to show on the radar display may be hills some distance inland. Ordinary buildings give good echoes, but smoothly contoured structures do not.

Due to the width of the radar beam, objects like ships or islands appear on the display as wider than they really are. For the same reason harbour entrances may not always be evident from seaward, although they should appear as the range is reduced.

Because radar ranges are more accurate than radar bearings, it is often preferable to obtain a radar range and visual bearing of an object in order to get a fix: be sure that the same object is observed on both occasions. Often a very good fix can be obtained from radar ranges of three different objects, suitably distributed.

Proper use of the range scales helps maintain a certain distance from any danger. As an example, if it is desired to pass 3 miles from a headland select the most appropriate range scale, and make sure that the 3 mile range ring does not reach the point concerned.

The bearing cursor can be used to determine the course to steer relative to an object such as a buoy, in order to offset the effect of tidal stream. Set the bearing cursor over the buoy and watch its progress. If its tail is along the bearing cursor, and the cursor continues to cover it as the range is closed, then the relative bearing is steady and the boat will arrive at the buoy. If the buoy drifts either side of the bearing cursor, course can be corrected accordingly.

When navigating by radar in poor visibility, do not forget to watch for echoes other than buoys etc, which may be approaching (or overtaking) ships.

4.6.5 Radar beacons (Racons)

A Racon is a transponder beacon, triggered by the emissions of a vessel's radar set, and sending out a distinctive signal which appears on the display of the set. They are fitted to a number of light-vessels, buoys and lighthouses, and are marked on the chart.

In most cases the Racon flash on the display is a line extending radially outwards from a point slightly beyond the actual position of the Racon, as shown in Fig. 4(8), due to the slight delay in the response of the beacon apparatus. Thus the distance to the mark of the Racon flash is a little more than the vessel's real distance from the Racon. Some Racons give a flash composed of a Morse identification signal, often with a tail to it, the length of the tail depending on the number of the Morse characters.

The maximum range of a radar beacon is usually about 10 nautical miles, but may be more. In practice, picking up a Racon at greater distances depends also on the effective range of the boat's radar. With abnormal radio propagation, a spurious Racon flash may be seen at much greater distances than the beacon's normal range, appearing at any random position along the correct bearing on the display. Only rely on a Racon flash if its appearance is consistent, and the boat is believed to be within its range. At short range a Racon sometimes causes unwelcome interference on the radar display, and this may be reduced by adjusting the rain clutter control on the set.

The characteristics of radar beacons around the coasts of Great Britain, and the adjacent coasts of Europe, are given each year in chapter 4 of *The Macmillan & Silk Cut Nautical Almanac*. Details shown include:

(1) Reference number.
(2) The type of radar beacon. Unless otherwise stated, all radar beacons sweep the frequency range of marine 3cm (X-band) radar emissions. A few, where indicated, respond to 10cm (S-band) emissions. The term F Racon indicates a fixed frequency Racon, transmitting on a frequency outside the marine radar band, so that by tuning to that frequency the Racon flash is selected to the exclusion of normal echoes. Some in-band Racons are called frequency agile. Their response is within the band width of a yacht's radar, and they may cease to respond for a short period to allow echoes otherwise obscured by the Racon signal to be seen.
(3) Name of the station.
(4) Latitude and longitude.
(5) The time, in seconds, for a slow-sweep radar beacon to sweep the frequency range of the marine radar band.
(6) The sector within which signals may be received, bearings being towards the beacon, clockwise from 000° to 359°. 360° indicates all round operation.
(7) Approximate range, in nautical miles. This also depends on the effective range of the yacht's radar set.
(8) The form of the beacon's flash on the radar display. Morse signals are shown alphabetically, and are often followed by a 'tail'. Racons coded 'D' are used to mark new dangers.

Chapter 5

Astro-navigation

Contents

5.1 Introduction to astro-navigation

5.1.1 General

Astronomical navigation, astro-navigation (or just astro, as it is widely called), remains the most basic method of fixing a vessel's position offshore out of sight of land. To some extent modern electronic fixing aids, including satellite navigation, have lessened its usefulness but it remains a system that is universally available, self contained and free; further, it is controlled by a non-political body! It continues to fascinate most navigators, perhaps largely because of its independence of outside influence.

The astro-navigator's tools are the sextant, with which to measure the altitude of a heavenly body above the horizon, the chronometer which gives the precise time of the observation, the ephemeris which gives the body's co-ordinates at that time and some form of reduction process (typically tables or a calculator) with which he works up the sight. A programmed calculator will yield latitude and longitude of the position so fixed, but with tables position will normally be established by plotting.

In this chapter the sextant is first of all described, with its errors and adjustments. To simplify the explanation of subsequent notes a summary of the principles of nautical astronomy is then given and, for those who want to go more deeply into the matter, a glossary giving definitions of the principal terms used in astro-navigation. The sextant altitude corrections are then described and illustrated.

The standard tabular method of reduction recommended is the *Sight Reduction Tables for Air Navigation*, published in the United Kingdom as AP 3270 and in the United States as Pub No 249. The tables, in three volumes, are of the direct-entry kind and cater for all bodies to a precision sufficient for all practical purposes at sea. They contain full explanations of use.

A dedicated calculator or computer undoubtedly offers the most convenient form of sight reduction because the navigator is, so to speak, always in the right book and always at the right page; with the latest types of calculator neither almanac nor reduction tables are necessary. However, computers can go wrong or get broken or be lost overboard, and it is only prudent to provide for such an eventuality. The tables reproduced in section 5.10 are intended primarily as a back-up of this kind, although they can, of course, be used as the primary method provided their limitations are understood. The principal limitation of the standard method applies to sights within 10–15° of the prime vertical circle. The standard method should not therefore be used, for example, to work up an early morning Sun sight taken more or less as a stand-by should it cloud over later. Apart from this the limitation is navigationally not a serious one, at any rate so far as the Sun is concerned, because for successive observations of the same body (Sun-run-Sun) the requirement is for the minimum run combined with the maximum change of bearing. This is best achieved by observations taken on either side of the meridian.

Methods of plotting are then discussed with ways of analysing the plot to establish the most

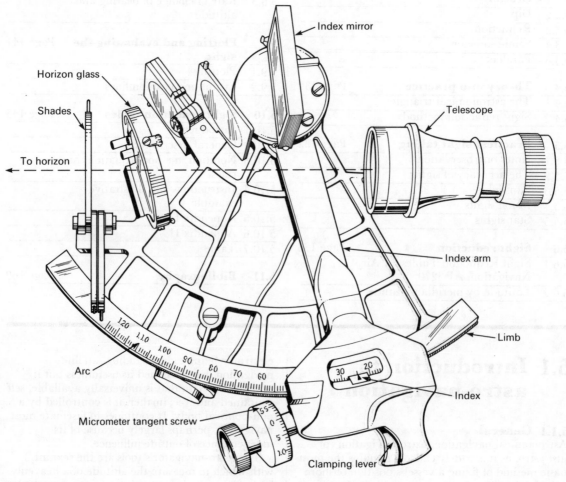

Fig. 5(1) The sextant.

Index mirror

Horizon glass

Shades

To horizon

Telescope

Index arm

Limb

Index

Arc

Micrometer tangent screw

Clamping lever

probable position. Finally there are some general notes on sight-taking, the height of altitudes, angle of intersection etc.

Whether star recognition for sights is by using the star tables of AP 3270 or by planisphere, or even by star globe, most navigators like to achieve a familiarity with the sky at night that will enable them, and indeed other members of the crew, to pick out the principal constellations, the main navigational stars and the planets. The star chart shown in Fig. 5(9) and the accompanying text are intended specifically for that purpose.

5.1.2 The sextant

The marine sextant is shown in a simplified form in Fig. 5(1). The telescope and horizon glass are fixed with respect to the frame although minor adjustments can be made by means of adjusting screws. The index mirror is similarly fixed with respect to the index arm. The latter rotates about the centre of curvature of the arc, and at its lower end carries an index against which the graduated arc is read. The index mirror and horizon glass should be parallel when the index reads zero.

The arc of the sextant subtends an angle of 60° but, because of the principle of double reflection, the scale is graduated to 120°. Older sextants carry a vernier scale on the index arm opposite the arc to facilitate reading fractional parts of the smallest graduations on the scale. Most modern instruments have micrometer tangent screws, or drums, which serve the same purpose and are far easier to read.

5.1.3 Sextant errors and adjustments

Sextants are subject to certain errors. Instrument error cannot be corrected by the navigator and, where it exists, is usually tabulated by the manufacturer and applied as corrections to different altitudes. The three principal sources of instrument error are centring error from a faulty location of the pivot of the index arm, graduation error on the scale, and prismatic error where the two sides of the mirrors or shades are not parallel. Instrument error in a good sextant is normally small enough to be ignored.

The errors adjustable by the navigator are perpendicularity, side error, index error and collimation error. Because of their interdependence they should normally be corrected in the order given.

Perpendicularity error

Perpendicularity error arises when the index mirror is not perpendicular to the frame. It is checked by holding the sextant horizontally and sighting the arc simultaneously through the mirror and directly. If the reflected and direct views of the arc do not appear as a single unbroken line there is perpendicularity error. The error is removed by means of a screw at the back of the mirror.

Side error

Side error is strictly speaking another form of perpendicularity error, arising from the fact that the horizon glass is not perpendicular to the frame. It may be checked by setting the index to zero and sighting the horizon which should appear as a continuous straight line in both the direct and double reflected views. If either moves up or down with respect to the other when the sextant is rotated about the line of sight, side error exists. It is corrected by means of a screw near the base of the glass. An alternative way of checking side error is to use a low-flying (low altitude) star. With the index set to zero two images of the star side by side show side error.

Index error

Index error occurs when the index mirror and horizon glass are not parallel when the index is at zero. It may be determined in the same manner as side error, observing the horizon with the sextant vertical. The horizon glass and index mirror will be parallel when the index reads zero and the direct and reflected image of the horizon appear as a continuous straight line. Several readings should be taken, the sextant being offset in different directions each time. An alternative way of determining index error is by observing the Sun *on* and *off* the arc, the limbs of the two Suns visible just touching in either case. The index error will be half the sum of the two readings, and a useful check on the accuracy of the observations is that the sum should be four times the semi-diameter of the Sun as given in the nautical almanac. Perhaps the best way of all is to use a low flying star and one that is not too bright, which will allow of greater accuracy and be less tiring than using the Sun.

Index error may be corrected by means of the screw or screws at the base of the horizon glass. Since it will directly affect the angles measured, index error should be checked each time the sextant is used. However, adjusting the sextant each time index error is found would tend to wear the thread of the adjusting screws and it is customary to allow errors up to 2′ or 3′ of arc as a correction to the observations. If the index correction is *on* the arc of the sextant the reading will be too high by that amount and must be subtracted to get the observed altitude, and of course added if it is *off* the arc. An easy way to remember the sign of the correction is the phrase 'If its on it's off, and if it's off it's on'.

Collimation error

Collimation error is caused by the telescope not being parallel to the frame and will result in greater angles being measured than the correct values. To determine the error the sextant is placed horizontally on a flat surface and a mark made on the wall or bulkhead opposite in line with the line of sight along the upper surface of the frame. Another mark is made above it corresponding to the distance between the frame and the telescope, and the two will be parallel when the second mark is in the centre of the field of view of the telescope. Where there is provision for correction, adjustment is by a pair of screws on the collar of the telescope.

Regular checks

In the normal course of events the only errors which need to be checked with any regularity are index error and side error; unless it exceeds about 2′ the former is generally included as a correction to the altitude, while the latter will so far as possible be eliminated by adjustment.

5.1.4 Sextant handling

The sextant is a delicate instrument that requires careful handling and treatment. It should only be lifted by the frame or the handle, never by the arc, and should always be replaced in its box after use. The glasses and mirrors should be wiped dry with a clean bit of soft chamois leather or linen to prevent moisture damaging the silvering. Wiping the glasses should be done with great care to avoid altering their adjustment. A bag of silica gel in the sextant box will help stave off moisture. A little light oil applied from time to time to the worm gear at the back of the arc is the only lubrication necessary.

Many modern sextants are made of aluminium alloys which confer a considerable advantage in terms of weight. Plastic sextants are both light and cheap but require careful treatment to prevent the possibility of warping or distortion. The question of telescopes is to some extent a matter for the individual but there is much to be said for having a single telescope suitable for all bodies in preference to a range of telescopes for different purposes (star, inverting etc).

5.2 Principles of nautical astronomy

5.2.1 Introduction

In order to grasp the basic principles of astro-navigation certain concepts and relationships must be understood. It is assumed throughout this chapter that the Earth is spherical; and in practice the navigator will not need to introduce corrections for its oblateness since these are taken into account in the charts, tables etc.

For the purposes of navigation the distances of the heavenly bodies are irrelevant. It is therefore permissible to envisage all of them as lying on the inner surface of a sphere concentric with the Earth which we call the celestial sphere. This is a purely notional device to facilitate the interpretation of position and apparent movement of the heavenly bodies in relation to the Earth's surface.

The plane of any great circle on a sphere will pass through the centre of the sphere dividing it into two equal parts (hemispheres).

The celestial horizon (sometimes called the rational horizon) is the great circle whose plane is horizontal to the observer which cuts the celestial sphere midway between the zenith and nadir.

The true altitude of a heavenly body is the angle at the centre of the Earth between that body and the celestial horizon.

The nautical mile is the average length of a great circle of the Earth which subtends an angle of one minute of arc at its centre. Since the radius of the Earth is known, so is the length on its surface of 1 minute of arc. Minor differences have arisen through accepting different values for the size (and shape) of the Earth and the International Nautical Mile has now been standardized as 1852m (6076ft); this fact, as such, has no navigational significance.

The counterparts of terrestrial latitude and longitude on the celestial sphere are declination, measured north or south, and hour angle, conventionally measured west from a chosen meridian (not east and west as is longitude). GHA, however, increases with the rotation of the Earth whereas longitude clearly does not, see Fig. 5(3).

The geographical position (GP) or sub-point of a heavenly body is where an imaginary line from the centre of the Earth to the body would cut the Earth's surface. To an observer at that point the body would be at the zenith, right overhead. The latitude of that position would be the body's declination, north or south and the longitude its Greenwich hour angle expressed in angular measure west of the Greenwich meridian.

5.2.2 Angular measure and geographical distance

Fig. 5(2) shows how the measurement of a body's altitude gives the observer's distance from the body's geographical position in nautical miles. The observer at O on the Earth's surface measures, after correction, the altitude of the body X above the celestial horizon H′CH. This measurement in arc subtracted from 90° gives the angle XCZ between the body (X) and the zenith

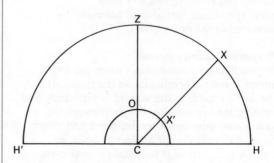

Fig. 5(2) Arc and distance on the Earth's surface.

(Z). The arc XZ on the celestial sphere is clearly the same as the arc X'O on the Earth's surface and, since the radius of the Earth is known, this angular measure in degrees and minutes gives the linear distance in nautical miles. This relationship is the basis of all nautical astronomy.

5.2.3 Time and hour angle

If the heavenly bodies were all stationary on the celestial sphere the element of time would not feature in astro-navigation. However, the rotation of the Earth on its polar axis gives the stars, which because of their immense distances we regard as fixed, an apparent motion from east to west across the celestial sphere of one complete cycle approximately every 23 hours, 56 minutes, 4 seconds, the length of a sidereal (or star) day.

The Earth, of course, not only rotates on its axis but also revolves about the Sun completing one revolution every year. This makes the solar day slightly longer than the sidereal day, by about one part in 365.

The movement of the apparent Sun in its orbit is not, for various reasons, entirely regular and for timekeeping the concept of a mean Sun whose passage over successive meridians takes exactly 24 hours has been introduced. The difference between mean time and apparent time is the equation of time given on the daily pages of *The Nautical Almanac*.

Both time and longitude are measured conventionally from the Greenwich or prime meridian and since the Earth rotates 360° relative to the Sun in 24 hours, 15° of longitude is equivalent to 1 hour of time. For every 15° of longitude west of Greenwich the local mean time will be 1 hour earlier than Greenwich Mean Time. (To preserve the Greenwich date an international date line runs, with certain detours round islands, along the meridian 180° E and W). The entries on the daily pages of the ephemeris are tabulated for Greenwich Mean Time but the navigator will in general be more directly concerned with local time.

For various reasons the longitude of a heavenly body is specified by its hour angle, that is the angle along a parallel of declination west of a celestial meridian. When the Greenwich or prime meridian is the celestial meridian chosen, the angle will be the Greenwich hour angle (GHA); if it is the observer's meridian it will be the local hour angle (LHA). The ephemeris tabulates GHA of the Sun, Moon and planets. This is converted to LHA by subtracting westerly or adding easterly longitude.

$$\text{LHA} = \text{GHA} \quad \begin{array}{l} + \text{ observer's longitude east} \\ \text{or} \\ - \text{ observer's longitude west} \end{array}$$

(where necessary adding or subtracting 360°) Fig. 5 (3) illustrates these relationships.

Because the stars may be regarded as fixed, whereas the bodies of the solar system move

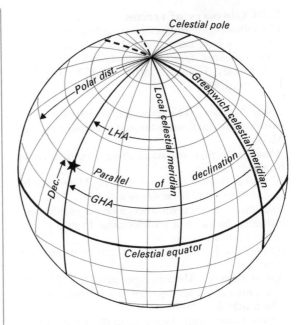

Fig. 5(3) Celestial coordinates relative to the Earth.

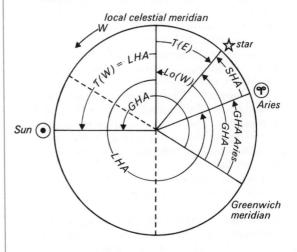

Fig. 5(4) Time diagram (viewed from above the South Pole) showing the relationship between time (T) and hour angle.

rapidly on the celestial sphere, the GHA of each navigational star is not usually tabulated in the ephemeris. Instead the GHA of the First Point of Aries, a fixed point in the sky, is given and for each (navigational) star sidereal hour angle (SHA) is tabulated. GHA Aries added to SHA gives the GHA of the star. The time diagram in Fig. 5(4) shows the connection between GHA, LHA and SHA.

The ephemeris in Chapter 5 of *The Macmillan & Silk Cut Nautical Almanac* each year provides the essential astronomical data required for navigational purposes.

5.2.4 Glossary of terms

The following definitions relating to nautical astronomy have been adapted, with permission, from *Navigation Afloat: A Manual for the Seaman* by A.B. Moody (Hollis & Carter and U.S. Naval Institute, 1980).

Age of the Moon   The elapsed time, usually expressed in days, since the last previous new Moon.

Altitude   Angular distance, along a vertical circle, from the horizon.

Altitude difference   (1) Intercept. (2) Difference in consecutive tabular entries of altitude.

Amplitude   Angular distance, along a parallel of altitude, clockwise or anticlockwise from the prime vertical.

Apogee   An Earth satellite's orbital point farthest from the Earth.

Apparent motion   Motion, especially of astronomical bodies, relative to a reference point which may itself be in motion.

Apparent time   Time based upon the rotation of the Earth relative to the apparent, or true, Sun.

Astronomical triangle   The navigational triangle solved in sight reduction.

Astronomical twilight   The period of incomplete darkness following sunset or preceding sunrise when the centre of the Sun is not more than 18° below the celestial horizon.

Atmospheric pressure correction   The value applied to a sextant altitude to correct for non-standard atmospheric pressure.

Autumnal equinox   That equinox at which the Sun crosses the celestial equator from north to south.

Augmentation   The increase in apparent semi-diameter of an astronomical body with increased altitude, because of reduced distance of the body from the observer.

Azimuth   Angular distance, along a parallel of altitude, eastward from the principal vertical circle.

Azimuth angle   Angular distance, along a parallel of altitude, clockwise or anticlockwise from the direction of the elevated pole, or occasionally from either this or the reciprocal direction, whichever is nearer.

Back sight   An observation of an astronomical body made facing *away* from the body.

Calculated altitude   Altitude of an astronomical body as determined by calculation or equivalent means.

Celestial equator   The intersection of the plane of the Earth's equator and the celestial sphere.

Celestial horizon   The celestial-sphere great circle midway between the zenith and nadir.

Celestial meridian   A great circle through the celestial poles and the zenith.

Celestial pole   Either of the two points of intersection of the celestial sphere and the extension of the Earth's rotational axis.

Celestial sphere   An imaginary sphere of great radius concentric with the Earth, and on which all astronomical bodies other than the Earth are imagined to be projected.

Civil twilight   The period of incomplete darkness following sunset or preceding sunrise when the centre of the Sun is no more than 6° below the celestial horizon.

Computed altitude   Calculated altitude.

Co-ordinated universal time (UTC)   A time approximating to UT_2 used for uniformity of time signals.

Corrected sextant altitude   Observed altitude.

Declination   Angular distance north or south of the celestial equator.

Dip   The vertical angle between the horizontal and the line of sight to the visible horizon.

Diurnal circle   The apparent daily path of an astronomical body.

Ecliptic   The apparent annual path of the Sun round the celestial sphere.

Elevated pole   The celestial pole above the horizon.

Equation of time   The difference between mean time and apparent time.

Equinoctial   Celestial equator.

Ex-meridian observation   An observation of the altitude of an astronomical body near the celestial meridian, for conversion to a meridian altitude.

First point of Aries   Vernal equinox.

Geographical pole   Either intersection of the surface of the Earth and the Earth's axis of rotation.

Geographical position   (1) Sub-point. (2) A position defined by geographical co-ordinates, usually latitude and longitude.

Geometrical horizon   The intersection of the celestial sphere and an infinite number of straight lines from the eye of the observer tangent to the surface of the Earth.

Great circle   The intersection of the surface of a sphere with a plane through its centre.

Greenwich apparent time   Apparent time on the Greenwich meridian.

Greenwich hour angle (GHA)   Angular distance, along a parallel of declination, west of the Greenwich celestial meridian.

Greenwich mean time (GMT)   Mean time on the Greenwich meridian.

Greenwich sidereal time   Sidereal time at the Greenwich meridian.

Horizon   That great circle of the celestial sphere midway between the zenith and nadir, or a line approximating this circle.

Horizontal parallax   Geocentric parallax of an astronomical body on the horizon.

Hour angle   Angular distance, along a parallel of

declination, west of a reference celestial meridian or hour circle.

Hour circle A semi-great circle of the celestial sphere connecting the celestial poles and another fixed point on the surface of the sphere.

International nautical mile The linear unit internationally accepted as the nautical mile; 1852m or 6076ft.

Local apparent noon The instant of upper transit of the apparent Sun.

Local apparent time Apparent time at a specified meridian.

Local hour angle (LHA) Angular distance, along a parallel of declination, west of a specified celestial meridian.

Local mean time (LMT) Mean time at a specified meridian.

Local sidereal time Sidereal time at a specified meridian.

Lower transit The passage of an astronomical body across the lower branch of a celestial meridian.

Lunar distance The angle between the Moon and another astronomical body.

Lunar month One revolution of the Moon around the Earth.

Mean Sun A fictitious Sun conceived as moving eastward along the celestial equator at the average rate of the apparent Sun along the ecliptic.

Mean time Time based upon rotation of the Earth relative to the mean Sun.

Meridian altitude Altitude of an astronomical body on the celestial meridian.

Meridian transit The passage of an astronomical body across a celestial meridian.

Nadir That point of the celestial sphere vertically below the observer.

Nautical mile (n mile) Generally, the length of 1′ of arc of a great circle of the Earth. Specifically, the international nautical mile of 1852m or 6076ft.

Nautical twilight The period of incomplete darkness following sunset or preceding sunrise when the centre of the Sun is not more than 12° below the celestial horizon.

Navigational triangle The spherical triangle solved in sight reduction or great-circle sailing.

Nutation Irregularities in precession of the equinoxes.

Observed altitude Actual altitude of an astronomical body above the celestial horizon.

Parallactic angle The navigational triangle angle at the astronomical body or destination.

Parallax Difference in apparent position of an object as viewed from different positions.

Parallax in altitude Geocentric parallax of an astronomical body at any specified altitude.

Parallel of altitude A circle of the celestial sphere parallel to the plane of the celestial horizon.

Parallel of declination A circle of the celestial sphere parallel to the plane of the celestial equator.

Parallel of latitude Parallel.

Polar circle The parallel (N or S) equal to the maximum co-declination of the Sun.

Polar distance Angular distance from a celestial pole.

Polar motion Wobbling motion of the geographical poles of the Earth, affecting measurement of universal time.

Precession of the equinoxes Conical motion of the Earth's rotational axis about the vertical to the plane of the ecliptic, caused by the attractive force of other bodies of the solar system on the equatorial bulge of the Earth, and resulting in a slow drift of the equinoxes and solstices.

Prime meridian The meridian from which longitude is reckoned.

Prime vertical circle The vertical circle through the east or west point of the horizon.

Principal vertical circle The vertical circle through the true north point of the horizon.

Proper motion The component of motion of an astronomical body perpendicular to the line of sight.

Refraction Change in direction of a ray of radiant energy as it passes obliquely into a medium of different density.

Retired (transferred) position line A position line moved back to allow for motion of the observer between the earlier time to which the line is retired and the time of observation.

Right ascension Angular distance, along a parallel of declination, east of the hour circle of the vernal equinox.

Sea-air temperature difference correction The correction applied to a sextant altitude to correct for error in tabulated dip because of difference in the temperature of the water and air at their interface.

Sensible horizon A small circle of the celestial sphere marking the intersection of a plane parallel to the plane of the celestial horizon, through the eye of the observer.

Sextant altitude Altitude of an astronomical body as measured by a sextant.

Sidereal Of or pertaining to stars.

Sidereal hour angle Angular distance, along a parallel of declination, west of the hour circle of the vernal equinox.

Sidereal time Time based upon rotation of the Earth relative to the vernal equinox.

Summer solstice The solstice occupied by the Sun about June 21.

Time sight Observation of an astronomical body for determination of longitude by calculation of

meridian angle and its comparison with Greenwich hour angle; and, by extension, the data.
True altitude   Observed altitude.

Upper branch   That half of a celestial meridian through the zenith.
Upper transit   The passage of an astronomical body across the upper branch of a celestial meridian.

Vernal equinox   That equinox at which the Sun crosses the celestial equator from south to north.
Vertical circle   A semi-great circle joining the zenith and nadir.

Zenith   That point of the celestial sphere vertically overhead.
Zenith distance   Angular distance from the zenith.
Zone description   The number, with its sign, applied to zone time to convert it to the corresponding GMT.
Zone time   Mean time at a standard reference meridian whose time is kept throughout a designated area.

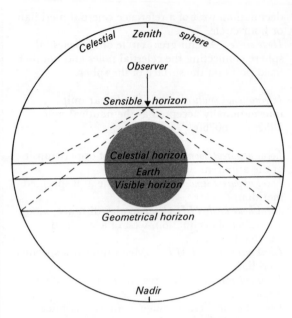

Fig. 5(5) Horizon systems used in astro-navigation.

5.3 **Altitude corrections**

5.3.1 **General**
The altitude read off the sextant is corrected first of all for any known instrument error including index error and, where appropriate, for personal error (where the observer has been able to establish the amount he habitually over- or under-reads the sextant). The resultant altitude, the sextant altitude (Hs for Height sextant) is then corrected for altitude corrections to give the true altitude or in modern parlance (which came in with the adoption of direct entry tables) observed altitude (Ho for Height observed). The altitude corrections are applied to the sextant altitude as appropriate for dip, refraction, semi-diameter and parallax. Only semi-diameter and parallax vary with the body concerned. In most methods of sight reduction the true or observed altitude so obtained is compared with the calculated altitude (Hc for Height computed) given in the tables to give an intercept. In using the correction tables the sextant altitude is first corrected for index error and dip to give an apparent altitude with which the table of correction for refraction and semi-diameter is entered. The altitude corrections will be considered in turn. The various horizon systems are illustrated in Fig. 5(5).

5.3.2 **Dip**
Dip of the sea horizon arises from the fact that the observer's eye level will be above the surface of the sea which causes the horizon to dip (be depressed) below the horizontal plane at the observer's eye. The correction, which is always subtractive, increases numerically with height. Anomalous conditions, such as a large difference between sea and air temperature, can introduce errors into the calculated dip values. Taking sights on opposite horizons or equally spaced round the horizon are one way of overcoming this difficulty. The dip correction includes an allowance for the fact that light from the horizon will be affected by terrestrial refraction.

5.3.3 **Refraction**
Astronomical refraction is the angular difference between the true and apparent direction of a heavenly body. The light travelling from a heavenly body into the Earth's atmosphere is progressively bent towards the vertical by the variation of the density of the medium which causes the body to appear higher in the sky than it would otherwise be, Fig. 5(6). The density of

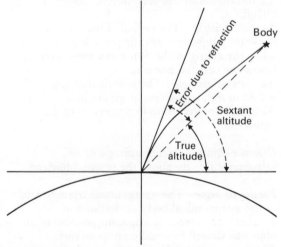

Fig. 5(6) Refraction and measured altitude.

the air is affected by temperature and atmospheric pressure and the mean refraction corrections given in the almanac are for temperature 10°C and pressure 1010mb. Refraction decreases with altitude, from about 34′ at the horizon to zero at the zenith. The correction is always subtractive. Anomalous conditions such as will affect the dip also affect astronomical refraction; however since refraction decreases rapidly with altitude, the effect will be minimised by avoiding low altitude sights, say below 10°. An additional table for non-standard atmospheric conditions is provided in some almanacs and may be used with low altitude sights.

5.3.4 Semi-diameter
Semi-diameter corrections apply only to the Sun and Moon, and arise from the fact that the coordinates for astronomical bodies given in the almanac relate to the centre of each body whereas in the case of the Sun and Moon one or other limb will have been observed. Stars and

Fig. 5(7) Parallax, only significant for the Moon, will be zero when it is at the zenith (M$_Z$) and maximum at Horizontal Parallax (M$_H$).

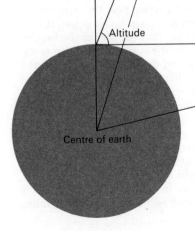

planets appear in the sextant telescope as points of light, although Venus at its nearest approach has in fact a semi-diameter of over 0′.5. Semi-diameter will vary with the body's altitude and its distance from the Earth but only in the case of the Moon, with its nearness to Earth, is this augmentation navigationally significant.

5.3.5 **Parallax**
Parallax is the angle between the direction of a body seen from somewhere on the Earth's surface and the place it would occupy if seen from the centre of the Earth. Parallax is zero at the zenith and increases as the altitude decreases to a maximum on the observer's sensible horizon, Fig. 5(7). This value is known as the horizontal parallax (HP). Corrections for parallax are taken into account in the altitude correction tables for the Sun, Moon, Venus and Mars; only in the case of the Moon, because of its proximity to the Earth, is horizontal parallax used as an entering argument in the tables. For stars any correction would be negligible and is ignored.

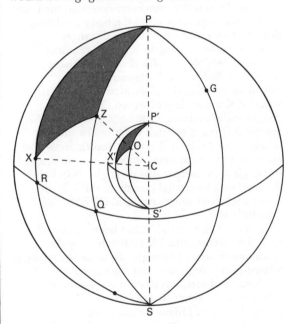

Fig. 5(8) The astronomical triangle.

5.4 Theory into practice

5.4.1 The astronomical triangle

Since, as we have seen (5.2.2), zenith distance measured in arc can be equated with distance on the Earth's surface in nautical miles, it follows that an observation of a heavenly body whose geographical position (5.2.1) can be established will locate the observer on a circle of position whose centre is the geographical position and radius the zenith distance. In Fig. 5(8) the outer hemisphere represents the celestial sphere, the inner one the Earth. The altitude subtracted from 90° gives the zenith distance ZX and the arc OX′ expressed in nautical miles is the distance on the Earth's surface.

For the instant of observation the navigator extracts from the ephemeris the body's coordinates (declination and hour angle) which will enable him in principle to plot its geographical position and describe a circle of position somewhere along which the observer must lie. In practice, however, except in the case of very high altitudes when the body is within a degree or two of the zenith, the distances involved make plotting to the scale required totally impossible. It is for this reason that resource is had to the navigational or astronomical triangle, illustrated in Fig. 5(8), where ZX is the body observed, X′ its geographical position, O the observer and Z his zenith; RQ is the celestial equator. In the triangle, the angle at Z is the azimuth angle, the angle at P the local hour angle of X from Z and the angle at X the parallactic angle. PGS being the Greenwich celestial meridian, GPX is the Greenwich hour angle of X and GPZ the longitude of Z.

In the triangle, 90°–XZ has been measured with the sextant, and PX established by the chronometer and ephemeris. To solve the triangle a third part is required, and the various mathematical methods of sight reduction make different approaches to this end.
In the Marcq St Hilaire or intercept method which, in a wide variety of forms, is virtually universal today, an approximate position (generally either the DR position or a position near it suitable to the reduction method in use) is assumed for Z which gives two sides and the included angle; the zenith distance of the position chosen is then calculated and compared with the zenith distance observed. The difference is the *intercept* which is applied from the chosen position towards or away from the body according to whether the position is nearer or further away from it. Unless the radius of the position circle is very small, as it will be with very high altitudes, the portion of it in the vicinity of the observer can be treated without sensible error as a straight line at right angles to the body's bearing.

5.4.2 Sight reduction methods

There are a large number of tabular solutions for the intercept method, each with its advantages and drawbacks. Compact tables, for example, may not be universally applicable, or involve special rules, or too much arithmetic, or not attain the required accuracy and so on. Tables otherwise impeccable may be too bulky for most requirements, or involve too many steps.

For most purposes there is little doubt that the modern direct entry or inspection tables provide the most convenient form of tabular sight reduction. In general for a range of values of assumed latitude, declination and hour angle they provide the (computed) altitude and azimuth angle. Auxiliary tables facilitate interpolation. Those proposed as the standard method of sight reduction are the *Sight Reduction Tables for Air Navigation* produced jointly in the United Kingdom (as AP 3270) and the United States (as Pub No 249). The tables have at any rate marginal advantages over *Sight Reduction Tables for Marine Navigation*, also produced jointly in the United Kingdom (as NP 401) and the United States (as Pub No 229), which are similar in principle but tabulate altitude to 0′.1 instead of 1′ and azimuth angle to 0°.1 instead of 1°. The air tables, which are to a precision which is sufficient for all practical purposes at sea, are in three volumes instead of six, and provide a particularly handy solution for stars.

In section 5.10, however, is given a brief and simple method of sight reduction, which may be used if other tables are not available.

The use of electronic calculators for sight reduction is described in 5.7.5.

5.5 Practical sight taking

5.5.1 Notes on observation

In a small boat there is generally little option about the height from which sights will be taken. For the purpose of altitude corrections, the observer's height of eye will be the height of the deck above the sea surface plus the observer's height. However, all things being equal, it is worth remembering that the higher the height of eye the less rapidly the correction for dip of the horizon changes and thus the more reliable the observation. Further, in anything like a seaway the horizon is often hidden from view by the wave tops. On the other hand in thick weather it is often possible to obtain satisfactory observations by getting close to the sea surface where the horizon shrinks to within the range of visibility. Thus at 2ft above the surface, which might be obtained by taking sights from a companionway, or in calm weather from a dinghy, the horizon will only be about 1¼ miles.

The best situation for taking sights is somehow to be wedged from the waist down with both hands free without the fear of falling overboard. An observation is made by bringing the heavenly body down to the point on the horizon immediately below it. In the case of the Sun the lower limb will generally be used and with the Moon whichever limb is fully visible. The point of tangency is defined by swinging the sextant through an arc of about 20° on either side of the line of sight.

Considerable practice is required in the technique of using the sextant from such an unsteady platform as a small boat. To begin with, the advice of an experienced observer can be helpful. There are a number of ways of bringing the body down to the horizon, including initially holding the sextant upside down to allow the horizon to be brought up to the body. With the Sun, and occasionally Moon, quite a good dodge is to half close the eye and be guided by the ambient light as to when the body is in the field of view. Clearly one should be careful not to be blinded.

The random error of the mean of a number of observations, we are told, is reduced as the square root of the number. Averaging a series of observations will not necessarily reduce the error by this amount because the errors will not all be random. However, because of the difficulties of taking sights in small vessels, with rapid accelerations and a low height of eye, it is customary to take a series of observations and mean the times and altitudes. If the sights are more or less evenly timed, a series of three or five (or even seven) observations allows the middle one to be treated as a yardstick as to how good the series is; the time and altitude should be close to the mean.

It is a great convenience to have another member of the crew as a timekeeper who will record the time of each sight and the altitude the navigator gives him. The time should be recorded to the nearest second, which represents 0.25 minute of arc. It is of course perfectly possible to take accurate times on one's own (as indeed single-handers have to) but it is inconvenient to the extent that sights will not normally be taken in the place where they are most easily recorded. The skill in taking one's own time, which can be acquired with practice, is in counting down accurately in seconds from the time of the observation to the moment the time is read.

Nowadays quartz crystal clocks or wrist watches have almost universally replaced clockwork chronometers or deck watches. Their accuracy is extremely high, they are reliable, and can be water resistant and virtually shockproof. The most convenient sort for navigation has a dual display, one analogue which can be kept on ship's time, the other digital kept on GMT for sights. With a digital display there is little chance of a gross reading error.

5.5.2 **The accuracy of sights**

Many navigators tend to exaggerate the accuracy of sights at sea, perhaps because of some confusion between the accuracy attainable, which is quite high, and the accuracy which on average one might be led to expect. The first thing therefore is to reach an understanding of what is meant by accuracy.

Obviously, by a combination of circumstances any sextant observation can be accurate to within the limits to which the altitude and time can be read, and the resultant position line will then pass near enough through the observer's position. In investigating accuracies the point to establish therefore is on how many occasions is this, or any other predicted result, likely to happen. This confidence level is usually expressed in terms of a percentage. The level with which practising navigators are normally most concerned is the 95 per cent level which defines the number of occasions out of every 100 on which the error is unlikely to exceed the stated value. To say, for example, that the 95 per cent level accuracy of sextant observations at sea is 4 miles is to say that out of every 100 observations only five may be expected to have an error exceeding 4 miles.

The next point is to establish whether the accuracy in question is what may be attained or is that which may be expected in the course of every day seafaring. Unless it is for some special purpose, such as survey, practising navigators will be more interested in the latter.

In 1957 the Royal Institute of Navigation, with the cooperation of the Royal Navy and the Royal Netherlands Navy and of a number of British shipping companies, conducted an investigation into the accuracy of astronomical observations at sea which gave the following results (from an analysis, by HM Nautical Almanac Office, of some 4000 observations).

Percentage error	Average observer	Best observer	Error exceeded in
50	0′.7	0′.5	10 out of 20
90	2 .4	1 .4	2 out of 20
95	3 .1	2 .0	1 out of 20

The errors in question are of course position-line errors not errors in position.

Although the observers in this investigation were for the most part professional seamen observing from a comparatively steady platform and an elevated height of eye, there is no reason to think that results from experienced yachtsmen would differ substantially.

Besides being a useful guide for the navigator these results shed light on the precision requirement for almanacs and tables. Almanacs and tables for marine navigation are normally tabulated to a precision of 0′.1 of altitude and 0°.1 of azimuth, mainly because the next convenient unit is 1′ or 1°. It can be shown however that where there is an inescapable error, in this case that of observation, little is gained by reducing other sources of error beyond a certain point. It is for that reason that the standard method of sight reduction proposed in this Handbook is the combined British and American *Sight Reduction Tables for Air Navigation* (respectively AP 3270 and Pub No 249) tabulated to 1′ of altitude and 1° of azimuth, a precision sufficient for all practical purposes at sea.

5.5.3 Sun sights

The Sun is the body most frequently observed at sea, generally in successive observations with an allowance for the run between sights.

Except when it is hidden by cloud the lower limb of the Sun will normally be observed. When the upper limb is brought to the horizon the altitude correction for semi-diameter will, clearly, be subtractive. Very occasionally the outline of the Sun is so blurred that it will be easier to estimate when the centre of the disk is on the horizon than to use either limb. In this case the altitude correction may be obtained from the combined altitude correction table by taking the mean of the corrections for the upper and lower limbs.

A firm horizon considerably facilitates accurate observation although it can occur in conditions conducive to abnormal dip. There are generally tell-tale signs of abnormal atmospheric conditions such as the distortion of the outlines of ships on the horizon.

5.5.4 Moon sights

Whether the upper or lower limb of the Moon is observed will depend on which is the more complete. The altitude correction tables for the Moon with argument horizontal parallax give separate corrections for either limb. In general Moon sights will only be taken in daylight when the resulting position line can often usefully be crossed with a position line from the Sun to give a fix. The Moon takes rather longer than other bodies to cross the same meridian and to that extent is marginally easier to observe.

5.5.5 Star sights

Star sights are normally taken in the morning and evening when the Sun is about 8° or 10° below the horizon in the interval between civil and nautical twilights. The limits last about 24 minutes on the equator, longer as latitude increases. In this period of incomplete darkness the brighter stars will be visible in the sextant telescope while the horizon will be firm enough for sight taking. In general stars to the eastward will appear first in the evening and disappear first in the morning. The brightest star should normally be taken first in the evening and last in the morning.

It is usual to plan star sights beforehand by working out the time of twilight for the dead reckoning position, from data given in the nautical almanac, and then by means of a star globe or planisphere or the Selected Star Tables of AP 3270 to calculate the altitudes and azimuths for the approximate time. The stars may then be observed by setting the approximate altitude on the sextant rather than attempting the more difficult task of bringing them down to the horizon.

Although single observations should be the exception rather than the rule, the time for taking stars is limited by the light, and it will generally be better to take single observations of a larger number of stars well distributed in azimuth than to take several shots of a smaller number.

It is sometimes possible to take star sights by moonlight but the results should be accepted with some caution because the horizon can be deceptive. Venus is occasionally visible in daylight through the sextant telescope and can be crossed with a position line from the Sun or Moon. Because of the difficulty of picking it up it is usual to observe Venus at its meridian altitude. Jupiter too is often visible long after sunrise or before sunset.

Because several stars can generally be observed more or less simultaneously, star sights tend to yield the most accurate astro-fix at sea. In principle two well observed stars at a reasonable angle of cut suffice for a fix, but a third will enable any errors in the observation or reduction in either sight to be detected and thus add reliability. Four stars or more, provided the plot is intelligently analysed (see 5.9.2), give the best chance of an accurate and reliable fix.

Star identification

The stars are identified by their constellation, a catalogue designation (within the constellation) and in some cases a name. Their apparent brightness is measured in terms of magnitude: the lower the magnitude, the brighter the star. The constellations, of which there are nearly 90, are groups of stars which appeared to different cultures to resemble mythical figures or objects; for the most part their names are Arabic, Greek or Latin. The designation of a star attaches to the Latin name of its constellation a lower-case Greek letter in descending order of brightness; thus α Leonis would be the brightest star in the constellation Leo, β Leonis the second brightest, and so on. The principal navigational stars have names, so that navigators seldom need bother with constellation and catalogue designations.

There are some 20 stars of the first magnitude, and in good conditions stars down to the sixth or even seventh magnitude are visible to the naked eye. In the normal course of events the navigator will not require to use more than about 20 of the 57 'selected' navigational stars, although there are occasions when it is convenient to be able to identify and observe some of the lesser used bodies.

Fig. 5(9) Star chart – northern stars.

Of the planets Venus, Jupiter, and sometimes Mars, are of negative magnitude. The navigational planets Venus, Mars, Jupiter and Saturn are easy enough to pick out in the sky since they are relatively bright and shine with a steady light, as opposed to the twinkling light of a star. All planets stay fairly close to the ecliptic. Mercury is sometimes confused with the navigational planets when it is near its maximum elongation (angle from the Sun).

Fig. 5(9) is a star chart of the northern sky, and shows in terms of declination and hour angle, the relative positions of the stars as seen from Earth. The projection obviously distorts the places of the stars near the equator, and the equatorial stars can be displayed separately. The

lines joining certain stars show the shapes of the constellations devised by the ancients, and the key gives the meaning of the ways of depicting stars on the chart.

For the beginner, in the northern hemisphere, the simplest way to locate stars is first of all to establish the pole of the heavens, marked approximately by Polaris, the Pole Star, around which the firmament appears to rotate. This is most easily done by identifying *Ursa Major*, the Great Bear or Plough, and following the line of the two Pointers at the 'front' end of the Plough, from the lower one Mirak through the brighter Dubhe (one of the selected navigational stars) which leads very close to Polaris. Polaris is itself part of *Ursa Minor*, a constellation very similar to

135

Ursa Major, which rotates anticlockwise round the Pole with Polaris as its (approximate) pivot. Following round the extension of the handle of the Plough leads to the first-magnitude Arcturus, a reddish star and, continuing the arc, to another first magnitude star, the bluish-white Spica.

On a summer evening, to an observer in the northern hemisphere the Plough will lie west of Polaris with the Pointers nearly horizontal. The brightest star in the northern hemisphere, Vega, a brilliant blue-white, will be visible to the east with Altair, an equatorial star, just about midway between the two Guardians which point towards it. The 'summer triangle' of Altair, Vega and Deneb is conspicuous. Antares, a noticeably red, first-magnitude star, will be found in the constellation of *Scorpius* at about this time, fairly low in the southern sky. In the sky, though not on the star chart, the resemblance to a scorpion is obvious.

In the autumn, the Plough will be low in the northern sky in the evenings, and Cassiopeia's Chair will be picked out on the other side of the Pole at about the same distance. On winter nights the Plough will lie to the right of Polaris, and Cassiopeia to its left. At this season Orion's Belt, with Betelgeuse, a bright yellowish-red star, to the north-east, and Bellatrix, a fainter, white star to the south-west, can be seen to the south. Rigel, a bright bluish star, lies south-west of the Belt. Continuing the line of the Belt south-eastward leads to Sirius, a brilliant blue-white star, the brightest in the heavens.

Undoubtedly the quickest way to become familiar with the night sky is to identify one or two of the constellations and the brightest stars within them, and to follow their progress across the sky, first hour by hour and then night by night. With the aid of the star chart more bodies can be added as time goes on, until recognition becomes virtually automatic once a pattern in the sky is discernible.

5.6 Sight reduction

5.6.1 Sight Reduction Tables for Air Navigation, AP 3270

Volume I of the tables is for star sights only and gives, for seven selected stars, for integral degrees of latitude, with argument LHA Aries, the computed altitude (Hc), to the nearest minute of arc, and azimuth to the nearest degree. The stars are chosen for brightness and angle of cut. Because of precession of the equinoxes and nutation, Volume I is published every five years and a correction table gives corrections to be applied to the fix for years other than the year for which they are computed. Volumes II and III can be used for stars with a declination of not more than 29°, should there be a requirement.

Volumes II and III of the tables are similar in method, and give for the nearest integral degree of latitude, with argument LHA of the body, and integral degree of declination: computed altitude to the nearest minute of arc (Hc), a quantity *d* which is the difference between the tabulated altitude and the altitude for a declination 1° greater, and azimuth angle to the nearest degree. An interpolation table enables the altitude to be corrected for increments of declination. Volume II cover latitudes 0° to 39°, and Volume III covers latitudes 40° to 89°.

Each volume carries full and clear instructions for its use. An assumed position is chosen such that the latitude is a whole degree and the longitude when combined with the GHA gives a whole degree of LHA. The tables are entered as indicated by the latitude and declination of the body, and the computed altitude and azimuth angle are extracted. By means of the interpolation table, Hc is then corrected for the increments of declination; comparison with the true altitude gives the intercept.

5.6.2 Latitude by meridian altitude

By far the simplest form of sight is the determination of latitude by observation of the meridian altitude, usually of the Sun. It is also an easy sight to take because during the period of meridian passage the altitude changes very slowly. At the time of transit the Sun appears to hang in the sky for a period of a minute or two.

The approximate time of meridian passage, generally to the nearest minute, is calculated by applying to the GMT of meridian passage given in the ephemeris the DR longitude at noon converted into hours and minutes. In west longitudes meridian passage will be later than on the Greenwich meridian, in east longitudes, earlier.

In some circumstances a timed altitude, generally to the nearest minute, is preferable to judging the maximum altitude but it is common practice at sea to observe the meridian altitude by taking a series of, say five, sights over two or three minutes when the Sun appears to be at its highest, before it dips. In that case the sight is not timed and no plotting is involved.

The altitude corrections are applied in the usual way and the zenith distance (90° minus true altitude) added to the declination when it is the same name as the latitude and subtracted when it is not. This gives the observer's latitude.

5.6.3 Latitude by the North Star

Polaris, the Pole Star, is easily picked out in the night sky by following the line of the pointers at the leading end of the Plough. It is not quite in line with the axis of the Earth's rotation and a correction to its altitude has to be made to obtain the latitude, which otherwise would correspond precisely with the true altitude. The star revolves very slowly around the pole of the heavens at an angular distance of about 1°. Its apparent

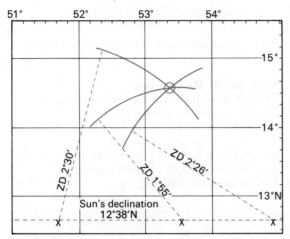

Fig. 5(10) Plotting the Sun's geographical position, a method only available in the tropics, illustrates the principle of astro-navigation. Were the zenith distances not so great in normal circumstances, the method could be employed universally.

movement is only about 1′ in 3 min so that an observation for latitude need only be timed to the nearest minute. For the time of the sight GHA Aries is extracted from the almanac and the longitude applied to form LHA Aries. With this as argument the Pole Star tables, as in *The Macmillan & Silk Cut Nautical Almanac*, give a correction to the altitude to give the latitude.

When the star is above or below the pole of the heavens, near the meridian, its altitude will change least and time be less important. Half an hour either side of meridian altitude, the change in altitude will only be about 1′ and this is the best time to observe so that a series of shots can be averaged to eliminate random error.

5.6.4 Plotting the Sun's geographical position

In the tropics when the Sun's declination is not more than about 2° from the latitude it is possible to obtain an extremely accurate fix by plotting the Sun's geographical position as it passes the meridian and from it describing two (or more) arcs with radius the zenith distance. At about 5 to 10 minutes before noon, and at about the same time after it, timed altitudes are taken in the normal fashion. The geographical position of the Sun at these times is then plotted with declination as latitude and GHA as longitude (360° minus GHA for easterly longitudes). From the three positions (the meridian altitude can conveniently form the third) as centre, arcs are described with zenith distance as radius; where they intersect constitutes the fix. Fig. 5(10), in tropical latitudes and easterly longitudes, illustrates an example. If it is necessary to transfer the first position circle for the course and distance sailed, as it might be at high speeds, this is most conveniently done by shifting the first geographical position the course and distance made good.

5.6.5 Equal altitudes

In certain circumstances, when the difference between the observer's latitude and the Sun's declination does not exceed about 10°, longitude may be determined by taking equal altitudes of the Sun on either side of the meridian. The latitude may at the same time be conveniently determined by meridian altitude, thus giving a fix. A correction must be made for the change in declination between the successive observations and for any change in latitude between the sights. In this case the assumption that meridian passage takes place at maximum altitude will not lead to significant error. Serious errors will be introduced if the method is used outside the rather confined limits in which it is valid. These are that the Sun should be not less than 20° in bearing from the meridian, not more than 10° in hour angle and at an altitude of not less than 70°.

The time of meridian passage is first worked out in the normal way and the first altitude taken, typically, about 15 minutes before it, and the time noted. The altitude corrections need not be applied, provided the afternoon sight is taken from the same height of eye. The meridian altitude is then observed as usual and (unless a second sextant has been available) the altitude of the first sight is set on the sextant again. At about the same interval after meridian passage the time is noted when the Sun is at the altitude set on the sextant. The mid-time of the observations is obtained by adding the two times together and dividing by 2; the GHA of the Sun for that time is the longitude west (or 360° minus GHA, the longitude east).

If the observer's latitude has changed and/or the Sun's declination has changed between the sights a correction is made to the first altitude to obtain the second. The quantity *d* given on the daily pages of *The Nautical Almanac* is the change of declination, north or south, in an hour; change of latitude will be obtained by working out a DR for the time of the second observation, or from the traverse table. The corrections can be combined and will be added to the first altitude if the Sun is getting nearer to the observer and subtracted if it is getting further away.

5.7 The use of calculators

5.7.1 Calculators – general

Instead of using tables for extracting the calculated altitude and azimuth, it is possible to solve the astronomical triangle using a calculator. One of the prime advantages of the calculator over tabular methods is that all sights can be worked from one position and it is unnecessary to round off the latitude or LHA to the nearest whole degree.

To be a useful aid for navigation, a calculator should meet certain requirements. It should be able to work in degrees, minutes and seconds of arc (DDMMSS or DMS), as well as degrees and decimals (D.d). It should have adequate memory storage and recall facilities. The suggested minimum requirement for celestial purposes is a minimum of six memory stores additional to any already used for statistical summation purposes. More detail notes on calculators appear in 3.3.16.

For astronomical navigation, a programmable or dedicated calculator (built for the purpose) is virtually essential in order to remove repetitive operations and reduce potential errors resulting from numerous key operations.

5.7.2 Dip

Dip corrections to the observed altitude (see 5.3.2) are always negative ($-$), and may be calculated from:–

Dip (in mins) $= 1'.76 \times \sqrt{HE}$ (in metres)
or/ $\qquad = 0'.97 \times \sqrt{HE}$ (in feet)

5.7.3 Refraction

For notes on refraction see 5.3.3. The correction is always subtractive, and may be calculated from the formula:

$$R_M = \frac{74}{h + 2} - 0.7$$

where: R_M is mean refraction in minutes of arc, h is observed altitude in degrees at sea level air temperature 10°C and atmospheric pressure 1010 millibars.

The accuracy of the above formula is:
In the range   0°– 3°,   maximum error 1'.8
In the range   3°–15°,   maximum error 0'.3
In the range 15°–90°,   maximum error 0'.1

Second, there is an additional correction factor (f) which may be applied under abnormal temperature or atmospheric pressure conditions. When non-standard conditions apply, multiply the Standard Altitude Correction (SAC) by f.

$$f = 1 + 0.001 \, (P - 1010) - 0.0036 \, (T - 10) + 0.000009 \, (T - 10)^2$$

where: P = Pressure in millibars
        T = Temperature (°C)

The total refraction correction (R), is the SAC (R_M) multiplied by f, and should be subtracted from the apparent altitude (Ha) to give the observed altitude (Ho). Do not forget to convert from degrees and decimals (D.d) into degrees, minutes and decimals (DMS) before using the answers.

5.7.4 Amplitudes

Amplitude is the bearing of a body measured from true east or west when it is on the horizon i.e. rising or setting. It is useful for checking compass accuracy, as described in 3.1.8.

$$\sin \text{Amplitude} = \frac{\sin \text{Declination}}{\cos \text{Latitude}}$$

Note: Amplitudes should not be used in high latitudes.

5.7.5 Sight Reduction

The following methods may be used to give calculated altitude and azimuth angle:
(1) sin Alt = (sin Lat × sin Dec) + (cos Lat × cos Dec × cos LHA)
where: Dec is positive if the SAME name as Lat, and negative if CONTRARY name
For the azimuth angle (Z):–

$$\tan Z = \frac{\sin \text{LHA}}{(\cos \text{Lat} \times \tan \text{Dec}) - (\sin \text{Lat} \times \cos \text{LHA})}$$

where: the sign conventions are (1) if Lat & Dec are of contrary name, Dec is treated as a negative quantity. (2) The rules for Zn are: If Z and sin LHA have the same sign, then $Zn = Z + 180°$; if Z is negative ($-$) and LHA is less than 180°, then $Zn = Z + 360°$.
(2) Using a different method, the procedure with a simple scientific calculator begins with loading the variable information into the memory stores.

(a)   Key in LHA, convert if necessary to (D.d), and put into STO 1
(b)   Key in DEC, convert if necessary to (D.d). If it is CONTRARY name to latitude, change its sign in the display to negative: Put into STO 2
(c)   Key in DR Lat, convert if necessary to (D.d), and put into STO 3
then proceed as follows:–

RCL 1 cos ÷ RCL 2 tan = inv
tan SUM 3 sin × RCL 1 tan ÷
RCL 3 cos = inv tan

The display will now show the azimuth angle (Z). Note Z and its sign ($+$) or ($-$), and continue as follows:–

cos × RCL 3 tan = inv tan
inv 2nd DMS

The display now shows the calculated altitude (Hc). Note the sign of the final display, and establish the true azimuth (Zn) from Z above according to these rules:–

(a)   If the final display is ($+$), in NORTH latitudes $Zn = 360° - Z$, and in SOUTH latitudes $Zn = 180° + Z$.
(b)   If the final display is ($-$), in NORTH latitudes $Zn = 180° - Z$, and in SOUTH latitudes $Zn = 360° + Z$.

Note: Remember that if (Z) was displayed as negative, you must apply the usual arithmetic rules when adding or subtracting.
(3) The best sight reduction method is available for calculators with the facility of rectangular to polar conversions, using the following formulae:

HP.41CV (also HP.67 & 97 with small mods.)	TI. 58 & 59
LHA ⬚ ENTER LAT ⬚ ENTER DEC ⬚ ENTER ⬚1 P ⟶ R XEQ ALPHA R↑ ALPHA x ⇄ y P ⟶ R XEQ ALPHA R↑ ALPHA STO 01 x ⇄ y P ⟶ R XEQ ALPHA x □ cos □ tan ALPHA 01 XEQ ALPHA R↑ ALPHA P ⟶ R XEQ ALPHA x □ cos □ tan ALPHA 01 + XEQ ALPHA x □ cos □ tan ALPHA 01 − R ⟶ P R↓ 180° + (= Zn ⬚ DDD.d) RCL 01 XEQ ALPHA ASIN ALPHA (= Hc ⬚ DD.d)	LHA ⬚ STO 01 LAT ⬚ STO 02 DEC ⬚ x ⇄ t ⬚1 x ⇄ t 2nd P ⟶ R 2nd EXC 01 2nd P ⟶ R 2nd EXC 02 STO 03 2nd P ⟶ R 2nd EXC 01 x ⇄ t 2nd EXC 03 2nd P ⟶ R SUM 03 2nd EXC 01 − x ⇄ t = x ⇄ t RCL 02 INV 2nd P ⟶ R + 180° = Zn ⬚ DDD.d RCL 03 INV 2nd sin (= Hc ⬚ DD.d)

Note: LHA, LAT and DEC should be entered in DDD.d format, or appropriate conversion keys pressed before ENTER.

Z = R→P (cos Dec × sin Lat × cos LHA − cos Lat × sin Dec, sin LHA × cos Dec)

Zn = Z + 180°.

Hc = sin⁻¹ (sin Dec × sin Lat + cos Dec × cos LHA × cos Lat)

A suitable key sequence for calculating Zn and Hc together on an HP.41CV or TI 59 is shown above.

Note: LHA, LAT and DEC should be entered in DDD.d format, or appropriate conversion keys pressed before ENTER.

5.7.6 Fix from two position lines

If two sights are reduced to give two values of the true azimuth (Zn), calculated altitude (Hc) and intercept (a), a fix can be calculated directly. In the formula below, NORTH latitudes and EAST longitudes are (+), and SOUTH latitudes and WEST longitudes are (−). Intercepts are (+) if TOWARDS, and (−) if AWAY.
The basic equations are:–

Another method of producing the fix takes advantage of the RPN calculator facilities which can be seen when using sight reduction method (3) above. Similarly, computation of the geographical fix from two celestial position lines is equally simple and rapid. For this procedure, intercepts are converted from minutes and decimals into decimals of a degree. Towards is (+) and Away is (−). You are simply calculating a correction to the DR/EP used for sight reduction.
The key sequence for a typical RPN calculator is as follows:–

Zn₁ ⬚ ENTER a₂ ⬚ ⟶ R

Zn₂ ⬚ ENTER a₁ ⬚ ⟶ R

x ⇄ y R↓ − R↓ − CHS R↑ ⟶ P

Zn₁ ⬚ ENTER Zn₂ ⬚ − sin ÷ ⟶ R
(= departure for △ d. Long correction)

x ⇄ y ⟶ HMS
(= read △ d. Lat correction)

$$\text{Fix Latitude} = \text{DR Lat} - \frac{\text{Intercept}_2 \times \sin Zn_1 - \text{Intercept}_2 \times \sin Zn_2}{60 \times \sin (Zn_2 - Zn_1)}$$

$$\text{Fix Longitude} = \text{DR Long} + \frac{\text{Intercept}_2 \times \cos Zn_1 - \text{Intercept}_1 \times \cos Zn_2}{\sin (Zn_2 - Zn_1) \times 60 \times \cos \text{Fix Latitude}}$$

The d.Lat correction can be applied directly to the DR/EP Latitude in the required direction. The departure must first be converted into d.Long before applying the correction to the DR/EP longitude using the formula:

d.Long = Departure ÷ cos Mean Latitude.

Worked example of celestial fix

DR Lat 48°30′.0N (48.500°) Long 08° 48′.0W (8.800°)
Sight No.1 225° ($\mathcal{Z}n_1$) Intercept (a_1) 3′.0
Towards (0°.050)
Sight No.2 267° ($\mathcal{Z}n_2$) Intercept (a_2) 2′.6
Towards (0°.0433)

Using the key sequence for a typical RPN calculator produces the results as follows:

△ d.long 0.0418 (departure)
△ d.lat − 0.0289 → HMS − 01′.7S

Convert the departure 0.0418 into d.long using standard formula gives 0.0631 → HMS = 3′.8W

DR Lat	48°30′.0N	long	08°48′.0W
d. lat	1′.7S	d. long	3′.8W
Fix	48°28′.3N		08°51′.8W

Note: The above calculation makes no provision for the motion of the observer between the sights.

5.8 The position line

5.8.1 The use of a single position line
A single astronomical position line can be used in conjunction with other information such as a line of soundings or a bearing (whether visual, radio DF or, for instance by Consol) to produce a fix. The accuracy of the fix will, clearly, depend upon both the accuracy of the information and the angle of cut. The accuracy of a visual bearing will depend on the distance of the object; the accuracy of radio bearings on that of the system used.

A useful fix can often be obtained by observing a planet or bright star shortly before sunrise, and crossing it later with an altitude of the Sun when it has reached at least 10°; the angle of cut should be at least 30°. In this way the uncertainty in the course and distance used to transfer the first position line will be minimised.

A single position line can also be used to clear a point or danger in the same way that a visual bearing can, due allowance being made for the accuracy of the observation. Where appropriate the position line can be shifted to clear the danger by the required distance; the direction and distance the line has been shifted will then be the course and distance to make good.

5.8.2 Angle of cut
For a two-body fix, whether Sun, Moon, star or planet (and whether obtained from simultaneous or successive altitudes) the optimum angle of cut is 90°, at which angle the effect of errors in either position line will be minimised. However, the error introduced by smaller angles of cut decreases so slowly that for all practical purposes any angle between about 60° and 120° will be as good as the right angle. See Fig. 5(11) and the accompanying table. With three position lines the optimum angle of cut is 60° and with four, as with two, 90°.

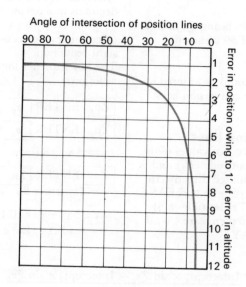

Angle °	Error ′
90	1.0
85	1.0
80	1.0
75	1.0
70	1.1
65	1.1
60	1.2
55	1.2
50	1.3
45	1.4
40	1.5
35	1.7
30	2.0
25	2.4
20	2.9
15	3.9
10	5.8
5	11.5

Fig. 5(11) The effect of angle of cut on fix accuracy.

5.8.3 Rate of change of bearing and altitude

In terrestrial navigation it is evident from the practice of doubling the angle on the bow that rate of change in bearing increases until the object is abeam. The maximum rate of change will be on the beam. The same principle applies to a celestial body as it approaches the meridian. The altitude on the other hand changes most rapidly when the body is rising or setting, and very slowly around the time of culmination. Further, the higher the altitude (in other words the closer the declination is to the latitude) the faster the change in bearing. In low latitudes it is thus possible on occasions to obtain a right-angled cut by successive observations of the Sun on either side of the meridian within the space of a comparatively few minutes.

For historical reasons that go back to before 'the problem of longitude' was solved, the noon position is always logged as the principal position for the day. However, noon is, navigationally, far from the best time to take a fix and whenever possible successive observations should be taken either side of the meridian. The important criterion is the shortest possible run between sights consistent with a sufficient change in bearing.

5.9 Plotting and evaluating the sight

5.9.1 Plotting

In oceanic navigation the chart in daily use will generally not be on a scale suitable for the accurate plotting of sights and for analysing the plot to obtain the most probable position. Plotting sheets on the Mercator projection for different bands of latitude are available from the Hydrographic Department but they are bulky and represent an unnecessary expense. Navigational charts of an appropriate scale can be used to plot sights, provided they are in the right latitude belt, by simply altering the longitude labels.

When the sight is worked from the DR, as opposed to an assumed position, as it is with some methods, the simplest form of plotting sheet is ruled paper used in conjunction with a protractor and ruler. The dead reckoning positions in successive observations are calculated from the first DR and the sights all plotted from the same position, with no transferred position lines (the transfer having been made by working the DRs one from the other.) A perpendicular up the page

Fig. 5(12) The 'Universal' plotting sheet is converted into a blank Mercator chart by joining the outer figures round the compass rose, north and south of the central latitude line, corresponding to the DR latitude. In DR latitude 50° (north or south), for example, joining the two fifties on the outer graduation east of the central meridian (one north and one south of the central parallel) establishes the meridian east of the central one etc.

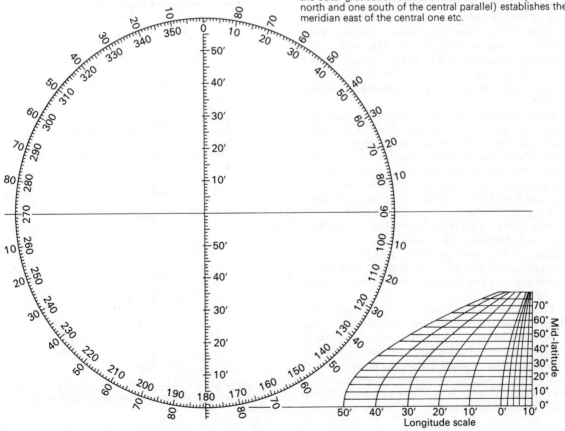

represents the meridian and the ruled lines can represent the latitude scale. The fix can either be transferred to the chart in terms of a bearing and distance from the DR or, preferably, read off the diagram in terms of difference of latitude and departure, the departure being converted into difference of longitude by the traverse or any other suitable table.

The most convenient form of plotting sheet for use with direct entry tables such as AP 3270 which use an assumed position is undoubtedly the universal plotting sheet (Fig. 5(12)) issued by the US Naval Oceanographic Office and published privately by a number of firms on either side of the Atlantic. Essentially it consists of a blank Mercator chart for small areas with a central compass rose, a central meridian graduated with a scale of nautical miles and blank latitude lines to be filled in according to the latitudes in question. The compass rose is graduated on the inside from 0 to 360° and on the outside from 0 to 90° from the central latitude line north and south. To convert the sheet into a Mercator chart, joining the graduations north and south corresponding to the latitude establishes the longitudinal meridians. A scale printed at the bottom of the sheet enables departure, for value of mid. latitude, to be converted into difference of longitude.

5.9.2 Evaluating position lines
The evaluation of position lines to establish the most probable position plays an important part in the art of astronomical navigation at sea. A plot of six star sights, for example, may show position lines intersecting at nine separate points within reasonable distance of the DR, and some method will be required to analyse the plot and see which of the lines is likely to be the more reliable and to detect the presence of gross errors or blunders.

Observational errors are of course an integral part of navigation and the first thing to realise is that a position line more accurately represents a band of position the width of which corresponds to the probable error of the observation. Thus if the error from all causes in an observation is estimated, to a given confidence level, to be, say, half a mile, the observer's position should lie within a band of position a mile wide (i.e. half a mile on either side of the position line). The confidence level most generally used in navigation is the 95 per cent level at which the stated error will be exceeded only once in twenty occasions.

When two position lines cross at an angle other than 90°, the bands will form a diamond of error which may conveniently be drawn as an ellipse. When the angle of cut is 90°, assuming equal reliability in each position line, the error configuration will be a box which is generally represented by a circle or ellipse of error of radius slightly larger than the position-line error.

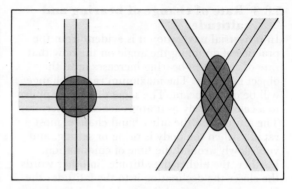

Fig. 5(13) Error configuration and angle of cut.

Fig. 5(13) illustrates examples. In practice these configurations will seldom be drawn on the chart but the experienced navigator will always think of position lines as bands with a certain width and of the resultant fix as a small area within which his ship lies rather than as a point.

When three position lines intersect at an angle of about 120°, the in-centre of the cocked hat is generally assumed to be the position. This will be so if the errors in each sight are equal and in the same direction, as they usually are; however, if there is a blunder in one of the position lines, the position may well lie outside the triangle.

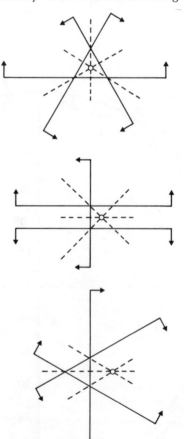

Fig. 5(14) The bisector method of establishing the most probable position. The arrows point toward the body observed.

There are several ways of analysing the astro plot, all of which involve marking on each position line, generally by a small arrow, the bearing of the body observed. The bearing will of course be at right angles to the position line. Unless there is an abnormal cause of error the arrows should all point towards or away from the centre of the figure described by the position lines. In the bisector method the (external) angle between two position lines whose azimuth arrows both point either towards or away from each other is bisected (by eye); the intersection of the bisectors is taken as the fix. The use of bisectors, which are in fact position lines obtained from equal differences of altitude, eliminates systematic error and averages random errors in the observations. However, there are constraints on the method. The best bisector will be derived from sights separated in azimuth by 180° but, because of the slow variation of the sine curve, this figure can be extended to 150°. The method should not be used where the difference in azimuth is less than 60°.

An alternative to the bisector method is to shift all the position lines the same amount and in the same direction, either towards or away from the body observed, thus closing or opening out the pattern, until they meet at a point. This will both eliminate systematic error and reveal gross errors or a blunder. The two methods are illustrated in Figs. 5(14) and 5(15).

Two position lines constitute a fix. A third line, however, will increase the reliability of the fix; it will not, though, enable the navigator to distinguish between any systematic errors and blunders. A 'cartwheel' fix of four stars whose bearings differ by 45° will give a more reliable fix, but four stars 90° apart will often indicate, by the spacing of the two sets of reciprocal position lines, the size of the systematic error and the probable size of the random error. On the other hand since the bisector method eliminates systematic error, the soundest procedure is to take four stars 90° apart and analyse the plot by that method which will indicate whether the set has been influenced by random error. A fifth sight as a stand-by, which need not be worked up, can indicate a blunder if that is suspected.

5.10 Sight reduction table

5.10.1 Introduction

The method of sight reduction described below is intended for use when other methods are not available. It has been chosen in spite of the limitation that it is not suitable for the reduction of sights of bodies within about 15° of the prime vertical. For occasional use the brevity and simplicity of the method compensates for this limitation.

When necessary to observe bodies within 20° of due east or due west, the alternative method described in Appendix II may be used.

Errors arising through the sight reduction are unlikely to exceed 2 miles.

It is assumed that the following data are available:
(a) An approximate position (latitude L_A, longitude λ_A) of the observer at the GMT of the sight. If observations are to be combined, a knowledge of the speed and course will also be required.
(b) The corrected observed altitude (H) and, for the GMT of the sight, the Greenwich Hour Angle (GHA) and the declination (D) of the observed body. If taken from the ephemeris in *The Macmillan & Silk Cut Nautical Almanac* the figures must be converted to degrees and minutes.

5.10.2 General description

Each sight is 'reduced' to provide a segment of the position line close to the approximate position of the observer. The latitude (L) of the point on the position line in longitude λ_A is calculated, together with an azimuth angle (z). The position line is then drawn, on the chart or plotting sheet, through the plotted position L, λ_A in the direction determined by z.

The limitation arises because, for bodies within about 15° of the prime vertical (i.e. for z less than 15°) the length of the segment of the position line may be larger than convenience or accuracy permits.

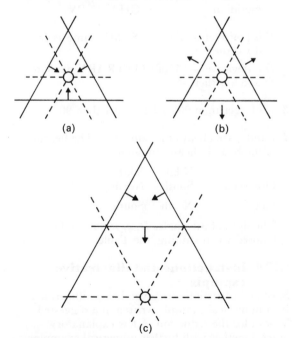

Fig. 5(15) Shifting astro-position lines an equal amount towards or away from the bodies observed to establish the most probable position from a cocked hat.

A single table, given in 5.10.7, contains tabulations of the three functions:

$$S(\theta) = k \log \sin \theta \qquad \text{for } k = -3 \times 10^4$$
$$T(\theta) = k \log \tan \theta \qquad \text{with argument}$$
$$C(\theta) = k \log \cos \theta \qquad \theta = 0° \text{ (interval 1') } 45°.$$

Although the columns are headed by the letters S, T, C alone, the notations such as $S(P)$, $T(D)$, $C(H)$ are used to indicate the function and its argument; they are convenient for equations and instructions.

To avoid interpolation between tabulated values of the functions, the Table is entered (directly) with angles as argument only when they are exact multiples of 1'. When the table is entered (inversely) with a function value (e.g. $C(z)$ in Step 5) the nearer of the two corresponding arguments is to be adopted for the angle (e.g. z).

A description of the Table, and of its use to provide function values for all arguments of θ from $-90°$ to $+180°$ is given on the first page thereof. It should be noted that, although $S(\theta)$ and $C(\theta)$ are always positive $(+)$, $T(\theta)$ may also be negative $(-)$.

5.10.3 Notation, method, equations and rules

The following notation is used:

L = latitude, designated N or S
λ = longitude, designated E or W
P = local hour angle (meridian angle), designated E or W
D = declination, designated N or S
H = corrected observed altitude
z = an azimuth angle, designated $+$ or $-$
x,y = auxiliary angles, designated $+$ or $-$

The only subscript used is A, in L_A, λ_A, P_A to denote values corresponding to the approximate position. In this method P_A is the only value of P that is used, so the subscript is omitted in the equations.

The navigational spherical triangle P (pole), Z (zenith), X (observed body) is divided into two right-angled spherical triangles by a perpendicular XL from X to PZ (produced as necessary), as in the figure.

In the triangle PXL,
$$PX = 90° - D \qquad PL = 90° - x \qquad LPX = P$$

In the triangle ZXL,
$$ZX = 90° - H \qquad ZL = y \qquad LZX = 90° - z$$

Since $PZ = PL - ZL$, $L = x + y$

The relevant equations are:

1 $T(x) = T(D) - C(P)$ to give x
2 $C(z) = C(D) - C(H) + S(P)$ to give z
3 $T(y) = S(z) - T(H)$ to give y
4 $L = x + y$ to give L
5 $S(D) - S(H) = S(x) - C(y)$ as a check

Equation 5 is used only as a check on the arithmetic, and may be omitted if desired. x, z, y are determined from the function values $T(x)$,

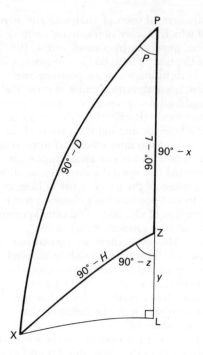

Fig. 5(16) Navigational spherical triangle.

$C(z)$, $T(y)$ and are rounded off, with a maximum error of 0'.5, before being used in subsequent equations.

The following rules concerning signs and quadrants apply:

1 Body east $\qquad P(E) = 360° - GHA - \lambda(E)$
of meridian $\qquad\quad = 360° - GHA + \lambda(W)$

Body west $\qquad P(W) = GHA + \lambda(E)$
of meridian $\qquad\quad\; = GHA - \lambda(W)$

2 D is positive $(+)$ if of the SAME name as L; and x is then $+$

D is negative $(-)$ if of CONTRARY name to L; and x is then $-$

3 x is larger than 90° if P is larger than 90°

4 y and z are always the same sign. The bearing of the body indicates the sign:

		N lats	S lats	y,z
Observed	to:	South	North	$+$
body		North	South	$-$

5 The signs of the angles D, x, y, z are to be ignored when entering the Table.

5.10.4 Instructions and illustrative example

Specific instructions are given below, illustrated by a numerical example written in a suggested lay-out for the reduction. A few explanatory notes, together with further numerical examples to illustrate various combinations of quadrants and signs, are given in Appendix I.

Provision is made for the numerical check provided by equation 5. Although exact agreement cannot be expected (because of the rounding off of x, y) it is recommended that it be used; it adds little to the amount of calculation.

Instructions and illustrative example

Enter basic data, including an indication of the bearing of the observed body.

Step

1 Enter Table with D, and copy $T(D)$, $C(D)$ and $S(D)$

2 Enter Table with H, and copy $C(H)$, $T(H)$ and $S(H)$

3 Form $A = C(D) - C(H)$ and
   $B = S(D) - S(H)$

4 Enter Table with P, and copy $C(P)$ and $S(P)$

5(a) Form $C(z) = A + S(P)$
 (b) Enter Table with $C(z)$, and copy z, $S(z)$; z is rounded

6(a) Form $T(x) = T(D) - C(P)$
 (b) Enter Table with $T(x)$, and copy x, $S(x)$; x is rounded

7(a) Form $T(y) = -T(H) + S(z)$
 (b) Enter Table with $T(y)$, and copy y, $C(y)$; y is rounded

8(a) Form $L = x + y$
 (b) Form true bearing of position line:

N lat	S lat	$\begin{cases} 180° - z \\ 360° - z \end{cases}$
P West	P East	

N lat	S lat	$\begin{cases} z \\ 180° + z \end{cases}$
P East	P West	

where z is to be applied with its sign

9 Form $S(x) - C(y)$ and compare with B.

Date	198 - August 7	Latitude	L_A N/S 53 10		Longitude	λ_A E/W 14 17
GMT	About 17ʰ	Corr. Obs. Alt.	H 31 35		GHA Body	73 47
Body	Sun LL; W by S	Declination	D N/S 16 28		LHA	P E/W 59 30
Step						
1	D +/− 16 28	+T(D) +/− 15880	+C(D)+ 546			+S(D)+ 16425
2	H 31 35		− C(H)− 2089	−T(H) − 6338		−S(H)− 8427
3			A ± 1543			B + 7998
4	P E/W 59 30	−C(P)− 8836	+S(P)+ 1940			
5	z + 14 04	←C(z) 397		+S(z)+ 18429		
6	x + 30 13	←T(x) + 7044				+S(x)+ 8946
7	y + 21 34			←T(y) + 12091		−C(y)− 946
8	L 51 47	Direction of p.l. W 14°; 166°/346°(T)				Sum ± 8000

The position line is drawn through the point latitude L (51° 47′), longitude λ_A (W 14° 17′) in the direction $180° - z/360° - z$ (166°/346°(T)), as illustrated in Fig. 5(17). Entries in the check column may be omitted if a check on the arithmetic is not required.

5.10.5 Appendix I

Although the arithmetical operations involved in the sight reduction are basically simple, they are subject to error in practice, especially when the calculation is unfamiliar. It is better to take care to avoid error rather than have to find and correct it when the check calculation does not agree. However, *small* differences in the check sum – arising mainly from the rounding off of x and y – are to be expected.

Particular care is required in the use of the Table, with its semi-quadrantal arrangement. A full description of the Table, and of the manner of its use for all angles between 0° and 180°, is given on the first page of the Table; there are adequate examples of its use. Little difficulty should be met with the functions $S(\theta)$ and $C(\theta)$, which are always positive (+), but $T(\theta)$ may be either positive or negative according to the semi-quadrant (+ for $\theta = 0°$–45°, 135°–180°; and −

Fig. 5(17) Position line, as plotted for the illustrative example on p.145. In the standard method the position line is plotted from A; in the alternative method either from B or by the usual intercept method from the DR position. The close agreement is fortuitous, since errors of 1′ can easily occur, and the long position line should be curved.

for $\theta = 45°-90°$, $90°-135°$. The suggested lay-out includes alternative signs for the application of $T(D)$, $T(H)$, $T(x)$ and $T(y)$; the upper sign relates to the ranges $0-45°$, $135°-180°$ and the lower to the range $45°-135°$. The unwanted signs should be deleted; the two components of each sum are then to be combined with the signs that precede them.

Illustrative examples

The four examples below contain, between them and the one in the main text, illustrations of most of the combinations of signs and quadrants that can occur.

Details of date and time of observation, used to derive the GHA and Declination, are not given. On the diagrams showing the position line as drawn on the chart, the point with longitude λ_Λ and calculated latitude L is marked as A; and the point for which the altitude was calculated is marked O. The approximate position of the observer is marked DR; but the 'errors' in L_Λ and λ_Λ from the 'true' position O are arbitrary choices.

A summary of the main features of the five examples follows:

No.	Lat	Long	LHA(P)	D	x	y	z
0	N	W	W, < 90°	N,+	+,< 90°	+	+,small
1	N	E	W, > 90°	N,+	+,> 90°	−	−,large
2	N	W	E, < 90°	S,−	−	+	+,large
3	S	E	E, > 90°	S,+	+,> 90°	−	−,medium
4	S	W	E, < 90°	N,−	−	+	+,medium

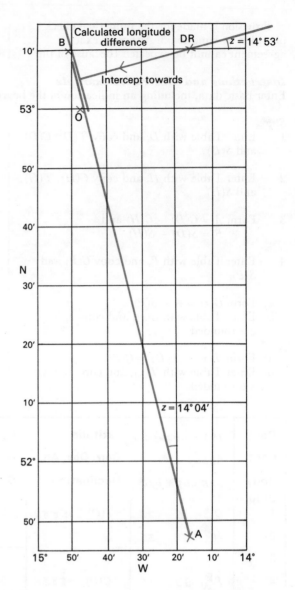

Example 1

Date	Not given	Latitude	L_A	N/S 36° 10′	Longitude	λ_A	E/W 15° 50′
GMT		Corr. Obs. Alt.	H	21 41	GHA Body		137 00
Body	Kochab; N by W	Declination	D	N/S 74° 13′	LHA	P	E/W 152 50
Step							
1	$D \pm$ 74 13	$+T(D) \pm$ 16462	$+C(D)+$ 16963				$+S(D)+$ 501
2	H 21 41		$-C(H)-$ 956	$-T(H) \mp$ 12016			$-S(H)-$ 12972
3			$A \pm$ 16007				$B \pm$ 12471
4	P E/W 152 50	$-C(P)-$ 1523	$+S(P)+$ 10214				
5	$z \pm$ 82 19		$\leftarrow C(z)$ 26221	$+S(z)+$ 117			
6	$x \pm$ 104 07	$\leftarrow T(x) \pm$ 17985					$+S(x)+$ 400
7	$y \mp$ 68 08		$\leftarrow T(y) \pm$ 11899	$-C(y)-$ 12868			
8	L 35 59	Direction of p.l. E 82°; 082°/262°(T)					Sum $\pm$ 12468

Example 2

Date		Latitude L_A $\frac{N}{S}$ 55 50		Longitude λ_A $\frac{E}{W}$ 6 50	
GMT	Not given	Corr. Obs. Alt. H 23 32		GHA Body 350 25	
Body	Sun LL ; S by E	Declination D $\frac{N}{S}$ 8 57		LHA P $\frac{E}{W}$ 16 25	
Step					
1	$D \frac{+}{-}$ 8 57	$+T(D) \pm 24082$	$+C(D)+$ 160		$+S(D)+24242$
2	H 23 32		$-C(H)-$ 1131	$-T(H) \mp 10830$	$-S(H)-11962$
3			$A \frac{+}{-}$ 971		$B \pm 12280$
4	$P \frac{E}{W}$ 16 25	$-C(P)-$ 542	$+S(P)+$ 16464		
5	$z \pm$ 72 16		$C(z)$ 15493	$+S(z)+$ 634	
6	$x \frac{+}{-}$ 9 19	$T(x) \pm 23540$			$+S(x)+23723$
7	$y \pm$ 65 26			$T(y) \pm 10196$	$-C(y)-11435$
8	L 56 07	Direction of p.l. E 72°; 072°/252°(T)			Sum· ± 12288

Example 3

Date		Latitude L_A $\frac{N}{S}$ 41 00		Longitude λ_A $\frac{E}{W}$ 25 40	
GMT	Not given	Corr. Obs. Alt. H 15 49		GHA Body 211 03	
Body	Canopus ; SE	Declination D $\frac{N}{S}$ 52 41		LHA P $\frac{E}{W}$ 123 17	
Step					
1	$D \frac{+}{-}$ 52 41	$+T(D) \pm 3537$	$+C(D)+$ 6521		$+S(D)+$ 2984
2	H 15 49		$-C(H)-$ 503	$-T(H) \frac{-}{+} 16433$	$-S(H)-16936$
3			$A \frac{+}{-}$ 6018		$B \pm 13952$
4	$P \frac{E}{W}$ 123 17	$-C(P)-$ 7818	$+S(P)+$ 2334		
5	$z \pm$ 58 13		$C(z)$ 8352	$+S(z)+$ 2117	
6	$x \frac{+}{-}$ 112 43	$T(x) \pm 11355$			$+S(x)+$ 1050
7	$y \pm$ 71 34			$T(y) \pm 14316$	$-C(y)-15001$
8	L 41 08	Direction of p.l. E 58°; 058°/238°(T)			Sum ± 13951

Example 4

Date	Not given	Latitude L_A $\frac{N}{S}$ 9 10		Longitude λ_A $\frac{E}{W}$ 14 30	
GMT		Corr. Obs. Alt. H 24 57		GHA Body 334 13	
Body	Deneb; NE	Declination D $\frac{N}{S}$ 45 14		LHA P $\frac{E}{W}$ 40 17	
Step					
1	$D \pm$ 45 14	$+T(D) \pm$ 106	$+C(D)+$ 4569		$+S(D)+$ 4463
2	H 24 57		$-C(H)-$ 1276	$-T(H) \frac{-}{+} 9970$	$-S(H)-11246$
3			$A \frac{+}{-}$ 3293		$B \pm 6783$
4	$P \frac{E}{W}$ 40 17	$-C(P)-$ 3527	$+S(P)+$ 5682		
5	$z \frac{+}{-}$ 59 51		$C(z)$ 8975	$+S(z)+$ 1894	
6	$x \pm$ 52 53	$T(x) \pm 3633$			$+S(x)+$ 2950
7	$y \frac{+}{-}$ 61 43			$T(y) \pm 8076$	$-C(y)-$ 9731
8	L 8 50	Direction of p.l. W 60°; 120°/300°(T)			Sum $\pm$ 6781

Example 1

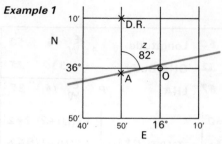

Example 2

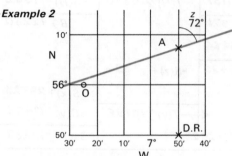

Example 3

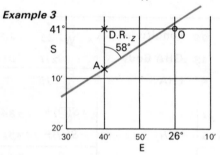

Example 4

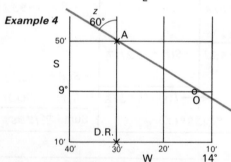

Fig. 5(18) Position lines plotted for Examples 1-4 (Appendix I).

5.10.6 Appendix II
ALTERNATIVE METHOD FOR USE FOR SIGHTS OF BODIES WITHIN ABOUT 20° OF THE PRIME VERTICAL

Using equations 1–5 in the form:

1	$T(x) = T(D) - C(P_\Lambda)$	to give x
4	$y = L_\Lambda - x$	to give y
5	$S(H_\Lambda) = S(D) - S(x) + C(y)$	to give H_Λ
3	$S(z_\Lambda) = T(H_\Lambda) + T(y)$	to give z_Λ
2	$C(z_\Lambda) = C(D) - C(H) + S(P_\Lambda)$	as a check

the altitude H_Λ and azimuth angle z_Λ may be calculated for the approximate position L_Λ, λ_Λ. When z_Λ is small (say, less than 15°), the intercept $H_\Lambda - H$ can readily be converted to a longitude difference, thus giving the longitude corresponding to the latitude L_Λ. Alternatively, the position line can be plotted by the usual intercept method, though it might well be simpler to draw a line through the approximate position in the direction given by z_Λ, and then to draw the position line parallel to it.

It will be seen that the notations H_Λ and z_Λ are used; but H_Λ itself is the only quantity that need be so specified in the calculation.

It is essential that $S(x)$ used in equation 5 should be consistent with the value of $T(x)$ obtained in equation 1. Small differences of up to 3 between $T(x)$ and the nearest tabular value can be ignored, but larger values may occur when x is small. Consistency may be achieved by:

either choosing $C(P)$ so that $T(x)$ is, or is close to, a tabular value, with adjustment of P_Λ and λ_Λ accordingly;

or, if x is less than about 20°, using
$$S(x) = T(x) + C(x) = T(D) - C(P_\Lambda) + C(x)$$

For example, if $T(D) = +17573$ with $P_\Lambda = 28°59'$, then $T(x) = +17573 - 1743 = +15830$. The nearer tabular value is 15824, corresponding to: $x = 16°32'$, $S(x) = 16374$, $C(P) = 1749$, $P = 29°01'$. An adjustment of 2′ can then be made to λ_Λ.

Alternatively, $C(x)$ for $x = 16°32'$ is 550, so that
$$S(x) = +15830 + 550 = 16380$$
which corresponds to $T(x)$ and to P_Λ and λ_Λ.

Even if not to be used, it is recommended that, where x is less than 30°, $C(x)$ be copied in step 3 as a matter of routine.

This difficulty does not arise with the standard method, since $S(x)$ enters only into the check calculation, giving rise to a rather larger check difference.

The standard method may be used, either deliberately or not, for sights within 15° of the prime vertical; and, if the DR longitude is not too much in error, it will lead to a satisfactory position line. If it does not do so, some parts of the calculation can be utilised for the alternative method.

The rules concerning signs and quadrants are the same as for the standard method, with the following addition for the bearing of the observed body, measured from the North through East:

	LHA (P)	
Latitude	East	West
North	$90° + z$	$270° - z$
South	$90° - z$	$270° + z$

where z is to be applied with its sign.

Instructions and illustrative example — alternative method

Enter basic data, including an indication of the bearing of the observed body.

Step

1 Enter Table with D, and copy $T(D)$, $C(D)$ and $S(D)$

2 Enter Table with P, and copy $C(P)$ and $S(P)$

3(a) Form $T(x) = T(D) - C(P)$
 (b) Enter Table with $T(x)$, and copy x, $S(x)$ and $C(x)$ if necessary (see above); x is rounded

4(a) Form $y = L_A - x$
 (b) Enter Table with y, and copy $T(y)$ and $C(y)$

5 Form $B = S(x) - C(y)$ and copy $-B$

6(a) Form $S(H_A) = S(D) - B$
 (b) Enter Table with $S(H_A)$, and copy H_A, $C(H)$ and $T(H)$; H_A is rounded

7(a) Form intercept $= H_A - H$ Away
 or $= H - H_A$ Towards
 (b) Form $A = C(D) - C(H)$

8(a) Form $S(z) = T(H) + T(y)$
 (b) Form $C(z) = A + S(P)$
 (c) Check consistency of $S(z)$, $C(z)$ in the Table, and copy z; z is rounded

9 Enter direction of position line (p.l.) or intercept.
 The position line is to be drawn:

 (a) as a parallel, offset by the intercept Away from or Towards the observed body, to the 'position line' (corresponding to altitude H_A) throught the point, latitude L_A longitude λ_A; or
 (b) by the usual intercept method; or
 (c) by converting the intercept to a longitude difference.

The following illustrative example uses the same data as that in the main text, and the same printed lay-out. The resulting position line is plotted in the figure in the main text.

In the example the following manuscript changes to the printed pro-forma have been made to facilitate its use for the alternative method:
(a) Modified step numbers have been inserted.
(b) The sign $-$ has been changed to $+$ for $T(H)$ and $S(H)$ in line 2 (step 6), and inserted before B in line 3.
(c) 'Int' has been inserted in column 1 of line 3

(step 7).
(d) $C(x)$ has been inserted in column 3 of line 6 (step 3). (Its value has been copied, although its use was unnecessary).
(e) An arrow has been inserted before $S(H)$, and the arrow before $T(y)$ crossed out.

It will be noted that, although steps 1, 2, 3, are the same as steps 1, 4, 6 of the standard method, equations 3, 4 and 5 are re-arranged. The column containing $C(D)$, $C(H)$, A, $S(P)$ and $C(z)$ is used as a check, and all the entries in it may be omitted if desired.

Date	198 - August	Latitude	L_A	N 8 53	10	Longitude	λ_A	E W 14	17
GMT	About 17^h	Corr. Obs. Alt.	H	31	35	GHA Body		73	47
Body	Sun LL; W by S	Declination	D	N 8 16	28	LHA	P	E W 59	30

Step							
~~1~~ 1	D 16 28	$+T(D)$ 15880	$+C(D)+$ 546		$+S(D)+16425$	
~~2~~ 6	H_A 31 15		$-C(H)-$ 2042	$+T(H)$ 6508	$+S(H)+$ 8553	
~~3~~ 5,7	Int. 20' Towards		A 1496		$-B$ 7872	
~~4~~ 2	P E W 59 30	$-C(P)-$ 8836	$+S(P)+$ 1940			
~~5~~ 8	z 14 53		$C(z)$ 444	$+S(z)+$ 17704		
~~6~~ 3	x 30 13	$T(x)$ 7044	$C(x)$ 1903		$+S(x)+$ 8946	
~~7~~ 4	y 22 57			$T(y)$ 11196	$-C(y)-$ 1074	
~~8~~ 9	L_A 53 10	Direction of p.l. Int. 255°(T)			Sum $\pm$	

Note: Measurement on the chart shows that a distance of 20' in latitude 53° corresponds to a longitude difference of 33' (which for $z = 15°$ should strictly be increased by about 3%) leading to a longitude, corresponding to L_A, of 14°51' which is point B in Fig.5(17).

5.10.7 Table

In the Table, the functions

$$S(\theta) = -3 \times 10^4 \log \sin \theta$$
$$T(\theta) = -3 \times 10^4 \log \tan \theta$$
$$C(\theta) = -3 \times 10^4 \log \cos \theta$$

are tabulated, for each minute of arc, in the range $\theta = 0° - 45°$, with complementary and supplementary arguments to extend the range from $0° - 180°$.

When entered directly with an angle (such as D) the tabulated values S, T, C are taken out without interpolation and designated $S(D)$, $T(D)$, $C(D)$. When entered inversely with a function, such as $C(z)$, the angle z is the nearer of the two values, and, in most cases, other function values of z are the corresponding tabulated values.

The lay-out used for both the standard and alternative methods allows both angles and functions to be taken out from the same line of the Table and copied on the same line of the lay-out.

There are four ranges of angle, each with a distinct arrangement of entry and function values.

Range	Position of degrees	Position of minutes	Order (left to right) of function values
0°–45°	Top	Left, downwards	S $+T$ C
90°–45°	Bottom	Right, upwards	C $-T$ S
90°–135°	Top	Left, downwards	C $-T$ S
180°–135°	Bottom	Right, upwards	S $+T$ C

The angles D, x, y, z may be negative, but the sign is to be ignored when entering the Table.

It should be noted that $S(\theta) = T(\theta) + C(\theta)$, allowing for rounding-off, so that $S(\theta)$ is larger than $C(\theta)$ when $T(\theta)$ is positive, and smaller than $C(\theta)$ when $T(\theta)$ is negative. $S(\theta)$ and $C(\theta)$ are always positive. Care should be taken to ensure that the correct angles and columns have been used; it is easy to make a mistake.

The following extracts illustrate the various uses of the Tables; the entering angle or function value is printed in blue.

	Angle ° ′	S	T	C
D	− 9 14	23839	+ 23669	170
D,H,P	+ 32 27	8111	+ 5899	2212
D,H,P	+ 57 33	2212	− 5899	8111
P	117 36	1574	− 8450	10024
P	164 07	16883	+ 16376	507
z	± 17 23	15740	+ 15131	609
z	± 50 41	3344	− 2602	5943
$x*,y$	± 16 32	16374	+ 15830	550
$x*,y$	± 27 41	9988	+ 8408	1584
$x*,y$	± 62 19	1584	− 8406	9988
H	49 05	3649	− 1863	5514

*If P is greater than 90°, x will be 163°28′, 152°19′, 117°41′.

To each function value (S, T or C) there may correspond an angle in each of the quadrants $-90°$ to $0°$; $0°$ to $90°$; and $90°$ to $180°$.

z and y are both } $-90°$ to $0°$ {if the observed} towards {the elevated
in the quadrants } $0°$ to $90°$ {body is } away from {pole

A check on the sign is provided by $L = x + y$.
x is $-$ if D is $-$; x is in the quadrant $90°$–$180°$ if P is greater than $90°$. H is always in the quadrant $0°$ to $90°$.

	INFIN	0	INFIN
		S/C	
	52744	2	52742

	0°		
	S	**+T**	**C**
↓ **90°**			
Min.	**C**	**−T**	**S**

Min.	S	+T	C	′
00	INFIN	INFIN	0	60
01	106088	106088	0	59
02	97057	97057	0	58
03	91775	91775	0	57
04	88026	88026	0	56
05	85119	85119	0	55
06	82744	82744	0	54
07	80735	80735	0	53
08	78996	78996	0	52
09	77461	77461	0	51
10	76088	76088	0	50
11	74846	74846	0	49
12	73713	73713	0	48
13	72670	72670	0	47
14	71704	71704	0	46
15	70806	70805	0	45
16	69965	69965	0	44
17	69175	69175	0	43
18	68430	68430	0	42
19	67726	67725	0	41
20	67057	67057	0	40
21	66422	66421	0	39
22	65816	65815	0	38
23	65236	65236	0	37
24	64682	64682	0	36
25	64150	64150	0	35
26	63639	63639	0	34
27	63147	63147	0	33
28	62674	62673	0	32
29	62216	62216	0	31
30	61775	61774	0	30
31	61348	61347	1	29
32	60934	60933	1	28
33	60533	60532	1	27
34	60144	60143	1	26
35	59766	59766	1	25
36	59399	59399	1	24
37	59042	59042	1	23
38	58695	58694	1	22
39	58357	58356	1	21
40	58027	58026	1	20
41	57705	57704	1	19
42	57391	57390	1	18
43	57085	57083	1	17
44	56785	56784	1	16
45	56492	56491	1	15
46	56206	56205	1	14
47	55926	55924	1	13
48	55651	55650	1	12
49	55383	55381	1	11
50	55120	55118	1	10
51	54862	54860	1	09
52	54609	54607	1	08
53	54360	54359	2	07
54	54117	54115	2	06
55	53878	53876	2	05
56	53643	53641	2	04
57	53413	53411	2	03
58	53186	53184	2	02
59	52963	52961	2	01
60	52744	52742	2	00

S	+T	C	Min.
		179°	
C	−T	S	
		89°	

	52744	2	52742
	S/C		±T
	31791	50	31741

Min.	1° S	+T	C	2° S	+T	C	3° S	+T	C	4° S	+T	C	
	91° C	−T	S	92° C	−T	S	93° C	−T	S	94° C	−T	S	
00	52744	52742	2	43715	43707	8	38436	38418	18	34692	34661	32	60
01	52529	52527	2	43607	43599	8	38364	38346	18	34638	34606	32	59
02	52317	52315	2	43500	43492	8	38292	38274	18	34585	34552	32	58
03	52109	52107	2	43394	43386	8	38221	38202	18	34531	34498	33	57
04	51904	51901	2	43288	43280	8	38150	38131	19	34477	34445	33	56
05	51702	51699	2	43184	43175	9	38079	38060	19	34424	34391	33	55
06	51503	51500	2	43080	43071	9	38009	37990	19	34371	34338	33	54
07	51307	51304	2	42977	42968	9	37939	37920	19	34319	34285	34	53
08	51114	51111	3	42875	42866	9	37870	37850	19	34266	34232	34	52
09	50924	50921	3	42774	42764	9	37801	37781	20	34214	34179	34	51
10	50736	50733	3	42673	42664	9	37732	37712	20	34162	34127	34	50
11	50551	50549	3	42573	42564	9	37664	37644	20	34110	34075	35	49
12	50369	50366	3	42474	42465	10	37596	37576	20	34058	34023	35	48
13	50190	50187	3	42376	42366	10	37528	37508	21	34006	33971	35	47
14	50012	50009	3	42278	42268	10	37461	37440	21	33955	33919	36	46
15	49837	49834	3	42182	42172	10	37394	37373	21	33904	33868	36	45
16	49665	49662	3	42085	42075	10	37328	37306	21	33853	33817	36	44
17	49495	49491	3	41990	41980	10	37261	37240	21	33802	33766	36	43
18	49326	49323	3	41895	41885	11	37195	37174	22	33752	33715	37	42
19	49161	49157	3	41801	41791	11	37130	37108	22	33702	33665	37	41
20	48997	48993	4	41708	41697	11	37065	37043	22	33651	33614	37	40
21	48835	48831	4	41615	41604	11	37000	36977	22	33602	33564	38	39
22	48675	48671	4	41523	41512	11	36935	36913	23	33552	33514	38	38
23	48517	48513	4	41432	41421	11	36871	36848	23	33502	33464	38	37
24	48361	48357	4	41341	41330	11	36807	36784	23	33453	33414	38	36
25	48207	48203	4	41251	41239	12	36743	36720	23	33404	33365	39	35
26	48055	48051	4	41162	41150	12	36680	36657	23	33355	33316	39	34
27	47904	47900	4	41073	41061	12	36617	36593	24	33306	33267	39	33
28	47755	47751	4	40984	40972	12	36554	36530	24	33257	33218	40	32
29	47608	47604	4	40897	40884	12	36492	36468	24	33209	33169	40	31
30	47462	47458	4	40810	40797	12	36430	36405	24	33161	33120	40	30
31	47319	47314	5	40723	40711	13	36368	36343	25	33113	33072	41	29
32	47176	47171	5	40637	40624	13	36306	36282	25	33065	33024	41	28
33	47035	47031	5	40552	40539	13	36245	36220	25	33017	32976	41	27
34	46896	46891	5	40467	40454	13	36184	36159	25	32970	32928	41	26
35	46758	46753	5	40383	40369	13	36124	36098	25	32922	32880	42	25
36	46622	46617	5	40299	40286	13	36063	36037	26	32875	32833	42	24
37	46487	46482	5	40216	40202	14	36003	35977	26	32828	32786	42	23
38	46353	46348	5	40133	40119	14	35943	35917	26	32781	32738	43	22
39	46221	46216	5	40051	40037	14	35884	35857	26	32734	32691	43	21
40	46090	46085	6	39969	39955	14	35824	35798	27	32688	32645	43	20
41	45960	45955	6	39888	39874	14	35765	35738	27	32642	32598	44	19
42	45832	45826	6	39808	39793	14	35707	35680	27	32595	32551	44	18
43	45705	45699	6	39727	39713	15	35648	35621	27	32549	32505	44	17
44	45579	45573	6	39648	39633	15	35590	35562	28	32503	32459	45	16
45	45455	45448	6	39569	39554	15	35532	35504	28	32458	32413	45	15
46	45331	45325	6	39490	39475	15	35474	35446	28	32412	32367	45	14
47	45209	45202	6	39412	39396	15	35417	35388	28	32367	32321	45	13
48	45088	45081	6	39334	39319	16	35360	35331	29	32322	32276	46	12
49	44968	44961	7	39257	39241	16	35303	35274	29	32277	32231	46	11
50	44849	44842	7	39180	39164	16	35246	35217	29	32232	32185	46	10
51	44731	44724	7	39104	39088	16	35190	35160	29	32187	32140	47	09
52	44614	44607	7	39028	39011	16	35133	35104	30	32142	32095	47	08
53	44498	44491	7	38952	38936	17	35078	35048	30	32098	32051	47	07
54	44383	44376	7	38877	38861	17	35022	34992	30	32054	32006	48	06
55	44270	44262	7	38803	38786	17	34966	34936	30	32010	31962	48	05
56	44157	44150	7	38729	38711	17	34911	34880	31	31966	31917	48	04
57	44045	44038	8	38655	38638	17	34856	34825	31	31922	31873	49	03
58	43934	43927	8	38581	38564	17	34801	34770	31	31878	31829	49	02
59	43824	43817	8	38509	38491	18	34747	34715	32	31835	31785	49	01
60	43715	43707	8	38436	38418	18	34692	34661	32	31791	31741	50	00
	S	+T	C	S	+T	C	S	+T	C	S	+T	C	Min.
			178°			177°			176°			175°	
	C	−T	S	C	−T	S	C	−T	S	C	−T	S	
			88°			87°			86°			85°	

31791   50   31741
    S/C   161 ±T
24170   161   24009

Min.	**5°** S	+T	C	**6°** S	+T	C	**7°** S	+T	C	**8°** S	+T	C	
	95° C	−T	S	**96°** C	−T	S	**97°** C	−T	S	**98°** C	−T	S	
00	31791	31741	50	29423	29351	72	27423	27326	97	25693	25566	127	60
01	31748	31698	50	29387	29315	72	27392	27294	98	25666	25538	128	59
02	31705	31654	50	29351	29279	72	27362	27263	98	25640	25511	128	58
03	31662	31611	51	29315	29242	73	27331	27232	99	25613	25484	129	57
04	31619	31568	51	29280	29206	73	27300	27201	99	25586	25456	130	56
05	31576	31525	51	29244	29170	74	27270	27170	100	25559	25429	130	55
06	31534	31482	52	29208	29134	74	27239	27139	100	25533	25402	131	54
07	31491	31439	52	29173	29099	74	27209	27108	101	25506	25375	131	53
08	31449	31397	52	29138	29063	75	27179	27077	101	25479	25348	132	52
09	31407	31354	53	29102	29027	75	27148	27047	102	25453	25321	132	51
10	31365	31312	53	29067	28992	76	27118	27016	102	25426	25294	133	50
11	31323	31270	53	29032	28956	76	27088	26985	103	25400	25267	133	49
12	31281	31228	54	28997	28921	76	27058	26955	103	25374	25240	134	48
13	31240	31186	54	28963	28886	77	27028	26924	104	25348	25213	134	47
14	31198	31144	54	28928	28851	77	26998	26894	104	25321	25186	135	46
15	31157	31102	55	28893	28815	78	26968	26864	105	25295	25160	136	45
16	31116	31061	55	28859	28780	78	26939	26834	105	25269	25133	136	44
17	31075	31019	55	28824	28746	79	26909	26803	106	25243	25106	137	43
18	31034	30978	56	28790	28711	79	26879	26773	106	25217	25080	137	42
19	30993	30937	56	28755	28676	79	26850	26743	107	25191	25053	138	41
20	30953	30896	57	28721	28641	80	26820	26713	107	25165	25027	138	40
21	30912	30855	57	28687	28607	80	26791	26683	107	25139	25000	139	39
22	30872	30814	57	28653	28573	81	26761	26653	108	25113	24974	139	38
23	30831	30774	58	28619	28538	81	26732	26624	108	25088	24948	140	37
24	30791	30733	58	28585	28504	81	26703	26594	109	25062	24921	141	36
25	30751	30693	58	28552	28470	82	26674	26564	109	25036	24895	141	35
26	30711	30653	59	28518	28436	82	26645	26535	110	25011	24869	142	34
27	30671	30612	59	28484	28402	83	26616	26505	110	24985	24843	142	33
28	30632	30572	59	28451	28368	83	26587	26476	111	24960	24817	143	32
29	30592	30532	60	28418	28334	84	26558	26446	111	24934	24791	143	31
30	30553	30493	60	28384	28300	84	26529	26417	112	24909	24765	144	30
31	30514	30453	60	28351	28267	84	26500	26388	112	24884	24739	144	29
32	30474	30413	61	28318	28233	85	26472	26359	113	24858	24713	145	28
33	30435	30374	61	28285	28200	85	26443	26330	113	24833	24687	146	27
34	30396	30335	62	28252	28166	86	26414	26300	114	24808	24662	146	26
35	30358	30296	62	28219	28133	86	26386	26271	114	24783	24636	147	25
36	30319	30256	62	28186	28100	87	26358	26243	115	24758	24610	147	24
37	30280	30217	63	28153	28066	87	26329	26214	115	24733	24585	148	23
38	30242	30179	63	28121	28033	88	26301	26185	116	24708	24559	148	22
39	30203	30140	63	28088	28000	88	26273	26156	116	24683	24534	149	21
40	30165	30101	64	28056	27967	88	26244	26127	117	24658	24508	150	20
41	30127	30063	64	28023	27935	89	26216	26099	117	24633	24483	150	19
42	30089	30024	65	27991	27902	89	26188	26070	118	24608	24457	151	18
43	30051	29986	65	27959	27869	90	26160	26042	119	24583	24432	151	17
44	30013	29948	65	27927	27837	90	26132	26013	119	24559	24407	152	16
45	29976	29910	66	27895	27804	91	26104	25985	120	24534	24382	153	15
46	29938	29872	66	27863	27772	91	26077	25956	120	24510	24356	153	14
47	29900	29834	66	27831	27739	92	26049	25928	121	24485	24331	154	13
48	29863	29796	67	27799	27707	92	26021	25900	121	24460	24306	154	12
49	29826	29759	67	27767	27675	92	25993	25872	122	24436	24281	155	11
50	29789	29721	68	27736	27643	93	25966	25844	122	24412	24256	155	10
51	29752	29684	68	27704	27611	93	25938	25816	123	24387	24231	156	09
52	29715	29646	68	27673	27579	94	25911	25788	123	24363	24206	157	08
53	29678	29609	69	27641	27547	94	25884	25760	124	24339	24181	157	07
54	29641	29572	69	27610	27515	95	25856	25732	124	24314	24157	158	06
55	29605	29535	70	27578	27483	95	25829	25704	125	24290	24132	158	05
56	29568	29498	70	27547	27452	96	25802	25676	125	24266	24107	159	04
57	29532	29461	70	27516	27420	96	25775	25649	126	24242	24082	160	03
58	29495	29425	71	27485	27389	97	25747	25621	126	24218	24058	160	02
59	29459	29388	71	27454	27357	97	25720	25593	127	24194	24033	161	01
60	29423	29351	72	27423	27326	97	25693	25566	127	24170	24009	161	00
	S	+T	C **174°**	S	+T	C **173°**	S	+T	C **172°**	S	+T	C **171°**	Min.
	C	−T	S **84°**	C	−T	S **83°**	C	−T	S **82°**	C	−T	S **81°**	

	24170	161	24009
	S/C		±T
	19437	338	19099

Min.	**9°** S	+T	C	**10°** S	+T	C	**11°** S	+T	C	**12°** S	+T	C	
	99° C	−T	S	**100°** C	−T	S	**101°** C	−T	S	**102°** C	−T	S	
00	24170	24009	161	22810	22610	199	21582	21340	242	20464	20176	288	60
01	24146	23984	162	22788	22588	200	21563	21320	242	20446	20157	289	59
02	24122	23960	163	22767	22566	201	21543	21300	243	20428	20139	289	58
03	24098	23935	163	22746	22544	201	21524	21280	244	20410	20120	290	57
04	24075	23911	164	22724	22522	202	21504	21260	245	20393	20101	291	56
05	24051	23887	164	22703	22500	203	21485	21240	245	20375	20083	292	55
06	24027	23862	165	22682	22478	203	21466	21220	246	20357	20064	293	54
07	24004	23838	166	22660	22456	204	21446	21200	247	20339	20046	294	53
08	23980	23814	166	22639	22434	205	21427	21179	248	20322	20027	294	52
09	23956	23790	167	22618	22412	206	21408	21159	248	20304	20009	295	51
10	23933	23766	167	22597	22391	206	21389	21140	249	20287	19991	296	50
11	23910	23741	168	22576	22369	207	21369	21120	250	20269	19972	297	49
12	23886	23717	169	22555	22347	208	21350	21100	251	20251	19954	298	48
13	23863	23693	169	22534	22325	208	21331	21080	251	20234	19936	298	47
14	23839	23669	170	22513	22304	209	21312	21060	252	20216	19917	299	46
15	23816	23646	171	22492	22282	210	21293	21040	253	20199	19899	300	45
16	23793	23622	171	22471	22260	210	21274	21020	254	20182	19881	301	44
17	23770	23598	172	22450	22239	211	21255	21001	254	20164	19862	302	43
18	23746	23574	172	22429	22217	212	21236	20981	255	20147	19844	303	42
19	23723	23550	173	22408	22196	212	21217	20961	256	20129	19826	303	41
20	23700	23527	174	22387	22174	213	21198	20941	257	20112	19808	304	40
21	23677	23503	174	22366	22153	214	21179	20922	257	20095	19790	305	39
22	23654	23479	175	22346	22131	214	21160	20902	258	20077	19772	306	38
23	23631	23456	176	22325	22110	215	21141	20883	259	20060	19753	307	37
24	23608	23432	176	22304	22088	216	21123	20863	260	20043	19735	308	36
25	23585	23409	177	22284	22067	217	21104	20843	260	20026	19717	308	35
26	23563	23385	177	22263	22046	217	21085	20824	261	20008	19699	309	34
27	23540	23362	178	22243	22025	218	21066	20804	262	19991	19681	310	33
28	23517	23338	179	22222	22003	219	21048	20785	263	19974	19663	311	32
29	23494	23315	179	22201	21982	219	21029	20766	263	19957	19645	312	31
30	23472	23292	180	22181	21961	220	21010	20746	264	19940	19627	313	30
31	23449	23269	181	22161	21940	221	20992	20727	265	19923	19609	313	29
32	23427	23245	181	22140	21919	221	20973	20707	266	19906	19592	314	28
33	23404	23222	182	22120	21898	222	20955	20688	267	19889	19574	315	27
34	23381	23199	182	22099	21877	223	20936	20669	267	19872	19556	316	26
35	23359	23176	183	22079	21856	224	20918	20649	268	19855	19538	317	25
36	23337	23153	184	22059	21835	224	20899	20630	269	19838	19520	318	24
37	23314	23130	184	22039	21814	225	20881	20611	270	19821	19502	318	23
38	23292	23107	185	22018	21793	226	20862	20592	270	19804	19485	319	22
39	23270	23084	186	21998	21772	226	20844	20573	271	19787	19467	320	21
40	23247	23061	186	21978	21751	227	20825	20553	272	19770	19449	321	20
41	23225	23038	187	21958	21730	228	20807	20534	273	19753	19431	322	19
42	23203	23015	188	21938	21709	229	20789	20515	274	19736	19414	323	18
43	23181	22992	188	21918	21689	229	20770	20496	274	19720	19396	324	17
44	23159	22970	189	21898	21668	230	20752	20477	275	19703	19378	324	16
45	23136	22947	190	21878	21647	231	20734	20458	276	19686	19361	325	15
46	23114	22924	190	21858	21627	231	20716	20439	277	19669	19343	326	14
47	23092	22902	191	21838	21606	232	20698	20420	277	19653	19326	327	13
48	23070	22879	192	21818	21585	233	20679	20401	278	19636	19308	328	12
49	23049	22856	192	21798	21565	234	20661	20382	279	19619	19291	329	11
50	23027	22834	193	21779	21544	234	20643	20363	280	19603	19273	330	10
51	23005	22811	193	21759	21524	235	20625	20344	281	19586	19256	330	09
52	22983	22789	194	21739	21503	236	20607	20326	281	19569	19238	331	08
53	22961	22766	195	21719	21483	236	20589	20307	282	19553	19221	332	07
54	22940	22744	195	21700	21462	237	20571	20288	283	19536	19203	333	06
55	22918	22722	196	21680	21442	238	20553	20269	284	19520	19186	334	05
56	22896	22699	197	21660	21422	239	20535	20251	285	19503	19168	335	04
57	22875	22677	197	21641	21401	239	20517	20232	285	19487	19151	336	03
58	22853	22655	198	21621	21381	240	20499	20213	286	19470	19134	337	02
59	22831	22633	199	21602	21361	241	20481	20194	287	19454	19116	337	01
60	22810	22610	199	21582	21340	242	20464	20176	288	19437	19099	338	00
	S	+T	C	S	+T	C	S	+T	C	S	+T	C	Min.
			170°			169°			168°			167°	
	C	−T	S	C	−T	S	C	−T	S	C	−T	S	
			80°			79°			78°			77°	

```
19437        338          19099
       S/C              ±T
16022        582          15440
```

Min.	13° S	+T	C	14° S	+T	C	15° S	+T	C	16° S	+T	C	
	103° C	−T	S	104° C	−T	S	105° C	−T	S	106° C	−T	S	'
00	19437	19099	338	18490	18097	393	17610	17158	452	16790	16275	515	60
01	19421	19082	339	18475	18081	394	17596	17143	453	16777	16261	516	59
02	19405	19065	340	18459	18065	395	17582	17128	454	16763	16247	517	58
03	19388	19047	341	18444	18049	396	17568	17113	455	16750	16232	518	57
04	19372	19030	342	18429	18032	397	17554	17098	456	16737	16218	519	56
05	19356	19013	343	18414	18016	398	17540	17083	457	16724	16204	520	55
06	19339	18996	344	18399	18000	399	17526	17068	458	16711	16190	521	54
07	19323	18979	344	18384	17984	400	17512	17053	459	16698	16175	522	53
08	19307	18961	345	18369	17968	400	17497	17038	460	16685	16161	523	52
09	19290	18944	346	18354	17952	401	17483	17023	461	16671	16147	525	51
10	19274	18927	347	18339	17936	402	17469	17008	462	16658	16133	526	50
11	19258	18910	348	18324	17920	403	17456	16993	463	16645	16119	527	49
12	19242	18893	349	18309	17904	404	17442	16978	464	16632	16104	528	48
13	19226	18876	350	18294	17888	405	17428	16963	465	16619	16090	529	47
14	19210	18859	351	18279	17873	406	17414	16948	466	16606	16076	530	46
15	19194	18842	352	18264	17857	407	17400	16933	467	16593	16062	531	45
16	19177	18825	352	18249	17841	408	17386	16918	468	16580	16048	532	44
17	19161	18808	353	18234	17825	409	17372	16903	469	16567	16034	533	43
18	19145	18791	354	18219	17809	410	17358	16888	470	16554	16020	535	42
19	19129	18774	355	18204	17793	411	17344	16873	471	16541	16006	536	41
20	19113	18757	356	18189	17777	412	17330	16858	472	16528	15992	537	40
21	19097	18740	357	18175	17762	413	17317	16843	473	16515	15978	538	39
22	19081	18724	358	18160	17746	414	17303	16829	474	16503	15964	539	38
23	19065	18707	359	18145	17730	415	17289	16814	475	16490	15950	540	37
24	19050	18690	360	18130	17714	416	17275	16799	476	16477	15936	541	36
25	19034	18673	361	18116	17699	417	17262	16784	477	16464	15922	542	35
26	19018	18656	361	18101	17683	418	17248	16769	478	16451	15908	543	34
27	19002	18640	362	18086	17667	419	17234	16755	480	16438	15894	545	33
28	18986	18623	363	18071	17652	420	17220	16740	481	16425	15880	546	32
29	18970	18606	364	18057	17636	421	17207	16725	482	16413	15866	547	31
30	18954	18589	365	18042	17620	422	17193	16710	483	16400	15852	548	30
31	18939	18573	366	18027	17605	423	17179	16696	484	16387	15838	549	29
32	18923	18556	367	18013	17589	424	17166	16681	485	16374	15824	550	28
33	18907	18539	368	17998	17573	425	17152	16666	486	16361	15810	551	27
34	18891	18523	369	17984	17558	426	17138	16652	487	16349	15796	552	26
35	18876	18506	370	17969	17542	427	17125	16637	488	16336	15782	554	25
36	18860	18490	371	17954	17527	428	17111	16622	489	16323	15769	555	24
37	18844	18473	371	17940	17511	429	17098	16608	490	16311	15755	556	23
38	18829	18456	372	17925	17496	430	17084	16593	491	16298	15741	557	22
39	18813	18440	373	17911	17480	431	17071	16578	492	16285	15727	558	21
40	18798	18423	374	17896	17465	432	17057	16564	493	16272	15713	559	20
41	18782	18407	375	17882	17449	433	17044	16549	494	16260	15700	560	19
42	18766	18390	376	17867	17434	434	17030	16535	495	16247	15686	561	18
43	18751	18374	377	17853	17418	435	17017	16520	496	16235	15672	563	17
44	18735	18357	378	17839	17403	436	17003	16506	498	16222	15658	564	16
45	18720	18341	379	17824	17388	437	16990	16491	499	16209	15644	565	15
46	18704	18325	380	17810	17372	438	16976	16477	500	16197	15631	566	14
47	18689	18308	381	17795	17357	439	16963	16462	501	16184	15617	567	13
48	18674	18292	382	17781	17341	440	16950	16448	502	16172	15603	568	12
49	18658	18276	383	17767	17326	441	16936	16433	503	16159	15590	569	11
50	18643	18259	383	17752	17311	442	16923	16419	504	16147	15576	571	10
51	18627	18243	384	17738	17295	443	16909	16404	505	16134	15562	572	09
52	18612	18227	385	17724	17280	444	16896	16390	506	16122	15549	573	08
53	18597	18210	386	17710	17265	445	16883	16376	507	16109	15535	574	07
54	18581	18194	387	17695	17250	446	16869	16361	508	16097	15521	575	06
55	18566	18178	388	17681	17234	447	16856	16347	509	16084	15508	576	05
56	18551	18162	389	17667	17219	448	16843	16332	510	16072	15494	577	04
57	18535	18145	390	17653	17204	449	16830	16318	511	16059	15481	579	03
58	18520	18129	391	17638	17189	450	16816	16304	513	16047	15467	580	02
59	18505	18113	392	17624	17174	451	16803	16289	514	16034	15453	581	01
60	18490	18097	393	17610	17158	452	16790	16275	515	16022	15440	582	00
	S	+T	C 166°	S	+T	C 165°	S	+T	C 164°	S	+T	C 163°	Min.
	C	−T	S 76°	C	−T	S 75°	C	−T	S 74°	C	−T	S 73°	

	16022	582		15440
		S/C		±T
	13370	895		12475

Min.	17° S	+T	C	18° S	+T	C	19° S	+T	C	20° S	+T	C	
	107° C	−T	S	108° C	−T	S	109° C	−T	S	110° C	−T	S	
00	16022	15440	582	15301	14647	654	14621	13891	730	13978	13168	810	60
01	16010	15426	583	15289	14634	655	14610	13879	731	13968	13156	812	59
02	15997	15413	584	15277	14621	656	14599	13866	733	13958	13144	813	58
03	15985	15399	586	15266	14608	658	14588	13854	734	13947	13133	815	57
04	15972	15386	587	15254	14595	659	14577	13842	735	13937	13121	816	56
05	15960	15372	588	15242	14582	660	14566	13829	736	13927	13109	817	55
06	15948	15359	589	15231	14570	661	14555	13817	738	13916	13097	819	54
07	15935	15345	590	15219	14557	662	14544	13805	739	13906	13086	820	53
08	15923	15332	591	15208	14544	664	14533	13793	740	13895	13074	822	52
09	15911	15318	593	15196	14531	665	14522	13780	742	13885	13062	823	51
10	15899	15305	594	15184	14518	666	14511	13768	743	13875	13051	824	50
11	15886	15291	595	15173	14505	667	14500	13756	744	13864	13039	826	49
12	15874	15278	596	15161	14493	669	14489	13744	746	13854	13027	827	48
13	15862	15265	597	15150	14480	670	14479	13732	747	13844	13015	828	47
14	15850	15251	598	15138	14467	671	14468	13719	748	13834	13004	830	46
15	15837	15238	600	15127	14454	672	14457	13707	750	13823	12992	831	45
16	15825	15224	601	15115	14442	674	14446	13695	751	13813	12980	833	44
17	15813	15211	602	15104	14429	675	14435	13683	752	13803	12969	834	43
18	15801	15198	603	15092	14416	676	14424	13671	754	13793	12957	835	42
19	15789	15184	604	15081	14404	677	14413	13659	755	13782	12945	837	41
20	15777	15171	606	15070	14391	679	14403	13646	756	13772	12934	838	40
21	15764	15158	607	15058	14378	680	14392	13634	758	13762	12922	840	39
22	15752	15144	608	15047	14365	681	14381	13622	759	13752	12911	841	38
23	15740	15131	609	15035	14353	682	14370	13610	760	13741	12899	842	37
24	15728	15118	610	15024	14340	684	14360	13598	762	13731	12887	844	36
25	15716	15105	611	15012	14328	685	14349	13586	763	13721	12876	845	35
26	15704	15091	613	15001	14315	686	14338	13574	764	13711	12864	847	34
27	15692	15078	614	14990	14302	688	14327	13562	766	13701	12853	848	33
28	15680	15065	615	14978	14290	689	14317	13550	767	13691	12841	850	32
29	15668	15052	616	14967	14277	690	14306	13538	768	13680	12829	851	31
30	15656	15038	617	14956	14264	691	14295	13526	770	13670	12818	852	30
31	15644	15025	619	14944	14252	693	14284	13513	771	13660	12806	854	29
32	15632	15012	620	14933	14239	694	14274	13501	772	13650	12795	855	28
33	15620	14999	621	14922	14227	695	14263	13489	774	13640	12783	857	27
34	15608	14986	622	14910	14214	696	14252	13477	775	13630	12772	858	26
35	15596	14972	623	14899	14202	698	14242	13465	776	13620	12760	859	25
36	15584	14959	625	14888	14189	699	14231	13453	778	13610	12749	861	24
37	15572	14946	626	14877	14176	700	14220	13441	779	13600	12737	862	23
38	15560	14933	627	14865	14164	701	14210	13429	780	13589	12726	864	22
39	15548	14920	628	14854	14151	703	14199	13417	782	13579	12714	865	21
40	15536	14907	629	14843	14139	704	14189	13406	783	13569	12703	867	20
41	15524	14894	631	14832	14126	705	14178	13394	784	13559	12691	868	19
42	15512	14881	632	14821	14114	707	14167	13382	786	13549	12680	869	18
43	15501	14867	633	14809	14101	708	14157	13370	787	13539	12668	871	17
44	15489	14854	634	14798	14089	709	14146	13358	789	13529	12657	872	16
45	15477	14841	635	14787	14077	710	14136	13346	790	13519	12645	874	15
46	15465	14828	637	14776	14064	712	14125	13334	791	13509	12634	875	14
47	15453	14815	638	14765	14052	713	14115	13322	793	13499	12623	877	13
48	15441	14802	639	14754	14039	714	14104	13310	794	13489	12611	878	12
49	15430	14789	640	14742	14027	716	14094	13298	795	13479	12600	880	11
50	15418	14776	642	14731	14014	717	14083	13286	797	13469	12588	881	10
51	15406	14763	643	14720	14002	718	14073	13274	798	13459	12577	882	09
52	15394	14750	644	14709	13990	719	14062	13263	799	13449	12566	884	08
53	15382	14737	645	14698	13977	721	14052	13251	801	13439	12554	885	07
54	15371	14724	646	14687	13965	722	14041	13239	802	13430	12543	887	06
55	15359	14711	648	14676	13953	723	14031	13227	804	13420	12531	888	05
56	15347	14698	649	14665	13940	725	14020	13215	805	13410	12520	890	04
57	15336	14685	650	14654	13928	726	14010	13203	806	13400	12509	891	03
58	15324	14673	651	14643	13915	727	13999	13192	808	13390	12497	893	02
59	15312	14660	653	14632	13903	729	13989	13180	809	13380	12486	894	01
60	15301	14647	654	14621	13891	730	13978	13168	810	13370	12475	895	00
	S	+T	C	S	+T	C	S	+T	C	S	+T	C	Min.
			162°			161°			160°			159°	
	C	−T	S	C	−T	S	C	−T	S	C	−T	S	
			72°			71°			70°			69°	

13370   895   12475
　　S/C　　　　±T
11222   1282   9940

Min.	21° S	+T	C	22° S	+T	C	23° S	+T	C	24° S	+T	C	
	111° C	−T	S	112° C	−T	S	113° C	−T	S	114° C	−T	S	Min.
00	13370	12475	895	12793	11808	985	12244	11164	1079	11721	10543	1178	60
01	13360	12463	897	12783	11797	987	12235	11154	1081	11712	10532	1180	59
02	13350	12452	898	12774	11786	988	12226	11143	1082	11704	10522	1181	58
03	13341	12441	900	12765	11775	990	12217	11133	1084	11695	10512	1183	57
04	13331	12429	901	12755	11764	991	12208	11122	1086	11687	10502	1185	56
05	13321	12418	903	12746	11753	993	12199	11112	1087	11678	10492	1187	55
06	13311	12407	904	12737	11742	994	12190	11101	1089	11670	10481	1188	54
07	13301	12396	906	12727	11731	996	12181	11091	1091	11661	10471	1190	53
08	13291	12384	907	12718	11721	997	12172	11080	1092	11653	10461	1192	52
09	13282	12373	909	12709	11710	999	12164	11070	1094	11644	10451	1193	51
10	13272	12362	910	12699	11699	1000	12155	11059	1095	11636	10441	1195	50
11	13262	12351	912	12690	11688	1002	12146	11049	1097	11627	10431	1197	49
12	13252	12339	913	12681	11677	1003	12137	11038	1099	11619	10420	1198	48
13	13242	12328	914	12671	11666	1005	12128	11028	1100	11611	10410	1200	47
14	13233	12317	916	12662	11656	1007	12119	11017	1102	11602	10400	1202	46
15	13223	12306	917	12653	11645	1008	12111	11007	1103	11594	10390	1204	45
16	13213	12294	919	12644	11634	1010	12102	10997	1105	11585	10380	1205	44
17	13204	12283	920	12634	11623	1011	12093	10986	1107	11577	10370	1207	43
18	13194	12272	922	12625	11612	1013	12084	10976	1108	11568	10360	1209	42
19	13184	12261	923	12616	11602	1014	12075	10965	1110	11560	10350	1210	41
20	13174	12250	925	12607	11591	1016	12067	10955	1112	11552	10340	1212	40
21	13165	12238	926	12597	11580	1017	12058	10944	1113	11543	10329	1214	39
22	13155	12227	928	12588	11569	1019	12049	10934	1115	11535	10319	1216	38
23	13145	12216	929	12579	11558	1021	12040	10924	1117	11527	10309	1217	37
24	13136	12205	931	12570	11548	1022	12031	10913	1118	11518	10299	1219	36
25	13126	12194	932	12561	11537	1024	12023	10903	1120	11510	10289	1221	35
26	13116	12183	934	12551	11526	1025	12014	10892	1121	11502	10279	1222	34
27	13107	12171	935	12542	11515	1027	12005	10882	1123	11493	10269	1224	33
28	13097	12160	937	12533	11505	1028	11996	10872	1125	11485	10259	1226	32
29	13087	12149	938	12524	11494	1030	11988	10861	1126	11477	10249	1228	31
30	13078	12138	940	12515	11483	1032	11979	10851	1128	11468	10239	1229	30
31	13068	12127	941	12506	11473	1033	11970	10841	1130	11460	10229	1231	29
32	13059	12116	943	12497	11462	1035	11962	10830	1131	11452	10219	1233	28
33	13049	12105	944	12487	11451	1036	11953	10820	1133	11443	10209	1234	27
34	13039	12094	946	12478	11440	1038	11944	10810	1135	11435	10199	1236	26
35	13030	12083	947	12469	11430	1039	11936	10799	1136	11427	10189	1238	25
36	13020	12072	949	12460	11419	1041	11927	10789	1138	11418	10179	1240	24
37	13011	12060	950	12451	11408	1043	11918	10779	1140	11410	10169	1241	23
38	13001	12049	952	12442	11398	1044	11910	10768	1141	11402	10159	1243	22
39	12991	12038	953	12433	11387	1046	11901	10758	1143	11394	10149	1245	21
40	12982	12027	955	12424	11376	1047	11892	10748	1145	11385	10139	1247	20
41	12972	12016	956	12415	11366	1049	11884	10737	1146	11377	10129	1248	19
42	12963	12005	958	12406	11355	1050	11875	10727	1148	11369	10119	1250	18
43	12953	11994	959	12396	11344	1052	11866	10717	1150	11361	10109	1252	17
44	12944	11983	961	12387	11334	1054	11858	10706	1151	11352	10099	1254	16
45	12934	11972	962	12378	11323	1055	11849	10696	1153	11344	10089	1255	15
46	12925	11961	964	12369	11313	1057	11840	10686	1155	11336	10079	1257	14
47	12915	11950	965	12360	11302	1058	11832	10676	1156	11328	10069	1259	13
48	12906	11939	967	12351	11291	1060	11823	10665	1158	11320	10059	1261	12
49	12896	11928	968	12342	11281	1062	11815	10655	1160	11311	10049	1262	11
50	12887	11917	970	12333	11270	1063	11806	10645	1161	11303	10039	1264	10
51	12877	11906	971	12324	11260	1065	11797	10635	1163	11295	10029	1266	09
52	12868	11895	973	12315	11249	1066	11789	10624	1165	11287	10019	1268	08
53	12859	11884	974	12306	11238	1068	11780	10614	1166	11279	10009	1269	07
54	12849	11873	976	12297	11228	1070	11772	10604	1168	11270	9999	1271	06
55	12840	11862	977	12288	11217	1071	11763	10594	1170	11262	9989	1273	05
56	12830	11851	979	12279	11207	1073	11755	10583	1171	11254	9979	1275	04
57	12821	11840	980	12270	11196	1074	11746	10573	1173	11246	9970	1276	03
58	12812	11830	982	12262	11186	1076	11738	10563	1175	11238	9960	1278	02
59	12802	11819	983	12253	11175	1078	11729	10553	1176	11230	9950	1280	01
60	12793	11808	985	12244	11164	1079	11721	10543	1178	11222	9940	1282	00
	S	+T	C 158°	S	+T	C 157°	S	+T	C 156°	S	+T	C 155°	Min.
	C	−T	S 68°	C	−T	S 67°	C	−T	S 66°	C	−T	S 65°	

11222	1282	9940
	S/C	±T
9433	1745	7687

Min.	25° S / C	+T / −T	C / S	26° S / C	+T / −T	C / S	27° S / C	+T / −T	C / S	28° S / C	+T / −T	C / S	Min.
	115°			116°			117°			118°			
00	11222	9940	1282	10745	9355	1390	10289	8785	1504	9852	8230	1622	60
01	11213	9930	1283	10737	9345	1392	10281	8776	1506	9845	8221	1624	59
02	11205	9920	1285	10729	9335	1394	10274	8766	1507	9837	8211	1626	58
03	11197	9910	1287	10721	9326	1396	10266	8757	1509	9830	8202	1628	57
04	11189	9900	1289	10714	9316	1398	10259	8748	1511	9823	8193	1630	56
05	11181	9890	1291	10706	9307	1399	10251	8738	1513	9816	8184	1632	55
06	11173	9881	1292	10698	9297	1401	10244	8729	1515	9809	8175	1634	54
07	11165	9871	1294	10690	9287	1403	10237	8720	1517	9802	8166	1636	53
08	11157	9861	1296	10683	9278	1405	10229	8710	1519	9795	8157	1638	52
09	11149	9851	1298	10675	9268	1407	10222	8701	1521	9788	8148	1640	51
10	11141	9841	1299	10667	9259	1409	10214	8692	1523	9781	8139	1642	50
11	11133	9831	1301	10660	9249	1411	10207	8682	1525	9774	8129	1644	49
12	11124	9821	1303	10652	9239	1412	10200	8673	1527	9767	8120	1646	48
13	11116	9812	1305	10644	9230	1414	10192	8664	1529	9759	8111	1648	47
14	11108	9802	1307	10637	9220	1416	10185	8654	1531	9752	8102	1650	46
15	11100	9792	1308	10629	9211	1418	10178	8645	1533	9745	8093	1652	45
16	11092	9782	1310	10621	9201	1420	10170	8636	1535	9738	8084	1654	44
17	11084	9772	1312	10613	9192	1422	10163	8626	1537	9731	8075	1656	43
18	11076	9762	1314	10606	9182	1424	10156	8617	1539	9724	8066	1658	42
19	11068	9753	1316	10598	9173	1426	10148	8608	1541	9717	8057	1660	41
20	11060	9743	1317	10590	9163	1427	10141	8598	1542	9710	8048	1663	40
21	11052	9733	1319	10583	9154	1429	10134	8589	1544	9703	8039	1665	39
22	11044	9723	1321	10575	9144	1431	10126	8580	1546	9696	8029	1667	38
23	11036	9714	1323	10568	9134	1433	10119	8571	1548	9689	8020	1669	37
24	11028	9704	1325	10560	9125	1435	10112	8561	1550	9682	8011	1671	36
25	11020	9694	1326	10552	9115	1437	10104	8552	1552	9675	8002	1673	35
26	11012	9684	1328	10545	9106	1439	10097	8543	1554	9668	7993	1675	34
27	11004	9674	1330	10537	9096	1441	10090	8533	1556	9661	7984	1677	33
28	10996	9665	1332	10529	9087	1442	10082	8524	1558	9654	7975	1679	32
29	10988	9655	1334	10522	9077	1444	10075	8515	1560	9647	7966	1681	31
30	10980	9645	1335	10514	9068	1446	10068	8506	1562	9640	7957	1683	30
31	10973	9635	1337	10507	9058	1448	10061	8496	1564	9633	7948	1685	29
32	10965	9626	1339	10499	9049	1450	10053	8487	1566	9626	7939	1687	28
33	10957	9616	1341	10491	9039	1452	10046	8478	1568	9619	7930	1689	27
34	10949	9606	1343	10484	9030	1454	10039	8469	1570	9612	7921	1691	26
35	10941	9596	1344	10476	9021	1456	10031	8459	1572	9605	7912	1693	25
36	10933	9587	1346	10469	9011	1458	10024	8450	1574	9598	7903	1695	24
37	10925	9577	1348	10461	9002	1460	10017	8441	1576	9591	7894	1697	23
38	10917	9567	1350	10454	8992	1461	10010	8432	1578	9584	7885	1700	22
39	10909	9558	1352	10446	8983	1463	10003	8423	1580	9577	7876	1702	21
40	10901	9548	1353	10438	8973	1465	9995	8413	1582	9571	7867	1704	20
41	10893	9538	1355	10431	8964	1467	9988	8404	1584	9564	7858	1706	19
42	10886	9528	1357	10423	8954	1469	9981	8395	1586	9557	7849	1708	18
43	10878	9519	1359	10416	8945	1471	9974	8386	1588	9550	7840	1710	17
44	10870	9509	1361	10408	8935	1473	9966	8377	1590	9543	7831	1712	16
45	10862	9499	1363	10401	8926	1475	9959	8367	1592	9536	7822	1714	15
46	10854	9490	1364	10393	8917	1477	9952	8358	1594	9529	7813	1716	14
47	10846	9480	1366	10386	8907	1479	9945	8349	1596	9522	7804	1718	13
48	10838	9470	1368	10378	8898	1480	9938	8340	1598	9515	7795	1720	12
49	10831	9461	1370	10371	8888	1482	9930	8331	1600	9508	7786	1722	11
50	10823	9451	1372	10363	8879	1484	9923	8321	1602	9501	7777	1724	10
51	10815	9441	1374	10356	8870	1486	9916	8312	1604	9495	7768	1727	09
52	10807	9432	1375	10348	8860	1488	9909	8303	1606	9488	7759	1729	08
53	10799	9422	1377	10341	8851	1490	9902	8294	1608	9481	7750	1731	07
54	10791	9412	1379	10333	8841	1492	9895	8285	1610	9474	7741	1733	06
55	10784	9403	1381	10326	8832	1494	9887	8276	1612	9467	7732	1735	05
56	10776	9393	1383	10318	8823	1496	9880	8266	1614	9460	7723	1737	04
57	10768	9383	1385	10311	8813	1498	9873	8257	1616	9453	7714	1739	03
58	10760	9374	1387	10303	8804	1500	9866	8248	1618	9447	7705	1741	02
59	10753	9364	1388	10296	8794	1502	9859	8239	1620	9440	7696	1743	01
60	10745	9355	1390	10289	8785	1504	9852	8230	1622	9433	7687	1745	00
	S	+T	C	S	+T	C	S	+T	C	S	+T	C	Min.
			154°			153°			152°			151°	
	C	−T	S	C	−T	S	C	−T	S	C	−T	S	
			64°			63°			62°			61°	

```
9433    1745        7687
    S/C           ±T
7917    2292        5624
```

Min.	29° S +T C / 119° C −T S			30° S +T C / 120° C −T S			31° S +T C / 121° C −T S			32° S +T C / 122° C −T S			
00	9433	7687	1745	9031	7157	1874	8645	6637	2008	8274	6126	2147	60
01	9426	7679	1748	9024	7148	1876	8639	6628	2010	8268	6118	2150	59
02	9419	7670	1750	9018	7139	1878	8632	6620	2013	8262	6109	2152	58
03	9412	7661	1752	9011	7131	1881	8626	6611	2015	8256	6101	2154	57
04	9406	7652	1754	9005	7122	1883	8620	6602	2017	8249	6093	2157	56
05	9399	7643	1756	8998	7113	1885	8613	6594	2019	8243	6084	2159	55
06	9392	7634	1758	8992	7104	1887	8607	6585	2022	8237	6076	2162	54
07	9385	7625	1760	8985	7096	1889	8601	6577	2024	8231	6067	2164	53
08	9378	7616	1762	8979	7087	1892	8594	6568	2026	8225	6059	2166	52
09	9372	7607	1764	8972	7078	1894	8588	6560	2029	8219	6051	2169	51
10	9365	7598	1767	8965	7069	1896	8582	6551	2031	8213	6042	2171	50
11	9358	7589	1769	8959	7061	1898	8576	6543	2033	8207	6034	2174	49
12	9351	7580	1771	8952	7052	1900	8569	6534	2035	8201	6025	2176	48
13	9344	7572	1773	8946	7043	1903	8563	6525	2038	8195	6017	2178	47
14	9338	7563	1775	8939	7035	1905	8557	6517	2040	8189	6008	2181	46
15	9331	7554	1777	8933	7026	1907	8551	6508	2042	8183	6000	2183	45
16	9324	7545	1779	8926	7017	1909	8544	6500	2045	8177	5992	2185	44
17	9317	7536	1781	8920	7008	1911	8538	6491	2047	8171	5983	2188	43
18	9311	7527	1783	8913	7000	1914	8532	6483	2049	8165	5975	2190	42
19	9304	7518	1786	8907	6991	1916	8526	6474	2052	8159	5967	2193	41
20	9297	7509	1788	8900	6982	1918	8519	6466	2054	8153	5958	2195	40
21	9290	7500	1790	8894	6974	1920	8513	6457	2056	8147	5950	2197	39
22	9284	7492	1792	8888	6965	1923	8507	6449	2058	8141	5941	2200	38
23	9277	7483	1794	8881	6956	1925	8501	6440	2061	8135	5933	2202	37
24	9270	7474	1796	8875	6948	1927	8495	6432	2063	8129	5925	2205	36
25	9263	7465	1798	8868	6939	1929	8488	6423	2065	8123	5916	2207	35
26	9257	7456	1801	8862	6930	1931	8482	6414	2068	8117	5908	2209	34
27	9250	7447	1803	8855	6922	1934	8476	6406	2070	8111	5899	2212	33
28	9243	7438	1805	8849	6913	1936	8470	6397	2072	8105	5891	2214	32
29	9237	7430	1807	8842	6904	1938	8464	6389	2075	8099	5883	2217	31
30	9230	7421	1809	8836	6896	1940	8457	6380	2077	8094	5874	2219	30
31	9223	7412	1811	8830	6887	1943	8451	6372	2079	8088	5866	2222	29
32	9216	7403	1813	8823	6878	1945	8445	6363	2082	8082	5858	2224	28
33	9210	7394	1816	8817	6870	1947	8439	6355	2084	8076	5849	2226	27
34	9203	7385	1818	8810	6861	1949	8433	6346	2086	8070	5841	2229	26
35	9196	7377	1820	8804	6852	1952	8427	6338	2089	8064	5833	2231	25
36	9190	7368	1822	8797	6844	1954	8420	6329	2091	8058	5824	2234	24
37	9183	7359	1824	8791	6835	1956	8414	6321	2093	8052	5816	2236	23
38	9176	7350	1826	8785	6826	1958	8408	6312	2096	8046	5808	2238	22
39	9170	7341	1828	8778	6818	1961	8402	6304	2098	8040	5799	2241	21
40	9163	7332	1831	8772	6809	1963	8396	6295	2100	8034	5791	2243	20
41	9156	7324	1833	8765	6800	1965	8390	6287	2103	8028	5783	2246	19
42	9150	7315	1835	8759	6792	1967	8384	6279	2105	8022	5774	2248	18
43	9143	7306	1837	8753	6783	1970	8377	6270	2107	8016	5766	2251	17
44	9137	7297	1839	8746	6774	1972	8371	6262	2110	8011	5758	2253	16
45	9130	7288	1841	8740	6766	1974	8365	6253	2112	8005	5749	2256	15
46	9123	7280	1844	8734	6757	1976	8359	6245	2114	7999	5741	2258	14
47	9117	7271	1846	8727	6749	1979	8353	6236	2117	7993	5733	2260	13
48	9110	7262	1848	8721	6740	1981	8347	6228	2119	7987	5724	2263	12
49	9103	7253	1850	8714	6731	1983	8341	6219	2121	7981	5716	2265	11
50	9097	7244	1852	8708	6723	1985	8335	6211	2124	7975	5708	2268	10
51	9090	7236	1854	8702	6714	1988	8328	6202	2126	7969	5699	2270	09
52	9084	7227	1857	8695	6706	1990	8322	6194	2128	7964	5691	2273	08
53	9077	7218	1859	8689	6697	1992	8316	6185	2131	7958	5683	2275	07
54	9070	7209	1861	8683	6688	1994	8310	6177	2133	7952	5674	2278	06
55	9064	7201	1863	8676	6680	1997	8304	6169	2136	7946	5666	2280	05
56	9057	7192	1865	8670	6671	1999	8298	6160	2138	7940	5658	2282	04
57	9051	7183	1868	8664	6663	2001	8292	6152	2140	7934	5649	2285	03
58	9044	7174	1870	8657	6654	2003	8286	6143	2143	7928	5641	2287	02
59	9037	7166	1872	8651	6645	2006	8280	6135	2145	7923	5633	2290	01
60	9031	7157	1874	8645	6637	2008	8274	6126	2147	7917	5624	2292	00

S +T C / 150°			S +T C / 149°			S +T C / 148°			S +T C / 147°			Min.
C −T S / 60°			C −T S / 59°			C −T S / 58°			C −T S / 57°			

Min.	33° S	+T	C	34° S	+T	C	35° S	+T	C	36° S	+T	C	'
	123° C	−T	S	124° C	−T	S	125° C	−T	S	126° C	−T	S	
00	7917	5624	2292	7573	5130	2443	7242	4643	2599	6923	4162	2761	60
01	7911	5616	2295	7568	5122	2445	7237	4635	2602	6918	4154	2764	59
02	7905	5608	2297	7562	5114	2448	7231	4627	2604	6913	4146	2767	58
03	7899	5600	2300	7556	5106	2450	7226	4619	2607	6908	4138	2770	57
04	7893	5591	2302	7551	5098	2453	7221	4611	2610	6903	4130	2772	56
05	7888	5583	2305	7545	5090	2456	7215	4603	2612	6897	4122	2775	55
06	7882	5575	2307	7540	5081	2458	7210	4595	2615	6892	4114	2778	54
07	7876	5566	2310	7534	5073	2461	7204	4587	2618	6887	4106	2781	53
08	7870	5558	2312	7528	5065	2463	7199	4579	2620	6882	4098	2783	52
09	7864	5550	2314	7523	5057	2466	7194	4571	2623	6877	4091	2786	51
10	7859	5542	2317	7517	5049	2468	7188	4563	2626	6871	4083	2789	50
11	7853	5533	2319	7512	5041	2471	7183	4555	2628	6866	4075	2792	49
12	7847	5525	2322	7506	5032	2474	7178	4547	2631	6861	4067	2794	48
13	7841	5517	2324	7500	5024	2476	7172	4538	2634	6856	4059	2797	47
14	7835	5509	2327	7495	5016	2479	7167	4530	2636	6851	4051	2800	46
15	7830	5500	2329	7489	5008	2481	7161	4522	2639	6846	4043	2803	45
16	7824	5492	2332	7484	5000	2484	7156	4514	2642	6840	4035	2806	44
17	7818	5484	2334	7478	4992	2486	7151	4506	2644	6835	4027	2808	43
18	7812	5475	2337	7473	4984	2489	7145	4498	2647	6830	4019	2811	42
19	7807	5467	2339	7467	4975	2492	7140	4490	2650	6825	4011	2814	41
20	7801	5459	2342	7461	4967	2494	7135	4482	2652	6820	4003	2817	40
21	7795	5451	2344	7456	4959	2497	7129	4474	2655	6815	3995	2819	39
22	7789	5442	2347	7450	4951	2499	7124	4466	2658	6809	3987	2822	38
23	7783	5434	2349	7445	4943	2502	7119	4458	2661	6804	3979	2825	37
24	7778	5426	2352	7439	4935	2505	7113	4450	2663	6799	3971	2828	36
25	7772	5418	2354	7434	4927	2507	7108	4442	2666	6794	3963	2831	35
26	7766	5409	2357	7428	4918	2510	7103	4434	2669	6789	3955	2833	34
27	7761	5401	2359	7423	4910	2512	7097	4426	2671	6784	3948	2836	33
28	7755	5393	2362	7417	4902	2515	7092	4418	2674	6779	3940	2839	32
29	7749	5385	2364	7412	4894	2518	7087	4410	2677	6773	3932	2842	31
30	7743	5377	2367	7406	4886	2520	7081	4402	2679	6768	3924	2845	30
31	7738	5368	2369	7401	4878	2523	7076	4394	2682	6763	3916	2847	29
32	7732	5360	2372	7395	4870	2525	7071	4386	2685	6758	3908	2850	28
33	7726	5352	2374	7390	4862	2528	7065	4378	2688	6753	3900	2853	27
34	7720	5344	2377	7384	4854	2531	7060	4370	2690	6748	3892	2856	26
35	7715	5335	2379	7379	4845	2533	7055	4362	2693	6743	3884	2859	25
36	7709	5327	2382	7373	4837	2536	7050	4354	2696	6738	3876	2861	24
37	7703	5319	2384	7368	4829	2538	7044	4346	2698	6733	3868	2864	23
38	7698	5311	2387	7362	4821	2541	7039	4338	2701	6727	3860	2867	22
39	7692	5302	2389	7357	4813	2544	7034	4330	2704	6722	3852	2870	21
40	7686	5294	2392	7351	4805	2546	7028	4322	2707	6717	3845	2873	20
41	7681	5286	2394	7346	4797	2549	7023	4314	2709	6712	3837	2876	19
42	7675	5278	2397	7340	4789	2552	7018	4306	2712	6707	3829	2878	18
43	7669	5270	2400	7335	4781	2554	7013	4298	2715	6702	3821	2881	17
44	7664	5261	2402	7329	4772	2557	7007	4290	2717	6697	3813	2884	16
45	7658	5253	2405	7324	4764	2559	7002	4282	2720	6692	3805	2887	15
46	7652	5245	2407	7318	4756	2562	6997	4274	2723	6687	3797	2890	14
47	7646	5237	2410	7313	4748	2565	6992	4266	2726	6682	3789	2893	13
48	7641	5229	2412	7307	4740	2567	6986	4258	2728	6677	3781	2895	12
49	7635	5220	2415	7302	4732	2570	6981	4250	2731	6672	3773	2898	11
50	7630	5212	2417	7297	4724	2573	6976	4242	2734	6667	3765	2901	10
51	7624	5204	2420	7291	4716	2575	6971	4234	2737	6662	3758	2904	09
52	7618	5196	2422	7286	4708	2578	6965	4226	2739	6656	3750	2907	08
53	7613	5188	2425	7280	4700	2581	6960	4218	2742	6651	3742	2910	07
54	7607	5179	2427	7275	4692	2583	6955	4210	2745	6646	3734	2912	06
55	7601	5171	2430	7269	4684	2586	6950	4202	2748	6641	3726	2915	05
56	7596	5163	2433	7264	4675	2588	6944	4194	2750	6636	3718	2918	04
57	7590	5155	2435	7259	4667	2591	6939	4186	2753	6631	3710	2921	03
58	7584	5147	2438	7253	4659	2594	6934	4178	2756	6626	3702	2924	02
59	7579	5139	2440	7248	4651	2596	6929	4170	2759	6621	3694	2927	01
60	7573	5130	2443	7242	4643	2599	6923	4162	2761	6616	3687	2930	00
	S	+T	C	S	+T	C	S	+T	C	S	+T	C	Min.
			146°			145°			144°			143°	
	C	−T	S	C	−T	S	C	−T	S	C	−T	S	
			56°			55°			54°			53°	

6616   2930   3687
    S/C   ±T
5492   3667   1825

Min.	37° S +T C 127° C −T S			38° S +T C 128° C −T S			39° S +T C 129° C −T S			40° S +T C 130° C −T S			'
00	6616	3687	2930	6320	3216	3104	6034	2749	3285	5758	2286	3472	60
01	6611	3679	2932	6315	3208	3107	6029	2741	3288	5753	2278	3476	59
02	6606	3671	2935	6310	3200	3110	6024	2733	3291	5749	2270	3479	58
03	6601	3663	2938	6305	3192	3113	6020	2726	3294	5744	2263	3482	57
04	6596	3655	2941	6300	3184	3116	6015	2718	3297	5740	2255	3485	56
05	6591	3647	2944	6296	3177	3119	6010	2710	3300	5735	2247	3488	55
06	6586	3639	2947	6291	3169	3122	6006	2702	3303	5731	2239	3491	54
07	6581	3631	2950	6286	3161	3125	6001	2695	3306	5726	2232	3495	53
08	6576	3624	2952	6281	3153	3128	5996	2687	3310	5722	2224	3498	52
09	6571	3616	2955	6276	3145	3131	5992	2679	3313	5717	2216	3501	51
10	6566	3608	2958	6271	3138	3134	5987	2671	3316	5713	2209	3504	50
11	6561	3600	2961	6267	3130	3137	5983	2664	3319	5708	2201	3507	49
12	6556	3592	2964	6262	3122	3140	5978	2656	3322	5704	2193	3511	48
13	6551	3584	2967	6257	3114	3143	5973	2648	3325	5699	2186	3514	47
14	6546	3576	2970	6252	3106	3146	5969	2641	3328	5695	2178	3517	46
15	6541	3568	2973	6247	3099	3149	5964	2633	3331	5691	2170	3520	45
16	6536	3561	2975	6242	3091	3152	5959	2625	3334	5686	2163	3524	44
17	6531	3553	2978	6238	3083	3155	5955	2617	3337	5682	2155	3527	43
18	6526	3545	2981	6233	3075	3158	5950	2610	3340	5677	2147	3530	42
19	6521	3537	2984	6228	3067	3161	5945	2602	3344	5673	2139	3533	41
20	6516	3529	2987	6223	3060	3164	5941	2594	3347	5668	2132	3536	40
21	6511	3521	2990	6219	3052	3167	5936	2586	3350	5664	2124	3540	39
22	6506	3513	2993	6214	3044	3170	5932	2579	3353	5659	2116	3543	38
23	6501	3506	2996	6209	3036	3173	5927	2571	3356	5655	2109	3546	37
24	6496	3498	2999	6204	3029	3176	5922	2563	3359	5650	2101	3549	36
25	6491	3490	3001	6199	3021	3179	5918	2555	3362	5646	2093	3552	35
26	6486	3482	3004	6195	3013	3182	5913	2548	3365	5641	2086	3556	34
27	6481	3474	3007	6190	3005	3185	5908	2540	3368	5637	2078	3559	33
28	6476	3466	3010	6185	2997	3188	5904	2532	3372	5633	2070	3562	32
29	6472	3458	3013	6180	2990	3191	5899	2525	3375	5628	2063	3565	31
30	6467	3451	3016	6176	2982	3194	5895	2517	3378	5624	2055	3569	30
31	6462	3443	3019	6171	2974	3197	5890	2509	3381	5619	2047	3572	29
32	6457	3435	3022	6166	2966	3200	5885	2501	3384	5615	2040	3575	28
33	6452	3427	3025	6161	2959	3203	5881	2494	3387	5610	2032	3578	27
34	6447	3419	3028	6156	2951	3206	5876	2486	3390	5606	2024	3582	26
35	6442	3411	3031	6152	2943	3209	5872	2478	3393	5602	2017	3585	25
36	6437	3404	3033	6147	2935	3212	5867	2471	3397	5597	2009	3588	24
37	6432	3396	3036	6142	2927	3215	5863	2463	3400	5593	2001	3591	23
38	6427	3388	3039	6137	2920	3218	5858	2455	3403	5588	1994	3595	22
39	6422	3380	3042	6133	2912	3221	5853	2447	3406	5584	1986	3598	21
40	6417	3372	3045	6128	2904	3224	5849	2440	3409	5579	1978	3601	20
41	6412	3364	3048	6123	2896	3227	5844	2432	3412	5575	1971	3604	19
42	6408	3357	3051	6119	2889	3230	5840	2424	3415	5571	1963	3608	18
43	6403	3349	3054	6114	2881	3233	5835	2417	3419	5566	1955	3611	17
44	6398	3341	3057	6109	2873	3236	5831	2409	3422	5562	1948	3614	16
45	6393	3333	3060	6104	2865	3239	5826	2401	3425	5557	1940	3617	15
46	6388	3325	3063	6100	2858	3242	5821	2393	3428	5553	1932	3621	14
47	6383	3317	3066	6095	2850	3245	5817	2386	3431	5549	1925	3624	13
48	6378	3310	3069	6090	2842	3248	5812	2378	3434	5544	1917	3627	12
49	6373	3302	3072	6085	2834	3251	5808	2370	3438	5540	1909	3630	11
50	6368	3294	3075	6081	2826	3254	5803	2363	3441	5535	1902	3634	10
51	6364	3286	3077	6076	2819	3257	5799	2355	3444	5531	1894	3637	09
52	6359	3278	3080	6071	2811	3260	5794	2347	3447	5527	1886	3640	08
53	6354	3270	3083	6067	2803	3263	5790	2339	3450	5522	1879	3644	07
54	6349	3263	3086	6062	2795	3267	5785	2332	3453	5518	1871	3647	06
55	6344	3255	3089	6057	2788	3270	5781	2324	3457	5514	1863	3650	05
56	6339	3247	3092	6053	2780	3273	5776	2316	3460	5509	1856	3653	04
57	6334	3239	3095	6048	2772	3276	5772	2309	3463	5505	1848	3657	03
58	6329	3231	3098	6043	2764	3279	5767	2301	3466	5500	1840	3660	02
59	6325	3224	3101	6039	2757	3282	5762	2293	3469	5496	1833	3663	01
60	6320	3216	3104	6034	2749	3285	5758	2286	3472	5492	1825	3667	00
	S	+T	C	S	+T	C	S	+T	C	S	+T	C	Min.
			142°			141°			140°			139°	
	C	−T	S	C	−T	S	C	−T	S	C	−T	S	
			52°			51°			50°			49°	

		5492		3667			1825
			S/C			±T	
		4515		4515			0

Min.	41° S	+T	C	42° S	+T	C	43° S	+T	C	44° S	+T	C	
	131° C	−T	S	132° C	−T	S	133° C	−T	S	134° C	−T	S	
00	5492	1825	3667	5235	1367	3868	4987	910	4076	4747	455	4292	60
01	5487	1817	3670	5230	1359	3871	4982	903	4080	4743	447	4296	59
02	5483	1810	3673	5226	1352	3875	4978	895	4083	4739	440	4299	58
03	5479	1802	3676	5222	1344	3878	4974	888	4087	4735	432	4303	57
04	5474	1794	3680	5218	1336	3881	4970	880	4090	4731	425	4307	56
05	5470	1787	3683	5214	1329	3885	4966	872	4094	4727	417	4310	55
06	5466	1779	3686	5209	1321	3888	4962	865	4097	4723	409	4314	54
07	5461	1772	3690	5205	1314	3892	4958	857	4101	4719	402	4318	53
08	5457	1764	3693	5201	1306	3895	4954	850	4105	4716	394	4321	52
09	5453	1756	3696	5197	1298	3899	4950	842	4108	4712	387	4325	51
10	5448	1749	3700	5193	1291	3902	4946	834	4112	4708	379	4329	50
11	5444	1741	3703	5189	1283	3905	4942	827	4115	4704	371	4332	49
12	5440	1733	3706	5184	1275	3909	4938	819	4119	4700	364	4336	48
13	5435	1726	3710	5180	1268	3912	4934	812	4122	4696	356	4340	47
14	5431	1718	3713	5176	1260	3916	4930	804	4126	4692	349	4343	46
15	5427	1710	3716	5172	1253	3919	4926	796	4129	4688	341	4347	45
16	5422	1703	3720	5168	1245	3923	4922	789	4133	4684	334	4351	44
17	5418	1695	3723	5163	1237	3926	4918	781	4137	4680	326	4355	43
18	5414	1687	3726	5159	1230	3930	4914	774	4140	4677	318	4358	42
19	5409	1680	3730	5155	1222	3933	4910	766	4144	4673	311	4362	41
20	5405	1672	3733	5151	1215	3936	4906	758	4147	4669	303	4366	40
21	5401	1665	3736	5147	1207	3940	4902	751	4151	4665	296	4369	39
22	5396	1657	3740	5143	1199	3943	4898	743	4154	4661	288	4373	38
23	5392	1649	3743	5139	1192	3947	4894	736	4158	4657	280	4377	37
24	5388	1642	3746	5134	1184	3950	4890	728	4162	4653	273	4380	36
25	5384	1634	3750	5130	1176	3954	4886	720	4165	4649	265	4384	35
26	5379	1626	3753	5126	1169	3957	4882	713	4169	4646	258	4388	34
27	5375	1619	3756	5122	1161	3961	4878	705	4172	4642	250	4392	33
28	5371	1611	3760	5118	1154	3964	4874	698	4176	4638	243	4395	32
29	5366	1603	3763	5114	1146	3968	4870	690	4180	4634	235	4399	31
30	5362	1596	3766	5110	1138	3971	4866	683	4183	4630	227	4403	30
31	5358	1588	3770	5105	1131	3975	4862	675	4187	4626	220	4406	29
32	5354	1580	3773	5101	1123	3978	4858	667	4190	4622	212	4410	28
33	5349	1573	3776	5097	1116	3982	4854	660	4194	4619	205	4414	27
34	5345	1565	3780	5093	1108	3985	4850	652	4198	4615	197	4418	26
35	5341	1558	3783	5089	1100	3988	4846	645	4201	4611	190	4421	25
36	5336	1550	3786	5085	1093	3992	4842	637	4205	4607	182	4425	24
37	5332	1542	3790	5081	1085	3995	4838	629	4208	4603	174	4429	23
38	5328	1535	3793	5076	1078	3999	4834	622	4212	4599	167	4433	22
39	5324	1527	3797	5072	1070	4002	4830	614	4216	4596	159	4436	21
40	5319	1519	3800	5068	1062	4006	4826	607	4219	4592	152	4440	20
41	5315	1512	3803	5064	1055	4009	4822	599	4223	4588	144	4444	19
42	5311	1504	3807	5060	1047	4013	4818	591	4226	4584	136	4448	18
43	5307	1497	3810	5056	1040	4016	4814	584	4230	4580	129	4451	17
44	5302	1489	3813	5052	1032	4020	4810	576	4234	4576	121	4455	16
45	5298	1481	3817	5048	1024	4023	4806	569	4237	4573	114	4459	15
46	5294	1474	3820	5044	1017	4027	4802	561	4241	4569	106	4463	14
47	5290	1466	3824	5040	1009	4030	4798	553	4245	4565	99	4466	13
48	5285	1458	3827	5035	1002	4034	4794	546	4248	4561	91	4470	12
49	5281	1451	3830	5031	994	4037	4790	538	4252	4557	83	4474	11
50	5277	1443	3834	5027	986	4041	4786	531	4255	4553	76	4478	10
51	5273	1435	3837	5023	979	4044	4782	523	4259	4550	68	4481	09
52	5268	1428	3841	5019	971	4048	4778	516	4263	4546	61	4485	08
53	5264	1420	3844	5015	964	4051	4774	508	4266	4542	53	4489	07
54	5260	1413	3847	5011	956	4055	4770	500	4270	4538	45	4493	06
55	5256	1405	3851	5007	948	4059	4767	493	4274	4534	38	4497	05
56	5252	1397	3854	5003	941	4062	4763	485	4277	4531	30	4500	04
57	5247	1390	3858	4999	933	4066	4759	478	4281	4527	23	4504	03
58	5243	1382	3861	4995	926	4069	4755	470	4285	4523	15	4508	02
59	5239	1375	3864	4991	918	4073	4751	462	4288	4519	8	4512	01
60	5235	1367	3868	4987	910	4076	4747	455	4292	4515	0	4515	00
	S	+T	C	S	+T	C	S	+T	C	S	+T	C	Min.
			138°			137°			136°			135°	
	C	−T	S	C	−T	S	C	−T	S	C	−T	S	
			48°			47°			46°			45°	

161

5.11 **Bibliography**

Admiralty Manual of Navigation (HM Stationery Office).

American Practical Navigator, originally by Nathaniel Bowditch, US Pub. No. 9 (US Government Printing Office).

Celestial Navigation for Yachtsmen by Mary Blewitt (Stanford Maritime).

Ocean Yacht Navigator by Kenneth Wilkes (Nautical Books).

The Complete Nautical Astronomer by Charles C Cotter (Hollis and Carter).

Celestial Navigation by Frances W Wright (Cornell Maritime Press).

Lecky's Wrinkles in Practical Navigation, 23rd edition by G Cobb (George Philip).

Navigation Afloat by Alton B Moody (Hollis and Carter).

The Yacht Navigator's Handbook by Norman Dahl (Ward Lock).

Chapter 6

Communications

Contents

6.1 Communications – general

While yachtsmen may not need to be able to communicate at sea with the same facility as professional seamen, it is still very useful to be able to understand and pass simple messages. There is also an increasing need for yachts to be able to communicate with shore stations which control commercial harbours.

Yachtsmen may, for example, wish to receive signals relating to weather forecasts, time signals, navigational matters including radio aids, safety or distress messages from (or concerning) another vessel, personal or business matters, or signals connected with yacht racing.

There are fewer reasons for yachtsmen wishing to send signals, but they include distress messages, being able to communicate with another boat when either is in some kind of trouble, arranging a rendezvous, and passing personal messages. Various methods of signalling are available, as will be explained. Some are slow, but simple and suitable for short distances: others are quicker but more complicated, and usually more expensive.

6.2 International Code of Signals

6.2.1 Explanation

The basis of most forms of communication afloat is the *International Code of Signals*, published by HM Stationery Office. In the following pages is given sufficient information for yachtsmen to understand its working and to pass simple messages. For comprehensive use of the code it is necessary to hold the complete code book.

Although the International Code caters for the increasing use of plain language communication (by voice on VHF radiotelephone for example), it provides for safety of navigation and of persons, particularly where there are language problems. By its use, seamen of nine nations can communicate with each other without knowing any foreign language.

Before explaining the various methods of signalling, and how the code works, it is helpful to establish certain important definitions.

Definitions

Addressee. The authority to whom a signal is addressed.

Group. One or more letters and/or numerals which together comprise a signal.

Hoist. In flag signalling, one or more groups displayed from a single halyard. A hoist or signal is *at the dip* when hoisted about half way, and is *close up* when hoisted to the full extent of the halyards.

Identity signal, or call sign. A group of letters and figures assigned to each station by its administration.

Numeral group. A group consisting of one or more numerals.

Originator. The authority who orders a signal to be sent.

Procedure. Rules drawn up for the conduct of signalling.

Sound signalling. Any method of passing Morse signals by siren, whistle, foghorn or other sound apparatus.

Station. A ship, aircraft, survival craft or any place at which communications can be effected.

Tackline. In flag signalling, a length of halyard used to separate groups of flags.

Time of origin. The time at which a signal is ordered to be made.

Visual signalling. Any method of communication, the transmission of which is capable of being seen.

Some of the above definitions are repeated elsewhere, when describing different methods of signalling.

Methods of transmission

The code can be transmitted in the following ways:

(1) *By flags* (see colour section page 191) displayed in groups (or singly for the most important signals), and interpreted in nine different languages. This method is rather slow, and requires good visibility.

(2) *By flashing light*, using the Morse code of dots and dashes (see 6.2.4). This can be transmitted by light (day and night, given a powerful light and good visibility). Messages can be passed in plain language (for preference) or by code groups in the event of language difficulties.

(3) *By sound signalling*, using the Morse code, with the boat's fog horn for example. This is rather slow, and it can cause confusion in poor visibility, when its use should be restricted to the minimum.

(4) *By voice* over a loud hailer. Whenever possible plain language should be used, but in the event of language difficulties groups from the International Code can be transmitted, using the phonetic spelling tables described later.

(5) *By radiotelegraphy*, using the Morse code. Not applicable to the very great majority of yachtsmen, but very high speeds can be achieved by professional operators, over big distances.

(6) *By radiotelephone* – by voice over radio circuits, normally in plain language, but again International Code groups are useful in the event of language difficulties.

(7) *By hand flags* (or arms) using the Morse code.

Types of signals

The present International Code, which came into effect in 1969, provides for nine languages – English, French, German, Greek, Italian, Japanese, Norwegian, Russian and Spanish. Signals consist of:

(1) Single-letter signals which are very urgent, important, or very common.
(2) Two-letter signals in the General Section.
(3) Three-letter signals beginning with the letter 'M' in the Medical Section.

Complements

In principle the Code provides that each signal should have a complete meaning. In some cases however complements are used to supplement the available groups. As explained in the examples below, complements may express variations in the meaning of the basic signal, questions concerning the same subject, answers to a question or a request, or more detailed information on the basic signal.

Example (a) Variations in meaning
'KT'   = 'You should send me a towing hawser'
'KT 1' = 'I am sending towing hawser'

Example (b) Questions concerning the basic signal
'CV'   = 'I am unable to give assistance'
'CV 4' = 'Can you assist?'

Example (c) Answers to a question or request
'IB'   = 'What damage have you received?'
'IB 3' = 'I have not received any damage'

Example (d) Supplementary, specific or detailed information
'CB'   = 'I require immediate assistance'
'CB 4' = 'I require immediate assistance: I am aground'

Complements which appear in the text more than once are grouped in Tables I, II and III which appear in 6.2.6. These should be used only as and when specified in the Code.

Example (e) Use of complements tables
'K'   = 'I wish to communicate with you'
'K'   = 'I wish to communicate with you by (with one ...
numeral) (Complements table I)'

Reference to complements table I shows that it lists the various methods of signalling.

In some groups words appear in brackets. These are either alternatives or information which may be included if it is available, or explanations of the text.

The code is arranged under these headings: Distress, Emergency, Casualties, Damage; Aids to Navigation, Navigation; Manoeuvres; Miscellaneous; Meteorology; Communications; Pratique; Medical.

6.2.2 General instructions

(1) *Numbers* are signalled as follows. By flag signalling – by numeral pendants: by light – usually by Morse numerals, but spelt if important: by R/T or loud hailer – by phonetic code words (see 6.2.4).
(2) *Decimal point* is indicated by flags – by Answering Pendant: by light – by '$\overline{AAA}$': by voice by word 'Decimal'.
(3) *Depths* are signalled in figures followed by 'F' for feet (not fathoms) or 'M' for metres.
(4) *Azimuth or bearing*, signalled in three figures, denoting degrees from 000 to 359. Unless stated to the contrary bearings are True.
(5) *Course* – as for Azimuth with figures prefixed by 'C'.
(6) *Dates* – signalled by two, four or six figures preceded by 'D' (for Date). The first two figures show day of month, the next two months of year, and the final two (when six are signalled) the last two figures of the year.

Example: D1002 means 10 February; D 211081 means 21 October 1981.

(7) *Latitude* – signalled by four figures preceded by 'L' and followed by 'N' or 'S', which may be omitted where obvious. The first two figures indicate degrees, and the second two indicate minutes.

Example: L 5146 N = Latitude 51°46′N.

(8) *Longitude* – signalled by four (or five) figures preceded by 'G' and followed by 'E' or 'W'. The last two figures show minutes and the first two (or three) show degrees.

Example: G 12117 W = Longitude 121°17′W.

(9) *Distance* – signalled by figures (in nautical miles) preceded by 'R'.
(10) *Speed* – signalled by figures preceded by 'S' (for knots) or by 'V' (kilometres per hour).
(11) *Time* – signalled by 24 hour clock. Preceded by 'T' for Local Time or by 'Z' for GMT.
(12) *Local Signal Codes* (when applicable) are preceded by the group 'YV1' – 'The groups which follow are from the local code'.

6.2.3 Yachtsmen and the International Code

Yachtsmen are most likely to use the International Code by Morse or, in the event of language or spelling difficulties, by using phonetic spelling with plain language messages (as by radiotelephone, for example). It is also important to know the meanings of the single-letter signals, which can be made by any method of signalling and which comprise messages which are either of special importance or which are commonly used.

The Morse code, phonetic alphabet and single-letter signals are shown in 6.2.4. Also shown is the figure-spelling table: in practice it is normally only necessary to use the last component of each code word in the figure-spelling table.

6.2.4 Morse code, phonetic alphabet and single-letter signals

Letter	Morse	Phonetic spelling (Emphasise syllables in italics)		Single-letter meaning (May be made by any method of signalling. * see note (1) below.)
A	·—	Alfa	*AL* FAH	I have a diver down; keep well clear at slow speed.
B	—···	Bravo	*BRAH* VOH	* I am taking in, or discharging, or carrying dangerous goods.
C	—·—·	Charlie	*CHAR* LEE	* Yes (Affirmative or 'The significance of the previous group should be read in the affirmative').
D	—··	Delta	*DELL* TAH	* Keep clear of me; I am manoeuvring with difficulty.
E	·	Echo	*ECK* OH	* I am altering my course to starboard.
F	··—·	Foxtrot	*FOKS* TROT	I am disabled; communicate with me.
G	——·	Golf	GOLF	* I require a pilot. (By fishing vessels operating in close proximity it means 'I am hauling nets').
H	····	Hotel	HOH *TELL*	* I have a pilot on board.
I	··	India	*IN* DEE AH	* I am altering my course to port.
J	·———	Juliett	*JEW* LEE ETT	I am on fire and have dangerous cargo on board; keep well clear of me.
K	—·—	Kilo	*KEY* LOH	I wish to communicate with you.
L	·—··	Lima	*LEE* MAH	You should stop your vessel instantly.
M	——	Mike	MIKE	*My vessel is stopped and making no way through the water.
N	—·	November	NO *VEM* BER	No (Negative or 'The significance of the previous group should be read in the negative'). This signal may be given only visually or by sound. For voice or radio transmission the signal should be 'NO'.
O	———	Oscar	*OSS* CAH	Man overboard.
P	·——·	Papa	PAH *PAH*	In harbour: All persons should report on board as the vessel is about to proceed to sea. At sea: By fishing vessels means 'My nets have come fast upon an obstruction.'
Q	——·—	Quebec	KEH *BECK*	My vessel is healthy and I request free pratique.
R	·—·	Romeo	*ROW* ME OH	
S	···	Sierra	SEE *AIR* RAH	* I am operating astern propulsion.
T	—	Tango	*TANG* GO	* Keep clear of me; I am engaged in pair trawling.
U	··—	Uniform	*YOU* NEE FORM	You are running into danger.
V	···—	Victor	*VIK* TAH	I require assistance.
W	·——	Whiskey	*WISS* KEY	I require medical assistance.
X	—··—	X-ray	*ECKS* RAY	Stop carrying out your intentions and watch for my signals.
Y	—·——	Yankee	*YANG* KEY	I am dragging my anchor.
Z	——··	Zulu	*ZOO* LOO	* I require a tug. By fishing vessels operating in close proximity it means 'I am shooting nets'.

Notes:
(1) * When made by sound, must comply with *International Regulations for Preventing Collisions at Sea*.
(2) 'K' and 'S' have special meanings as landing signals for small boats. See 6.4.4.

Figure-spelling table

Figure	Morse	Word	Pronounced
0	− − − − −	NADAZERO	NAH-DAH-ZAY-ROH
1	· − − − −	UNAONE	OO-NAH-WUN
2	· · − − −	BISSOTWO	BEE-SOH-TOO
3	· · · − −	TERRATHREE	TAY-RAH-TREE
4	· · · · −	KARTEFOUR	KAR-TAY-FOWER
5	· · · · ·	PANTAFIVE	PAN-TAH-FIVE
6	− · · · ·	SOXISIX	SOK-SEE-SIX
7	− − · · ·	SETTESEVEN	SAY-TAY-SEVEN
8	− − − · ·	OKTOEIGHT	OK-TOH-AIT
9	− − − − ·	NOVENINE	NO-VAY-NINER
Decimal point		DECIMAL	DAY-SEE-MAL
Full stop		STOP	STOP

Note: In the figure-spelling table, each syllable should be equally emphasised. The last component of each code word (e.g. 'Zero') is the code word used for figures in the Aeronautical Mobile Service.

6.2.5 Procedure signals

Certain procedure signals are laid down, and are designed to facilitate the conduct of signalling. Certain procedure signals are reserved for certain types of signalling, but the majority can be used for any form of transmission.

A bar over the letters of a signal means that the letters are joined together and made as one symbol.

(1) Procedure signals for voice transmissions (RT or loud hailer)

Signal	Pronunciation	Meaning
Interco	IN-TER-CO	International Code group(s) follow(s)
Stop	STOP	Full stop
Decimal	DAY-SEE-MAL	Decimal point
Correction	KOR REK SHUN	Cancel my last word or group. The correct word or group follows.

(2) Procedure signals for Morse by light

$\overline{AA}\ \overline{AA}\ \overline{AA}$ etc. Call for unknown station or general call.

$\overline{EEEEEEE}$ etc	Erase signal.
$\overline{AAA}$	Full stop or decimal point.
$\overline{TTTT}$ etc	Answering signal.
T	Word or group received.

(3) Procedure signals for flags, radiotelephony and radiotelegraphy transmissions.

CQ Call for unknown station(s) or general call to all stations.

Note: When this signal is used in voice transmission, it should be pronounced in accordance with the letter-spelling table (i.e. Charlie Quebec).

(4) Procedure signals for use where appropriate in all forms of transmission

AA	'All after ...' (used after the 'Repeat' signal (RPT) – see below – means 'Repeat all after ...').
AB	'All before ...' (used after the 'Repeat signal (RPT) – see below – means 'Repeat all before ...').
$\overline{AR}$	Ending signal, or End of Transmission or signal.
$\overline{AS}$	Waiting signal or period.

BN	'All between ... and ...' (used after the 'Repeat' signal (RPT) – means 'Repeat all between ... and ...').	6.	Towing
		7.	Survival craft
		8.	Vessel to stand by
C	Affirmative – YES or 'The significance of the previous group should be read in the affirmative'.	9.	Ice breaker

Table III

0. Direction unknown (or calm)
1. North-east
2. East
3. South-east
4. South
5. South-West
6. West
7. North-West
8. North
9. All directions (or confused or variable)

CS 'What is the name or identity signal of your vessel (or station)?'

DE 'From ...' (used to precede the name or identity signal of the calling station).

K 'I wish to communicate with you' or 'Invitation to transmit'.

NO Negative – NO or 'The significance of the previous group should be read in the negative'. When used in voice transmission the pronunciation should be 'NO'.

OK Acknowledging a correct repetition or 'It is correct'.

RQ Interrogative or 'The significance of the previous group should be read as a question'.

R 'Received' or 'I have received your last signal'.

RPT Repeat signal 'I repeat' or 'Repeat what you have sent' or 'Repeat what you have received'.

WA 'Word or group after ...' (used after the 'Repeat' signal (RPT) means 'Repeat word or group after ...').

WB 'Word or group before ...' (used after the 'Repeat' signal (RPT) means 'Repeat word or group before ...').

Notes:
1. The procedure signals 'C', 'NO' and 'RQ' cannot be used in conjunction with single-letter signals.
2. When these signals are used by voice transmission the letters should be pronounced in accordance with the letter-spelling table, except that 'NO' is pronounced 'NO'.

6.2.6 Tables of complements

Table I
1. Semaphore
2. Morse signalling by hand flags or arms
3. Loud Hailer (or megaphone)
4. Morse signalling lamp
5. Sound signals
6. International Code flags
7. Radiotelegraphy, 500kHz
8. Radiotelephony, 2182kHz
9. VHF Radiotelephony – Channel 16

Table II
0. Water
1. Provisions
2. Fuel
3. Pumping equipment
4. Fire-fighting appliance
5. Medical assistance

6.2.7 Single-letter signals with complements

These signals bear no relation to the single-letter signals already described in 6.2.4. Some have already been mentioned in 6.2.2. They may be made by any method of signalling.

A with three numerals	AZIMUTH or BEARING
C with three numerals	COURSE
D with two, four or six numerals	DATE
G with four or five numerals	LONGITUDE (the last two numerals denote minutes and the rest degrees)
K with one numeral	I wish to COMMUNICATE with you by ... (Complements table I)
L with four numerals	LATITUDE (the first two figures denote degrees, the others minutes)
R with one or more numerals	DISTANCE in nautical miles
S with one or more numerals	SPEED in knots
T with four numerals	LOCAL TIME (the first two figures denote hours, the others minutes)
V with one or more numerals	SPEED in kilometres per hour
Z with four numerals	GMT (the first two figures denote hours, the others minutes)

6.2.8 Selected groups from the International Code

AC I am abandoning my vessel.
AE I must abandon my vessel.
AF I do not intend to abandon my vessel.
AN I need a doctor.
CB I require immediate assistance.

CB4 I require immediate assistance; I am aground.

CB5 I require immediate assistance; I am drifting.

CB6 I require immediate assistance; I am on fire.

CB7 I require immediate assistance; I have sprung a leak.

CJ Do you require assistance?

CK Assistance is not (or is no longer) required by me (or vessel indicated).

CV I am unable to give assistance.

DX I am sinking.

ED Your distress signals are understood.

EF SOS/MAYDAY has been cancelled.

FA Will you give me my position?

IL I can only proceed at slow speed.

IM I request to be escorted until further notice.

IT I am on fire.

IW Fire is under control.

IX Fire is gaining.

IZ Fire has been extinguished.

JG I am aground. I am in a dangerous situation.

JH I am aground. I am not in danger.

JI Are you aground?

JL You are running the risk of going aground.

JO I am afloat.

JW I have sprung a leak.

JX Leak is gaining rapidly.

KM I can take you in tow.

KN I cannot take you in tow. (See also 15.4.3)

LO I am not in my correct position (to be used by a lightvessel).

MG You should steer course . . .

NC I am in distress and require immediate assistance.

NG You are in a dangerous position.

NH You are clear of all dangers.

PD Your navigation light(s) is (are) not visible.

PH You should steer as indicated.

PI You should maintain your present course.

PP Keep well clear of me.

QO You should not come alongside.

QP I will come alongside.

QR I cannot come alongside.

QT You should not anchor. You are going to foul my anchor.

RA My anchor is foul.

RB I am dragging my anchor.

RN My engines are out of action.

RY You should proceed at slow speed when passing me (or vessels making signal).

SC I am under way.

SD I am not ready to get under way.

SQ You should stop or heave to.

UM The harbour or port is closed to traffic.

UN You may enter harbour immediately.

UO You must not enter harbour.

UW I wish you a pleasant voyage.

VJ Gale is expected from direction indicated. ⎫
⎬ (Complements table III)
VK Storm is expected from direction indicated. ⎭

YT I cannot read your . . . (Complements table I)

YU I am going to communicate with your station by International Code.

YV The groups which follow are from the International Code of Signals.

ZD2 Please report me to Lloyd's London.

ZK I cannot distinguish your signal. Please repeat it by . . . (Complements table I).

ZL Your signal has been received but not understood.

ZM You should send (or speak) more slowly.

6.2.9 Flag signalling

The International Code flags (see colour section page 191) consist of 26 alphabetical flags, 11 pendants (numerals 0-9 plus the Answering Pendant or Code Flag), and three triangular flags – the First, Second and Third Substitutes.

Some definitions already mentioned in 6.2.1 are important. *Group* – one or more continuous letters and/or numerals comprising a signal. *Hoist* – one or more groups on one halyard. *At the dip* – a signal half-hoisted. *Close up* – a signal fully hoisted. *Tackline* – a line separating two groups. *Superior* – a flag or group above another. *Inferior* – a flag or group below another. *Class* – whether a flag is alphabetical or numeral.

The Answering Pendant is used to answer or acknowledge signals from another vessel. It may also be used as a decimal point.

Substitutes allow for the repetition of one or more letters (or numerals) within a group. The First Sub. repeats the first flag of the group in the class immediately superior to it. The Second Sub. repeats the second flag of that class, and the Third Sub. repeats the third.

A substitute can only repeat a flag of the same class as that immediately preceding it. The Answering Pendant used as a decimal point is disregarded in deciding which substitute to use.

Procedure

The basic procedure is that the sending ship hoists the identity signal of the ship she is calling: or she hoists the group 'VF' ('You should hoist your identity signal') or 'CS' ('What is the name or identity signal of your vessel/station') – at the same time hoisting her own identity signal.

The sending ship then hoists her message, and when sighted the receiving ship hoists her Answering Pendant at the dip – and close up when the signal has been understood. The procedure is repeated for subsequent hoists.

6.2.10 Morse code by light

The most likely method for yachtsmen to use the Morse code is by light. It helps to have a good light with a proper flashing key or trigger.

When making Morse it is most important to get the right rhythm and spacing. If a dot is taken as the unit of time, the correct spacing is as follows:

Dot	1 unit
Dash	3 units
Space between each dot or dash in a letter	1 unit
Space between each letter or symbol	3 units
Space between each word or group	7 units

Procedure (Morse by light)
The procedure signals used when sending Morse by light are given in (2) of 6.2.5. Other procedure signals, common to all forms of signalling, are given in (4) of 6.2.5. It should be remembered that where a bar is placed above the letters, they are run together.

A signal made by flashing light comprises the following:

(1) *The call.* This may be either the general call (AA AA $\overline{AA}$ etc) if it is required to attract the attention of all stations within sight or of a station whose identity is not known, or it may be the identity signal of a known station to be called. The call is repeated until response is made in the form of the answering signal ($\overline{TTTTTT}$ etc) which is repeated until the call stops.

(2) *The identity.* The transmitting station then makes 'DE' followed by its identity signal or name. This is repeated back by the receiving station, which then signals its own identity signal or name. This in turn is repeated back by the transmitting station.

(3) *The text.* This may consist of plain language or code groups, the latter being preceded by the signal 'YU'. Plain language may be included in code groups for the names of places etc. The receiving station acknowledges the receipt of each word or code group by the letter 'T'.

(4) *The ending.* The transmitting station indicates the end of the signal with the letters '$\overline{AR}$', which are acknowledged by the receiving station with the signal 'R', meaning 'Received' or 'I have received your last signal'.

The erase signal ('$\overline{EEEEE}$' etc) indicates that the last word or group was signalled incorrectly. It is answered by the same signal. When answered the transmitting station repeats the last word or group, and then proceeds with the rest of the message.

The repeat signal ('RPT') is used by the transmitting station to indicate that it is going to repeat. If such a repetition does not follow immediately, the signal should be interpreted by the receiving station as a request to repeat the signal received. If used by the receiving station the repeat signal is a request for a repetition of the signal transmitted.

The special repetition signals 'AA', 'AB', 'WA', 'WB' and 'BN' are made by the receiving station as appropriate, after the repeat signal 'RPT'.

A correctly received repetition is acknowledged by the signal 'OK'.

The transmitting station makes the signal 'CS' when requesting the name or identity signal of the receiving station.

The waiting signal, or period signal '$\overline{AS}$', when made independently or after the end of a signal indicates that the other station must wait for further communications; when inserted between groups it separates them to avoid confusion.

The signal 'C' is used to indicate an affirmative statement or an affirmative reply to an interrogative signal. The signal 'RQ' is used to indicate a question. For a negative reply or for a negative statement, the signal 'N' should be used in visual (or sound) signalling. The signals 'C', 'N' or 'RQ' cannot be used in conjunction with single-letter signals. When the signals 'N' or 'RQ' are used to change an affirmative signal into a negative statement or a question, they are transmitted after the main signal.

Examples:

'CY'	— 'Boat(s) is (are) coming to you'
'CY N'	— 'Boat(s) is (are) not coming to you'
'CW'	— 'Boat/raft is on board'
'CW RQ'	— 'Is boat/raft on board?'

6.2.11 **Foreign Morse symbols**
The following foreign Morse symbols may be met, as for example with the identification signals for certain foreign radiobeacons:

Ä (German) or AE (Danish)	· — · —
Á (Spanish) or Å (Scandinavian)	· — — · —
Ch (German or Spanish)	— — — —
É (French)	· · — · ·
Ñ (Spanish)	— — · — —
Ö (German) or Ø (Danish)	— — — ·
Ü (German)	· · — —

6.2.12 **Radiotelephony (RT)**
Plain language is normally used for communication by radiotelephone, and the procedures are described in 6.6.8. However, in the event of language difficulties it may be necessary to use the International Code, in which case the following procedures apply. Letters and figures are spelt in accordance with the spelling tables (6.2.4).

(1) *Method of calling.* The call consists of the call sign or name of the station called, not more than three times at each call; the group 'DE' (DELTA ECHO); and the call sign or name of the calling station, not more than three times at each call. Difficult names should be spelt. Once contact is established the call sign or name need not be sent more than once.

(2) *Reply to call.* The form of reply consists of the call sign or name of the calling station, not

more than three times; the group 'DE' (DELTA ECHO); and the call sign or name of the station called, not more than three times.

(3) *Calling all stations.* The group 'CQ' (CHARLIE QUEBEC) is used to call all stations in the vicinity, but not more than three times at each call.

(4) *Code groups.* The word 'INTERCO' indicates that International Code groups follow. Words of plain language may also be in the text as names, places etc. In this case the group 'YZ' (YANKEE ZULU) meaning 'The words which follow are in plain language' is inserted if necessary.

(5) *Waiting.* If the station called is unable to accept traffic immediately, it transmits the signal 'AS' (ALFA SIERRA), adding if possible the duration of the waiting time in minutes.

(6) *Receipt.* Receipt of a transmission is indicated by the signal 'R' (ROMEO).

(7) *Repetition.* If the transmission is to be repeated in total or in part, the signal 'RPT' (ROMEO PAPA TANGO) is used, supplemented as necessary by:

AA (ALFA ALFA) – all after ...
AB (ALFA BRAVO) – all before ...
BN (BRAVO NOVEMBER) – all between ... and ...
WA (WHISKEY ALFA) – word or group after ...
WB (WHISKEY BRAVO) – word or group before ...

(8) *End of transmission.* The end of transmission is indicated by the signal 'AR (ALFA ROMEO).

6.2.13 Morse code by hand flags, or arms

The method of signalling the Morse code by hand flags or arms is shown in Fig. 6(1). A dot is made by raising both flags (arms) above the head, and a dash by extending them horizontally at shoulder level. Between dots and dashes the flags (arms) are brought in front of the chest. To separate letters, groups or words the flags (arms) are extended downwards at 45° from the body. Circular motion of the flags (arms) overhead indicates the erase signal if made by the transmitting station, or a request for repetition if made by the receiving station.

A station wishing to communicate with another by this method signals 'K2', or makes the usual general call for Morse 'AA AA AA etc.' On receipt of the call the station addressed should make the answering signal ('TTTT etc'), or, if unable to communicate by this method the signal 'YS2' by any means.

Both arms should be used, but where this is difficult or impossible only one need be used.

The signal concludes with the ending signal 'AR'.

1. *Raising both hand-flags or arms*

'dot'

2. *Spreading out both hand-flags or arms at shoulder level*

'dash'

3. *Hand-flags or arms brought before the chest*

   Separation of 'dots' and/or 'dashes'

4. *Hand-flags or arms kept at 45° away from the body downwards*

   Separation of letters, groups or words

5. *Circular motion of hand-flags or arms over the head*

   Erase signals, if made by the transmitting station. Request for repetition if by the receiving station

Note: The space of time between dots and dashes and between letters, groups or words should be such as to facilitate correct reception

Fig. 6(1) Morse signalling by hand-flags or arms.

6.3 Sound signals

6.3.1 Sound signals – International Code

Sound signalling is one of the ways of using the International Code, but because of the equipment used (whistle, siren, foghorn etc) it is necessarily slow. Also if misused it can cause serious confusion. Sound signalling in poor visibility should be reduced to a minimum, and signals other than the single-letter ones should be used only in extreme emergency, and never where there is other traffic around.

The signals should be made slowly and distinctly. They may be repeated, if necessary, but at sufficiently long intervals to ensure that no confusion can arise.

The single-letter signals of the Code, which are marked with an asterisk, when made by sound must only be made in accordance with Rules 34 and 35 of the *International Regulations for Preventing Collisions at Sea* (see the relevant rules in 2.1).

6.3.2 Sound signals in restricted visibility

The requirement for ships to make sound signals in fog, mist, heavy rain or other conditions restricting visibility (whether by day or night) are in Rule 35 of the *International Regulations for Preventing Collisions at Sea*, which are stated in 2.1.

By Rule 33 a vessel of 39ft (12m) or more in length shall be provided with a whistle and a bell. A smaller vessel is not obliged to carry these but must have other means of making an efficient sound signal.

A prolonged blast is four to six seconds' duration. A short blast is about one second.

Sound signals in restricted visibility are:

Power vessel making way through the water	A prolonged blast at intervals of not more than 2 minutes.
Power vessel under way, but stopped (i.e. not at anchor)	Two prolonged blasts at intervals of not more than 2 minutes.
Vessel at anchor	Bell rung rapidly for about 5 seconds, at intervals of not more than 1 minute.
Vessel over 328ft (100m) at anchor	In addition to above sound, a gong aft at similar intervals.

(In addition a vessel at anchor may sound 'R' on her fog-horn to warn an approaching vessel.)

Vessel towed	One prolonged blast followed by three short, every two minutes.
Vessel aground	As for at anchor, plus three separate and distinct strokes of bell before and after.
Pilot vessel on duty	Four short blasts.

Vessel under sail or not under command, or constrained by her draught or engaged in fishing or towing, sounds one prolonged followed by two short blasts ('D') at least every two minutes.

6.3.3 Sound signals by vessels in sight of each other

Rule 34 of the Collision Regulations prescribes the following:

One short blast – 'I am altering course to starboard.'
Two short blasts – 'I am altering course to port.'
Three short blasts – 'I am operating astern propulsion.'

When either of two vessels approaching each other fails to understand the actions or intentions of the other, or is doubtful that sufficient action is being taken to avoid a collision, she shall give at least five short and rapid blasts.

The whistle signals above may be supplemented by an all-round white light, with the number of flashes equivalent to the number of blasts.

In a narrow channel when overtaking can only occur if the overtaken vessel takes action to permit safe passing, a vessel intending to overtake shall indicate her intention by the following whistle signals.

Two prolonged blasts followed by one short – 'I intend to overtake you on your starboard side.'
Two prolonged blasts followed by two short – 'I intend to overtake you on your port side.'

If in agreement the overtaken vessel sounds one prolonged, one short, one prolonged and one short blast and takes the necessary steps. If in doubt she may sound five or more short rapid blasts.

Warning signal

Under Rule 34(e), a power driven vessel is required to sound one prolonged blast as a warning when approaching a blind bend in a river or channel.

6.3.4 Sound signals for distress purposes

Under Annex IV of the Collision Regulations the following constitute distress signals and must not be used for any other purpose.

(1) A gun or other explosive signal fired about every minute.
(2) The continuous sounding of any fog-signalling apparatus.

6.4 Miscellaneous signals

6.4.1 Radio time signals

When seagoing it is necessary to understand the system of standard times, whereby the world is divided in 24 zones, each with a width of 15° of longitude. In each zone, the same time (Zone Time) is kept. The Greenwich meridian is the reference centre of the system, and of Zone 0. Zones to the east of Zone 0 are numbered − 1, − 2, − 3 etc, and those to the west + 1, + 2, + 3 etc. The twelfth zone is divided into two by the International Date Line, the part to the west being − 12, and the part to the east + 12. Ashore, zones are adapted to suit geographical areas. For example, all France keeps Zone − 1 (− 0100) as Standard Time.

The zone number shows the number of hours by which Zone Time must be decreased (east of Greenwich) or increased (west of Greenwich) to obtain Greenwich Mean Time (GMT). Zone Time may also be indicated by letters. GMT is Z (zero): zones to the east are lettered A to M (omitting J), and those to the west are lettered N to Y.

The International Date Line is a modification of the 180° meridian, drawn so as to include islands of particular groups on the same side of the line. When crossing the Date Line heading east, assume yesterday's date: when heading west, assume to-morrow's date.

The standard times kept in different countries, together with indications as to whether or not individual countries observe Daylight Saving Time (DST), are shown in *The Macmillan & Silk Cut Nautical Almanac*, as are the details of time signals broadcast by the British Broadcasting Corporation (BBC). These are transmitted at roughly hourly intervals from 0500–2400 on one of the following: BBC Radio 1, BBC Radio 2, BBC Radio 3 or BBC Radio 4. BBC time signals consist of six pulses representing successive seconds – five pulses each of one-tenth of a second, followed by a final half-second pulse. The start of the final, longer pulse marks the minute.

For details of other systems of time signals, world wide, reference should be made to *Admiralty List of Radio Signals, Vol. 5*.

6.4.2 Pratique messages

All yachts, whether carrying dutiable stores or not, arriving in the United Kingdom from abroad (including the Channel Islands) are subject to Customs, Public Health and Home Office (Immigration Department) requirements. Details are given in Customs Notice No. 8, which is summarised in 2.3 and is obtainable from any Customs and Excise office or from HM Customs and Excise, Kent House, Upper Ground, London, SE1 9PS. For these purposes Customs Officers normally act for the Immigration and Health authorities.

The following Health Clearance Messages, from the *International Code of Signals*, apply:

'Q' or 'ZS'	My vessel is 'healthy' and I request free pratique. (Note: Customs Notice No. 8 requires 'Q' to be flown on entering UK territorial waters, and to be suitably illuminated at night).
'QQ' (i.e. flag 'Q' over First Substitute) or by night a red light over a white light.	I require health clearance.
ZT	My Maritime Declaration of Health has negative answers to the six health questions.
ZU	My Maritime Declaration of Health has a positive answer to question(s) … (indicated by an appropriate number(s))
ZW	I require Port Medical Officer. ZW 1 Port Medical
	Officer will be available at (time indicated).
ZY	You have health clearance.
ZZ	You should proceed to anchorage for health clearance (at place indicated). ZZ 1 Where is the anchorage for health clearance?
AL	I have a doctor on board.
AM	Have you a doctor?

Health clearances may be given wholly in plain language, partly in the above signal code and the remainder in plain language, or wholly in the above code.

6.4.3 Distress signals

A complete list of distress signals, as in Annex IV of the *International Regulations for Preventing Collisions at Sea*, is given in Section 2.1. Those which are more appropriate for yachts and small crafts are given in 8.3.10, together with notes on their use. It must be emphasised that distress signals must only be used when the boat is in serious and immediate danger, and when help is urgently required. If help is needed but the boat is not in immediate danger, the proper signal is 'V' (Victor) in the International Code, meaning 'I require assistance'. (See also 6.2.8 for selected groups from the International Code.)

6.4.4 Visual signals between UK shore stations and ships in distress

The following signals should be used if a vessel is in distress, or stranded off the coast of the United Kingdom.

(1) Acknowledgement of distress signal

By day. Orange smoke signal or combined light and sound signal (thunderlight) consisting of three single signals fired at about one minute intervals.
By night. White star rocket consisting of three single signals fired at about one minute intervals.

'You are seen – assistance will be given as soon as possible'. (Repetition has the same meaning)

If necessary the day signals may be given at night, or the night signals by day.

(2) Landing signals for small boats with persons in distress

By day. Vertical motion of a white flag or the arms, or signalling the code letter 'K' (− · −) by light or sound.
By night. Vertical motion of a white light or flare, or signalling the code letter 'K' (− · −) by light or sound. An indication of direction may be given by

'This is the best place to land'

'This is the best place to land'

placing a steady white light or flare at a lower level and in line with the observer.

By day. Horizontal motion of a white flag or arms extended horizontally, or signalling the code letter 'S' ($\cdots$) by light or sound.	'Landing here is highly dangerous'
By night. Horizontal motion of a white light or flare, or signalling the code letter 'S' ($\cdots$) by light or sound.	'Landing here is highly dangerous'
By day. Horizontal motion of a white flag, followed by the placing of it in the ground and the carrying of another white flag in the direction indicated, and/or a white star–signal in the direction of a better landing place. Or signalling the code letter 'S' ($\cdots$) followed by the code letter 'R' ($\cdot-\cdot$) if a better landing place is more to the right in the direction of approach, or by code letter 'L' ($\cdot-\cdot\cdot$) if a better landing place is more to the left in the direction of approach.	'Landing here highly dangerous. A more favourable location for landing is in the direction indicated'
By night. Horizontal motion of a white flare or light, followed by the placing of the white light or flare on the ground and the carrying of another white light or flare in the direction to be indicated, and/or a white star–signal in the direction towards the better landing place. Or signalling the code letter 'S' ($\cdots$) followed by the code letter 'R' ($\cdot-\cdot$) if a better landing place is more to the right in the direction of approach, or by code letter 'L' ($\cdot-\cdot\cdot$) if a better landing place is more to the left in the direction of approach.	'Landing here highly dangerous. A more favourable location for landing is in the direction indicated.'

(3) *Signals used in connection with shore life–saving apparatus*

By day. Vertical motion of a white flag or the arms *By night*. Vertical motion of a white light or flare.	In general 'Affirmative' Specifically – 'Rocket line is held' 'Tail block is made fast' 'Man is in breeches buoy' 'Haul away'
By day. Horizontal motion of a white flag or arms extended horizontally.	In general 'Negative' Specifically –

By night. Horizontal motion of a white light or flare.	'Slack away' 'Avast hauling'

(4) *Signals to be used to warn a vessel standing into danger*

The International Code signals 'U' or 'NF', or the letter 'U' ($\cdot\cdot-$) flashed by lamp or made by foghorn, whistle etc.	'You are running into danger'

If necessary the attention of the vessel may be called to these signals by a white flare, a rocket showing white stars on bursting, or an explosive signal.

6.4.5 **Signals used by aircraft on SAR operations**

With the increasing use now made of aircraft in search and resue (SAR) it is important that yachtsmen can recognise and understand certain signals which may be used.

Search procedures

The pattern of search and the spacing between tracks flown by an aircraft depends upon the visibility, the characteristics of the object being searched (e.g. yacht or liferaft) and the type, if any, of electronic search aid used. Unless distressed personnel can indicate their position to the aircraft the search may be valueless.

An aircraft normally flies through the search area at 3000–5000ft (900–1500m), or below cloud, firing a green Very cartridge approximately every five to ten minutes and at each turning point. When a green flare is sighted it is most important that the following action is taken:

(1) Wait for the glare of the green flare to die out.
(2) Fire one red flare.
(3) Fire another red flare after about 20 seconds (this enables the aircraft to line up on the bearing).
(4) Fire a third red flare when the aircraft is overhead, or appears to be going badly off course.

It is important to note that, in order to comply with the above, a boat or life-raft should carry at least three red flares. Should the aircraft be diverted to the search from another task it may fire flares of another colour (except red).

RAF aircraft diverted to SAR are equipped with some or all of UHF, VHF, HF WT/RT and MF. Royal Navy SAR helicopters carry VHF/UHF RT equipment, and other Royal Navy aircraft carry UHF RT. RAF search aircraft on SAR operations usually maintain the following continuous watches:

(1) HF WT communications with Rescue Co-ordination Centre, 5695 or 3095kHz.

(2) MF watch (with DF) on 500kHz. This is a listening watch only, the aircraft cannot transmit on this frequency.

(3) RT watch on 121.5 or 243MHz. The aircraft also have homing facilities on 243MHz and in some cases on 121.5MHz and Marine Band FM frequencies.

Designated SAR helicopters in the UK can communicate with RNLI lifeboats, HM Coastguard, Coast Radio Stations etc on the VHF/FM marine distress calling and safety frequency Ch 16, and on working frequencies.

Directing signals

The following signals may be used by SAR aircraft to direct ships towards another ship, aircraft or person in distress.

(1) In sequence, the aircraft circles the ship at least once. It then crosses low, ahead of the ship, opening and closing the throttle or changing the propeller pitch. Finally it heads in the direction in which the ship is to be directed. The signal may be repeated.	The aircraft is directing the ship towards the ship or aircraft in distress.
(2) The aircraft passes close astern of the ship, at low altitude, opening and closing the throttle or changing the propeller pitch. The signal may be repeated.	The aircraft is indicating that the assistance of the ship is no longer required.

6.4.6 Port signals

General

On the Continent signals to control port or harbour traffic are to some extent standardised, but not at present in the United Kingdom. Signals for individual harbours are shown in Chapter 10 of *The Macmillan & Silk Cut Nautical Almanac*. A new system of International Port Traffic Signals is to be introduced – see 6.4.7 – but the process will be gradual.

Increasing use is being made of VHF radio for port operations, pilot services and traffic management; VHF channels used for individual harbours are shown in Chapter 10 of *The Macmillan & Silk Cut Nautical Almanac*. Where appropriate, call on the indicated working frequency – usually Ch 12 or Ch 14. Radiotelephone procedures are discussed in Section 6.6.

The following groups in the *International Code of Signals* refer to port operations:

UH   Can you lead me into port?
UL   All vessels should proceed to sea as soon as possible owing to danger in port.

UM   The harbour (or port indicated) is closed to traffic.
UN   You may enter harbour immediately (or at time indicated).
UO   You must not enter harbour.
UP   Permission to enter harbour is urgently requested. I have an emergency case.
UQ   You should wait outside the harbour (or river mouth). UQ 1 You should wait outside the harbour until daylight.
UR   My estimated time of arrival (at place indicated) is (time indicated). UR 1 What is your estimated time of arrival (at place indicated)?
RZ 1 You should not proceed out of harbour/ anchorage.
RV 2 You should proceed into port.

British Isles

The Ministry of Defence might, in certain circumstances, control entry to special ports, and institute an Examination Service for vessels which approach them. In such cases, signals as follows may be displayed ashore or by Examination Vessels or by Examination Vessels or Traffic Control Vessels in the approaches:

By day	By night	Meaning
Three red balls shown vertically	Three flashing red lights shown vertically	Entry to port prohibited
	Three green lights shown vertically	Entry to port permitted
A blue flag	Red, green, red lights shown vertically	Movement of shipping within the port or anchorage prohibited

Vessels of the Examination Service wear a special flag, with a blue border and a square in the centre – the top half white and the bottom half red.

France and Belgium

The following signals are in general use in France and Belgium. There are two systems – the simplified code, used where there is not much traffic, and the full code.

(1) *Simplified code.*

By day	By night	Meaning
A red flag	A red light	Entry prohibited
A green flag	A green light	Departure prohibited
A red flag above a green flag	A red light above a green light	Entry and departure prohibited

(2) *Full code.* Each of the following signals is displayed vertically, and should be read accordingly:

By day	By night	Meaning
A cone, point up between two balls	A white light, between two red lights	Entry prohibited
Two cones, points together, above another cone point down	A white light between two green lights	Departure prohibited
Two cones, points together, above a ball	A white light above a red light and below a green light	Entry and departure prohibited

(3) In addition to the usual traffic signals, the following special signals may be shown:

By day	By night	Meaning
Three red balls, vertically	Three all-round flashing red lights, vertically	Port closed (emergency signal)
The appropriate International Code signal	Three all-round green lights, vertically	Port open

Netherlands
In the event of government control of entry to Dutch harbours, the following signals indicate that entry is prohibited, and that a yacht should proceed towards the examination vessel flying the same signal.

By day	By night
Three red balls, disposed vertically or:	Three red lights, disposed vertically or:
Two cones point together, over a ball	Three lights, disposed vertically, green over red over white

West Germany
The following signals are commonly used in the Federal Republic of Germany.

Signals at fixed bridges	Meaning
Two diamonds red and white in halves	Indicate limits of navigable width
Yellow diamond over centre of passage	Passage permitted in both directions
Two yellow diamonds, horizontally disposed	Passage permitted in one direction; traffic coming from opposite side stopped.

Sound signals at moveable bridges, locks etc	Meaning
. . . .	Passage or entry forbidden.
– –	Please open bridge or lock, or raise lift bridge to first step.
– – .	Please open lift bridge to full extent.
– – . –	Vessel proceeding seawards may pass or enter.
– – . . –	Vessel proceeding inwards may pass or enter.
– – – – –	Channel is closed.

Light signals (*R – red, W – white, G – green*)

		Meaning
R	R	Passage or entry forbidden.
	R	Be prepared to pass or enter.
W R	R	Bridge closed or down; vessels which can pass under the available clearance may proceed, but beware of oncoming traffic which may have a right of way.
W R	W R	Lift bridge will remain at first step; vessels which can pass under the available vertical clearance may proceed.
G	G	Passage or entry permitted; oncoming traffic stopped.
W G	G	Passage permitted, but beware of oncoming traffic which may have right of way.
	R	Bridge, lock or flood barrage closed to navigation.
	R	Exit from lock forbidden.
	G	Exit from lock permitted.

6.4.7 International Port Traffic Signals
An international system of port signals is being gradually introduced, but their general adoption is likely to take many years, and some existing signals may be retained indefinitely.

The rules for the new system, which is illustrated on page 62, are as follows:
(1) The main movement message given by a port traffic signal shall always comprise three lights, disposed vertically. No additional light shall be added to the column carrying the main message. (The fact that the main message always consists of three vertical lights allows the mariner to recognise it as a traffic signal, and not lights of navigational significance).

(2) Red lights indicate 'Do not proceed'.
(3) Green lights indicate 'Proceed, subject to the conditions stipulated'.
   Note that, to avoid confusion, red and green lights are never displayed together.
(4) A single yellow light, displayed to the left of the column carrying main messages Nos 2 or 5, at the level of the upper light, may be used to indicate that 'Vessels which can safely navigate outside the main channel need not comply with the main message'. This signal is of obvious significance to yachtsmen.
(5) Signals which are auxiliary to the main message may be devised by local authorities. Such auxiliary signals should employ only white and/or yellow lights, and should be displayed to the right of the column carrying the main message.

From the above it is evident that the basic signals are simple, and easy to memorise. Ports with complex entrances and much traffic may need many auxiliary signals, which will have to be documented: but smaller harbours with less traffic may only need one or two of the basic signals, such as 'Vessels shall not proceed' and 'Vessels may proceed, two way traffic'.

Some signals may be omni-directional – exhibited to all vessels simultaneously: others must be directional, and be shown either to vessels entering or to vessels leaving harbour.

Signal No 5 is based on the assumption that some other means of communication such as VHF radio, signal lamp, loud hailer, or auxiliary signal will be used to inform a vessel that she may specifically proceed.

The 'Serious Emergency' signal must be flashing, at least 60 flashes per minute. All other signals must be either fixed or slow occulting (the latter useful when background glare is a problem). A mixture of fixed and occulting lights must not be used.

6.4.8 Visual storm signals
Visual gale warning signals are displayed at places around the British Isles when a gale is expected within 12 hours, or is already blowing, in the adjacent sea area. The signals consist of black cones, point up for a gale from a northerly quarter or point down for a gale from a southerly quarter. Further details are given in 7.6.16.

It is likely that official visual storm signals will be discontinued in UK, but that they may still be shown in a few places by private arrangement.

Continental storm signals, as displayed in France, Belgium, Holland and the Federal Republic of Germany, are of a uniform type and are described in 7.6.17.

6.4.9 Tide signals
At some French and Belgian ports tide signals are displayed, indicating the height of the tide above chart datum. The signals are shown by three different shapes (or lights by night) as follows:

By day	At night	Meaning
A cone, point down	A green light	0.2m (or about 8in)
A cylinder	A red light	1.0m (or about 3.3ft)
A ball	A white light	5.0m (or about 16.4ft)

The three different shapes are disposed horizontally with cones to the left, and balls to the right of the cylinders when viewed from seaward; if more than one of each shape is used they are disposed vertically. Thus three cones, three cylinders, and one ball signify 8.6m. The night signals are disposed in a similar way.

Other signals are used to indicate the state of the tide, as follows:

By day	By night	Meaning
An elongated cone, point up	A green light over white light	Tide rising
A white flag with a black St Andrew's cross	Two white lights, horizontally	High water
An elongated cone, point down	A white light over green light	Tide falling
A blue pendant	Two green lights, horizontally	Low water

6.5 Radio receivers

6.5.1 Requirements for seagoing yachts
The advantages and uses of radiotelephones are discussed in Section 6.6, but any seagoing yacht should at least have a radio receiver. The very minimum requirement is to receive the shipping forecasts broadcast by the BBC on 200kHz (1500m). In many yachts this facility is provided by a set which is also used for direction finding. A 'Ship (Receiving Only) Licence' is required, and can be obtained from the Department of Trade and Industry, Marine Licensing Section, Radio Regulatory Division, Waterloo Bridge House, Waterloo Road, London, SE1 8UA. A separate licence is needed for a television receiver.

6.5.2 Frequencies
It is becoming increasingly common to specify a radio transmission by its frequency rather than its wavelength; this has been the practice in commercial and marine radio for many years, and it is useful to understand the relationship between the two descriptions.

Frequencies are expressed in kiloHertz (kHz), which used to be called kilocycles per second. For frequencies higher than 3000kHz, the term MegaHertz (MHz) is used. One MHz = 1000kHz.

Wavelength (metres) × Frequency (kHz) = 3×10^5

From this formula it can be seen, for example, that 1500 metres equals 200kHz, and that 200 metres equals 1500kHz.

The various frequency bands in use in marine radio are:

Frequency	Band	Wavelength (metres)
Low (LF)	30–300kHz	10,000–1000
Medium (MF)	300–3000kHz	1000–100
High (HF)	3–30MHz	100–10
Very High (VHF)	30–300MHz	10–1

Typical frequencies (in kHz) covered by a yacht's radio receiver are: 150–400 for radiobeacons, shipping forecasts and Consol; 550–1600 for 'Medium Wave' broadcast stations; 1600–4000 for receiving radiotelephone messages (e.g. from British Telecom Coast Radio Stations – see 6.6.9).

6.5.3 Weather bulletins
Full details of the various methods of receiving weather information from the radio are given in Section 7.6.

6.5.4 Radio installation
Marine radios need proper, professional installation if they are to perform efficiently. Bad aerials are often a cause of trouble. Attention must also be given to the suppression of electrical equipment in the boat; alternators, pumps, fluorescent lighting, windscreen wipers, ignition systems, revolution counters, and even rotating propeller shafts can all cause interference.

6.6 Radiotelephony

6.6.1 Radiotelephones – introduction
The radiotelephone is the modern way to communicate at sea, and there are four distinct types of concern to yachtsmen:
(1) Long Range High Frequency (HF) Service. World-wide communication is provided through Portishead Radio, but HF sets are large and costly so they are only appropriate for yachts making extended cruises.
(2) Medium Frequency (MF) equipment has a range of 200 miles (322km) or more, operating in the 2MHz band, and was once commonly fitted in yachts. But now MF sets must be single sideband (SSB) and are very expensive. Double sideband transmissions are prohibited except for emergency-only sets on 2182kHz. For modes of emission see 6.6.6, and for SSB see 6.6.7.

(3) Very High Frequency (VHF) equipment has a range rather more than line of sight between the aerials concerned, but is much cheaper than MF (or HF), simple to install, and also relatively free from interference. The number of VHF shore stations is steadily increasing. See 6.6.4.
(4) Citizens Band (CB) radio is not a real substitute for VHF afloat, because it has less range and because the CB emergency channel 09 is not monitored in the same way as VHF Channel 16 (see 6.6.4). But legal (CB 27/81) CB radio can be useful for club purposes in organising events, and for social chat. For further details see 6.6.18.

Similar considerations to those for radio receivers (6.5.4) apply in the installation of a radiotelephone. A good aerial is most important. Since the power of a VHF transmitter is limited to 25w it is desirable to use an antenna which will transmit the maximum beam in a horizontal direction, and not up into the sky. This, however, can be overdone, so that there is a loss in signal strength when the boat heels appreciably. The antenna must be matched to the transmitter, with the right impedance, expressed in terms of the 'voltage standing wave ratio' which should be as near unity as possible over the range of frequencies employed. Connecting cables must be kept as short as possible (consistent with placing the antenna as high as possible), and be of good co-axial cable: this should normally be $\frac{1}{4}$in (6.5mm), although $\frac{1}{2}$in (13mm) may be required for some masthead installations. In the event of dismasting, it should be possible to use an emergency aerial rigged on deck.

Good suppression of all electrical equipment is essential, and should meet the requirements of BS1597, which defines the permitted interference over a frequency range of 15kHz to 100MHz.

The set itself should be mounted where it is accessible, but protected from spray and dampness. A waterproof extension speaker is useful at the steering position.

The battery should be as high as possible, remote from bilge water or from possible fire in the engine compartment, and it must be kept well charged.

MF and HF radiotelephones require some form of earthing arrangement, usually a metal plate in the bottom of the boat.

6.6.2 Radiotelephones – licences
A licence is required for any radio apparatus which is installed or used on board. There are four types of licence:
(1) *Ship Licence.* A Ship Licence authorises the installation and use of a sending and receiving station.
(2) *Ship (Receiving Only) Licence.* This authorises the establishment and use of a receiving station for receiving messages from coast and certain other stations in addition to normal

broadcast programmes.

Provided that the renewal fees are paid on or before the anniversary of the date of issue, these two Licences continue in force until revoked.

(3) *Ship (Emergency Only) Licence.* This licence authorises a sending and receiving station for use only in emergency.

(4) *CB Radio Licence.*

Apply for Licences 1–3 above to the Department of Trade and Industry, Marine Licensing Section, Radio Regulatory Division, Waterloo Bridge House, Waterloo Road, London, SE1 8UA.

It is a condition of the licence that the set complies with certain performance specifications in the 'MPT' series, issued by the Secretary of State for the Home Department. The address above will advise whether particular equipment conforms.

Authorised radio installations (other than CB) must be controlled by an operator holding an appropriate certificate of competence: the minimum standard is the Restricted Certificate of Competence, for which a candidate is required:

(1) To produce evidence of British, British Commonwealth or Irish Republic Nationality;

(2) To operate a radiotelephone installation, including changing frequency, varying the power of the transmitter, and charging the batteries;

(3) To possess a knowledge of radiotelephone procedure in general and the distress regulations in particular;

(4) To maintain a radiotelephone log;

(5) To send and receive messages by telephone.

For most yachtsmen the appropriate certificate is the Certificate of Competence, Restricted VHF Only. The Royal Yachting Association (RYA) is responsible for the conduct of this examination. Full details of the syllabus and of the examination procedure, together with an application form, are given in RYA booklet G26, obtainable from the RYA (£1.50).

The completed form, with an examination fee of £13.00, must be sent to the nearest examination centre listed. At the examination it is essential to produce evidence of British nationality, and a passport-size photograph.

Enquiries for operators' certificates for MF or HF should be made to Examination Duty, Maritime Radio Services, British Telecom International, 43 Bartholomew Close, London, EC1A 7HP.

After application for a Ship Licence, an official will visit the boat to inspect the radio installation, and ensure that the conditions of the Licence have been met. The Licence shows the name and call sign of the yacht, the frequencies and the type of emission and power for transmission, and the conditions under which the station must be operated. There are stiff penalties for any contravention.

Subject to the approval of the owner, the Ship Licence permits crew members to use sound radios for receiving programmes from authorised broadcasting stations: it does not cover television, for which a separate licence is required.

Yacht clubs and marinas may set up radio stations operating on Channel 'M' (157.85MHz). Yachts so fitted may communicate with the base station of any club or marina on matters related to their activities or business. Ch M must not be used for intership working – communication between two boats. Application forms for this service can be obtained from the Department of Trade and Industry, Marine Licensing Section, Radio Regulatory Division, Waterloo Bridge House, Waterloo Road, London, SE1 8UA.

6.6.3 Radiotelephones – general provisions

Apart from the licensing arrangements described in 6.6.2, there are various regulations governing RT (other than CB radio) afloat. They are contained in the *Handbook for Radio Operators* (HMSO). Here is a brief summary.

(1) Operators are required to preserve the secrecy of correspondence, and not to divulge the contents of any transmissions which they may receive or intercept.

(2) Stations *must* identify themselves when transmitting. Coast stations (see 6.6.9) are normally identified by their geographical names followed by the word 'Radio', e.g. Northforeland Radio. Ship stations are identified by the name of the vessel, amplified where necessary to explain her nationality or occupation. Yacht call signs may be prefaced by the word 'Yacht', e.g. Yacht Seabird, when this information is relevant.

(3) A yacht with a radiotelephone must carry the Ship Licence; a copy of Section 11 of the Post Office (Protection) Act, 1884; the certificate(s) of the operator(s); a Radiotelephone Log; a list of coast stations with which communications are likely to be conducted, showing watchkeeping hours, frequencies and charges; the *Handbook for Radio Operators*.

(4) Except in cases of distress, coast stations control communications in their areas, and their instructions should be complied with. For a vessel in distress close to the coast, the nearest MRCC or MRSC becomes the co-ordinating station for the incident – see 8.4.2. and 8.4.7.

(5) While at sea a yacht may call other vessels, and she may call shore stations (or aircraft stations). Messages must not be transmitted to an address ashore except through a coast radio station (see 6.6.9). When in harbour she may not communicate with other vessels, but only with shore stations

– (including any local Port Operations Service, or station authorised to use Channel M). Intership calls in harbour are allowed only on matters concerning safety.

(6) It is most important that operators do not interfere with the working of other stations. Before transmitting, an operator must listen on the appropriate frequency or channel to ensure that it is not already in use.

(7) It is forbidden to transmit unnecessary or superfluous signals. Test transmissions must not interfere with other stations, and must include the vessel's call sign.

(8) Absolute priority must be given to distress calls and messages. The transmission of false distress, safety or identification signals is strictly prohibited.

(9) The transmission of profane, indecent or obscene language is strictly forbidden.

(10) Under the regulations any vessel fitted with a radiotelephone should keep a radiotelephone log. The following entries should be made:
— the operator's name
— the time of arrival at and departure from ports, with names
— a summary of any communications relating to distress, urgency and safety traffic
— a record of communications exchanged with coast stations and other ship stations
— a reference to any important service incidents (breakdowns of the apparatus)
— the boat's position, at least once each day.

6.6.4 VHF radio

The general subject of VHF radiotelephones for yachtsmen is well covered in RYA booklet G22, which gives the various procedures in detail.

VHF is limited to ranges slightly better than the line of sight between the aerials, so the yacht's aerial needs to be sited as high as possible. The maximum permitted output of a VHF set is 25 watts, and it pays to fit an efficient aerial in order to get the best performance. A low power output, normally one watt, is used for close range communication.

Most UK coast stations, and an increasing number of commercial and yachting harbours, are now fitted with VHF. So are the principal Coastguard stations and other elements of the rescue services.

The frequencies allocated by international agreement for marine VHF are in the range 156.00–174.00MHz. Channel 16 (156.80MHz) is used for distress and safety purposes, and for calling and answering. Once communication has been established the stations concerned must switch to an appropriate working frequency, except for safety matters.

All vessels at sea equipped with VHF are encouraged to keep watch on Ch 16, for safety reasons.

Although there are a total of 57 channels in the international marine VHF band, a small boat needs only about a dozen.

Basic VHF sets are 'simplex' which means that they transmit and receive on the same frequency – so that it is not possible to speak and listen at the same time; the 'transmit' button blots out all reception. 'Semi-duplex' sets transmit and receive on two different frequencies, while fully 'duplex' sets can do this simultaneously – so that conversation is normal.

There are three main groups of frequencies, as shown below in order of preference. Certain channels can be used for more than one purpose.

(1) *Public correspondence* (for use with British Telecom coast radio stations). All these can be used for duplex working if the set is so equipped: Ch 26, 27, 25, 24, 23, 28, 4, 1, 3, 2, 7, 5, 84, 87, 86, 83, 85, 88, 61, 64, 65, 62, 66, 63, 60, 82.

(2) *Inter-ship*. These are all simplex channels: Ch 6, 8, 10, 13, 9, 72, 73, 69, 67, 77, 15, 17.

(3) *Port operations* (pilotage, tugs etc). The simplex channels are: Ch 12, 14, 11, 13, 9, 68, 71, 74, 10, 67, 69, 73, 17, and 15. Channels which can be used for duplex are: Ch 20, 22, 18, 19, 21, 5, 7, 2, 3, 1, 4, 78, 82, 79, 81, 80, 60, 63, 66, 62, 65, 64, 61, 84.

It should be explained that the original VHF channel spacings were 50kHz. In 1972 this was reduced to 25kHz, and additional frequencies were interleaved between the existing ones; this has resulted in the rather odd channel designations, since channels between 29 and 59 are allocated to other services.

Channel 70 is reserved for digital selective calling for distress and safety purposes.

Channel 0 (Zero), which is 156.00MHz, is a special channel reserved for communication between HM Coastguard and other rescue services such as lifeboats. It may only be fitted in a yacht if specially authorised by the Home Office for an Auxiliary Coastguard (Afloat).

Two other frequencies are of particular interest to yachtsmen. 157.85MHz, normally referred to as Channel M, is allocated to yacht clubs and marinas. A special letter of authorisation is needed to use this frequency: it is obtainable from the Marine Licensing Section, Radio Regulatory Division, Waterloo Bridge House, Waterloo Road, London SE1 8UA.

Ch 67 (156.375MHz) is an inter-ship channel allocated in this country to communications relating to yacht and small craft safety. The principal coastguard stations are fitted with this channel, which is accessed via Ch 16. When calling HM Coastguard, use the title of the local centre followed by 'Coastguard'. For example: 'Solent Coastguard'.

VHF sets

As can be understood from the number of different channels which are available for VHF communication, to take full advantage of the system a set should be chosen which can use a reasonable number – depending on the intended area of operation. If a boat is only to be used in one locality, then a dozen channels (which are the sort of number fitted in less expensive sets) can be sufficient, if they are sensibly selected.

It is mandatory to have Ch 06 as well as Ch 16. Most boats will probably need Ch 12 and Ch 14 for port operations. Ch M can be very useful if the boat is kept in a marina which operates this frequency. Ch 67, the Small Craft Safety Channel, is a great benefit in a boat which is used for coastal cruising. In a 12-channel set this leaves six further channels to be chosen – say Ch 08 as an alternative inter-ship channel, and the others from the public correspondence (ship-shore) channels depending on which coast stations are most likely to be used.

A refinement available with some sets is 'dual watch facility', whereby two channels can be monitored by the receiver at the same time: one of these should be Ch 16, and the other can be selected as required. It is also possible to obtain an attachment which will scan a larger number of channels.

Another operational extra available is selective calling (Selcall), which dispenses with the need to

Channel	Transmitting frequencies (MHz) Ship stations	Coast stations	Inter ship	Port operations Single frequency	Two frequency	Public correspondence
60	156.025	160.625			•	•
01	156.050	160.650			•	•
61	156.075	160.675			•	•
02	156.100	160.700			•	•
62	156.125	160.725			•	•
03	156.150	160.750			•	•
63	156.175	160.775			•	•
04	156.200	160.800			•	•
64	156.225	160.825			•	•
05	156.250	160.850			•	•
65	156.275	160.875			•	•
06	156.300		•			
66	156.325	160.925			•	•
07	156.350	160.950			•	•
67	156.375	156.375	•	•		
08	156.400		•			
68	156.425	156.425		•		
09	156.450	156.450	•	•		
69	156.475	156.475	•	•		
10	156.500	156.500	•	•		
70	156.525		•			
11	156.550	156.550		•		
71	156.575	156.575		•		
12	156.600	156.600		•		
72	156.625		•			
13	156.650	156.650	•	•		
73	156.675	156.675	•	•		
14	156.700	156.700		•		
74	156.725	156.725		•		
15	156.750	156.750	•	•		
75	Guard band 156.7625–156.7875 MHz					

Channel	Transmitting frequencies (MHz) Ship stations	Coast stations	Inter ship	Port operations Single frequency	Two frequency	Public correspondence
16	156.800	156.800	DISTRESS Safety and Calling			
76	Guard band 156.8125–156.8375 MHz					
17	156.850	156.850	•	•		
77	156.875		•			
18	156.900	161.500				•
78	156.925	161.525			•	•
19	156.950	161.550				•
79	156.975	161.575				•
20	157.000	161.600				•
80	157.025	161.625				•
21	157.050	156.050 or 161.650				•
81	157.075	161.675				•
22	157.100	161.700			•	•
82	157.125	161.725			•	•
23	157.150	156.150 or 161.750				•
83	157.175	156.175 or 161.775				•
24	157.200	161.800				•
84	157.225	161.825			•	•
25	157.250	161.850				•
85	157.275	161.875				•
26	157.300	161.900				•
86	157.325	161.925				•
27	157.350	161.950				•
87	157.375	161.975				•
28	157.400	162.000				•
88	157.425	162.025				•

NOTES

1. For intership communication, those channels (i.e. Ch 06, 08, 72 and 77) assigned solely for this purpose should be used in preference to other frequencies. Ch 06 may however be used by ships and aircraft on SAR operations, when its use for other purposes must be avoided.
2. Ch 10, 67 and 72 may be used by ships, aircraft and land stations for SAR co-ordination and for anti-pollution operations.
3. In the UK, Ch 67 is allocated as a Small Craft Safety Channel, for use by small craft and HM Coastguard. 157.85 MHz is a private channel, referred to as Ch M, for communication between yachts and marinas/yacht clubs.
4. Ch 70 is reserved for digital selective calling in connection with the Future Global Maritime Distress and Safety System (FGMDSS).

monitor traffic lists and allows the set to be used almost like a telephone ashore. When a message is to be passed to the yacht, the coast station concerned transmits a specially coded signal which alerts a decoder attached to the receiver, triggering an audible alarm and an indicator light. In addition to alerting vessels for individual calls, a special signal also gives warning of 'All Ships' calls for safety and urgency messages about to be transmitted by coast stations.

When Selcall is to be fitted to existing equipment, application must be made to the Radio Regulatory Division at Waterloo Bridge House for a Selcall number, or with a new set it can be requested when applying for the licence. Coast stations keep on file the Selcall numbers for all vessels so allocated.

Using special equipment (IRMA), telephone numbers can be direct-dialled through French VHF coast stations.

6.6.5 MF and HF radio

It is convenient to consider Medium Frequency (MF) and High Frequency (HF) together, because there are basic similarities and because sets are available which overlap the MF band (1.6–4.2MHz) and the HF band (4–25MHz). MF radiotelephones provide communication at ranges of up to 200 miles (320km) or more – considerably greater than can be achieved by VHF. An HF set can give world wide coverage. But MF/HF sets are larger and heavier than VHF, consume more power, and are considerably more expensive.

As explained in 6.6.7, MF/HF sets must now be single sideband (SSB), and must be type-approved for a licence to be obtained. As for VHF sets, a large number of channels are available at different frequencies. The MF international RT distress frequency is 2182kHz, and is used for distress calls and traffic, signals of emergency position-indicating radiobeacons, the urgency signal and urgency messages, the navigational warning signal, and for the safety signal. UK and many foreign coast stations keep watch on 2182kHz. There is a silence period on this frequency for three minutes commencing every hour and half-hour. During these silence periods all transmissions except distress, urgency and safety communications must cease on 2182kHz.

6.6.6 Modes of emission

As already discussed in 4.2.7, intelligence is impressed upon a radio signal in various ways – by employing different modes of emission. New designations for modes of emission came into force on 1 January 1982, and examples of those most commonly used in marine radio are given below (with the previous designation in brackets).

A1A	(A1)	Continuous wave telegraphy, Morse code.
A2A	(A2)	Telegraphy by the on-off keying of a tone modulated carrier, Morse code: double sideband.
H2A	(A2H)	Telegraphy by the on-off keying of a tone modulated carrier, Morse code: single sideband, full carrier.
A3E	(A3)	Telephony using amplitude modulation: double sideband.
R3E	(A3A)	Telephony using amplitude modulation: single sideband, reduced carrier.
J3E	(A3J)	Telephony using amplitude modulation: single sideband, suppressed carrier.
H3E	(A3H)	Telephony using amplitude modulation: single sideband, full carrier.
F3E	(F3)	Telephony using frequency modulation.
F1B	(F1)	Telegraphy using frequency modulation; Narrow band direct printing (Telex).
F3E	(F3)	Telephony using frequency modulation.
FXX	(F9)	Cases not covered by F1B, F3E nor frequency modulation facsimile, in which the main carrier is frequency modulated.

6.6.7 Single sideband (SSB)

Except for distress purposes, it is now illegal to use double sideband (DSB) transmissions. The old DSB signal consisted of three components – the carrier wave and two speech information sidebands, one on each side of the carrier, thus occupying a fairly broad band. In single sideband (SSB), the carrier and one sideband (usually the lower) are suppressed, thus reducing the width to the upper sideband only. This therefore reduces the band width, and greatly reduces interference with adjacent channels. Also, whereas previously the output power of a transmitter was divided between three components, it is now concentrated on the one sideband, thus effectively increasing power output.

A3E (previously A3) DSB transmissions are now prohibited on all channels, except for Emergency-Only equipment using 2182kHz.

H3E (previously A3H) full carrier SSB working should be used for calling and listening on 2182kHz, and for all casualty working between ship and shore.

R3E (previously A3A) reduced carrier SSB working is seldom used in practice. It is permitted, but tends to be used only at the request of a receiving station which has difficulty in resolving an incoming signal. The injection of partial carrier allows a finer tune on the carrier. It is then usual to request return to J3E (A3J) – see below.

J3E (previously A3J) fully suppressed carrier, SSB working is compulsory on all working frequencies. This includes the United Kingdom supplementary calling channel of 2381kHz, and the United Kingdom Coast Radio Station answering frequency of 1792kHz.

All Casualty and other broadcasts on 2182kHz are made in the H3E (A3H) mode. All other broadcasts (i.e. Weather Bulletins, Gale Warnings and Navigational Warnings) on working channels are made in the J3E (A3J) mode, as are all link calls and other transmissions on working channels.

In the event of having to make a Distress Call, you are permitted to use any means at your disposal to attract attention. This means that an old DSB set can still be used for Distress working, but only for this purpose. All modern sets are arranged so that H3E (A3H) is used when 2182kHz is selected.

If using French documentation, the term for SSB is BLU (Bandes Latérale Unique); and for Dutch it is EZB (Enkel Zyband).

6.6.8 General procedures
The following procedures in general apply to all radiotelephones (other than CB). Except for distress, urgency or safety messages, communications between a ship and coast station are controlled by the coast station; ship stations must comply accordingly. Between two ship stations, the station called controls the working, but if a coast station intervenes both ship stations must comply with its instructions.

Before transmitting, a station must first listen to ensure it will not interfere with communications already in progress, and if necessary await an appropriate break. Apart from distress, urgency or safety communications, calling and signals preparatory to the exchange of traffic must not exceed one minute when using 2182kHz (MF) or Ch 16 (VHF).

Calling procedure
To make a call, the calling station must use a frequency on which the other station keeps watch. Normally a ship station calls a coast station, and the frequencies/channels to be used are given in *The Macmillan & Silk Cut Nautical Almanac*.

However a coast station may call a ship station for which it has traffic if it knows the ship is within its area.

A call consists of:
— the name or identification of the station(s) called, not more than three times;
— the words THIS IS (or DE spoken as DELTA ECHO in case of language difficulties);
— the name or identification of the calling station, not more than three times.

For VHF communication the name of the station called need only be given once, and that of the calling station twice. When contact is made the name need only be transmitted once.

If a station does not reply, the call may be repeated at three-minute intervals – assuming that this does not interfere with any communication in progress. Where reliable VHF communication is practicable, the calling ship station may repeat the call as soon as it is known that other traffic has terminated.

Replying to calls
A reply is made on the frequency upon which the calling station keeps watch, unless it has specified another frequency. The exchange of identities is made in a similar form to the initial call. If the station is unable to accept traffic immediately it instructs the other station accordingly – 'WAIT ... MINUTES', or if other ships are waiting, 'YOUR TURN IS NUMBER ...'

When a station receives a call intended for it, but is uncertain of the identity of the calling station, it replies as follows:
— 'STATION CALLING ...' (insert name of called station). 'THIS IS ...' (insert name of called station). 'REPEAT YOUR CALL – OVER'.

Agreement on working frequency/channel
If the station called agrees with the working channel proposed by the calling station, in the reply to the call it should indicate that from then on it will listen on that working channel, and also state the working channel which it will itself use. If it does not agree with the working channel proposed it should indicate a suitable alternative.

'All Ships' broadcasts
Information about gale warnings, navigational warnings etc. for general promulgation from coast stations is generally addressed to 'All Ships' or 'All Stations'. Such a message does not require any reply or acknowledgement.

Voice communication
Before making a radiotelephone call it is important to decide exactly what needs to be said; for those who are inexperienced it is advisable to write the message down, rather as one would write out a telegram. Clear and distinct speech is very important. The voice should be pitched a little higher than normal for best results, avoiding any tendency to drop the pitch at the ends of phrases. Speak directly into the microphone, held a few inches from the face, about as loud as for normal conversation. Speak clearly, and emphasise weak syllables. The rate of speaking should be steady, but complicated words or figures should be given more slowly than other parts of the message – particularly if they need to be written down the other end – and may be repeated.

Names or important words should be spelled out by the phonetic table given in 6.2.4. It is normally not necessary to use the full phonetic spelling for figures, as in 6.2.4, but the following pronunciations are helpful:

Numeral	Pronunciation	Numeral	Pronunciation
0	ZE-RO	5	FIFE
1	WUN	6	SIX
2	TOO	7	SEV-en
3	TREE	8	AIT
4	FOW-er	9	NINE-er

Prowords (procedure words)

In RT communication it is important to know certain prowords, which have the following meanings:

ACKNOWLEDGE	'Have you received and understood?'
CONFIRM	'My version is . . . is that correct?'
CORRECTION	Spoken during a message, means 'An error has been made in this transmission; the correct version is . . .'
I SAY AGAIN	'I repeat' (normally important words or numerals in the message).
I SPELL	'I will spell out the next part of the message phonetically'
OUT	End of work
OVER	'I have completed this part of my message and am inviting you to reply'
RECEIVED	Receipt acknowledged
SAY AGAIN	Repeat your message (or portion indicated)
STATION CALLING	Used when a station is uncertain of the identity of a station which is calling

6.6.9 **Coast Radio Stations**

British Telecom operates a number of Coast Radio Stations at strategic places around the British Isles: details of their frequencies and services and fuller information is given in *Notice to Ship Wireless Stations*. Similar facilities are provided in other countries. Details of all Coast Radio Stations, worldwide, are contained in the *Admiralty List of Radio Signals, Vol 1*. Those in North-West Europe are given in *The Macmillan & Silk Cut Nautical Almanac*.

Coast stations control their respective areas and serve as a link between ship stations and the telephone network. They also transmit routine traffic lists (notifying ships of traffic for them), navigational warnings (of wrecks, lights not functioning etc) for sea regions lettered A–N around the British Isles, and weather bulletins. Gale warnings are broadcast at the end of the next silence period and at other scheduled times. Details of these services are given in *The Macmillan & Silk Cut Nautical Almanac*.

Coast stations have an important role to play in respect to distress, urgency, safety and medical messages, which are described in 6.6.16.

Most of the major coast stations in the United Kingdom operate on both MF and VHF, and some control one or more unmanned, remote VHF stations, in order to extend the area of VHF coverage.

MF calls to United Kingdom coast stations are made on 2381kHz 0900–1700 (local time) Monday–Saturday, and on 2182kHz at all other times. The coast station always answers on 1792kHz. Once communication is established both the coast station and the ship station transmit on selected working frequencies. To save time, a yacht should indicate in her call which working channels she has available: the coast station will tell her which to use.

MF calls to French coast stations may be made on 2321kHz, if 2182kHz is busy.

Except in the case of distress, urgency or safety messages all United Kingdom VHF coast stations should be called directly on a working channel. Where possible avoid using a station's broadcast channel, particularly around the times of scheduled broadcasts.

The yacht should monitor each working channel in turn until a free one is located, with no transmissions. A channel in use is indicated by either speech or by an engaged signal – a series of pips being transmitted. Having selected a free channel, the call should last at least five seconds in order to activate equipment at the coast station, whereupon the engaged signal indicates that the call has been accepted. The radio officer will then speak, although not perhaps immediately since he may be occupied with another call on another channel.

If you do not succeed in 'switching on' a coast station's transmitter you may be out of range. Try another channel or another station, or call again when closer.

VHF coast stations which use direct calling on working channels continue to keep watch on Ch 16 for distress, urgency and safety purposes, and give preliminary announcements of traffic lists etc on this channel.

Queries or comments regarding United Kingdom coast radio stations should be addressed to Maritime Radio Services, British Telecom, 43 Bartholomew Close, London, EC1A 7HP.

French and German coast stations should be called on VHF on the appropriate working channel. The calling channel for Belgian and Dutch coast stations depends on the geographical position of the yacht.

6.6.10 **'TR' organisation**

A radiotelephone provides the best and most convenient way for a yacht to be kept in touch with somebody ashore. Any boat leaving harbour for more than a few hours sailing in local waters – say if she is coastal cruising, or bound foreign –

is advised to call the nearest coast station and give the boat's name, her current position, destination, and estimated time of arrival, or return to harbour. This not only enables the coast station to know how to set about passing any traffic to the boat, but it could be vital information if the boat becomes overdue or is involved in a distress situation. It also serves as a test for the boat's radiotelephone, and is an opportunity to train members of the crew in its use. It is equally important to report the boat's safe arrival at her destination.

This is done through what is known as the 'TR' organisation, and a call would take the following form after initial contact has been made with a coast station:

'LEWIS RADIO – THIS IS SEABIRD – TANGO ROMEO – DEPARTED OBAN – BOUND LERWICK – ETA ONE SIX JULY – OVER'.

On arrival at Lerwick *Seabird* reports to the nearest coast station (Shetland Radio):

'SHETLAND RADIO – THIS IS SEABIRD – ARRIVED LERWICK – CLOSING DOWN RADIO WATCH – OVER'.

Shetland Radio would then inform *Seabird* if there is any traffic for her.

6.6.11 Radiotelephone link calls

Radiotelephone services are available, through coast radio stations, from ship stations to telephone subscribers not only in the United Kingdom but also in other countries of the international telephone network. It is possible to make personal calls to certain countries and collect (transferred charge) calls to the United Kingdom.

World-wide accounting for calls made through coast stations is arranged by quoting the 'Accounting Authority Indicator Code' (AAIC). For all British yachts and small craft this is GB 14. Thus, when making a link call, the AAIC 'GULF BRAVO ONE FOUR' must be included, together with the yacht's call sign. However, as an alternative arrangement it is possible to have a VHF link call from a yacht or small craft through a British coast station to a telephone number in the United Kingdom, the Channel Islands or the Isle of Man, charged to the owner's home telephone account. To do this, the Accounting Authority Indicator Code 'YTD' must be quoted, followed by the telephone number to which the call is charged.

Example: To set up a link call from the yacht *Seabird* to a number in the United Kingdom. The yacht calls the nearest coast radio station, say Lewis Radio, on Ch 16 (or on a working channel where this is permitted):

'LEWIS RADIO – THIS IS SEABIRD – SEABIRD – LINK CALL PLEASE – OVER'.

Lewis Radio replies, indicating the working channel to be used:

'SEABIRD – THIS IS LEWIS RADIO –

CHANNEL FIVE – STAND BY – OVER'.

Seabird acknowledges as follows:

'LEWIS RADIO – THIS IS SEABIRD – CHANNEL FIVE – OVER'.

Seabird then switches to Ch 05 and listens for Lewis Radio, which calls back:

'SEABIRD – THIS IS LEWIS RADIO – WHAT NUMBER PLEASE – OVER'.

Seabird replies (on Ch 05), giving her AAIC. Assuming that the call is to be charged to the owner's home account, the procedure would be:

'LEWIS RADIO – THIS IS SEABIRD – YANKEE TANGO DELTA – ZERO ONE – THREE EIGHT FIVE – SIX ONE FOUR THREE – LINK CALL TO ZERO NINE SIX – TWO SEVEN EIGHT – THREE ZERO THREE – OVER'

If communications are good, it should not be necessary to repeat the numbers, but do so if in doubt or if so requested.

The coast station would then ring the number required, and when it is obtained make the connection to the yacht. When radio channels are congested calls may be limited to six minutes. The coast station decides the duration of the call for charging purposes, and normally informs the ship station at the end of the conversation with the land number.

6.6.12 Weather information by radiotelephone

The various sources of weather information are given in Section 7.6, and the proper use of a radiotelephone can be an advantage in this respect. For example, as detailed in 7.6.10, it is possible to make a link call through any United Kingdom coast station.

Similarly, reports on actual weather conditions in local areas can be obtained by link calls to Coastguard Stations and Lighthouses which make weather observations for the Met. Office. When within VHF range, reports on local weather conditions may be obtained direct from principal Coastguard Stations using Ch 67 – the Small Craft Safety Channel (see 6.6.4). Ch 67 is accessed via Ch 16.

6.6.13 Medical help by radiotelephone

Medical advice can be obtained by requesting 'Medico' service through any United Kingdom or Irish coast station, which will connect the yacht with a suitable medical authority – usually the nearest hospital. If medical help is needed in the form of a doctor, or if a serious casualty has to be off-lifted, the call will be passed to the Coastguard. In either case the message is passed free of charge, and where appropriate the Urgency Signal PAN PAN may be used (see 6.6.16).

Similar arrangements apply in other European countries. Calls to French coast stations should be in French, prefixed 'Radiomédical'. For Belgium call Oostende coast station in English, French,

Dutch or German using the address 'Radiomédical Oostende'. For Netherlands call Scheveningen coast station in English, Dutch, French or German, using the address 'Radiomédical Scheveningen'. For the Federal Republic of Germany, call the nearest coast station in English or German, prefixing the call 'Funkarzt' (see also 8.6.27).

6.6.14 Special broadcasts to yachtsmen

A service is available through United Kingdom medium range (MF) or short range (VHF) coast station for broadcasting urgent business or personal messages to yachts or other small craft with radio receivers. The messages are broadcast immediately after the morning and evening weather messages.

Persons ashore should telephone any urgent message to the coast station nearest to the best known position of the boat, asking for 'Yachting Radio Messages' and giving the name of the yachtsman, the name of the yacht, and the area where the yacht is expected to be. The service (in 1983) costs 38p per word, plus £1.50 per message. Receipt of a one-way broadcast message can never be certain. If a yacht picks up a message for a nearby yacht which may not have received it, it is helpful if the message can be passed on. The telephone numbers of the coast stations concerned are shown below:

Land's End Radio (plus Start Point, Scillies and Pendennis Radio) – 073687 363.

Niton Radio (plus Weymouth Bay Radio) – 0983 730495.

Northforeland Radio (plus Hastings, Thames and Orfordness Radio) – 0843 220592.

Humber Radio (plus Bacton and Grimsby Radio) – 0521 73447.

Cullercoats Radio (plus Whitby Radio) – 091 253 1318.

Wick Radio (plus Cromarty, Orkney, Shetland and Collafirth Radio) – 0955 2271.

Stonehaven Radio (plus Forth, Buchan, Hebrides, Lewis, Skye Radio) – 0569 62917.

Portpatrick Radio (plus Clyde and Islay Radio) – 077 681 311.

Anglesey Radio (plus Morecambe Bay and Cardigan Bay Radio) – 0407 830541.

Ilfracombe Radio (plus Celtic and Severn Radio) – 0271 63453.

6.6.15 Port operations

Many commercial ports and harbours now have radiotelephone facilities, operating on VHF. A few also operate on MF, mostly in connection with pilotage services which are not normally the concern of yachtsmen.

Certain VHF channels, most commonly Ch 12 and Ch 14, are allocated for port operations. Communications on such channels must be restricted to those relating to operational handling, the movement and the safety of ships and, in emergency, to the safety of persons. They must not be used for public correspondence messages.

In harbour a radiotelephone must only be used on port operations channels, on private channels authorised by the Home Office (e.g. Ch M), and for communication with the nearest coast station. Intership communication is only allowed for safety purposes.

It is very useful to be able to communicate with harbour authorities by VHF – particularly in busy commercial ports where permission is sometimes needed to leave or enter, or in strange harbours when local information is needed on moorings or other facilities.

Call on Ch 16 or, where possible, on a nominated working channel, but since the Port Radio is likely to be listening out on more than one channel it is helpful, when calling, to state the channel being used, e.g. 'Orkney Harbour Radio – This is Seabird, Seabird – on Channel 20 – over'.

Useful information can often be obtained merely by listening out on the appropriate channel in a commercial harbour. In some ports regular information on local traffic, weather and tidal conditions is broadcast at specified times. It is most important that yachts do not use those working channels which are reserved for port operations – berthing/unberthing, ship/tug, pilot/berthing master messages etc.

6.6.16 Distress messages and procedures

One of the greatest advantages of having a radiotelephone on board a yacht is that it is easy to call for help if things go wrong. In such an important matter there are, however, strict procedures to be followed. All the crew should know what they are, and how to use the set in an emergency.

The frequencies of 2182kHz MF and Channel 16 (156.8MHz)VHF are internationally recognised for passing Distress, Urgency and Safety messages. Many stations, ashore and afloat, keep continuous watch on these frequencies.

The distress signal MAYDAY by radiotelephone indicates that a ship, aircraft or other vehicle is threatened by grave and imminent danger, and requests IMMEDIATE ASSISTANCE. The procedure is as follows:

Check that the yacht's main battery switch is 'on'. Switch on the set, and in the case of VHF ensure that it is on 'high power'. Switch the transmitter to Ch 16 or 2182kHz, as appropriate.

If the boat carries an alarm signal generator (few yachts do), operate this device for a least 30 seconds. Then speak slowly and distinctly, transmitting–

MAYDAY MAYDAY MAYDAY

THIS IS (name of boat spoken three times)

MAYDAY (name of boat spoken once)

MY POSITION IS ... (Latitude and longitude, or true bearing and distance from a known point)

Nature of distress ...

Type of assistance required ... OVER

The yacht's position is of vital importance, and should be repeated if time allows. It is also helpful to state the number on board. Do not forget to release the 'transmit' button on completion of the message.

An immediate acknowledgement should be expected anywhere in coastal waters, either from another vessel or from a shore station. If not, check the set and repeat the distress call and message. When using MF, and if there is difficulty in passing a distress message, try during one of the three minutes silence periods which start on each hour and half hour, and which are intended for this purpose. During these silence periods all transmissions on 2182kHz, except for Distress or Urgency traffic, must cease. There is no equivalent on Ch 16.

Use of distress signal (MAYDAY) imposes general radio silence,which is maintained until the vessel concerned or some other authority cancels the distress. A distress signal should be cancelled as soon as (but not before) the emergency is over.

A distress message is acknowledged in the following form:

MAYDAY

The name of the station sending the distress message, spoken three times

THIS IS ... (name of the station acknowledging, spoken three times)

RECEIVED MAYDAY

A yacht which hears a distress message from a vessel in her immediate vicinity and is able to give assistance should acknowledge accordingly, but only after giving an opportunity for the nearest shore station or some larger vessel to acknowledge. If a yacht hears a distress message from some more distant vessel, and if it is apparent that it has not been acknowledged, then the yacht should do everything possible to pass on the distress message. The intercepted distress message is preceded by the words:

MAYDAY RELAY, MAYDAY RELAY, MAYDAY RELAY

THIS IS ... (name of vessel re-transmitting the distress message, spoken three times)

Followed by the intercepted distress message

Control of distress traffic

Should it be necessary, the station controlling distress traffic may impose radio silence by transmitting:

SEELONCE MAYDAY, followed by its own name or other identification,on the frequency being used for distress purposes

If any other station nearby believes it essential to do likewise, it may transmit:

SEELONCE DISTRESS, followed by its own name or other identification

When complete silence is no longer necessary on a frequency being used for distress traffic, the station controlling traffic may relax the silence by a signal in the following form, indicating that restricted working may be resumed:

MAYDAY

HELLO ALL STATIONS (spoken three times)

THIS IS (the name or identification of the station sending the message)

The time

The name of the station in distress

PRU-DONCE (pronounced as the French word 'prudence')

When distress traffic has ceased, the controlling station lets all stations known that normal working may be resumed, as follows:

MAYDAY

HELLO ALL STATIONS (spoken three times)

THIS IS (the name or identification of the station)

The time

The name of the station which was in distress

SEELONCE FEENEE

Urgency Signal

The Urgency Signal consists of the words PAN-PAN, spoken three times, and indicates that the station has a very urgent message to transmit concerning the safety of a ship, aircraft or other vehicle, or the safety of a person. Messages prefixed by the Urgency Signal take priority over all messages except distress, and are sent on either or both of the international distress frequencies, 2182kHz or Ch 16 – or on any other frequency which may be used in case of distress. In the case of 2182kHz transmit a long message or the repetition of one on a working frequency.

The Urgency Signal is appropriate when urgent medical advice or attention is required, or when someone has been lost overboard. It should be cancelled by the station concerned when the urgency no longer exists.

Safety Signal

The Safety Signal consists of the word SÉCURITÉ (pronounced SAY-CURE-E-TAY) spoken three times, and indicates that the station is about to transmit a message containing an important navigational or meteorological warning, e.g. a drifting buoy, an extinguished light, a wreck, or a gale warning. Such messages usually originate from coast stations, and are transmitted on a working frequency after an announcement on the distress frequency.

Portable RT equipment

Portable RT sets, operating on 2182kHz or on Ch 16, are mentioned in 8.3.10, together with Personal Locator Beacons (PLBs) and Emergency Position Indicating Radio Beacons (EPIRBs).

6.6.17 INMARSAT

Although at present only of indirect benefit to most yachtsmen, the introduction of a global maritime satellite communication system has opened a new era for marine communications, and it is only a matter of time before this will extend to yachts.

INMARSAT (International Maritime Satellite organisation) provides satellites and their associated control systems ('the space segment'), which allow national telecommunication authorities to offer maritime satellite communications to their customers, and British Telecom is a major INMARSAT shareholder.

Access to the space segment is via maritime coast earth stations (CES) such as Goonhilly in Cornwall, and thence via one of several satellites to ship earth stations (SES), which are terminals purchased or leased by ship owners or operators.

SES comprise a parabolic antenna, about 4ft (1.2m) in diameter, with a protective radome, which is connected to a transmitter/receiver with handset and teleprinter below decks. Ships so equipped can enjoy direct dialling to over 100 countries, automatic ship-to-ship calls, telex services, data and facsimile transmission, and virtually instantaneous connection to HM Coastguard's Maritime Rescue Co-ordination Centre at Falmouth.

6.6.18 Citizens' Band Radio

CB radio afloat is not a substitute for proper marine band VHF, if only for the fact that there is no official monitoring procedure for the CB emergency channel (Ch 09) in the way that numerous stations keep watch on VHF Ch 16. Nevertheless it should be recognised that CB radio can be useful in certain circumstances – as a relatively cheap method of communicating between a yacht and a shore station such as a yacht club or marina – or even with the owner's house if within range. In particular CB radio can be used for some of the social talk for which marine VHF is not intended.

The *CB Code of Practice* includes the following instructions:

(1) Read the licence carefully.
(2) Listen before transmitting, with the Squelch control turned down (and Tone Squelch turned off if you have Selective Call facilities), to make sure that the channel is clear.
(3) Keep transmissions and conversations as short as possible.
(4) Leave a pause before replying, so that other stations may join the conversation.
(5) Use plain language.
(6) At all times and on all channels give priority to calls for assistance. Leave Ch 09 clear for emergencies. If you hear a call for help, wait. If no regular volunteer monitor answers, then offer help if you can.
(7) In emergency, if there is no answer on Ch 09,

try Ch 14 or 19.
(8) The calling channel is Ch 14. Once contact is established move to another channel.

6.7 Flag Etiquette

6.7.1 Flags concerned

The flags which may be displayed by a yacht include the national (maritime) ensign, the club burgee or flag officer's flag of a yacht club, a house flag, a courtesy flag when abroad, and flags connected with signalling or racing.

6.7.2 Ensign

For British yachts this is normally the Red Ensign (*never* the Union Flag). The Union Flag is flown at the bows of warships at anchor or secured alongside, and this is the only occasion when it is correct to refer to it as the Union Jack. Certain clubs (see the *Navy List*, HMSO) have the privilege of using a special Ensign, under strict regulations. There are stiff penalties for contravening them. The special Ensign for a yacht may be the White Ensign (Royal Yacht Squadron only); the Blue Ensign; the Blue Ensign defaced, i.e. with a badge; or the Red Ensign defaced. A special Ensign may only be worn under a warrant issued prior to 1 April 1985, or under a Permit subsequently issued to the owner by his club and in accordance with the following rules.

The yacht must be registered under either Part I of the Merchant Shipping Act 1894, or the Merchant Shipping Act 1983. She must be not less than 2 tons gross if registered by tonnage, or 7 metres overall if registered by length. The owner(s) must be British and be member(s) of the club concerned. The yacht must be a cruising boat (not a houseboat) and must not be used for any commercial purpose. Her name must not incorporate a name, product or trademark used for business purposes. The Permit must be carried on board, and a special Ensign may only be worn if the owner is on board or ashore nearby, and if the club's burgee (or Flag Officer's flag) is flown.

If an owner belongs to more than one club eligible to wear a special Ensign, then he must apply for a separate Permit for each Ensign. The loss or theft of a Permit must be reported immediately, and if the owner ceases to be a member of the club or if the yacht is sold the Permit must be returned forthwith to the secretary of the club.

Charterer's Warrants are no longer issued, but a Permit may be issued for short periods in respect of a yacht on charter to a club member. Further details of the issue and conditions for Permits for special Ensigns are available from secretaries of clubs concerned.

The Ensign, being the yacht's national colours, should be worn in the most prominent position – normally at a staff on the stern. In sailing yachts however this may be impossible: then in gaff-rigged yachts it is usually worn at the peak of the sail on the after mast (if more than one), in bermudan yawls and ketches on a staff at the mizzen masthead, and in others at a position two-thirds of the way up the leech of the aft sail. In power-driven yachts with a gaff on an aft mast, the Ensign may be worn at the peak of this gaff at sea.

The Ensign should be worn when entering or leaving harbour, and must be worn when a yacht arrives at or departs from a foreign port. At sea it need not be worn except when meeting other craft or when coming near to land – especially when passing coastguard or signal stations etc. Yachts which are racing do not normally wear Ensigns.

In harbour the Ensign should be hoisted, if people are on board, at 0800 (0900 between 1 November and 14 February). It should be lowered at sunset (or 2100 local time if earlier), or when the crew go ashore if before that time. It is bad form to leave the Ensign flying overnight in harbour.

In a yacht with a Permit for a special Ensign, the Red Ensign should be hoisted in the morning if the owner is not present – being replaced by the special Ensign when he arrives. Similarly if the owner departs from the yacht and the port, the special Ensign must be lowered, and should be replaced by the Red Ensign if the yacht is still manned.

Ensigns should only be used ashore at yacht clubs, where they should be hoisted and lowered at the same times as above.

The maritime Ensigns of the principal yachting and maritime countries are shown on pages 199–202, together with general examples of flag etiquette on page 192.

On occasions of private or national mourning colours are half-masted. This is done by first hoisting them close up, and then lowering them to the dipped position: similarly before hauling them down they are first raised to the masthead. For national mourning only the Ensign is half-masted: for private mourning both the Ensign and burgee.

6.7.3 Courtesy flag

It is customary in a foreign harbour to fly the maritime Ensign of the country being visited – normally at the starboard crosstrees. Some countries insist on this practice. The courtesy Ensign is a small version of the country's maritime Ensign – in the case of yachts visiting Britain, the Red Ensign (not the Union Flag).

Care must be taken that a courtesy flag is not flown inferior to (i.e. below) any flag other than the yacht's own Ensign (if, for example, worn at the mizzen masthead) and burgee (or flag officer's flag).

6.7.4 Burgee

Each club has its own burgee – a triangular flag which can be flown on members' yachts. The design is optional provided it does not conflict with official signals or other established flags. A yacht should normally fly not more than one burgee, (see also 6.7.6).

It must be understood that the burgee signifies that the owner, or person in charge of the yacht, is a member of that club, and a club burgee must never be flown under any other circumstances (see also 6.7.6).

6.7.5 Flag officers' flags

Most clubs authorise their flag officers to fly special swallow-tailed flags – of a similar design to the club burgee. The Vice- and Rear-Commodore's flags are distinguished from the Commodore's by one and two balls respectively in the cantons next to the hoist.

Some clubs also provide for their past Commodores to fly a special flag at the masthead. This flag incorporates the design of the club burgee but is either a different shape (e.g. rectangular) or has some other distinguishing feature.

6.7.6 Flying burgees etc

Anybody lent or chartered a yacht flies a burgee of a club of which he is a member – not a burgee of the absent owner. In harbour a burgee should be flown at the same times as the Ensign: where a special Ensign is worn the related club burgee should be flown. In recent years, however, the practice has developed of leaving the burgee flying at night in harbour, when the owner is either on board or ashore in the immediate vicinity. At sea a burgee is normally flown in sight of land or other ships.

A flag officer's flag is flown day and night while the owner is on board or in effective control. Yachts which are racing do not fly a burgee or a flag officer's flag.

Normally a flag officer of a club always flies his flag officer's flag (with appropriate special ensign, if any) in preference to the burgee of some other club of which he is a member. But special occasions may arise when it is appropriate to depart from this general rule – as for example when another club stages a rally or regatta which he is attending.

An owner who is not a flag officer of any club but who belongs to a club in the harbour where his boat is lying should use the burgee (and special ensign, if any) of that club. If he belongs to more than one local club he should use the burgee (and special ensign, if any) of the senior one, unless one of the other clubs is holding a regatta or similar function.

6.7.7 House flag

Some owners have a private, distinguishing flag, square in shape, which is normally flown at the starboard crosstrees, but in harbour only. It should be hoisted and lowered at the same times as the burgee and Ensign. The design of a house flag must not conflict with that of any other official or existing flag. The general practice is that a house flag is only flown when the owner is on board.

6.7.8 Yacht racing

The various flags and signals connected with yacht racing are detailed in the rules – RYA booklet YR1.

6.7.9 Salutes

It is customary for yachts to salute all Royal Yachts and all warships, and flag officers of the club whose burgee the yacht is flying (but normally only once a day). Salutes are made by dipping the Ensign (only) – lowering it about two-thirds of the way, but to a position where it will still fly. The salute is acknowledged by the other vessel dipping and re-hoisting her Ensign, when the saluting yacht then re-hoists hers.

6.7.10 Dressing ship

Ships can be dressed in two ways – overall (only in harbour), or with masthead flags (normally only when under way in or near a harbour, but may be used as an alternative to dressing overall in vessels not fitted with dressing lines).

Dressing overall is done by flying the flags of the International Code (only) from stem to masthead, from masthead to masthead if there is more than one mast, and down to the taffrail. The triangular flags and pendants should be spaced out between the rectangular flags. The recommended order of flags, from forward, is:

E, Q, p3, G, p8, Z, p4, W, p6, P, p1, I, Code, T, Y, B, X, 1st Sub, H, 3rd Sub, D, F, 2nd Sub, U, A, O, M, R, p2, J, p0, N, p9, K, p7, V, p5, L, C, S.

The Ensign should be worn at its normal position, and there should be a flag (normally another similar Ensign) at each masthead.

For British national festivals (see below) a British Ensign is worn at each masthead, and at the main masthead the Ensign and club burgee fly side by side. But if the owner is a flag officer he flies his flag at the masthead without an Ensign. The principal occasions for dressing ship in this country are currently: Accession Day, Coronation Day, HM The Queen's Birthday, Commonwealth Day, HM The Queen's Official Birthday, HRH The Duke of Edinburgh's Birthday and HM The Queen Mother's Birthday.

For foreign national festivals (at home or abroad), the Ensign of the country concerned is flown – at the masthead alongside the burgee in single-masted yachts, at the mizzen masthead (in place of a British Ensign) in ketches and yawls, and at the fore masthead (in place of a British Ensign) in a schooner-rigged yacht. In the case of a flag officer, flying his flag (alone) at the masthead of a single-masthead yacht, the foreign Ensign should be flown at the starboard crosstrees.

When dressing ship for a local occasion (e.g. a regatta) the club burgee should be flown at the main masthead, and no Ensign. An Ensign should be worn at any other masthead. On all occasions of dressing ship it is important that the same design of Ensign is worn in different parts of the vessel.

Dressing with masthead flags is carried out by wearing Ensign(s) at the masthead(s), as described above, without dressing lines.

6.7.11 Mourning

Mourning is indicated by wearing the Ensign and (in the case of private mourning only) the burgee at half mast. When colours are hoisted to the half mast position they should first be hoisted close up, and after a pause lowered to the dipped position. When they are to be lowered they should first be hoisted close up, before being lowered to the deck.

National mourning is observed on such occasions as the death of a member of the Royal Family. The Ensign (only) is half masted when news is received, and kept at half mast until sunset; or if news is received at night, then the Ensign is flown at half mast throughout the next day. Colours are again half masted while the funeral is in progress.

HM Ships half mast Ensigns and jacks when the funeral of an officer or rating takes place in a port where they are lying. Yachts present should conform.

Private mourning may be observed when the owner of a yacht dies, or when for example a flag officer or a past flag officer of a club dies. On such occasions both the Ensign and burgee are half masted, the procedure otherwise being similar to national mourning described above.

International Code of Signals

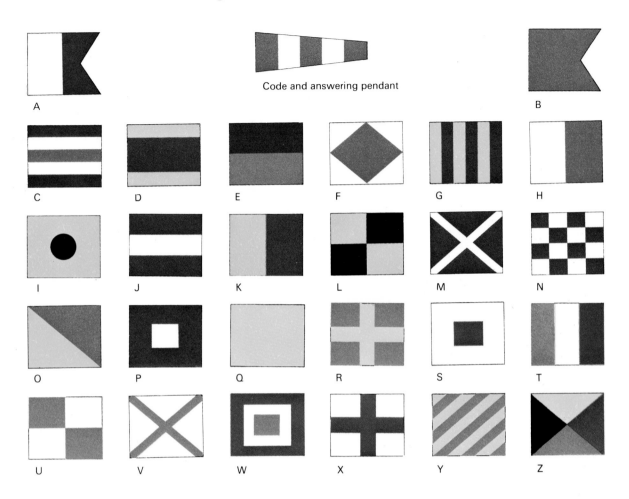

Code and answering pendant

A B

C D E F G H

I J K L M N

O P Q R S T

U V W X Y Z

Numeral pendants

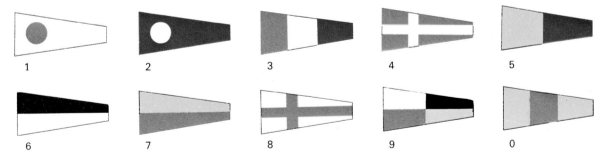

1 2 3 4 5

6 7 8 9 0

Substitutes

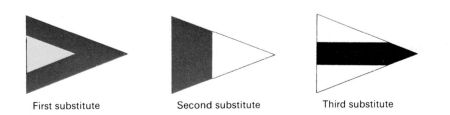

First substitute Second substitute Third substitute

Flag Etiquette

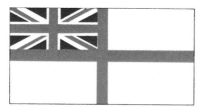

White Ensign

Blue Ensign

Red Ensign

Defaced Blue Ensign

Defaced Red Ensign

Club Burgee

Commodore's Flag

Vice-Commodore

Rear-Commodore

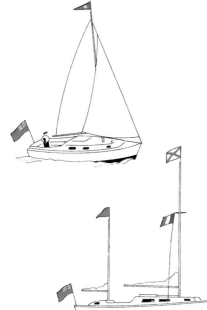

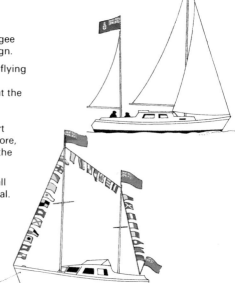

Left, yacht flying club burgee and wearing the Red Ensign.

Right, ketch-rigged yacht flying a Flag Officer's flag, and wearing a special ensign at the mizzen masthead.

Left, yacht in a foreign port flying a house flag at the fore, with a courtesy ensign at the starboard yardarm.

Right, yacht dressed overall for a British national festival.

Yacht Club Burgees

Aldeburgh Yacht Club

Alexandra Yacht Club

Association of Thames Yacht Clubs

Ballyholme Yacht Club

Bar Yacht Club

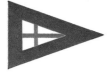
Barry Yacht Club

Bembridge Sailing Club

Benfleet Yacht Club

Birdham Yacht Club

Blackpool & Fleetwood Yacht Club

Blackwater Sailing Club Ltd

Bosham Sailing Club

Brading Haven Yacht Club

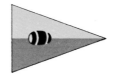
Brandy Hole Yacht Club

Brighton Marina Yacht Club

Britannia Yacht Club

British Kiel Yacht Club

Brixham Yacht Club

Burnham-on-Sea Yacht Club

Burry Port Yacht Club

Cabot Cruising Club

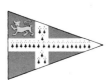
Cambridge University Cruising Club

Chichester Yacht Club

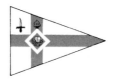
City Livery Yacht Club

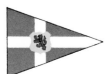
Clyde Corinthian Yacht Club

Clyde Cruising Club

Colne Yacht Club

Crouch Yacht Club

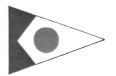
Cruising Association

Dale Yacht Club

Yacht Club Burgees

 Deauville Yacht Club

 Deben Yacht Club

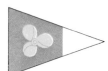 Eastney Cruising Association

 Erith Yacht Club

 Essex Yacht Club

 Fishguard Bay Yacht Club

 Forth Corinthian Yacht Club

 Guernsey Yacht Club

 Hamble River Sailing Club

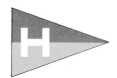 Hardway Sailing Club

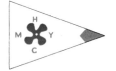 Harleyford Motor Yacht Club

 Hartlepool Yacht Club

 Household Division Yacht Club

 House of Commons Yacht Club

 House of Lords Yacht Club

 Howth Yacht Club

 Humber Yawl Club

 Ilfracombe Yacht Club

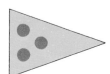 Imperial Poona Yacht Club

 Irish Cruising Club

 Island Cruising Club

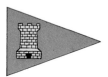 Island Sailing Club

 Isle of Man Yacht Club

 Itchenor Sailing Club

 Junior Offshore Group

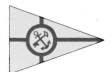 Keyhaven Yacht Club

 Koninklijke Jacht Club Oostende en Motor Jacht Club van Belgie

 Koninklijke Nederlandsche Motorboot Club

 Koninklijke Nederlandsche Zeil-en Roeivereeniging

 Koninklijke Roei-en Zeilvereeniging 'De Maas'

Yacht Club Burgees

Law Society Yacht Club

Little Ship Club

Lloyd's Yacht Club

London River Yacht Club

Lough Erne Yacht Club

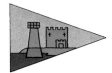
Lough Foyle Yacht Club

Madoc Yacht Club

Maldon Little Ship Club

Maldon Yacht Club

Margate Yacht Club.

Medway Cruising Club

Medway Yacht Club

Merioneth Yacht Club

Middle Thames Yacht Club

Minima Yacht Club

Mudhook Yacht Club

Multihull Offshore Cruising & Racing Association

Mumbles Yacht Club

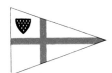
Mylor Yacht Club

National Yacht Club

Newhaven Marina Yacht Club

Norfolk Broads Yacht Club

North Devon Yacht Club

Orwell Yacht Club

Parkstone Yacht Club

Penarth Yacht Club

Penton Hook Yacht Club

Poole Harbour Yacht Club

Poole Yacht Club

Portrush Yacht Club

Yacht Club Burgees

 Royal Air Force Yacht Club

 Royal Anglesey Yacht Club

 Royal Artillery Yacht Club

 Royal Belgian Sailing Club

 Royal Burnham Yacht Club

 Royal Channel Islands Yacht Club

 Royal Cinque Ports Yacht Club

 Royal Corinthian Yacht Club

 Royal Cork Yacht Club (incorporating Royal Munster Yacht Club)

 Royal Cornwall Yacht Club

 Royal Cruising Club

 Royal Dart Yacht Club

 Royal Dorset Yacht Club

 Royal Engineer Yacht Club

 Royal Findhorn Yacht Club

 Royal Forth Yacht Club

 Royal Fowey Yacht Club

 Royal Gourock Yacht Club

 Royal Harwich Yacht Club

 Royal Highland Yacht Club

 Royal Irish Yacht Club

 Royal London Yacht Club

 Royal Lymington Yacht Club

 Royal Mersey Yacht Club

 Royal Motor Yacht Club

 Royal Naval Club & Royal Albert Yacht Club

 Royal Naval Sailing Association

 Royal Norfolk & Suffolk Yacht Club

 Royal Northern & Clyde Yacht Club

 Royal North of Ireland Yacht Club

Yacht Club Burgees

Royal Northumberland Yacht Club

Royal Ocean Racing Club

Royal Plymouth Corinthian Yacht Club

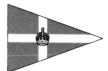
Royal St George Yacht Club

Royal Scottish Motor Yacht Club

Royal Solent Yacht Club

Royal Southampton Yacht Club

Royal Southern Yacht Club

Royal Tay Yacht Club

Royal Temple Yacht Club

Royal Thames Yacht Club

Royal Torbay Yacht Club

Royal Ulster Yacht Club

Royal Victoria Yacht Club

Royal Welsh Yacht Club

Royal Western Yacht Club

Royal Western Yacht Club of England

Royal Yacht Club de Belgique

Royal Yachting Association

Royal Yacht Squadron

Royal Yorkshire Yacht Club

Salcombe Yacht Club

Seaview Yacht Club

Segelkameradschaft 'Das Wappen von Bremen'

Severn Motor Yacht Club

Société des Régates du Havre

Société Nautique de la Baie de St Malo

Solway Yacht Club

South Caernarvonshire Yacht Club

Starcross Yacht Club

Yacht Club Burgees

St Helier Yacht Club

Strangford Lough Yacht Club

Sunderland Yacht Club

Sussex Motor Yacht Club

Sussex Yacht Club

Teign Corinthian Yacht Club

Thames Estuary Yacht Club

Thames Motor Yacht Club

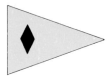

The Arun Yacht Club Ltd

The British Motor Yacht Club

The Dartmouth Yacht Club

Thorpe Bay Yacht Club

Thurrock Yacht Club

Union National Pour La Course Au Large

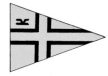

Vlaamse Vereniging Voor Watersport

Walton & Frinton Yacht Club

Watersportvereniging 'Haringvliet'

Welland Yacht Club

West Lancashire Yacht Club

West Mersea Yacht Club

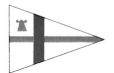

West Stockwith Yacht Club Ltd

Whitby Yacht Club

Whitstable Yacht Club

Yacht Club de ·Cherbourg

Yacht Club de France

Yacht Club de Morlaix

Yacht Club de Nieuwpoort

Yacht Club du Nord de la France

Yacht Club du Trieux

Yealm Yacht Club

National Maritime Flags

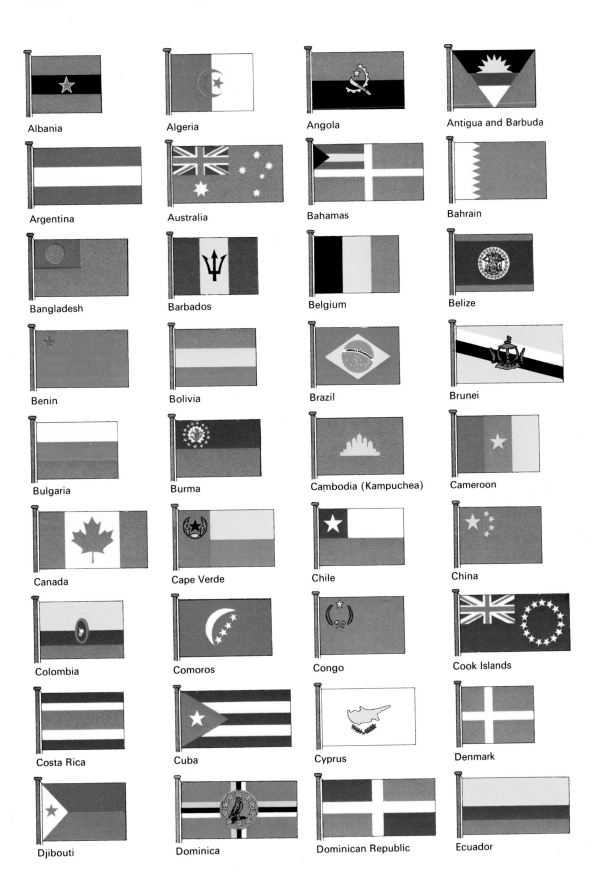

Albania

Algeria

Angola

Antigua and Barbuda

Argentina

Australia

Bahamas

Bahrain

Bangladesh

Barbados

Belgium

Belize

Benin

Bolivia

Brazil

Brunei

Bulgaria

Burma

Cambodia (Kampuchea)

Cameroon

Canada

Cape Verde

Chile

China

Colombia

Comoros

Congo

Cook Islands

Costa Rica

Cuba

Cyprus

Denmark

Djibouti

Dominica

Dominican Republic

Ecuador

National Maritime Flags

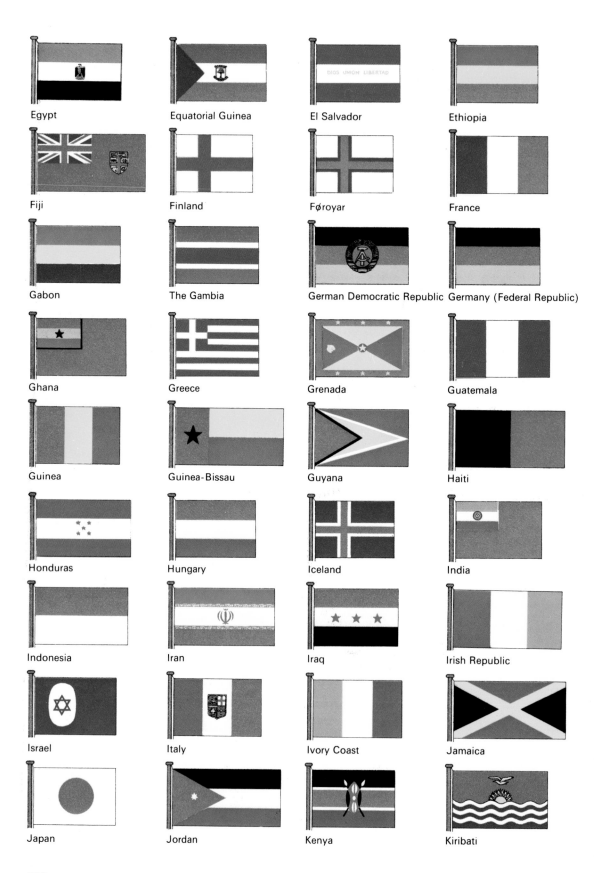

Egypt

Equatorial Guinea

El Salvador

DIOS UNION LIBERTAD

Ethiopia

Fiji

Finland

Føroyar

France

Gabon

The Gambia

German Democratic Republic

Germany (Federal Republic)

Ghana

Greece

Grenada

Guatemala

Guinea

Guinea-Bissau

Guyana

Haiti

Honduras

Hungary

Iceland

India

Indonesia

Iran

Iraq

Irish Republic

Israel

Italy

Ivory Coast

Jamaica

Japan

Jordan

Kenya

Kiribati

National Maritime Flags

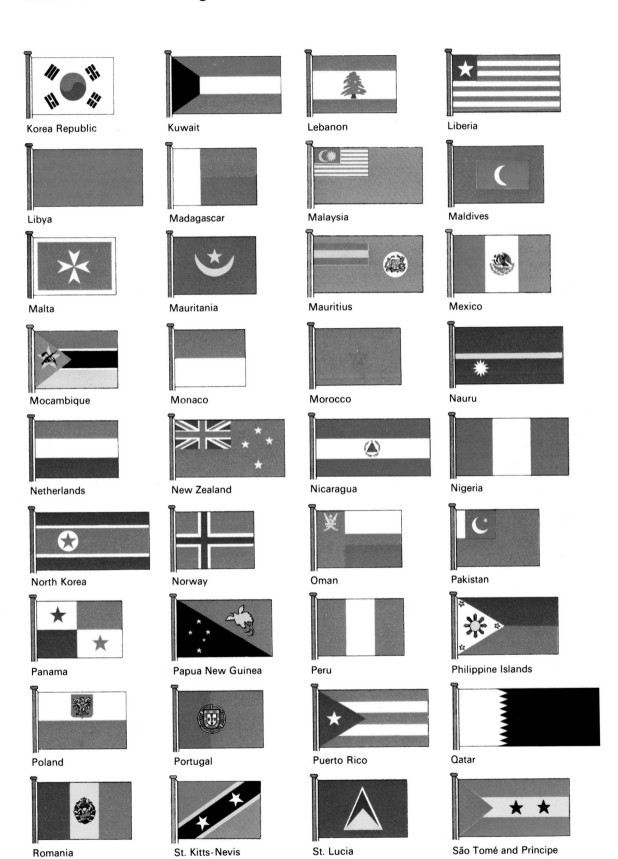

Korea Republic	Kuwait	Lebanon	Liberia
Libya	Madagascar	Malaysia	Maldives
Malta	Mauritania	Mauritius	Mexico
Mocambique	Monaco	Morocco	Nauru
Netherlands	New Zealand	Nicaragua	Nigeria
North Korea	Norway	Oman	Pakistan
Panama	Papua New Guinea	Peru	Philippine Islands
Poland	Portugal	Puerto Rico	Qatar
Romania	St. Kitts-Nevis	St. Lucia	São Tomé and Príncipe

National Maritime Flags

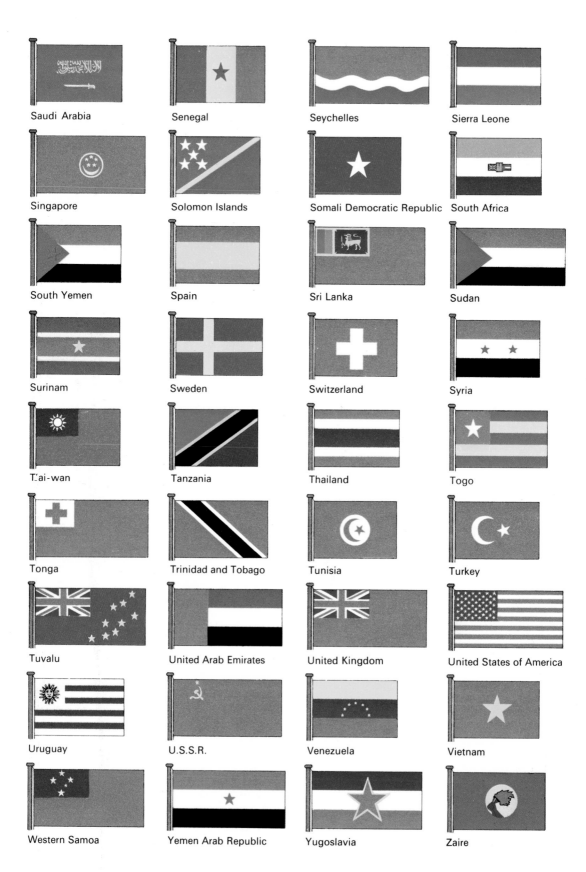

Saudi Arabia

Senegal

Seychelles

Sierra Leone

Singapore

Solomon Islands

Somali Democratic Republic

South Africa

South Yemen

Spain

Sri Lanka

Sudan

Surinam

Sweden

Switzerland

Syria

T'ai-wan

Tanzania

Thailand

Togo

Tonga

Trinidad and Tobago

Tunisia

Turkey

Tuvalu

United Arab Emirates

United Kingdom

United States of America

Uruguay

U.S.S.R.

Venezuela

Vietnam

Western Samoa

Yemen Arab Republic

Yugoslavia

Zaire

Distress Signals

Note: Only to be used if the vessel is in serious and immediate danger, and help is urgently required

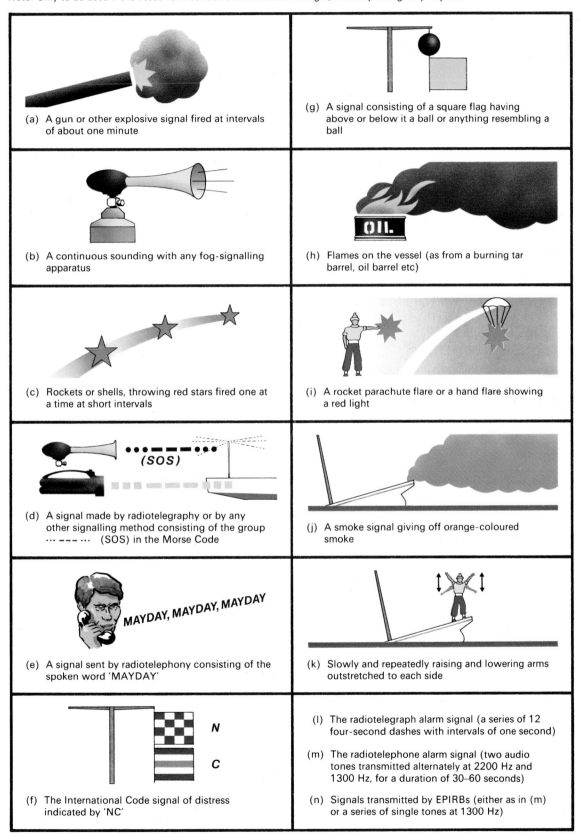

(a) A gun or other explosive signal fired at intervals of about one minute

(b) A continuous sounding with any fog-signalling apparatus

(c) Rockets or shells, throwing red stars fired one at a time at short intervals

(d) A signal made by radiotelegraphy or by any other signalling method consisting of the group ... --- ... (SOS) in the Morse Code

(e) A signal sent by radiotelephony consisting of the spoken word 'MAYDAY'

(f) The International Code signal of distress indicated by 'NC'

(g) A signal consisting of a square flag having above or below it a ball or anything resembling a ball

(h) Flames on the vessel (as from a burning tar barrel, oil barrel etc)

(i) A rocket parachute flare or a hand flare showing a red light

(j) A smoke signal giving off orange-coloured smoke

(k) Slowly and repeatedly raising and lowering arms outstretched to each side

(l) The radiotelegraph alarm signal (a series of 12 four-second dashes with intervals of one second)

(m) The radiotelephone alarm signal (two audio tones transmitted alternately at 2200 Hz and 1300 Hz, for a duration of 30–60 seconds)

(n) Signals transmitted by EPIRBs (either as in (m) or a series of single tones at 1300 Hz)

1. Typical Cirrus (Mares' Tails) invading the sky, and heralding a warm front when moving rapidly from the North West or West.

2. When Cirrus is thinning out it indicates fine weather, but here Cirrus and Cirrocumulus are increasing and thickening from the West.

3. 8/8 Cirrostratus and a 22° halo round the sun – one of the surer signs of deteriorating weather in the offing.

4. Clouds now thicker and lower – Altocumulus in several layers and gradually increasing, with signs of Altostratus in the distance.

5. Thin Altostratus with a watery sun. The first few spots of rain are felt, and the wind is increasing from the South East or South.

6. 8/8 Nimbostratus – a grey layer of cloud blotting out the sun, and bringing continuous rain with it.

Pictures 1–6 above illustrate a typical sequence of clouds seen with an approaching warm front.

7. Now in the warm sector – 8/8 Stratus; sometimes sea fog too, when the air is moist and warmer than the water.

8. Stratocumulus in the warm sector, well to the south of the depression. This cloud occurs of course with other air streams.

9. Large Cumulus and Cumulonimbus herald the approach of a vigorous cold front. Be prepared for squalls and a veering wind.

10. Small, fair weather Cumulus shows little sign of growth as the day proceeds. Most Cumulus clouds originate over the land.

11. Typical large Cumulus (Mediocris) in cold air. This type of cloud gives warning of showers occuring, with squally winds.

12. Cumulonimbus and heavy showers, often with rapid wind changes and squalls as the shower passes. Here expect a line squall, with a definite veer.

Pictures 7 and 8 show warm sector weather; 9 the approach of a cold front; and 10–12 the growth of Cumulus.

Lifesaving Signals

(1) Landing signals for the guidance of small boats with crews or persons in distress

Manual signals	*Light signals*	*Other signals*	*Meaning*

Vertical motion of a white flag (or white light or flare by night) or of the arms

Green star signal

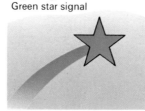

International Code letter '**K**' by light or sound

— • —

'This is the best place to land'
(An indication of direction may be given by a steady white light or flare at a lower level)

Horizontal motion of a white flag (or white light or flare by night) or of the arms extended horizontally

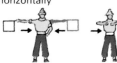

Red star signal

International Code letter '**S**' by light or sound

• • •

'Landing here is highly dangerous'

Horizontal motion of a white flag followed by
2. the placing of the white flag in the ground and
3. by the carrying of another white flag in the direction to be indicated.
   By night white lights or flares are used instead of white flags

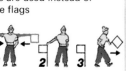

1. Red star signal fired vertically and
2. a white star signal in the direction towards the better landing place

1. Signalling the code letter '**S**' (• • •), followed by the code letter '**R**' (• — •) if the better landing place is more to the right in the direction of approach, *or*
2. Signalling the code letter '**S**' (• • •), followed by the code letter '**L**' (• — • •) if the better landing place is more to the left in the direction of approach

'Landing here is highly dangerous. A more favourable location for landing is in the direction indicated'

(2) Signals to be employed in connection with the use of shore life-saving apparatus

Vertical motion of a white flag (or white light or flare by night) or of the arms

Green star signal

In general: affirmative.
Specifically: rocket line is held – tail block is made fast – hawser is made fast – man is in the breeches buoy – haul away

Horizontal motion of a white flag (or white light or flare by night) or of the arms

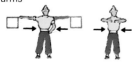

Red star signal

In general: negative.
Specifically: slack away – avast hauling

(3) Replies from life-saving stations etc. to distress signals made by a ship or person

Pyrotechnic signals
Orange smoke signal

White star rocket – three single signals fired at intervals of about one minute

Combined light and sound signal – three single signals fired at intervals of about one minute

'You are seen – assistance will be given as soon as possible'

Chapter 7

Weather

Contents

7.1 What makes the weather

7.1.1 Introduction

The yachtsman or inshore fisherman needs to understand something about the weather for two good reasons. First so that he can better interpret the forecast he receives by radio or other means, and second so that when he is at sea he can relate what he actually experiences in the way of weather to the forecast, and thereby fill in some of the gaps in it or explain any local variations.

Weather forecasting, despite modern aids such as computers and satellite pictures, is anything but an exact science. Weather systems do not always move as predicted, or they may do so more quickly or more slowly than anticipated. The area covered by an individual forecast is very big (sea area Sole, for example, is over 50,000 square miles) and at any moment the weather can be quite different in various parts of it. It is therefore important that the yachtsman at sea knows enough about the subject to be able to monitor what is happening around him, so that he can detect any departure from the general weather pattern that has been forecast, and anticipate what is likely to occur in his own local area in the immediate future.

A third requirement for a yachtsman is to be fully aware of all the various sources of weather information that are available to him, either in harbour or at sea, and to be able to record radio shipping forecasts in a form which will be of use to him subsequently.

The general principles of weather forecasting are not too difficult to understand because it is a subject that can be studied and practised every day. A great deal can be learned from a regular study of the weather map, listening to one of the better radio forecasts (such as Radio 3 each morning), checking the barometer and a thermometer outside, and then watching the sky and the weather from time to time during the day. But first it is necessary to have some insight into the various factors which make and alter the weather around us – the changes of temperature, pressure and humidity in the atmosphere, maybe hundreds of miles away, which are going to affect the wind and weather tomorrow or perhaps next week.

7.1.2 Transfer of heat

The transfer of heat is the key to an understanding of how weather systems develop on both global and local scales. Most of the world's weather occurs in a relatively thin layer of air above the earth called the troposphere, which extends to a height of about 10 miles (16km) at the equator and 5 miles (8km) at the poles. In this region the air temperature usually decreases with increase of altitude (although it is possible to have temporary so-called inversions, as for example when air close to the ground is cooled as the earth's heat is radiated on a clear winter's night when there is little or no wind).

Above the troposphere the next higher layer in the atmosphere is called the stratosphere, in which temperature increases with height. This increase in temperature with height (inversion) restricts vertical movement of the air, and without vertical movement there is very little weather as we know it.

The sun is, of course, the prime source of heat energy that drives the 'weather machine'. This energy is available by day, and much of it is absorbed by the earth's surface, but throughout the 24 hours heat is lost into the atmosphere by radiation. At the poles the sun's rays are spread over a greater area than elsewhere, and hence less energy is received than in lower latitudes. There is more energy lost by radiation at the poles than is received from the sun, whilst the reverse is the

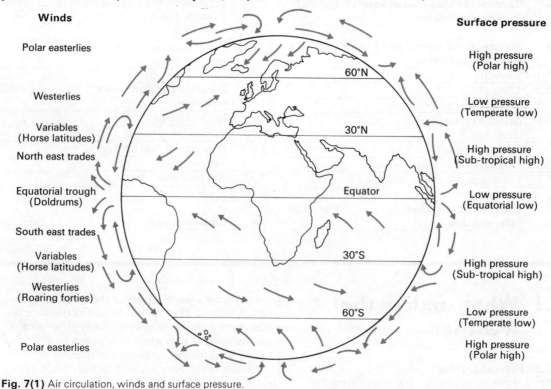

Winds

Polar easterlies

Westerlies

Variables (Horse latitudes)

North east trades

Equatorial trough (Doldrums)

South east trades

Variables (Horse latitudes)

Westerlies (Roaring forties)

Polar easterlies

60°N

30°N

Equator

30°S

60°S

Surface pressure

High pressure (Polar high)

Low pressure (Temperate low)

High pressure (Sub-tropical high)

Low pressure (Equatorial low)

High pressure (Sub-tropical high)

Low pressure (Temperate low)

High pressure (Polar high)

Fig. 7(1) Air circulation, winds and surface pressure.

case at the equator. On these considerations alone, the poles would become progressively colder, and the equator increasingly hotter. The major weather systems around the globe are a result of Nature's way of correcting this potential imbalance.

The excess heat at the equator is carried upwards through the troposphere by convection, whereupon the air then travels north and south. After a time the air becomes cooler and sinks back to earth, where some of it returns to the equatorial region and some moves to higher latitudes. At the same time, dense cold air near the surface is travelling away from the poles to meet the warmer air in lower latitudes, where they rise to set up other vertical circulation patterns. These major vertical circulations transfer heat around the globe. Fig. 7(1) shows these circulations in a simplified form. It can be seen that where the air rises the surface pressure is low, while descending air is associated with high surface pressure.

Whereas the temperature over the land can show a considerable daily (diurnal) change, the temperature of the sea and of the air blowing over it changes only slowly.

As stated above, the temperature in the troposphere normally decreases with height, the rate of decrease being important in deciding the type of weather on any occasion. When air is heated from below (by passing over a warmer surface) it will rise by convection and also cool as it expands. The rising parcel of air will continue to rise provided that in spite of its own cooling it remains warmer than its surroundings. When the decrease of temperature with height is sufficient to allow this process to take place the air is called 'unstable'. On the other hand when the decrease of temperature with height is much less, the rising parcel of air will soon acquire a temperature similar to that of its surroundings and will rise no further – the air is then called 'stable'.

Whether a mass of air is stable or unstable has an effect on the type of wind it produces. Stable air gives winds which may be strong but which are steady. Unstable air gives winds which are more variable, and often blustery or squally.

The type of air aloft can be seen from the clouds. Those which mark unstable air are the cumulus type – heaped up clouds with much vertical development, often well separated from each other. In a stable air mass this type of cloud does not appear – the clouds are spread out in a layer, often covering a large area. These of course are broad distinctions, and we will have more to say on the general subject of clouds (see 7.1.8).

7.1.3 World weather

A study of the more local weather pattern starts with a look at the broader picture – the general distribution of pressure over the whole world, caused by the differences in temperature between the two poles at the extremes and the equator

round the middle. These temperature differences and the rotation of the earth combine to produce areas of high atmospheric pressure (as a general rule) over the poles and in subtropical belts around the earth, with lower pressures in the mid-latitudes and equatorial regions in between.

In practice however the various land masses, with their predominantly north-south orientation, considerably disturb this theoretical system. The belts of high pressure in about latitudes 30°N and 30°S are split into separate regions of high pressure – commonly situated over the eastern part of each ocean – as for example the Azores high. Similarly the belt of low pressure round the world in about 60°N is divided into two regions of low pressure near Iceland and the Aleutians. In the southern hemisphere the belt of low pressure does extend more or less round the world because there are no major land masses in this latitude.

Other factors distort the theoretical picture. Over large land masses pressure tends to build in the winter and to fall in the summer, and these seasonal changes can considerably modify the wind system over nearby oceans – as for example the monsoon winds which blow over the Indian Ocean. Then the belts of high and low pressure drift somewhat north and south during the year, following the sun. To a lesser extent, ocean currents (discussed in 9.11.15) affect the pressure over the world's surface, as they transfer some heat from place to place.

Fig. 7(2) shows the principal regions of high and low pressure, and the main wind systems, throughout the world in January and July, but in the following discussion remarks are confined to the Atlantic Ocean. The Equatorial Trough (Doldrums) represented by the heavy dotted line, is a low pressure area between the NE trade winds north of the equator and the SE trades to the south of it. Although renowned for their light winds, the Doldrums have very changeable weather; their width varies greatly, but is typically 200–300 miles (322–483km).

The NE and SE trade winds blow persistently, mostly about Force 4 and sometimes stronger, but seldom of gale force. The weather is usually fair, with small detached cumulus clouds, described in 7.1.8, rather wetter on the western side of the Atlantic. The amount of cloud and rain experienced increases towards the Equatorial Trough. Normally the barometer is steady, apart from the diurnal variation described in 7.1.5, but if this diurnal rise and fall ceases, or if the barometer rises or falls to any marked degree, it may portend a tropical disturbance (see 7.1.15).

On the polar side of the trade wind belts lie areas of anticyclones called The Variables (or the Horse Latitudes), with calms, or light to moderate winds variable in direction. Here the weather is usually fine, with only small amounts of cloud and rain.

North of 35°N, and south of 35°S, the winds

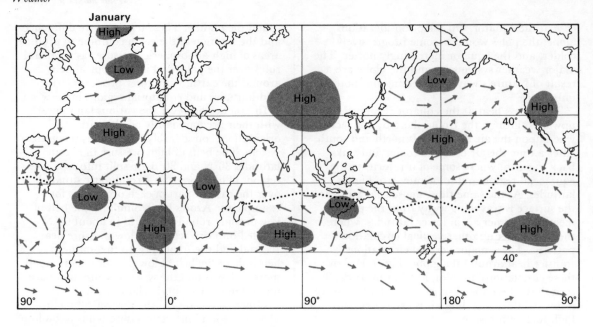

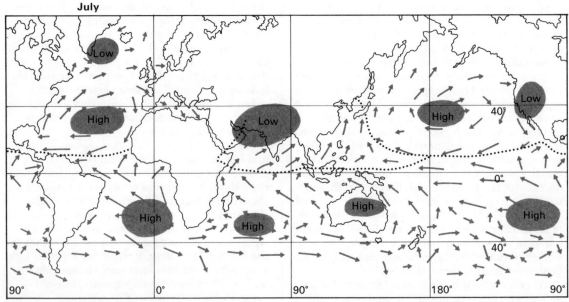

Fig. 7(2) Pressure distribution and wind systems in January and July. The dotted line indicates the Equatorial Trough. The relative strength of wind is shown by the length of the arrows.

become more predominantly westerly as latitude increases – more especially in the southern hemisphere where the significance of the Roaring Forties needs little explanation. In the northern hemisphere the westerlies in the North Atlantic are in general lighter and not so constant in direction, due to the large land masses and the effects of the depressions which form along the polar front (see 7.1.9 below). Fog is common in summer on the western side of the North Atlantic.

The polar regions are largely unnavigable due to ice. The wind is generally easterly, and the weather often cloudy with frequent fog in summer.

In some parts of the world, particularly the Indian Ocean and the West Pacific, the general distribution of pressure described above is very much influenced by the seasonal heating and cooling of the adjacent land masses.

7.1.4 Air masses

Prevailing weather conditions, and forecasts of what is likely to happen in the future, depend largely upon the vertical temperature profile of the air.

When air has originated from a polar source it is naturally cold, and a simplified temperature/height graph of such air might look like the solid blue line in Fig. 7(3). If that air is then carried to

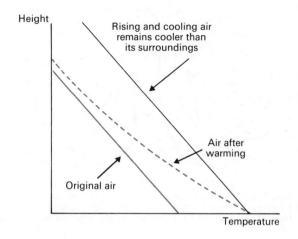

Fig. 7(3) Cold air warmed from below to make it unstable.

lower latitudes (for example in the wake of a cold front) the temperature of the lower layers will be increasingly raised by the warmer underlying surface, thus changing the shape of the graph as indicated by the dotted line. If further heating is applied to the air at the surface – perhaps by sunshine – the air will rise by convection. The rising air cools, but provided that it remains warmer than its environment it will continue its upward motion. This condition is known as 'unstable' air, and is associated with good visibility, cumuliform cloud and gusty wind.

The reverse process occurs when a large mass of air is taken to higher latitudes, as indicated in Fig. 7(4). A situation is reached when any parcel of rising air will soon cool to the temperature of its surroundings, and can rise no further unless mechanically lifted – as it may be by turbulence, or by passing over a mountain range. This condition is known as 'stable' air, which often brings layered cloud, fairly steady winds, and sometimes poor visibility.

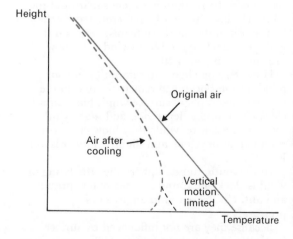

Fig. 7(4) Warm air cooled from below, making it stable.

Tropical maritime air is typically warm and humid, liable to cause fog and cloud, usually of the stratus variety as described in 7.1.8. Initially it is unstable, but as it travels towards us over the sea it is cooled from below and becomes more stable.

Polar maritime air is air of Arctic origin which has been over the ocean for a little while, and it often influences the weather in Britain and NW Europe. It will have absorbed moisture and become warmer over the sea, and its characteristics are instability and showers, combined with good visibility.

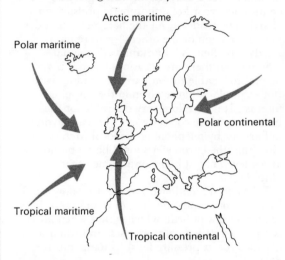

Fig. 7(5) The various types of air masses which influence our weather have widely different characteristics, depending upon their origins.

Arctic maritime air comes straight off the polar ice cap, and is initially cold, dry and stable. As it travels south over warmer seas it becomes unstable and can cause strong winds and squalls.

Polar continental air is from higher latitudes, but has travelled to us over the Continent bringing mostly fair weather. Summer heating can create some instability, but in the winter the low temperatures will create stability at least in the lower layers of the atmosphere.

Tropical continental air, coming to us from (say) North Africa, is initially dry and stable, and usually brings very warm and hazy weather; but it can pick up moisture as it crosses any sea, and strong summer sunshine over land can cause some instability.

There is often a well defined boundary between air masses with different characteristics. The boundary is called a 'front', and these are discussed in 7.1.9.

7.1.5 **Atmospheric pressure**

Due to gravity air exerts a force, and at ground level we are subjected to atmospheric pressure equal to the weight of the column of air above us. The modern unit for measuring atmospheric pressure is the millibar (mb), which equals 100 Newtons per square metre. 1000mb is equivalent to the force needed to support a column of mercury about 29½in or 750mm high.

The mean value of atmospheric pressure at sea level is about 1013mb. Atmospheric pressure in certain places round the world is semi-permanently higher than this mean figure, and these are referred to as regions of high pressure (such as polar regions). In other places the atmospheric pressure is semi-permanently lower than the mean figure and these are regions of low pressure (such as the equator).

Any seagoing yacht should carry an aneroid barometer (or a barograph, which gives a continuous record of atmospheric pressure on a chart). The tendency for the barometer to move in one direction or the other – or to remain steady – is often as important as the actual reading, but there are occasions when it is very helpful to be able to compare the reading with (for example) a figure given in the shipping forecast. It is therefore very desirable for the instrument to be correctly set. This can be done in harbour by telephoning the local Met. office. Note that the barometer should be set on board, at sea level, not at home or at some other altitude.

It has been mentioned how heat is transferred by radiation, conduction or convection but there is another law of heat, which is that when air is compressed its temperature rises, and when it expands (or its pressure falls) its temperature drops.

Atmospheric pressure is not uniform over the surface of the globe and it also decreases with altitude (reminding us that all problems relating to air masses are three-dimensional). So, as air masses move from place to place, or are made to rise or fall, they are expanded or compressed by varying amounts, and are cooled or heated accordingly.

The pressure distribution over the surface of the globe is vital information for the meteorologist, and is displayed on an isobaric or synoptic chart (commonly called a weather map). An isobar is a line joining places which have equal barometric pressure at any one time. At any place, even in settled weather, it should be noted that the barometer does not read quite the same all day, tending to fall slightly between 1000 and 1600, and between 2200 and 0400, and to rise at other times – due to what is called diurnal variation.

On a synoptic chart isobars are usually drawn at equal intervals either side of 1000mb, which is about the average atmospheric pressure at sea level. The spacing of the isobars depends upon the scale of the synoptic chart.

In some places the isobars totally encircle areas of either relatively low pressure or relatively high pressure. These areas are termed depressions and anticyclones respectively, and they can each have a big influence on the weather we experience at sea.

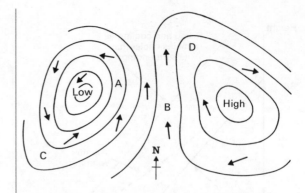

Fig. 7(6) How isobars depict an area of low pressure, (depression) on the left, and an area of high pressure (anticyclone) on the right. The arrows show typical wind circulations.

7.1.6 Wind

Isobars are like contours on a map. When contours are close together the gradient is steep: when isobars are close together the pressure gradient is steep – or pressure is changing rapidly. Since wind is caused by air moving due to changes of pressure it follows that stronger winds will be experienced where the isobars are closely spaced, whereas few isobars which are well spaced out indicate light winds. Thus in Fig. 7(6) the winds at A could be expected to be stronger than at B.

The curvature of the isobars also has an effect on the wind speed. When the isobars are curved cyclonically, i.e. round a depression, the wind speed is less for the same spacing of isobars than round high pressure. Although in Fig. 7(6) the isobars at C and D are of the same spacing, the wind at D will be much stronger.

Air would like to move directly from an area of high pressure to one of low pressure, but it only does this near the equator. Elsewhere, due to the rotation of the earth (Coriolis Force), it is deflected to the right in the northern hemisphere and to the left in the southern.

It was a Dutchman called Buys Ballot who recognised the relation between isobars and the wind. His law can best be remembered by the fact that if in the northern hemisphere you stand with your Back to the Blast (wind), the Low pressure is on your Left.

However you choose to retain this in your mind, it is important to remember that in the northern hemisphere surface winds blow anti-clockwise round a depression and slightly in towards the centre, while they blow clockwise round an anticyclone and slightly outwards as in Fig. 7(6).

In the southern hemisphere the circulation of wind is clockwise round an area of low pressure, and anti-clockwise round an area of high pressure.

Because they are not influenced by surface friction, winds at about 2000ft (600m) are veered about 20° from the surface wind and blow roughly parallel to the isobars. This is the general direction in which low clouds (see 7.1.8) will be moving.

On some weather maps there is a geostrophic scale against which the spacing of isobars at 2mb intervals (usually) can be read, to give the approximate wind speed or Beaufort force as shown in Fig. 7(7). The scale is placed at right angles to the isobars at the place required, with the highest end of the scale on one isobar, and the reading taken where the next isobar (2mb higher or lower) cuts the scale. Such charts for yachtsmen give the wind speed at sea level, but those used by meteorologists give the wind speed at 2000ft (600m). In this case the wind at sea level is likely to be about $\frac{2}{3}$ the speed shown, due to surface friction.

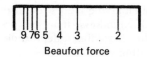

Beaufort force

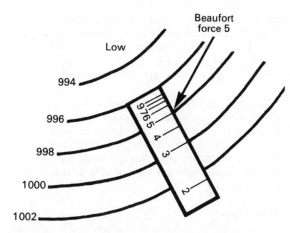

Fig. 7(7) Scale for deriving the Beaufort force from isobar spacing on a RYA weather map.

This raises the point that the wind speed over the open sea can be twice what it is over the land, which needs to be borne in mind when you are in harbour, trying to decide whether or not to put to sea. It applies particularly in sheltered harbours with off-shore winds. It should also be remembered that the wind is less at sea level or ground level than it is even 30ft (9m) above.

Wind strengths are commonly expressed in forecasts and for other purposes in terms of the Beaufort scale (see 7.3). This originated as an attempt to relate the strength of the wind (when there were no instruments to measure its speed) to the amount of sail a ship could carry, and later to the effect of the wind on the sea state. It should not be imagined that terms such as 'Force 5' or 'Force 7' have any direct significance in respect of the physical force of the wind – on a

sail for example. The actual force exerted on a sail is proportional to the square of the wind speed. Hence a wind of Force 7 (say 30 knots) would have more than twice the weight of a wind of Force 5 (say 20 knots). This explains why even a fairly small increase in wind speed can have a significant effect on a sailing yacht.

7.1.7 **Humidity**

We have mentioned the temperature of the air, and atmospheric pressure, but there is one more way by which any particular parcel of air can be identified – by its humidity.

All air contains some water vapour, although sometimes it is more evident than others. Without it there would be no clouds or rain. It is collected, for example, by evaporation as the air passes over the sea, so south-westerly winds which come to us across the Atlantic are likely to be more moisture laden than south-easterlies from the Continent.

The lower the air temperature, the less moisture the air can hold without some of it condensing into water droplets. For example air at 32°F (0°C) can only hold half as much water in vapour form as air at 50°F (10°C). The temperature at which this condensation occurs is called the dew point.

So when air is cooled – by passing over colder surfaces of land or sea, or by being lifted over hills or by thermal currents, or where different air masses meet – the moisture is likely to be released in some form. For example fog at sea is normally caused when the sea temperature is equal to or less than the dew point of the air, resulting in condensation of water vapour. The opposite happens when the air temperature rises – dew or rain puddles evaporate, and the moisture is re-absorbed into the atmosphere once more.

The most comon manifestation of moisture in the atmosphere is however the presence in the sky of the clouds which we see almost every day. They are described in some detail in 7.1.8.

7.1.8 **Clouds**

Recognition of the different types of cloud, and knowledge of how they form, move, change and decay, is a great help when studying the local weather or making your own forecast. When observing clouds the extent of cover, the heights and types of cloud present, and their directions of movement should all be recorded. If this is too daunting a task, try to determine the dominant types of upper and lower cloud.

There are four different types of cloud, depending on how the air is made to ascend and is therefore cooled so that the dew point is reached.

Convection clouds

In unstable conditions rising air is cooled to its dew point and forms heaped up cumulus cloud described later.

Clouds due to turbulence

Over the sea turbulence may extend to about 2000ft (600m) when the wind is strong. If the air is sufficiently damp to be cooled to its dew point at this height, a sheet of stratus cloud may be formed.

Orographic clouds

This is the type of cloud formed when damp air is forced up or over the top of a hill. By its nature it is not of much direct consequence to yachtsmen.

Frontal cloud

This is caused by a mass of relatively warm air meeting a mass of cooler air, so that the warm air, being lighter, climbs up over the cold air (or is forced upwards by the cold air driving underneath).

Basically clouds are divided into three levels – high, medium and low levels depending on the height of their base. In some cases it may not be easy to decide the actual heights of clouds, but it is usually simple to decide their other main feature – whether they have vertical development and individual form (cumulus type) or whether they are a shapeless type of spreading cloud (stratus type).

Main cloud types

Cirrus	Ci	High clouds	Typically above 22,000ft (6700m)
Cirrocumulus	Cc		
Cirrostratus	Cs		
Altocumulus	Ac	Medium clouds	7000–20,000ft (2135–6100m)
Altostratus	As		
Nimbostratus	Ns	Low clouds	Usually below 7000ft (2135m)
Stratus	St		
Stratocumulus	Sc		
Cumulus	Cu	ditto	but these may extend vertically into High clouds
Cumulonimbus	Cb		

Where appropriate read the following descriptions of the ten more common types of cloud listed above in conjunction with the coloured cloud pictures on pages 204–205. These pictures show:

1–6   A typical warm front sequence (cirrus, cirrocumulus, cirrostratus, altocumulus, altostratus, nimbostratus)
7–8   Warm sector weather (stratus, stratocumulus)
9   Cold front (cumulus, cumulonimbus)
10–12 The growth of cumulus cloud

In studying cloud types it is helpful to understand the meaning of certain terms:

Cirrus	—	feathery
Stratus	—	layers or sheets
Cumulus	—	heaped
Alto	—	medium level cloud
Nimbus	—	rain bearing
Fracto	—	broken

High cloud

Cirrus (Ci) White, feathery, isolated clouds of ice crystals which cast no shadow. When thin and tufted they are often called 'mares' tails'. Usually indicate strong wind at altitude. Thin, high level cirrus means good weather, but when it thickens and consolidates into cirrostratus and altostratus, it foretells an advancing depression or frontal system.

Cirrocumulus (Cc) Banks or rows of small white flakes, sometimes rippled or patterned (mackerel sky). Thicker than cirrostratus and usually contrasted against the blue sky. May indicate changeable weather. A transient form of cloud which often develops from cirrus or cirrostratus, and then changes back to these or other forms.

Cirrostratus (Cs) A thin white veil of transparent cloud, often giving haloes round the sun and moon. Often follows cirrus and precedes altostratus, heralding a depression and deteriorating weather.

Medium cloud

Altocumulus (Ac) Longish layers or patches of white or pale grey cloud, usually in groups or lines. Rather similar to cirrocumulus, but larger and thicker, with a darker pattern. If much vertical development is evident it is a sign of instability which may give rise to thunderstorms.

Altostratus (As) A sheet of cloud which may follow cirrostratus (although it is lower and thicker), in which case rain almost invariably follows with an approaching front. Altostratus often varies in density – dark in some parts but the sun can be seen through others. It may cover the whole sky.

Low cloud

Nimbostratus (Ns) A dense grey layer of low cloud which forms below altostratus, covering the whole sky and giving steady precipitation; often with scud detached from the main cloud layer.

Stratus (St) Low sheet of uniform grey cloud, like fog not resting on the ground. The sun can sometimes be seen through it. It may cover the whole sky, or only be patches trailing over the sea. Often associated with drizzle and poor visibility.

Stratocumulus (Sc) Irregular masses or rolls of large puffy clouds, with varying degrees of darkness, and often a thick wavy appearance. Common in winter, bringing drizzle rather than rain.

Cumulus (Cu) Clouds with clear outlines, separated from each other. They have flat, grey bottoms; white, puffy sides; and billowing tops, with considerable vertical development. Cumulus comes in all sizes. Small puffy cumulus indicates fair weather.

Cumulonimbus (Cb) Towering and forbidding storm clouds; when well developed, marked by anvil tops indicating powerful rising air currents – often producing squally winds with rain, heavy showers of hail or snow, and frequently thunder. Often embedded in intense cold fronts and vigorous troughs.

7.1.9 Depressions and fronts
Depressions which affect the British Isles mostly originate from a distortion of the polar front (although there are other types of low which can start, for example, from thundery conditions). All frontal depressions have a finite life: some persist longer than others, some become deeper and more vigorous, while others quickly disappear. But during their varying lives the Atlantic

depressions are all continually changing as they meet up with or absorb other air masses in their general movement, which is often in an ENE direction passing northward of the British Isles.

Around a depression are formed marked boundaries between the different types of air masses which have helped to get it established. Warm air is lighter than cold, so where a warm air mass advances towards colder air the warm air tends to rise up over the cold before any significant mixing takes place. This is called a warm front, see Fig. 7(8). As the warm air is forced upwards it is cooled and is likely to produce cloud and possibly rain.

Behind the warm front, where colder air is overtaking warm, is formed a cold front – with the cold air driving in under the warm in a wedge action – pushing the warm air upwards even more vigorously. Sometimes the cold air lifts all the warm air off the surface of the land or sea, in which case the front is called occluded.

There are two types of occlusion, depending on whether the air ahead of or behind the occluded front is the colder. With the cold front type of occlusion, as in Fig. 7(10), cold air has overtaken a warm air mass, lifting it off the surface, and has then caught up air which is cool but not so cold as itself. This usually results in rain from the warm front, which continues for a while after the front has passed, followed by characteristic cold front wind and cooler weather. This is the more common type of occlusion experienced in the region of the British Isles.

A warm front occlusion, shown in Fig. 7(11), is where the overtaking air is cool but not so cold as the air ahead of the front. The front is not so

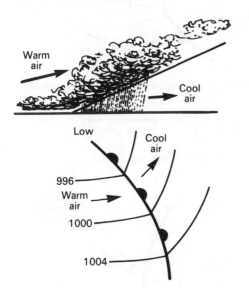

Fig. 7(8) Section and plan view of a warm front.

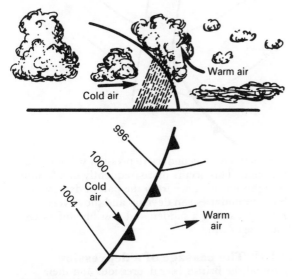

Fig. 7(9) Section and plan view of a cold front.

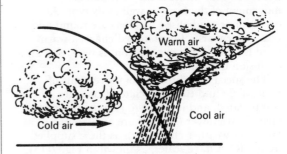

Fig. 7(10) Cross section of an occlusion (cold front type).

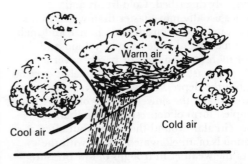

Fig. 7(11) Cross section of an occlusion (warm front type).

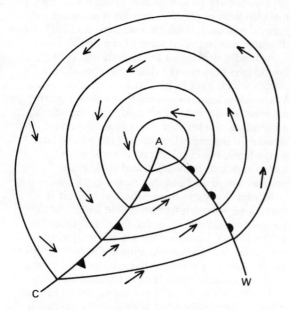

Fig. 7(12) Model depression, showing warm front (AW) and cold front (AC). The arrows indicate wind directions.

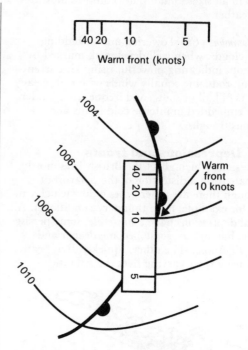

Fig. 7(13) Speed of front scales. Above, for warm front. Below, for cold front or occlusion.

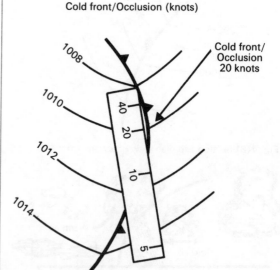

active as a cold front occlusion, and is followed by somewhat warmer air.

Fig. 7(12) shows a typical or 'model' depression with its associated warm and cold fronts. AW (indicated by the rounded marks) is the warm front and AC (with the spiked marks) is the cold front. Between them is the warm sector, behind the warm front. The arrows indicate the probable wind directions. The frontal symbols are placed on the forward side of a front so they indicate the direction of movement of the front as well as its type. An occlusion is symbolised by alternate round and triangular marks. On coloured charts a warm front is marked red, a cold front is blue, and an occlusion is purple.

The speed and direction of movements of depressions and their associated fronts are complicated, and it is best to rely on information given in whatever forecasts are available. However weather charts such as those supplied by the RYA have scales, as shown in Fig. 7(13), with which the speeds of warm and cold fronts can be estimated in a similar way to wind speeds, as previously described. Cold fronts and occlusions usually move faster than warm fronts.

Depressions vary considerably in size and their speed of movement. They can be a thousand miles or more in diameter, or barely cover a shipping forecast area. They can travel at over 50 knots, but the depressions which cover a large area are usually the slower moving ones. With the simplest form of depression the isobars are roughly circular around the centre, but often a depression is of an elongated shape, with the worst of the weather in troughs of low pressure extending from the centre. All fronts lie in a trough, but not all troughs are 'frontal'.

Sometimes a secondary depression will form in a trough. This occurs more frequently in a frontal trough some distance from the parent depression. Such secondaries can develop and move very rapidly, causing a sudden and possibly unforseen increase of wind.

7.1.10 The passage of a depression
Around the British Isles depressions and their associated fronts typically approach from the west

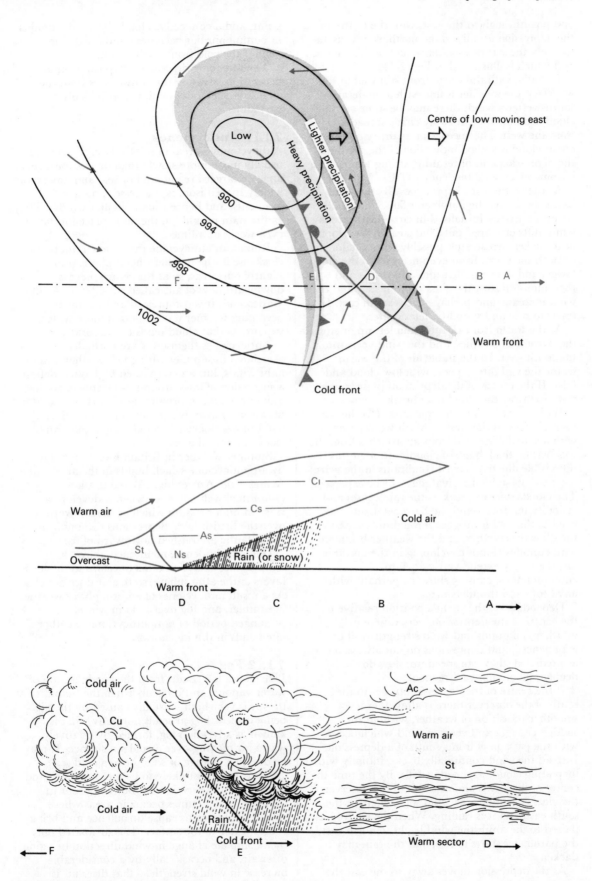

Fig. 7(14) The passage of a depression.

and pass through to the east, with the centre of the depression usually to the north, so it is useful to study the sort of weather sequence this causes, and which is illustrated in Fig. 7(14).

Initially, with the warm front still well to the west (A), the weather is fine with a moderate south-westerly wind; there may be some cumulus cloud around, and probably cirrus spreading from the west. The speed and quantity of the cirrus cloud is a good indication of the depth of the depression and of resulting strong winds. The barometer shows a tendency to fall.

As the warm front approaches (B) the wind backs southerly, the barometer falls, and cloud cover increases – initially thin cirrus with streaky white tufts or mares' tails, but steadily developing into thicker cirrostratus, possibly with a halo.

With the warm front even nearer (C) the cloud lowers and thickens, first into altostratus and then nimbostratus; the glass drops faster, and the wind increases and perhaps backs south east. It starts to rain and visibility deteriorates.

At the warm front (D) the rain lets up or stops, the barometer steadies, and the wind veers into the south west. In the stable air of the warm sector the visibility is poor, with low cloud and mist. If the centre of the depression passes some distance away the cloud may break.

With the passing of the cold front (E) the wind veers sharply to the west or north west, perhaps with a squall. The cold front approaches from the west with a thick bank of cloud, but often this is not visible due to overcast conditions in the warm sector, so its sudden arrival may not be expected. The clouds start to break as the rain ceases and visibility improves, and the barometer starts to rise. As the cold front goes through to the east (F) the glass rises further, and the weather brightens with cumulus clouds developing in the unstable air; these may extend vertically into cumulonimbus, causing showers, perhaps with anvil tops and thunderstorms.

Depending on the yacht's position relative to the centre of the depression, very different weather conditions and wind strengths will be experienced, and depressions do not always move as predicted: they can speed up, slow down, deepen, fill or change direction.

If the centre of the depression passes to the south of the observer there is altogether a smoother transition of weather, without the sudden changes and veers of wind which occur with the passage of fronts south of a depression. Instead the wind continually backs, initially with increasing cloud, as the glass falls. By the time the centre of the low is almost south of the observer the glass is steadier, the wind somewhere in the south east, and it is raining. When the centre has passed to the south the wind backs to north east, the barometer starts to rise, and the rain may slacken.

As the depression moves away to the east the wind backs through north to a north-westerly point, and a convective cloud system of cumulus or cumulonimbus becomes established – as behind the cold front further south.

The foregoing describes a 'typical' frontal depression, crossing the British Isles from the west, but each one is unique, with its own variations.

7.1.11 Anticyclones

Anticyclones – areas of relatively high pressure – usually move more slowly than depressions, cover an even larger area of land or sea, and have more widely spaced isobars (i.e. lesser pressure gradients, and hence usually lighter winds). They can remain roughly in the same place for days or even weeks at a time.

Round an anticyclone the wind circulation is clockwise in the northern hemisphere, and slightly outwards, so at the centre there is a downward flow of air, called subsidence. As this air descends it is compressed and warmed; becoming warmer it can contain more water vapour, so that cloud tends to evaporate.

Anticyclones themselves are normally associated in summer with good weather and light winds, but an established high often deflects a succession of lows around its periphery so that quite pronounced pressure gradients can build up between the two, which act in concert (since the wind blows clockwise round a high and anti-clockwise round a low).

Summer weather in Britain is often influenced by an anticyclone which builds in the area of the Azores – the Azores high. When this is established well north, or when it develops a ridge of high pressure which extends towards or over the British Isles, depressions coming from the Atlantic are pushed northward of us.

Due to subsidence, mentioned above, a temperature inversion often develops in the lower layers of the atmosphere, so the air does not clear. As a result anticyclones often bring hazy weather in summer, and fog over land in winter. A prolonged period of hot, anticyclonic weather often ends in thunderstorms.

7.1.12 Fog

Like cloud, fog results from the condensation of water vapour, and it occurs when the humidity of the air is very high – usually caused by the air being cooled. Fog at sea is normally what is known as advection fog, formed by relatively warm air moving over a cold sea surface. It may be due to a change of wind or to a cold sea current. It is most likely to be met in winter and spring when the sea is cold, but can occur in summer. It sometimes occurs in areas where strong tidal streams cause turbulence and bring colder water to the surface. It is dissipated only by a complete change in wind direction bringing drier air, and occasionally by a considerable increase in wind strength so that drier air is brought down from above. A feature of sea fog is that, unlike fog over land, it can persist in quite strong winds.

Another type which may be met at sea, but which does not normally persist for long, is fog associated with the passage of a front. Fog or poor visibility is often experienced in the warm sector after a warm front has passed.

Over land, radiation fog is what causes the trouble on still nights, with clear skies over low-lying parts of the country. As the earth radiates its heat into space, mist forms close to the ground and gradually thickens. Radiation fog may drift out to sea, but since the water temperature is usually higher than that required to form fog over land it normally soon disperses.

Fog sometimes forms in estuaries where cold river water runs into the sea.

7.1.13 Sea and land breezes

Since many yachtsmen cruise largely in coastal waters, special mention must be made of these particular thermal winds which can play an important part in the local weather pattern, especially in respect of sea breezes during the months when most yachtsmen are afloat.

Sea breezes

The theory of the sea breeze is simple – the sun heats up the land so that it is warmer than the sea, because the two have different thermal properties. The land warms and cools more quickly than the sea. So on a sunny morning the land warms, quickly heating the air above it, which rises so that cooler air from over the sea is drawn in to replace it, thus initiating a wind blowing in towards the land. Fig. 7(15).

The effect depends upon there being little or no cloud over the land; if there is more than half cloud cover the likelihood of a sea breeze developing is remote.

The timing and strength of the sea breeze, and its subsequent behaviour, depend however on other factors. First, and most important, on what wind is already blowing in the morning. If the wind, due to the gradient of isobaric pressure, is already on-shore the sea breeze will intensify it, and by mid-afternoon there may be quite a strong wind blowing. If the gradient wind is off-shore the sea breeze will work in opposition to it,

and may or may not prevail. If the off-shore wind is only moderate in strength there is likely to be a period of calm before the sea breeze gets established. If the off-shore wind is more than about 15 knots over the sea then it is likely to continue to blow, but with less force. If the gradient wind is force 5 or more it will inhibit the vertical circulation described and a sea breeze is unlikely to develop.

Sea breezes are encouraged by low coastal areas with hills behind rather than by high cliffs, and are more pronounced on days when the atmosphere is unstable than stable. They start earlier in the absence of cloud over the land, or in the absence of an existing off-shore wind, or on coasts facing east rather than west since they get warmed up more quickly.

The sea breeze begins along the shore, and gradually spreads seawards. Visible evidence of its onset may be the build up of a line of cumulus cloud along the coast and gradually moving inland – formed by the air drawn in from the sea rising by convection over the warm shore – combined with vanishing cloud over the sea, where the air is sinking to feed the on-shore wind which is developing.

Under favourable conditions a sea breeze may be felt 10 miles (16km) or so offshore, although probably not until early afternoon(or later if it has had to overcome an offshore wind), but its effect may reach much further in some areas.

By early evening, as the power of the sun is reducing, the sea breeze starts to drop and it will be gone by sunset – perhaps earlier due to an increase in the off-shore gradient wind or the spread of cloud across the land.

In British waters sea breezes are most common in late spring, but they are also experienced in summer and early spring.

Land breezes

Land breezes work at night, in the opposite way to sea breezes by day, but they do not usually blow so strongly. They are caused by the land cooling more quickly than the sea – by radiation on a clear night, as often happens in anticyclonic conditions. These off-shore breezes may start a couple of hours after sunset and blow until dawn, or a bit later. Since they depend on the temperature difference between the land and the sea they are more likely to occur in autumn (when the sea is warmest) than in spring or early summer. Their effect does not extend so far offshore as the sea breeze by day – usually not more than about five miles from the coast.

The air which rises over the sea may form some cloud of a cumulus type, while the upper air flowing back inshore and sinking over coastal areas helps to keep them clear of cloud.

The land breeze may be strengthened in some areas by a katabatic wind – caused by air being cooled on the slopes of coastal hills and mountains in settled weather with clear skies, and

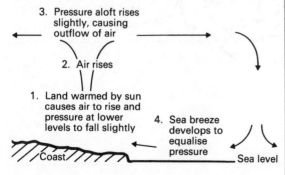

Fig. 7(15) How a sea breeze develops.

draining down the valleys to the sea. The effect is local and is usually not very strong in British waters, except in steep-sided estuaries such as Scottish lochs.

Diurnal weather variation

Related to the sea and land breezes described above are the daily changes in the weather that can occur on shore during the day – more particularly in the summer if the weather is fine and settled.

As the sun heats the land in the morning, the air above it is heated and rises by convection, making the lower layers of the atmosphere less stable. If the morning dawned with a clear sky, this may give rise to some cumulus cloud, under which the wind will be puffy and variable: if there is considerable development of cumulus cloud they may produce some rain. Convection also tends to bring down, nearer the earth's surface, wind from aloft which (due to lack of surface friction) has been blowing more strongly than the wind at ground level – so that by early afternoon the wind speed has increased to its maximum for the day.

In the evening, the earth's surface starts to cool by radiation – cooling the lower levels near the ground, but not the air higher up. This causes an inversion, which prevents convection, and so the wind decreases in strength – perhaps to a complete calm before dawn, when the temperature is lowest and there is the possibility of fog. In the morning the sun heats up the land

again, breaks the inversion, and the cycle is repeated.

7.1.14 Thunderstorms

Thunderstorms are intense local disturbances which can be accompanied by very strong winds, heavy rain or hail, and the discharge of electricity (lightning). They are most common in the tropics. In higher latitudes they are caused when an air mass becomes unstable at a great height, and they occur more often over land than over the sea where they develop mainly along fronts – usually cold fronts.

A thunderstorm can be anticipated by strongly developing cumulus cloud, with well defined heads. Cumulus clouds are created by convection and contain strong up-currents of wind, causing gusty conditions.

The conditions particularly suited to the development of cumulus lead to cumulonimbus, which can cause precipitation. Large cumulonimbus can produce thunderstorms with towering banks of threatening clouds eventually topped by an anvil-shaped layer, orientated along the direction in which the thunderstorm is moving. Cumulonimbus clouds are composed of cells, each one having its own area of strong vertical air currents.

As the rolling clouds along the base of the cumulonimbus come overhead the yacht will experience gusty down-draughts and big wind shifts, and then rain or hail. Behind the thunderstorm the wind is likely to be light – with

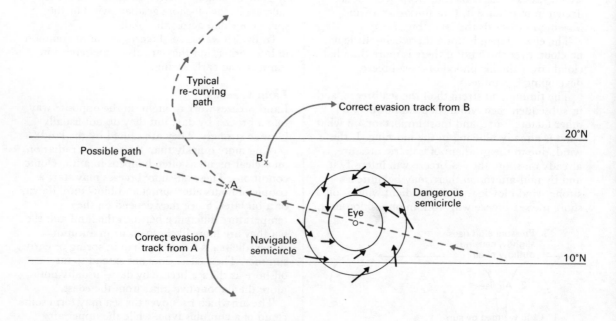

Fig. 7(16) Typical path of a hurricane, showing the dangerous and navigable semicircles.

little rain, lower temperatures and less humidity. If a yacht sails away from a thunderstorm it is only likely to prolong the time it is overhead. At sea the best course is to steer, if possible, across the path of an approaching storm but leaving the centre to port.

The cumulonimbus anvil head is composed of ice crystals at a height of 25,000ft (7600m) or more, spreading outwards at the upper limit of convection. It is the effect of the shattering of frozen drops of water within a cloud which leads to the creation of a static charge of electricity. Thunder is caused by the sudden expansion of air as it is heated by a flash of lightning. The distance of a thunderstorm (in miles) can be estimated by timing the interval (in seconds) between the lightning and the thunder, and dividing the figure by five. Damage to a yacht as a result of possible lightning strike can be minimised by connecting a metal mast to a metal earthing plate in the boat's bottom.

7.1.15 Tropical storms

Tropical storms are intense depressions which develop in low latitudes. They are of much smaller diameter than a deep depression in (say) the North Atlantic (although covering a larger area than a tornado) and hence the isobars are much more closely spaced and the winds speeds greatly increased. In a tropical storm the wind spirals in towards the centre (anti-clockwise in the northern hemisphere) at all heights, whereas with a normal depression in higher latitudes the winds eventually conform to the higher wind above.

At the centre, or eye, of the storm there is a temporary lull, but near the centre the wind blows at hurricane force, the visibility is almost nil, and the seas are extremely high and confused. Gale force winds are likely to be encountered within 100 miles (161km) of the storm centre.

In general, tropical storms occur on the western sides of oceans. The following remarks apply to the North Atlantic, the Caribbean and the Gulf of Mexico where such storms are known as hurricanes. Hurricanes originate as a rule between 7° and 15°N, but sometimes nearer the equator. Initially they move in a WNW direction, at speeds of 10–15 knots. When in about 25°N they are likely to re-curve to the north and north-east, and to increase their speed of advance to about 25 knots. They may continue, gradually diminishing in intensity, for a long way. Some severe gales off NW Europe originated as hurricanes. The hurricane season is from July to September, but tropical storms can occur at other times.

When sailing in low latitudes beware of abnormally low barometric pressure for the time of year. For example, 5mb below the normal mean pressure should arouse suspicion of a tropical disturbance, and it is important to take careful readings of the barometer at hourly intervals, allowing for diurnal variation. Other warning signs are: a significant change in wind speed or direction; swell from a direction indicating the storm centre; cirrus cloud, followed by altostratus and broken cumulus.

With the advent of weather satellites the identification and tracking of hurricanes has improved, and regular information is broadcast by radio. This may allow even a slow-moving yacht to avoid the storm centre. Fig. 7(16) shows the typical path of a hurricane, and identifies the dangerous and navigable semicircles. The dangerous semicircle is on the right of the storm's path, because here the wind is strongest and a yacht tends to be blown into the eye of the storm: also, should the hurricane re-curve, the eye of the storm may pass over the yacht. If the wind is steadily veering, it can be assumed that the yacht is in the dangerous semicircle.

Tropical storms are known as cyclones in the Indian Ocean and Bay of Bengal, and as typhoons in the Western Pacific.

7.2 Glossary of meteorological terms

Anemometer Instrument for measuring wind speed.

Anticyclone An area of high barometric pressure, with isobars encircling the centre of the 'high'.

Aurora Borealis The 'northern lights' – bright streaks of light in the northern sky, caused by electrical discharges in the atmosphere.

Backing A change in the direction of the wind, in an anti-clockwise direction.

Clouds Collection of minute water droplets, or ice, suspended in the atmosphere. For descriptions of different types of cloud see 7.1.8.

Cold front The boundary line which marks advancing cold air in the passage of a depression.

Coronae Coloured rings around the sun or moon, due to diffraction of light by water droplets.

Cyclone The name given to a tropical revolving storm occuring in the Indian Ocean, Arabian Sea or Bay of Bengal.

Cyclonic Anti-clockwise circulation over an area associated with a depression.

Depression A discrete area of low barometric pressure.

Dew Water drops formed by condensation of water vapour in the air on surfaces cooled by radiation at night.

Dew point The lowest temperature to which the air can be cooled before condensation (e.g. dew) is formed.

Equinoctial gales A phrase sometimes used in the mistaken belief that gales occur with greater severity and frequency near the equinoxes than at other times of the year.

Eye of the storm The area of light winds and often broken cloud in the centre of a tropical revolving storm.

Eye of wind The direction from which the wind blows (now rarely used).

Front A zone on or above the earth's surface, separating cold and warm air masses.

Further outlook A brief description of the general weather conditions for a period following that covered by a more detailed forecast.

Geostrophic wind The wind that would theoretically blow if only the spacing of the isobars is considered (disregarding friction, curvature of the isobars, latitude, and other local effects).

Gust A rapid fluctuation in the strength of the wind, mainly caused by turbulence or eddies.

Haar A name given to sea fog in some eastern parts of Scotland and England.

Hail Small, hard pellets of ice from cumulo-nimbus clouds – often associated with thunderstorms.

Halo Phenomenon caused by refraction or reflection of light from the sun or moon.

Hurricane A wind of force 12 on the Beaufort scale; also the name given to a tropical revolving storm in the West Indies or off the American seaboard.

Inversion When air temperature (contrary to the usual case) increases with altitude. Sometimes a cause of fog.

Isobars Lines on a synoptic chart or weather map joining places of equal barometric pressure.

Isotherms Lines joining places of the same temperature.

Katabatic wind A wind that blows down mountain slopes, due to cooling by radiation.

Land and sea breezes Off-shore and on-shore winds caused respectively by the land cooling and heating up more quickly than the sea under clear skies.

Line squall A sudden, violent squall often associated with a cold front; usually identifiable by the low line of black cloud from which it takes its name. Apart from a sudden increase in wind and change of wind direction, its passing is accompanied by a rise of the barometer, a fall in temperature, and usually heavy rain, hail or thunder.

Mackerel sky A sky with cirrocumulus or high altocumulus arranged in a regular pattern like mackerel scales.

Mirage The appearance in the sky of images which are in reality over the horizon, due to abnormal refraction.

Occlusion When the warm sector of a depression has been raised from the surface of the land or sea by the advance of the cold front behind it, the depression is said to be occluded.

Polar front A line of discontinuity in the global weather system where polar air and subtropical air meet, and where as a result depressions often originate.

Precipitation Particles of water or ice which fall from clouds, e.g. rain, drizzle, snow, sleet or hail.

Recurvature Describes the typical track of a tropical cyclone, e.g. in the northern hemisphere such storms, after tracking roughly west, usually swing round to a north-easterly course.

Ridge The extension of an area of high pressure (similar to a ridge running out from a mountain).

Scud Seaman's term for fractostratus cloud – low fragments of racing cloud, often beneath rain clouds.

Sea breeze See land breezes.

Sea fret Used in parts of North-East England to describe sea fog.

Secondary depression An offshoot from a parent depression, often formed by a distortion of isobars along a front, which can cause a quick and unexpected deterioration in the weather.

Showers Periods of rain from cumuliform cloud, interspersed with fair weather and clearer skies.

Sleet Precipitation of snow and rain.

Snow Precipitation of ice crystals, in formations of varying size.

Squall A sudden increase of wind lasting several minutes, usually caused by fronts and large convective clouds, and often associated with a change in wind direction.

Synoptic chart A weather map, showing the distribution of barometric pressure and the principal weather features over a large area for a certain time.

Thunder and lightning Thunder is the noise made by lightning which is a discharge of static electricity within clouds or from a cloud to earth. Most thunderstorms form in cumulo-nimbus clouds and may result in squalls, hail and heavy rainstorms.

Tornado A violent whirl usually cyclonic and associated with thunderstorm clouds.

Trade winds Winds which blow from the sub-tropical high pressure belts towards the equator – NE winds in the northern hemisphere and SE winds in the southern hemisphere.

Trough An extension of a depression shown on a weather chart by isobars with increased curvature. A front always lies in a trough. As the trough passes a place the barometer falls and then rises.

Typhoon The name given to a tropical revolving storm in the Western Pacific.

Veer A change in the direction of the wind, in a clockwise direction.

Ventimeter A small hand held instrument for measuring wind speed or force.

Warm front, warm sector The boundary between cooler air in front of a depression and the warmer air (warm sector) on its equatorial side is called the warm front.

Waterspout A cone or cloud extending from the base of cumulonimbus cloud to the sea. Often occurs with a tornado.

Wedge An alternative word for ridge (of high pressure). Now rarely used.

7.3 Beaufort Scale

Force	Mean speed (knots)	Description	State of sea (description in brackets)	Ashore	Probable wave height ft/m	Probable max. wave height ft/m
0	0–1	Calm	Like a mirror (calm)	Calm; smoke rises vertically	0/0	0/0
1	1–3	Light air	Ripples only (calm)	Direction of wind shown by smoke	0/0	0/0
2	4–6	Light breeze	Small wavelets, not breaking (smooth)	Wind felt on face; leaves rustle	0.7/0.1	1/0.3
3	7–10	Gentle breeze	Large wavelets, crests begin to break; a few white horses (smooth)	Leaves in constant motion; wind extends light flag	1.2/0.4	3/1
4	11–16	Moderate breeze	Small waves growing longer; fairly frequent white horses (slight)	Raises dust; small branches moved	3/1	5/1.5
5	17–21	Fresh breeze	Moderate waves, taking more pronounced form; many white horses, perhaps some spray (moderate)	Small trees in leaf begin to sway, crested wavelets on inland waters	6/2	8/2.5
6	22–27	Strong breeze	Large waves forming; white foam crests more extensive; probably some spray (rough)	Large branches in motion; telephone wires whistle	10/3	13/4
7	28–33	Near gale	Sea heaps up; white foam streaks begin blowing from crests (very rough)	Whole trees in motion; difficult to walk into wind	13/4	18/5.5
8	34–40	Gale	Moderately high waves of greater length; crests break into spindrift, with foamy streaks (high)	Twigs break off trees; wind impedes progress	18/5.5	25/7.5
9	41–47	Severe gale	High waves with tumbling crests; dense streaks of foam; spray may affect visibility (very high)	Slight structural damage occurs (e.g. slates, chimney pots)	23/7	33/10
10	48–55	Storm	Very high waves with long overhanging crests and dense streaks of foam making surface of sea white; heavy tumbling sea; visibility affected (very high)	Seldom experienced inland; trees uprooted, structural damage occurs	30/9	41/12.5
11	56–63	Violent storm	Exceptionally high waves; sea completely covered with long white patches of foam along direction of wind; visibility affected (phenomenal)	Very rarely experienced; wide spread damage caused	36/11	52/16
12	64 plus	Hurricane	Air filled with foam and spray; sea white with driving spray; visibility very seriously affected (phenomenal)	—	46/14	—

Note: The wave heights above are only a guide to what may be expected in the open sea, away from land.

7.4 Barometer and thermometer conversion scales

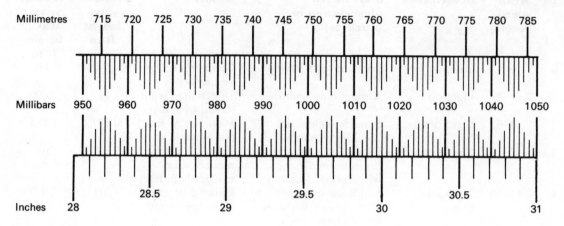

Fig. 7(17) This scale shows the relationship between millibars, inches of mercury, and millimetres of mercury for atmospheric pressure.

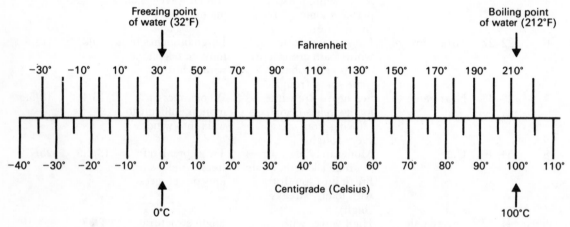

Fig. 7(18) The relationship between temperatures in degrees Fahrenheit and Centigrade (Celsius).

7.5 Meanings of terms used in weather bulletins

In order to be able to understand a forecast it is essential to know the meanings of certain terms which are regularly used – apart from some of those in the glossary in section 7.2. The following are often used in shipping forecasts.

7.5.1 Visibility

Good	More than 5 miles
Moderate	5–2 miles
Poor	2 miles – 1100yds (1000m)
Fog	Less than 1100yds (1000m)

7.5.2 Timing

Imminent	Within 6 hours of time of issue
Soon	6–12 hours
Later	12–24 hours

7.5.3 Speeds (of weather systems)

Slowly	0–15 knots
Steadily	15–25 knots
Rather quickly	25–35 knots
Rapidly	35–45 knots
Very rapidly	Over 45 knots

7.5.4 Barometric pressure changes (tendency)

Now falling) Pressure
Rising more slowly (or now steady)) higher than
Rising) 3 hours ago
Steady Change less than 1mb in 3 hours
Now rising Pressure lower or the same as 3 hours ago
Falling more slowly) Pressure lower than
Falling) 3 hours ago

'Rising' and 'Falling' may be qualified by:

Slowly	Change less than 1.6mb in 3 hours
Quickly	Change 3.5–6mb in 3 hours
Very rapidly	Change more than 6mb in 3 hours

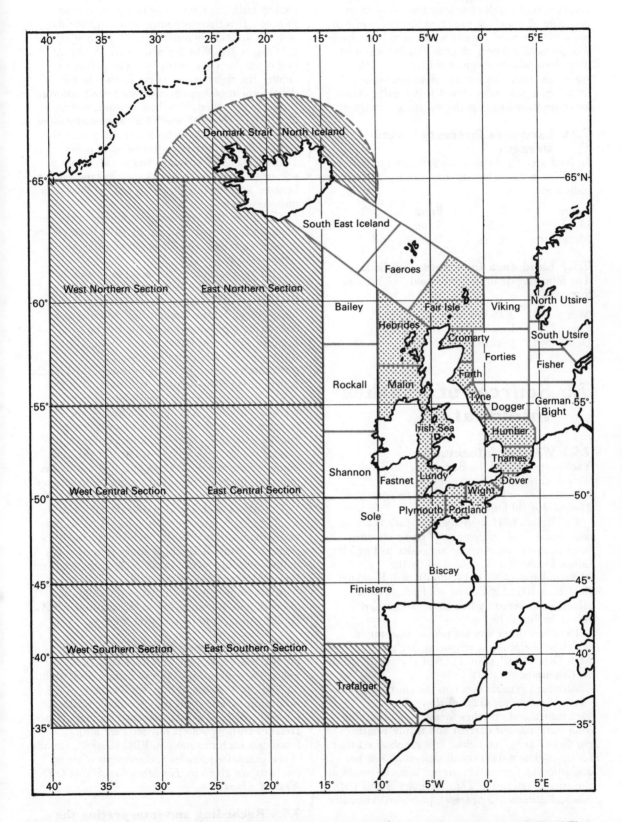

Fig. 7(19) British Sea Forecast Areas. The stippled sea areas are those for which visual gale warnings are displayed. The hatched areas, plus Biscay, Sole and Finisterre, are included in the Atlantic Weather Bulletin which is transmitted by WT (Morse code) by Portishead Radio. The other areas (stippled and plain) are included in bulletins broadcast by the BBC and by British Telecom coast stations.

7.5.5 Gale warnings

Indicate that winds of at least force 8 or gusts reaching 43 knots are expected somewhere in the area. 'Severe gale' implies winds of at least force 9 or gusts of 52 knots. 'Storm' implies winds of force 10 or above, or gusts of 61 knots. Gale warnings remain in force until amended or cancelled ('gales now ceased'). If a gale persists for more than 24 hours the warning is re-issued.

7.5.6 Land area forecasts – wind strength

In land area forecasts winds are given in the following terms, which relate to Beaufort forces as indicated:

Calm	0	Fresh	5
Light	1–3	Strong	6–7
Moderate	4	Gale	8

7.5.7 Land area forecasts – visibility

The following definitions are used in land area forecasts:

Mist	200–1100yds (183–1000m)
Fog	Less than 200yds (183m)
Dense fog	Less than 50yds (46m)

7.6 Sources of weather information

7.6.1 Weather information

Yachtsmen around the British Isles are well served with various sources of weather information – all of which originates from the Meteorological Office.

Full details of *Weather Bulletins, Gale Warnings and Services for the Shipping and Fishing Industries* (and of course yachtsmen) are contained in Met. Office Leaflet No. 3, published by the Meteorological Office, London Road, Bracknell, Berkshire, RG12 2SZ. The sea forecast areas which are covered by British broadcasts are shown in Fig. 7(19).

Details of other services provided, some of which are helpful to yachtsmen, are given in Met. Office Leaflet No. 1, titled *Weather Advice to the Community*.

Although general notes on the contents of the two leaflets above, so far as they affect yachtsmen, and on other methods of obtaining information about current and future weather conditions are given below, it is emphasised that for up-to-date details on all aspects of weather and shipping forecasts reference must be made to the current edition of *The Macmillan & Silk Cut Nautical Almanac* (Chapter 7), published annually.

7.6.2 BBC Radio Shipping Forecasts

Shipping forecasts, primarily designed to give guidance to commercial vessels on passage, necessarily cover very large sea areas, and the spoken bulletins have to be compressed into five minutes. It is therefore impossible, in the time allotted, to include much detail – particularly that associated with the many variations that can and often do occur near land. The ability to convey the right degree of confidence in the development of a particular weather situation is similarly restricted. For these reasons, forecasts for 'Inshore Waters' (see 7.6.3) are usually more helpful to yachtsmen who are cruising near the coast. These forecasts are intended to cover up to 12 nautical miles offshore, and to take some account of local phenomena such as land and sea breezes, and the funelling effect of the land over inshore waters.

The times, frequencies and contents of the shipping forecasts broadcast by BBC Radio 4 are given in detail in *The Macmillan & Silk Cut Nautical Almanac*.

VHF reception may be useful in certain local areas (such as in the West of Scotland) where 200kHz or medium frequency reception is not satisfactory. A little booklet *BBC television and radio stations*, published annually by the Engineering Information Department of the BBC, gives details and locations of all transmitters. A similar booklet is published by the Independent Broadcasting Authority.

The bulletins include a summary of gale warnings in force; a general synopsis of the weather for the next 24 hours and expected changes within that period; forecasts for each coastal sea area (in a given order) for the next 24 hours, giving wind direction and speed, weather and visibility; and the latest reports from selected stations.

The size of each sea area and the fact that the whole bulletin lasts only five minutes mean that many details of interest to yachtsmen have to be excluded. Some skill and practice is needed to make a sensible record of the facts presented, and this is discussed further in 7.6.4.

Apart from being included in the shipping forecast, gale warnings are broadcast in the BBC Radio 4 programme soon after receipt.

7.6.3 BBC Inshore Waters Forecasts

Forecasts are given for inshore waters (up to 12 miles/19km offshore) of Great Britain each night on English, Welsh and Scottish Radio 4 programmes, and on Radio Scotland. Radio Ulster broadcasts similar forecasts for Northern Ireland. Inshore waters forecasts are also broadcast each morning on BBC Radio 3. Details of the times, frequencies and contents of these forecasts are given in *The Macmillan & Silk Cut Nautical Almanac*.

7.6.4 Recording and interpreting the shipping forecasts

Just to hear the shipping forecast for a particular area may be better than nothing, but much more benefit can arise if the whole of the shipping forecast is recorded and analysed in some detail. This applies particularly when a series of forecasts at six hour intervals are treated in the same way, because it is then possible to study how a weather pattern is developing and how the local situation relates to what is being forecast for a very much bigger area.

The first requirement is to be able to write down all the essential details of the forecast – any gale warnings in force, the general synopsis (so easy to miss), the forecasts for all sea areas (not just the local ones), and the 'actuals' from the various stations round the coast.

In order to achieve this it is vital to start off with some kind of form on which to write down or tick off the details which are broadcast. Various types are available; one is the Metmap jointly published by the Royal Meteorological Society and the Royal Yachting Association. Pads of 25 can be purchased from the RYA, Shaftesbury Road, Gillingham, Dorset, SP8 4LJ.

Next it is essential to devise some form of shorthand which will allow all the details to be recorded in the very limited time available. This can be a matter of personal choice, although there is an advantage in using the standard international weather map symbols because it is then possible to interpret bulletins which are posted up at harbour offices and other places. A selection of some of the more commonly used symbols is given below.

Wind symbols

Wind direction is shown by arrows, flying in the direction of the wind. The international convention is that each long feather indicates 10 knots, and each half feather indicates 5 knots. A solid triangular feather indicates 50 knots, at which point the long and half feather notation recommences. The examples below show westerly winds.

Symbol	Knots	Symbol	Knots
	1– 2		43– 47
	3– 7		48– 52
	8–12		53– 57
	13–17		58– 62
	18–22		63– 67
	23–27		68– 72
	28–32		73– 77
	33–37		78– 82
	38–42		103–107

Other useful wind symbols include:

Calm	⊙
Variable force 3	V3
Cyclonic variable force 4	④

Weather symbols

	Beaufort notation	Plotting symbols
Rain	r	●
Drizzle	d	،
Shower	p	▽
Snow	s	✳
Hail	h	△
Thunderstorm	t	⟁
Fog	f	≡
Mist	m	=
Haze	z	∞

The symbols may be combined, or elaborated as in the example for rain below:

	Beaufort	Plotting
Intermittent slight rain	r_0	●
Continuous slight rain	$r_0 r_0$	● ●
Intermittent moderate rain	r	●●●
Continuous moderate rain	r r	●●●●
Intermittent heavy rain	R	●●●●
Continuous heavy rain	R R	●●●●●

Have everything ready well before the time that the bulletin is going to start, and it is useful to refer to the previous forecast because then one is ready to record the sort of details which are likely in the general synopsis. Once the forecast begins just concentrate on writing down all the details, without trying to analyse them in any way – that comes later. Remember that it is important to write down the various times stated – the time of the forecast and the time at which the actual weather at coast stations was recorded. These are easy to miss.

For navigational purposes it is a good rule to check the time signal which often follows the shipping forecast, and this gives time to draw breath before starting to interpret what has been written down so hurriedly.

It is easiest to construct your own weather map for the time of the actuals recorded. These are usually about two hours before the broadcast. So these reports from coastal stations can be plotted directly on to the chart – wind strength and direction, weather and pressure.

Then plot the information contained in the general synopsis, but with the movements of centres and fronts advanced by the time between the forecast and the time of the actuals on the basis of the speeds given in the forecast.

Finally add the wind, weather and visibility forecasts for the various sea areas. Concentrate on the 'at first' forecasts if there are other predictions for 'later'.

Now all the information is available to start drawing in the isobars, but sketch lightly because almost certainly there will be some rubbing out to do. Begin by joining up the coastal stations with equal pressure, conforming to the general pattern indicated by whatever lows or highs have been given in the general synopsis. More isobars can then be added at suitable angles to the forecast wind directions over the open sea, and at spacings which conform to the geostrophic chart for the forecast wind strengths. Remember that at troughs or fronts the isobars should change direction. It is largely a matter of trial and error, but practice helps to speed up the process so that a very useful weather map can be produced in a few minutes. Armed with this it is much easier to understand what is happening to the weather in one particular small area of sea.

When interpreting the resulting synoptic chart, remember that if the yacht is not far offshore the weather may be affected by a number of variations due to the land. Sea and land breezes are obvious examples, and have already been discussed in 7.1.13. But wherever there is a large lump of land the wind will tend, where possible, to flow round it rather than over the top, and particularly when air conditions are stable. So off large headlands, or in rivers or estuaries, allowance must be made for significant changes in wind speed and direction. The wind can also be greatly affected by purely local cloud conditions.

7.6.5 BBC General Forecasts

Land area forecasts can be useful to yachtsmen in as much as they include the outlook period (up to 48 hours beyond the detailed forecast and the shipping forecast) and often some reference to weather along the coasts. They may also give more recent information which was not available in the previous shipping forecast. The more detailed land area forecasts are broadcast on Radio 4 on 200kHz (1500m).

7.6.6 Local Radio Stations – Forecasts

The details and values of forecasts broadcast by local radio stations vary considerably; some give no more than an indication of the present weather conditions. However, many local radio stations in coastal areas now participate in a scheme for broadcasting 'Small Craft Warnings' when winds of Force 6 or more are expected within the next 12 hours on the coast or up to five miles offshore. These warnings are handled in a similar way to gale warnings on Radio 4, being broadcast at the first programme junction after receipt and then repeated on the next hour or after the next news bulletin.

Details of weather forecasts from local radio

stations in coastal areas which are of particular interest to yachtsmen are given in *The Macmillan & Silk Cut Nautical Almanac*.

7.6.7 British Telecom Coast Radio Stations – Weather bulletins by RT

Forecasts originating from the Meteorological Office (usually those for adjacent sea areas from the latest shipping forecast) are broadcast twice daily – at 0803 and 2003 (GMT) or at 0833 and 2033 (GMT). Details of stations, frequencies, times and forecast areas are given in *The Macmillan & Silk Cut Nautical Almanac*.

British and Irish Coastal Radio Stations transmit gale warnings at the end of the next R/T (MF) silence period after receipt. These silence periods are from 00 to 03 and from 30 to 33 minutes past each hour. Gale warnings are repeated at the next of the following times: 0303, 0903, 1503, 2103 GMT. Gale warnings are preceded by the R/T Safety Signal 'SECURITE' (pronounced 'SAY-CURE-E-TAY').

Gale warnings remain in force unless amended or cancelled. If the gale persists for more than 24 hours from the time of origin, the gale warning is re-issued.

7.6.8 Television Forecasts, Prestel

An increasing number of television forecasts now include a synoptic chart, which together with the satellite weather pictures can be a useful guide to the general weather situation at the start of a passage.

The use of teletext television receivers is slowly increasing, the systems being Ceefax operated by the BBC and Oracle by ITV. Oracle shows the latest Shipping Forecast.

Prestel

Prestel (operated over a telephone link by British Telecom) has a great deal of meteorological data supplied by the Meteorological Office. The following is a summary of information of particular interest to yachtsmen. Frame charges are indicated in brackets.

Main index page, key 209: land areas 2091; shipping and sailing 2093: actual weather in UK 20940: actual weather world-wide 2094: aviation Fcsts 20971: European Fcsts 20915: UK regional weather 20912.

Caption chart for 24h, 4 times/day 20911 (3p): text for 24h, 4 times/day 20910 (3p): 3 day outlook 20913 (6p).

Coastal areas/sailing Fcsts (4p). Essex, Kent & Sussex 209171: Anglesey/N Wales 209173: S Wales 209177: W Coast of Scotland 209179: Poole Bay to Selsey Bill 209353: English Channel (Solent to Cherbourg & Channel Islands) 209354: Thames Estuary 209351: Channel coast 209352.

Shipping Fcsts (4p) 4 times/day. Synopsis 209300. Viking, Forties, Cromarty & Forth

209301: Tyne, Dogger, Fisher & German Bight
209302: Humber, Thames, Dover & Wight
209303: Portland, Plymouth, Biscay & Finisterre
209304: Sole, Lundy, Fastnet & Irish Sea
209305: Shannon, Rockall, Malin & Hebrides
209306: Bailey, Fair Isle, Faeroes & SE Iceland
209307. Gale warnings, since latest Shipping
Fcst, 20931. Sea crossings, 3 times/day. Southern
North Sea 209330: Dover Strait 209331: English
Channel (East) 209332: St Georges Channel
209333: Irish Sea 209334.

7.6.9 Reports on current weather

Reports on actual weather conditions can be
obtained from certain Meteorological Office
stations, Coastguard stations and lighthouses
around the coast of the British Isles. These are
listed, with their telephone numbers, in *The
Macmillan & Silk Cut Nautical Almanac*.

7.6.10 Special forecasts for sea areas

Forecasts for areas within the region 65°N to
35°N, and 40°W and the coast of Europe
(including the Mediterranean) may be obtained
by yachts at sea by contacting the appropriate
Meteorological Office forecasting centre. These
are listed, with telephone numbers, in *The
Macmillan & Silk Cut Nautical Almanac*. No charge is
made by the Meteorological Office, but a normal
RT link call charge is levied by British Telecom.

Alternatively, the request may be addressed to
the nearest Coast Radio Station. Such a call
might be in the form: 'North Foreland Radio.
Request weather forecast next 24 hours for sea
areas Dover and Wight on passage Ramsgate to
Cherbourg, Yacht Nonsuch'.

When telephoning a forecasting centre it must
be realised that during busy periods, such as
occasions of bad weather, the staff may be fully
occupied and there is likely to be a delay before
an answer is obtained.

If a forecast is required for some future
occasion or period, or if the forecast is to be kept
under review and up-dated, the request should be
addressed to The Director-General,
Meteorological Office, Met.02a, London Road,
Bracknell, Berks, RG12 2SZ, giving full details of
the service required and the address to which the
account is to be forwarded. Cheques in payment
of charges should be crossed and made payable to
'Met. Office HQ. Public a/c'.

7.6.11 Automatic Telephone Weather Service (Marineline)

Marineline is a taped message service of British
Telecom, sponsored by the RYA, HM
Coastguard and *Practical Boat Owner*, covering the
British Isles. Forecasts, updated daily at 0600 and
1900 (local time), include a general synopsis,
strong wind and gale warnings, inshore forecast,
and outlook for 48 hours. Telephone numbers for
the 13 areas are in *The Macmillan & Silk Cut
Nautical Almanac*.

7.6.12 Facsimile Broadcasts

Weather facsimile receivers are available for
yachts. They will receive and reproduce the
various charts (isobaric, isothermal, wind
direction etc) which are broadcast at specific
times. While the technique is long-standing, it is
only in recent years that the price, size and
weight of facsimile equipment has made it
suitable for use in yachts. It is simply a method of
receiving weather maps by radio. Information
from many meteorological stations is sent to
major centres such as Bracknell (England), Paris
(France) and Offenbach (Germany) where it is
processed by computer, codified, and sent out as
a radio signal. In the yacht the equipment
comprises a suitably stable radio receiver
(normally part of the facsimile unit) and a
recorder which converts the radio signals into
pictures. The correct scanning speed and index of
co-operation (ratio of scanning speed to paper
feed) must be set on the recorder, but some
machines do this automatically.

Each station broadcasts on certain frequencies
and at certain times, as promulgated in *Admiralty
List of Radio Signals, Vol 3*, and transmits a
number of different charts during the day, some
of which are unintelligible to the average
yachtsman since they require skilled
interpretation. Most useful are the Surface
Analysis charts, which show the weather map
with depressions, anticyclones and fronts drawn
in. There are also forecast charts for 24, 48 and
72 hours ahead.

7.6.13 Volmet

Volmet is a continuous VHF broadcast of
weather information at airfields, for aircraft. It
gives wind directions and speed, atmospheric
pressure, and other information on visibility,
weather and cloud cover as appropriate.

The principal British broadcasts are on
126.6MHz, 128.6MHz and 135.375MHz.
These frequencies cannot be received on an
ordinary marine VHF set, and require a special
licence.

7.6.14 W/T Transmissions from Coast Radio Stations

These are intended for ocean going vessels, and
the average yachtsman will have neither the
equipment nor the ability to receive the
information at the speed it is transmitted by
W/T. Details are available in the *Admiralty List of
Radio Signals Vol. 3*.

7.6.15 Press Forecasts

The delay between the time of issue and the time
they are available the following day make press
forecasts of limited value to yachtsmen. However
the better papers publish weather charts which
may include a forecast of the synoptic chart for
noon on the day of publication. In the absence of
any other chart this can be helpful when

interpreting the shipping forecast on first putting to sea.

7.6.16 Visual storm signals (British Isles)

Visual gale warnings signals are displayed at a few vantage points around the coasts of Britain when a gale is expected within 12 hours, or is already blowing, in the coastal sea area adjacent to the station displaying the signal.

Official signals as hitherto displayed by Coastguard stations, lighthouses, light-vessels etc are now discontinued. A few visual storm signals are still shown by private arrangement, but such signals should be treated with caution, since they may not be up to date.

The signal is lowered when the wind is below gale force if a renewal of gale force winds is not expected within six hours. Thus it is left flying during a temporary lull if a renewal is expected.

The signals consist of black cones. The North cone, point upwards, indicates gales from a point north of the east-west line. The South cone, point downwards, indicates gales from a point south of the east-west line.

A few stations display night signals consisting of a triangle of lights, which are used in the same way as the cones.

7.6.17 Visual storm signals (Continental)

Visual storm signals of similar types are displayed in France, Belgium, Netherlands and the Federal Republic of Germany. They consist of cones, flags and balls with the following meanings.

Gale expected from	By day	By night
North-west	A black cone point up.	Two red lights shown vertically
South-west	A black cone point down	Two white lights shown vertically
North-east	Two black cones, one above the other, points up.	A red light above a white light
South-east	Two black ones, one above the other, points down.	A white light above a red light
Near gale (any direction)	A black ball	A white light above a green light

A single black or red flag displayed with any of the above signals indicates that the wind is expected to veer. Two red, or two black, flags indicate that the wind is expected to back.

7.6.18 Weather information broadcast in English from radio stations in Western Europe

A number of foreign radio stations broadcast weather information in English which is helpful to cruising yachtsmen. Details of these stations including frequencies, times of forecasts, contents and areas covered are given in *The Macmillan & Silk Cut Nautical Almanac*. A glossary of some of

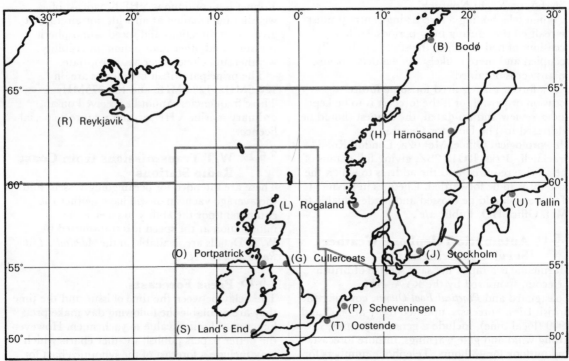

Fig. 7(20) European NAVTEX transmitters and areas served from 1st January, 1984. (Station identity code letters in brackets)

the more common terms in English, French, German and Dutch is given in 7.6.20.

7.6.19 NAVTEX

Certain coast stations in Northern Europe broadcast weather and navigational information by teleprinter. This service, known as NAVTEX, is the basis of a world-wide system. The area served from 1 January 1984, and the stations concerned, are shown in Fig. 7(20).

All broadcasts are on a single frequency of 518 kHz, which allows the use of a relatively simple, dedicated installation consisting of a receiver and a printer which uses 'cash-roll' paper less than 4in (102mm) wide. Such receivers are manufactured by Lo-kata Ltd, Falmouth, Cornwall, TR10 8AE, and by West Electronics, 3 Balena Close, Creekmoor Industrial Estate, Poole, Dorset, BH17 7 DB. The NAVTEX receiver is switched on continuously, but may be programmed to receive only selected stations and/or categories of message. A microprocessor ensures that routine messages already received are not reprinted.

All messages are prefixed by a four-character group. The first character is the identity code of the station. The second indicates the category of the message. The third and fourth are serial numbers, from 01 to 99, and then starting again at 01. The serial number 00 denotes urgent traffic, and will always be printed – regardless of how the receiving equipment has been programmed.

Station identity codes and transmission times

R — Reykjavik, Iceland. 0318 0718 1118 1518 1918 2318

B — Bodφ, Norway.

L — Rogaland, Norway. 0148 0548 0948 1348 1748 2148

J — Stockholm, Sweden. 0330 0730 1130 1530 1930 2330

H — Härnösand, Sweden. 0000 0400 0800 1200 1600 2000

U — Tallin, USSR. 0030 0430 0830 1230 1630 2030

P — Scheveningen, Netherlands. 0348 0748 1148 1548 1948 2348

T — Oostende, Belgium. 0248 0648 1048 1448 1848 2248

G — Cullercoats, United Kingdom. 0048 0448 0848 1248 1648 2048

O — Portpatrick, United Kingdom. 0130 0530 0930 1330 1730 2130

S — Niton, United Kingdom. 0018 0418 0818 1218 1618 2018

F — Brest-Le Conquet, France.

Message categories

A — Navigation warnings
B — Gale warnings
C — Ice reports (unlikely to apply in UK)
D — Search and Rescue information – distress alerting
E — Weather bulletins (twice daily)
Z — No messages on hand at scheduled time

7.6.20 Four language glossary of weather terms

English	French	German	Dutch
Anticyclone (High)	Anticyclone (haut)	Hoch	Hoge drukgebied
Area	Région	Gebiet	Gebied
Backing	Vent refuse	Krimpen	Krimpend
Calm	Calme	Stille/Kalme	Stil
Centre	Centre	Zentrum	Centrum
Clouds	Nuages	Wolken	Wolken
Cold	Froid	Kalt	Koud
Cold front	Front froid	Kalt front	Koud front
Cyclonic	Cyclonique	Zyklonisch	Cyclonisch
Decrease	Affaiblissement	Abnahme	Afnemen
Deep	Profond	Tief	Diep
Deepening	Creusement	Vertiefend	Verdiepend
Depression (Low)	Dépression (bas)	Depression (Tief)	Depressie
Direction	Direction	Richtung	Richting
Dispersing	Se dispersant	Zerstreuend	Verstrooiend
Drizzle	Bruine	Sprühregen	Motregen
Extending	S'étendant	Erstreckend	Uitstrekkend
Extensive	Étendu	Verbreitet	Uitgebreid
Falling	En baisse	Fallend	Vallend
Filling	Comblement	Auffüllend	Vullend
Fine	Beau	Schönwetter	Mooi
Fog	Brouillard	Nebel	Mist
Frequent	Fréquent	Häufig	Veelvuldig
Frost	Gelée	Frost	Vorst
Gale	Coup de vent	Sturm	Stormachtig
Gale warning	Avis de coup de vent	Sturmwarnung	Stormwaarschuwing

English	*French*	*German*	*Dutch*
Good	Bon(ne)	Gut	Goed
Gusty	Vent à rafales	Böig	Buiig
Hail	Grêle	Hagel	Hagel
Heavy	Abondant	Stark	Zwaar
Increasing	Augmentant	Zunehmend	Toenemend
Isolated	Isolé	Einzelne	Verspreid
Lightning	Éclair	Blitz	Bliksem
Local	Locale	Örtlich	Plaatselijk
Mist	Brume legère	Dunst	Nevel
Moderate	Modéré	Mässig	Matig
Moving	Se déplacant	Bewegend	Bewegend
Occasional (showers)	Éparse(s)	Gelegentlich	Nu en dan
Overcast	Couvert	Bedeckt	Geheel bewolkt
Poor	Mauvais	Schlecht	Slecht
Precipitation	Précipitation	Niederschlag	Neerslag
Pressure	Pression	Druck	Druk
Quickly	Rapidement	Schnell	Zeer snel
Rain	Pluie	Regen	Regen
Rough	Agité(e)	Stürmisch	Guur
Scattered	Sporadiques	Verstreut, vereinzelt	Verspreide
Shower	Averse	Schauer	Stort bui
Slowly	Lentement	Langsam	Langzaam
Squall	Grain	Bo	Bui
Stationary	Stationnaire	Stationär, ortsfest	Stationair, stilstand
Steadily	Regulièrement	Stetig, ständig	Regelmatig
Storm	Tempête	Sturm	Storm
Strong	Fort	Stark	Sterk
Swell	Houle	Dünung	Deining
Thunder	Tonnerre	Donner	Donder
Thunderstorm	Orage	Gewitter	Onweer
Variable	Variable	Veränderlich	Veranderlijk
Veering	Vent adonne	Rechtsdrehend	Ruimend
Wind force	Force du vent	Windstärke	Windkracht

7.7 Forecasting your own weather

7.7.1 Introduction

In preceding sections of this chapter are described the general mechanisms which affect the two weather elements of greatest concern to the yachtsman – wind and visibility. With this knowledge it is possible for the yachtsman to attempt his own predictions using the various sources of weather information available to him, in conjunction with his own observations and any synoptic charts to which he may have access or be able to construct for himself. Strictly speaking this is not weather forecasting but a close and intelligent monitoring of forecasts and weather changes, so that a yachtsman has a greater awareness of how the elements may affect him, and enable him to react to and anticipate weather changes. The professional weather forecaster has at his disposal data acquired from instrumented sites over a large area of the globe, and also from instruments launched into space and into the earth's atmosphere. A yachtsman has at his disposal two highly sophisticated instruments – the eye coupled to the human brain. Use of these together with sound basic knowledge and information can help him anticipate problems. It should be remembered that there is a reason for everything that is observed; that reason may not be immediately apparent, but careful observation and thought can lead to better decision making and understanding of the weather.

7.7.2 Barometric pressure

Generations of mariners have observed 'the glass' to give them some indication of forthcoming weather changes, and regular and systematic barometer readings remain a useful weather guide. The ideal instrument is a barograph which continually records the pressure on a paper covered drum so that the changes of pressure can be readily seen – and it is the changes which are of most importance. Although barographs are now being made for yachts it is not always easy to site them in a small boat so that the boat's movement does not create a blurred and unreadable trace. However a properly set (see 7.1.5) dial type aneroid barometer of reasonable quality is adequate, provided that regular readings are taken and noted. The most convenient way of recording the readings is probably to plot them on graph paper, and on a cruising or offshore racing boat this could become part of a routine log entry and thus provide a record similar to that from a barograph.

A steadily falling pressure can confirm a forecast of the approach of a depression or frontal system with the usual worsening of conditions they bring. Conversely a steady rise of pressure occurs whilst such systems are moving away. Frequently the rate of pressure change is linked to the intensity of a system – the greater the fall (or rise) the stronger are the accompanying winds likely to be. As a general guide strengthening winds can be expected if the pressure change is more than three millibars in three hours, and gales are probable if a pressure change of more than five millibars in three hours is recorded. Past weather records show that gales rarely fail to develop at a place after a pressure change of ten millibars in three hours has occured. A falling barometer is a better indicator of strong winds to come, because with a rising barometer they are often already being experienced.

It should be emphasised that a steady barometer does not preclude a significant increase in wind. The boat could be between an anticyclone and an advancing depression, so that although the barometric pressure at the place is steady the pressure gradient is increasing.

7.7.3 **Wind speed and direction**
It is also useful to note the wind speed and direction so that any changes can be readily detected and put in the context of the weather chart. Measuring the wind is easily done if masthead equipment is installed but on any boat under way it should be remembered that it is the apparent wind that is measured, and allowance for the boat's course and speed should be made. Simple hand held instruments such as a ventimeter and a hand bearing compass can be used to measure the wind, taking care to do this on the windward side.

7.7.4 **Temperature**
This weather element is usually of no great concern to a yachtsman but it is possible to obtain both the dew point and sea temperature to assess whether the conditions are near to those necessary for the formation of fog. The dew point is usually obtained by measuring the dry and wet bulb temperatures. A convenient instrument is the whirling psychrometer which is a frame holding two thermometers, the bulb of one being kept moist by dampened muslin. After the instrument has been whirled like a football rattle, the difference in the thermometer readings is noted, and from tables the dew point is obtained.

7.7.5 **Weather lore**
Seamen, and especially longshoremen, have traditionally judged the weather outlook in terms of certain visible signs – the only method once available. In any one place the local weather lore may well have some validity, but what applies on, say, the East Coast may have little relevance on the West Coast of Scotland or in the English Channel. So, as generalisations, many of the well known sayings are not to be trusted. There are however a few signs whose meanings are a little more reliable, and which – if used sensibly in the context of the general weather situation – may prove helpful.

There are several sayings which link the forthcoming weather with the colouring of the sky – especially a red sky. As Shakespeare has it,

'A red morn that ever yet betoken
Wreck to the seaman, tempest to the field,
Sorrow to shepherds, woe unto the birds,
Gust and foul flaws to herdman and to herds'.

A reddening of the sky at sunrise could mean an increase of water vapour in the upper troposphere, perhaps also a high level inversion and some cirrus cloud. In other words a frontal depression might be approaching, causing rain and strong winds by and after dusk with the seaman having to navigate under poor conditions in darkness whilst the shepherd has the problem of gathering a dispersed flock at night. The implications of a red sky at dusk are that any rain and strong winds are more likely to occur during daylight. Sayings that refer to a low or high dawn and dusk (whether the sun is visible on the horizon or not) come into a similar category to the red sky. These sayings are straws in the wind, but could alert a yachtsman to observe more closely any changes in wind and cloud.

One of the most reliable of old saws is 'Backing winds and mare's tails make tall ships carry low sails'. The twisted sheaves of cirrus cloud called 'mares' tails' are caused by the strong winds at upper levels which are often associated with a vigorous frontal depression which, if it is approaching, usually causes the wind to back.

Another reasonably reliable predictor is 'The moon with a circle brings water in her beak'. The circle in this saying is the lunar halo. Remember that the halo occurs around the sun just as frequently as around the moon, but is noticed less often because of the glare. Observing clouds on a bright day is much easier when using sun glasses, and often helps to see cloud formations that cannot be seen with the naked eye.

'Warmth in spring, sea fog will bring' contains an element of truth. As we have seen (7.1.7) air can hold a greater quantity of water vapour with higher temperatures, and in the spring when the sea temperatures have only just started to recover after the winter the air at the surface could be cooled to the dew point – in other words, form fog.

All such sayings should be used with caution although the basis for some can be scientifically explained and can be used by the yachtsman to alert him to possible developments. Listening to the various weather bulletins that are available, drawing a synoptic chart, recording pressure and wind together with careful observation of the sky is the best method of predicting what the weather has in store.

7.7.6 Sea state

Although sea state is the result and not the cause of weather conditions, the subject is of special interest to yachtsmen and is covered in Chapter 9 (9.11).

7.8 Bibliography

The following books are suggested for a fuller discussion on various aspects of weather as it affects the seagoing yachtsman:

Meteorology for Mariners (HMSO). A detailed textbook for the professional seaman.

Interpreting the Weather by Ingrid Holford (David and Charles). A practical guide to general weather forecasting.

The Yachtsman's Weather Guide by Ingrid Holford (Ward Lock). An economical description of weather for the yachtsman.

Weather for Yachtsmen by Captain W. H. Watts (Bosun Books). A good, simple description of the subject.

The Yachtsman's Weather Map by Frank Singleton and Keith Best (Royal Yachting Association). An excellent teaching aid, particularly for analysing the shipping forecast.

Weather Forecasts (Booklet G5) by David Houghton (Royal Yachting Association). Basic guidance on shipping forecasts and other weather information for yachtsmen. Useful pocket reference.

Wind Pilot by Alan Watts (Nautical Books). A comprehensive survey of wind conditions in European waters.

Cruising Weather by Alan Watts (Nautical Books). How the cruising yachtsman can best take advantage of what the weather offers.

Clouds, Formation and Types; Clouds and Weather Photographs and notes by R. K. Pilsbury (BP Educational Services) available on slides, charts, cards or filmstrips.

Cloud Types for Observers (Meteorological Office).

Weather Observation by Bill Giles (E P Publishing Ltd.). Good basic information.

A Course in Elementary Meteorology by H. Heastie (HMSO). An excellent general textbook.

Wind and Sailing Boats by Alan Watts (Adlard Coles Ltd.). Good treatment of local sailing weather, mainly for dinghy and inshore sailing.

Teach Yourself Weather Forecasting for Sailors by Frank Singleton (Hodder & Stoughton).

Meteorology at Sea by Ray Sanderson (Stanford Maritime). A useful basic textbook for the yachtsman.

Your own weather map by M. W. Stubbs (Royal Meteorological Society). A useful guide to constructing a synoptic chart.

The following leaflets are available from the Meteorological Office (Met 07a), London Road, Bracknell, Berkshire, RG12 2SZ.

Met. O. Leaflet No. 1. Weather Advice to the Community.

Met. O. Leaflet No. 3. Weather Bulletins, Gale Warnings and Services for the Shipping and Fishing Industries.

Chapter 8

Safety

Contents

8.1 Introduction

Assuming that a boat is handled sensibly and prudently, implying that good seamanship is used, safety afloat is ultimately a matter of preparation – making sure that the boat is well found and properly fitted out, and that the skipper and his crew are ready to cope with any emergency by knowing exactly how to use the appropriate equipment.

Prevention is always better than cure, and at sea it is easier to forestall an accident than to retrieve the situation. Fire prevention is infinitely preferable to fire fighting: careful pilotage is more satisfactory than having to kedge off the shore: listening to the weather forecast (and interpreting it correctly) is a lot more comfortable than getting caught out unexpectedly in gale force winds: and proper engine maintenance is safer and cheaper than a tow into harbour. However accidents can sometimes happen even on board the best organised boat, and on such occasions it is vital that all on board know how best to deal with the particular emergency, and the correct procedures for seeking help should it be required. In this area the skipper has an important responsibility for the proper management and training of his crew.

In earlier years most yachtsmen and yachtswomen learned the basic skills of seamanship and navigation by being afloat in boats belonging to relatives or friends, often from an early age. Now this is not so common, and newcomers to the sport are encouraged to obtain details of the various proficiency and training schemes which are administered by the Royal Yachting Association. These cover every aspect of the sport – dinghy sailing, ski-boats and runabouts, coastal cruising under either sail or power, and the RYA/DoT Yachtmaster Certificates for those who go offshore.

The skipper is responsible for the safety of the boat and all on board. He must be prepared to make quick decisions on all matters, and must learn to anticipate what the next problem may be.

Every boat should have a number of built-in safety factors. First is her basic design and construction, which must be suitable for her intended purpose. Second, she must be maintained in proper condition. Third, she must have a competent crew, with some reserve of strength for unforeseen events. Fourth, she must be fitted with suitable gear which will withstand all conditions likely to be met. Fifth, in the event of some accident, the necessary emergency equipment must be carried for the crisis to be overcome, and the crew must know how to use it. All these matters are the direct and inescapable responsibility of the owner or skipper.

Individual crew members of a seagoing boat have a responsibility for taking with them certain personal items of equipment, some of which are discussed in more detail below. For comfort and for the safety of the individual, and ultimately of the entire crew, it is essential to be properly clothed at sea. Non-slip shoes or sea boots should be worn by everybody on board, and even in mid-summer all should be in possession of foul weather clothing with close fastenings at neck, wrists and ankles, and with a hood or sou'wester hat. At least two changes of sailing clothing should be carried, including warm sweaters and towelling strips as neck scarves. Other personal items include a sailor's knife and spike, on a lanyard; a waterproof electric torch, and a personal supply of anti-seasickness pills for those particularly afflicted.

Lifejackets and safety harnesses (which are discussed in 8.3.6 and 8.3.7) are usually supplied on board, but some individuals prefer to take their own. If this is the case the owner or skipper should be satisfied that they are to the required standard.

8.2 Safety equipment – general

8.2.1 Safety equipment – legal requirements

There are certain legal requirements in respect of the safety equipment to be carried in yachts. Owners of larger yachts – 45ft (13.7m) or more in overall length – must conform to the requirements in the *Merchant Shipping (Life Saving Appliances) Rules 1965* and the *Merchant Shipping (Fire Appliances) Rules 1965*, which are obtainable from HM Stationery Office.

All yachts must be equipped with the necessary navigation lights and means of giving sound signals as required by the International Regulations for Preventing Collisions at Sea (see Section 2.1).

Yachts which are racing are usually required to carry at least a certain minimum of safety equipment, as prescribed by the class, club or organisation involved. For example yachts competing under the International Offshore Rule (IOR) must normally comply with special safety regulations prescribed by the Offshore Racing Council (ORC), available from the Royal Ocean Racing Club Rating Office, Seahorse Building, Bath Road, Lymington, Hants, SO4 9SE. Tel: Lymington (0590) 77030.

8.2.2 Safety equipment – recommendations for sea-going yachts of 18ft (5.5m) to 45ft (13.7m) overall length

The following is a summary of general recommendations, agreed by the Department of Trade and Industry, but precise requirements vary with the type of craft, where she is used, and the season of the year. As indicated, certain items of equipment are dealt with in more detail below. The suggested type and scale of equipment applies to seagoing boats; lesser requirements may be suitable for inshore use or for inland waters.

(1) Normal equipment
For operation and safe navigation.

(2) Personal safety equipment
One lifejacket to BS 3595 or of Department of Trade accepted type for every person on board, kept in a safe but accessible place. (For further details on lifejackets see 8.3.6). One safety harness (BS 4224) for each person in a sailing yacht; one or more should be provided in motor cruisers for use when working on deck, but experience has

shown that a harness may be dangerous if a person goes overboard at speeds greater than about eight knots. In sailing yachts safety harnesses should be worn on deck in bad weather, or at night; they must be properly adjusted, and clipped to a suitable strongpoint. (For further details see 8.3.7.)

(3) Rescue equipment for man overboard

At least two lifebuoys, one within easy reach of the helmsman and with a self-igniting light for use at night. A buoyant line, 100ft (30m) in length and with a minimum breaking strain of 250lb (115kg), should be within the helmsman's reach.

(4) Flotation equipment

For boats going more than three miles offshore (summer or winter), a liferaft of Department of Trade type (or equivalent) should be carried on deck or in a locker opening to deck, *or* a rigid dinghy with permanent buoyancy fitted should be carried on deck, *or* an inflatable dinghy should be stowed inflated on deck. Of these three the liferaft is to be preferred (see 8.3.9) but it must be serviced annually: dinghies should have oars and rowlocks secured in them.

For boats going not more than three miles out in winter an inflatable liferaft (or the dinghy alternatives above) is recommended. In well sheltered waters the summer scale, below, may be adequate. Liferafts may not be necessary in angling boats operating in organised groups when the boats are continually close to each other.

For boats not going more than three miles offshore in summer months (1 April to 31 October), lesser provisions in the form of lifebuoys, buoyant seats etc would be acceptable.

(5) General Equipment

Anchors – two, each with warp or chain of appropriate size and length. Where warp is used there should be at least 3 fathoms (5.5m) of chain between the anchor and the warp.

Efficient compass, and spare.

Charts, covering the intended area of operation.

Daylight distress (smoke) signals (see 8.3.10).

Distress flares (red) – six, with two parachute rockets (see 8.3.10)

Tow rope – of adequate length, say 30 fathoms (50m).

First aid box – with anti-seasick pills (see 8.6.28).

Radio receiver – sufficient for weather/shipping forecasts (see Section 7.6).

Water-resistant torch.

Radar reflector of adequate performance – as large as can be conveniently carried, and mounted at least 13ft (4m) above sea level. (See 8.3.1).

Line suitable for general purposes, such as inboard lifeline in bad weather.

Engine tool kit (see 13.5.2).

Name or number, prominently displayed. These should be painted on the vessel or on dodgers in letters or figures at least 9in (220mm) high.

(6) Firefighting equipment

For boats over 30ft (9m) in length and those with powerful engines – two extinguishers each of not less than 3lb (1.4kg) capacity, of the dry powder type or equivalent, and one or more similar additional extinguisher of not less than 5lb (2.3kg) capacity.

For boats of up to 30ft (9m) in length, with cooking facilities and engines – two extinguishers each not less than 3lb (1.4kg) of the dry powder type or equivalent.

For boats up to 30ft (9m) in length, with cooking facilities only or with engine only – one extinguisher of the dry powder type or equivalent, of not less than 3lb (1.4kg) capacity.

Carbon dioxide (CO_2), or foam extinguishers of equivalent capacity are alternatives to dry powder. BCF (bromo-chloro-difluoro-methane) or BTM (bromo-trifluoro-methane) are acceptable but the crew must be warned that fumes from them are dangerous in a confined space, and a notice to this effect should be displayed by each extinguisher.

All craft should also carry a couple of buckets, with lanyards attached, and a small bag of sand for containing or extinguishing a burning spillage of fuel or lubricant.

Your boat should have been designed and built to keep fire risks to a minimum, but the arrangements can be checked by referring to the Home Office pamphlet *Fire Precautions in Pleasure Craft* (HMSO).

Further details on fire prevention and fire fighting in 8.3.5 below.

8.3 Safety equipment – details and usage

8.3.1 Radar reflectors

Objects made of steel or aluminium (the most likely metals encountered in yacht construction) will reflect a radar beam if they are hit at the correct angle, but timber and glassfibre return no worthwhile echo at all. So the average yacht can be considered almost invisible to radar since, due to its shape, even a metal mast is a very poor reflector.

To avoid collision a ship should be able to identify and plot an echo from a boat at a range of at least 5 miles (8km), and to achieve this sort of detection it is essential that the boat has an efficient radar reflector.

Most yachts rely on a simple octahedral reflector, consisting of three metal surfaces (usually aluminium sheet) mounted at right angles to each other. This type of reflector has six points around it, and eight internal corners each of which forms what is called a re-entrant trihedral. When a radar beam encounters one of these re-entrant trihedrals it is reflected off the sides (usually all three) and is reflected back in a direction parallel to that from which it came.

Maximum reflection is obtained when the radar beam is directed into a corner within a cone, as shown in Fig. 8 (1). In an octahedral reflector there are eight such corners, and hence eight such cones for maximum reflection. Within these eight cones reflection is good; elsewhere it is not so satisfactory.

To give the best reflection for 360° all round the boat, an octahedral reflector should be mounted in what has come to be called the 'catch rain' position (the attitude it adopts when standing on a level surface). But in this position it can be seen that one of the optimum cones is pointing straight upwards and one is pointing straight downwards. The other six point sideways, three of them angled 20° above the horizontal and three of them 20° below. So that, when the boat is upright, none of the six reflecting corners are working at maximum efficiency.

If a polar diagram is plotted to show the strength of reflection for the complete 360° around the boat, this will typically indicate six equally spaced sectors of about 35° each where reflection is good, with gaps in between where reflection is considerably reduced. A different pattern will emerge when the boat is heeled.

To give adequate responses an octahedral reflector needs to be quite large, with a minimum diagonal length of 18in (460mm), so that each reflecting corner has sides of 9in (230mm). It must be stoutly made so that the plates remain flat and perpendicular to each other. The reflector must be hoisted in the 'catch rain' attitude already described, and at a height of at least 13ft (4m) above the waterline.

Some octahedral reflectors have circular (rather than pointed) corners, formed by the intersection of three circular plates at right angles to each other, instead of three square plates. These have some advantage because the reflecting ability is increased relative to overall size.

Other, more sophisticated types of reflectors are available to overcome some of the shortcomings of the standard octahedral. These more elaborate reflectors are however heavier and more expensive. One is the Firdell Blipper 300, consisting of an array of reflecting corners stacked vertically and enclosed in a cylindrical plastic case for protection and to reduce windage.

The most uniform reflection throughout 360° of azimuth (right round the horizon) is provided by the Lensref reflectors, which work on the principle of the Luneberg dielectric lens. This consists of a spherical lens, so constructed that the density of the material is graded as a function of the radius, being greatest in the centre. This has the effect of focusing an incoming radar beam onto a reflecting band, which is fitted round the 'equator' of the sphere and returns the beam along a path parallel to that on which it arrived. The width of the reflecting band dictates the

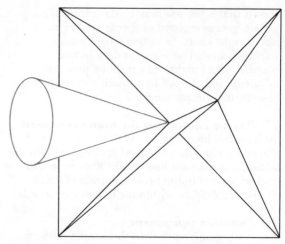

Fig. 8(1) In each of the eight re-entrant trihedrals (reflecting corners) of a standard octahedral reflector, the best reflections are given when the incoming beam is contained within an imaginary cone, as depicted in this diagram.

angle of heel which the device can accommodate, but the width cannot be too much or it blanks off an undue proportion of the incoming beam. Performance is very good up to 15° of heel, but then falls off sharply.

8.3.2 Bilge pumps

Modern glassfibre boats should not normally take water into the bilge, but for any boat it is essential that adequate pumping arrangements are provided, and periodically tested, in case they are ever needed for emergency use.

Any seagoing boat should be fitted with at least two suitable pumps, which can be operated off the engine, electrically driven or worked manually. If an engine driven or electrical pump is fitted it must be supplemented with a powerful manual pump in case no power is available. An electrical pump does however have the advantage that it can be float controlled, and therefore cope with any accumulation of water when the boat is lying idle.

A manual bilge pump must be sited where it is easy to use, remembering that considerable and prolonged effort may be called for in an emergency, and also so that it can be conveniently dismantled for cleaning and inspection. The diaphragms, seals and valves of manual pumps should be examined at least once a season, and it is sensible to carry spares for these parts.

Any bilge pump should be fitted with a good strainer in the bilge, and this must be easily accessible for cleaning.

Any opening below the waterline is a threat to the watertight integrity of the boat, and must be fitted with a seacock which can be shut in the event of any failure of pipes or fittings. It is important that these are kept free, and are easy to get at. A few soft wood plugs of different sizes are useful for stopping leaks.

Limber holes in the bilges must be kept clear so that water can drain to the pump suction. Any dirt which is allowed to accumulate in the bilges will soon cause a blockage, and for this reason alone it is important that bilges be kept clear of all forms of dirt and debris.

8.3.3 Underwater damage

Although thankfully it is not common, it is not unknown for a yacht to suffer underwater damage – perhaps due to collision with submerged wreckage, or even a whale. Large baulks of timber are particularly dangerous. If such impact damage results in cracks or splits in the hull, it should be possible to stem most of the inflow of water by driving in small, soft wood wedges wrapped with pieces of rag – always provided that the damaged area is accessible.

If the hull is actually punctured, rather than just cracked or split, a very large quantity of water will start to pour into the boat, far above the capacity of any pumps installed. For example, a hole 6in (150mm) square at 2ft (0.6m) below the waterline will admit about 500 gallons (2275 litres) of water a minute, which is sufficient to sink a small yacht within a couple of minutes. At this point it should be noted that certain smaller yachts (such as the Etap range, built in Belgium, and the Sadler 26 in this country) have two skins with foam buoyancy in between them, to make the boat unsinkable – a commendable safety feature. The survival of an ordinary yacht, however, will depend on the very rapid location of the damage, and immediate steps to reduce the rate of flooding to something that can be controlled by the pumps.

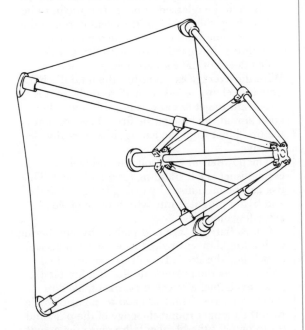

Fig. 8(2) The Subrella leak-stopping device can be pushed through a hole in the hull and then opened on the outside, to make a seal.

Collision mats were invented more than a century ago, and have proved their efficiency on many occasions. Traditionally made of heavy canvas with ropes at each corner, a collision mat can be drawn over the outside of the hull so that it covers the damaged area, whereupon the pressure of the seawater presses it tightly against the hull, to stem at least most of the leak. It is obvious, however, that this would need to be done very quickly indeed to cope with a hole of any significant size.

More practical for speedy deployment is a device called the Subrella, made in three sizes by Damage Control Gear (UK) Ltd, 1 Longfellow Road, Banbury, Oxon, OX16 9LB. This consists of something looking rather like an umbrella, which is pushed through the hole and then opens on the outside (see Fig. 8(2)). Water pressure spreads the patch over the hole and forms an effective seal. Should it prove impossible to get at the hole from inboard, due to parts of the boat's structure, the Subrella can also be used from outboard. To be effective, it is important that the Subrella be stowed where it is instantly available – not at the bottom of a cockpit locker.

8.3.4 Guardrails

A seagoing boat should have double guardrails, the top one not less than 2ft (0.6m) above the deck, well supported by stanchions at intervals of not more than about 7ft (2.15m). The heel fittings of the stanchions must be through bolted, so that they are securely fitted. The guardrails should be kept taut by bottlescrews or lanyards.

A solid pulpit forward gives much needed security for sail changing or anchor work. It too needs to be firmly bolted through the deck. In cruising boats it is usually feasible to fit some similar arrangement aft, around the stern of the boat. This can be utilised for fitting lifebuoys, and weather cloths with the boat's name clearly painted port and starboard.

8.3.5 Fire prevention and fire fighting

Any boat contains a lot of flammable equipment – even discounting such potential hazards as fuel and bottled gas. Hence fire prevention is the first priority. Provided that those who smoke are well disciplined, and that fuel and gas systems are properly installed and maintained, and sensibly used, the risks are not too great.

Gas systems

Bottled gas (normally butane) is the most common galley fuel in British boats. Propane is similar, but can be used in lower temperatures than butane. Both are heavier than air, so if they escape they sink to the bottom of a space or into the bilge, where they can collect until an explosive mixture (about 2% by volume) is built up. It is a sensible precaution to fit a gas detector which will give warning of any leak before a dangerous concentration is reached. The sensor should be fitted down in the lowest part of the bilge, but above the normal level which any bilge water might reach. Gas detectors should be wired up so that they can be switched on before any other electrical equipment in the boat is used.

The gas cylinder must be fitted outside the accommodation – in a cockpit locker for example with a drain venting overboard above the waterline. Gas piping must be stainless steel or seamless copper, mounted high in the boat and well clipped. Flexible connections should only be used at the cylinder end or at a gimballed stove, and must conform to BS 3212 *Flexible Tubing or Hose for Use in Butane/Propane Gas Installations.*

Gas appliances (water or cabin heaters as well as galley stoves) must be designed for butane/propane gas and conform to the relevant British Standards. Appliances with pilot lights, such as water heaters, should incorporate a flame failure device to shut off the gas supply if the pilot light is extinguished. Adequate ventilation must be provided to prevent a build up of carbon monoxide or carbon dioxide. When a stove or similar appliance is not in use, and always before leaving the boat, the gas should be turned off at the bottle.

If gas is smelt prevent all naked lights and smoking, do not run any electrical equipment or the engines, and ventilate the boat thoroughly. It will be necessary to bail the gas from the bilges, or pump it out with a manual diaphragm type bilge pump. Give the entire gas system a careful check for leaks by testing all pipe unions with soapy water, and do not use it until the defect has been rectified.

Fuel systems

A boat's fuel system is the other major fire risk, particularly if the fuel is petrol. Even the smallest leak must be eliminated, and care must be taken with spills when refuelling. The fuel filler must be on deck so that any overflow does not go into the bilges, and so that fumes displaced from the tank are vented into the fresh air. The air vent from the tank should go to a protected place on deck and be covered with a gauze.

There must be a shut off valve (easily accessible) on the fuel line where it leaves the top of the tank, and the entire fuel system should be professionally fitted using materials of approved standards.

Particular care must be taken when refuelling or when working on any part of the fuel system – cleaning filters for example. At such times it is essential to stop smoking and have no naked lights in the vicinity. On completion of the work make quite certain that all joints are tight. In the event of a spill mop up as much fuel as possible and thoroughly ventilate the area.

Before starting an engine, always first run the engine compartment exhaust fan (where fitted) for five minutes, and inspect the engine space for any smell of fuel.

Firefighting

Fire extinguishers work by cooling the fire down, by smothering it, or by reacting with it chemically – or sometimes by a combination of these methods.

Water is an excellent medium for cooling down a fire, and in a boat there is always a plentiful supply, even if just using a couple of buckets with lanyards. Water is less damaging than chemicals to the interior of a boat, and it does not produce harmful fumes. Water can also be useful to prevent re-ignition of a fire which has been temporarily extinguished by other means. But water must not be applied to burning liquids such as fuel or cooking fat since a violent reaction will occur, spreading the fire in every direction. Also, since water is heavier than fuels or cooking fat, the latter will float on the water and continue burning. Neither must water be used on electrical fires where high voltage is present, due to the danger involved.

For general purposes dry powder is best for use below deck since it does not give off any dangerous fumes, does not conduct electricity, is non-corrosive and is suitable for most types of fire. It does make rather a mess, however, although not as much as foam. The powder works chemically to stop combustion, and it also absorbs some heat as it melts, thereby giving at least some cooling effect. When released, the powder emerges as a fine jet which should travel at least 6ft (2m), and when this hits the flames it causes dense white smoke, which can be alarming in the confines of a boat.

Dry powder extinguishers are operated by pressure from a CO_2 bottle, and the best type has a controlled discharge so that all the contents do not have to be released at once. It is useful to be able to keep some back in the event of re-ignition – always something to be watched for when firefighting, but particularly with dry powder, which does not have good cooling properties. With the average extinguisher the total discharge time is likely to be less than 10 seconds, so it is important to get as close as possible and take good aim at the base of the fire, to ensure that the first burst from the extinguisher is really effective.

The powder may consolidate inside if the extinguisher is left standing for a long time. This risk can be minimised by giving it a good shake and by tapping it firmly with a piece of wood every few months.

Galley flare ups are best tackled by smothering with a fire blanket, stowed near (but not above or behind) the stove. Do not use water, which only scatters the burning liquid. If a fire blanket is not available, a towel or blanket soaked in water will serve. Make as good a seal as possible with the blanket round the edge of the pan, and try to prevent the blanket falling into the actual liquid. Leave the blanket in place until the pan and its contents are thoroughly cooled.

Foam extinguishers are best for burning liquids. They form a blanket over the surface, which cuts off the supply of oxygen needed to support combustion and also cools the surface, but generally their use in boats is rather limited.

Vaporising liquids such as halon 1211, or BCF (bromo-chloro-difluoro-methane) and halon 1301, or BTM (bromo-trifluoro-methane) are alternative and good extinguishants, but users must understand that fumes given off by them can be dangerous in the confined spaces of a boat.

Carbon dioxide is good for extinguishing fires of liquids or of electrical equipment, although it acts by blanketing the fire and has no cooling effect. But it needs to be stored under high pressure, and the weight of the cylinders makes it unsuitable for small boats. In larger craft it is often used (like BCF) for fixed installations in machinery spaces. In the event of a fire in the engine compartment of a small yacht, stop the engine(s) plus any ventilation fan(s) fitted, turn off the fuel at the tank, blank off (if feasible) the air inlets to the engine space, and then operate any extinguisher fitted in that compartment. A petrol-engined boat should have an automatic BCF extinguisher in the engine space: heat from the fire activates the sensing head to operate the extinguisher, which floods the compartment with gas. In the event of fire, this eliminates any need to open up the engine space, which can only make matters worse. It is important that the extinguisher should have sufficient capacity in relation to the volume of the space. Manufacturers seem to be divided on this point, but 3lb (1.4kg) of BCF are suggested for every 100 cubic feet (2.8 cubic metres) of engine compartment (no deduction being made for space occupied by engines etc).

Speed is essential in firefighting, so it is important that there should be an extinguisher ready to hand in each compartment of a boat, and that the crew should all know how to use them. A minimum scale is suggested in para (6) of 8.2.2, but one or two extra extinguishers are strongly recommended.

If a serious fire develops, head the boat in a direction so that the wind will not spread the flames further along the boat.

Fire extinguishers do not remain efficient, or even operable, if left indefinitely in a marine environment. Some (more expensive ones) are fitted with pressure gauges, which should be checked regularly. BCF or BTM extinguishers can be checked by weight, but this is no good for dry powder extinguishers where a leak only causes loss of the propellant, which has negligible weight compared to the powder. It is therefore recommended that extinguishers of this type should be discharged and replenished about every five years.

8.3.6 Lifejackets

Any seagoing boat should carry a lifejacket which conforms to BS 3595 for every person on board – see Fig. 8(3). This specification requires that a lifejacket has a minimum buoyancy of 35lb (16.4kg) for adults, and 20lb (9.4kg) for children. It must also support the head of an unconscious person so that the mouth is clear of the water, and turn an unconscious or exhausted person from being face down onto his back in five seconds. Another requirement is a lifting becket for raising the wearer from the water.

There are five different types of lifejackets available, as follows:

(1) *Inherent buoyancy only.* These are bulky lifejackets of the 'Mae West' variety – simple, cheap and durable, but very awkward to wear and normally only found in commercial ships.

(2) *Part inherent buoyancy, and part oral inflation.* A typical lifejacket of this type might have about 15lb (6.8kg) of built-in buoyancy, which can be increased to a total of 35lb (16kg) by oral inflation. This is a good compromise – reasonably comfortable to wear, and the inherent buoyancy is enough to bring the wearer to the surface if he goes over the side. But oral inflation is needed to give the full support required by BS 3595.

(3) *Full oral inflation.* This type has no inherent buoyancy, and has to be inflated by mouth to produce any support. Some can be worn partially inflated in reasonable comfort. These are the most compact and also the cheapest lifejackets conforming to BS 3595, and are available in vest or halter types.

(4) *Manual gas inflation.* Similar to (3), but with the added facility of inflation from a small CO_2 cylinder, manually operated. Oral inflation available as a stand-by. Gas inflation must not be used if the lifejacket has already been inflated orally.

(5) *Automatic gas inflation.* Similar to (4), except that the lifejacket inflates automatically on entering the water. Alternatively gas inflation can be operated manually, or the lifejacket can be inflated orally. But note that the lifejacket must not be inflated orally before entering the water. This is the most expensive type, but it has the significant advantage that the lifejacket will inflate itself even if the wearer is unconscious on entering the water.

When buying a lifejacket inflate it and try it on. It should provide firm support to the neck, and should not allow the head to fall forward. Special sizes are available for children.

Most lifejackets are a bright orange colour, which makes them more visible in the water. It is a good idea to fit them with strips of reflective tape around the collar. They should also be fitted with a whistle attached to a lanyard, and preferably have some form of automatic light which is switched on when immersed in water.

Lifejackets should be stowed in a dry place, which is known to the crew, where they are easily accessible if required. They should be checked periodically. The straps should be properly

Fig. 8(3) Putting on a lifejacket – first read the instructions. Hold the jacket up in front of you, put your head through the hole, and secure the waistband at the side or front as appropriate.

adjusted to suit individual wearers, and this is particularly important in the case of young persons.

For inland waters, where help is readily at hand for a person who goes overboard, a lesser standard of flotation provided by a garment called a Personal Buoyancy Aid (PBA) is acceptable. A PBA is more comfortable to wear than the average lifejacket, but it does not provide so much flotation and is intended to provide buoyancy for a conscious person to help them reach safety.

Good lifejackets are not particularly cheap but they are essential items of equipment for any sea-going boat, and they should be worn when conditions are bad, or by non-swimmers whenever they are on deck or in the cockpit of a boat at sea. Another occasion when lifejackets may well save lives is when proceeding to or from shore in a small tender in a tideway – particularly at night or in adverse weather.

8.3.7 **Safety harnesses**
In bad weather or at night it is doubly important to prevent any crew member falling over the side; so the skipper must ensure that those on deck are wearing safety harnesses, and that these are clipped to suitable strong points – not to the guardrails or parts of the standing or running rigging.

Safety harnesses should conform to BS 4224/82 (BS 4474 for children) or some other recognized standard which requires minimum sizes and strengths for all the component parts – the webbing straps, the securing line, and the snap

hook at the end. Apart from being strong enough the metal fittings must be non-magnetic. A harness must be properly adjusted for the wearer, so that the point of attachment for the safety line is high on the chest.

It is useful if the harness has two clips, one on short stay and one on a longer line for working on deck. In poor conditions a crew member should be hooked to a fixed part of the boat's structure before emerging from the cabin into the cockpit. Jackstays rigged along the deck can allow people to move forward and aft without the need to continually alter their attachment to the boat.

The Tupper Latchway system provides the means for a crew member to walk round the yacht, connected by his personal lifeline, with the minimum of restriction. A stainless steel wire is secured round the deck by special fittings. The Latchway 'Transfastener', to which the personal safety line is attached, runs along the wire and traverses the fittings without being detached, see Fig. 8(4). It can therefore give an uninterrupted run, from one end of the boat to the other. All the components meet the requirements of BS 4224/82, and the fittings have a tensile strength in excess of 4840lb (2200kg).

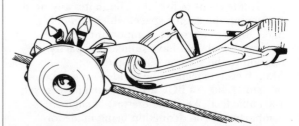

Fig. 8(4) The Latchway safety system permits movement the length of the boat by a crew member attached to a personal safety line.

Some sailing jackets incorporate a built-in harness (sometimes an inflatable lifejacket too). These garments help overcome the problem of ensuring that people on deck are wearing harnesses when the weather deteriorates.

Harnesses need to be checked regularly to ensure that there is no wear or damage to the webbing or the safety line. In particular the adjusting buckles and the snap hook need to be kept free and in good condition, and the hinges lightly oiled.

There is not the same requirement for safety harnesses in motor boats, but one or two should be carried in case it is necessary to work on deck in bad weather. It should be remembered however that anybody wearing a safety harness and going over the side at more than about 8 knots is liable to injury.

An experienced crew knows when it is sensible to be hooked on, but often it falls to the skipper or whoever is in charge on deck to insist that everybody conforms.

8.3.8 Man overboard – gear and drill

If, despite all normal precautions, somebody should go over the side, it is important not only to have the necessary gear at hand to help locate and recover him, but to have some prior understanding of the procedure to be followed depending on the circumstances.

The first necessity is to give the alarm, so that all hands are alerted to the emergency. 'Man overboard, port (or starboard) side' should bring everybody on deck immediately. One of the crew on deck, preferably whoever saw him go over the side, should be detailed to keep a continuous watch on the person in the water for as long as possible. Another should release the lifebuoy(s) which should be carried near the stern – preferably fitted with dan buoy and flag, self-igniting light, whistle, dye-marker, and drogue to reduce drift Fig. 8(5). The sooner this can be done the nearer it will be to the person in the water.

In a sailing yacht, particularly when running down wind or almost down wind, it may be helpful to start the auxiliary engine if fitted, but before the clutch is engaged care must be taken that no sheets or lines which might foul the propeller are trailing over the side. Great care must be taken with the use of the engine when manoeuvring close to anybody in the water, to avoid injury by the propeller.

Meanwhile, until the boat is fully under control in respect of handling sails etc, so as to be able to return to the place of the disaster, the helmsman should steer a very steady course which he must memorise.

With a well crewed yacht, under sail, the recognised manoeuvre when beating to windward or reaching is to bear away, gybe, and then luff back onto a course which will take the boat back to the required spot. The yacht then approaches the person in the water nearly on a close-hauled course, in order that speed may be more easily adjusted to round up alongside him. If stopped just to windward of the person, the yacht will drift down towards him and form a lee for the recovery operation, but there is a danger that the boat may either be thrown onto him by a sea, or sail over the top of him. These risks are avoided if the boat is brought to rest immediately to leeward of the man in the water, but in this case it is essential to establish contact with him (see below) before the boat drifts away to leeward. Practice is needed in different wind strengths and on different points of sailing to get this manoeuvre right, and it is vital that the sails are trimmed and handled according to the orders of the skipper or helmsman.

If a yacht is running under spinnaker, even with a competent crew, it may be five minutes before the boat is ready to come on the wind and beat back to the place where the man went overboard – perhaps half-a-mile away. Here some accurate plotting is needed to make sure that the tacks which are made will bring the boat as near as possible to the scene.

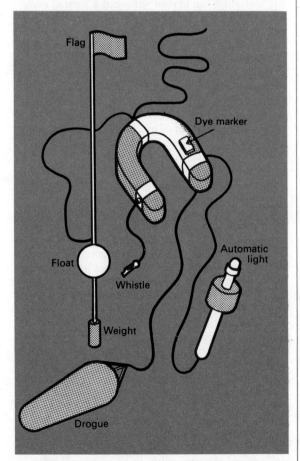

Fig. 8(5) Lifebuoy with dan buoy and flag, automatic light, whistle, dye marker, and drogue.

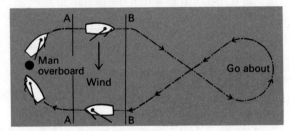

Fig. 8(6) Man overboard drill for a family cruiser, going to windward. The first step is to get the boat on a reach, while getting everything ready to tack and return on a reciprocal course.

In a boat such as a family cruiser which is probably not strongly crewed, it may be safer to get the boat onto a reach initially, while things are sorted out, and then go about and return on the opposite tack, sailing a reciprocal course. The distances from the place of the incident to the position of tacking, and from there back to the person – represented by AB in Fig. 8(6) are equal, which may be useful to remember particularly at night. Counting may help. This is mentioned because it is sometimes not feasible to return immediately – if, for example, a spinnaker

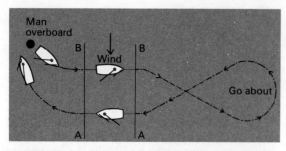

Fig. 8(7) As for Fig. 8(6), but with the boat on a broad reach. In both cases the times to sail from A to B, and from B to A, are equal – useful at night or in poor visibility.

is set, or a foreguy is rigged on the main boom, or if a mizzen staysail is set in a two-masted boat. Success is more likely to be achieved by keeping control of the boat in such situations, than by precipitate action which may leave her helpless.

When running or broad reaching, especially in a lot of wind, it is probably best to luff gradually until the wind is about on the beam (lowering the spinnaker beforehand, if it is set), and then come about so as to return on a roughly close hauled course (if originally running) or on more of a reach (if originally on a broad reach), as in Fig. 8(7).

In a motor boat it is normally not too difficult to turn the boat round and return to somebody who has gone over the side. If the helmsman sees the incident, or if sufficiently early warning is given by somebody else, the helmsman should apply helm so as to swing the stern away from the person, and thereby reduce the risk of injury from the propeller(s).

As in a sailing boat, a lifebuoy should be released as quickly as possible and somebody should be detailed to watch the person in the water continuously.

Depending on the type and speed of boat the quickest way of getting back to the scene is using the Williamson turn. After the initial helm has been applied to swing the stern away from the person in the water, continue altering in that direction until about 60 degrees off the original course. Then apply full opposite rudder until the boat is steadied on a reciprocal course to that originally being steered. The person should then

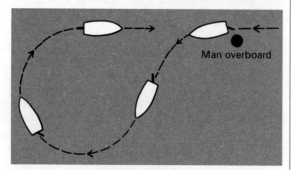

Fig. 8(8) In a motor boat the Williamson turn, pictured here, is a good method of returning with reasonable certainty to a person in the water.

be right ahead, and it is important not to run him down. With practice in one's own boat this manoeuvre can be made quite precisely. See Fig. 8(8).

Having returned to the immediate vicinity of the person in the water, the next step is to establish contact with him quickly, before the boat starts to drift away. Have two or three lines ready to throw to him, and a lifebuoy if he has not already got one and is not wearing a lifejacket. To reach a person who is more than a few feet from the boat there is a device called the Balcan Emergency Life Line (BELL), which consists of a capsule into which is packed a 130ft (40m) line, which can be thrown quickly and accurately.

Once the person has been got alongside the boat, the next stage of the rescue is to get him inboard. In a boat with any substantial amount of freeboard this can be quite a problem. The first requirement is to get him secured by the becket of his lifejacket or safety harness, or with a bowline round his chest – so that he can't drift away. Some boats have a bathing ladder aft, usually with a hinged lower section which projects down into the water; this is very useful, but remember it is close to the propeller(s). Alternatively a boarding ladder amidships can be used, but since this is unlikely to reach even to the waterline the person will need a loop of rope about 2ft (0.6m) below water, into which he can put one or both of his feet so as to get onto the bottom rung of the ladder. A rope ladder, or any other type of ladder, can be pressed into service.

By this time however he is likely to be cold and exhausted, and will probably need assistance. A strong crew may be able to haul him aboard with the aid of the line already mentioned but otherwise some form of mechanical assistance will be needed. Possibilities include unshackling the lower block of the mainsheet and securing this to his harness/lifejacket, and then winching him in with the topping lift set up: using a small handy billy tackle (preferably fitted with snap hooks each end) attached to him and the main boom for the same purpose: or utilising the falls of davits in the same way. Another suggested method is to lower the jib partly over the side so that the person can be manoeuvred into the bight of the sail and then bowsed inboard by the sheet winch, together with an auxiliary halyard transferred to the clew of the sail.

If none of these methods is practicable an inflatable dinghy or even a liferaft secured alongside the boat will serve to get the person out of the water for the first part of the rescue. In this event it may help to remove the guardrails round that part of the boat in order to transfer him inboard.

It can be seen that such an emergency needs consideration and planning in advance. In order to avoid delay it is essential that all the crew understand the procedure to be used, and know where the requisite gear is stowed.

8.3.9 Liferafts

If because of some disaster it is necessary for the crew to abandon ship (and there are good reasons not to do so prematurely), a liferaft which will accommodate all on board should ensure their safety for a considerable period. Because of the shelter it provides and the survival equipment which it should contain, a liferaft is much better than either a rigid or inflatable dinghy, and is therefore recommended even for coastal waters. It is essential that the raft should be capable of carrying the entire crew. Large yachts may need more than one raft.

Liferafts are stowed in either a valise or a canister, which should be secured by quick release lashings in a place where it can be easily got over the side. The inboard end of the painter must be firmly secured to the boat. Once the valise or canister is in the water (preferably on the leeward side of the boat) the painter is given a really strong jerk or series of jerks, whereupon the liferaft will automatically break out of its container and inflate itself. Don't worry about the subsequent wailing sound, which is only surplus gas escaping so that the raft is not over inflated. It is possible that the raft may inflate upside down, but this is easy to rectify although it may mean somebody entering the water. It is better if the crew can enter the liferaft directly from the yacht, and therefore keep dry, rather than via the water. In any case it is extremely difficult to climb into a liferaft when wearing an inflated lifejacket.

When first inflated a liferaft is unstable because it is unloaded, the water ballast pockets have not had time to fill, and the drogue has not been streamed. In bad weather the liferaft should be boarded as soon as possible after inflation, and the weight of the crew should be evenly distributed.

Even a loaded liferaft can become unstable in bad weather. Factors which influence instability include the shape of the canopy in very strong winds, the design and strength of water ballast pockets, the position of the access hatch in the canopy, and (particularly) the design of the drogue. These and other factors have been the subject of detailed investigation following the unsatisfactory performance of liferafts in the 1979 Fastnet Race.

Liferafts are available with a choice of survival equipment, and the scale carried depends upon what sort of cruising is intended. Obviously more items are desirable for an ocean voyage than for a passage across the North Sea or the English Channel. As a very minimum it is necessary to carry water, flares, a pair of bellows for topping up the raft, repair equipment and a first aid kit, see Fig. 8(9).

Some yachts sensibly carry a 'panic bag' containing such items as food, clothing, extra flares, fishing gear and a signalling mirror, which can be taken into the raft on abandoning ship.

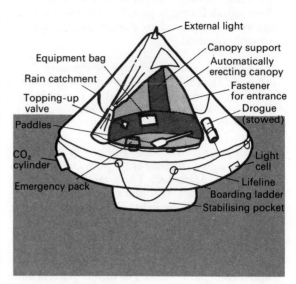

Fig. 8(9) Inflated liferaft.

Information about abandoning ship and the use of a liferaft is given in 8.4.8.

Liferafts and the survival equipment which they contain require annual servicing to ensure that they will function correctly in an emergency.

Since cases have occurred of liferafts being found at sea, sometimes being lost from the parent craft in error, it is recommended that the raft should have the yacht's name painted clearly on it in order to assist identification (which otherwise can only be done through the serial number, which takes some time).

It should be noted that for occasional offshore cruises it is possible to hire a liferaft for quite a modest sum.

8.3.10 Distress signals

If (and only if) a situation develops where a boat is in serious and immediate danger, and help is urgently required, a distress signal should be made, as described below.

For a lesser emergency an urgency signal (as described in 6.6.16 and in sub para (e) below) may be appropriate. If help is needed but the boat is not in immediate danger, the proper signal is 'V' ('Victor') in the International Code, which means 'I require assistance'. This can be sent as a flag signal (a white flag with a red St Andrew's cross), or by light or sound in Morse code ($\cdots-$). Certain other signals of an 'emergency' nature are contained in the International Code, and a selection is given among the two-letter groups shown in 6.2.8.

A full list of the recognised distress signals is given in Annex IV to the *International Regulations for Preventing Collisions at Sea*, stated in full in Section 2.1. The following are those which are most likely to be appropriate for yachts and small craft, together with some notes on their use. (The letters of the sub-paragraphs refer to Annex IV, mentioned above). Note that the use of any of these signals is strictly prohibited unless a vessel is in serious and immediate danger, and help is urgently required.

(b) *Continuous sounding with any fog signalling apparatus.* In order to avoid any doubt as to the intention, the continuous sounding should be in the form of a succession of letters SOS ($\cdots$ $---$ $\cdots$) in Morse.

(d) *A signal made by radiotelegraphy or by any other signalling method consisting of the group* $\cdots$ $---$ $\cdots$ *(SOS) in the Morse Code.* For a yacht the most likely methods are by sound signal as in (b) above, or by flashing light. The latter is of course particularly effective at night.

(e) *A signal sent by radiotelephony consisting of the spoken word MAYDAY.* The procedure is fully described in para 6.6.16. For ease of reference the basic rules are repeated briefly below. The distress frequencies are 2182kHz (MF) and Ch 16 (VHF). Speak clearly and distinctly, as follows:–
    MAYDAY MAYDAY MAYDAY
    THIS IS (name of boat, repeated three times)
    MAYDAY
    (Then restate the boat's name, followed by her position, the nature of the emergency, what assistance is required, and any other helpful information such as the number of persons on board.)
    OVER.
Listen for a reply, and if none is heard repeat the procedure. If transmitting on 2182kHz (MF) the distress call should be repeated during the three-minute silence period at each hour and half-hour.

An Urgency Signal indicates a lesser emergency than a Distress Signal, and should be used when there is a very urgent message to transmit concerning the safety of a ship, aircraft of other vehicle, or the safety of a person. The message, which in other respects is similar in format to a distress message, is prefaced by the words 'PAN PAN' spoken three times (instead of 'MAYDAY'). The signal, which has priority over all traffic except distress, should be made on 2182kHz or Ch 16. In the case of a long message, such as when requesting medical advice, it is appropriate to transfer to a working frequency once communication has been established.

Portable, emergency radiotelephones, operating either on 2182kHz or on Ch 16, are available. These are useful because as well as being operable from the yacht they can be taken into the liferaft.

Also available are Personal Locator Beacons (PLBs) and Emergency Position Indicating Radio Beacons (EPIRBs) which operate on 121.5 and 243MHz. These are primarily for aeronautical purposes, and the maritime search

and rescue authorities such as the Coastguard do not keep watch on these frequencies. Reception depends on an aircraft flying nearby and monitoring these channels, and this cannot be relied on. Consequently these devices are of limited use to yachtsmen, and for British coastal waters VHF or MF radios are a better proposition. Moreover the wrong or accidental use of PLBs or EPIRBs can raise problems, particularly in the event of any aircraft being in difficulties in the area. So, if carried, it is important that they are stowed carefully, out of the reach of unsupervised children, and only operated when a distress signal is fully justified. Like any other radio transmitting equipment, PLBs and EPIRBs must have a licence, obtained from the Radio Regulatory Department, Home Office, Waterloo Bridge House, Waterloo Road, London, SE1 8UA.

(f) *The International Code signal of distress 'NC'.* This can be made by flag hoist, N being a blue and white chequered flag and C one horizontally striped blue, white, red, white, blue.

(g) *A signal consisting of a square flag having above or below it a ball or anything resembling a ball.* This should not be too difficult to contrive from any square flag or piece of material, and from a round fender or anchor ball.

(i) *A rocket parachute flare or a hand flare showing a red light.* Undoubtedly a red flare is the most effective visual distress signal at night. Flares are needed for two purposes – first to raise the alarm and then to pinpoint the boat's position so as to guide rescuers to her. Within about three miles from land a hand flare, which gives a brilliant red light for one minute, will do both tasks. At greater distances a red parachute rocket which projects a suspended flare to more than 1000ft (300m) and burns for more than 40 seconds is needed to raise the alarm, but hand flares are useful to indicate the boat's position.

(j) *A smoke signal giving off orange-coloured smoke.* By day orange smoke signals (hand held for short distances, or the larger buoyant type for greater range) are more effective than flares, although the smoke disperses quickly in a strong wind.

The following table indicates suggested minimum outfits of flares for different sorts of usage of a boat. More should be carried by ocean cruising yachts.

White flares are not distress signals, but are used to indicate the presence of a boat – to another vessel sighted on a collision course for example. An outfit of four is suggested for boats which make night passages. Shield your eyes when using them, to prevent loss of night vision.

Flares must be stowed where they are easily accessible, but protected from damp. In good storage conditions they should have a life of three years: replace them by the expiry date. Examine them regularly for any signs of deterioration. All the crew should know where the flares are stowed, and how to use them. Hold hand flares firmly downwind. Rockets turn into the wind: fire them vertically in normal conditions, or aimed about 15° downwind in strong winds. Do not aim them into the wind, or they will not gain altitude. If there is low cloud, fire rockets at 45° downwind so that the flare burns under the cloud.

	Inshore (within three miles of coast)	Coastal (within seven miles of coast)	Off-shore (more than seven miles from coast)
Red hand flares	2	2	4
Red parachute rockets	—	2	4
Hand held orange smoke	2	2	—
Buoyant orange smoke	—	—	2

(k) *Slowly and repeatedly raising and lowering arms outstretched to each side.* The arms should be raised and lowered together, above and below the horizontal.

It must be emphasised that the use of any of the above signals except for genuine distress purposes is strictly forbidden. Even then they should only be made with the authority of the skipper, and only if in serious and imminent danger and needing immediate assistance, or on behalf of another vessel in such danger which for some reason is unable to make a distress signal.

If subsequently the danger is overcome, the distress call must be cancelled by whatever means are available.

8.4 Search and rescue (SAR) organisation – United Kingdom

Around the coasts of Britain we are lucky to have excellent rescue services, manned by skilled and dedicated personnel, and any seagoer should have some understanding of how these various resources are organised and co-ordinated.

When a vessel (or aircraft) is in distress off our coasts, help may be given not only by other vessels but by the authorities shown in 8.4.1 to 8.4.6.

8.4.1 Coast Radio Stations

These are operated by British Telecom, and part of their duties is listening to the international radio distress frequencies. Eleven stations keep continuous watch on 500kHz (the radiotelegraphy distress frequency) and on 2182kHz (the Medium Frequency radiotelephone distress frequency). A total of 28 keep watch on Ch 16, which is the VHF distress frequency. If a distress signal is heard it is broadcast on all distress frequencies to ships at sea, and authorities ashore such as HM Coastguard are also notified. Radio distress calls and distress traffic have priority over all other transmissions.

Full details of Coast Radio Stations are published each year in Chapter 6 of *The Macmillan & Silk Cut Nautical Almanac.*

8.4.2 HM Coastguard

HM Coastguard is responsible for initiating and co-ordinating all civil maritime search and rescue around the United Kingdom and over a large part of the eastern Atlantic (between latitudes 45° and 61°N and out to longitude 30°W). The area is divided into six Maritime Search and Rescue Regions (SRRs), supervised by Maritime Rescue Co-ordination Centres (MRCCs) at Aberdeen, Great Yarmouth, Dover, Falmouth, Swansea and the Clyde. It also includes 'Shannon' area which is the responsibility of the Republic of Ireland. Each region is divided into Districts, each with a Maritime Rescue Sub-Centre (MRSC).

The relevant telephone numbers of the MRCCs and MRSCs are published each year in Chapter 10 of *The Macmillan & Silk Cut Nautical Almanac.*

Within each district there is an organisation of Auxiliary Coastguard watch and rescue stations, grouped within Sectors under the management of Regular Coastguard Officers.

All MRCCs and MRSCs keep constant watch on VHF Ch 16, monitor 2182kHz, and are connected to telephone and telex. A visual lookout is maintained when necessary. Some stations have a radar watch facility and the Channel Navigation Information Service (CNIS) keeps a constant radar watch on the Dover Strait, with broadcasts on Ch 10 at 10 and 40 minutes past each hour. Also there are about 100 Auxiliary Watch Stations, where watch is set in bad weather. There are some 550 Regular Coastguard Officers, backed up by more than 8000 Auxiliaries on call for emergencies. HM Coastguard also have a cliff and beach rescue role.

Some HM Coastguard stations operate VHF direction-finding equipment, which is for emergency use only and is intended for locating a vessel which is in distress or in difficulty. Details are given in Chapter 4 of *The Macmillan & Silk Cut Nautical Almanac* each year. A yacht should transmit on Ch 16 (distress only) or on Ch 67 for the station to determine the bearing. The yacht's bearing from the station is transmitted on Ch 16 (distress only) or on Ch 67.

Yacht and Boat Safety Scheme

HM Coastguard Yacht and Boat Safety Scheme aims at providing useful information for the Coastguard to be able to mount a successful Search and Rescue operation, and at promoting closer links with small boat users. Owners can obtain a post-paid card (Form CG66) from the local Coastguard station, harbour master or marina, on which to fill in details of their boat and her equipment. The information includes club or association, type of boat or rig, colours of hull and sails, sail number, speed and endurance under power, any special identification features, liferaft and serial number, dinghy type and colour, details of safety equipment, radio type and call sign, name of boat and how or where displayed, usual base or mooring, where normally operated, shore contact's name and address and telephone number, owner's name and address and telephone number. It is useful if a recent photograph of the boat can be provided.

This card is then posted to the local Coastguard Rescue Centre, where it is retained so that information on the boat is on file if she becomes overdue or in distress. There is a tear-off section which can be given to a shore contact, such as a reliable friend or relative, so that they will know the Coastguard station to contact if they are concerned for the boat's safety.

It is obviously not easy for the Coastguard to maintain continuous watch for small boats on coastal passages, but they will record any information received by phone before departure, or from intermediate ports, or while on passage by visual signals or VHF Channel 67, which is the small craft safety channel. Access to Ch 67 is via Ch 16. When using Ch 67 for safety messages it is requested that yacht gives the name of the Coastguard Rescue Centre holding the boat's Safety Scheme card.

The Coastguard must be advised of any change to the planned movements of the boat, if they have been informed of previous intentions. This can be done by telephone, or by visual or radio signals.

Raising the alarm

If you are ashore and see an accident afloat, dial 999 on the nearest telephone and ask for the 'Coastguard'. You will be asked to make a report of the incident, and possibly to stay near the telephone for further communications.

If at sea you pick up a distress signal, or get information about any vessel or aircraft in distress, you are obliged to proceed with all speed to give assistance (assuming you are in a position to do so), unless or until you are specifically released.

When alerted, by whatever means, the Coastguard summons the most appropriate assistance available. They might direct a Coastguard Shore Boat or an Auxiliary (Afloat) if there was one in the vicinity; they might request the launch of a RNLI lifeboat or inflatable lifeboat; the Royal Navy or the Royal Air Force could be asked to send an SAR helicopter; other Coastguard stations might be contacted; or shipping might be alerted through nearby Coast Radio Stations.

8.4.3. Royal National Lifeboat Institution (RNLI)

The RNLI (founded in 1824) is a charitable organisation, supported entirely by voluntary contributions. There are about 200 RNLI stations around the coasts of the United Kingdom, the Republic of Ireland, the Isle of Man and the Channel Islands. From them are deployed about 130 lifeboats and a similar number of inflatable lifeboats. Some of the latter are only in service during the summer months. The location of RNLI lifeboat stations in Great Britain and the Republic of Ireland is shown on the 'Diagram of Radiobeacons, Air Beacons, lifeboat stations etc' at the start of each relevant Area in Chapter 10 of *The Macmillan & Silk Cut Nautical Almanac*.

Lifeboats are manned by volunteer crews. At each station there is normally one full-time RNLI servant who may be a motor mechanic or a coxswain-mechanic.

Yachtsmen can help support the activities of the RNLI by joining Shoreline – full details of which can be obtained from the RNLI, West Quay Road, Poole, Dorset, BH5 1HZ.

When launched on service offshore lifeboats keep watch on 2182kHz and Ch 16. They can also use other frequencies for contacting other vessels, SAR aircraft, Coastguard, Coast Radio Stations or other authorities concerned with SAR. Inflatable lifeboats are fitted with VHF. All lifeboats now show a quick-flashing blue light.

8.4.4 Royal Navy

The Royal Navy assists casualties by means of ships and aircraft, including helicopters (see also 'Helicopter rescue', 8.4.9).

8.4.5 Royal Air Force

The Royal Air Force operates through Rescue Co-ordination Centres at Edinburgh and Plymouth, providing search and rescue facilities for Service and civil aircraft in and around the United Kingdom, but also helping where possible with other casualties by means of rotary and fixed wing aircraft.

8.4.6 Air Traffic Control Centres

These often first know about aircraft in distress, but they may also be involved in asking aircraft to keep a watch for vessels in trouble.

8.4.7 Response to a distress call

The action taken for any particular incident depends on whether a vessel or aircraft is involved, and the position and whereabouts of the casualty. In the case (for example) of a yacht drifting ashore, the Coastguard may have seen her or have observed her distress signals, or have received a report from a Coast Radio Station. The Coastguard informs the local RNLI Secretary, who decides whether to launch the lifeboat, and also musters the local Coastguard Auxiliary Service with its rescue equipment at the scene. The Coastguard may also request a helicopter, or send a radio-equipped rescue vehicle to the spot.

For a yacht or vessel in trouble offshore, some other ship is most likely to answer her distress call. The Coast Radio Station will re-broadcast a distress message on all the distress frequencies and also inform the Coastguard, the appropriate Area Flag Officer, Lloyd's, RNLI, and the appropriate Rescue Co-ordination Centre at Edinburgh or Plymouth. Each of these authorities will decide whether it can, or should, assist.

It should be remembered that any vessel (including a yacht) which sees or hears a distress signal from some other craft is legally obliged to proceed with all speed to her assistance, unless she is unable to do so in the particular circumstances, or unless and until she is released from such an obligation by other ships or the vessel in distress.

8.4.8 Abandon ship

Although preparations should be made, it is unwise to leave a yacht until it is certain that she is doomed. A boat is a much better target for rescue craft than a liferaft and while it is possible to remain on board it may be feasible to use her various resources (such as the radiotelephone for distress calls) to good effect and to select equipment which can be taken into the liferaft, or perhaps be securely lashed into the dinghy – which should be taken too if circumstances permit.

Action needed, if time permits, before entering the raft and cutting it adrift from the yacht:

(1) If a radiotelephone is available, send out a distress message (Mayday call) stating that the crew are abandoning ship in the liferaft, and giving the position. If an emergency radiotelephone is carried it should of course be taken in the liferaft.
(2) Dress warmly with sweaters etc under oilskins and lifejackets on top. Take extra clothes.
(3) Collect any available containers with screw tops or similar, and fill them about ¾ full of fresh water, so that they will float.
(4) Collect any additional food that is ready to hand, including tins and a can opener.
(5) Collect any equipment which will help to navigate and manage the liferaft – such as charts, hand bearing compass, pencils and

paper, torch, extra flares, bucket, length of line, first aid kit, knife, fishing gear.
(6) If possible, salvage such items as passports, money and ship's papers.

Sea Survival – A Manual by Dougal Robertson (Paul Elek) is recommended reading.

In the liferaft

Around the British Isles it is unlikely that survivors would be adrift in a liferaft for any length of time, but it is best to plan for the worst from the outset. If there has not been time to collect useful items from the parent vessel, there will probably be the opportunity to salvage all sorts of flotsam when she sinks. Almost any item could prove to be useful, but beware of any sharp objects or pieces of wreckage which might pierce the raft.

(1) Get and keep the inside of the raft as dry as possible. In our northern latitudes cold is likely to be a problem even in summer – keep close together for warmth. Close the opening to the raft as necessary, but always keep a lookout for shipping.
(2) Stream the drogue if it is desired to stay near to the scene of abandoning ship, or if the weather is bad.
(3) Ration fresh water to ¾ pint (½ litre) per person per day. Do not drink sea water or urine. Collect any rain water with the arrangements provided.
(4) Use flares sparingly, and only on the skipper's orders. See 6.4.5 and 8.3.10.
(5) Seasickness is likely to be a problem – issue pills as soon as possible.

8.4.9 Helicopter rescue

In the event of a helicopter coming to the rescue of the crew of a yacht in distress, it is essential to understand the procedure. Helicopters have limited endurance and limited lifting capacities (depending on the type) and for safety reasons they cannot hover close to a yacht with a mast.

While hovering the pilot has limited vision of a boat or a survivor below him, and has to rely on instructions from his navigator/winch operator. Normal hovering height is about 25ft (8m) but aircraft may hover lower than this on occasions. Some helicopters have a Hi-Line lifting capability to 300ft (90m), and only larger helicopters can operate at night or in bad weather.

It is essential that the yacht in distress can be identified from the air, particularly if other craft are in the vicinity. An accurate position (latitude and longitude, or range and bearing from some charted object) in the yacht's MAYDAY distress message is the first requirement, so that the helicopter goes to the right area. Dodgers with the boat's name or sail number, an upturned dinghy with the name on the bottom, or the boat's name clearly painted on the hull or superstructure are all aids to identification.

When the helicopter is sighted by a boat in

distress, either a flare or a daylight orange smoke signal will assist recognition; even an Aldis lamp trained on the helicopter and flashing SOS will help. If the boat is fitted with VHF radio this may be used to pass a message to the aircraft via the nearest Coast Station or Coastguard station, or via a lifeboat if one is in the vicinity.

Once the helicopter is approaching, final preparations for rescue must be made. In the case of a yacht with a mast it is necessary for survivors to be picked up from a dinghy or liferaft streamed at least 100ft (30m) away from the yacht. It is helpful if the drift of the yacht can be reduced by a sea anchor, or by streaming the anchor and cable over the bows. In a small sailing yacht which does not have any form of dinghy, survivors (who should in any case be wearing lifejackets) may have to take to the water at the end of a long warp so that they can be picked up. This problem does not arise in the case of a motor boat with no mast, or a small sailing dinghy. The latter should however, if still upright, lower any sails so as to minimise the considerable downdraught from the helicopter's rotor.

Never secure the winch wire to the boat, and beware that it may carry a lethal static charge if not dipped (earthed) in the sea before handling.

The normal way of lifting a survivor is in a strop, as shown in Fig. 8(10). The strop is put over head and shoulders, and fitted under the arm pits with the padded part in the small of the back. The sliding toggle in the front is then pulled down towards the body to tighten the strop. A thumbs up sign indicates that the survivor is ready for the lift to commence. The survivor's arms should be kept extended downwards, close to the sides of the body. Sometimes two strops may be offered simultaneously, so that two survivors may be raised in one lift.

If the winchman descends to the yacht, or to rescue somebody from a liferaft or from the

Fig. 8(11) Winchman with survivor in double lift.

water, follow his instructions exactly and as quickly as possible, since time may be precious. A winchman will accompany a survivor in a double lift, as illustrated in Fig. 8(11). The survivor in his strop faces the winchman, who puts his legs round the survivor's waist. An injured person is lifted in a Neil-Robertson stretcher, into which he or she is strapped, accompanied by the winchman. Small children are lifted by being carried by the winchman, or by another adult.

If it is not possible to lower the winchman and a strop to the yacht, a Hi-Line technique may be used. The Hi-Line consists of a nylon rope 150ft (46m) in length. At its upper end, where it is secured to the hook on the end of the helicopter's normal winch wire, it has a weak link, intended to break at a load of 200lb (90kg). At its lower end it has a weight, to help it hang as vertical as possible. In effect the Hi-Line is a rope extension to the winch wire. On occasions two Hi-Lines may be joined together, to give double the length.

The helicopter hovers well above the yacht, and the Hi-Line is lowered across the deck. It should be taken in by the crew as the helicopter pays out the winch wire. Do not make the Hi-Line fast, but coil it down carefully and keep it clear of snags. The Hi-Line is used to guide the winch wire, with its hook and strop, to the yacht. Keep it just taut, but do not pull it in more quickly than the winch wire is lowered, or the weak link will part, with consequent delay. The helicopter pays out the winch wire and descends, while the yacht's crew take in the slack of the Hi-Line (taking care to keep it outboard and clear of all obstructions) until the winch hook and strop are on board.

The winchman may or may not be lowered with the strop. Two strops may be offered together. When the survivor is secured in the strop, and the thumbs up signal is passed, the helicopter ascends and takes in the wire. Pay out

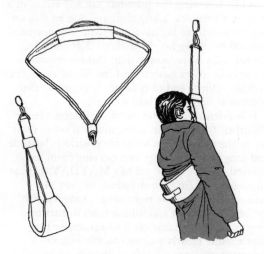

Fig. 8(10) The strop used in helicopter rescue lifts.

the Hi-Line, keeping it just taut, until the end is reached, when it should be cast off well clear of the yacht. If, however, a further lift is to be made, the end of the line should be retained on board if possible (but not made fast) in order to facilitate the recovery of the strop for the next lift.

On arrival at the door of the helicopter, obey the instructions of the winchman and/or the winch operator. Once the survivor is inside the aircraft the strop will be removed, and the survivor will be directed to a seat where he should strap himself in.

When alighting from a helicopter it is important to obey the instructions of the crew, since it is easy to walk into the tail rotor.

8.5 Search and rescue (SAR) organisation – North-West Europe

In North-West Europe similar SAR arrangements exist as are described in 8.4 for the United Kingdom.

These are summarised in notes about the countries concerned, which appear in Section 7 of the relevant Areas in Chapter 10 of *The Macmillan & Silk Cut Nautical Almanac* each year. Republic of Ireland – Area 12; France – Area 14; Belgium, Netherlands – Area 19; Federal Republic of Germany – Area 20. The location of lifeboat stations in these countries is shown on the 'Diagram of Radiobeacons, Air Beacons, lifeboat stations etc' at the start of each relevant Area in Chapter 10 of the Almanac.

Distress signals and procedures are internationally recognised. In the event of language difficulties, use the International Code: selected groups which include emergency signals are given in 6.2.8.

8.5.1 Republic of Ireland

The Marine Rescue Co-ordination Centre for the Irish Republic is situated at Shannon Airport. Tel: (061) 61219 and (061) 61969. If engaged call Air Traffic Control, Shannon (061) 6111, or Cork (021) 26552, or Dublin (01) 376 4971. In emergency dial 999. The centre can call on the RNLI, Coast Life Saving Service, Irish Army Air Corps helicopters, civil aircraft, the Irish lighthouse service, and the Garda Siochana. The centre liaises with the United Kingdom and France, and acts as a clearing house for all messages received during rescue operations within 100 miles of the Irish coast.

The Irish Coast Life Saving Service is staffed by volunteers who are trained in first aid and equipped with breeches buoys, cliff ladders etc. The telephone number (of the Leader's residence) is given for places quoted in Areas 12 and 13 in Chapter 10 of *The Macmillan & Silk Cut Nautical Almanac* each year.

8.5.2 France

SAR in French waters is controlled by the CROSS organisation (Centres Régionaux Opérationnels de Surveillance at de Sauvetage). CROSS can be alerted by telephone, through French Coast Radio Stations (e.g. St Nazaire, Brest-Le Conquet, Boulogne), through 'Semaphore' stations of the French Navy, through the Gendarmerie Nationale, or through Affaires Maritimes. Navigational warnings (e.g. lights extinguished, buoys out of position) are broadcast and weather bulletins can be provided.

CROSSA (A for Atlantic) covers the west coast of France from the Spanish border to Pointe du Raz (48°02′N 4°45′W). Stations at Soulac (45°31′N 1°07′W) and at Etel (47°39′N 3°12′W) keep watch on VHF Ch 16, and on 2182kHz.

CROSSCO (CO for Corsen-Ouessant) covers the north-west coast from Pointe du Raz to Mont St Michel (48°38′N 1°31′W). A station at Corsen (48°25′N 4°48′W) keeps watch on VHF Ch 16 and 11, and on 2182kHz.

CROSSMA (MA for Manche – English Channel) covers the French coast from Mont St Michel to the Belgian border. Stations at Jobourg (49°41′N 1°54′W) and at Cap Gris Nez (50°52′N 1°35′E) keep watch on VHF Ch 16 and 11, and on 2182kHz.

Further details (e.g. telephone numbers) of the CROSS organisation are given in *The Macmillan & Silk Cut Nautical Almanac* each year.

The French lifeboat service is administered by the Société Nationale de Sauvetage en Mer (SNSM), 9 Rue de Chaillot, 75116 Paris. Tel: 723.98.26.

8.5.3 Belgium

The Sea Rescue Co-ordination Centre is at Oostende, telephone numbers 70.10.00, 70.11.00, 70.77.01 or 70.77.02. Belgian lifeboats are administered by the Ministerie van Verkeerswezen, Aarlenstraat 104, 1040 Brussels. Tel: (02) 233.12.11. SAR Sea King helicopters of the Belgian Air Force are based as Koksijde.

8.5.4 Netherlands

Lifeboats in the south of the Netherlands are administered by the Koninklijke Zuid-Hollandsche Maatschappij tot Redding van Schipbreukelingen, Westerkade 11A, 3016 CL, Rotterdam. Tel: 010–364742.

In the north, lifeboats are administered by the Koninklijke Noord-en Zuid-Hollandsche Redding-Maatschappij, Spinonzastraat 1, 1018HD, Amsterdam.

There is an SAR helicopter base near Den Helder.

8.5.5 Federal Republic of Germany

The SAR service is operated by the Maritime Rescue Co-ordination Centre, Bremen (MRCC Bremen) as a part of Deutsche Gesellschaft zur Rettung Schiffbrüchiger, Werderstrasse 2, 2800

Bremen 1. Tel: (0421) 50.43.93. The larger German lifeboats are equipped with 'daughter boats' which are used, for example, for rescues in shallower water.

German military SAR helicopters are operated by the Rescue Co-ordination Centre (RCC) at Glücksburg, and are based at Kiel-Holtenau, Borkum, Helgoland and Sylt.

8.6 First Aid afloat

The objectives of first aid at sea are to preserve life, to prevent further damage, to relieve pain and distress, and to deliver a live casualty ashore.

8.6.1 Emergency life support

(1) If unconscious, check breathing passages. Clear mouth of teeth or debris with fingers. Tilt head backwards, using neck lift or chin support to maintain clear airway – Fig. 8(12). Place in coma position if breathing – Fig 8(13).

Fig. 8(12) Ensuring clear airway: head tilted and chin supported.

Fig. 8(13) Coma position.

Fig. 8(14) Mouth to mouth resuscitation: Pinch nose and support chin. Blow into victim's mouth; watch chest rise.

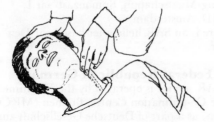

Fig. 8(15) Place to feel for the carotid pulse.

(2) If not breathing, start mouth to mouth resuscitation – Fig. 8(14). Kneel beside patient, maintain head tilt, pinch nostrils. Blow four rapid full breaths into patient's mouth. Feel carotid pulse – Fig. 8(15).If pulse present, continue one inflation every five seconds.

(3) If pulse absent, encourage circulation by external cardiac massage. Lay patient on hard, flat surface. Kneel beside patient; place heel of one hand just below middle of breastbone – Fig. 8(16). Place other hand on top of this hand. Depress breastbone $1\frac{1}{2}$–2in (40–50mm) – Fig. 8(17).

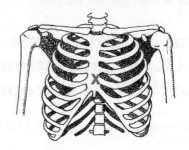

Fig. 8(16) Cardiac massage: hand position on breastbone.

Fig. 8(17) Cardiac massage: body and hand position.

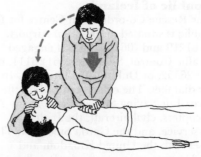

Fig. 8(18) One operator: cardiac massage rate 80/min, two quick breaths every 15 compressions.

One operator:
– Fig. 8(18) 80 chest compressions per minute. Two quick breaths after every 15 compressions.
Two operators:
– Fig. 8(19) 60 chest compressions per minute. One breath every five compressions.

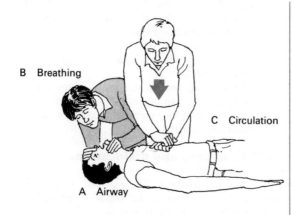

Fig. 8(19) Two operators: cardiac massage rate 60/min, one breath every 5 compressions.

Do not stop. Continue resuscitation until pulse and breathing return, or qualified help arrives, or patient is obviously dead (skin cold and pale, pupils widely enlarged, no breathing, no pulse, no heartbeat). Exception: hypothermia victim.

8.6.2 Resuscitation – further points
(1) Children. Blow into both mouth and nose if necessary: use a faster breathing rate, one inflation every three seconds. For external cardiac massage use gentle compression with one hand only, or just fingers for a baby; use a faster compression rate, 80–100 per minute.
(2) Damaged mouth. If mouth to mouth resuscitation impossible because of injury, use mouth to nose resuscitation, making certain the mouth is kept closed.
(3) Blockage of airway (choking). If blockage by a foreign body is suspected, turn victim on to side and give a hard blow between shoulder blades. If this fails, administer four quick chest thrusts (identical to external cardiac massage) in an attempt to expel the object. Clear mouth. Attempt lung inflation. Do not give up. If the victim is conscious you may wrap both arms around his waist from behind, and then give four sharp upward thrusts into solar plexus. Infants and small children may be held upside down whilst the back is slapped.
(4) Bulging stomach. This may result from swallowed air (e.g. during immersion), or from resuscitation efforts. Turn onto side, exert pressure on stomach.
(5) Vomiting. This occurs commonly during resuscitation (especially after immersion). To prevent vomit entering the lungs, turn the patient rapidly onto his side. Clear the airway before recommencing resuscitation.
(6) Cardiac compression. External cardiac massage moves blood around the body by directly compressing the heart, and by increasing the pressure in the chest cavity.

Use your whole body weight to compress the breastbone, do not lift your hands between compressions and do not press anywhere but directly on the breastbone. If the ribs break, do not stop but ensure that the heel of your hand is in the correct position.
(7) Drowning and hypothermia. These casualties may exhibit all the signs of apparent death, yet may still be completely revived. Abandon resuscitation reluctantly and only after attempts have been made to warm the victim.

8.6.3 Shock
Shock can result from almost any accident or medical emergency and, depending upon the cause, may range in severity from a simple faint to near death. The mechanical cause is impaired delivery of oxygen to the tissues because of inadequate or inefficient circulation of the blood. Possible causes include:
(1) Loss of blood – internal or external bleeding.
(2) Loss of fluid – diarrhoea, peritonitis, burns.
(3) Heart failure – heart attack.
(4) Lung failure – drowning.
(5) Brain failure – stroke, head injury.
(6) Illness – diabetes.

Signs and symptoms
Pale, cold, clammy skin; then, weak, rapid pulse; rapid, shallow breathing; apathy; nausea; dull, sunken eyes; bluish lips; thirst; sweating; restlessness leading to collapse.

Management
(1) Airway, breathing, circulation (see 8.6.1).
(2) Control bleeding.
(3) Lie flat; elevate legs to 20°. Exceptions:
  (a) Bleeding from mouth – coma position.
  (b) Unconscious – coma position.
  (c) Chest injury – sitting.
  (d) Neck or spinal injury – do not move.
(4) Splint fractures; avoid movement.
(5) Avoid chilling.
(6) Relieve pain – give pain killers. Exceptions:
  (a) Head injury with impaired consciousness.
  (b) Cases with breathing difficulty.
(7) Reassure.
(8) Fluids. Although thirst is a prominent symptom, fluids taken by mouth may be harmful. Avoid if:
  (a) Medical help is nearby.
  (b) Patient unconscious or having convulsions.
  (c) Severe abdominal pain or internal abdominal injury.

Fluids may be life saving in cases of dehydration (e.g. diarrhoea, vomiting, severe burns). Give half a glass of water at 15 minute intervals. Add a pinch of salt and a little sugar. Never give alcohol.

Collapse after an accident when external blood loss is absent or slight, must suggest internal injuries. Clues may be few. The patient may cough or vomit blood, or pass blood in urine or from bowel. He may complain of worsening pain in abdomen or chest. Urgent help needed.

Medical illnesses, such as diabetes, severe infection or heart disease, may produce shock without giving many clues as to the cause. Urgent help needed. Acquaint yourself with any medical problems of crew before a long passage. There should be a record on board of any medication being taken by any member of crew, including skipper (see 8.6.21).

8.6.4 Bleeding – open wound
Bleeding often dramatic, but always controllable.

Management
(1) Firm, continuous direct pressure; bandage on a large pad. If bleeding continues, bandage more pads on top of initial pads; press directly over wound for 10 minutes (blood takes this time to clot).
(2) Elevation if wound is on a limb.
(3) If spurting vessel visible (e.g. in a deep wound) pinch with fingers or forceps. If possible tie a firm reef knot round the vessel.
(4) Only use tourniquet to prevent a patient bleeding to death.

8.6.5 Bleeding – internal (closed injury)
May follow fractured bones, crush injuries, or damage to internal organs. Urgent help needed.

8.6.6 Nose bleed
Sit forwards: pinch the soft part of the nose firmly for 10 minutes; do not blow nose or try to remove clot. If bleeding continues insert as much 2in (50mm) gauze bandage (moistened with water) as you can. Use forceps to feed the bandage into the nose. Urgent help needed.

8.6.7 Cuts and wounds
Clean thoroughly with antiseptic. Remove dirt or other foreign bodies in the wound.
(1) Small clean cuts can be closed using Steristrips. Skin must be dry. Use as many Steristrips as necessary to keep the skin edges together. Leave for five days at least. See Fig. 8(20).
(2) Larger deep cuts may require special suture techniques. Unless experienced, do not attempt at sea – apply a dressing and seek help.

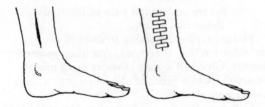

Fig. 8(20) Use of Steristrips to close a superficial wound.

(3) Ragged lacerations or very dirty wounds. Do not attempt to close these; dead tissues may have to be trimmed away to prevent infection. Clean as well as possible, sprinkle antibiotic powder in wound and apply a dressing. Seek help.

In general, wounds are best left open to the air if they can be kept clean and dry. If contemplating an extended passage, seek tuition in suturing.

8.6.8 Fractures and dislocations – general
Fracture – broken bone. Dislocation – displaced joint. Both result from major trauma and will give pain (worse on attempted movement), localised swelling, abnormal shape compared to other side, and grating feeling when fracture present. The tissues around the bone or joint may be damaged also: skin – may produce considerable swelling; nerves and blood vessels – the part of the limb below the fracture may be cold and discoloured, or numb.

To minimise these complications and reduce pain, splint and elevate the injured part where possible.

8.6.9 Common fractures and dislocations
(1) Collar bone. Support arm in sling – Fig. 8(21).

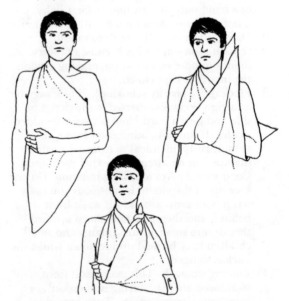

Fig. 8(21) Sling.

(2) Dislocated shoulder. If this has happened before, the patient may reduce the dislocation himself; otherwise do not attempt reduction in case a fracture exists. Seek help.
(3) Upper arm. Support the arm with a collar and cuff inside his shirt. Tie a clove hitch around the wrist, loop the ends behind his neck – Fig. 8(22).

Fig. 8(22) Collar and cuff.

(4) Forearm and wrist. Splint (e.g. with battens or inflatable splint). Do not bandage tightly. Elevate or support in a sling.
(5) Fingers. Elevate hand and, unless badly crushed, leave unbandaged; try to move. If unstable, bandage to adjacent finger.
(6) Thigh. Shock may be considerable. Splint by strapping to other leg with padding between. Do not bandage too tightly.
(7) Lower leg. Pad very well. Splint using oar, broom or inflatable splint.
(8) Ankle. Fracture or severe sprain may be indistinguishable. Immobilise in neutral position with foot at right angles.

To be really effective a splint should be rigid and extend to the joint above and below the fracture. This is not always possible. The splint must be very well padded. Inflatable splints offer great advantages.

If the limb beyond the bandage or splint becomes swollen or discoloured, the bandage must be loosened to improve circulation. If you improvise a fibre glass splint, be careful not to enclose the whole limb.

8.6.10 Special fractures
(1) Skull. See head injury (8.6.12).
(2) Nose. Control bleeding by pinching. Straighten immediately after the accident if possible.
(3) Jaw. Beware of associated brain or spine injury. Remove blood and teeth fragments; leave loose teeth in place. Ensure airway is clear. Commence regular antiseptic mouth washes and antibiotics. Support jaw with bandage over top of head. Give only fluids by mouth.
(4) Spine (including neck). May result from a direct blow, a fall or a whiplash type injury. If conscious patient may complain of pain, tingling, numbness or weakness in limbs below the injury. Mishandling may damage the spinal cord, resulting in paralysis or death. Avoid movement and support head continuously. Immobilise by wrapping a folded towel around the neck. If movement is necessary then lift as one rigid piece, never allowing the spine to sag or the neck to bend. Urgent help needed.
(5) Ribs. See chest injury (8.6.13).

(6) Compound fractures. If bone ends are visible, either in an open wound or protruding through the skin, clean thoroughly with antiseptic. Do not try to close the wound or replace the bone ends. Cover with sterile dressing. Help needed soon.

8.6.11 Strains and sprains
Torn ligaments, pulled muscles and other injuries. Rest the injured part; elevate if possible; apply ice packs (wrapped in a towel) if possible; paracetamol. If in doubt, treat as a fracture and immobilise.

8.6.12 Head injury
A blow to the head, with or without fracture, may result in immediate unconsciousness or more delayed effects.

Management
(1) Immediate unconsciousness but quick recovery with slight drowsiness or headache. Prescribe rest and watch carefully.
(2) Immediate unconsciousness, no sign of recovery. Put in coma position (beware of associated spine injury). Check airway. Observe and record every 15–20 minutes: pulse rate, pupil size (both sides), responses to verbal command; response to firm pinching. Urgent help needed.
(3) Delayed deterioration (either not unconscious at time of accident, or apparently recovering). Increasing drowsiness, change in mental state and eventually unconsciousness. Treat as (2) above. Urgent help needed.

Scalp wounds bleed profusely. Control with very firm pressure; cut away hair, and close using Steristrips if no fracture beneath. If in doubt seek help. Avoid giving drugs to head injury cases.

8.6.13 Chest injury
May result in fractured ribs. These are very painful, and breathing may be uncomfortable and shallow. The fractured ribs may puncture the lung, or if a number of ribs are broken in two places (e.g. after crushing) then the isolated mobile segment of the chest so created will further affect breathing. A hole in the chest wall will open the lungs to the atmosphere.

Management
(1) Airway, breathing, circulation.
(2) Patient may be more comfortable sitting up.
(3) Plug any hole with a pad if air is sucking in and out.
(4) Support any unstable chest segment with your hand.
(5) For fractured ribs prescribe rest and analgesics.

In general, light strapping restricts breathing even further.

Urgent help needed.

8.6.14 Eye injury

All eye injuries or illnesses are potentially serious. Never put old, previously used, ointment or drops into an eye. Serious infection could result.

(1) Foreign body. Flush the eye with clean water, pull the bottom lid out to inspect, remove object with a clean tissue. To inspect beneath upper lid, pull the lid out and then roll it upwards over a matchstick. After removal, instil sterile antibiotic ointment inside pulled out lower lid. Cover with pad.

(2) Corrosive burns. Continuous flushing with water for 15 minutes. Pain killers; antibiotic ointment; cover with pad; seek help as soon as possible.

(3) Infection. A sticky, weeping eye with yellow discharge. Antibiotic ointment 2/3 times per day.

8.6.15 Burns and scalds

(1) If smoke has been inhaled, move into fresh air.

(2) Stop the burning – dip the whole of the burnt part into cold water for 10/15 minutes. Seawater is excellent but may be very painful.

(3) Remove only loose clothing. Do not pull off clothing stuck to the skin.

(4) Cover with sterile dressing. If skin broken or blistered, use sterile paraffin gauze beneath the dressing. Keep burnt fingers separate with paraffin gauze.

(5) Do not prick blisters or apply ointments.

(6) Elevate burnt limb.

(7) Give pain killers liberally.

(8) Treat shock – give frequent drinks of half a cup of water.

(9) Commence antibiotics if help days away.

(10) If burns extensive or deep, urgent help needed.

Sunburn may be very severe. Treat as for any other burn. If skin unbroken, apply calamine lotion; give analgesics. For prevention use only certified ultra-violet filter preparations (e.g. Uvistat).

8.6.16 Drowning

The resuscitation of an apparently drowned person may be complicated by two factors. First, a sudden illness (e.g. a stroke) or an accident (e.g. a blow to the head) may have precipitated the fall into the water. Second, the time spent in the water may have produced marked hypothermia. The water around the British Isles is rarely warmer than 60°F (15°C).

Management

(1) Clear the airway – seaweed, false teeth etc.

(2) If not breathing start mouth to mouth resuscitation as soon as possible (in the water if practicable).

(3) If unable to inflate lungs, airway may be blocked; see Choking – 8.6.2 (3).

(4) If pulse absent, start cardiac massage as soon as aboard.

(5) If stomach bulging, turn on to side and press to empty, or he may vomit large quantities of swallowed water.

(6) Remove wet clothes; wrap in blankets to warm.

(7) Continue resuscitation until victim revives or death is certain. Hypothermia may mimic death. Do not abandon resuscitation until person has been warmed.

(8) On recovery, put in coma position – Fig. 8(13).

(9) Any person rescued from drowning may collapse in next 24 hours as the lungs react to inhaled water. Take to hospital as soon as possible.

8.6.17 Hypothermia

Lowered body temperature may follow immersion in sea – Fig. 8(23) or prolonged exposure on deck. Symptoms include: unreasonable behaviour followed by apathy and confusion; unsteady gait, stumbling, slurring of speech; pale, cold skin; slow, weak pulse; slow breathing; shivering early on, which leads to collapse, unconsciousness and ultimately death.

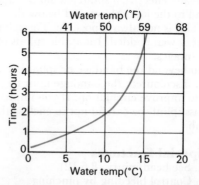

Fig. 8(23) Estimated survival time after which only 50% of immersion victims would still be alive. Adult males in conventional dress. (By kind permission Surg. Cdr. Frank St. C. Golden, R.N.)

Management

(1) Airway control; put in coma position.

(2) If not breathing, start mouth to mouth resuscitation.

(3) It is probably unwise to use cardiac massage.

(4) Remove wet clothing. Dry and wrap in blankets or sleeping bag with another person to generate heat.

(5) Immersion in warm bath – 110°F (43°C) is ideal.

(6) Do not give alcohol, or rub the skin, or place very hot objects against skin.

8.6.18 Frostbite

Usually affects toes, fingers, ears or nose. The affected part may be very painful, numb, stiff and discoloured. Warm gently (e.g. on someone else's back). Immersion in water less than 110°F (43°C) is satisfactory; higher temperatures will increase the damage. Do not rub the affected part with anything.

8.6.19 Poisoning

Poison may reach the body when swallowed, inhaled or injected through the skin (e.g. bites and stings).

(1) For swallowed poison the container may have instructions or suggest antidote(s). For corrosive or petroleum products (e.g. acids, alkalis, bleach, detergent, petrol) do not induce vomiting, administer copious fluids (e.g. milk). For other substances (e.g. pills, medicines) induce vomiting – tickle back of throat, or give *one* glass of very salty water. If collapsed or unconscious, urgent help needed.

(2) Poison may be inhaled from sources such as carbon monoxide or other exhaust fumes, bottled gas which has leaked into bilge, or fire extinguisher gas. Carbon monoxide inhalation produces a cherry red skin. Move into fresh air immediately. If breathing absent, commence resuscitation. Urgent help needed.

(3) Injected poison from bites and stings usually only causes local swelling and discomfort, but some individuals may react severely. For insect stings, resuscitate if collapse occurs; otherwise give rest, analgesics, antihistamines (e.g. Avomine), Waspeze. In warmer water, sea snakes and various sea stingers can inject extremely deadly poison: prevent drowning, resuscitate if necessary; if sting caused by jelly fish or Portuguese Man O' War etc, pour vinegar or strong alcohol onto sting to reduce further poison release. If the victim becomes weak and breathless, apply a tourniquet above the bite or wrap a tight bandage around the whole limb to delay spread of poison. Urgent help needed.

Many large cities maintain a 24-hour poison information centre. Use the radio for advice.

8.6.20 Seasickness

Basically an inner ear disturbance caused by motion. Previous nautical experience and time at sea modify likelihood of being sick. Fear, anxiety, fatigue and boredom aggravate the condition.

Avoid very acidic or spicy foods, and too much alcohol. Take small amounts of food (e.g. biscuits) frequently if you feel ill. Avoid fatigue; sleep will often relieve the sick feeling. Keep warm. Stay on deck, and concentrate on some task. Anybody on deck being sick must be secured by lifeline. If vomiting frequent, prescribe rest, encouragement and frequent small sips of sweet drinks.

No one remedy is suitable for every person. Try the various tablets available until you find one effective with minimum side effects. All cause

tiredness and a dry mouth to some degree. Take the first tablet up to 24 hours before sailing, and then regularly for as long as necessary. Take a tablet just before a sleep period if possible. Available tablets include: Dramamine (dimenhydrinate), Avomine (promethazine), Marzine (cyclizine), Stugeron (cinnarizine), Kwells (hyoscine).

8.6.21 Sudden illness

Acquaint yourself with any medical problems of crew before a long passage. Seek medical advice. Unless forewarned, diagnosis may be very difficult at sea.

(1) Stroke. Sudden unconsciousness, paralysis or weakness on one side of body, slurring of speech. Coma position, airway control. Urgent help needed.

(2) Convulsions. Patient may be a known epileptic. Insert twisted cloth between teeth to protect tongue. Try to prevent him injuring himself. Coma position; protect airway (he may still look very blue). After fit, allow him to sleep. Urgent help needed.

(3) Heart attack. Severe central chest pain; may spread to shoulders, neck or arms. Sweating, bluish lips, then collapse. Breathing and heart may stop (no pulse in neck).
   (a) Early symptoms: rest, reassure. Urgent help needed.
   (b) If unconscious: coma position; observe breathing and pulse.
   (c) If breathing stops or pulse absent, commence mouth to mouth breathing and cardiac massage immediately and *do not stop.*

(4) Diabetes. A diabetic may become unconscious if his blood sugar is too high or too low. For hyperglycaemia (too much sugar) insulin is needed urgently. Hypoglycaemia (too little sugar) may be caused by too much insulin, unusual stress or exercise, or too little food. In either case give sweets, sugar, soft drinks. Urgent help needed if recovery not rapid.

(5) Abdominal pain (minor)
   (a) Upper abdomen, intermittent, burning, no tenderness, otherwise well. May follow large alcohol intake. Eased by milk or antacid. Bland meals. No alcohol.
   (b) More generalised, cramping or colicky pain, no tenderness, may have diarrhoea or vomiting. May be gastroenteritis or food poisoning. Prescribe fluid with a pinch of salt added. Avoid dehydration.

(6) Abdominal pain (major). Severe abdominal pain, usually constant and generalised. Abdomen may be rigid or very tender to touch, fever may be present, rapid pulse rate, generally unwell, nausea and vomiting. Make him comfortable, give pain relief (injection if possible). Give nothing to eat or drink. Urgent help needed.

(7) Diarrhoea. Can become serious, especially in young children if much fluid is lost. Stop food, give plenty of fluid. Kaolin may be useful. Lomotil tablets very effective in adults.

(8) Fever. May be associated with anything from common cold, appendicitis, heat stroke to an infected toe. Except for major abdominal problems, prescribe copious fluids, paracetamol or aspirin – and antibiotics if infection is present.

(9) Heat stroke. Cool patient by sponging with cold water; encourage drinking (one teaspoon of salt per pint of water). If patient stops sweating, has a rapid pounding pulse and is becoming unconscious, seek help urgently.

8.6.22 Toothache
If a hole is obvious, insert cottonwool soaked in oil of cloves. Pain killers: paracetamol or stronger. Give antibiotics if abcess present, jaw swollen or temperature elevated. Your dentist may help with a suitable kit before a long voyage.

8.6.23 Children
Children may become ill with alarming rapidity. Ear and throat infections are especially common. Children also more susceptible to effects of dehydration, so if ill encourage to drink a lot. Reduce drug dosage to a proportion of adult dose based on weight. Average adult 155lb (70kg).

8.6.24 Drugs

Paracetamol 500mg tablets	pain or fever	1–2 4 hourly
Codeine 30mg tablets	more serious pain	1–2 4 hourly
Fortral (pentazocine) 25mg tablets	severe pain	1–2 4 hourly
Aludrox	indigestion	as directed on box
Lomotil tablets	diarrhoea	2–4 tablets, then 2 every 6 hours until controlled
Senokot tablets	constipation	2–4 tablets daily
Tetracycline 250mg	antibiotic	1 capsule 4 times daily
Stenetil suppositories	severe seasickness	1 as required
Chloramphenicol eye ointment		inside lower lid

8.6.25 Injections
A doctor's prescription is required for injections of pain-killing drugs. Probably only warranted for long passages. It is safest to inject into the muscle on outer part of the front of mid thigh. Clean the area, then plunge the needle swiftly an inch or so through the skin, pull back on the plunger to ensure that a blood vessel has not been entered, then slowly complete the injection.

8.6.26 Normal measurements
(1) Pulse rate.   Adults 60–80/min.
                        Children up to 100/min.
(2) Breathing.   12–15/min
(3) Temperature.   98.4°F (36.7°C).

8.6.27 Seeking medical advice
International Code single letter signal W (Whisky) means 'I require medical assistance'. Use any method of signalling. Medical advice can be obtained through Coast Radio Stations as below. The Coast Station communicates with the most appropriate medical authority. There is no charge. Use the urgency signal Pan Pan (three times) in serious cases.

(1) *United Kingdom and Ireland*. Call nearest Coast Radio Station, requesting 'Medico' service. If medical assistance is required (e.g. a doctor, or off-lifting a patient) the request will be passed to the Coastguard.

(2) *France*. Call nearest Coast Radio Station, with address 'PAN PAN (three times) Radiomédical ... (name of Coast Station)'. French language should be used.

(3) *Belgium*. Call Oostende Radio, using address 'Radiomédical Oostende'. English may be used.

(4) *Netherlands*. Call Scheveningen Radio, using address 'Radiomédical Scheveningen'. English may be used.

(5) *Federal Republic of Germany*. Call nearest Coast Radio Station, using address 'Funkarzt ... (name of Coast Station)'. English may be used.

For radio procedures see Chapter 6. Before calling it is best to write down as many details as you can about the patient (e.g. pulse rate, breathing rate, temperature, skin colour, conscious state, site and description of any pain, site and type of any injury, amount of blood lost).

8.6.28 Suggestions for a first aid kit
Your doctor or chemist may suggest alterations. Prescriptions are needed for many of the drugs. Out of date drugs are dangerous – destroy them. Special preparations are available for children. Secure items in a waterproof container.

Triangular bandage × 2 (double as bandage or sling)
Crepe bandage 75mm × 2
Gauze bandage 50mm × 2
Elastoplast 75mm × 1
Band Aids (or similar) various shapes and sizes
Wound dressing BPC, 1 large, 1 medium
Sterile non-adhesive dressing (Melolin) × 5
Paraffin gauze sterile dressings – 5 packs
Steristrips – 5 packs
Cottonwool

Scissors and forceps – good stainless steel
Safety pins
Thermometer
Antiseptic solution (e.g. Savlon)
Ultraviolet filter cream (e.g. Uvistat)
Cicatrin antibiotic powder
Tinaderm powder (athlete's foot)
Calamine lotion (bites, stings and sunburn)
Individual choice of antiseasick tablets
Drugs – see 8.6.24

Additional items for extended cruising
Inflatable splint

Syringes 2ml × 2 (if carrying injections)
Oil of cloves (toothache) and dental kit
Moisture cream (for cracked hands and lips)

8.6.29 Recommended books
First Aid. Manual of St John Ambulance Assoc.
The Ship's Captain Medical Guide. (HMSO). A little dated but covers the subject comprehensively.
The Emergency Book by Bradley Smith and Gus Stevens (Penguin).
The Yachtsman's Doctor by Dr R. Counter (Nautical).

Chapter 9

Tides and the sea

Contents

9.1 Tides – general

9.1.1 General theory

The tide is the periodical rise and fall of sea level caused by the gravitational attraction of the Moon and, to a lesser extent, of the Sun. The gravitational effect of the Moon is not uniform over the earth's surface. At a point nearest to the Moon it is greater than at the centre of the earth, where it is in turn greater than at a point on the far side of the earth. This causes the sea level to be raised at the points nearest to the Moon and furthest from it – at A and B in Fig. 9(1).

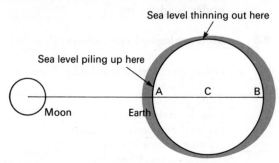

Fig. 9(1) Diagrammatic sketch showing the exaggerated effect of the Moon's gravitational pull on the sea.

When the Moon and the Sun are in the same straight line as the earth their combined gravitational effect is greatest, and this produces the largest rise and fall of tide. These are called spring tides, and occur just after new moon and full moon – see Fig. 9(2).

When the Moon and the Sun form a right angle with the earth their respective gravitational

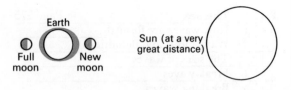

Fig. 9(2) When the Moon and Sun lie in a straight line with the earth, their gravitational forces act in conjunction, and result in a large rise and fall in sea level (spring tides).

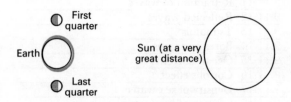

Fig. 9(3) When the Moon and Sun form a right angle with the earth, their combined effect is minimised, resulting in a smaller rise and fall in sea level (neap tides).

effects are acting at places which are one-quarter of the earth's circumference apart, and hence their combined effect is minimised. This results in a smaller rise and fall in sea level, or neap tides which occur just after the first and last quarters.

Since the earth is rotating on its axis every 24 hours, the actual areas nearest to and furthest from the Moon are continually changing. Hence the level of the sea at any point is also continually changing.

A lunar day (the time between two successive passes of the Moon across a given meridian) is about 24 hours 50 minutes. In the Atlantic Ocean, and along the coasts of North-West Europe, two complete tidal cycles occur every lunar day. These are called semi-diurnal tides, with a period of about 12 hours 25 minutes between successive high waters.

Some parts of the world have diurnal tides, with only one high water and one low water every 25 hours or so. Diurnal tides usually have very little rise and fall.

Other parts of the world experience mixed tides, which are partly semi-diurnal and partly diurnal in character. Mixed tides, like semi-diurnal tides, have two complete tidal oscillations per day but often one of the cycles is much more pronounced than the other.

Tides are influenced by the physical details of ocean basins and the surrounding land. For example in the Mediterranean and the Baltic there is virtually no tide, because the entrances to these seas are too narrow to allow the flow of water necessary to create any significant rise and fall in the time available. On open coasts the tide usually rises and falls at about the same rate on any given day, but in estuaries it normally rises more quickly than it falls.

The height of the tide is measured against a reference level called chart datum, as defined in 9.2.1. Predictions for the times and heights of high water and low water at places all over the world are published annually in tide tables, which include constants for calculating times and heights at intermediate ports.

Tide refers to the vertical rise or fall in sea level. This in turn causes horizontal movements of water, called tidal streams. Information on the strength and direction of tidal streams is available from various sources, as described in 9.10.

9.1.2 Local tidal conditions

Physical details of the coast and the sea bed can cause local tidal conditions which depart substantially from the semi-diurnal (or diurnal) pattern. Often there is no simple explanation for such phenomena, of which a good example is the complex tidal regime between Swanage and the Nab Tower on the south coast of England, and the double high waters which occur at places in that area.

The Coriolis force (induced by the earth's rotation on any object which moves on the surface of the earth, except at the equator) can also affect local tidal conditions, and helps to explain (see 9.11.16) why the French side of the English Channel has bigger tides than the English coast opposite.

Other tidal phenomena, such as bores (or eagres), together with non-tidal changes in sea level caused by abnormal meteorological conditions, are mentioned in 9.8 and 9.11.14.

9.1.3 Equinoxes and solstices

Twice a year, at about the times when the Sun is over the equator at the vernal equinox on 21 March and the autumnal equinox on 23 September, spring tides are larger than normal. These are called Equinoctial Spring Tides, and they occur when all the factors which contribute to big tides – such as the phase of the Moon, the Moon's declination and the Sun's declination – are working in concert. Around the solstices (21 June and 22 December) the tides are smaller than normal.

9.1.4 Tide tables

The Hydrographer of the Navy publishes the *Admiralty Tide Tables* in three volumes. Vol 1 covers all Europe, the Mediterranean and the Black Sea; Vol 2 covers the East Coasts of North and South America including the Caribbean, Greenland, all the coasts of Africa except the Mediterranean, the coasts of Asia up to Singapore and the Malacca Strait; Vol 3 covers the West Coasts of North and South America, Australasia, the Asian coasts east of Singapore, and all the Pacific. Vols 2 and 3 include tidal stream predictions.

Vol 1 is divided into three parts. Part 1 gives tidal predictions for the Standard Ports, being the times and heights of high water and low water for each day of the year, computed by the Institute of Oceanographic Sciences or the Hydrographer for United Kingdom ports, and by the appropriate authorities for foreign ports. Part 2 gives data for predictions at a large number of Secondary Ports in the form of time and height differences referred to one of the Standard Ports in Part 1. Part 3 gives the harmonic constants for use with the Admiralty method of tidal prediction (NP 159), as discussed in 9.9.5.

All the information from Vol 1 which a yachtsman needs for the United Kingdom, Eire or the coast between the Loire and the Elbe is given in *The Macmillan & Silk Cut Nautical Almanac*, published annually.

9.2 Definitions

9.2.1 Chart Datum (CD)

Chart datum is the level to which soundings and drying heights on a chart are referred. The height of the tide at any time is the vertical distance of

sea level above (or very occasionally below) chart datum. To find the actual depth of water, the height of the tide at a particular time is added to the depth shown on the chart at the place concerned.

Tidal predictions for British ports are based on Lowest Astronomical Tide – LAT, see 9.2.13. Admiralty metric charts of the British Isles use LAT as chart datum but most fathom charts, of which there are still a small number, were drawn with a chart datum that approximated to Mean Low Water Springs (MLWS). Since MLWS is slightly higher than LAT, it is necessary to make a small correction when using *Admiralty Tide Tables* with most fathom charts. Check the tidal information panel on the chart against the heights given in Part II of *Admiralty Tide Tables* to see if a correction is needed. Any such correction must be subtracted from the predicted height, and may be as much as 0.5 metres.

9.2.2 Charted depth

The charted depth shown on the chart is the vertical distance of the sea bed at that place below chart datum. Depths are shown in metres and tenths of metres on modern metric charts where, for example, 5_2 indicates 5.2 metres. Depths will still be found expressed in fathoms and/or feet on some older charts, where 5_2 would indicate five fathoms and two feet. It is very important to make sure which units are used. Admiralty metric charts have DEPTHS IN METRES printed in magenta in the margins, top and bottom.

9.2.3 Co-tidal and co-range lines

Co-tidal lines are drawn on a special chart through points where Mean High Water occurs at the same time. Co-range lines are drawn through points of equal Mean Spring Range. They enable the height of tide to be predicted at places well offshore, whereas tide tables only give predictions for coastal places (see 9.9.4 for further details).

9.2.4 Depth (actual)

The actual depth of water at any place is the sum of the charted depth and the height of the tide at that time and place. If there are no errors in the chart, or in the tidal prediction, the depth as so calculated should correspond to a sounding obtained by lead line or by an accurate echo sounder.

9.2.5 Drying height

The drying height is the vertical distance of the top of any feature which is occasionally covered by water above chart datum. Figures for drying heights are underlined on the chart – in metres and tenths of a metre on metric charts, and in feet on older charts. For example, on a metric chart, $\underline{5_2}$ indicates that the place concerned dries 5.2 m above CD. The actual depth of water at such a place is the height of the tide at the time minus the drying height indicated. If the result is minus, then that place is exposed at the time selected.

9.2.6 Duration
The duration of a tide is the time between high water and the previous low water, and is normally slightly more than six hours where semi-diurnal tides apply as around the coasts of North-West Europe. The duration can be used to calculate the time of low water where only the time of high water is given in tide tables.

9.2.7 Ebb
The ebb is the movement of tide as it recedes from high water. With semi-diurnal tides it is about six hours' duration and is divided into three parts – the 'first of the ebb', the 'strength of the ebb' and the 'last of the ebb'.

9.2.8 Elevation of lights etc
The elevations of lights or other structures such as bridges are expressed (in metres on metric charts) above the level of Mean High Water Springs, as is shown in Fig. 9(4).

9.2.9 Equinoctial spring tides
As explained in 9.1.3, unusually big tides can be expected with spring tides at about the equinoxes, which occur on 21 March and 23 September.

9.2.10 Flood
The flood is the movement of tide as it rises from low water. It is about six hours in duration and is divided into three parts, the first two hours being described as the 'young flood', the middle two hours as the 'main flood' and the last two hours as the 'last of the flood'.

9.2.11 Height of tide
The height of the tide is the vertical distance between chart datum and sea level at a given time. In *Admiralty Tide Tables* and in *The Macmillan & Silk Cut Nautical Almanac* the heights of tide at High Water and at Low Water are shown in metres and tenths of metres for the Standard Ports quoted.

9.2.12 Interval
The interval is the time between any given time and the time of high water, expressed in hours and minutes before (−) or after (+) high water (HW).

9.2.13 Lowest Astronomical Tide (LAT)
LAT is the lowest sea level predicted to occur under average meteorological conditions and under any combination of astronomical conditions. It is only reached very occasionally, but it must be noted that it is not the extreme level. Abnormal meteorological conditions (see 9.8) may cause lower sea levels.

Lowest Astronomical Tide is used as chart datum for Admiralty metric charts of the British Isles. Lowest Astronomical Tide is also the reference level for *Admiralty Tide Table* predictions for ports in Great Britain.

As already noted in 9.2.1, older (fathom) charts were drawn with a chart datum which approximated to Mean Low Water Springs (MLWS). Corrections must therefore be applied to predictions from *Admiralty Tide Tables* when used with most fathom charts.

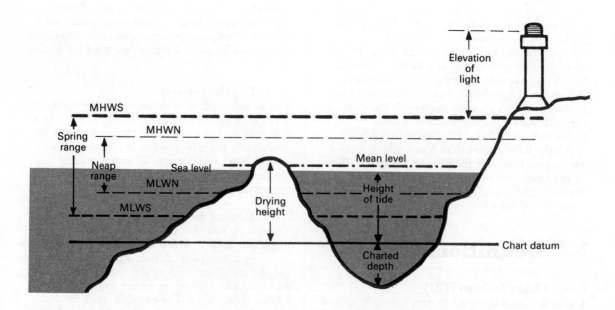

Fig. 9(4) This diagram shows the more important terms used in tidal predictions and calculations.

9.2.14 Making

At neaps the range of a tide (the difference in height between high water and low water, as in 9.2.17) is relatively small. At springs the range is relatively big. As the range increases from neaps to springs, the tide is said to be making. The opposite is 'taking off'.

9.2.15 Mean Level (ML)

The mean level (ML) at a place is the average height of Mean High Water Springs (MHWS), Mean High Water Neaps (MHWN), Mean Low Water Neaps (MLWN) and Mean Low Water Springs (MLWS). There are seasonal changes in Mean Level, and the monthly variations are shown in Part 2 of *Admiralty Tide Tables*. Where the variation is less than 0.1m it is entered as 'negligible'. For short periods the Mean Level may vary by as much as 0.3m above or below the predicted figures.

The term 'Mean Level' is also used to describe mean sea level, or the average of a large number of hourly heights. This can produce a different figure.

9.2.16 Neap tides (neaps)

Neap tides occur between spring tides, at the first and last quarters of the moon when (as explained in 9.1.1) the influences of the Sun and Moon are at right angles. At neaps the range of the tide is smallest, i.e. high water is lower and low water is higher than at springs.

9.2.17 Range

The range of the tide is the difference in height between successive high and low waters. Spring range is the difference between MHWS and MLWS. Neap range is the difference between MHWN and MLWN.

9.2.18 Secondary Ports

The term 'Secondary Port' does not imply that the place concerned is of secondary importance. Tidal predictions for Secondary Ports are made by applying time and height differences to predictions for a selected Standard Port (see 9.2.22). The Standard Port chosen is not necessarily the nearest, but one with tidal characteristics which are similar to those of the Secondary Port.

9.2.19 Slack water

Slack water is the period between the completion of the flood and the commencement of the ebb, or similarly at low water between the end of the ebb and the start of the flood. At high water it is also known as the 'stand'.

9.2.20 Sounding

The term 'sounding' is used in two senses. Strictly it means the depth of water as obtained by echo sounder or lead line, but it is also used for the figures on a chart showing the depth of water

(below chart datum), because these figures are derived from actual soundings which are adjusted for the height of tide at the time they are taken. To avoid confusion it is best to refer to a sounding on the chart as 'charted depth' (see 9.2.2).

9.2.21 Spring tides (springs)

At springs the tide rises highest and falls lowest from the Mean Level, i.e. the range is greatest. Spring tides occur when the Moon and Sun are acting in conjunction, as described in 9.1.1. During spring tides the tidal streams run more strongly.

9.2.22 Standard Ports

For certain selected Standard Ports, the predicted time and height of every high and low water throughout the year are given in *Admiralty Tide Tables*, and in *The Macmillan & Silk Cut Nautical Almanac*. Predictions are based on observations over a period of at least a year, and usually much longer. Daily predictions for the following Standard Ports are to be found each year in *The Macmillan & Silk Cut Nautical Almanac*: Devonport, Dartmouth, Poole (low water only), Southampton, Portsmouth, Shoreham, Dover, Sheerness, London Bridge, Harwich, Lowestoft, Immingham, Tees, Leith, Aberdeen, Lerwick, Ullapool, Oban, Greenock, Liverpool, Milford Haven, Avonmouth, Cork (Cobh), Dublin, Belfast, Galway, Pointe de Grave, Brest, St Helier (Jersey), Cherbourg, Le Havre, Dieppe, Flushing (Vlissingen), Hook of Holland (Hoek van Holland), Helgoland.

9.2.23 Taking off

'Taking off' is the opposite to 'making' (see 9.2.14). The tide is said to be taking off as the range decreases from its maximum during springs to its minimum during neaps.

9.3 Calculations of times of high and low water

9.3.1 Standard Ports

Daily times of HW and LW for Standard Ports are given in tide tables. Zone times are shown. In the United Kingdom, GMT is used throughout, so one hour must be added during BST. Similar action is required for other daylight saving times (e.g. France), as is explained in 9.3.3.

9.3.2 Secondary Ports

For Secondary Ports, the approximate times of HW and LW are calculated by adding (when +) or subtracting (when −) the time difference shown, to (or from) the time of HW or LW at the Standard Port indicated. Predictions for times falling between those given for the Standard Port at the top of each column must be interpolated. For example, the tidal information for St. Peter Port:

Standard Port   ST HELIER

Times				Height (metres)			
HW		LW		MHWS	MHWN	MLWN	MLWS
0900	0300	0200	0900	11.1	8.1	4.1	1.3
2100	1500	1400	2100				

Differences   ST PETER PORT

+0012	0000	−0008	+0002	−2.1	−1.4	−0.6	−0.3

If HW St Helier is at about 0900 or 2100, the time difference to be applied to obtain HW St Peter Port is +0012 (plus 12 mins). If HW St Helier is at about 0300 or 1500, no correction is needed. For times of HW at St Helier between (say) 0900 and 1500, the time difference is obtained by interpolation. Hence for HW St Helier at 1200, it would be +0006.

The same principle applies to time of LW. If LW St Helier is at about 0200 or 1400, LW St Peter Port is 8 minutes earlier; if LW St Helier is at about 0900 or 2100, LW St Peter Port is 2 minutes later. As for HW, the corrections for intermediate times of LW St Helier must be interpolated. If for example LW St Helier is at 1600, LW St Peter Port will be about 5 minutes before LW St Helier.

9.3.3 Zone Time and time difference

There are twenty-four Time Zones in the world each of which covers 15° of longitude. The 'zero' time zone, in which the Standard Time corresponds to Greenwich Mean Time, is centred on the prime meridian and extends from $7\frac{1}{2}$°E to $7\frac{1}{2}$°W. The other zones, in which the time kept differs from GMT by an integral number of hours, are sequentially numbered and have either a negative prefix if east of Greenwich or a positive prefix if west of Greenwich. The demarcation of these time zones is adjusted to suit geographical areas. For example, all France keeps Zone −0100 as Standard Time.

To convert Zone Time to GMT, the number of hours as given by the zone number is added to (if positive) or subtracted from (if negative) the Zone Time, e.g. in Zone −0100 the time kept is one hour in advance of GMT, and so 2000 local time is 1900 GMT.

During winter months in the United Kingdom, clock time is GMT.

During summer months in the United Kingdom, clock time is BST which is Zone −0100, i.e. one hour ahead of GMT.

During the winter months in France, Belgium, Netherlands and West Germany, local (clock) time is Zone −0100. In all four countries, daylight saving time (DST) operates from the last Sunday in March until the last Saturday in September. During this period, local (clock) time

Greenwich Mean Time (GMT) Tide tables for UK, Ireland and Channel Isles	Zone -0100 British Summer Time, (BST) from last Sun in March to 4th Sat in Oct Standard Time in France, Belgium, Netherlands and West Germany. Used for tide tables in these countries	Zone -0200 Daylight Saving Time (DST) from last Sun in March to last Sat in Sept, for France, Belgium, Netherlands and West Germany
0000	0100	0200
0100	0200	0300
0200	0300	0400
0300	0400	0500
0400	0500	0600
0500	0600	0700
0600	0700	0800
0700	0800	0900
0800	0900	1000
0900	1000	1100
1000	1100	1200
1100	1200	1300
1200	1300	1400
1300	1400	1500
1400	1500	1600
1500	1600	1700
1600	1700	1800
1700	1800	1900
1800	1900	2000
1900	2000	2100
2000	2100	2200
2100	2200	2300
2200	2300	2400
2300	2400	0100
0000	0100	0200

Fig. 9(5) Table showing relation between GMT, BST, and the standard and daylight saving times (DST) kept in Western Europe.

is −0200, or two hours ahead of GMT. BST (British Summer Time) is Zone −0100. The relationships between GMT, Zone −0100 and Zone −0200 are shown in the table in Fig. 9(5).

The tide tables take no account of BST or other Daylight Saving Times.

The times of Standard Port predictions are given in the normal Standard Time kept by the port. When using the tables it should be verified that this is the same as the time *which is actually being kept*. Changes in Zone Times are not always reported in sufficient time for inclusion in the tide tables.

Time differences for Secondary Ports, when applied to the printed times of high and low water at Standard Ports, will give times of high and low water at the Secondary Ports in the *Zone Time tabulated for the Secondary Port*. Any change in Zone Time at the Standard Port, or any difference between Zone Times at Standard and Secondary Ports has no significance; *the predicted values tabulated for the Standard Port must be used unaltered*. Only changes in Zone Time at the Secondary Port, where different from those tabulated, may be corrected for. It should be verified that the Zone Time tabulated for the

Secondary Port is the same as the time being kept. For example, Binic (in France, Zone −0100) is quoted on the Standard Port of St Helier (keeping Zone 0, i.e. GMT). When adding the time differences to St Helier times, the result gives the time of HW or LW at Binic for Zone −0100, the hour's difference being allowed for (but not any correction for daylight saving).

9.4 Calculations of heights of high and low water

9.4.1 Standard Ports
For Standard Ports the daily heights of HW and LW are shown in metres, referred to chart datum at the port concerned.

9.4.2 Secondary Ports
For Secondary Ports heights of HW or LW are found by applying the height differences, given in the tidal information for each harbour, to the height of HW or LW at the Standard Port indicated. These average differences are shown

for Mean Spring and Mean Neap levels, heights for intermediate dates being obtained by interpolation. The resulting heights are referred to chart datum at the Secondary Port concerned.

Referring to the tidal data for St Peter Port in 9.3.2, the height of MHWS at St Peter Port is $11.1 - 2.1 = 9.0$m. The height of MLWN is $4.1 - 0.6 = 3.5$m. To determine the height (say) of LW at St Peter Port midway between springs and neaps, take the mean of 4.1 and 1.3 (2.7m) to give the predicted height of LW St Helier, and subtract the mean of 0.6 and 0.3 (a correction of -0.45m), giving a height of 2.25m.

The height differences shown for Secondary Ports are average values, and predicted heights so obtained are approximate.

9.5 Calculations of depths of water at specific times

9.5.1 Tidal curves – procedure
As shown in Fig. 9(4), the depth of water is the height of the tide plus the charted depth. To

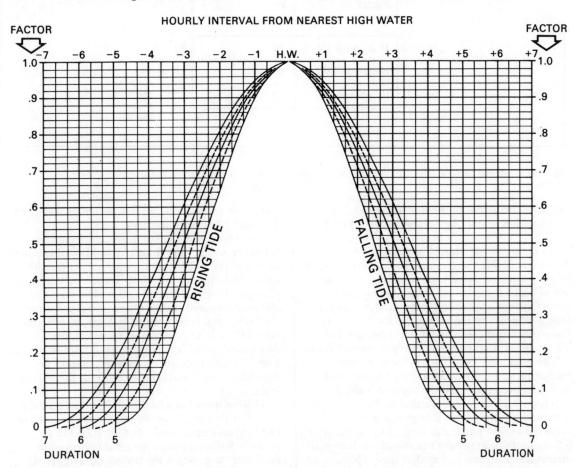

Fig. 9(6) Standard tidal curves for finding the height of tide at times between high water and low water. Note that where special curves are given for individual Standard Ports, these special curves should be used.

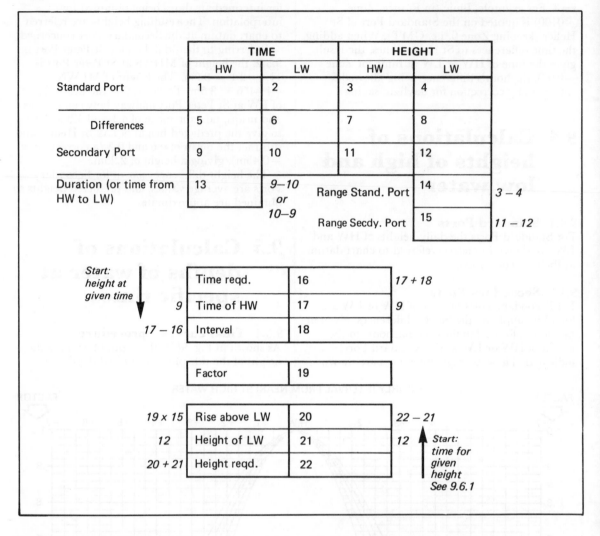

	TIME		HEIGHT	
	HW	LW	HW	LW
Standard Port	1	2	3	4
Differences	5	6	7	8
Secondary Port	9	10	11	12

Duration (or time from HW to LW): 13 | 9–10 or 10–9

Range Stand. Port: 14 | 3 – 4
Range Secdy. Port: 15 | 11 – 12

Start: height at given time

9 | Time reqd. | 16 | 17 + 18
| Time of HW | 17 | 9
17 – 16 | Interval | 18

| Factor | 19 |

19 x 15 | Rise above LW | 20 | 22 – 21
12 | Height of LW | 21 | 12
20 + 21 | Height reqd. | 22 | *Start: time for given height See 9.6.1*

Fig. 9(7) Pro-forma for tidal calculations when using *Admiralty Tide Tables* or *The Macmillan & Silk Cut Nautical Almanac*.

calculate the height of the tide at times between high and low water, the following procedure is used.

A number of Standard Ports shown in *The Macmillan & Silk Cut Nautical Almanac* are covered by the Standard Tidal Curves in Fig. 9(6), the use of which is explained below. Where these curves are not applicable, individual curves are shown adjacent to the tide tables for Standard Ports concerned (see also 9.6.1). *Admiralty Tide Tables* give a tidal curve for every Standard Port.

The Standard Tidal Curves show, on the horizontal scale, the times in hours before and after high water and, on the vertical scale, the 'Factor' which may be regarded as the percentage of the Mean Range which has occurred at that particular time. Thus a factor of 0.5 means that 50 per cent of the Mean Range in metres has been reached at that time. Hence 1 at the top of the scale is high water and 0 at the bottom is low water. Three curves are given for

durations (times between low and high water) of 5, 6 and 7 hours respectively.

The appropriate curve must be selected by reference to the time from LW to HW (duration) or from HW to LW, as appropriate, in the tide table. Multiplying the Mean Range by the factor gives the height of the tide above low water at the time required. From the required point on the horizontal scale (before HW on the left and after HW on the right) take a vertical line downwards until it cuts the appropriate curve (5, 6 or 7 hours' duration or an interpolation as necessary), and read off the factor on the vertical scale.

This information can then be used to find the height of tide at any given time. For this purpose, use the pro-forma shown in Fig. 9(7). Fill in boxes 1–8 directly from the tidal information available, to produce the times and heights of high and low water at the Secondary Port required, and to enable calculation of the duration and ranges. Then proceed as shown in the diagram, going down the left hand side of the bottom section.

9.5.2 Example

To find the height of the tide at Teignmouth at 0300 GMT on 21 May – see Fig. 9(8).

Tidal information for Teignmouth (as given for 1983 in *The Macmillan & Silk Cut Nautical Almanac*) is as follows:

Standard Port DEVONPORT

Times				Height (metres)			
HW	LW			MHWS	MHWN	MLWN	MLWS
0100	0600	0100	0600	5.5	4.4	2.2	0.8
1300	1800	1300	1800				

Differences TEIGNMOUTH
+0025	+0040	0000	0000	−0.7	−0.8	−0.3	−0.2

This means that when HW Devonport is at 0100 or at 1300, HW Teignmouth is 25 minutes later. When HW Devonport is at 0600 or at 1800, HW Teignmouth is 40 minutes later. Between these times, the difference between HW Devonport and HW Teignmouth can be interpolated. In this particular example there is no difference between the times of LW Devonport and LW Teignmouth.

So far as heights are concerned, at MHWS the height of the tide at Teignmouth is 0.7m less than at Devonport (5.5m). At MLWS the height of the tide at Teignmouth is 0.2m less than at Devonport (0.8m).

As shown above, the Standard Port for Teignmouth is Devonport, and the Devonport predictions for the day concerned are:

Devonport	0023	4.7
21	0654	1.7
SA	1322	4.4
	1926	1.8

	TIME		HEIGHT		
	HW	LW	HW	LW	
Standard Port *Devonport*	¹0023	²0654	³ 4.7	⁴ 1.7	
Differences	⁵+0026	⁶0000	⁷ −0.8	⁸ −0.3	
Secondary Port *Teignmouth*	⁹0049	¹⁰0654	¹¹ 3.9	¹² 1.4	
Duration (or time from HW to LW)	¹³0605	9–10 or 10–9	Range Stand. Port	¹⁴ 3.0	3 – 4
			Range Secdy. Port	¹⁵ 2.5	11 – 12

Start: height at given time ↓ 9	Time reqd.	16 **0300 (GMT)**	17 + 18
17 – 16	Time of HW	17 **0049**	9
	Interval	18 **+0211**	
	Factor	19 **0.74**	
19 × 15	Rise above LW	20 **1.85**	22 – 21
12	Height of LW	21 **1.4**	12
20 + 21	Height reqd.	22 **3.25**	Start time for given height see 9.6.1

Fig. 9(8) Calculating the height of the tide at a Secondary Port.

(1) Insert these figures as appropriate in boxes 1, 2, 3 and 4 in Fig. 9(8). The time differences are + 0040 for HW Devonport at 1800, and + 0025 for HW Devonport at 0100. By interpolation, the difference for HW Devonport at 0023 is + 0026 (insert in box 5). The time differences for LW are 0000, so insert this figure in box 6.

(2) Examination of the tide tables in this particular example would show that the date is soon after neaps, so the height differences can be taken as:

HW − 0.8 (insert in box 7)
LW − 0.3 (insert in box 8).

(3) Thence calculate the predicted times and heights at Teignmouth by taking the figures in boxes 1, 2, 3 and 4 and adding or subtracting the figures in boxes 5, 6, 7 and 8, entering the results in boxes 9, 10, 11 and 12.

(4) Then calculate the ranges. For the Standard Port, Devonport, the range is box 3 minus box 4, and the result is entered in box 14. For the Secondary Port, Teignmouth, the range is box 11 minus box 12, and the result is entered in box 15.

Next work down the bottom part of the diagram, and insert:

(5) In box 16, time required   0300
(6) In box 17, time of HW
Teignmouth   0049 (box 9)
(7) In box 18, the interval   0211 (box 16 minus box 17)

If the Standard Port had no special tidal curve, one of the Standard Curves in Fig. 9(6) would be used – taking the correct curve for the interval between HW and LW on the Falling Tide side of the diagram. In this case, however, special curves are available for Devonport, as shown in Fig. 9(9), and should be used. Since the tides are nearer neaps than springs, select the neap curve (the lower one).

(8) In box 19, the factor 0.74
from neap curve, for
interval + 2^h 11^m
(9) In box 20, the factor   1.85 (box 19
multiplied by range   multiplied by
at Secondary Port   box 15)
(10) In box 21, the   1.4 (box 12
height of LW
(11) In box 22, the   3.25 (box 20 plus
height required at   box 21)
0300 GMT

Because the date is between springs and neaps, a more accurate prediction could be obtained by also working out the same calculation but using the spring curve. This gives a height of 3.35m at 0300. Interpolating, the predicted height at Teignmouth at 0300 GMT on 21 May is 3.28m (say 3.3m). Note that this height is referred to chart datum at Teignmouth.

DEVONPORT
MEAN SPRING AND NEAP CURVES

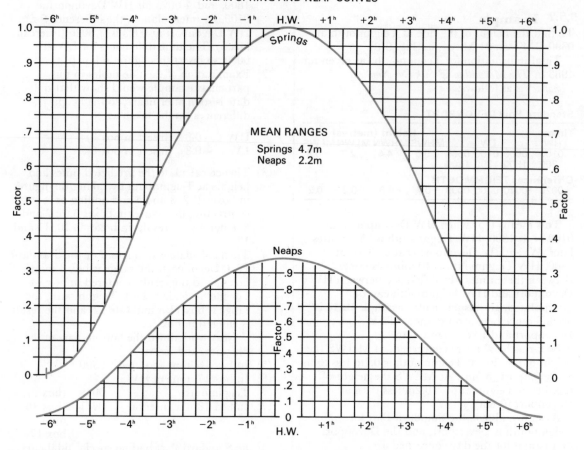

MEAN RANGES

Springs 4.7m
Neaps 2.2m

Fig. 9(9) Special tidal curves for Devonport.

9.6 Calculations of times at which tide reaches certain heights

9.6.1 Tidal curves – procedure

The depth of water is the height of the tide plus the charted depth. If it is required to calculate when there will be, say, 4 metres at a certain point, and the depth on the chart is 2.5 metres, it is possible to calculate, as shown below, when the height of the tide will be 1.5 metres, giving the required depth.

In Fig. 9(7), carry out the same steps on the top half as when calculating the height at a given time. On the lower half of the diagram, start at the bottom right corner. Insert the height required (in the example above 1.5 metres) in box 22, height of LW in box 21 (obtained from box 12) which gives the rise above LW (22–21). Enter the factor, which is the rise above LW (box

20) divided by the range (box 15). From the appropriate curve on the Standard Tidal Curves (selected and interpolated if necessary according to the duration (box 13)) read off the interval. If the Standard Port concerned has special tidal curves provided, these should be used instead of Fig. 9(6). Then from the factor on the vertical scale, run across horizontally until meeting the selected curve. From this point move vertically upwards and read off the interval on the horizontal scale. The time of HW (box 9 or 17) plus or minus the interval gives the time at which the required depth will be reached.

Tidal curves for individual ports are given for springs and neaps. Select the appropriate curve according to the predicted range that day. Usually the factor from the spring curve suffices, but, where necessary, greater accuracy can be obtained by interpolating between the two curves, using the range at the Standard Port as argument.

9.6.2 Example

To find the time at which tide will reach a height

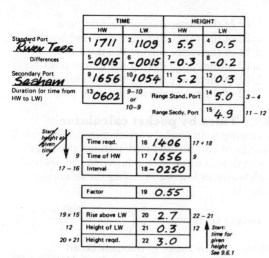

	TIME		HEIGHT	
	HW	LW	HW	LW
Standard Port **River Tees**	¹1711	²1109	³5.5	⁴0.5
Differences	⁵-0015	⁶-0015	⁷-0.3	⁸-0.2
Secondary Port **Seaham**	⁹1656	¹⁰1054	¹¹5.2	¹²0.3
Duration (or time from HW to LW)	¹³0602	9–10 or 10–9	Range Stand. Port	¹⁴5.0 3–4
			Range Secdy. Port	¹⁵4.9 11–12

Start height at given time 9	Time reqd.	16 **1406**	17+18
17–16	Time of HW	17 **1656**	9
	Interval	18 **–0250**	

	Factor	19 **0.55**	

19 x 15	Rise above LW	20 **2.7**	22–21
12	Height of LW	21 **0.3**	12 Start: time for given height See 9.6.1
20+21	Height reqd.	22 **3.0**	

Fig. 9(10) Calculating the time at which the tide will reach a specific height.

of 3m some time after 1000 GMT at Seaham on 12 July, as illustrated in Fig. 9(10).

Standard Port predictions:

River Tees	0435	5.5
(entrance)	1109	0.5
12 July	1711	5.5
	2326	0.9

Insert times and heights in boxes 1, 2, 3 and 4. From the information given for Seaham, insert the differences in boxes 5, 6, 7 and 8. As it happens, the time differences for Seaham are all the same; otherwise interpolation would be necessary, as explained in 9.5.2. Since the date is close to springs, the height differences for MHWS and MLWS can be assumed. Then enter the predicted times and heights for Seaham in boxes 9, 10, 11 and 12:

Then fill in:

(1) Duration (difference in time between box 9 and box 10) in box 13.
(2) Range at Standard Port (height of HW, box 3, minus height of LW, box 4) in box 14.
(3) Range at Secondary Port (height of HW, box 11, minus height of LW, box 12) in box 15.

Then, working up from the bottom of the diagram, insert:

(4) In box 22, height required — 3.0
(5) In box 21, height of LW at Seaham — 0.3 (box 12)
(6) In box 20, the rise above LW — 2.7 (box 22 minus box 21)
(7) In box 19, the factor — 0.55 (rise, box 20, divided by range, box 15)
(8) In box 18, the interval — –0250 (from the rising tide curve in Fig. 9(6) for 6h duration and factor of 0.55)

(9) In box 17, time of HW — 1656 (box 9)
(10) In box 16, the time when tide reaches 3m — 1406 (box 17 minus box 18)

To facilitate such calculations, a perspex sheet or a sheet of tracing paper can be placed over the blank diagram in Fig. 9(7).

9.7 Calculations of clearances under bridges etc.

It is sometimes necessary to calculate whether a boat can pass underneath such objects as bridges or power cables. The heights of such objects are shown on the chart above MHWS, so the clearance will nearly always be greater than the figure shown. The height is shown in metres on metric charts, but in feet on older charts. It is sometimes useful to draw a diagram, as illustrated in Fig. 9(11), which shows how the measurements are related to chart datum.

Clearance = (Elevation of object + height of MHWS) – (height of tide at the time + height of mast above water).

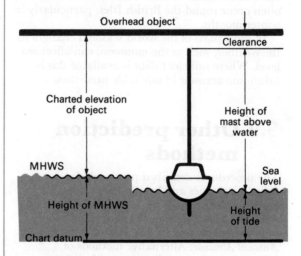

Fig. 9(11) Calculating clearance under bridges etc.

9.8 Meteorological conditions

Meteorological conditions can have a significant effect on tides and tidal streams. Sea level tends to rise in the direction towards which the wind is blowing, and to be lowered in the other direction. The stronger the wind and the longer it blows, the greater the effect. If the wind changes direction significantly – say from south to north – it can cause an oscillation of sea level that greatly affects predicted heights of tide.

271

Strong winds blowing along a coast can establish long waves which raise sea level at their crest and lower it at their trough. Under exceptional conditions this can raise the height of the tide by two or three metres in what is known as a storm surge; conversely a negative surge can lower the height of low water by one or two metres, which may be more serious for yachtsmen. The southern North Sea is an area which is particularly affected by storm surges and by negative surges, especially in winter months.

Tidal heights are predicted for average barometric pressure. When the barometer is high, tidal heights are likely to be lower than predicted, and vice versa. A change of 34 millibars (1in (2.5cm) of mercury) can cause a change of 1ft (0.3m) in the height of sea level, although this may not occur immediately. Severe conditions giving rise to a storm surge, as described above, are likely to be caused by a deep depression, and the low barometric pressure tends to raise sea level still more. The result of these abnormal conditions is naturally more devastating at springs than at neaps.

An intense depression or the passage of a line squall can have local effects on the height of water by setting up what is known as a seiche, which can raise or lower sea level a metre or more in the space of a few minutes. Seiches quite often occur round the British Isles, particularly in winter months.

In some parts of the world seasonal changes in the weather, such as the monsoon, can affect sea level. Where sufficient data is available this is taken into account in tide table predictions.

9.9 Other prediction methods

The procedures described previously for calculating times and heights etc of tides are based on the methods recommended when using *Admiralty Tide Tables*, or the equivalent tables published each year in *The Macmillan & Silk Cut Nautical Almanac*. Alternative methods of calculating tides are given below. In other countries, tide tables may employ different methods for calculating heights at intermediate times and resolving similar problems.

9.9.1 Twelfths Rule
To obtain a rough approximation to the height of the tide between high water and low water, it is possible to use the 'Twelfths Rule'. It must be remembered, however, that unless the tide at the place in question follows a regular pattern (as indicated by the curves in Fig. 9(6), where the rate of rise and fall is proportional to the interval, defined in 9.2.12) the method can be very misleading. The rule assumes that the rise and fall of the tide is:

1/12 of the range during the first hour
2/12 of the range during the second hour
3/12 of the range during the third hour
3/12 of the range during the fourth hour
2/12 of the range during the fifth hour
1/12 of the range during the sixth hour

9.9.2 Tides by pocket calculator
Assuming a sinusoidal variation in tide height, a calculator can be used to determine the height correction to be applied relative to the nearest high water or low water, using the following formula:

$$\text{Height correction} = \frac{R}{2}\left(1 - \cos\frac{180 \times t}{T}\right)$$

where
R = range of tide concerned
t = interval from nearest HW or LW
T = duration of rise or fall

More advanced scientific calculators can be programmed to provide heights of tide for a limited number of places at any time required.

A calculator can also be used for applying the Admiralty method of tidal prediction, which is described in 9.9.5.

9.9.3 French tidal coefficients
In France a coefficient is used to show the size of each tide on each day of the year. These figures are based on a scale for which the reference coefficients are as follows:

C = 120 for the biggest range of tide
C = 95 for Mean Spring tides
C = 70 for an average range of tide
C = 45 for Mean Neap tides
C = 20 for the smallest range of tide

These coefficients are used both for tidal calculations and also for estimating the rate of tidal streams.

In the scale above it is apparent that the range of the biggest spring tide is six times the range of the smallest neap tide.

Apart from the table of coefficients, French tide tables provide similar information to that contained in *Admiralty Tide Tables*, if in a different form. The French also publish a very useful table which gives the height of tide every 15 minutes at certain places where the tidal regime is irregular.

The terms shown in the table below are useful in order to understand tidal information displayed in French ports:

High water	Pleine mer (PM)
Low water	Basse mer (BM)
Springs	Vives-eaux (VE)
Neaps	Mortes-eaux (ME)
Chart datum	Zero des cartes
MHWS	Pleine mer moyenne de VE
MHWN	Pleine mer moyenne de ME
MLWN	Basse mer moyenne de ME
MLWS	Basse mer moyenne de VE
GMT	Temps universel (TU)

9.9.4 Co-tidal and co-range charts

These charts show lines of equal times and equal range of tides for certain selected areas, including the United Kingdom (chart 5058), Dungeness to Hoek van Holland (chart 5057), and the southern North Sea (chart 5059).

Some tidal systems centre round what is called an amphidromic point, where the range is very small but increases in an outward direction, while the times of high and low water progress in either a clockwise or anti-clockwise direction round this centre. A system of this type is centred in the southern North Sea.

Near the amphidromic points the range of tide may change quite considerably in only a short distance – as for example in the North Sea by as much as 3ft (1m) in 15 nautical miles. Co-tidal and co-range charts enable predictions for the times and heights of tide at positions offshore to be obtained, whereas tide tables only provide predictions for coastal places.

The actual lines on the chart show Mean High Water Interval, defined as the mean time interval between the passage of the Moon over the Greenwich meridian and the time of the next high water at the place concerned, and Mean Spring Range, defined as the difference in level between Mean High Water Springs and Mean Low Water Springs. Instructions for use are given on the charts.

9.9.5 Harmonic constituents

Harmonic constants are quoted in Part 3 of *Admiralty Tide Tables* for a large number of Secondary Ports, and are for use with the Admiralty Method of Tidal Prediction (NP 159). Harmonic constants are also given for Standard Ports. These figures enable the most accurate prediction possible to be made, both in times of high and low water and in hourly heights between. The degree of accuracy produced by this method is not normally needed by yachtsmen, since meteorological conditions probably produce a greater difference to the prediction which he already has, than the increased accuracy provided by this method. The following brief summary is for interest or for the purist.

The study of tides has been considerably facilitated by the fact that tidal movements are to all intents and purposes linear with respect to the tide generating forces. This means that the resultant tide is the direct sum of all the constituents; for example, if the lunar tide is calculated and then the solar tide is calculated, the resultant tide will be the direct sum of the two, there being no inter-action between the two. The *Admiralty Method of Tidal Prediction* is given in full in NP 159 where a graphic method is used, and a variation on this is given in the introduction to *Admiralty Tide Tables* for those who prefer to use a pocket calculator. The harmonic method of tidal analysis and prediction is based on the principle that a complex curve can be broken down into a number of sine curves and that these can be calculated for future dates, reassembled in their correct relationships and so give predictions of hourly heights of the tide. From these values it is possible to determine the times and heights of the turning points of the curve, which are, of course, high water and low water. The four most important constituents are:

M_2 The Lunar semi-diurnal constituent
S_2 The Solar semi-diurnal constituent
K_1 The Luni-Solar diurnal constituent
O_1 The Lunar diurnal constituent

These four are the ones used for the Admiralty method. Many others can be discovered and normally up to 60 are used in calculating tidal predictions for a Standard Port; in some complex cases up to 120 are used. Distortions of the tidal curve are included by the use of higher harmonics of the basic constituents usually consisting of the Quarter and Sixth diurnals. These are allowed for in the Admiralty method by the use of F_4, f_4, F_6 and f_6.

As the Admiralty method provides hourly or half-hourly heights, details of the shape of the tidal curve can be found. In some cases programs have been written for programable machines so that the user has only to insert the program, insert the data and then run off hourly heights. As this method is universal, it has been used for ports where no suitable Standard Port is available.

9.9.6 Tidal data on Admiralty charts

Large scale charts of the British Isles have a panel which shows the mean heights of high and low water at springs and neaps (i.e. MHWS, MHWN, MLWS and MLWN). This indicates the approximate depths that may be expected at springs and neaps under average conditions, but on occasions the range may be increased by 20 per cent or more.

9.9.7 Establishment of a port

For many centuries seamen have understood that there is a connection between the Moon and the tide. In the Middle Ages mariners predicted the tide from the bearing of the Moon, and in principle this method continued until quite recent times.

Although now only of historical interest, a port's establishment refers to the interval between meridian passage of the Moon and the next high water at the port, and the associated terms (described briefly below) may be found in old pilot books or on charts. Since this interval is nearly constant for any port, it allowed the approximate time of high water to be determined from the age of the Moon.

High Water Lunitidal Interval (HWI) was normally considered to be the time between the local transit of the Moon and local high water. The mean value of this figure over a lunation of

29 days was defined as the Mean High Water Interval (MHWI), or the corrected establishment.

High Water Full and Change (HWF&C), otherwise referred to as the establishment or the vulgar establishment of the port, was the high water lunitidal interval on the days of full and new moon. Though often used, this quantity was not so convenient as MHWI, but it could be obtained from fewer observations.

9.10 Tidal streams

9.10.1 Tidal streams – general

Tidal streams are the horizontal movement of water caused by the vertical rise and fall of the tide. With semi-diurnal tides, as occur around the British Isles, the tidal streams reverse their direction every six hours or so, and can be predicted by reference to a suitable Standard Port. Tidal streams are quite distinct from ocean currents, which run for long periods in the same direction and are described in 9.11.15.

Tidal streams are important to yachtsmen in many parts of North-West Europe, because they often run at about two knots, and much more strongly in a few areas and at spring tides. In some places they can attain rates of six to eight knots.

Along open coasts the turn of the tidal stream does not necessarily occur at high or low water, but more often near half-tide. The stream usually turns earlier inshore than offshore, sometimes resulting in significant eddies. In open waters round the British Isles, non-tidal currents are not included in tidal stream predictions. However, in rivers and estuaries there is often a permanent current caused by the flow of river water, and such currents are included in tidal stream predictions.

Tidal streams (and currents) are described by the direction towards which they flow, i.e. a tidal stream setting 180° is flowing from north to south.

9.10.2 Tidal stream atlases

For North-West Europe the rate (strength) and set (direction) of tidal streams is shown in 15 booklets of Admiralty *Tidal Stream Atlases*. Each atlas has a set of 13 charts covering the same area, and each chart shows the rate and set of the tidal streams for each hour before and after high water at a Standard Port (usually Dover). It should be remembered that tidal atlases cannot show details of inshore eddies, and that the tide often sets towards the coast in bays.

The set of the stream is shown by arrows which are graded in weight to indicate the rate. Thus → indicates a weak stream, and ⟶ indicates a strong stream. The figures against the arrows give the mean neap and mean spring rates in tenths of a knot. Thus 19,34 indicates a mean neap rate of 1.9 knots, and a mean spring rate of 3.4 knots. The comma indicates the approximate position at which the observations were taken.

For predictions referred to HW Dover it is possible to compute the rate at times between neaps and springs by using the table shown in Fig. 9(12). This table assumes that rates vary directly with the range of tide at Dover. First extract the mean spring and neap rates from the tidal atlas for the position and time required. Then obtain the range of the tide at Dover that day from the tide tables. Join the dots

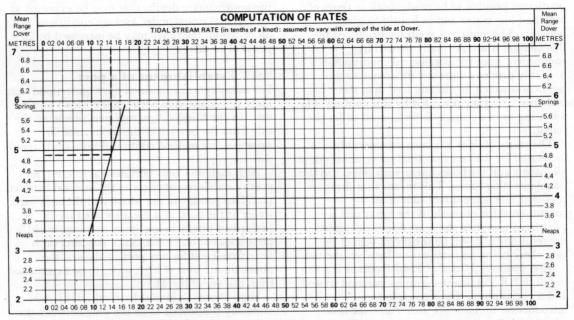

Fig. 9(12) Table for computing tidal stream rates at times between neaps and springs, for tidal stream predictions referred to HW Dover.

representing the mean neap and spring rates with a ruler, and find the point where the ruler intersects the horizontal line representing the range at Dover that day. From that point follow the vertical line to the top or bottom scale and, read off the rate.

Example

It is required to predict the rate of the tidal stream off the northerly point of the Isle of Skye at 0420 on a day when the tidal predictions for Dover are:

0328	1.4
0819	6.3
1602	1.1
2054	6.4

The range of tide is therefore 6.3−1.4 = 4.9m. The appropriate chart in the *Tidal Stream Atlas* NP 218, or in Chapter 10 Area 8 of *The Macmillan & Silk Cut Nautical Almanac*, is that for '4 hours before HW Dover' and this gives a mean neap and a mean spring rate of 09 and 17 respectively (0.9 and 1.7 knots). Referring to the table in Fig. 9(12), Computation of Rates, on the horizontal line marked Neaps, mark the dot above 09 on the horizontal scale; similarly on the line marked Springs, mark the dot below the figure 17 on the horizontal scale. Join these two dots with a straight line. On the vertical scale 'Mean Range Dover', find the range 4.9. From this point follow across horizontally until the pencil line just drawn is cut; from this intersection follow the vertical line to the scale of Tidal Stream Rates, either top or bottom, and read off the predicted rate – in this example it is 14, or 1.4 knots.

A perspex sheet or a sheet of tracing paper can be used on top of the table so as to preserve it for future use.

9.10.3 Tidal stream diamonds on Admiralty charts

On some Admiralty charts there are diamonds to indicate the rate and set of tidal streams at the positions concerned. On the chart a diamond is shown with a letter inside it, thus: ◇B. In a box insert, under a similar diamond, there is shown the latitude and longitude of the position where the observations were made and a table which gives the set, spring rate and neap rate for each hour before and after HW at the Standard Port nominated. Where appropriate the normal river current is included.

The example shown in Fig. 9(13) is for position ◇A on chart 3247, where tidal streams are referred to HW at Milford Haven.

9.10.4 Tidal stream predictions in tide tables

In some parts of the world, tidal streams are not related to the predicted times of high water at any Standard Port, or are completely unrelated to the tidal pattern. For such places daily predictions of maximum rates, slack water and

		◇A	51°41'.8N 5°05'.5W			◇B
	Hours	Dir	Rate Sp	(kn) Np		Dir
Before HW	6		slack			
	5	013	0.3	0.1		
	4	023	0.8	0.4		
	3	027	1.1	0.5		
	2	023	1.0	0.5		
	1	017	0.7	0.		
HW		354	0.3			
After HW	1	214	0.5			
	2	207	0.9			
	3	207				

Fig. 9(13) Tidal stream information on Admiralty chart.

set are given in *Admiralty Tide Tables*, Vols 2 and 3. The information also includes typical tidal stream curves (dominant semi-diurnal, mixture of semi-diurnal and diurnal, and dominant diurnal), and any currents not included in the predictions.

9.10.5 Tidal stream information in Sailing Directions

General descriptions of tidal streams for the areas concerned are given in Admiralty Sailing Directions. In these volumes time references are in four-figure groups, where the first two figures are hours and the last two are minutes. Such references are usually to the nearest five minutes. Those preceded by a minus (−) sign are intervals before HW; those preceded by a plus (+) sign are intervals after HW.

9.11 The sea

9.11.1 How waves are formed

Any sensible yachtsman prefers to sail in smooth water, but once at sea it is inevitable that waves will be encountered. A little knowledge of the subject helps to understand their behaviour and their possible dangers.

Waves are created by wind. Friction between the water and the air moving over it causes energy to be transferred from the wind to the surface of the sea. This energy manifests itself by forming waves, and is the reason that wind speed at sea level is less than at the top of a mast. When wind first starts to blow over a calm sea, small ripples are formed. These result in pressure fluctuations and turbulence above the surface of the water, both of which help to increase the size of the ripples into wavelets and eventually into proper waves. The windward side of each wave is more affected by the wind than the leeward side, and hence each wave collects extra energy from the wind, causing it to grow in size.

The wave making process does not continue indefinitely however. As the size of a wave increases so does its speed of movement, which reduces the speed of the wave relative to the wind, and energy is lost within the wave itself due to the motion of the water, particularly if the wave breaks. So there comes a time when a state of equilibrium is reached, and unless the wind speed changes or the wave reaches shallow water or some other obstruction the wave will continue at a steady size.

9.11.2 Wave forms and definitions

Although waves at sea comprise an infinite variety of sizes and types, it is necessary to consider a train (succession) of theoretical waves in order to study their form and behaviour. Initially it is also necessary to consider waves in deep water, not influenced by the bottom of the sea.

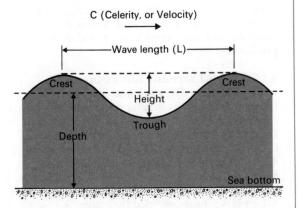

Fig. 9(14) Diagrammatic representation of a wave.

Fig. 9(14) shows in diagrammatic form a wave, and some of the key terms and dimensions which are used to describe it.

In the diagram, C is the celerity (velocity) in ft/sec of the wave, which is moving from left to right. The period of a wave (T) is the time in seconds between two successive crests passing a given point. If the wave length in feet is L,

$$C = \frac{L}{T}$$

In deep water it can be shown that:

$$C = \sqrt{\frac{gL}{2\pi}}$$

(where g = 32.2ft/sec/sec, and π = 3.14) and hence

$$C = 2.26 \times \sqrt{L}$$

From the equations above it follows that:

$$L = 5.12 \times T^2 \quad \text{and}$$
$$C = 5.12 \times T$$

Thus it is shown that whereas the celerity (velocity) of a wave varies directly with its period, its length varies as the square of the period.

If celerity is expressed in knots

$$C = 3.03 \times T$$

Fig. 9(15) shows the relationships between celerity (knots) and wavelength (feet) with wave period (seconds).

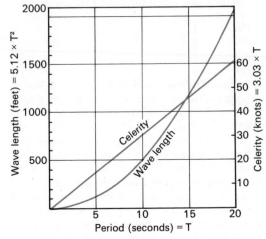

Fig. 9(15) Relationships between celerity and period, and wave length and period of waves.

When a wave passes, any particle of water on or near the surface moves in nearly a circular orbit. Although the wave moves forward, the surface of the sea does not – or only very slightly. If the movement of an object, such as a floating can, is observed it will be seen to move in an almost closed orbit, in a vertical plane: not quite a closed orbit because, as suggested above, there is a small movement of the surface water in the direction of wind and wave.

Particles below the surface also prescribe orbits, the end of each orbit being approximately the same as its starting point. The size of these orbits decreases very quickly with depth below the surface, and becomes negligible at a depth equal to $\frac{3}{4}$ x the wave length.

9.11.3 The sizes of waves

In the open sea, the sizes of waves that are encountered depend on the strength of the wind, the length of time for which it has blown, and the fetch (distance upwind of the observer) over which it is blowing. Thanks to data collected and published by the Marine Information and Advisory Service, of the Institute of Oceanographic Sciences, who have kindly agreed to the publication of Figs. 9(16), 9(17) and 9(18), it is possible to predict wave heights and periods with reasonable accuracy. Such predictions must, however, be for some kind of average value and, as explained below, larger waves can be expected to appear from time to time.

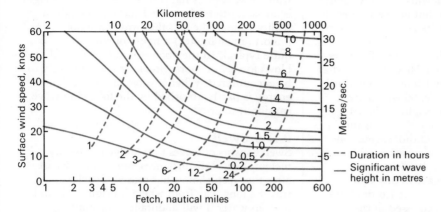

Fig. 9(16) Wave height prediction graph for coastal waters (depth typically 20–200m).

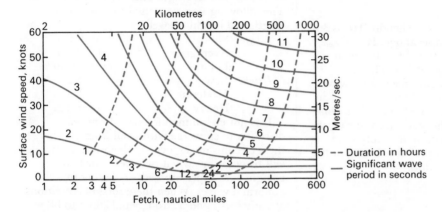

Fig. 9(17) Wave period prediction graph for coastal waters (depth typically 20–200m).

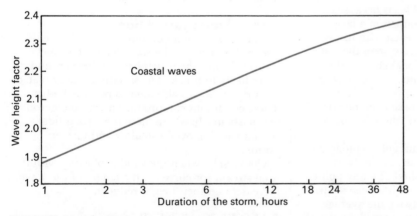

Fig. 9(18) Curve relating wave height factor to duration of storm (coastal waves).

Sometimes strong winds blowing for only a short duration produce higher waves than lesser winds blowing for a long time: on other occasions moderate winds blowing for a considerable time produce larger waves. To use Fig. 9(16), enter the diagram on the left with the surface wind speed in knots. Follow a horizontal line until it meets either the dotted curve for the appropriate duration (in hours) or the vertical line corresponding to the fetch (in nautical miles) as shown on the bottom scale, whichever is reached

first. The predicted height in metres is read from the solid curve intersected at that point. As an example, consider a 30 knot wind blowing for 12 hours over a fetch of 60 nautical miles. Entering the diagram on the left at 30 knots, and moving horizontally to the right, the 60 mile fetch line is reached before the duration of 12 hours, and the resulting height is 3m. Fig. 9(17) is used in a similar way to determine the period. Both these graphs give predictions for coastal waters, with depths typically 20–200m. Except in very strong winds the predicted wave heights are only slightly too small for deeper waters, but in deep water the wave periods will be about 10–20 per cent longer than suggested by Fig. 9(17).

The predicted height (H$_S$) obtained from Fig. 9(16) is the 'Significant Wave Height', defined as the average value of the heights of the one-third highest waves. If, for example, 60 waves are observed, H$_S$ is the average height of the 20 biggest. The 'Significant Wave Period' is the average value of the periods of those same (one-third highest) waves. Theory, together with actual measurements at sea, show that on average the highest single wave in any ten-minute period is likely to be about 1.6 times the significant wave height, as expressed in the formula:

$$H_{max(10\ min)} = 1.6 \times H_S$$

Hence, if the significant wave height (H$_S$) is 3m, as determined in the example above, H$_{max(10\ min)}$ will be 4.8m. Having calculated this figure, it is then possible to refer to Fig. 9(18). This is a graph of 'Wave Height Factor' for coastal waves plotted against the duration of gale conditions in hours. If, as in the example used above, the wind has blown for 12 hours, the factor from the curve is 2.23 and this figure is used to multiply H$_{max(10\ min)}$ to give the most probable height of the highest wave in the storm, thus:

$$4.8 \times 2.23 = 10.7m.$$

9.11.4 Freak waves

Observation at sea makes one realise that waves vary considerably in height. This is because any individual wave in practice consists of a large number of wave components, each with its own height and period. In any wave system the faster components (with longer periods) continually overtake the slower components. When crests get into step with each other, exceptionally large waves occur. When crests of some components coincide with troughs of others, there is a brief spell of relative calm.

In a small yacht it is very difficult to judge the heights of waves with any accuracy, but wave recording stations are established at many points around the United Kingdom. It has been shown that about one wave in 23 is twice the average height, and one in 1175 is three times the average height. Only about one wave in 300,000 (the equivalent of about a month at sea) exceeds four times the average height, and such a wave is very seldom encountered by yachtsmen or recorded on any instrument. In the foregoing it should be noted that average height corresponds to about 0.6 times the significant wave height, as defined previously.

9.11.5 Breaking waves

As the wind speed increases, some waves become too steep, and tend to break. In a theoretical train of waves this happens when the wave height is one-seventh of the wave length, although in reality (due to the fact that waves are not uniform in character) a figure of one-twelfth is quite typical. In the open sea, once the wind blows force 7 or more, breaking seas are likely to be encountered. When a wave breaks, its kinetic energy is partly absorbed by the following wave, causing it to grow.

9.11.6 Swell

Swell consists of waves that are generated by meteorological disturbances, and which persist after that disturbance has ceased. Swell can travel a long way from where it originated, and in deep water it will maintain a constant direction. With distance travelled its height decreases, but its length and speed stay the same. The following terms are used to describe the length and height of swell:

Length –	Short	0–100 m
	Average	100–200 m
	Long	over 200 m
Height –	Low	0–2 m
	Moderate	2–4 m
	Heavy	over 4 m

It is not uncommon for swell from one direction to converge with swell from another. In these circumstances, even in deep water, there will be occasions when two crests (or two troughs) are superimposed – resulting in abnormal waves. When these sorts of conditions already exist, and a strong wind starts to blow from some other direction, a very confused and dangerous sea is likely to result.

9.11.7 Wind against tide

When a wave system encounters an adverse tidal stream (or current) the wave length becomes shorter. Hence the waves become steeper, and more likely to break. The situation is aggravated because the waves also tend to become higher. These conditions can produce a very dangerous sea, particularly where there is a strong tidal stream running over a shallow and uneven bottom.

Conversely, when the wind is blowing with the tidal stream (or current), the length of the waves increases and their height reduces.

9.11.8 Waves in shallow water

When waves move into shallow water they start to feel the effect of the sea bottom once the depth equals three-quarters of the wave length. Due to friction against the bottom, the orbiting movement of the water beneath the wave is upset and the celerity of the wave is reduced.

Because C = L/T (see 9.11.2 above) the wave length is reduced, and the waves become steeper – to the point where they break, a process which is also greatly assisted by the diminishing depth of water.

When a wave breaks upon a beach its total

energy content is destroyed, as anybody who has experienced heavy surf can testify. The force generated by breaking waves can be very considerable, and has been known to shift structures weighing hundreds of tons. As a wave starts to break some of the surface water moves forward with the wave form itself. In the open sea this energy, from a breaking wave, is transferred to other overtaking waves, but when approaching a beach the whole accumulated force is spent upon the shore. This moving mass of water is called a 'wave of translation'.

A special situation arises when waves of translation are approaching an estuary. As they meet the outflowing river current the breaking wave can continue for a great distance upstream as a special form of bore – see 9.11.14.

9.11.9 Bars
When, due to the local configuration of the shelving bottom, waves tend to break repeatedly at a certain distance from the shore, a bar may be formed. Smaller waves may pass over the bar without breaking, but they are affected by the shallow water, which shortens their wave length. Larger waves break on the bar, throwing large quantities of water over it so that there is a tendency for the sea level inshore of the bar to rise. This water has to return seawards, often through one or more channels scoured through a narrow part of the bar – an extremely dangerous area for boats and swimmers.

Many popular yachting harbours are fronted by a bar. In moderate weather most such bars do not present any great hazard, but it is normally advisable to cross them before (and not after) local high water. Some bars are potentially very dangerous however, and a stretch of harmless-looking water can soon be transformed into a death trap once the ebb starts to run, particularly if there is any strength of wind blowing onshore.

9.11.10 Overfalls and tide races
Some of the worst sea conditions that can be experienced occur quite close to land – off headlands where the tidal stream runs strongly. Any promontory (or a narrow channel, say between two islands) constricts the natural flow of the tidal stream, and hence speeds it up. If at the same time the sea bottom is irregular in depth, considerable turbulence can be created in the area concerned. These factors, combined with wind blowing against the tidal stream, can create tide races where very dangerous overfalls are formed – conditions naturally being worst at spring tides and in gale force winds.

The more significant tide races can be unpleasant for a small yacht even in good conditions and should be avoided at all times. Others are passable in safety in good weather at the right state of the tide – usually at slack water. Any tide race, or area where there are heavy overfalls, should be given a wide berth in bad

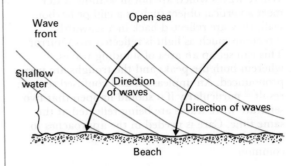

Fig. 9(19) Refraction of waves approaching a beach.

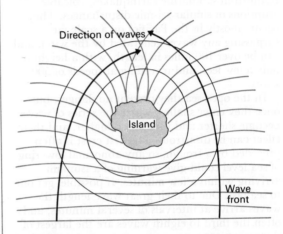

Fig. 9(20) Refraction of waves round an island.

weather, or when wind of any strength is against the tide.

9.11.11 Refraction of waves
When waves pass from one depth of water to another – as happens when they met a coastline at an angle, or when they pass the end of a headland, or down either side of an island – they are refracted (or bent) in much the same way as a ray of light is bent when passing from one medium to another.

The most common example of this is where a train of waves approaches a beach at an angle, as illustrated in Fig. 9(19). As soon as the inshore end of a wave gets into shallow water, it slows down, so that the whole wave train eventually alters course somewhat, and the waves approach the shore roughly parallel to it.

Refraction can be very pronounced round the sides of an island. Where the two refracted wave trains meet on the leeward side of the island there can be an uncomfortable stretch of confused water, just where a peaceful lee might have been anticipated, see Fig. 9(20).

The diffraction of waves occurs as waves spread out after passing an obstruction such as a pronounced headland or a breakwater, tending in general to reduce wave height.

9.11.12 Reflected waves

Where waves which are not in shallow water meet a vertical object such as a cliff or harbour wall, they are reflected back in a seawards direction, much as light is reflected by a mirror. This can set up an area of standing waves, wherein both the peaks and the troughs are very pronounced. An unpleasant and confused sea can result – particularly if it should happen that two separate wave trains are being reflected at the same time. Care is needed in the approaches to harbours, where these conditions are relatively common.

9.11.13 Tsunamis

This Japanese name is given to waves which result from submarine earthquakes, volcanic eruptions or similar seismic disturbances. They occur (mostly in the Pacific) on a scale far surpassing any waves generated by the wind, and can be over 100 miles in length, with a height of only a few feet, and travelling at speeds of 500 knots.

In the open sea they present no danger, but once they enter shallow water the series of waves become shorter and very much higher, and their effect can be disastrous. The first crest is often preceded by a trough, so any abnormal lowering of sea level could give warning of a tsunami arriving within a few minutes. If possible, get out to sea fast. Due to their great wave length the waves arrive at intervals of several minutes, and often the third to eighth waves are the largest of the series.

9.11.14 Bores or eagres

A bore, or eagre, is a form of wave induced by resonant tidal oscillations, which rolls up certain estuaries and rivers. In simple terms they are caused either by the meeting of two tides or, more commonly, by the general constriction of the advancing tide into a narrowing and shelving channel. The effect is increased by spring tides, previous heavy rainfall, following winds and low barometric pressure.

The most impressive bores occur on the Rivers Hooghli, Amazon, Petticodiac (Bay of Fundy), and Chien Tang Kiang in China. In Europe the most noteworthy bore used to be the *mascaret* on the lower Seine, but this is now much reduced due to improvements in the channel and is only significant at springs between Villequiers and Rouen. In Britain the Severn bore starts above Sharpness, but does not fully develop until it reaches Longney, 9 miles (14km) from Gloucester, where it rushes upstream at a height of some 3–5ft (1–1.5m) and is dangerous to boats where it breaks along the banks. The eagre on the River Trent is only slightly less impressive.

9.11.15 Ocean currents

Currents are movements of water that are not caused by the tide. In the navigational context we are concerned with horizontal movement, although out at sea sub-surface currents may have vertical components. Currents are caused by either seasonal or more permanent wind systems blowing over the sea, or by changes in the density of sea water brought about by differences in temperature (rather like air temperature affects the wind). The set of a current is described by the direction in which it flows, so a westerly current flows *to* the west whereas a westerly wind blows *from* the west.

The established atmospheric circulations over the oceans, such as the north-east and south-east trade winds which blow either side of the equator, are the principal causes of currents – the north equatorial currents and the south equatorial currents which flow in the Atlantic, Pacific and Indian Oceans and which in turn result in the flow of compensating counter-currents.

A simplified diagram of the principal currents of the world is shown in Fig. 9(21). This indicates how, in the Atlantic, the north equatorial current is augmented by a split in the south equatorial current off the coast of Brazil, and flows into the Caribbean and the Gulf of Mexico before swinging north up the east coast of North America to form the Gulf Stream. Off Newfoundland the Gulf Stream is deflected by the cold Labrador current, and swings towards Europe. In the North Atlantic part of it divides to form the Canaries current and then to rejoin the north equatorial drift. The rest flows past the British Isles towards Norway.

In southern latitudes there are no land masses to disrupt the west wind drift caused by the Roaring Forties, resulting in a general current running in an easterly direction round the bottom of the world.

Currents are important considerations for major passage making, and more detailed information is available in *Ocean Passages for the World* and in *Meteorology for Mariners*. Notes for particular areas are contained in Admiralty Sailing Directions.

9.11.16 Coriolis effect

Except at the equator, any body moving on the earth's surface is affected by the earth's rotation, and this applies to the water in both ocean currents and tidal streams. This effect, called the Coriolis force, deflects moving water to the right in the northern hemisphere and to the left in the southern hemisphere. The effect is greater in higher latitudes, and in practice typically results in a deflection of 20°. It is the reason that north-flowing currents such as the Gulf Stream and the Kuro Siwo current off Japan, or the south-flowing ones like the Brazil and Agulhas currents, drift away from their respective coasts.

The Coriolis force also influences the bigger range of tide on the French side of the English Channel. Coming up Channel the flood is

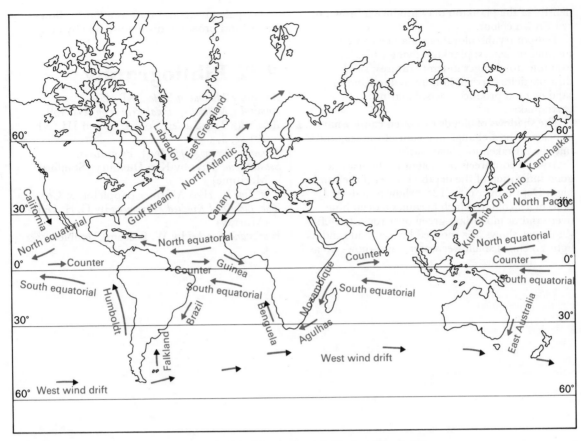

Fig. 9(21) Principal ocean currents of the world (solid arrowheads indicate cold currents).

diverted to the right – towards the French coast. Conversely, on the ebb it is diverted towards the English coast.

9.11.17 Density of sea water

The density of sea water depends on temperature, pressure and salinity. As temperature rises, the density decreases; as pressure rises (with depth below the surface), the density increases; as salinity rises, the density increases.

For normal calculations the density of fresh water at surface level is taken as 1000 kg/m³. Sea water varies from about 1021 kg/m³ in equatorial regions to about 1027 kg/m³ at the poles (at surface level). In general the density of sea water is less in coastal regions than in the open sea. In the depths of the ocean it can reach 1070 kg/m³.

For convenience, density is often expressed in the form *sigma-t*, where:

$$sigma\text{-}t = (\text{density in kg/m}^3 - 1000)$$

Hence a density of 1025.6 kg/m³ has a value of 25.6 in *sigma-t* terms.

9.11.18 Salinity of sea water

For our purposes, the salinity of water may be defined as the amount of dissolved solids present, expressed in parts per thousand. In fresh water the figure is zero, and in the open sea it is typically 35 parts per thousand and generally within the 33–37.5 range. The salinity is less in higher latitudes, in regions of high rainfall, or where there is dilution by rivers or melting ice. Where there is considerable evaporation the figure may reach more than 40 parts per thousand.

The North Atlantic has a higher salinity than the South Atlantic, and the Atlantic as a whole is more saline than the Pacific Ocean.

In estuaries, where rivers and streams flow into the sea, changes in salinity have a great influence on plant and animal life. Salinity fluctuates with the tides, and with the prevailing weather conditions. The well-defined zones in which different species live and breed depend largely on the tolerance of the species concerned to varying degrees of salinity. Nature finds ways to meet these natural changes, but not to resist man's pollution of rivers and estuaries with sewage, pesticides, industrial chemicals, oil and other destructive matter.

9.11.19 The colour of the sea

In the open ocean the natural colour of the sea is a very intense blue, but this is modified in higher latitudes and in coastal regions to a green or blue/green colour due to the presence of plankton (very small animal and vegetable life, floating in the sea). In a few areas, such as the Red Sea, the density of the plankton may produce a brown or red/brown colour.

Temporary discolorations may be caused by a number of factors: plankton dying (due, for example, to changes in temperature); sand or dust particles carried offshore by the wind; or sand or mud produced by submarine earthquakes.

The shadows of clouds can often cause what appears to be a change in colour of the sea, and may be mistaken for shoal water.

Around coral reefs the colour of the sea is a good indication of the depth of water if the sun is high. Depths over 60ft (18m) show as a deep blue-black colour, which becomes a deep blue over sand or more dark green over rock. In 30ft (9m) rock shows as a mottled brown, and sand as light green. In shallower water, sand shows up as a very pale green, and rock as a light yellow-brown and probably distinguishable by eye.

9.12 **Bibliography**

Admiralty Manual of Tides (NP 120)
Admiralty Method of Tidal Prediction (NP 159)
Admiralty Tide Tables, Vols. I, II and III (NP 201, 2, 3)
Dynamic Oceanography by J. Proudman
Seastate and Tides by Ken Duxbury (Stanford Maritime)
The Tide by H. A Marmer (Appleton & Co)
The Tides and Kindred Phenomena by G. H. Darwin (Murray)
Waves and Beaches by W. Bascom (Doubleday & Co.)

Chapter 10

Hulls

Contents

10.1 Design considerations

In any discussion on hull types and forms it is
necessary to understand the meaning of terms like
displacement, centre of buoyancy, stability,
balance etc. Like many technical terms the jargon
obscures what is often simple and straightforward.

10.1.1 Displacement

This is simply the weight of the vessel in tons,
tonnes, pounds or kilogrammes, complete with
everything on board. That includes ballast,
stores, engine, water, fuel, personal gear etc, so
that a boat's displacement varies from day to
day. However, if a displacement is quoted it can
be assumed to mean the weight of the craft ready
for sea (excluding items of personal gear) with
half-full tanks.

If a boat were lowered into a tank brim full of
water, some of it would spill over the edge as the
craft settled down to its floating level. If the weight
of that displaced water were measured it would be

found to be the same as the weight of the boat. The denser the liquid in which a vessel is floating the smaller will be the amount (volume) required to equal the weight of the boat. Thus, since salt water is slightly denser (or heavier) than fresh water less volume will be required to support the craft which will consequently float slightly higher in the water.

10.1.2 Centres of buoyancy and gravity

If the water in that tank had been frozen solid after the boat had been lowered in, and she was then taken out again, a hollow would remain representing the shape of the underwater hull of the craft. That hollow must have a centre of area, both longitudinally and vertically. After all, if a cast of the shape were taken in concrete, for example, it would have a balancing point which would be its centre of area. The longitudinal position of that centre of area is called the longitudinal centre of buoyancy (LCB) and its vertical position, the vertical centre of buoyancy (VCB). Since the concrete balanced about that point, so must the boat, and her fore and aft centre of weight, the longitudinal centre of gravity (LCG), must fall in the same line as the LCB.

10.1.3 The lines plan

Of course a designer cannot rely on floating a model of his proposed creation in a tank and then finding the weight of water displaced. Nor can he fiddle with lumps of concrete trying to find a balance point (which would be very difficult anyway) so he draws the boat in three-dimensional form and does the necessary

calculations from that plan. This drawing is called the lines plan and Fig. 10(1) shows the basic lines of a simple 10ft (3m) dinghy. Three views are drawn: the profile (a view looking from one side of the boat which has been sliced down the middle); a plan view (looking down from above on to the deck); and a sectional view with the cross-section shape of the boat shown at various equally-spaced points (known as stations) along its length. Convention has it that the bow points to the right and one side only is drawn. The sections forward of 'midships and that of midships are shown on the right-hand side of the centreline, and the aft sections on the left-hand side.

Buttocks

It is assumed that the boat is again sliced longitudinally but at some specified distance out from the centreline. This slice will produce a definite shape on the profile view but will only be seen as straight lines on the other two views. One buttock is shown on the dinghy plan.

Waterlines

Sometimes called level lines, waterlines are the shapes produced if the boat were sliced longitudinally on a plane parallel to the line at which she floats. Waterlines will thus have a definite shape on the plan view but will show up only as straight lines on the profile and sectional views. Two waterlines, one above and one on the LWL (which is the load waterline and is the actual level at which the vessel is intended to float) are shown.

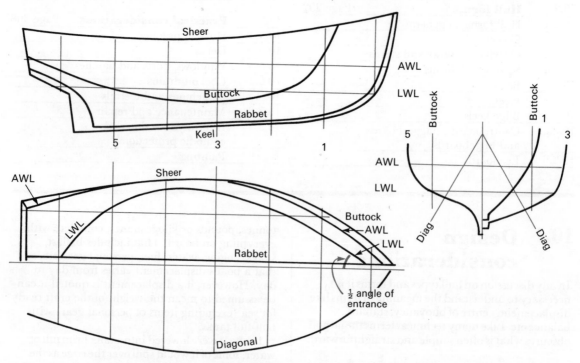

Fig. 10(1) An outline lines plan of a 10ft (3m) dinghy. This is a wooden boat and so the rabbet line is shown. That is where the planking joins the backbone of the vessel and is, presumably, a corruption of the word rebate.

Diagonals

Further slices may be taken running diagonally out from the fore and aft centreline, and one is shown. Their shape will normally be plotted on the plan view and their angle defined on the sectional view.

Fairing up

The general shape of the boat and of the buttocks, waterlines and so forth are drawn to suit the designer's beliefs as to what is required to get the best performance from the boat in whatever role she is cast. However, each of the different lines must be fair and smooth and agree with other lines. A buttock, for instance, must have a fair curve in profile but at the same time it has a definite height above or below the load waterline at each station along its length. The sections must correspond exactly. Waterlines must have a fair curve in plan view but they also have a definite width out from the centreline at each station. So a line drawn through the buttock heights and waterline widths must produce a fair and desirable curve at each section. The same principle applies to diagonals. Ensuring that all this is so is the basic task of the fairing processes that a designer has to go through.

Results

From the lines plan the area of the hull below LWL can be calculated in cubic feet or cubic metres and also the position of the LCB and VCB. The designer will have judged from past experience the best position of the LCB, and he will have totted up the various weights that comprise a boat to discover the probable actual displacement. This must agree with, or be near enough to, the displacement calculated from the lines plan. If he is wrong the boat will float higher or lower in the water than planned. Though at this stage he has probably not worked out exactly where the longitudinal centre of gravity of all the weights lies, he will have a good approximate idea and now knows how the final and shiftable weights will have to be disposed to put the LCG over the LCB. When that figure of volume in cubic feet below the LWL is known it can be divided by 35 to give tons displacement (in imperial units there are 35 cu ft of sea water to the ton). Using the metric system, one cubic metre of underwater volume represents 1000kg of displacement by weight.

10.1.4 Offsets

A lines plan itself is not of much use to a builder, who will not want to have to scale off dimensions from a small-scale plan. So the designer does the job for him, giving dimensions out from the centreline for the deck line and all waterlines: heights from a base line outside the vessel or above and below LWL for all the buttocks plus the keel and deck lines; and distances down the diagonals from centreline. The bow and stern profiles will also be dimensioned.

All these measurements are set down on what is known as an offset table. The builder then makes patterns from these or draws out the whole boat again, full size, on the mould loft floor. He can then make templates for anything he wants at any position he wants (not just at the stations drawn by the designer) off the floor. The designer will have been working to quite a small scale ranging, perhaps, from 1/5th to 1/8th full size on a dinghy to 1/24th or 1/25th full size on a biggish boat, so inaccuracies are bound to creep into his offsets.

10.1.5 Tonnage

As stated in 10.1.1, displacement is the actual weight of the boat in whatever state of readiness for sea has been decided upon. There are, however, other forms of tonnage, the principal ones being gross tonnage and register tonnage. Neither is a weight at all but is the estimated internal volume of the boat less exemptions and deductions. Either the internal volume in cubic feet is divided by 100 when using imperial units or the volume in cubic metres is divided by 2.83 to give the same result in notional tons. The word tonnage is confusing but probably derives from the fact that cargo vessels were once assessed on how many tuns, or casks, of wine they could carry. Anyway, from the total internal volume certain exempted spaces such as double bottom tanks and the wheelhouse are subtracted to give gross tonnage. From the gross figure are deducted spaces such as crews' quarters, chart room and so forth to give register tonnage. Passenger ship tonnages are normally quoted in gross tons.

Cargo ships, on the other hand, usually deal in what is called deadweight. This is the weight in tons, or tonnes, that a ship can carry when loaded to her maximum permitted draught and includes provisions, fuel and water as well as cargo. What a ship weighs when completely empty is called Lightship, and therefore Lightship + Deadweight = Load Displacement. When warship tonnages are quoted these are usually actual displacement tons but yachts were once measured in what was termed Thames Tonnage, which again had nothing to do with weight. For further information on tonnage measurement see Chapter 2(2.5).

10.1.6 Centre of lateral resistance

From the lines plan, or more specifically from the underwater profile, the centre of lateral resistance (CLR) can be found. In essence this is the centre of area of the underwater profile and is assumed to be the spot around which the vessel pivots under the influence of wind, waves or sail power. If that below-water profile were traced out on a piece of tracing paper and then cut out to shape, folded longitudinally a few times to stiffen it and then balanced on a compass point, that balancing point would be the centre of area, centre of lateral resistance or CLR.

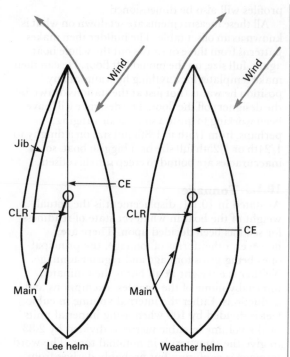

Lee helm   Weather helm

Fig. 10(2) The left-hand sketch shows a yacht with jib and mainsail set, but the centre of effort of the sail plan is so far forward that is causes lee helm. With the jib doused the situation changes and the boat has weather helm.

10.1.7 Centre of effort

The centre of effort (CE) is the combined, overall centre of area of all the sails and is taken to be the centre through which the wind pressure acts, though even a motor boat can have a centre of effort which would be the centre of profile area of hull and superstructure. On yachts the sails are assumed to be fore and aft as they would be shown on a profile drawing of the craft.

The distance between the centre of lateral resistance and the centre of effort is known as the 'lead' and is generally expressed as a percentage of the waterline length. Both these centres move with the boat under way and as Fig. 10(2) shows, for the boat to have 'weather helm' (that is, for the bows to have a bias towards turning into the wind) the centre of effort must be aft of the centre of lateral resistance. In fact when designing a sail plan the opposite is assumed to be the case for the CE is nearly always positioned well ahead of the CLR. The amount these two centres move is impossible to predict and the correct amount of 'lead' is judged by past results. A certain amount of weather helm is desirable because it causes the bows to swing into the wind once the helm is put down and so speeds tacking. The opposite would be the case with 'lee helm' where the bows want to swing away from the wind and have to be forced round when turning through the wind. Weather helm is also safer since if the tiller is abandoned the boat will come up into the wind and stop. A yacht with weather helm can also sail closer to the wind than one with lee helm.

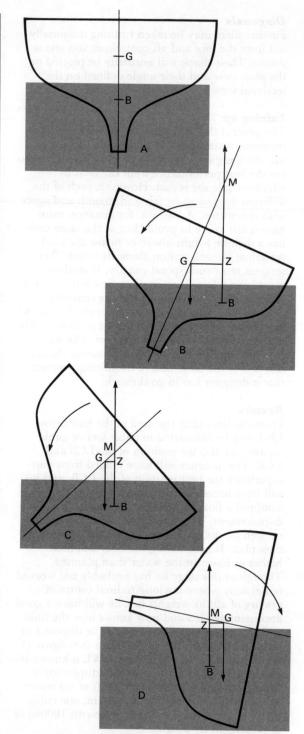

Fig. 10(3) A section through the midship section of a yacht showing the shift in the centre of buoyancy (B) at different angles of heel and its effect on stability. In the bottom, right-hand sketch the position of M has changed from being above G to being below it, and the twisting forces through G and B are now acting to capsize the vessel.

10.1.8 Aspect ratio

Technically this is the length of the chord of any surface measured normally to the direction of motion divided by the chord in the line of motion. In practice this means, for instance, that the aspect ratio of a rudder is its depth divided by its fore and aft length; of a sail, its vertical height (e.g. the luff) divided by its foot length; for a bilge keel, its depth into the water divided by its fore and aft length. Generally the higher the aspect ratio the more efficient the object will be. Thus a mainsail with a luff five times as long as its foot will be more efficient than one with a ratio of only 2:1, whatever its other disadvantages.

10.1.9 Stability

As a boat heels her underwater shape changes since a new length of hull is immersed and an original length emerges. The centre of buoyancy moves across to be the centre of area of this new immersed volume. Fig. 10(3) shows this on one section through the hull. The centre of buoyancy will move forward or aft too, since the boat will trim by bow or stern to accord with the entirely new underwater shape, but that is a complication best ignored at the moment. Only its transverse shift need be considered in this section on stability. The buoyancy of the water keeping the boat afloat will act vertically upwards through that centre of buoyancy (B) while the weight of the boat acts vertically downwards through its centre of gravity (G) and however much the boat heels, in theory at any rate, the centre of gravity does not shift. That implies that nothing breaks loose and falls to leeward and there is no loose water in the bilge. Anyway, those two forces through G and B are acting in opposite directions and trying to twist the boat upright or to capsize her.

10.1.10 Metacentric height

A vertical line (representing the forces of buoyancy) extended up through B, the centre of buoyancy, will cross the inclined centreline of the vessel at some point M, and that point is known at the metacentre. The distance between G (the centre of gravity) and M is called the metacentric height, or GM. As shown on Fig. 10(3) the distance from G to M will vary according to the angle of heel but as long as the twisting forces are acting to urge the boat back on to an even keel, she is stable. At some angle of heel on most craft, though, the forces change sides in relation to each other and the twisting moment they exert is trying to capsize the vessel, and she is then unstable.

10.1.11 Curves and range of stability

The distance from G to M may be plotted on a base of angle of heel and is known as a stability curve. A self-righting yacht would have positive stability up to 180° (that is, the twisting couple will always be trying to right her) and a representative curve showing such stability together with a curve for a more normal boat is shown on Fig. 10(4). The angle to which a yacht

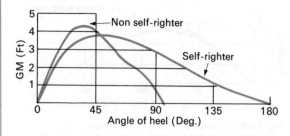

Fig. 10(4) A stability curve for self-righting and non self-righting craft. The latter would capsize at an angle of heel of greater than about 95 deg. The former would right herself from any angle of heel.

may heel before she becomes unstable is known as her range of stability.

10.1.12 Righting levers and moments

Though GM is a measure of stability, an even better one might be the distance between the lines through G and B, Fig. 10(3). This is GZ and is called the righting lever. The length GZ at different angles of heel may also be plotted on a base of heel angle. If the distance GZ were multiplied by the boat's displacement, the result would be called the righting moment and would be a measure of the force actually trying to twist the boat back upright (or to capsize her when she was past her range of positive stability).

10.1.13 Factors affecting stability
Height of centre of gravity
On any boat the lower the centre of gravity the better as far as stability is concerned, and Fig. 10(5) shows the stability curves for two

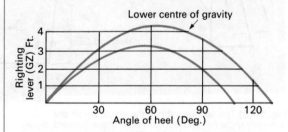

Fig. 10(5) The effect of lowering the centre of gravity (probably by adding weight to the keel or installing inside ballast on an unballasted boat) is nearly always to improve stability at all angles (the distance between the forces acting through G and B being greater) and to increase the range at which the craft is still stable.

vessels with different VCG heights. The marked effect on the righting levers can be seen. A low centre of gravity is normally achieved by installing ballast as low as possible and many yachts with a big outside ballast keel are self-righting in theory. The words 'in theory' are used advisedly since if, as the boat rolls, water can come aboard and flood the accommodation its effect will be to raise the position of the VCG once the boat is well heeled.

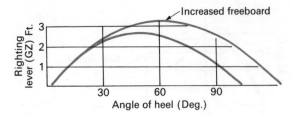

Fig. 10(6) Increasing freeboard – as long as it can be done without raising the height of the centre of gravity too much – generally increases stability a modest amount and, more importantly, lengthens the range of stability.

Freeboard

Increasing freeboard will normally give greater stability provided that the VCG does not rise too far in sympathy. As the boat heels, there are more topsides available than on a boat with lower freeboard to increase the buoyancy and strive to push her back on an even keel.
Fig. 10(6) shows the likely result of increasing freeboard on stability curves.

Beam

Increasing beam will also improve stability for much the same reason as increasing freeboard, but the usual effect is also to reduce the range of stability, see Fig. 10(7).

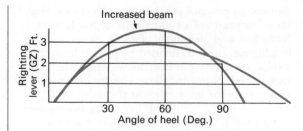

Fig. 10(7) Increasing beam normally gives better stability (the boat is stiffer) at normal angles of heel but reduces the range of stability.

Watertightness

It should be emphasised that the greatest aid to stability is watertightness. If hatches leak or are left open, if hatch boards collapse or are displaced, or if skylights or ports are broken during a knock-down to allow water to flood below, the most convincing self-righter in the world (on paper) may still capsize.

10.1.14 Hull balance

Though in the section on transverse stability (10.1.9) it was said that no account was taken of the fore and aft shift of the centre of buoyancy and change of trim as a boat heeled, in fact this trim change has a considerable effect on hull

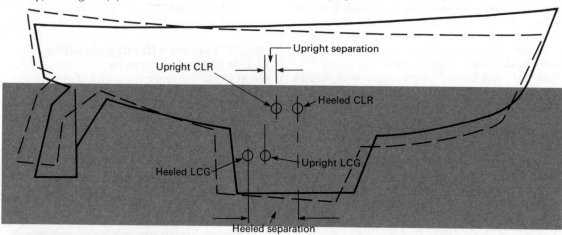

Fig. 10(8) The sections above the waterline aft are generally more full and buoyant than those forward. So as a yacht heels her stern tends to lift and the bow to drop, so that she is trimming bows down. This has the effect of moving the CLR forward and increasing the separation between the LCG and the CLR.

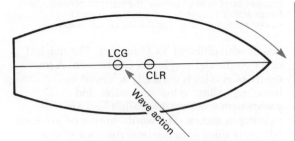

Fig. 10(9) External forces, such as waves, act through the LCG of a yacht but the vessel tends to pivot about her CLR.

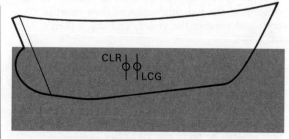

Fig. 10(10) With a full-length keel the CLR is often astern of the LCG when the boat is upright. Heeled, the CLR moves forward but its separation from the LCG should never be great.

balance and handling characteristics. Generally speaking as a modern yacht is heeled she trims bows down because above the LWL her aft sections are full and her bow sections fine. Thus a very buoyant length aft and less buoyant length forward is being pushed into the water, and the hull will adjust itself in the water accordingly. This change of trim has the effect of moving the centre of lateral resistance forward as in Fig. 10(8).

The CE (centre of effort) of the sail plan is nearly always ahead of LCG. It is also generally forward of the centre of area of the load waterline about which the vessel may be considered to pivot in a fore and aft direction. Thus, as the wind blows the sails tend to force the bows down, adding to the natural bow-down inclination of the heeled hull. Once the sheets are started the centre of effort of the sail plan will move further ahead and the trim will become greater, as will the separation between the centre of lateral resistance and centre of gravity. If for any reason a yaw, or turning moment, is set up (perhaps by a wave), the turning forces will act through the LCG while the boat pivots about its CLR, Fig. 10(9). Hence the craft will try and swing through a circle in the same direction as the induced yaw. This can only be counteracted by fierce rudder action and is the classic cause of broaching. Fig. 10(9) shows the forces causing the swing to be coming from off the bow and the more extreme racing yachts today can broach in these conditions, but the more common cause is a wave from the aft quarter overtaking the yacht and, acting through the LCG, causing the stern to swing round so that it ends up broadside to the seas.

Fig. 10(10) shows the profile of an old-fashioned sailing workboat with the keel line becoming progressively deeper all the way to the stern. The old-timer will probably have her CLR further aft than the modern craft and the tendency for it to move forward when heeled under sail will be far less dangerous, for its separation from the LCG will never be as great. The old boats, too, had better balanced ends than today's yachts in that neither bow nor stern were exaggerated in shape and the change in trim caused by heeling was less. All this partly explains why the long keel, classic underwater profile, tends to be easier on the helm and less liable to broach.

It is not only sailing craft that have unbalanced ends. The modern planing motor boat is a supreme example. The wide, deeply immersed transom, which is necessary for speed, is coupled with comparatively fine lines forward, and she can be a dreadful boat to handle in following seas when speed has had to be reduced. The overtaking sea lifts her great, buoyant transom and in doing so shoves her bows deep into the water where they act as a brake. The waves continue to travel forward and carry the stern along with them. The boat then pivots about the bow and swings round to lie broadside on to the seas – an unhappy situation.

10.1.15 Speed/length ratio

Speed on its own is not a valid comparison between two craft, length must also be taken into consideration. Hence speed and length are linked by the speed/length ratio which is $V/\sqrt{L}$ were V is speed in knots and L is waterline length, in feet. A yacht doing 6 knots on a waterline length of 25ft would thus have a speed/length ratio of $6/\sqrt{25} = 6/5 = 1.2$.

10.1.16 Resistance in general

As a boat moves through the water the passage of her hull creates waves (shown by the wash). If the energy contained in those waves could be measured it would be found to equal the amount of energy expended in making them. That is one type of resistance and is known, with unusual obviousness, as wave-making resistance. At the same time the friction of the water rushing past the bottom, rudder, shaft, propeller and so on has to be overcome. This is called frictional resistance. The two types of resistance to forward motion occur at the same time but the proportion of each to the total resistance varies with the speed/length ratio. Fig. 10(11) shows a typical example in graphical form, and note that the resistance is measured in lb per ton of displacement.

Most of the world's merchant fleets travel at speed/length ratios of not more than about 0.8 where total resistance may be around 7lb to 8lb per ton. Incidentally, a $V/\sqrt{L}$ of 0.8 for a 300-footer is $V = \sqrt{300} \times 0.8 = 13.8$ knots. Warships tend to be faster, as do some passenger liners and ferries, but no commercial vessel is likely to be

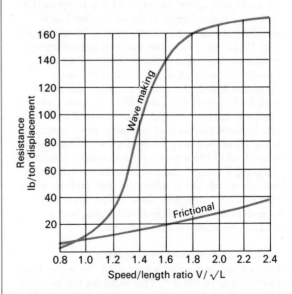

Fig. 10(11) At low speed/length ratios frictional resistance plays a greater part in overall resistance than wave-making but the situation changes as speeds climb.

economical at a ratio of more than 1 which is 17.3 knots on our mythical 300-footer. At this speed resistance has risen to 20lb per ton, or thereabouts. Yachts commonly sail at ratios of up to 0.8 to 1.0 (4 to 5 knots on a craft 25ft on the waterline) but may reach a speed/length ratio of 1.2 or 1.3 on rare occasions when resistance will be 50lb to 75lb per ton – or some 10 times its earlier value, which maybe explains the rarity of these bursts of speed. Certain yachts can exceed even these limits without resorting to surfing or other exceptional conditions but at, say, a speed/length ratio of 1.4 (7 knots on a 25-footer) resistance will have increased perhaps 14 times over that at 4 knots.

Resistance can be translated into horsepower; in this case brake horsepower or the power of an engine needed to push the boat along.

$$BHP = \frac{R \times V \times 2}{550}$$

For the sake of an example assume a 25-footer is displacing 5 tons. At 4 knots total resistance (R) will be about 8lb per ton so with a displacement of 5 tons resistance will be $5 \times 8 = 40lb$. At 7 knots it will rise to 108lb per ton or $5 \times 108 = 540lb$ total resistance for the 5-tonner. V is speed in feet per second and 4 knots = 6.8 ft/sec while 7 knots = 11.9 ft/sec.
So, for 4 knots,

$$BHP = \frac{40 \times 6.8 \times 2}{550} = 1.0$$

and for 7 knots

$$BHP = \frac{540 \times 11.9 \times 2}{550} = 23.3$$

Above those speed/length ratios come the majority of motor boats – even those of the notional slow speed variety – and way up in the realms of speed/length ratios of maybe 5 or 6 are the fast planing cruisers. As can be seen from Fig. 10(11) the resistance curve is flattening out from a speed/length ratio of about 1.7 and though it continues to rise inexorably with increased speed, the rate of increase will not be very high, partly because a planing boat (which commences true planing at a ratio of 2.5 to 3) lifts in the water so that her high speed waterline is significantly above its level at rest. Thus there is less hull in the water, and frictional resistance is reduced. Further, and as observation will show, as high speeds are reached the tremendous wash that has been dragged along at low speeds is considerably reduced, indicating that wave-making resistance is also reduced.

10.1.17 Frictional resistance

Everything that is in contact with the water leads to frictional resistance. This includes the bottom, keel, bilge keels, rudder, propeller shaft and the propeller itself. It also includes, on fast power boats, that part of the topsides that may be wetted by the sheets of water thrown up in high speed running. Hence the need for an abrupt change in shape between bottom and topsides on such craft. Water running up the bottom flies off into space at the corner, known as the chine, rather than attempting to climb up the sides. Spray rails along the bottom, which will be dealt with in greater detail under 10.3.4 are there mainly to reduce wetted surface.

The shape that gives least wetted surface (or area in contact with the water) for any given displacement is the arc of a circle. That means that for least frictional resistance a boat ought to have semi-circular bottom sections. That would be fairly hopeless in practice since it would produce a barrel-shaped craft that would roll like a barrel too, but some racing yachts have sections that approximate to a circular form underwater though towards the centreline they are generally flattened to give a shape with some resistance to rolling.

A long, inclined propeller shaft with a bracket towards its aft end, all exposed to the water, is quite a large contributor to wetted surface and frictional resistance. It also produces unwanted turbulence. In many cases sail drives, or outdrives in the case of motor boats, produce less resistance. That is one reason for their efficiency. Another is that they allow the propeller to be set with the blades vertical rather than at an angle to the water flow. This is an advantage when it comes to effective propulsion.

10.1.18 Fouling

An important element in reducing friction is the smoothness of the bottom. Back in the late 1800s William Froude, who made the first proper experiments in model testing and many of whose findings are still relevant today, towed a series of planks in his test tank. The planks were coated with a variety of substances ranging from varnish and enamel to coarse sand. He found that the latter produced double the frictional resistance of enamel and since a barnacle-encrusted and weed-festooned bottom is likely to be very much rougher than coarse sand, the importance of a clean bottom is obvious. In a year without docking, frictional resistance due to fouling can be expected to increase by 100 per cent in temperate waters and 200 per cent in tropical seas. Around the coasts of the United Kingdom resistance may increase by 0.5 per cent per day between July and September, when bottom growth is generally at its worst.

Even on a fast-moving vessel the bottom can become a home for unwelcome visitors, because a boat drags a thin film of water (known as the laminar film) along with her however fast she is moving. This film of water has just the same percentage of spores in it as the rest of the ocean, and these will make a home on the bottom without difficulty since the water is not moving in relation to the boat.

10.1.19 Wave-making resistance

Two principal wave forms are generated by a boat in her passage through water. The first is a divergent wave system running at some 30° to 40° to the bow, and to a lesser extent, the stern. The second, and generally more important, is the transverse wave system which can be seen running along the vessel's sides. This form commences with a wave crest near the bow, caused by increased pressure at this point, followed by a trough and then another crest.

The energy content of a wave is proportional to its length and to the square of its depth. In turn, wave length is governed almost entirely by its speed; and its height or depth by displacement and general hull form (the heavier the boat the bigger the wave she will make).

The following table shows the speed of a boat that produces a wave of a certain length, and since the faster she is travelling the longer the wave she makes, the more the power needed to produce it.

Speed (knots)	Wave length (feet)
3	5
4	9
5	14
6	20
7	27.2
8	35.6
9	45
10	55.6

Since wave length and speed are linked it is perfectly possible to judge the speed of a vessel by the distance between the wave crests, provided that the length of the boat is known and so can be used as a guide. If a boat 40ft (12.2m) was developing a transverse wave system that appeared to be about three-quarters as long as the boat between crests, Fig. 10(12), that would mean that the wave was some 30 ft long and the craft was consequently travelling at a bit over 7 knots. All this can most easily be seen on a heavy displacement vessel because her wave system will be deeper (and more power sapping) than on some lightweight flyer. It also shows up clearly on the weather side of a yacht heeled under sail.

The length of that transverse wave system governs the likely top speed of a conventional

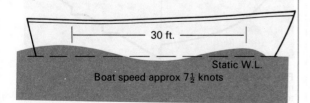

Fig. 10(12) The length of the transverse wave system is governed by the speed of the boat and this fact may be used to estimate the speed of a boat.

sailing boat. As speeds increase and the wave lengthens there comes a point where there is a crest at the bow and another at the stern. This occurs at a speed/length ratio of 1.34 (6.7 knots on a boat 25ft on the waterline; 7.3 knots on one 30ft and so on) and a further speed increase moves the aft crest past the stern. The boat is then beginning to settle with her bows on a crest and the stern in a trough – at 8 knots, for instance, the aft crest would be some 10ft beyond the stern of a 25-footer. In a sense she would now be sailing uphill and would need a wide, deeply immersed transom to give buoyancy plus plenty of power to be able to climb that hill. Not many sailing craft, other than dinghies where the crew balance the heeling effect of a large sail area and sit in a lightweight hull making a reasonably shallow wave formation, can manage to generate sufficient power for that struggle. The limiting speed dictated by speed/length ratio is sometimes known as displacement speed.

10.1.20 Towing speeds

Past sections have dwelt on hull balance and wave-making resistance. The two could now be combined for a brief aside as to why a yacht may tow so badly and even dangerously at speed. Let us assume that she is of normal sailing or slow motor boat shape (that is, high speeds were not envisaged in the design stage), is 25ft (7.6m) on the waterline and is being towed at 9 knots. The aft wave crest is now some 20ft (6m) behind her and the tow is pulling her up on to that forward wave crest with the consequence that the centre of lateral resistance moves forward, Fig. 10(13). The longitudinal centre of gravity remains where it always was and is now well aft of the CLR.

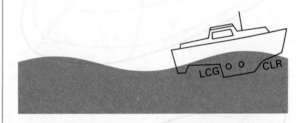

Fig. 10(13) A yacht being towed at greater speeds than her natural or displacement speed is hauled on to the forward wave of her transverse wave system. This causes her CLR to move forward and give rise to possible dangerous yawing from side to side.

The forces acting on the boat are concentrated at the LCG with the result that the slightest deviation off course will cause her to pivot about the CLR and sheer off violently to one side. The towing vessel will unceremoniously drag her back, only for the process to be repeated endlessly until damage is caused or speed is reduced. Ideally, towing speed should not exceed a speed/length ratio of about 1.3 on the towed craft.

10.2 Hull forms

10.2.1 Hull forms in general

Broadly speaking boats can be divided between those that have a V-bottom, or hard chine, form and those that are round bilged. The object of having a boat with a definite angle between the topsides and bottom may be to simplify construction when using a sheet material such as ply, steel or alloy; or it may be to achieve better performance on certain types of craft under certain conditions. The notion that a hard chine shape automatically has to have sections composed of straight lines is wrong – in fact there cannot be straight line sections in areas where there is a lot of curve and change in shape (such as towards the bow) without strenuous work being required to deform the sheet. It will naturally fall into concave curves in these regions and Fig.10(14) shows the general hull form of a single chine yacht. Fig.10(15) does the same for a double chine vessel and though it would be possible to build three chines or more, needlessly proliferating chines brings the cost close to genuine round bilge form. Though the curves in the sections below the waterline may be discerned, on such a small scale drawing it is difficult to see that most of the sections above the waterline have some shape to them, too.

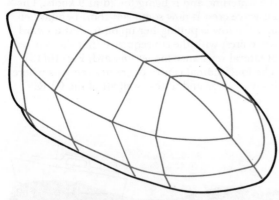

Fig. 10(14) A single chine double-ender.

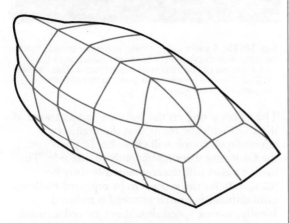

Fig. 10(15) A double chine craft with short counter stern.

A drawback to the chine sailing boat is that the abrupt change in shape between sides and bottom creates a certain amount of turbulence in the water flowing past and this increases drag to the detriment of speed. The difference between a chine boat's performance (especially of a double chine craft) and that achieved by its round bilge counterpart is quite small but significant when planning a racing machine. On the other hand, the V-bottom may be slightly faster downwind in the surges when the stern is starting to drop, simply because a flattish underwater surface will react to water rushing past it more positively than will a curved one. The water flow will have some upwards component which can act more readily on a flat surface to produce lift. Further, a bottom whose sections are formed of straightish lines will resist rolling better than if they were composed of curves.

Sometimes there is found a combination of round bilge and hard chine form. Forward, the bottom sections are rounded to give an easy motion as the bow slices into a head sea in bad weather. Aft, the shape changes to V-bottom to give a better downwind, or motoring, performance. This dual shape is most often seen on motor boats but it sometimes occurs on sailing craft.

On fast motor boats the V-bottom is almost mandatory, partly for frictional resistance reasons and partly to allow the water streaming under the bottom to generate maximum lift. If, for any reason, the hard chine form is not selected, spray rails run along the sides at a height that corresponds to the position of some notional chine to deflect water away from the sides. Spray rails are not really as effective as building in a change of shape, but are much better than nothing. Fig.10(16) illustrates a section towards the stern of two motor boats; one hard chine and the other round bilged with a spray rail.

The V of the V-bottom may be flattened out to give a completely flat bottom, and this allows very speedy and economical building. Flatties can be successful as sailing boats provided they are light and narrow (the length to beam ratio

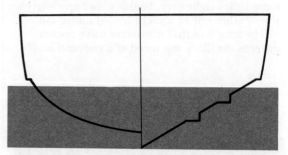

Fig. 10(16) Half sections through two craft; one with a round bottom and the other hard chine, but both intended to reach planing speeds. The chine rail of the round bottom boat will deflect water away from the topsides, though not as effectively as the same rail on a chine boat, while the bottom will clearly not allow as much 'lift' from the water streaming under it.

should not be less than 4:1, and 5:1 would be better) and have low freeboard including the superstructure. Since a boat heels under wind pressure, flatties present a corner to the water under sail and not their flat bottom, and so do not pound in head seas nearly as much as might be imagined. The same flat-bottomed form can be used for power boats, again provided that the craft is light and low. Motor flatties can be pushed along at quite high speeds and are widely used with outboard power by commercial fishermen in the USA.

10.2.2 Sheer

Conventionally, boats have a hollow sheer, or deck line, viewed in profile but sometimes reverse sheer is employed, Fig.10(17). The looks of this latter shape are unexpected but it has some

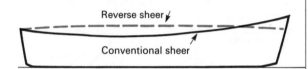

Fig. 10(17) Reverse sheer allows greater space in a boat before side decks intrude.

practical advantages. From the seagoing point of view the critical height above water is around the forward ending of the load waterline. What happens aft of this point will not affect weatherliness very much, and normally the deck line drops to a point about three-quarters of the length of the boat aft of the bow and then climbs again. However, if it went back some distance parallel to the waterline from that critical forward point, or even had a hump in it, the hull would be more spacious and perhaps allow for better accommodation. Another point in favour of reverse sheer is one connected with stability. Once the deck edge is submerged during heeling there is little further buoyancy available to shove the boat back upright again until the superstructure enters the water. So, if the moment the deck edge is immersed can be delayed by raising the freeboard at its lowest point, the better able to resist heeling the boat will be.

As a matter of aesthetics it is worth remembering that to an observer looking at a boat sideways on, the bow is further away from his eyes than the point of widest beam. Through optical illusion this makes the bow appear to be lower than it actually is. Boats drawn with straight sheerlines thus look as if the bow is drooping, and an illusion of straightness can only be achieved by drawing a slight conventionally-hollow deck edge. With reversed sheers the bow is often drawn as having a downwards slope and this feature is accentuated to the observer.

10.2.3 Overhangs, bows and sterns

At low speeds – up to a speed/length ratio of about 0.9 – resistance is mainly frictional (10.1.16) but above that figure wave-making resistance becomes the more important and thus length is the main factor in governing speed, with the longer the boat the higher the potential speed. This is the reason for building a boat with long overhangs, Fig.10(18). When the wind is light and the boat sailing reasonably upright there is comparatively little length of hull immersed, and so wetted area and frictional resistance are low. As the wind and heel increase a greater length is presented to the water and since length has increased so has potential speed. Also, for any given speed if length is increased the speed/ratio drops to reduce resistance. The reason why few boats are built with long overhangs today is simply that there is little useful space in these drawn-out ends, and so length is being paid for without compensating gains in accommodation. The theory behind overhangs is as sound these days as it ever was.

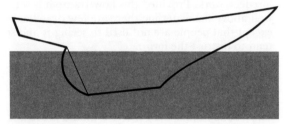

Fig. 10(18) This would have been quite a normal amount of overhang on a cruising yacht of the 1950s.

Clipper bows

There are various types of bow shape, the most famous of which is the clipper bow, Fig.10(19). This style is a natural adjunct to a bowsprit and is markedly hollow in profile. It needs to be carefully designed if it is not to look a mere affectation, and can be achieved either by incorporating the shape as a part of the hull lines and structure or by planting a knee on to the face of a normal stem.

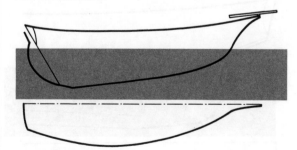

Fig. 10(19) A clipper bow matched with a raked transom stern.

Pram bow

Though quite often seen on dinghies the pram, or scow bow, Fig.10(20), has never been popular on yachts in the western world. It has the

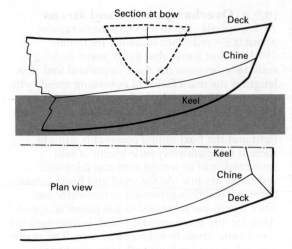

Fig. 10(20) Though pram bows are frequently used on dinghies, for no very good reason they are almost unknown in this country on bigger craft.

advantages that it gives plenty of interior space forward and, on bigger craft, a spacious area for foredeck work. Provided this bow transom is set well above the waterline there are few drawbacks except that people are not used to seeing it and so tend to distrust the form.

Transom stern

There are a variety of possible stern configurations. The cheapest to build in any construction other than where a mould is used, is the transom stern and it also gives the greatest interior and deck space for any waterline length. The boat is simply sawn off at the aft ending of the waterline (or close to it) though the transom may lie at quite a steep angle as shown on Fig.10(19).

Counter stern

If the body of the hull is continued past the aft waterline ending and then terminates in a transom, the result is a counter stern, Fig.10(21). This has an advantage over the pure transom

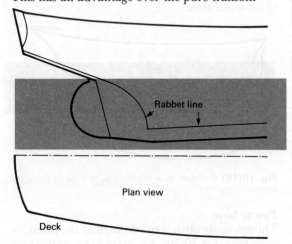

Fig. 10(21) Counter stern on a timber yacht.

stern that as the stern starts to drop at high speeds, or the boat heels, an additional length of hull is set down into the water to increase length and potential top speed as well as lowering the speed/length ratio and resistance. This is the same argument as that applied to the advantages of overhang, and a counter stern is the usual form used in association with an aft overhang.

Canoe stern

On the other hand, the aft overhang could consist of the stern drawn out beyond the aft waterline ending but terminating in a point. This would give a canoe stern, Fig.10(22), which is perhaps the most attractive of all the options from an aesthetic viewpoint. It is a waster of space both below and on deck but is reckoned by some to be the most seaworthy form of all. It provides a reasonable amount of reserve buoyancy aft, although not as much as that given by the counter stern, and balances the buoyancy of the bow quite well.

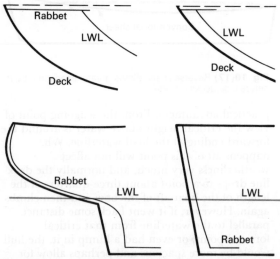

Fig. 10(22) On the left is a canoe stern and, on the right, a lifeboat stern. Both are shown in profile and plan views.

Lifeboat stern

If the hull had been chopped off at the aft waterline but the deck line ended in a point this would give a lifeboat stern, Fig.10(22), which, as its name implies, is the form traditionally used on lifeboats. Since it was also the type found on Viking ships it has a long and honourable history but it is not as popular now as it once was. Lifeboats and fishing boats increasingly use transom sterns without apparent loss in seaworthiness and, in fact, there is no 'best' bow or stern configuration. Prejudice comes into the reckoning as does the useful space that can be offered on a production boat.

Tumblehome and flare

An aft section that has a marked convex curve above the waterline is said to have tumblehome, Fig.10(23). That term can be applied to other parts of the boat as well, and is then used to denote how much a structure slopes in towards the centreline. A superstructure, for instance, would look as if it were leaning outwards if the sides were built vertically. Thus it slopes in and the amount of this slope is written, for instance, as 1:10 or 1:12 tumblehome. Bow sections that are markedly concave are said to be flared, Fig.10(23). A reasonable amount of flare tends to throw water downwards and keep the deck dry, but an exaggerated flare often leads to water running along the hollow until this dies away. The water then comes aboard over the deck edge.

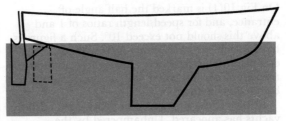

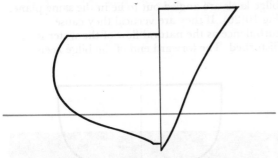

Fig. 10(23) On the left is a half section at the stern of a yacht with tumblehome and, on the right, a half section through a flared bow.

10.2.4 Sailing hull forms

Most production craft today are designed unashamedly around a combination of requirements and beliefs. First, the accommodation must be as spacious as possible within a given length, with length itself important since marina charges have to be taken into account. Secondly, the price must be competitive and since weight costs money, especially if achieved by heavy construction rather than by the addition of ballast, the boat must be light. Thirdly, it is believed that it is a selling feature if the hull form is recognisably similar to that used by successful competitors in the racing fleets. These constraints commonly lead builders to produce craft that are beamy (for superior accommodation and in deference to racing trends) and, because they are also light, to having small hull draught. That is, the main body of the hull has comparatively little depth in the water, whatever may be added to it afterwards in the way of keels or skegs. The hull will also have considerable freeboard to give headroom and the impression of space below. Since this combination of shallow hull draught and high freeboard would lead to a hopeless performance under sail – with the boat preferring to drift sideways rather than marching forward in the desired direction – a fin keel is added, so called to differentiate it from the traditional long keel. This also allows some ballast weight to be carried low down and so promotes stability. The weight may be an addition to the fin keel or it may be provided simply by the weight of the structure itself.

Fig. 10(24) Transom hung and spade rudders on a fin-keeler. A skeg-supported rudder is shown in Fig. 10(8). A spade rudder has no support other than the rudder stock.

The boat has to be steered and so a rudder is arranged. This is sometimes hung on the transom; sometimes emerges from the bottom of the hull with no external support, the bottom bearing being within the hull (in which case it is called a spade rudder); and sometimes has an external support incorporating a bearing. This support is in the form of a miniature fin keel and is called the skeg. Thus a hull with quite low wetted surface has been achieved and frictional resistance is low. Fig.10(24) and Fig.10(8) show the possible arrangements.

The speed of this boat is governed by her length and she enters speed/length ratios of about 0.8 and upwards, where wave-making resistance is climbing steeply, sooner than would a longer boat which would also have a higher top theoretical speed. Though it would be quite possible to build that longer boat, with the narrow beam that would be a further requirement for high ultimate speed, as cheaply as the typical beamy, shallow type, her accommodation would be poor by comparison and berthing charges would be higher. So a builder who wants to cash in on a worthwhile section of public demand has little choice.

Of course boats are still produced similar in form to the classic yachts of yesteryear and which, by having more headroom and beam than once would have been considered suitable, can have an accommodation quite as good as their more fashionable rivals. They are likely to be good to look at, steady on the helm and easy for a family crew to handle. But if of the same length as their competitors are likely to be not quite as fast, due to their greater wetted area, and to cost a bit more.

10.2.5 Beam

Where sheer speed has priority over everything else, narrow beam is desirable. The resultant boat may be hard to handle to windward where a good sail area will heel the boat uncomfortably and too much for efficiency, but off the wind the craft will come into her own. The reason why narrow beam pays is mainly that water does not like to be disturbed and the more it is forced apart by the boat's passage the greater will be the shock to it and the bigger the waves created. The power absorbed in making those waves leaves a little less available for driving the yacht forward.

On Fig.10(1) is marked the half angle of entrance, and for speed/length ratios of 1 and above this should not exceed 10°. Such a figure is hard to achieve on a beamy boat without compensating steep curves somewhere aft along the waterline, and water will not appreciate that big change in direction.

In the USA a new breed of lightweight offshore yachts has appeared. Unhampered by the International Offshore Rule (IOR) rating restrictions, they are remarkably narrow. On a waterline length of 24ft (7.3m) for example, beam may only be 5ft 8in (1.7m) and a 40-footer may have a beam of 8ft, a length/beam ratio of 5:1. This contrasts with the 3:1 ratio of more conventional craft. The combination of narrow beam and light weight is unbeatable. Nearer to home, for example the 17ft (5.2m) single-handed International Canoe with a beam of 3ft 2in (0.95m) and a sail area of about 107 sq ft (10 sq m) is as fast as the two-man Flying Dutchman which is nearly 3ft (0.9m) longer, far beamier and sets 190 sq ft (17.7 sq m) of sail.

10.2.6 Keels

As with sails, rudders, centreboards and the like, the higher the aspect ratio of a keel the better it will reduce leeway, and with less wetted area. A good example of such a keel may be expected to contribute only 25 per cent of the total drag of the hull (the main body of the hull causing the rest) while providing about 70 per cent of the lateral force acting against leeway. It need not be very thick – about 15 per cent as wide as it is long, fore and aft, being about right – and such types abound, wedded to shoal draught main hulls. They are, though, just necessary excrescences, adding to the draught without the redeeming feature of being wide enough to allow some accommodation to be dropped into them. The old-time yachts could have a low profile above water while still having headroom, because the cabin sole could be arranged in the wide keel which was much more a genuine part of the hull structure and form than it is on today's shapes. Fig.10(25).

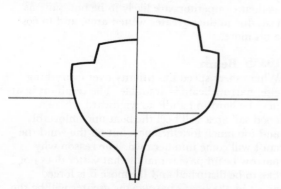

Fig. 10(25) The long keel form of the classic yacht allowed the cabin sole to be deeper in the hull and the overall height above the waterline to be lower than is possible on the shallow hull of the modern fin-keeler.

10.2.7 Bilge keels

In the place of a single, central keel, whether of the fin or full-length variety, two keels can be substituted, one under each bilge. Their function is exactly the same as for any keel – to reduce leeway and increase stability. Though two keels like this are not as efficient as one of the same total area their combined lateral plane should be sufficient to allow them to be less deep than a central keel. Thus draught is reduced without worsening leeway though at the expense of added surface area. Since the water flooding along the bottom runs roughly on a line with the diagonals, bilge keels are angled out to lie in the same plane, Fig.10(26). If they are vertical they cause turbulence as the natural flow of the water is disturbed. The forward end of the bilge keels

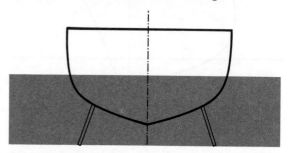

Fig. 10(26) Bilge keels provide resistance to leeway and the ability to take the ground reasonably upright.

toe-in a matter of a degree or two to help windward performance. Bilge keels have become associated with light, high-sided, beamy yachts at the cheaper end of the market, which naturally sag off to leeward under sail more readily than a heavier, deeper vessel. If bilge keels do not cure this condition entirely that is not a reflection on the scheme itself, for nothing would work any better except for a deep, central keel and this would immediately put paid to the shoal draught advantage. Bilge keels are also popular because in the right conditions of river or harbour bottom they allow the boat to sit upright, or nearly so, when dried out and balancing on her keels. It is worth remembering, though, that the LCG of the boat and all its equipment must lie approximately in line with the middle of the keels in profile, or the boat may tip backwards or forwards.

10.2.8 Centreboards, daggerboards and bilgeboards

For a genuinely shoal draught craft it is obvious that all appendages beneath the hull should be eliminated, and the keel replaced by something that can be lowered into the water to combat leeway only when needed. The amount of wetted area could then be adjusted to suit the course on which the yacht is sailing. On a run this movable wetted area could be lifted right up inside the boat; on a reach it would be set half-way down; and going to windward it would be fully lowered.

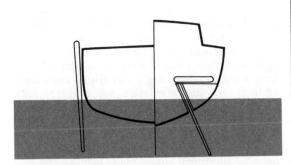

Fig. 10(27) A leeboard (on the left) is sited outside the hull but bilgeboards (on the right) are set in cases like a centreboard. If suitably planned the cases can form the berth or settee fronts for much of their length.

On a suitably designed hull the boat could take the ground more or less upright without the need to perform a balancing act on bilge keels. All the requirements of altering wetted area are provided by centreboards, which pivot about a bolt near their forward ends and are housed in a case; daggerboards (which slide straight up and down in their case with no pivot); and bilgeboards which either pivot or lift but whose cases are set out one each side of the centreline where they do not intrude badly into the accommodation. If the bilgeboards are canted as shown in Fig.10(27) one of them becomes vertical as the craft heels and so is more effective than a centreline board in reducing leeway. Unlike bilge keels, which they resemble, only one board need be lowered so that wetted area can be controlled. Still on bilgeboards, which deserve to be more popular than they are, the slots in the bottoms of their cases will be above keel level and so less likely to get clogged with stones and mud than where the case is set into the keel.

In some cases boards have ballast attached to their bottom face and this particularly applies to daggerboards. The ballast might be in the form of a bulb of iron or lead which recesses into a hollow built into the hull, or it might be that the bulb simply pulls up against the hull. The welcome addition of weight low down can also be achieved by making the board hollow and filling some part of it with a dense material, or by making the board of thick steel plate. In all cases the structure must be strong and able to resist the shock of a sudden grounding without bending and staying bent. The argument for having the board of wood is partly that it will break rather than bend in these circumstances. Also, since the board will naturally float up into the case it only requires light tackle to push it down into the water. If the tackle breaks, the board will house itself which can be advantageous.

Heavy centreboards, daggerboards and bilgeboards should have a built-in stop to prevent them dropping down out of their cases if the raising mechanism breaks. It should also be possible to lift them out of the tops of their cases,

rather than having to make some elaborate arrangements to drop them through the bottom when inspection, painting or repair is needed.

As with rudders, keels and all suchlike objects, boards with a high aspect ratio are most effective. That is, when lowered, they should be deep compared with their fore and aft length. Such theoretical advantages need to be approached with caution because the strength of the board must be of paramount importance. Sheer surface area, however inefficiently disposed, is better than none at all.

Centreboards and daggerboards are hardly ever of an area that enables them to equal the effectiveness of proper bilge keels or central keel, and so are best used on craft that present a low profile and thus have the least possible windage. They are sometimes used in conjunction with a shallow ballast keel – dropping down through a slot in the keel – and so allow a boat of modest draught to have a potentially good windward performance. Otherwise, in the case of non-ballasted boards, ballast is stowed inside the hull.

10.2.9 Leeboards
The best examples of these are found on Thames barges where boards, pivoting at the deck edge and set outside the hull, can be lowered to reduce leeway. A leeboard being wholly outboard does not take up any useful space and on craft designed to accept them can be quite effective. The pressure of water on the lee side holds them against the side of the vessel and they can be adjusted in a fore and aft position by tackles made fast to the board. The windward board in some cases is left to its own devices, in which case it will fan out from the boat's side and skitter across the surface. Otherwise it is hauled clear of the water on each tack, Fig.10(27).

10.2.10 Rudders
The rudder, in association with the keel or centreboard, acts to provide a transverse lifting force to counteract the sideways thrust of the sails. Thus it does more than simply steer the boat. A high aspect ratio is good for efficiency and may be as high as 5 on a deep draught yacht. Unlike other high aspect boards such as centreboards, a rudder can be supported down its leading edge from either the aft end of the keel or from a rudder skeg. A skeg, incidentally, allows a slightly smaller rudder to be used than would otherwise be needed.

Modern racing boats with their high speeds and somewhat wayward handling characteristics can place enormous strains on rudders and associated skegs. Unhappily the obsession with saving weight extends to these items and there have been many failures. Since a rudder can be thick and still be efficient, the soundest way to construct one is to take the stock right down to the bottom of the rudder and build up the blade round that. The stock is the bar or tube that extends up inside the boat, and to which the tiller or quadrant is fastened. Suitable scantlings for different sizes and types of rudder and stock are given by all the classification societies, so there is no excuse for failure. A rudder blade should be aerofoil shaped for efficiency. A flat blade slotted through the stock is cheap but not very effective. Two typical rudders are illustrated in Fig.10(24).

10.2.11 Multi-hulls

From what has been written so far on matters of beam, resistance and balance it would seem that a multi-hull, and especially a catamaran, should be the ideal sailing machine. She does tend to run straight, because of the long, widely spaced hulls, and so may not turn as promptly as a conventional single hull vessel and may present structural problems in joining up the hulls, but those two factors apart (and discounting the very real difficulty in ensuring that the craft can be righted after a capsize) the multi-hull has everything going for it.

Catamarans

The conventional yacht has more beam than is desirable, from the resistance point of view, to allow a generous sail area to promote speed without undue heeling. The catamaran's two hulls can be very narrow and efficient without prejudicing her ability to sail upright. On the same theme, bottom sections can approach the ideal of being semi-circular, for least wetted area, since they do not need to be shaped to resist heel. The huge initial stability of two hulls placed at some distance from one another means that ballast is not required, and so the boat can have a low overall weight – again disregarding the problems of righting after a capsize. And because a light, narrow hull will only have a shallow transverse wave system, she has the potential for velocities well above her displacement speed. The ends can also be reasonably symmetrical to make a well-balanced hull.

As with other yachts the catamaran, especially in the smaller sizes, may need some additional lateral plane to reduce leeway. This is commonly provided by a daggerboard in each hull, though there have been types built with fin keels. The justification for the latter would be that, in conjunction with a masthead float (of which more later), they can make for a boat that will

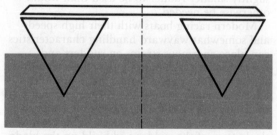

Fig. 10(28) The Wharram type of catamaran relies on steeply vee'd hulls to prevent excessive leeway.

right herself from any angle of heel. Other than in that role a fin keel is a nuisance since it adds draught and wetted surface at all times – even when not needed. A big catamaran may not even need daggerboards since her hulls can be very narrow in proportion to their length and so will have a reasonable draught and grip of the water on their own. Big catamarans, too, and especially those designed for racing will probably not have any accommodation planned for the bridge deck – the structure joining the two hulls – and so will have quite low windage. Again this reduces the need for additional lateral plane below water.

The catamarans designed by James Wharram deal with this problem in a different way. Apart from eliminating all structures on the bridge deck their hulls are V-shaped, Fig.10(28), which allows them to be deeper in the water and to resist leeway by that depth alone.

The structural difficulties of a catamaran have been mentioned. The strains on the connections between two widely spaced hulls can be enormous and are aggravated by additional stresses set up by the rigging. It can be appreciated that setting a mast on the bridge deck and then tightening up shrouds attached to the hulls tends to pull those hulls upwards, and some clever engineering may be needed to sort that problem out.

As far as stability is concerned it is fairly obvious that an upside-down catamaran is just as stable as one the right way up; more stable in fact, because the mast may be deep down in the water adding weight just where it is not needed. There have been many solutions or partial solutions to the problem of righting a capsized catamaran; the most usual being to attach a float to the top of the mast. Assuming the mast did not break during the capsize, the float will try to rise to the surface bringing the catamaran on her beam ends with it. In this attitude it may be possible to right the boat completely. The weight of a fin keel would assist in getting the craft upright, or it may be feasible to flood the upper hull for the same result. In some cases an inflatable bag replaces the permanent float at the masthead. This can be activated when required. Uninflated it does not have as much windage as the float but has potentially greater buoyancy, which is a good thing. High performance catamarans are also sometimes equipped with automatic sheet releases so that as the load on the mainsail approaches that at which it would capsize the craft, the sheet is let go and the load abruptly diminishes.

Trimarans

A catamaran carries its weight equally distributed between two hulls, but a trimaran's main load carrier is her central hull with the floats port and starboard acting more as balancing sponsons. A trimaran has fewer accommodation problems than a catamaran as, though the central hull will be narrower than on a monohull since it does not need to counter heel with its own beam, everything is under one roof, so to speak. Headroom in the hull is not difficult to achieve either as the main, weight carrying hull is likely to be quite deep. On a catamaran living quarters tend to be very elongated unless the bridge deck can be used. If it is, then excessive windage invariably follows since the floor of that accommodation starts at a fair distance above the waterline and then soars upwards.

Structural difficulties are less marked on a trimaran. The floats are comparatively close to a stout main hull and so are easily braced. Even righting after a knock-down does not present quite the same problems and, all in all, the trimaran has many virtues. She may not turn as swiftly as a monohull nor have quite the same accommodation or top speed potential as the catamaran, but will be comparatively safer and fast enough for virtually all purposes.

10.2.12 Motor sailers

The modern motor sailer has most of the characteristics of the true sailing yacht including, in some cases, a fin keel and skeg underwater form. The rig is generally slightly undersize by comparison, and windage is allowed to rise with the provision of a sheltered steering position or even a small wheelhouse-cum-deck saloon, but a reasonably powerful engine overcomes any difficulties. The craft will generally perform well under sail alone but the biggish motor is there for speedy passages or for when the wind drops. Used in conjunction with the sails when turning to windward it will permit greater speed and closer footing. However, as on all craft of sailing yacht form whose aft waterlines come to a point, top speed is limited to a speed/length ratio of 1.4 or thereabouts. Applying more power than is necessary to reach this speed simply causes the stern to drop and the uphill battle to commence. A slight increase in speed might be possible but at the cost of a huge waste of power and fuel.

The more traditional motor sailer, of which there are still examples being built, relies on the engine to do most of the work most of the time. Under sail only the boat will perform tolerably on a reach or a run and so in an emergency some harbour can be gained, even though it may not be the one originally envisaged. To windward the sails are usually trimmed flat and the engine provides virtually all the drive. On these occasions the sails act mainly as roll-dampers and, to a slight extent, fuel savers. The hulls of these motor sailers are generally of traditional yacht or slow motor boat form without much in the way of keels or other aids to reducing leeway. Since they are not usually expected to reach speed/length ratios over that magic 1.4, the aft waterlines will come to a point to allow an easy flow of water round the hull. Where slightly higher speeds are planned the transom may be lightly immersed for additional stern buoyancy but once this has been done all pretensions to a reasonable sailing performance disappear. A sailing boat develops little enough effective horsepower from its sails at the best of times. The extra drag and turbulence created by a transom being towed through the water is more than it can bear with equanimity.

10.3 Power craft

10.3.1 Motor boats

Vessels that rely purely on engines come in all speed ranges from those that plod along at a very economical speed/length ratio of 1 or a little over (these tend to be biggish craft where even a measured gait – 7½ knots on a 60-footer for example – is still a worthwhile speed) to those that commonly cruise at ratios of 3 or more and may be capable of reaching ratios of 6 or 7. Even these extremes leave out offshore racers where a boat 30ft (9.1m) on the waterline might be capable of 80 knots ($V/\sqrt{L} = 14.6$) in the right conditions, and record breakers where boat shape is as much affected by aerodynamics as hydrodynamics. It follows, then, that there must be a wider variation of hull shape than on sailing yachts. But, unlike them, the form of pure racing boats has comparatively little influence on those designed for more mundane uses.

As speeds increase from a speed/length ratio of about 1.4 up to ratios of 2.5 to 3 (when the boat may be considered to be planing) there is a pressing need for a wide buoyant transom to counteract sinkage of the stern. This transom is then dragging through the water creating a massive amount of turbulence and wash. Above planing speeds, though, the transom will run dry with wash and wave-making resistance greatly reduced. At the same time the boat will have risen bodily under the influence of the lifting component of the water rushing past the bottom, and so the wetted area of the bottom will also have been reduced. Consequently frictional resistance drops. A resistance curve of a planing boat will show a steep climb to the point where the craft is just about on the point of planing. Resistance will then suddenly drop before starting to climb again, though much less steeply than it did initially. The point of maximum resistance is sometimes called the hump speed – because there is a hump in the resistance curve.

10.3.2 Trim

In the course of its progress towards full planing a motor boat will behave in precisely the same way as any other boat. First it settles in the water with the bow usually sinking a little more than the stern. As the aft transverse wave crest passes the stern (speed/length ratio just over 1.34), the bow rises and the stern sinks but then things begin to change. Whereas the sailing vessel or low-speed power boat (which have very much the same sort of shape though the motor craft has no outside keel) would find themselves with an exaggerated bows-up attitude, the planing boat by virtue of its buoyant stern will lift and then start to flatten out. A speed/length ratio of 3.5 to 4 will now have been reached and from there on lift occurring at the LCG, which is normally well aft of midships, will raise the stern more than the bow and the boat will start to run almost level. Though this might seem to be a desirable state, in fact frictional resistance with all that length immersed will be higher than necessary and most planing boats run most efficiently with a bows-up attitude of 3° to 4°.

It is most important to get trim right if power is not to be wasted. A boat will normally plane earlier and thus be more efficient if an excessive bows-up attitude can be avoided. This can be accomplished either by the use of transom flaps which, pivoting on the transom, have their aft edges forced down into the water flow and thus try and lift the stern, or by wedges under the hull. Both are shown in Fig.10(29). The latter are effective but inflexible in that as speeds rise they will continue to depress the bow until the craft is running much too flat for efficiency. Transom flaps can be raised to allow the hull to assume its natural planing attitude at any time.

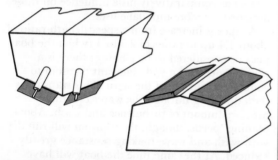

Fig. 10(29) On the left are transom flaps which may be hydraulically, electrically or even manually operated. On the right are wedges fastened to the boat's bottom to force her bows down at speed.

Flaps are useful, too, in bad weather. Going to windward a boat will be most comfortable and least liable to violent pounding if she is running level. Too level for greatest efficiency, perhaps, but at an attitude that the crew can stand. Downwind the bows should be high to bring the CLR (centre of lateral resistance) back towards the LCG (longitudinal centre of gravity) to aid handling. That high bows-up attitude is probably the one naturally adopted by the craft at moderate planing speeds and should not be spoilt with wedges.

10.3.3 Planing hull forms

Not all planing hull types have the same trim characteristics. Fig.10(30) shows the three main types with typical chine and keel lines. The first is

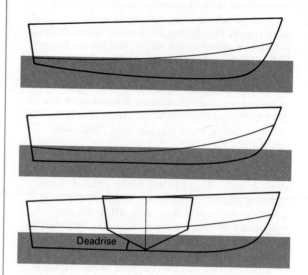

Fig. 10(30) Top, a warped bottom form; centre, a monohedron type; and bottom, a deep vee planing hull showing also what is meant by deadrise angle. This is the angle the bottom makes with a horizontal through the base of the keel.

the warped bottom type where the deadrise angle is lessening all the way aft to the transom. This shape produces a hull that tends to plane early but flattens out too quickly for really high speeds to be achieved with efficiency. The second type, the monohedron, has a fairly constant deadrise from a little way aft of midships back to the transom. This form generally planes later than the warped bottom type but never trims with quite such a bows-up attitude. The third type, known as a deep V, where the least deadrise angle is 22° or more, has a chine line similar to that of the monohedron – only higher of course. The steeply angled bottom produces less lift than the other two types and consequently the vessel planes later and less efficiently, but is what is known as a high trimmer. In other words the bows are high further along into the speed range. The warped bottom and monohedron forms will start to flatten out with an increase in resistance comparatively early in the speed range and just when the deep V is becoming efficient – having had too steep a bows-up attitude earlier on. Thus the deep V is suited to really high speeds.

10.3.4 Beam

Motor and sailing boats share many of the same criteria for best performance. Thus, for instance, a very narrow, lightweight power boat can reach high speeds efficiently despite not having a planing form. It is simply that she creates such low tranverse waves that it is no effort for her to break through the displacement speed barrier. But in general, while the shape of a motor boat will resemble that of a yacht without a keel at speed/length ratios below 1.4 or so, above that and up to a ratio of 3 or thereabouts, beam becomes increasingly important. The more of it,

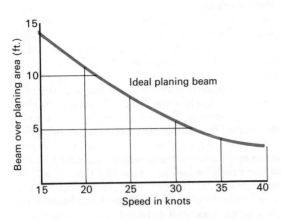

Fig. **10(31)** Ideal planing beam (maximum beam over the chine rails) plotted against boat speed for a craft 25ft (7.6m) on the waterline displacing 3 tons, and with an LCG 10ft (3m) forward of the transom.

within reason, the better. At higher ratios again the maximum beam of the planing surface ought gradually to reduce. Fig.10(31) shows what would be the ideal planing beam for a craft 25ft (7.6m) on the waterline, displacing 3 tons and with the LCG 10ft (3m) forward of the transom. The requirement has dropped from getting on for 15ft (4.5m) at 15 knots (which is ridiculously wide) to a little over 3ft (1m) at 40 knots. The latter beam would be impossible to attain on a monohull if the boat was not to be hair-raisingly unstable at rest and at low speeds. However, a deep V in conjunction with spray rails, Fig.10(32), can effectively reduce beam as speeds increase. The boat rises in the water as the throttles are opened and with a number of spray rails running along the bottom at various widths out from the centreline, one pair in succession will define the edge of the waterline beam. A more conventional boat with lower deadrise cannot manage this feat as water breaking away from one set of rails will re-form on the bottom a little higher up.

Consequently a deep V, despite its lack of lift compared with its flatter floored brethren, comes into its own at high speeds because it is a high trimmer and can effectively reduce its waterline beam. It will also have a slightly easier motion in a head sea since the narrow, steeply V'd forward sections will drop into the water without too much shock.

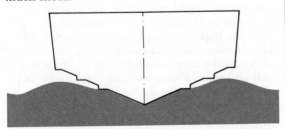

Fig. **10(32)** The spray rails on a deep vee hull can define a new, narrower waterline beam as speeds rise and the craft lifts in the water.

10.3.5 Windage
Though windage due to the hull and superstructure is considered an important feature in depressing the performance of a sailing yacht it is treated in a very cavalier fashion by designers and builders of fast motor boats, probably because it is believed that its power-sapping proclivities will pass unnoticed. It can be a significant factor, however, and on a 30-footer (9.1m) sporting a flying bridge for example, steaming at 25 knots into a 12 knot headwind the power absorbed in counteracting wind resistance alone would be about 50bhp. This might rise to 65bhp or thereabouts with the wind at 20° to 30° off the bow. Streamlining would have little effect on this total. It is interesting to reflect that only about 6bhp would have been expended in overcoming the wind resistance of the hull alone.

10.3.6 Catamarans
Twin-hulled forms have never made much of an impact on the fast cruising fraternity of the motor boat world. This is somewhat surprising since a power catamaran has advantages in reduced roll at low speeds and, incorporating the bridge deck, the potential for spacious accommodation. But catamarans show their paces in the racing world by exploiting the advantages of very narrow, steeply V'd hulls to the hilt, without having to worry about stability at rest and low speeds. Further, on those boats designed for inshore and sheltered water racing the bridge deck can be set low down so that the air being forced into the gap between the bridge deck and water surface has a strong upwards or lifting component. This is known as the ground effect and in action lifts the boat bodily upwards. These circuit racers at full speed run with daylight showing beneath their hulls, only the drive units of their outboards being immersed. Resistance is consequently at a minimum. The low bridge deck form is not so suitable for offshore work where rough water and the constantly changing trim of the boat reduces the ground effect. In addition, waves hammering on the underside of the bridge do it no good at all. Speed offshore can be obtained by relying on the narrow hulls and, forgetting ground effect, siting the bridge deck well above water level.

10.4 Construction

10.4.1 Construction – general
The construction of all boats may be loosely divided into two types – that where a mould is used (for example GRP, cold moulding and some forms of ferro-concrete construction) and that where it is not (such as with traditional timber, steel and alloy building). The former can be subdivided again into whether a female mould is used (as with GRP) or male (as with foam sandwich and cold moulding).

10.4.2 Moulds

When a female mould is required (where laying-up or whatever is done on the inside face of the mould) a wooden version of the boat is made first. The timber used must be as stable as possible so it does not shrink or swell too much in changing atmospheric conditions. This hull, known as the plug, is sanded and smoothed to as good a finish as can be achieved since every imperfection is likely to be faithfully reproduced on the production craft. The plug is then coated with a release agent, and layers of glassfibre and resin are laid over it in the normal moulding process until a sufficient thickness has been achieved. This laminated structure, known as the mould, is then lifted off the plug and with supports bonded to it is stood on the floor for work to commence.

Small boats moulds are normally made in one piece but for bigger craft they may be split longitudinally down the middle and bolted together so that after the hull has been laid up inside, it can be supported from above while the two halves of the mould are unbolted and moved apart. Such a split mould is also necessary if there is appreciable tumblehome in the sections. If a one-piece mould were used the hull could not be lifted out since it is wider at some distance below the deck line than it is at the deck line itself. Moulds are sometimes arranged so they can be tipped. This allows the men laying up the layers of glass and resin inside to work downhand from a staging projecting into the mould. Failing such a set-up they have either to scramble about in the bottom or work from stages lowered from above.

A mould has a limited life since it is sometimes damaged when a hull sticks while it is being lifted out – due, maybe, to the laminating resin penetrating the release agent. The damage can be repaired but it may be difficult to get the repair to match exactly the contours of the mould. Further, the mould is frequently polished to achieve a good finish on the hull taken from it and this polishing can wear flats into surfaces that were originally curved.

This description is, of course, of a female mould where the best surface will be that on the outside of the hull – the side that was in contact with the mould. The smoothness of the inside face depends entirely on the skill of the laminators.

Matched moulds

In a few cases another mould is made which represents the inside face of the hull, taking lay-up thickness into consideration. Dry glassfibre is laid between the two. Resin is then sucked up between the two moulds to permeate the glass and give a good finish to both inside and outside surfaces of the finished hull. Traditionally the difficulty with this scheme is determining whether the resin has actually penetrated every nook and cranny of the glassfibre and it is, or course, expensive in mould making costs.

Male moulds

A male mould is virtually the same thing as the plug used when creating a female mould, though it is built to give the hull shape to the inside of the skin and not the outside. It may be an accurate representation of the hull completely planked up, or it may consist of frame patterns covered in closely-spaced though not necessarily touching battens. Though it must be faired and cleaned off it is not usually necessary to bring it to the high degree of finish of a plug, since it acts more as a former against which veneers or sheets of foam may be laid and attached than as a genuine mould. Hence it is cheap by comparison. The finished hull is lifted off the mould which can then be used again if required.

10.4.3 GRP construction

The term GRP stands for glass reinforced plastic but since glass is not always used as the reinforcement, another term for it is fibre reinforced plastic (FRP). Nevertheless the basic materials are usually polyester resin and glass. The latter is in the form of glass strands about 0.004in (0.1mm) diameter either chopped up and randomly deposited to form a sheet held together with a high solubility binder (known as chopped strand mat), or bundled together and woven into a type of cloth (called woven rovings). Both types are available in various weights per square foot (or square metre). Rovings may also be obtained where the glass is laid to give strength in one direction only, that being known as uni-directional rovings. In a GRP laminate it is the glass that gives most of the strength; the resin being there to bind everything together and keep the water out. The ratio of resin to glass is important and a common figure is about 2:1 by weight. Though a lower ratio will probably give greater strength, the long-term weatherproof qualities of the structure will suffer.

Of the glass types mentioned, chopped strand mat is the cheapest and easiest to work, while woven rovings give more strength to a completed laminate but are expensive and call for more care in the laminating process. Though resin is easily worked through chopped strand mat to bind with other layers and form a homogeneous whole, it is less easily worked through the denser rovings. Thus it is unusual to find a boat built entirely of woven rovings whatever might be the theoretical strength or weight advantage. The scheme is generally to alternate layers of mat and rovings until the required thickness has been achieved. On the other hand many craft at the cheaper end of the market are built entirely of chopped strand mat and resin. This is perfectly satisfactory and indeed Lloyd's Rules for GRP yachts were originally based on that system being used. Where particular strains in one direction are anticipated uni-directional rovings may be incorporated. High strength is also provided by such exotic reinforcements as Kevlar and carbon fibres. These expensive materials are usually worked into a conventional laminate and not used alone. Weight saving is also achieved by employing a stiffening of aluminium alloy tubing. This is taken right round on the centreline to give fore and aft strength, and may be supplemented by a few transverse stiffeners. The alloy structure has come to be known as a space frame.

Resins

Though the resin used in GRP work is usually polyester, in some cases an epoxy resin is substituted. This has slightly higher strength but its main virtue is in its superior water-repelling qualities. The hull of a glassfibre polyester resin laminate will absorb a certain amount of water. Normally this does not matter too much, but if the laminate has not cured properly or has areas of dry glass where the resin has not wetted it completely, water may be drawn up the strands of glass as though up a wick. This can seriously prejudice strength, or lead to a laminate breakdown in the affected area. If voids are left in the lay-up then water drawn in will build up pressure through osmosis, and cause blistering. The blisters and surrounding parts have then to be ground off and left to dry. They are subsequently usually coated with an epoxy resin rather than a polyester.

If a resin/glass ratio of lower than 2:1 by weight is wanted, then an epoxy resin will prove more weatherproof and give a longer life than a polyester, though it will be considerably more expensive.

The resins used in boatbuilding commonly burn spectacularly as anyone who has seen a fire on a GRP vessel can testify. Self-extinguishing resins are available (that is, they will not support combustion and will stop burning once the source of the fire has been removed) but they are less waterproof than normal laminating resins. Their use in a boat hull is a matter of balance between the likelihood of fire set against the desirability of a long-lasting hull.

Resins may be clear or pigmented to the desired colour. Common practice is to use clear laminating resin throughout but to pigment the gel coat (the outside layer of resin) on the topsides. On the bottom even this coat may be clear since the bottom has to be painted anyway (with antifouling). The reason for using clear resins is that it is easier to spot dry patches as laminating is proceeding than with a pigmented resin.

The laminating process

Assuming a female mould, this is first polished and then coated with a release agent. As the name implies this is used to prevent the laminate sticking to the mould. After that, the gel coat is brushed or sprayed on. The durability of a GRP moulding is mainly dependent on the quality of its exposed surfaces, and every effort must be made to prevent the layers of reinforcement straying too close to that surface where they are liable to act as magnets for moisture. Thus a thick layer of resin is needed on the outside and this is called the gel coat. It may be reinforced with a thin surfacing tissue of glassfibre to hold the resin and help balance the laminate. After the gel coat has been applied and is sufficiently hard comes a coat of laminating resin, on which is laid the first layer of glassfibre reinforcement. Another coating of resin follows, worked past the glass strands by the combination of a stippling action with a paintbrush and rolling with a special roller to get rid of air bubbles. This done, further coats of glassfibre and resin are applied in the same way until the desired number of layers has been reached.

The weight of a laminate is usually defined by the glassfibre weight alone. Thus its final weight will be given as so many ounces per square foot or grammes per square metre. This weight will vary over different areas of the boat and is normally at its greatest along the keel. The bottom will be heavier than the sides, and the middle of the boat heavier than her ends. All this is achieved by adding layers of glass and resin to the basic laminate. In addition there is usually a length of heavier laminate at the top of the hull, extending a little way down the sides and extending over about half the length. When the shell has been laid up, stiffeners in the form of stringers and frames are added. These are usually formed from an expanded foam and glassed over to the required weight. Finally the inside of the hull may have a coat of surfacing tissue applied to hide the coarse weave of the glassfibre and to provide a reasonable surface for painting.

Though hull lay-ups are mostly defined by weight, a rough approximation of thickness can be made by taking 1oz of glass (combined with the appropriate amount of resin) as being 1/32nd of an inch thick. In metric terms that means that a 300 gramme per square metre laminate will be about 0.8mm thick. So, for example, an 8oz lay-up will be $8 \times 1/32 = 1/4$in thick.

As an alternative to this hand lay-up method the glass and resin may be sprayed on. Here the rovings are chopped up and fed out through the nozzle of a special gun. Resin is sprayed out simultaneously from the same gun in the correct proportions. Though the mixture still needs consolidating with rollers, labour costs are reduced. The difficulty, which can be overcome by a skilled operator, is in ensuring that a uniform thickness is achieved.

Foam sandwich construction

An alternative way of building a GRP vessel is to use a male batten mould and foam sandwich construction. Here a complete layer of some foamed plastic sheeting is laid over the mould and fastened down. Even string will do for this fastening, tying the foam tight to the battens from which it can eventually be cut. Over this foam is laid the appropriate weight of glass and resin. When this has cured the hull is lifted off the mould and further layers of glass and resin applied inside. The batten mould is comparatively cheap but, since neither GRP skin has been in contact with a smooth surface, there is a considerable amount of work involved in finishing off the hull to an acceptable standard of smoothness. This means that the final hull is not likely to be any cheaper than one made in a normal, female mould though this method is well suited to 'one-offs' where the cost of a conventional mould, which would have to be written off in the price of one boat, would be prohibitive.

Decks, superstructures and bulkheads

Decks and superstructures are generally laminated together in a single mould. The moulding will often incorporate the cockpit as well. Since GRP is not a very rigid material, areas which tend to be wide'but poorly supported, such as cabin tops, often incorporate some depth-giving material in the laminate. This might be foamed plastics, end-grain balsa wood or even honeycomb paper, and its object is to make the laminate deeper and stiffer without increasing weight dramatically. The core material is sandwiched between layers of glassfibre and resin. Reinforcing pads in the way of deck fittings and the like are also bonded into the laminate while it is still in the mould. The pads are generally of thick marine ply. The final moulding is bonded and bolted to some suitable connection on the hull.

Bulkheads are nearly always of marine ply. Though it would be possible to have them of a foam or honeycomb core construction (solid GRP would not be stiff enough without being excessively heavy), the weight saving is not normally considered worthwhile when set against the extra cost and complications.

10.4.4 Cold and hot moulded timber

In this construction a male mould is used. The hull is made up of several layers of thin ply or veneer (three thicknesses being the minimum) all bonded together with, these days, an epoxy glue or resin. The first layer of timber runs at about 45° to the keel; the second layer at right angles to the first; and the third, if the outermost layer, runs fore and aft or at right angles to the keel or in the same direction as the first, Fig.10(33).

The keel, stem and sometimes the transom framing are let into the mould which is covered with something to prevent the hull sticking to it – even newspaper will do. This is carried up to but not over the keel and stem. The first layer of planking is then close butted, glued to keel and stem and stapled to the mould. The planks will normally be not more than about 4in (100mm) wide so that there is not a lot of shaping to do. The staples are fastened through scraps of thin ply or straddle a piece of thin cord, so that by levering the ply or heaving the cord they can be easily removed. Another thickness of planking is stapled and glued to the first with the original staples being removed as work progresses. The next layer is completed the same way, and so on. Finally the hull is sanded down and probably given some coats of epoxy resin which permeate the outer fibres of the timber and give a hard, waterproof finish. The whole job has been most likely done upside down, so the hull is finally lifted off the mould and inverted for the framing to be added. The inside surface of the hull is also given a coat of epoxy.

The result is a boat of superior strength and one which comes out lighter than almost any other form of construction, barring foam sandwich GRP which might equal it. With the epoxy resins used, rot and water soakage no longer present the problems they did on traditionally-built timber hulls.

Boats like the Fairey Huntsman, Fisherman, Atalanta and others were built in a similar

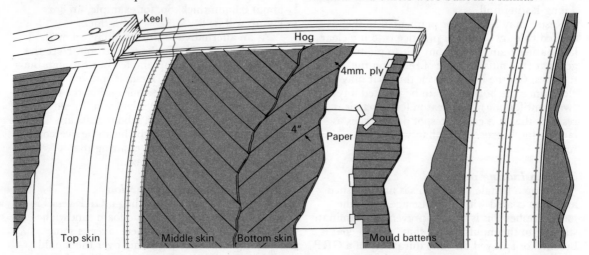

Fig. 10(33) Cold moulding consists of glueing several skins of veneer or thin ply together over a mould. Staples may be fastened over a cord for easy removal.

manner, though epoxy glues were not available in those days. The building process went one stage further in that a rubber bag was placed over the glued-up hull and the air inside exhausted. This created an even pressure over the whole hull and virtually ensured good contact between all timber/glue/timber faces. The boat and bag were then wheeled into an oven, or autoclave, into which steam was introduced to supply heat and more pressure, and to ensure that the glue permeated every crevice and finally set hard regardless of conditions in the workshop. This was an excellent form of construction but the cost of autoclave, rubber bag and heating equipment in the end made it uneconomic.

10.4.5 Ply construction
In the 1950s and 1960s, before the rise of GRP construction, marine plywood was widely used as a boatbuilding material. It is strong and light but to use it economically in sheet form demands a hard chine or V-bottom hull. There is little wrong with such a shape but today it is unfashionable. The use of epoxy resins and glues at all joints, scarphs and faying surfaces should cure the previous tendency of the ply to delaminate and then rot. Provided the ply is to BSS1088 (and preferably inspected during manufacture as being up to that standard) and epoxies are employed, a marine ply boat should have a long life. It can, of course, be sheathed in nylon or glassfibre as an additional precaution.

As a rule plywood boats are framed conventionally, with timber longitudinals at the keel, chine, and gunwale; but on small craft these are largely eliminated in favour of glassfibre and resin corner pieces. What happens is that the sheets of ply that form the hull of the boat are butted up and sewn together with twists of copper wire. Glassfibre tape or chopped strand mat is then laid over the sewn edges and coated with resin. The process of laminating can be done in as many layers as needed and duplicated on the inside of the craft. This angle of GRP sticks well to the ply and makes for a strong and lightweight structure. Polyester resins are usually used though the more expensive epoxies will do a slightly better job. If the ply forming the sides, bottom and deck is cut accurately from a template this is a simple and quick form of building. It is impossible to put a boat together in any but the intended form if the panels forming the hull are the correct shape.

10.4.6 Steel construction
Steel boats are slowly but steadily finding favour among the cruising fraternity. The reasons for this are that with modern coatings (epoxies or chlorinated rubber) applied after thorough shot blasting, maintenance requirements are low and rusting is no longer the problem it once was. Steel is very strong and will merely bend under an impact that would shatter a GRP or timber hull,

and which might tear a hole in aluminium alloy. With good design a 'one-off' single or double chine vessel in steel need cost no more than a production GRP yacht, because the material itself is comparatively inexpensive and is quickly converted to boat form with proper thought in the design and planning stages. Steel is stiff and on small craft the shell requires little additional stiffening or framing other than that which is needed to form the boundaries of bulkheads. But it is indisputably heavy. The hull will weigh maybe twice as much as one of GRP or alloy, and though the completed boat will not weigh twice as much, since fitting out weights will be similar on boats of every form of construction, the additional hull weight may not be acceptable on performance craft. Distortion can be a real problem when welding steel plates less than about $\frac{1}{8}$in (3mm) thick. This prevents steel boats competing with rivals built of lighter materials simply by cutting down on plate thickness. In the days of riveting though, very light plates could be and were used (the Thornycroft-built launch *Ariel* of 1863 vintage had iron hull plates 1/40in (0.6mm) thick) but today a riveted hull would be expensive as compared with welding, not least because rivets for very thin plating would probably have to be specifically made.

Steel used in boatbuilding is usually to BS4360 43A which is a fairly conventional mild steel. Special steels such as Corten, which has a low carbon content and additions of copper and manganese, have been tried but have not been found to offer sufficient advantages to outweigh their higher initial cost.

Framing on small craft is normally flat bar, and on bigger boats angle bar with the toe welded to the shell. The same types of section are used for the longitudinal stiffeners. Because large, flat areas of steel are unattractive to look at, may even be wavy and anyway are heavy, bulkheads are usually of marine ply. The exceptions are the forward collision bulkhead and possibly another just forward of the engine room. These will be steel and watertight. Decks and upperworks are often of steel, too, though an all-steel boat can have compass problems, especially if the compass cannot be mounted on the centreline. Though a compass adjuster can usually cope, if cost is not of primary importance there is a case for making the surrounding structure (such as the wheelhouse or indeed the whole superstructure) of timber or aluminium alloy. Failing that, the compass can always be mounted at some distance from magnetic materials, and it is normally happy enough set in a pedestal on deck.

Integral tanks are simple to arrange on steel boats but it is important to ensure that there are adequate manholes in them to allow inspection and repair as required. Too many steel boats are built without real thought, using traditional wood building as a basis for construction. This leads to a proliferation of unwanted objects such as chine, keel and stem bars. It is easier, cheaper and just as satisfactory simply to butt plates together in these areas and weld. Welding may be of the simple electric arc type, or the more sophisticated and slightly more expensive shielded arc process where the arc is shrouded in an inert gas such as CO. This last type of welding makes for less distortion.

10.4.7 Aluminium alloy construction

Despite its many attractions and advantages aluminium boats have never been very popular in this country. From time to time 'one-offs' have been built and occasionally some brave soul announces a limited production run, but generally the material is treated with grave suspicion or ignored altogether. This must be partly due to the attitude of the manufacturers who seem to make no serious effort to promote its use and who, by their complicated pricing structure, ensure that costing a boat in its early stages is as difficult as possible; waverers are thereby quickly eliminated.

Aluminium alloy cannot rust or rot. It needs painting, apart from antifouling, only for cosmetic purposes and it is light and strong. Its principal disadvantage is that it is incompatible with many other of the traditional non-ferrous materials used in boatbuilding, such as the brasses and bronzes. In their presence under water it is quickly eaten away through electrolytic or galvanic action (10.5.7). However it is generally possible to substitute some other material. Thus, seacocks may be bought made in aluminium alloy, and stainless steel (which produces no fierce reaction) can often be used. As a last resort just about anything can be hard chrome plated for complete protection. Aluminium alloy is popular with companies working in the less developed countries, where boats may have a bad time in the hands of unskilled crews and receive minimum maintenance.

Just like steel, an alloy vessel may be of any shape desired but if she is of single or double chine form labour costs will be reduced. Alloy is normally welded (with an inert gas type of welder), though it is often riveted on small boats to eliminate distortion and to allow thin plates to be used. A typical hull structure will weigh about half as much as steel and about the same as GRP. An alloy plate with equal resistance to bending as steel will be about 1½ times as thick, but about half as thick as ply or a GRP laminate. An alloy boat is built in very much the same way as a steel boat, with frames and longitudinals reducing unsupported panel size. Since it is non-magnetic, alloy presents no compass problems. The aluminium alloy used is normally a British Standard alloy 5083 and though a hull might cost two or three times as much as the steel

equivalent, the hull alone represents only a small percentage of complete boat cost and so this figure is not as damning as it first appears.

10.4.8 Ferro-concrete construction

This is a labour-intensive and somewhat heavy form of building that was once all the rage amongst amateur builders of cruising vessels, but which is now less so. The materials are cheap and since conscientious rather than particularly skilled work is required (up to the final stage where the concrete is plastered over the framework) it has its attractions for those who feel they cannot cope with the more traditional forms of boatbuilding. The plastering can be done by professional teams so that a good standard can be achieved at this vital stage, and since it is not really a lengthy process (it is generally reckoned that it is best completed in a single day) the cost involved is not prohibitive. If properly built, a ferro-concrete hull is strong and does not suffer from defects which can afflict other materials: it will not burn, rot, corrode, be eaten by worms, or develop osmosis. It is also easy to repair.

On the debit side, though the work is straightforward enough it is very time consuming and very hard as some builders discovered to their dismay. Secondly, since the actual building materials are cheap people are tempted to turn their hands to craft which are far too big for their pockets, forgetting that the hull alone represents only a fraction of overall cost and that fitting out a big boat is expensive regardless of its constructional material. Thirdly, the re-sale value of the amateur-built ferro-concrete yacht tends to be low since prospective buyers cannot judge the overall standard of workmanship. Everything is hidden under the concrete and that itself, since it has been made on site, might not be up to scratch. It is difficult, even with professional plastering, to ensure that there are no voids or cavities which can cause problems with corrosion, strength and leakage, and such faults are not easily disclosed by surveys. And finally, though conscientious work will produce a fair hull and one that accords with the designer's drawings, slipshod work will result in a bumpy abomination.

Ferro-concrete boats may be built on a full, male mould (that is, they are constructed on the outside of the mould); on a batten mould (though one that has considerably fewer battens than the type used in cold moulded timber); or the boat's own frames may be erected as a basis (as in traditional timber and steel construction). Basically the idea is that to a backbone of, generally, steel pipe, with pipe transverse frames and closely-spaced round bar longitudinals, several layers of chicken wire or similar steel mesh are fastened. This mesh is lashed to the framing with twists of wire, with the same scheme being used to tie the individual layers of mesh to each other. Everything is then faired and smoothed until it gives an accurate representation of the contours of the hull. The mesh acts as a reinforcement for the concrete and obviously can be formed to the correct shape more easily if it can be hammered against a full mould than if simply draped round a framework. However it is said that when the concrete is applied (and this is a very solid mix with a water/cement ratio of about 0.35 with $3\frac{1}{2}$ gallons of water to each 112lb bag of cement (15.4 litres per 50kg) and a sand/cement ratio of roughly 2:1 by weight) it is difficult to avoid air entrapment even where vibrators are used.

On this count the open batten or open frames methods where concrete is applied from inside and outside the hull are preferred. Various additions may be made to the cement/sand/water mix to delay curing (which may be important in hot weather); to reduce water requirement and so to increase strength; and by imparting minute air bubbles, to prolong the life of the concrete where alternate freezing and thawing cycles occur. But such additions are controversial and many builders prefer to use simple Portland cement and to rely on a good standard of workmanship for prolonging life and achieving adequate strength.

It is most important that none of the reinforcing mesh pierces the surface of the concrete or indeed comes very close to it, or it will start to rust and so bring about the eventual breakdown of the structure. Careful workmanship is thus very necessary. In addition the hull is normally painted with an epoxy resin to reduce water absorption.

Decks and even deckhouses may be ferro-concrete but more usually the latter are of timber bolted to a suitable flange formed in the structure. Slow curing is vital with this type of construction, and the hull should be kept moist for at least 28 days after concreting. This is normally achieved by tying sacks round the outside and draping other sacks inside. These are kept continuously moist with fine sprays of water. The water that collects in the hull drains out through previously prepared holes in the bottom into which can be rammed wooden plugs.

Some ferro-concrete boats are built commercially but their price, due to the large labour content in construction, is not very different from craft built in more conventional ways.

10.4.9 Timber construction

With timber planking various options are open. A close relative to cold moulding for instance, is the double diagonal planking once used throughout the RNLI fleet, on ships' lifeboats and on many small naval craft. Here the planking is put on in two layers, the first at about 45° to the keel and the second running at about 90° to the first. Between the two is laid a layer of unbleached calico soaked in thick white lead paint. The planking is fastened with copper nails and roves (rather like riveting over a washer) as Fig.10(34) demonstrates. This type of planking makes for a strong hull with only comparatively short lengths of planking needed. Another short plank method is long diagonal, where the planking runs up at an angle to the keel but there is only one skin. The scheme here is to butt succeeding planks against one another, run a spindle up the jointing faces to cut away wood and ensure a perfect fit, and then edge-glue.

When planking runs longitudinally it might be carvel (a flush outside surface with caulking cotton and white lead stopping between the plank edges) or clinker, where the planks overlap along their edges. Plank fastenings with the latter method are normally copper nails and roves. No stopping or caulking is used except along the planks which are fastened into the keel.

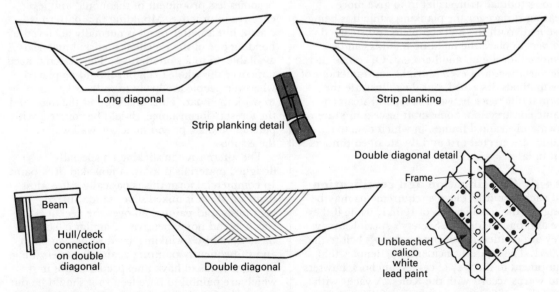

Fig. 10(34) Various types of flush timber planking are possible and three are illustrated here.

Everything depends upon a good fit and the natural swelling of wood in water.

Carvel planking has its own variations. In top class building the caulking between the planks is sometimes replaced by a thin strip of wood, glued into place. This is known as splined planking, while if the seams in the planking have a batten fastened along inside the hull to cover them this is called seam batten construction. Shortly before cold moulding became popular a common method of planking was to employ what is known as strip planking. With this the planking is in quite narrow strakes which may be rounded or hollowed, as shown in Fig.10(34), and is the method recommended by Lloyd's, or they may simply be accurately bevelled. All these glued and multi-skinned types of construction make for strong and watertight hulls where it is often possible to save weight in the framing but which are rather difficult to repair.

The two basic methods of framing are to use either sawn frames (originally sawn to shape from the solid, though using natural crooks and following the grain of the timber as far as possible, but now often laminated to shape) or steam bent timbers. In the former the keel, stem, transom and other items of the boat's backbone are erected on the shop floor and the frames next set in place and attached, via their floors, to the keel. They are then faired and the planking fastened. With steamed timbers the backbone is erected as before but in place of the frames are building patterns to give the shape of the hull at a few different positions along its length. If clinker planking is being used this is now set up and fastened. Only then are the closely spaced frames, which are quite small and steamed to make them supple and easy to bend, put in position.

On other forms of construction (such as double diagonal) the frame patterns may have ribbands or longitudinal stringers let in to give more bearing surface for the planking while it is being fastened. With the hull complete and steamed timbers in place the building moulds can be removed for use on another boat. Of course there are variations and even outright contradictions of the methods described, but they illustrate the normal difference between sawn and steamed frame construction. Some craft have a mixture of sawn and steamed frames, in which case the frames are erected first and the steamed timbers put in later.

10.4.10 Classification and certification
All yachts built to Lloyd's requirements may be assigned the classification of 100A1, while if they are also built under the Society's special survey they are entitled to put the symbol ✠ before the 100A1. The figure 1, incidentally, denotes that equipment in the way of cables, anchors, hawsers and warps accord with the Rules. A yacht with this full classification must have a full survey

every four years and intermediate biennial surveys to remain in class. A machinery classification, ✠ LMC or ★ LMC, may also be assigned.

Where owners do not want to get involved with these surveys their boats may have a Hull Construction Certificate and a Machinery Installation Certificate. If they have both of these then the craft carries a Lloyd's Register Building Certificate, or LRBC for short. Though there is no requirement for a survey (apart from that involved during construction) Lloyd's will carry out one at any time after completion if requested. More information on Lloyd's Register of Shipping is given in Chapter 1 (1.5.6).

10.5 Practical considerations

10.5.1 Hulls in practice
The previous sections have dealt with basic design considerations and brief descriptions of building methods. However, most owners are stuck with what they have and though with a bit of knowledge of hull balance, stability, resistance or trim, or any of the other subjects already covered, they may be able to improve their craft in various ways, they cannot profoundly change its in-built qualities. What they might be able to do, on the other hand, is to make minor changes to create, perhaps, a safer or even drier boat.

10.5.2 Decks
With GRP construction it is extremely difficult to mould in a really satisfactory non-slip deck surface. It is often tried but, though the result may be quite good on the first few craft of the production run, gradually the non-skid pattern becomes less prominent in the mould and less effective in practice. Moulding in a pattern is cheap, but a better result is normally achieved by bonding one of the excellent non-skid materials available on to a smooth deck. The material need not cover the whole deck but should be placed wherever people are likely to walk or be standing to work the boat. Thus areas round the mast and the forestay for instance, should be covered, with patches on deck providing a safe walkway to these spots.

The alternative to sticking on specially designed materials is to use a non-skid deck paint. In commercial form this is basically a low gloss paint in which is mixed silver sand. Stirred vigorously and painted all over the deck it is effective and not expensive. A similar effect can be achieved by sprinkling sawdust on wet paint and subsequently painting again over everything. Sawdust tends to have unexpected lumps in it which are painful to bare feet, so it should be put through a fine sieve before use. Deck paints work equally well on all surfaces, but a scrubbed wooden deck (preferably of teak) has built-in non-skid properties and does not need touching.

10.5.3 Windows, ports and hatches

Windows, especially when bent round the curve of the cabin side and then bolted to the non-uniform thickness of the average cabin side GRP moulding, tend to leak. This tendency is exaggerated if the windows have alloy frames, which become distorted in the bending, and if they were also designed to slide open. Cabin sides, ideally, are straight, changing angle occasionally to give the required side deck width, but generally all that can be done with a leaking window is to take it off and re-bed it.

Ports are generally smaller and better, and as their opening capability is achieved through top hinging plus side and bottom clamps, they can generally be persuaded to stay tight. Ports do not have to be round; there are rectangular versions available which work well. On steel, alloy and wood the tendency to leak is minimized by the fact that the cabin sides are uniformly thick.

Hatches tend to leak too, and the only type with a reasonable prospect of keeping all the water out even in bad weather is the double coaming type, Fig.10(35), originally developed by Maurice Griffiths.

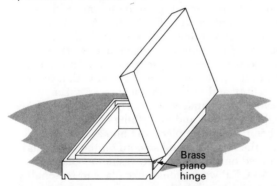

Fig. 10(35) The Maurice Griffiths type of hatch has two coamings with a gap and water drainage between the two.

10.5.4 Cockpit drains

Too many cockpit drains are based on standard household waste systems for reasons of economy, and are consequently hopelessly inadequate in area. According to the Norwegian authorities, all craft with cockpit soles 35cm (14in) or more above the waterline should have drains in accordance with the following formula:
Total drain area (sq cm) = 40 + (15 × area of cockpit sole in square metres).
That could be written in imperial units as:
Area of drains (sq in) = 0.155 × (40 + 1.4A) where A is the cockpit sole area in square feet.
If the cockpit sole was, for example, 6ft × 3ft (18sq ft) the drain area should be:
Area = 0.155 × [40 + (1.4 × 18)] = 0.155 × 65 = 10sq in

That means two drains each 2.5in diameter. They can be crossed if desired so that the port side drain exhausts on the starboard side and vice versa. This means that the leeward drain outlet, which may well be under water, will not flood the cockpit. On the other hand it will not drain it very well either. On a cockpit with its sole well above the waterline it is probably better to have straight-through drains with as short a pipe length as possible, exiting above the waterline. The two last suggestions are to help speed the flow of water through the pipe.

A rough guide to the length of time taken to empty a cockpit is given by the formula:

$$T = \frac{A \times \sqrt{D}}{2B}$$

where T is the time taken to empty, in seconds; A is the sole area of the cockpit in square feet; D is the depth of water to which it is flooded, in feet, and B is the drain area in square feet.

If a 6ft by 3ft cockpit were flooded to a depth of 2ft, two 3in diameter drains would empty it in about 2 minutes; with twin 1½in drains it would take about 10½ minutes; and with 1in drains about 21 minutes. The last two are clearly not very comforting figures.

Cockpit drains should have seacocks at their outlets.

10.5.5 Stanchions and toerails

These are safety items and need to be substantial and very well fastened. Stanchions below about 2ft in height (0.6m) are not a lot of use in preventing a body catapulted from one side of the deck to the other from going overboard. If they are 2ft 6in high (0.76m) they will be better and anything more is better still. The strains that a flailing body puts on the stanchion base fastenings are enormous, and they must be through-bolted, not screwed. On a GRP craft there must be thick and wide backing plates (usually of marine ply) under the bolts, which might otherwise be pulled straight through the deck. Toe rails bounding the deck edge are a safety feature too, and not merely to stop small items rolling over the side. They should be something like 2½in to 3in high (about 75mm) and again be through-bolted.

10.5.6 Maintenance and repair

If a boat is to have a long and useful life it pays to have a look at things in detail from time to time, rather than simply standing back and admiring the general picture. Small blemishes in paint or varnish work can turn into large blemishes unless attended to in their early stages, and the same applies to cracks in the gel coat of GRP craft. Stress cracks, like those that sometimes appear in regions of high stress – an instance being in the area round the chain plates – should be looked at by an expert and some remedial action taken. After all, these show that everything is not quite as it should be, and the chain plates might need to be lengthened or have arms welded to them to distribute their load over a wider area. Check that the bow roller runs freely in the stemhead fitting, or raising the anchor will be doubly difficult, while all shackles should be looked at to spot undue wear. The loss of a small and cheap item like a shackle can lead to the loss of a boat easily enough.

With the boat hauled out the opportunity should be taken to examine the sacrificial anodes (see also 10.5.7) for excessive wasting; to check on the state of the propeller shaft and its bearing (seize the prop and shake it violently – if there is much movement the shaft or bearing or both need renewing); and to check on rudder bearing wear. If these bearings are bolted to the hull the bolts themselves ought to be examined. Take a couple out and see if they are wasted, which may be the case if they are brass or stainless steel. If the bearing cannot be removed hit the heads of the bolts hard with a hammer to see if they fall off – they might! All sorts of afflictions can occur among metal items below the waterline, from rusting and stress corrosion to de-zincification. (See also 10.5.7).

Blisters on the bottom of a GRP vessel should be viewed with the gravest suspicion as they may well indicate the onset of osmosis (see also 10.4.3.) which needs quick remedial action. Pitting on the bottom plates of a steel boat probably means that the mill scale that is present on the surface of all steel plate after rolling was not properly removed during shot blasting, and a more thorough examination is indicated. On a wooden boat a sharp bradawl or something similar should be poked into the planking, especially along the length between wind and water and at the ends where the planking is rebated into the stem, keel and transom, to check for softness or rot. In fact, have a good look at everything that will all too soon be hidden from view again below the water. Seacock fastenings should be checked and, if possible, a keel bolt drawn for examination. If this cannot be done hit the heads with a hammer, as with the rudder bearings, to check on the state of the metal.

Leaks round deck erections are a curse on wooden boats and occur, too, on GRP craft which have timber deckhouses. Fresh water leaks can lead to rot and not just discomfort below. If the joint or connection is at all suspect clear away all the previous water-stopping treatment, which might take the form of an ineffective quarter-round beading lightly bedded on some compound, and glue a strip of nylon along the joint with resorcinal glue. Ordinary shirt nylon will do quite well, but an alternative is to use glassfibre tape, and polyester or epoxy resin. The nylon method is very effective on an all-wood structure but no use where GRP is concerned. Epoxy putties are great fillers of holes and dents in all materials, but take a great deal of sanding

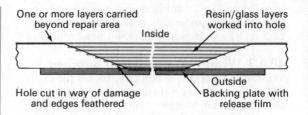

Fig. 10(36) If damage has penetrated right through a GRP hull, then it is best to work on the repair from the inside.

off afterwards so probably the car body repair kits are best for work on GRP construction. On major repairs to GRP the damage needs to be ground back to sound laminate and thoroughly cleaned out. When this has been done the area should be dried and de-greased. If the damage has not penetrated right through the hull the repair consists of filling the hole with resin and glassfibre mat – as if normal laminating were being carried out (10.4.3) – until the repair is slightly proud of the surface. Then a plastic sheet like cellophane is smoothed on and taped over the repair and everything is left to dry. Lastly the surface can be ground smooth and the appropriately-coloured two-pot polyurethane paint applied. If the damage extends right through the hull, it is best tackled from inside. The damaged area is ground out and feather-edged as indicated in Fig.10(36). A backing piece of ply or something similar is attached to the outside of the hull (or wedged against it). This is coated with a release agent and then, if possible, gel coated. The hole is made good with layers of glassfibre and resin with a few layers taken beyond the damaged area. This is covered with a cellophane film and everything allowed to dry, when the backing piece and film are removed and the repair ground smooth on the inside and painted outside if gel coat was not available.

All GRP work should take place in reasonably calm and certainly dry conditions. Warmth assists rapid resin cure, and an electric fire pointing at the repaired section will help things along. Plastic hulls respond well to regular washing off and polishing with one of the many proprietary polishes on the market, but avoid the silicone variety which is difficult to remove if the boat ever needs painting.

Repairs on other forms of construction consist of seeing how the job was done in the first place and then copying the method as far as possible. Much use can often be made of the modern gap-filling epoxy resins which will disguise many deficiencies in workmanship. They will easily fill gaps of up to 1/4in wide (6mm), and even more if extended with a suitable filler. Epoxy paints can be used on all forms of construction and are very waterproof and hard. After a while even wet and dry paper does not seem to touch them, but they do tend to 'chalk' quite quickly. For this reason a final coat of two-pot polyurethane is often applied over an epoxy where a good finish is wanted.

10.5.7 Electrolytic action

Sea water is an admirable electrolyte and that being so two dissimilar metals in close proximity under water tend to form a cell with the current flowing from one to another. This has the effect of wasting away the anodic or more base of the metals. The following table puts some typical boatbuilding metals in a rough electrochemical series with the noble, or cathodic materials at the top.

Galvanic series in sea water

Noble or cathodic end

> Stainless steel type 316 (2 per cent molybdenum)
> Stainless steel type 304
> Stainless steel type 321 (0.4 per cent titanium)
>
> Monel
> Gunmetal
> Phosphor bronze
> Admiralty brass
> Red brass
> Copper
> Naval brass
> Manganese bronze
> Muntz metal
> Lead
> Stainless steels with oxide destroyed
> Cast iron
> Mild steel
> Aluminium alloys
> Cadmium plating
> Galvanised steel
> Zinc
> Magnesium

Base or anodic end

Stainless steel appears in two positions in the table, which is confusing. As delivered, and in normal use with the oxide film that forms naturally to protect the metal intact, stainless steel is among the most noble and corrosion resistant of materials. However the maintenance of that oxide film requires the presence of oxygen which in certain places (such as under a barnacle) may be absent. In other areas as, for instance, where a shaft passes through a rubber bearing, the oxide film may be worn away and the oxygen prevented from reaching the surface. Here what is known as crevice corrosion may occur, and where this happens stainless steel drops down the galvanic series towards the base end and is liable to corrosion. The metal does not change; it is simply that its protective skin (which is formed in other alloys, such as aluminium alloy, in much the same way) is destroyed locally. The addition of molybdenum, as in the 316 alloys, minimises crevice corrosion. The presence of titanium, on the other hand, though it makes

for easier welding, reduces resistance to corrosion. If the oxide film is restored the material will again move to the noble end of the scale.

It is clear why zinc anodes are used. They will be attacked before any other of the usual metals and, that being so, will protect them. Magnesium anodes are generally preferred in fresh water, incidentally. The size, positioning and installation of all such sacrificial anodes is best left to the professionals. These anodes should never be painted. Paint acts as a protection against galvanic corrosion (and so is very important) but anodes are meant to be attacked and corroded. Even where cathodic protection is fitted, leakage from insulation faults in electrical circuits can cause rapid corrosion under water, see Chapter 13 (13.3.4).

When deciding on what metals to use underwater the distance they are apart on the galvanic series is one important factor (the greater the distance the more serious the action); the other is their relative bulk. Thus, for instance, if a yacht were copper sheathed and iron fastenings were used, the iron would be attacked which would be dangerous. On the other hand if for some reason gunmetal bolts were put through an iron keel, though the iron would still be wasted that would not be too serious. Taking an even more extreme example, stainless steel shafts are sometimes used in conjunction with aluminium alloy hulls, and though the aluminium will be attacked, because there is such a vast area compared with that of the shafts the effect is generally not serious. Aluminium alloy shafts in a stainless hull (if such a combination can be imagined) would be asking for trouble.

Mill scale on steel plating is another example of dissimilar metals in action. Mill scale, which occurs as the plates are being rolled, comprises various ferric oxides, among them magnetite. This is about as cathodic to iron as copper, and where paint has been removed and sea water can get at the scale, the plating will be attacked and eaten away. Thus the removal of mill scale by shot blasting or other means is most important on steel craft, just as is the maintenance of a protective film of paint.

Brass is an alloy of copper and zinc. It can be guessed that in the presence of sea water the zinc will be wasted away. This is called de-zincification and leaves the metal copper-coloured, crumbly and quite lacking in strength.

10.5.8 Painting

Painting is still extensively used on yachts, both to protect surfaces above and below the water and for cosmetic purposes. Even a GRP hull needs anti-fouling unless the boat is normally kept out of the water, and epoxy paint systems are being increasingly used on GRP hulls to combat osmosis, or to restore and protect the surface after osmosis has been treated (see 10.5.6).

Terms like two-pot polyurethane, wet edge time and pot life do sound rather forbidding, and modern paint systems are chemically very complex – so it is vital to follow in detail the instructions which are issued by paint makers. Nevertheless, there are some general rules which apply, no matter what paint or varnish is being used.

First, it is essential to choose a suitable paint covering for any particular application. Certain paints are not compatible with others, and cannot be satisfactorily applied on top of them, so it is important to keep a record of what products are used year by year on various parts of the boat – bottom, boottopping, topsides, upperworks, deck, spars, varnished surfaces, deck fittings, interior surfaces, chain locker, bilges etc. It is also necessary to use the right type of paint system for the material being covered, be it GRP, timber, alloy, steel or ferro-cement for example. All paint manufacturers provide literature on these matters, and if this is carefully read and followed there should be no problems, but do not hesitate to seek their advice if in doubt.

Good surface preparation is absolutely essential for all paintwork, and is likely to account for 75 per cent of the work involved, probably more when applying a single-coat, epoxy resin-based paint. The surface must be smooth, clean and free of grease. Depending on the paint being applied, it may be necessary to remove every trace of the previous paint film. Dust must be removed by washing with water or white spirit, and finally wiping off with a tack rag. The atmosphere must be dust-free; damp down the floor, and do not wear woollen garments which are liable to shed small particles of hair.

With most paint systems a primer or undercoat must be overcoated within a certain interval of time (say within 6-24 hours) which means that careful planning is needed. The weather and temperature must also be considered: never paint in damp conditions.

Paints and varnishes either contain, or need added to them, thinners which allow the covering to spread evenly in a thin film and which then evaporate. Consequently the final film may only be half as thick as the wet film that is applied – one reason that dust particles mysteriously appear when the paint dries. Make sure that the correct thinners are used, and in the right proportions. If a can of paint is to be used which has been previously opened, it is important to strain it carefully to remove any portions of skin which have formed. Mix the components of the paint and/or thinners as directed, and allow the pot to stand for a few minutes to get rid of any air bubbles.

Most paints can be applied by brush, roller or spray. Professional painters may use spray systems, for which proper equipment and precautions are essential. Paint spraying can be extremely dangerous unless proper safety precautions are taken. The amateur is therefore likely to use brush or roller; the latter is quicker but does not give such a good finish as a brush, properly used. Also a brush is better for priming coats, which need to be brushed well into the surface. Some paints can be applied satisfactorily with a pad.

Brushes must be best quality and, of course, scrupulously clean. Because speed is important in applying paint (a polyurethane, for example, sets quite quickly) it is necessary to use as large a brush as can be easily handled for the area concerned. If a roller is used, have one of the shaved mohair type.

It is essential to plan the work, dividing the area to be covered into manageable sizes, and working from one to another while the paint is still wet and the boundaries can merge together. Immerse the bristles of the brush not more than half-way into the paint, and do not wipe off the brush against the sides of the tin which causes loss of thinners from the paint running back into the tin. Transfer the paint to the surface as evenly as possible, using fast horizontal strokes, but finally laying off in one direction with the brush angled at about 45°. Do not reverse the brush while it is in contact with the paint film, or air bubbles will be trapped therein.

After about half-an-hour, paint may start to gel in the top of the brush, so either wash the brush with thinners or change brushes to prevent bits of dried paint getting to the paint film.

Brushes must be thoroughly washed out with thinners after use, and then with warm water and detergent. After rinsing and drying they should be wrapped in greaseproof paper and stowed carefully away, not left stuck in a tin.

Chapter 11

Spars, Rigging, Ropes and Sails

Contents

11.1 Spars

11.1.1 Masts – general

The mast of a sailing yacht supports the sails which drive her through the water. Most yacht masts depend on standing rigging to hold them in position, but a few are unstayed. In a typical cruising yacht the mast is relatively sturdy, and is kept as straight as possible by the standing rigging. But in a modern racing yacht the mast is made as light and thin as possible, and can be bent by varying amounts in order to optimise the set of the mainsail. This type of rigging is more complicated and must be carefully controlled since any error may cause dismasting.

11.1.2 Masts – manufacture

Originally masts were made of solid timber –

usually pine, or spruce for smaller racing yachts. It was not always easy to find suitable timber, and to ensure that it was of uniformly good quality, so as better glues were developed it became feasible to build up a mast in sections. Short lengths of timber which might have been a source of weakness could then be rejected, and by reversing the natural grain of the wood in adjacent sections it was possible to minimise the risk of distortion as the timber matured. Hollow wooden masts were developed.

Masts for large vessels, such as sailing ships and the bigger yachts, were built up from steel plates, originally rivetted together but later of welded construction.

Aluminium alloy began to be generally adopted for yacht masts in the 1950s, and is now in almost universal use. The material has a tensile strength of about 20 tons per square inch, and an alloy spar can be about two-thirds the weight of a hollow one laboriously fashioned in silver spruce. Masts are manufactured from extruded tubes of the required section, incorporating a track or groove for the mainsail as required. Spars for smaller yachts are made up from one extruded length, but bigger masts can be constructed from two or more sections joined together.

The top of a mast may be tapered, by removing a thin vee from each side of the spar, closing the gaps, and welding the seams so formed. Partly to resist the pull of the luff of the mainsail, but also because they have better support athwartships, masts are usually made with a bigger section (and hence more resistance to bending) fore-and-aft.

Special procedures have to be adopted for welding aluminium alloy, because the oxide film which gives the metal resistance to corrosion interferes with the fusion of the joint: consequently the welding process has to be performed within a shield of inert gas, usually argon, which isolates the area of the weld from atmospheric oxygen. Even minor repairs to masts (or other aluminium alloy spars) which involve welding must be done with equipment which is not likely to be available in the average boatyard.

Particular attention also has to be given to avoid dissimilar metals in contact with aluminium alloy, due to the the probability of galvanic action. No brass or other copper-based alloys must be used. Stainless steel fittings such as mast tangs and spreader heel fittings should be insulated from the mast with zinc chromate paste. Many winches have bronze bases, which

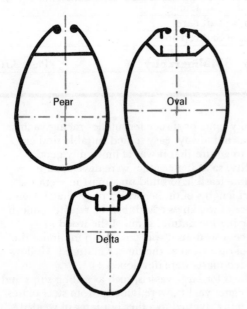

Fig. 11(1) Typical common mast sections. The dotted lines indicate the neutral axes of each section – about which the areas of material on either side balance. In general the pear and oval sections are preferred for masthead rigs, and the delta for fractional rigs because it gives more fore-and-aft flexibility.

must be isolated from the pad on which they are mounted by some suitably inert material such as Tufnol. Rivets should be monel metal or alloy, and stainless steel self-tapping screws should be avoided even for the lightest fittings.

After a mast has been polished and chemically etched it is anodised. This is an electrolytic process to prevent corrosion and to give a harder surface which will resist abrasion. Then the shroud and spreader fittings, winch pads, gooseneck, spinnaker fittings etc are attached, and internal halyards and electric wiring are fitted. The interior of the mast may be lined with polystyrene to reduce the noise from wire halyards.

11.1.3 **Booms and spinnaker poles**

The construction of a boom is similar to that of an alloy mast. The section used depends on the method of reefing (see 11.5.3). A round section should be used for roller reefing, since the sail rolls better and the boom has the same strength no matter in which direction it is rotated. Booms for slab reefing are not turned on their sides, so they can be thinner but taller in section.

Spinnaker poles are of circular section. The only point of note is to check and lubricate the end fittings at regular intervals.

11.1.4 **Standing rigging**

Standing rigging is intended to hold the mast straight and upright, or to control its required bend in the case of racing yachts. The rigging wires which hold the mast in the athwartships direction (sideways) are called shrouds: those which hold it fore-and-aft are stays.

The beam of a yacht in the neighbourhood of the mast, together with the height of the mast, determines what angle a shroud will make to the mast at its point of attachment. In order that the shroud may provide sufficient athwartships pull, this angle needs to be as large as can be arranged: otherwise the shroud tension must be increased, which puts undue compression on the mast. A mast is essentially a strut in compression and under well established mechanical laws it will buckle at a certain load – depending on its length, the moment of inertia (or strength) of its cross-section, the material, and how it is stepped (on the keel or on deck). The problem is exacerbated by the modern tendency to reduce the sheeting angle of headsails making it necessary to set the chain plates (to which the shrouds are attached at their lower ends) inboard from the deck edge, see Fig. 11(2).

Consequently it is necessary for shrouds which run to or near the masthead to be provided with spreaders (or crosstrees) in order to increase the angle which they make to the mast. In Fig. 11(3) it is evident that the tension of the shroud bearing against the end of the spreader is forcing the mast in the direction of the arrow. Hence, in order to keep the mast straight, it is essential for a lower shroud to be fitted at this point so that it

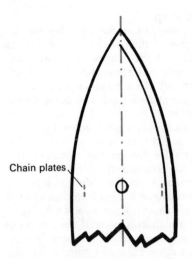

Fig. 11(2) Narrower sheeting angles for headsails require the chain plates to be set inboard from the deck edge, thereby narrowing the angle which a shroud makes with the mast aloft.

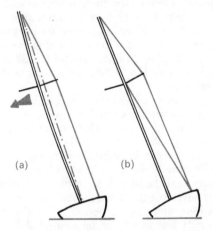

Fig. 11(3) In (a) the upper (cap) shroud bearing against the spreader bends the mast to leeward. The addition of a lower shroud (b), joining the mast at the spreader, holds the mast up to windward at that point, and keeps it straight.

holds the mast (and the spreader attached thereto) up to windward. In cruising yachts there are commonly two pairs of lower shrouds, one set leading to the deck slightly forward of the mast and the other set slightly aft of it.

Fig. 11(4) and Fig. 11(5) show typical rigging arrangements in cruising yachts, and the names of the various components. In Fig. 11(4) the mast has only one pair of spreaders, and this layout would be suitable for the average masthead sloop. In Fig. 11(5) two pairs of spreaders are provided, as would be appropriate for a larger yacht, or one with cutter rig (two headsails). In special cases, particularly for racing yachts or in the case of larger vessels, more than two pairs of spreaders may be used. These two diagrams also show the stays which hold the mast fore-and-aft. With the sloop rig this is done by the forestay and the backstay: in addition the lower shrouds help to steady the centre of the mast in the fore-and-aft plane, while an inner forestay (now usually referred to as a baby stay) may also be fitted to the height of the spreaders. The baby stay may be portable, so that it can be brought back to the mast in light to moderate conditions.

With a cutter rig it is necessary to have running backstays to hold the mast aft at the point where the forestay meets it. In order not to restrict the boom and mainsail, the running backstays (or runners) are set up in turn – the windward one being tensioned by a winch or lever, and the leeward one being slacked away. Racing yachts with bendy masts may also have one or more sets of runners to control the rig.

There are a few types of seagoing yacht which have unstayed masts – such as those with modified Chinese junk rigs, and cat rigged yachts as in Fig. 11(37) with no headsails. These unsupported masts must necessarily be bigger and heavier, even though they are not subject to the compression which rigging imposes on an ordinary mast.

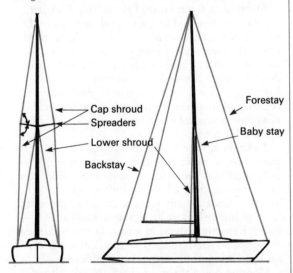

Fig. 11(4) Typical rigging suitable for a masthead sloop.

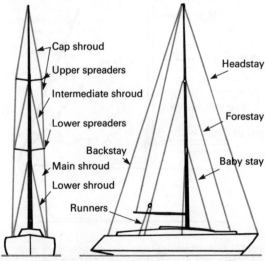

Fig. 11(5) Typical rigging suitable for a larger yacht, or one with cutter rig.

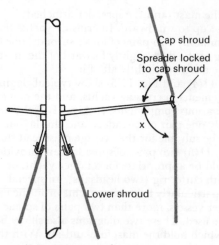

Fig. 11(6) It is important that the spreader bisects the angle of the cap shroud, and that it is locked to same.

11.1.5 **Spreaders**

The length of spreaders is usually determined by the need to clear overlapping headsails. Spreaders must be carefully designed, and well engineered in respect of their attachment to the mast. If they are firmly fixed to the mast the spreaders must be very strong, and consequently large and heavy. More usually they are arranged to swing fore-and-aft. It is most important that the outer end of the spreader is securely fixed to the cap shroud, and that it bisects the angle of the shroud, which means that it normally needs to be cocked up about 5° or 6° above horizontal, see Fig. 11(6). Some spreaders have clamps at the outer end for this purpose, otherwise bulldog grips can be used, well taped over to prevent any damage to sails.

Spreaders and their attachments should be items which are subjected to routine examination aloft, since spreader failure is a common cause of dismasting.

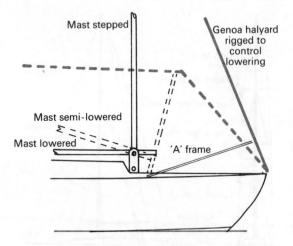

Fig. 11(7) 'A' frame rigged to control lowering of mast stepped on deck in tabernacle, using genoa halyard. The sideways movement of the mast must also be controlled as it is lowered.

11.1.6 **Mast step**

Most masts are stepped on the keel, thereby obtaining support at the partners where they pass through the deck. A mast stepped on deck needs to be a bigger section, but has the advantage of not passing through the accommodation, of eliminating leaks at deck level, and being shorter for transportation.

Some yachts have their mast stepped in a tabernacle or hinged heel fitting on deck, so that it can be lowered for passing under bridges etc. As the mast is lowered the effective angle of the forestay to the mast soon diminishes, so it is necessary to erect some kind of frame forward of the mast to serve as a strut, as is shown in Fig. 11(7). Also, as the mast is lowered the tension on the shrouds is removed, and so it is necessary to steady the mast athwartships in order to avoid damage to the tabernacle or heel fitting.

11.1.7 **Masts – maintenance**

During the sailing season there is little actual maintenance to be done on aluminium alloy spars, but there is a continual need for inspection aloft to ensure that all is in order and to prevent trouble developing. Maintenance of standing rigging is discussed in 11.2.5, and should be done at the same time.

For going aloft a good bosun's chair is needed, preferably one with a safety belt round to prevent the occupant slipping out. Modern bosun's chairs have handy pockets for tools and spares, but otherwise these can be hoisted separately in a bucket. Normally the main halyard is used – make sure that the shackle is properly screwed up. It is advisable to have a second halyard attached for safety, or the person going aloft may take a safety line which can be secured aloft. While anybody is aloft one of the crew should be permanently in attendance at the foot of the mast: it has been known for somebody else to come along and let go the halyard by mistake.

Starting at the masthead check that halyard sheaves are free and in good condition. Take the weight of the halyard off each sheave in turn, to check the clearances in the bearings. Worn bushes should be renewed before further trouble develops with jammed sheaves and worn halyards. A good wash down with fresh water to remove salt deposits from bearing surfaces will not come amiss, followed by the application of an aerosol lubricant.

Examine all the fittings secured at the masthead, to make sure that pins are in good order and that the holes through which they pass are not elongated. Check all split pins for security. Look for any signs of cracks in the mast itself or in castings or fittings attached thereto, and for any movement in screws or rivets. Unless these details are inspected methodically it is easy for something untoward to be overlooked.

Coming down the mast check the security of the mast track, if externally fitted, and wash out the track so that the slides can run freely. Inspect each shroud fitting, check the security of any through-mast bolts, and look for any sign of distortion to the mast itself.

At the spreaders, check that they bisect the shroud angle correctly, that the tips are secured to the shrouds where appropriate, and that anti-chafe arrangements are in place. See that the spreaders are secure in their sockets, and that the latter are properly attached to the mast with all securing arrangements tight and correct.

At deck level check round the main boom gooseneck, winch pads, cleats, sheave boxes etc, for any visual sign of deterioration. Only close inspection may detect a tiny crack in some weld or fitting of a mast, or an elongated hole which should be round, but these are the little details which might save your mast, or even your life.

When spars are laid up for the winter they should be washed with warm, fresh water to remove salt deposits. Use soap, but not detergents which may react with the alloy. When thoroughly dry, the spar can be polished with silicone wax. Lightly oil all moving fittings.

11.2 Standing Rigging

11.2.1 Standing rigging - materials

The materials most commonly used for standing rigging are stainless steel rod, 1×19 wire and 7×7 wire rope.

Cold drawn stainless steel rod is the simplest but most expensive type of standing rigging. It is usually round, but for use as shrouds it may be lenticular in section. The ends of the rod are threaded, and can be used with screwed or rotary-hammer-swaged terminals (see below). Rod rigging has very little stretch for a given strength, and because it is thin it has minimal windage. But it does have some disadvantages, apart from its high cost. Because it is very rigid it must be laid out straight or carefully coiled in a big circle, and it is more prone to fatigue than other types of rigging. It is also brittle, and even minor damage to the surface can cause loss of strength. Trying to straighten a bent stainless steel fitting or rod rigging is likely to lead to early failure.

Wire rigging can be manufactured from either galvanised wire or 316 specification stainless steel wire. Galvanised wire, which has a zinc coating, is much cheaper, rather stronger and more flexible than stainless steel wire. But it is not nearly so durable and does not look so nice.

Most yachts have standing rigging of 1×19 stainless steel wire, to specification 316. Stainless steel can in fact stain under certain conditions, and particularly if it is starved of atmospheric oxygen which initiates crevice corrosion: for this same reason rigging or terminals should not be taped over with adhesive tape. Stainless steel wire is weakened by bending or scratching it, and it is more liable to fatigue failure than galvanised wire. A slight rusty-brown discoloration of the material itself is not serious, and can easily be removed, but such symptoms from inside a terminal or any sign of a broken strand indicate that the rope has reached the end of its life at that point.

Details of the construction and strength of wire ropes are given in 11.4.15 – 11.4.18.

11.2.2 Wire rope terminals

Apart from splicing, which is not practicable for 1×19 wire, there are various ways of attaching terminals to wire rigging.

Swaged terminals are commonly used with stainless steel wire, and consist of a sleeve which fits closely over the end of the wire and which has an eye, or a fork or a threaded stud at its other end. The wire is then inserted into the sleeve, which is then squeezed onto the wire at very high pressure in a rotary-hammer machine. If the correct procedures are followed the joint is as strong as the wire, but sometimes salt water may cause corrosion along the grain boundaries of the work hardened stainless steel, so that after a period of service the swage (sleeve) develops hair-line cracks which will lead to failure. Salty moisture may also settle in the minute spaces between the terminal and the wire, creating hidden pockets of corrosion which will, however, be revealed by stains around the lip of the sleeve before they reach a critical stage. Hence it is most important to examine such fittings very carefully, and at regular intervals. At the same time look closely at the wire rope for any signs of flattened and shiny strands adjacent to the swage, which indicate failure at this point.

Swageless screwed terminals, as produced by Norseman, are good alternatives to swaged terminals for stainless steel wire. They are attached to the wire without cold working in a press or work hardening of the stainless steel – the main cause of stress corrosion problems – and they require no special tools or equipment, so they are ideal for use afloat. Routine inspection of the terminal can be done by dismantling the assembly. The complete fitting comprises the end portion (available with eye, fork or stud ends), a cone, a lock nut, and the terminal body. It is important to follow the fitting instructions, summarised in Fig. 11(8).

With the Talurit (or pressed ferrule) system the wire passes through a ferrule (copper for stainless steel wire, or light alloy for galvanised wire), round a thimble, and back into the collar in the reverse direction. The ferrule is then squeezed round both parts of the wire in a hydraulic press. Provided that the ferrule is correctly placed (not close against the thimble) and is not cracked, this system gives good results for rigging which is more lightly loaded, but it does not have the inherent strength of the systems described above.

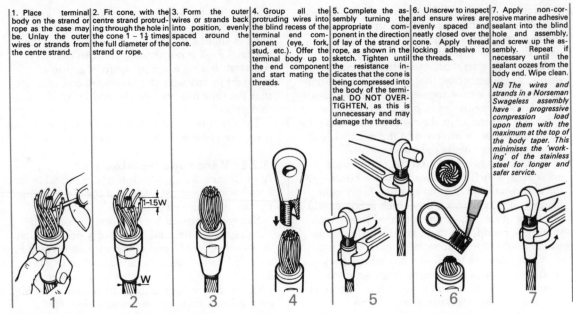

| 1. Place terminal body on the strand or rope as the case may be. Unlay the outer wires or strands from the centre strand. | 2. Fit cone, with the centre strand protruding through the hole in the cone 1 – 1½ times the full diameter of the strand or rope. | 3. Form the outer wires or strands, evenly spaced around the cone. | 4. Group all the protruding wires into the blind recess of the terminal end component (eye, fork, stud, etc.). Offer the terminal body up to the end component and start mating the threads. | 5. Complete the assembly turning the appropriate component in the direction of lay of the strand or rope, as shown in the sketch. Tighten until the resistance indicates that the cone is being compressed into the body of the terminal. DO NOT OVERTIGHTEN, as this is unnecessary and may damage the threads. | 6. Unscrew to inspect and ensure wires are evenly spaced and neatly closed over the cone. Apply thread locking adhesive to the threads. | 7. Apply non-corrosive marine adhesive sealant into the blind hole and assembly, and screw up the assembly. Repeat if necessary until the sealant oozes from the body end. Wipe clean.

NB The wires and strands in a Norseman Swageless assembly have a progressive compression load upon them with the maximum at the top of the body taper. This minimises the 'working' of the stainless steel for longer and safer service. |

Fig. 11(8) Norseman swageless terminal fitting instructions.

Security can be improved by using two ferrules per eye.

Emergency repairs to rigging can be done with bulldog grips. A seagoing yacht should carry a selection of these, in the correct sizes for the wire rope fitted. The grip, shown in Fig. 11(9), consists of a U-shaped clamp, the two legs of the U being threaded. A drilled cross piece fits over the legs of the U and is serrated on its inner edge to engage with the lay of the wire. The two lengths of wire within the U are compressed into the bend of the U by two nuts on the outside of the crosspiece. The short end of the wire should be against the U bend, and the standing part against the cross piece. Three grips should be fitted alongside each other, and it is important that they are the right size for the wire concerned.

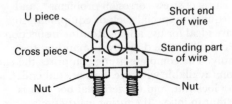

Fig. 11(9) Bulldog grip, for emergency rigging repairs. It is important that the wires be assembled as shown, with the short end in the U of the grip. The grip must be the right size for the wire concerned, and three should be fitted.

11.2.3 Rigging fittings

At their upper ends shrouds are secured to tangs, usually fitted to the mast with through bolts, by means of clevis pins. For a single tang the rigging wire must have a fork terminal, or for a double tang an eye terminal. Whichever arrangement is fitted the clevis pin, see Fig. 11(10), must be a

close fit in the holes, and must be held in position by a good split pin. Split pins for such essential services should not be re-used after rigging has been removed for any reason, but should be replaced with new. Added security is given by taping them over, which also avoids the posibility of sails or running rigging snagging on the ends of the split pin. All such fittings aloft should be examined at regular intervals.

Racing yachts may have a more sophisticated arrangement for shrouds whereby, in order to reduce windage and turbulence round the mast, the shrouds disappear through holes in the side of the mast and are secured inside.

Shrouds are tensioned at their lower ends by bottlescrews, which must be secured to the chainplates by toggles, as shown in Fig. 11(11). Chainplates must be carefully designed and engineered, securely fastened to the hull, and at the correct angle for the pull to be exerted on them. Like other rigging fittings, they are liable to wear and should be examined regularly.

A toggle, shown in Fig. 11(10), is a form of universal joint which allows the bottlescrew to

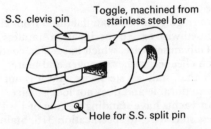

Fig. 11(10) Toggle with clevis pin. With all such rigging fittings it is most important that the clevis pin is an accurate fit within the toggle (or the fork end of a bottlescrew), and that it is also the correct length with the minimum longitudinal movement when secured by the split pin.

318

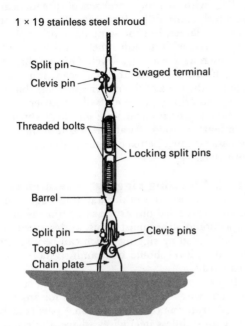

1 × 19 stainless steel shroud

Split pin — — Swaged terminal
Clevis pin —

Threaded bolts —
— Locking split pins

Barrel —

Split pin — — Clevis pins
Toggle —
Chain plate —

Fig. 11(11) Shroud – attachment to chain plate. The 1×19 stainless steel shroud ends with a swaged terminal. This is connected by a clevis pin (secured by a split pin) to the upper fork end of the bottlescrew. The lower fork end of the bottlescrew is connected to the chain plate by a toggle, which gives freedom of movement in all directions.

move in any direction – both to avoid damage to the bottlescrew and also to minimise fatigue in the rigging wire where it enters the terminal above the bottlescrew. The clevis pins in toggles must of course be secured by split pins and inspected as for those in mast tangs referred to above. Forestays should be fitted with toggles at their upper and lower ends.

Bottlescrews (otherwise referred to as rigging screws or turnbuckles) are available to various designs, and in different materials, but basically they all consist of a central body which is threaded internally, right-handed at one end and left-handed at the other, Fig. 11(11). Into this central body are threaded bolts which have either eye, fork or stud ends – to match up with the rigging and with the toggle attached to the chainplate. Obviously, one of these bolts is threaded right-hand, and the other is threaded left-hand. When the central body is turned, the threaded ends protruding from it are either pulled together or pushed apart. Some means must be provided to prevent the bottlescrew rotating under load: this may be arranged by lock nuts fitted on the threaded ends, but a more positive locking device (e.g. using split pins) is to be preferred.

In most sailing yachts the forestay is fixed (although some means may be provided for making adjustments to it, and hence to the rake of the mast), and the fore-and-aft tension of the rig is controlled by the permanent backstay. Modern rigs for racing yachts depend very much

on proper control of backstay tension – whereby mast bend, the shape of the mainsail and tension of the forestay (supporting the genoa) are correctly adjusted for optimum performance. In smaller yachts the backstay may be controlled by a simple purchase, but more commonly tension is adjusted by a handwheel, somewhat resembling the steering wheel of a car, which is screwed internally and carries a threaded shaft connected to the bottom of the backstay. Such tensioners are available in various sizes – from those suitable for backstays of $\frac{5}{8}$in circumference (5mm diameter) and capable of loading to 3500lb (1600kg), to those for 1$\frac{1}{8}$in circumference (9mm diameter) wire which will develop tensions of 17,200lb (7800kg).

More sophisticated are hydraulic backstay tensioners, with which even higher loadings can be achieved for larger yachts. It is important that such tensioners incorporate some form of pre-set maximum load device, to avoid possible damage to the rig by overloading.

11.2.4 Setting up rigging

These notes are not intended to apply to the more detailed tuning required for the mast of a racing yacht, which is a continuing process, but rather to give guidance on setting up the standing rigging for the average cruising yacht so that it is first of all safe and secure for any weather likely to be met, and second allows the sails to set as well as possible.

The exact procedure depends on the type of rig, and every yacht needs somewhat different treatment according to the type of mast, how it is stepped, and details of the rigging plan. For our purpose we will assume that the yacht is a masthead sloop, and that the mast has a single pair of spreaders with two pairs of lower shrouds.

There is only one way that standing rigging can be properly set up, and that is under sail in smooth water in a breeze of about force 3–4. But previously certain initial adjustments must have been completed in harbour.

First adjust the mast fore-and-aft so that it is standing with a slight rake aft – that is not quite perpendicular, but leaning very slightly aft. This can best be judged by letting the main halyard hang down the aft side of the mast, so that in a boat of 33ft (10m) length it lies about 8in (200mm) aft of the mast at deck level. This, it should be emphasised, is only an initial setting which may need adjusting later, and when checking it be sure that the boat is in normal trim – not down by the bow or by the stern. Tighten and lock the forestay and backstay accordingly: they should be quite tight, because the forestay has to support the luff of the genoa when sailing.

Now tighten the upper (cap) shrouds equally each side, so that they both have almost the same tension as the forestay, but not quite so much. Remember that if the rigging is new it is going to stretch somewhat as soon as the boat is sailing. At this point it is important to make sure that the mast is not leaning to port or starboard. This can easily be checked by taking the main halyard down to the chainplates on each side in turn, and adjusting the cap shrouds until the two measurements are the same. Then adjust the lower shrouds each side so that the forward pair are just taut, but with no real weight on them, and the aft pair are just slack.

If the mast is stepped on the keel it should now be chocked in position at the partners (where it passes through the deck). This can be done with specially shaped wooden wedges, carefully fitted so that they hold the mast evenly, but do not misalign it: alternatively hard rubber strips can be used, but they will need to be held in position in some way – by a large jubilee clip or similar strap.

Now the boat is ready to go sailing – as soon as conditions are suitable. If the rigging is new it will stretch, more especially the upper (cap) shrouds. Increase their tension alternately on the leeward side, as the boat sails on each tack in turn, until most of the slack is taken up in the lee rigging, but being careful to tighten both sides an equal amount by counting the turns of the bottlescrews. It then remains to adjust the lower shrouds so as to eliminate any bend in the mast – which can be checked quite easily by squinting up the mainsail groove or mast track from a position underneath the gooseneck. When the boat is on the wind most of the weight will be on the windward, forward shroud so far as the lowers are concerned: both the leeward lowers will be slack. If the mast falls away to leeward at the spreaders, then both the windward lowers need tightening: in a small yacht the effect of doing this can be judged by racking the two shrouds together. If, however, the mast bends to windward in the area of the spreaders, both the windward lowers need to be slackened.

Sail to windward on alternate tacks, adjusting the lowers on the lee side and then checking the result on the next tack. This can take some time to get right, and it is best to have one person doing the adjusting and one person looking up the mast, while a third sails the boat. During this procedure check the balance of the boat on the helm. Mast rake is not the only cause of weather (or lee) helm but it can be a major factor, and initial sailing trials may show that the masthead should be moved slightly forward or aft. Depending on the type of fitting, adjusting the forestay to achieve less or more rake may have to await return to harbour. When the best possible adjustments have been made to the lower shrouds be sure to lock all the bottlescrews, and to tape them over.

The rigging of a new boat takes a little time – and a good breeze or two of wind – to settle down. So it will certainly be necessary to repeat the above procedure for adjusting both the upper and lower shrouds while sailing.

Rigs with two (or more) sets of spreaders are obviously more difficult to tune, since there are more variables, but the same basic principles apply. To facilitate adjustments it is best if all bottlescrews are at deck level. The cap shrouds (which run to or near the masthead) must be fixed to the ends of the upper spreaders, but be free to run through the ends of the lower spreaders. The intermediate shrouds (which terminate on the mast at the height of the upper spreaders) must be fixed to the ends of the lower spreaders.

11.2.5 Standing rigging – maintenance

Routine inspections of the standing rigging aloft should be carried out at the same time as the inspection of other mast items, as described in 11.1.7. Standing rigging which can be inspected from deck level should be examined more frequently.

Inspection of standing rigging should cover:
(1) The wires themselves, to check for any signs of stranding or deterioration – particularly with stainless steel wires adjacent to rigging terminals, where flattened strands with a shiny appearance indicate failure. Whereas stainless steel wire requires no real maintenance, galvanised wire will have a longer life if it is washed down periodically, and treated with boiled linseed oil. Any wire which is rusty or has broken strands should be condemned, and the condition of galvanised wire can also be judged by bending it and seeing how it reacts: if it stays bent, or straightens very slowly, it should be replaced.
(2) Rigging terminals (swaged or swageless), for any signs of cracks, hole elongation, security of clevis pins and split pins.
(3) Winches, tackles or other tensioning devices for backstays.
(4) Chain plates, forestay fittings, backstay fittings – for general condition of securing arrangements, welds etc.

If the mast is unstepped for the winter the opportunity should be taken for a thorough examination of all the standing rigging. Ideally it should be labelled, removed from the mast, well washed and dried, and (for galvanised wire) treated with boiled linseed oil. Before storing away in the dry, examine each wire closely throughout its length, and bend it slightly where it enters the rigging terminals to see if there are any signs of broken strands.

11.2.6 Rigging failures and dismasting

In the event of a rigging failure the first action is to try to save the mast by minimising the strain on it. For example, if a weather shroud parts, go about on the other tack: if the forestay carries away, run off before the wind. Then attention must be given to reducing sail, and either repairing the damage or rigging a jury shroud or

11.3 Running rigging

11.3.1 Running rigging – general

Running rigging comprises the numerous lines such as halyards, sheets, guys, lifts, downhauls, outhauls etc (together with their various snap shackles, blocks, cleats and the like) which hoist and control the set of the sails of a yacht. In a small boat all of these can be controlled by hand, or with the benefit of simple tackles, but in larger yachts powerful winches and other mechanical devices have to be used. Fig. 11(13) shows a handy-billy tackle which can be used for a variety of tasks.

Descriptions of types of cordage and wire rope, together with their properties and strengths, and notes on their splicing, handling and maintenance, are given in 11.4.

An increasing variety of fittings are used with running rigging, all aimed to combine strength with lightness, and mechanical simplicity with ease of operation. For full details of what are currently on offer it is best to consult the illustrated catalogue of a good chandler. Fig. 11(14) shows just a few of the more common items of gear.

In Fig. 11(15) can be seen the principal running rigging of a modern masthead sloop. Some of the lesser items will be described separately. Halyards needs to maintain a uniform tension on the luff of a sail, often for long periods, so they should stretch as little as possible.

Fig. 11(12) Jury rigged mast – from spinnaker pole lashed to foot of broken mast, and stayed by lines leading to deck fittings such as samson post, spinnaker blocks etc. On such a mast could be set the yacht's smallest headsail, with its foot along the jury mast and the head of the sail attached to some kind of sheet.

stay. A genoa halyard can be set up as a temporary forestay, while the main halyard or even the topping lift might be utilised as a backstay. A halyard or the spinnaker pole lift can be pressed into service as a temporary shroud, sufficient to steady the mast on the leeward side while more permanent repairs are done.

Provided it can be reached, and this may be a problem, a break in a wire can be repaired by using bulldog grips to form loops at the two broken ends, and then shackling a hand-billy between the two loops and setting it up tight. If a mast fitting fails it may be possible to pass a strop round the mast and over a spreader, to provide a temporary anchorage for a jury shroud.

Often however, when an item of standing rigging fails, the mast will break and/or go over the side. If a mast is actually falling it is better to bear away so that it drops into the sea, than to luff so that it lands on deck and possibly injures somebody. The first priority is to try to recover the wreckage from the sea, so that it does not damage the hull. If this is not possible it must be cut adrift, for which purpose special wire cutters such as Felco should be carried onboard: try to salvage whatever is available for use as a jury rig. Do not start the engine until it is certain that all the rigging has been removed from the water, and there is no possibility of fouling the propeller.

What sort of jury rig can be contrived depends very much on what items, particularly spars, are available. If the mast has been lost completely it should be possible to use the spinnaker pole or perhaps the main boom as a jury mast (set up with shrouds rigged from sheets or warps), on which at least a small headsail can be set as a form of trysail.

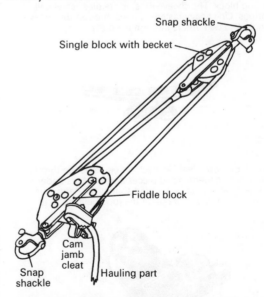

Fig. 11(13) A handy-billy (or luff tackle) is made up of a single block with a becket, to which is attached the standing part, and a fiddle block. That shown in the sketch has a cam jamb cleat on the fiddle block – a modern aid which replaces the old method of 'choking the luff' by jamming the hauling part across the sheave of the block. Snap shackles each end allow the handy-billy to be used easily for a number of tasks. When rigged to advantage (with the single block fixed) the mechanical advantage is 4:1. When rigged to disadvantage (with the fiddle block fixed) it is 3:1.

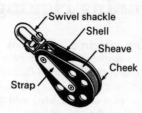

Single block with swivel. Modern blocks are typically manufactured from glass fibre filled nylon, with stainless steel reinforcement and sheaves mounted on ball bearings.

Fiddle block with fixed eye. Since the sheaves are in the same plane, this type of block is less likely to twist than a double block, if the sheaves turn in the same direction.

Turning block. The sheave runs on stainless steel ball bearings. One heavy fastening goes through the sheave spindle and two others through the body.

General purpose cleat. All deck fittings must be through bolted, with generous pad pieces and washers under the deck. A cleat should be secured so that the centreline is about 15° to the line of pull of the rope belayed to it.

Genoa sheet lead block – position adjustable on deck-mounted track. This type of block gets the sheet as near the deck as possible.

Fig. 11(14) Items of gear for use with running rigging.

Double block with swivel and becket. When choosing any type of block, make sure the sheave is wide enough for the tope, and that the diameter is sufficient to allow the rope to render round it easily. The sheave diameter should be at least five times the rope diameter for fibre cordage.

Snatch block with swivel. The shell is hinged so that one side can be opened to allow the bight of a rope to be inserted.

Snap shackle with swivel eye. Note the short lanyard attached to the ring which releases the plunger. Suitable for loads up to 7000lb (3200kg).

Fiddle block with swivel and becket. The standing part of the rope is made fast to the becket.

Consequently they are made up from wire, but for ease of handling they are fitted with a rope tail. The length of the wire should be such that four turns can be taken on the winch, and the wire to rope splice comes between the winch and the cleat when the sail is fully hoisted. Because wire rope for running rigging has to pass over sheaves and round winches, it needs to be much more flexible than the wire used for standing rigging. This is achieved by using a rope which has a larger number of smaller wires –typically 6×19 construction with a fibre core. Sheaves for this type of wire should be 12 times the diameter of the wire in the case of halyards.

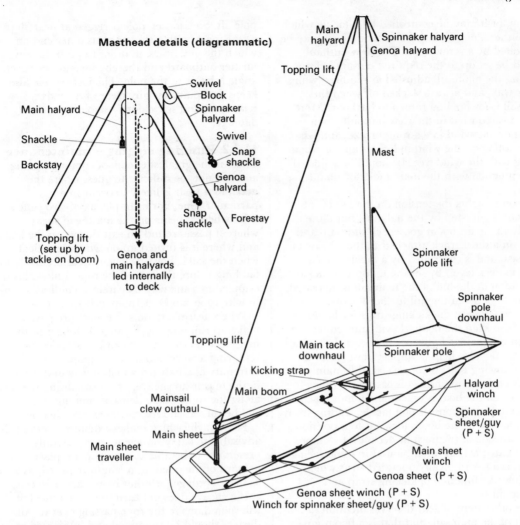

Masthead details (diagrammatic)

Swivel
Block
Spinnaker halyard
Swivel
Snap shackle
Genoa halyard
Snap shackle
Forestay

Main halyard
Shackle
Backstay
Topping lift (set up by tackle on boom)
Genoa and main halyards led internally to deck

Main halyard
Spinnaker halyard
Genoa halyard
Topping lift
Mast
Spinnaker pole lift
Spinnaker pole downhaul
Topping lift
Main tack downhaul
Spinnaker pole
Kicking strap
Halyard winch
Main boom
Spinnaker sheet/guy (P + S)
Mainsail clew outhaul
Main sheet
Main sheet winch
Main sheet traveller
Genoa sheet (P + S)
Genoa sheet winch (P + S)
Winch for spinnaker sheet/guy (P + S)

Fig. 11(15) Diagrammatic sketch showing the main items of running rigging of a 33ft (10m) masthead sloop. For clarity, standing rigging and other details are omitted. Running rigging which is duplicated port and starboard (P&S) is only shown on the starboard side.

The windage of halyards can be reduced by running them down inside the mast, and this is now common practice. The main halyard is shackled to the headboard of the mainsail, whereas genoa and spinnaker halyards are normally fitted with snap shackles: these need to be cleaned and lightly oiled from time to time to keep them free and secure.

Sheets have to be continually adjusted, so a slight amount of stretch is more acceptable. In any case they need to be easy to handle, so they must be made of rope – except for the largest yachts, where wire may be found. Sheets take a lot of wear, and this should be minimised, both for safety and economy, by making sure that blocks are of sufficient size (with sheaves at least five times the diameter of the rope), and correctly aligned for the direction of pull, and by fitting plastic tubing or similar anti-chafe protection round shrouds, bottlescrews and the like. It pays to buy sheets which are slightly overlength, because the points of wear can then be moved round to give a longer life.

The mainsheet must be sufficiently powerful to control the mainsail in all foreseeable conditions, with large sheaves in blocks which swivel as required to take up the necessary alignment according to the position of the boom. In modern yachts the lower block of the mainsheet is usually secured to a traveller, mounted on a track which runs athwartships. The position of the traveller can be controlled by tackles, and can have a considerable influence on the set of the mainsail. Going to windward in moderate conditions the traveller should be about the middle of the track, but in stronger winds or when reaching it should be moved to leeward. In light airs the traveller may be brought up to windward, and the mainsheet eased, to give more fullness in the mainsail. Other items of running rigging which control the set of the mainsail are the clew outhaul, the main tack (gooseneck) downhaul, and the kicking strap (or boom vang).

The main clew outhaul controls the tension in the foot of the mainsail, which has a big effect on the shape of the whole sail. It may be a simple lashing, or it may be controlled by a tackle which runs either along or inside the boom, or it may be controlled by a screw gear. The clew outhaul should be set up to the required tension before hoisting the mainsail, adjusted as required while under way, and always slacked off when the mainsail is lowered on return to harbour. More tension is required in the clew outhaul when sailing on the wind in a strong breeze, and less when sailing on the wind in lighter airs or when sailing with the wind free. It should be adjusted in conjunction with the main tack downhaul (see below).

In some yachts the tension on the luff of the mainsail is adjusted by the halyard, but more usually the main boom gooseneck slides up and down on a short track attached to the aft side of the mast, and is controlled by a tackle rigged down to deck level. By setting up on this tackle the tension in the luff of the mainsail is increased, pulling the flow in the sail further forward.

The function of the kicking strap (or boom vang) is to keep the boom down, and reduce the twist in the mainsail towards the head. In a small yacht it may also help to impart mast bend. So far as reducing twist is concerned, this mainly applies once the mainsheet is eased – in other words when the boat is reaching. In most yachts the kicking strap consists of a tackle, leading from the underside of the boom forward to a position on the aft side of the mast at deck level. A more sophisticated arrangement, found in some racing yachts, is a hydraulically operated strut which combines the function of kicking strap and topping lift.

One other item of gear deserves mention in respect of the mainsail, and that is a boom guy (or preventer) which is led from the end of the boom forward to a block near the bow, in order to steady the boom in a following wind and sea, and to prevent an accidental gybe.

Details of reefing systems and roller furling for headsails are given under 'Sails' in 11.5.3 and 11.5.4.

In smaller yachts the spinnaker sheets/guys are interchangeable, the windward one to the end of the spinnaker pole being called the guy and the leeward one to the clew of the spinnaker being the sheet. On the opposite gybe their roles are reversed. Larger yachts have separate guys (wire) and sheets (cordage). The sheets/guys are led outboard of all other rigging to blocks fitted right aft each side of the boat, and thence to winches.

The spinnaker pole is clipped to a traveller on a track secured to the forward side of the mast, so that the height of the heel of the pole can be adjusted according to the wind strength and the point of sailing. A lift and a downhaul control the height of the outer end of the spinnaker pole.

When the spinnaker pole is trimmed well forward, with the wind almost on the beam, the effective angle of pull of the guy is greatly reduced, making it difficult to pull the spinnaker

pole aft. So a jockey pole is rigged athwartships at the mast, with a sheave at its outer end on which the guy bears, in order to push the guy further outboard and thereby increase its effective angle relative to the pole. The jockey pole also keeps the spinnaker guy clear of shrouds, guardrails and stanchions – avoiding mutual damage.

11.3.2 Running rigging – maintenance

Chafe is the greatest enemy of running rigging, and it is not too difficult to guess where the maximum wear is likely to occur in any particular rope. For example, a halyard suffers most where it bears on the masthead sheave, where it passes round an exit sheave on the mast, and where it is turned up on winch and cleat when the sail is hoisted. These areas are likely to fail long before the rest of the rope, unless this is crippled in some way by careless handling – kinks in wire rope can be permanently damaging.

Where feasible to do so, it therefore pays to make up running rigging slightly longer in the first place, so that its life can be extended by removing a worn end, as for example the extremity of a halyard which suffers undue wear in the masthead sheave, or by equalising the wear along the rope. Some items of running rigging can be turned end for end to extend their life.

For a yacht which makes extended cruises it is advisable to carry sufficient wire (carefully preserved) to be able to make up a replacement halyard of the maximum length required, as well as spare cordage for other items such as sheets.

If a sheave does not turn freely in a block it will soon damage the rope passing over it. All sheaves should be examined and lubricated at frequent intervals.

If a halyard has to be removed from inside the mast, it should be replaced by a thin line as a messenger – so that the new halyard can be rove easily. If a halyard is broken inside a mast, and needs to be replaced, it will be necessary to pass a messenger through the mast for the purpose. This can be done using a short length of thin but flexible chain, which will pass over the masthead sheave and which can be attached to a suitable messenger to be pulled down the mast. First set up all other internal halyards as tight as possible, to avoid twists in the halyards inside the mast.

11.3.3 Winches

Winches provide the necessary power for hoisting and setting sails, and for other tasks connected with the running rigging of a yacht. The power which a winch develops is the relationship between the distance moved by the handle compared to the distance moved by the circumference of the drum. The power ratio of a simple direct action sheet winch in a small yacht might be 7:1. Power ratio is more meaningful than gear ratio, which is the number of turns of the handle for one turn of the drum.

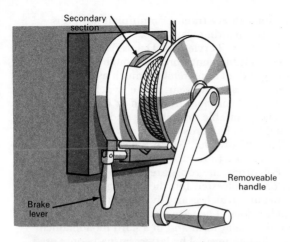

Fig. 11(16) Main halyard self-stowing winch. When hoisting, the turns must be led on evenly with the disengaged hand, and the final two or three turns must be led over the secondary section of the drum, nearest the mast. Remove the handle before releasing the brake to lower the sail.

Larger yachts need much more powerful winches to sheet home big genoas, for example. But a winch with a power ratio of, say, 30:1 would take a long time to take down the slack of a sheet before the higher power is really needed. So bigger sheet winches are two speed, or even three speed. A two speed winch might have power ratios of 7:1 and 30:1, obtained by rotating the handle in opposite directions. A three speed winch might give 5:1, 17:1 and 48:1, selected by a button on top of the winch drum in addition to reversing the direction of the handle.

Usually one person 'tails' the sheet or halyard, maintaining the tension of the rope round the drum, while another operates the winch handle. The lead of a rope onto and off the drum of a winch must be such as to avoid the risk of a riding turn – when a turn rides up over the one above it and jams. Often a riding turn can only be removed by taking the load off the winch. One way of doing this is by securing another line to the sheet with a rolling hitch, and then leading this line to another winch. Another method is by passing a stopper (see 11.4.8). Modern sheet

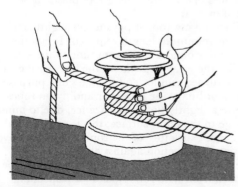

Fig. 11(17) Releasing a sheet. To loosen a taut rope, gradually reduce the tension on the tail while easing the turns slowly round the drum with the flat of the other hand.

winches are often 'self-tailing', whereby the sheet is automatically kept taut on the winch drum and the winch can then be operated entirely by one person.

Winches normally turn clockwise, viewed from above, and the turns must be put on in that same direction. When pulling in a sheet or hauling a halyard first take in as much slack as possible, then put on a single turn and continue to haul. Always keep your hands well away from the winch drum in case the rope takes charge and traps your fingers. As soon as any real strain comes on the rope put on a second turn, still hauling. Then put on a third and a fourth turn before inserting the winch handle. Putting on too many turns too soon is one way to encourage riding turns – as is pulling on the rope before it reaches the winch drum. When winching is completed, cleat up the rope, remove the winch handle, and place it in its proper stowage.

Main halyard winches are often self-stowing – the wire being reeled onto the drum as the sail is hoisted. These winches incorporate a brake, and the drum has a secondary section onto which the halyard should be led for the last few turns in order not to damage the wire, see Fig. 11(16). Unless operated correctly such winches can be dangerous, so it is important to familiarise yourself with the brake mechanism. The brake should be on except when lowering the sail.

When it is required to let go a sheet (say) which is under tension round a winch, be careful to keep tension on the tail while uncleating it. Then, still keeping tension on the tail, Fig. 11(17), gradually reduce it slightly while easing the turns round the drum with the flat of the other hand (with fingers clear of possible danger). Once the main load has been released from the winch the turns can be thrown off the drum by raising the tail vertically.

Winches are accurately machined, with close working fits, and to be reliable they must be regularly stripped down, cleaned and lubricated according to the maker's instructions. Manufacturers provide packs of spares for the internal parts of their winches, and it is sensible to carry these on board.

11.4 Ropes

11.4.1 Ropes – general
Rope is a vital material for yachtsmen. In one form or another it is used for mooring a boat, or for anchoring her safely, while sailing yachts of course rely on it in many ways for hoisting and setting their sails. There is also a fascination in its construction, and in the very many ways in which it can be used and knotted. Anybody going to sea needs to have some knowledge of rope – how to use and handle it, and how to take care of it. It is also necessary to understand what

Fig. 11(18) Three strand rope hawser laid – three strands twisted together to form a rope, normally right hand construction, with individual strands twisted left handed.

type and size of rope is required for a given task.

Technical information in compiling this section on ropes has been kindly supplied by Bridon Fibres and Plastics Limited, makers of Marina yacht ropes. The illustrations are taken from their *Marina Manual of Yacht Ropes*, available at most chandlers. The editors are grateful to Bridon for their kind co-operation.

11.4.2 Ropes – construction

Most yacht ropes, particularly mooring warps, are formed of three strands, made up from fibres twisted into yarns, and yarns twisted into strands. Usually they are hawser laid, which means that the strands are twisted together right-handed as in Fig. 11(18).

For sheets and other running rigging there is increasing use of plaited or braided ropes, made from inter-twined strands. Double braided rope is made up from two single braided ones, one inside as a core and the other forming an outer sheath. Fig. 11(19) shows a double braided rope, the braided sheath and core combining to give very high strength.

Fig. 11(19) Braidline — A double braided rope. A braided sheath and braided core combine to give very high strength.

11.4.3 Ropes and cordage – materials

Nowadays all yacht ropes are manufactured from synthetic fibres. Nylon was the first man-made fibre to be used for boats, and it is still the strongest rope available in general use, although more exotic (and much more expensive) materials have been developed for special applications in racing yachts. Nylon has excellent shock absorbing properties – which make it very suitable for anchor warps particularly in braidline or multiplait form. It is a soft rope, made from fine fibres, and is nice to handle; but it is too stretchy to be used for running rigging.

In either three-strand or multiplait form it is good for mooring warps.

Polyester (Terylene or Dacron) is also made from multifilament fibres; although slightly less strong it does not stretch so much as nylon. It has good resistance to wear, and is widely used for warps and cordage. In plaited or braidline form it is very suitable for halyards and sheets. In small boats halyards may be entirely of pre-stretched polyester, which is heat set during manufacture to reduce stretch in service.

Polypropylene ropes are of lower strength than nylon or polyester, but they are lightweight and buoyant – which is an advantage in some applications. They are available in soft, multifilament form and in a hard monofilament or split film form. The latter is usually only used for water ski lines. In its three-strand form polypropylene can be used for mooring warps but should be a slightly larger size than polyester for the same purpose. It also suffers rather more from light degradation (attack by the sun's rays).

Kevlar is a relatively new fibre which combines great strength with minimal stretch, but it is very expensive and not very resistant to chafe.

Various terms connected with ropes and their different parts are described in Fig. 11(20), and should be understood by any seaman. Although less likely to get damaged than natural cordage, even synthetic ropes must be used and handled carefully to give long service. Although they are waterproof and do not rot they should be stowed away from any source of heat. They can also be damaged by chemicals or dirt; even salt crystals can hurt the internal structure, so ropes should be washed with clean, fresh water (do not use detergents) and dried naturally.

Sheaves which are too small in diameter, or too narrow, will damage ropes passing over them. A seized sheave can ruin a rope very quickly, so it is important to check and lubricate all sheaves regularly.

Most damage to ropes is usually caused by chafe – at fairleads for example in the case of mooring warps. Wherever a rope may be exposed to a rough surface it should be protected by parcelling or by a short length of plastic hose slipped over it.

When buying rope it pays to get slightly more than the minimum length required. It can then be moved around a little from time to time, to equalise the wear and extend the life. A rope can also be turned end for end for the same purpose.

With ordinary use polyester and nylon ropes acquire a slightly fluffy appearance, due to minor damage to the outer surface; this is not harmful to the main structure of the rope and in fact gives additional protection against abrasion.

Periodically the servings (bindings) should be removed from wire rope splices for inspection, since water can be trapped here. If the splice is sound and not corroded, re-grease, parcel and serve.

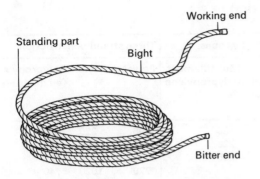

(a) Rope coiled down right-handed (clockwise). The bitter end is the extremity or inboard end of a line (or cable). The working end is used for knotting etc. The standing part is the fixed (as opposed to hauling) part, or the part of a rope about which the working end is turned to make a knot or hitch. A bight is an open loop in a rope.

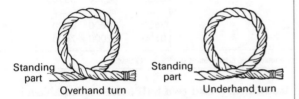

(b) The end of a rope looped over the standing part (left) forms an overhand turn. When looped under the standing part (right) it forms an underhand turn.

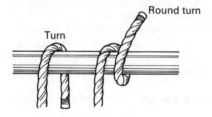

(c) When a rope is passed part way round an object, such as a bollard or a spar, it is said to form a turn. When it goes completely round the object it forms a round turn. However, the instruction 'Take a turn' (round a cleat or bollard, for example) normally implies taking a round turn.

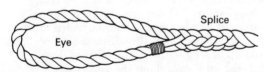

(d) An eye is formed in rope when the working end is brought back and secured to the standing part – either temporarily by a hitch, or more permanently by splicing or seizing.

Fig. 11(20) Rope terms.

11.4.4 Recommended sizes of rope

All rope is now measured by its diameter in millimetres. A diameter of 8mm corresponds to a circumference of one inch. The recommendations which follow should only be taken as a general guide; certain factors such as design, displacement, sail ratio, use etc. may necessitate variations.

Halyards

Overall length of boat (m)	Main	Jib	Spinnaker	Burgee
	mm	mm	mm	mm
5	6	6	6	3
7	8	8	8	3
10	10	10	8	3
12	12	12	10	3
15 and over	12	12	12	3

Sheets

Overall length of boat (m)	Main or jib	Genoa	Spinnaker	Light weather spinnaker
	mm	mm	mm	mm
5	10	10	8	6
7	10	10	10	6
10	10	12	12	8
12	12	14	14	8
15	12	16	16	10

Mooring warps

Overall length of boat (m)	Nylon	Polypropylene
	mm	mm
5	8	10
7	12	14
10	14	16
12	16	20
15	18	22
17	20	24
20	24	28

Anchor warps

The length of anchor chain carried should be three times the maximum depth of water for anchoring. If anchor warp is used, five times the depth should be carried. Always use at least 5 metres (3 fathoms) of chain between the anchor and the warp, to add weight and reduce chafe on the bottom.

Overall length of boat (m)	Nylon mm	Polyester mm	Anchor weight- Danforth or CQR kg	Anchor chain diam. mm	Kedge warp (nylon) mm
7	12	14	10	8	8
8.5	14	16	16	8	8
10	16	18	20	9	10
12	18	20	25	10	10
15	20	22	35	11	10
17	20	22	40	11	10
20	24		45	12	12

11.4.5 Yacht ropes – minimum breaking loads (kg)

Diam (mm)	Super braidline		Marina Hystrain Kevlar	Marina Squareline Nylon	Plaited dinghy ropes		Three strand construction		
	Super polyester braidline	Super nylon braidline			Polyester matt finish/ continuous filament	Multifilament polypropylene	Polyester	Nylon	Polypropylene (all qualities)
4	–	–	720	–	–	180	295	320	250
5	–	–	–	–	225	225	400	500	350
6	650	950	1050	–	295	295	565	750	550
7	–	–	–	–	–	–	770	1020	740
8	1175	1450	1750	–	565	565	1020	1350	960
9	–	–	–	–	635	635	1270	1700	1150
10	1800	2725	2500	2080	905	905	1590	2080	1425
12	2575	3400	5000	3000	1360	1250	2270	3000	2030
14	3650	4300	–	4100	–	–	3180	4100	2790
16	4525	5400	–	5300	–	–	4060	5300	3500
18	5675	7700	–	–	–	–	5080	6700	4450
20	–	–	–	–	–	–	6350	8300	5370
21	7925	9525	–	–	–	–	–	–	–
22	–	–	–	–	–	–	7620	10000	6500
24	10200	12700	–	–	–	–	9100	12000	7600

The above figures refer to Marina yacht ropes, from a table kindly supplied by their manufacturers, Bridon Fibres and Plastics Limited.

11.4.6 Useful knots, bends and hitches

A bend joins the ends of two ropes together, while a hitch makes a rope fast to some other object. A stopper knot is tied at the end of a rope to prevent unreeving, while a binding knot constricts a single object or holds two or more objects snugly together.

It is always important to use an appropriate knot, bend or hitch – first for security, and second so that it can be undone when required. It must be stressed that knots do reduce the breaking load of a rope – by as much as 50 per cent.

Sheet bend. A most useful general purpose bend, which does not damage the rope, and unties readily. If used to join ropes of different materials, the ends should be seized or the bend may spill.

Double sheet bend. No stronger than the sheet bend, but more secure. If the rope is stiff and large, seize the eye and reeve the working end twice.

Heaving line bend. Used when bending a heaving line to a hawser.

Figure of eight knot. The sailor's most usual stopper knot.

Stevedore knot. Another single strand stopper knot, more suitable for synthetic rope than a figure of eight.

Reef knot. An admirable binding knot, as for reefing sails, but not as a bend. If tied with ends of unequal size, or if one if stiffer or smoother than the other, the knot is almost bound to capsize.

Half hitch. Usually the first stage in tying a more elaborate hitch, and should not be used unsupported.

Round turn and two half hitches. Suitable for securing a rope to a bollard or pile. If employed aloft or in ground tackle, the working end should be seized to the standing part. It is easily untied.

Clove hitch. Often used as a binding knot, but it is not very secure for use afloat. Will unwind under a steady rotating pull.

Rolling hitch. Simple to tie, and the most reliable knot under a lengthwise pull in the direction of the round turn. When bending this knot to another rope, the round turns should be crossed.

Fisherman's bend. Very useful as an anchor bend.

Bowline. A popular and useful loop knot. When properly tied there is little or no danger of this knot capsizing before the breaking point of the rope is reached.

11.4.7 Handling ropes

Ropes should always be stored or stowed ready for immediate use. Three strand rope is normally laid up right handed, and should be coiled down right handed (clockwise). Braidline should be hanked up in a figure of eight, ensuring that subsequent turns cancel out the kinks caused by previous turns.

The tails of sheets or halyards, or the ends of warps, should be coiled so that the running part of the rope is on top, and not underneath or at the back of the coil. There are various techniques for making up a halyard on a cleat, but one simple method is shown in Fig. 11 (22). When the halyard has been coiled the inner loop is pulled forward through the centre of the coil, and twisted several times in a left handed direction. The loop so formed is slipped over the top of the

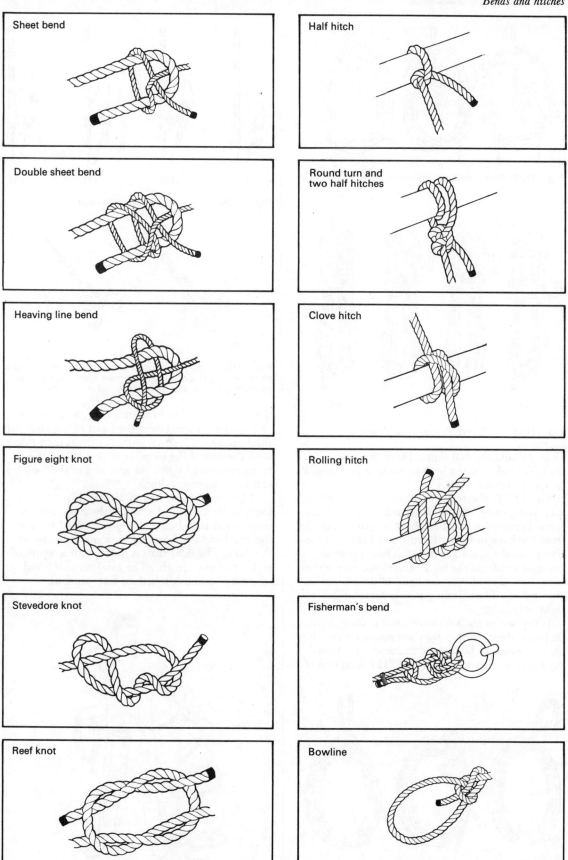

Fig. 11(21) Different types of bends and hitches.

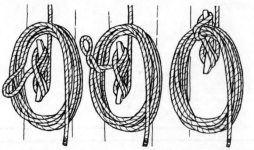

Fig. 11(22) Simple method for making up a halyard on a cleat.

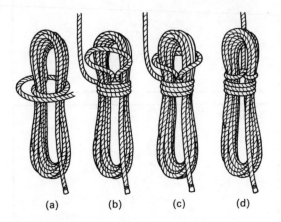

(a)   (b)   (c)   (d)

Fig. 11(23) Another way of securing a halyard.

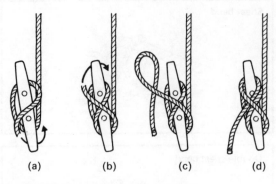

(a)   (b)   (c)   (d)

Fig. 11(25) How to belay a line to a cleat.

Fig. 11(26) Where a line with an eye spliced in the end is to be secured to a cleat with an open base, pass the eye through the base, and then put the loop over the horns.

cleat, to hold the coil tight. There must be sufficient twists in the loop to make it just possible to slip it over the cleat.

Fig. 11(23) illustrates another way of securing a halyard, suspended by its standing part. When it has been coiled down, a short length is brought from the back of the coil and turned three or four times round the coil, as in (a). Then a loop is brought out from the back of the coil, above the turns and slipped over the head of the coil, as in (b) and (c). The standing part is then pulled tight (d).

When warps etc are stowed away, they should be coiled down so that they are ready for use, but the coil needs to be secured in some way. One method is shown in Fig. 11(24). The final coil of

the rope is doubled to form a loop, as shown in (a), which is passed over the head of the coil and then up, under its own part. A turn is then taken with the end of the loop, as in (b). When the turns are pulled tight, the free end of the loop (c) can be hung over a hook.

When belaying a line to a cleat, Fig. 11(25), the first turn should be round the base, and by convention this should be right-handed in case the line has to be handled by somebody else in the dark. The next turn is made with a figure of eight, as shown in (b). The final turn, (c) and (d), may be half-hitched for lines such as

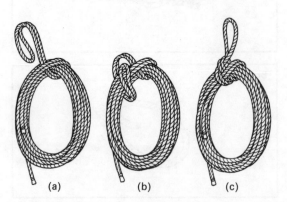

(a)   (b)   (c)

Fig. 11(24) Method of stowing a warp.

Fig. 11(27) Preparing to heave a line.

Fig. 11(28) Heaving a line.

halyards or mooring warps. For sheets the half-hitch should be omitted, and replaced by a final turn round the base.

When heaving a line, Fig. 11(27), do not rely on a previously coiled line being free of turns, but coil it down yourself into your left hand, in right-handed (clockwise) loops about 18in (450mm) in diameter. Plaited or braided rope may fall into figures of eight. Before heaving the line secure the standing part to a cleat or similar fitting, and make sure that the line is long enough for the job. For any lengthy throw it is advisable to use a light (heaving) line as a messenger, in order to pass across a heavier warp. These instructions assume that the rope has a right-hand lay, and that the thrower is right-handed. Before heaving, transfer about half the coil to the right hand, Fig. 11(28). Stand sideways to the direction of throw, bring the throwing arm well back, and swing it forwards with a round arm motion, or more overarm if a long throw is involved. Keep the coil in the other hand facing forward so that it can uncoil easily.

11.4.8 Passing a stopper
A stopper is used to take the strain on a rope temporarily, as for example when it is necessary to clear a riding turn from a winch. The stopper should be a smaller rope, and it should be applied so that the direction in which it pulls is as near as possible the same as the direction of the

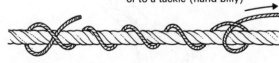

Stopper led to another winch, or to a tackle (hand billy)

Fig. 11(29) Passing a stopper.

rope which is to be relieved. If that is a laid rope a single stopper can be used, as shown in Fig. 11(29). First half-hitch the stopper round the rope against the lay, and then dog (wrap) it several times round the rope in the other direction so that the stopper lies closely into the lay of the rope: the end of the stopper can then be seized to the rope, or held against it by the hand.

If the rope under load is a plaited or braidline rope, without any lay, a double stopper must be used. One end of the stopper is half-hitched round the rope as for a single stopper, above. The other end is then half-hitched alongside it, but in the opposite direction. The two ends are then criss-crossed in opposite directions round the rope several times, and the two ends either seized to the rope or held round it as before.

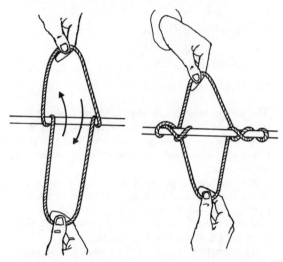

Fig. 11(30) An alternative method of passing a stopper.

An alternative way of passing a stopper is shown in Fig. 11(30), by using a loop of rope thinner than the rope to be relieved, and passing it round and round as illustrated. The relieving tackle should be shackled to both loops of the stopper.

11.4.9 Whippings
The end of a rope should always be neatly whipped, to prevent it unravelling. In most cases a whipping is better than a back splice, which may snarl up when a rope is required to run through a block or fairlead.

When synthetic rope is first purchased the ends of the strands and the strands themselves can be prevented from unravelling by securing them with waterproof boat tape and fusing the ends with a match. This should only be regarded as a temporary measure.

A sailor's whipping can be made by laying a short length of twine along the rope, and towards its end, as in Fig. 11(31). About half-a-dozen tight turns are taken round the rope and against its lay. The short length S can then be cut off.

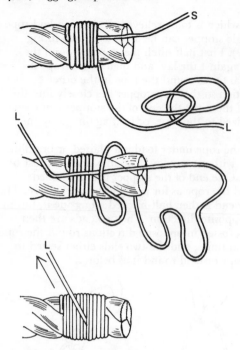

Fig. 11(31) Sailor's whipping.

The longer length L is then laid back along the rope, and further turns are continued with the loop so formed. Finally L is drawn tight (a pair of pliers may be useful) and cut off close to the turns on the rope.

A common whipping is made by laying a loop along the rope and making a number of turns over it. The working end is put through this loop and pulled back out of sight. The two ends are then cut off short. See Fig. 11(32).

The length of either of the above whippings should be about the same as the diameter of the rope.

A sailmaker's whipping is the most secure, but it really needs a palm and needle. These are items which should be on board any sailing boat.

Fig. 11(33) Sailmaker's whipping.

The end of the twine is first anchored by stitching it through a strand, after which turns are taken tightly round the rope – working towards the end and against the lay, as shown in Fig. 11(33). The needle is then passed under a strand, and brought back along the groove between strands so that the turns of whipping are frapped tight. It is then stitched under the next strand, and the procedure repeated with each groove in turn. The end of the twine is then secured by stitching it through a strand, and the end cut off short.

11.4.10 Eye splice – three strand rope

To make an eye splice in three strand rope, first apply a seizing at the point where the rope is to be unlaid. Five full tucks are necessary with synthetic ropes, and six inches of rope are allowed for every inch circumference: (A 8mm diameter rope is 1in in circumference). Secure the thimble (if one is to be used) in the bight of the rope, as in Fig. 1. The numbered instructions below refer to the appropriate diagrams.

1

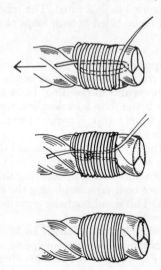

Fig. 11(32) Common whipping.

(2) Unlay the rope back to the seizing, and temporarily whip each strand. The centre strand will be tucked first. The back of the thimble has been marked black, so that rotation of the work can be followed.

2

(3) Insert the spike, with the lay of the rope, and open up the bight of the strand next to the one to be tucked; pass this strand through this bight from right to left, as looking back along the length of the rope, or in other words against its lay.

3

(4) Haul the centre strand taut, insert the left hand strand underneath the next bight to the left, and haul taut.

4

(5) Now turn the thimble over. Open up with the spike the remaining bight, and pass the remaining strand through, as indicated. All tucks are made from right to left, against the lay of the rope, keeping the lay of each strand correct and maintaining an even tension in the strands.

5

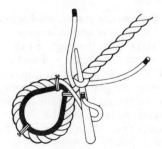

(6) Turning the thimble over again, haul taut on each strand to ensure that the splice fits snugly at the toe of the thimble.

6

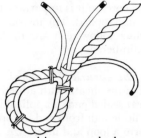

(7) Each strand is now tucked over the strand to its left and under the next one. Continue tucking over and under with each strand in turn until five full tucks are completed.

7

(8) Then unlay each of the ends, and divide into two. Each half is matched with its partner of the next strand, and seized together over the intermediate strand. The surplus tails are cut off, and the ends fused together. The stops holding the thimble are removed, and the splice rolled in the hands so as to even it out.

8

11.4.11 Eye splice – braidline

For splicing braidline a special fid and pusher are required, and can be obtained from chandlers. The fid must be the right size for the rope, e.g. size 10 for a 10mm rope.

Three marks must be made on the sheath, and three on the core. These are best done with a felt tip pen, using the fid as a measure. One fid is the overall length of the fid: one short fid is the distance between the two marks on the fid and the hollow end.

It is important during all stages of the splice that the slack in the sheath be removed, particularly after extracting the core and in completing the splice. Braidline is a balanced rope, with about half the strength in the sheath and half in the core, so it is important that the tension is equally applied. The instructions (1), (2), (3) etc which follow refer also to the diagrams so numbered.

(1) Marking the sheath (3 marks).

Tape the end of the sheath with adhesive tape, and cut off heat sealed end, if applicable. Measure one fid length from end of rope, and mark (R). Form a loop and mark size of eye required opposite the one fid length – X, where the core is extracted. For instructions when fitting a thimble see under (8). Measure about five fid lengths from core extraction point (X) and secure to cleat or similar. From R count ten double strands back towards the taped end, and mark all way round the rope (T). This is the crossover point.

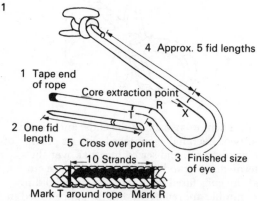

1

4 Approx. 5 fid lengths

1 Tape end of rope

Core extraction point

R X

2 One fid length

5 Cross over point

3 Finished size of eye

10 Strands

Mark T around rope   Mark R

(2) Extract core and mark (3 marks).

Take out the core at X by folding the rope and working the outer strands aside to expose the core. Pull out the core from the end of the rope, and tape the end. Holding the core, slide the sheath towards the knot and then smooth all of the slack of the sheath from the knot, back over the core. This ensures that all slack is removed from both core and sheath, and that tension is equal on both, which is most important. Mark the core where it comes out of the sheath (Mark 1). Slide the sheath back towards the knot and from mark 1 on the core measure towards the

2

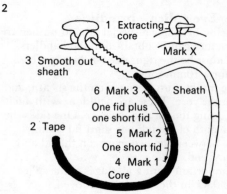

1 Extracting core

Mark X

3 Smooth out sheath

6 Mark 3

Sheath

One fid plus one short fid

2 Tape

5 Mark 2

One short fid

4 Mark 1

Core

knot one short fid length (Mark 2). From mark 2 measure one full fid length plus a short fid length (Mark 3).

(3) Insert sheath into core.

Lay the work out flat, and ensure the rope parts are not twisted. Place the fid into the core at mark 2, and carefully guide it through the centre and out at mark 3. Flatten the taped end of the sheath and fold it double; now place it in the hollow end of the fid, ensuring a smooth surface that will not catch the yarns as it is pushed through. Place the pusher into the hollow end of the fid, and slide the fid and sheath through the core. When the sheath protrudes at mark 3, remove the fid and pull the sheath through until mark 2 meets the crossover point (T).

3

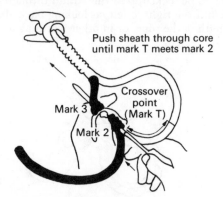

Push sheath through core until mark T meets mark 2

Crossover point (Mark T)

Mark 3

Mark 2

(4) Insert core into sheath.

Place the fid into the sheath at the crossover point (T), along the centre and out of the same hole that the core was extracted from. Place the end of the core into the fid, and pass the fid and all of the core through the sheath. Remove the fid.

4

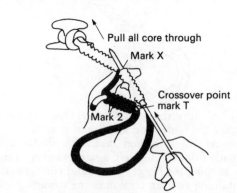

Pull all core through

Mark X

Crossover point mark T

Mark 2

(5) Lock crossover point, and taper sheath.

Important – the core end must now be pulled bunching the sheath back against the crossover point. Now pull the sheath end and bunch the core back to the crossover point, making sure that the crossover point is pulled tight. Take off the tape from the end of the sheath and unlay the sheath strands as far as possible. Take a quarter of the strands and cut off as far back as possible. Cut the next quarter of strands at two-thirds

5

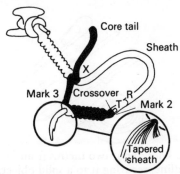

length, and the next quarter at one-third, leaving a quarter of strands at full length.

(6) *Smooth out eye.*

The slack parts of the rope are now smoothed out either side of the crossover point. Hold the crossover point as you do this making sure it does not slip. The tapered sheath will disappear into the core.

6

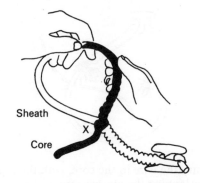

(7) *Bring back slack of sheath from knot.*

Hold the core in the right hand and maintain tension against the knot. The left hand smooths the slack of the sheath from the knot, over the core and the crossover point. The right hand maintains tension on the core at all times, and it is necessary to slide the hand back as the sheath progresses. If you cannot get the sheath over the crossover point, slide the sheath back towards the knot, and smooth out the eye from the crossover point as in (6), and continue as above. Go over the rope several times from the knot to ensure that all of the sheath slack is removed. Marks X and R should now coincide.

7

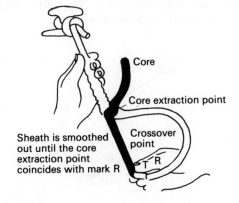

(8) *Finish the splice.*

Smooth out the eye towards the core, and cut off the core leaving a ¼in protruding. This is now tucked away into the throat of the splice. Fit thimble if required. Check once again that all of the sheath is smoothed out. Place a sailmaker's whipping on the neck of the splice, as near to the throat as practicable. Note that the taped end of the sheath and core must fit neatly into the fid so that they do not catch yarns as they are pushed

8

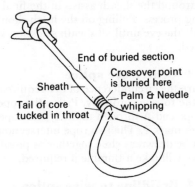

through. If difficulty is found in placing the taped end into the fid, several strands may be removed from the end – but do not cut off. Should the sheath distort or ruck during the splicing operations, this may be due to a joined strand. The strand ends at the join will be buried between the core and the sheath. Locate the join, and remove the strands by pulling out of the rope. Continue the splice. Smooth out the rucked area with the hands. When the splice is finished, bury the two join strands between the sheath and the core for a minimum distance of 125mm (5in) each way.

To fit a thimble in a braidline splice it is necessary to measure the size of eye around the thimble, as in (1) above, and continue the splice as instructed. Fit the thimble after cutting off the core (8). Carefully slide the sheath towards the knot just enough to insert the thimble. Now ensure that all of the slack is smoothed out towards the eye. Place a sailmaker's whipping at the neck of the splice. If it is found that slack remains in the sheath after the throat is tight on the thimble, then this slack must be worked out through the tail of the rope after whipping, as instructed.

11.4.12 Splicing used braidline rope

First soak the section of rope in water for several minutes, to lubricate and loosen the fibres. When extracting the core, as in (2) above, thoroughly loosen three to four sheath strands at point X, to obtain a large and flexible hole for the extraction.

Before burying the sheath at the crossover point, anchor the loop of slip knot to a firm object before starting to bury: both hands and weight of body can then be used to assist in burying sheath over core at crossover. Holding the crossover tightly, milk all the excess sheath from R to X. Cut off the core tail at X. Pull above crossover with one hand to reduce diameter of the crossover and core, then milk the sheath with the other hand. The use of a small cord in a rolling hitch around the sheath assists in the final burying process. Pulling on the hitch should be towards the eye until all sheath slackness is removed.

11.4.13 Centre eye splice

Measure the circumference of eye required, and mark the rope accordingly. Pierce the rope and pass rope end A through mark 2, and rope B through mark 1. The two rope intersections should be drawn as close together as possible. The eye will take a thimble if required.

11.4.14 Braidline to wire splice

This splice is simple and quick, and extremely strong because it does not rely on the tucks alone for strength but also on the hollow braids gripping the wire as tension is applied. See illustrations (1) and (2).

1

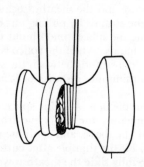

2

If neatly made, little bulk is formed, and the lay of the wire is disturbed to a minimum. Measurements are not critical, providing enough wire is covered and the core tuck is made sufficiently deep to allow enough length for the sheath splice and length of tucks for working. In this case a 6mm diameter 6 × 19 galvanised wire is spliced to a 10mm diameter Marina Super Polyester Braidline. The numbered instructions refer to the diagrams.

(3) The tools needed are a sharp knife, tape, and a hollow or Swedish fid to separate the wire strands. A Marina Braidline splicing fid will help, but is not essential.

3

(4) Tie a knot about two metres from the end of the braidline, securing it to a solid object. Bind the end of the wire with tape, and put a tape marker about 400mm (16in) along it. This amount of wire will be buried inside the rope. Lightly bind the rope about 25mm (1in) from the end and fray the strands out. Separating the core strands from the sheath, the sheath can be slid back along the core towards the knot, exposing about one metre (39in) of core.

4

(5) Bury the wire in the core, with the rope ends overlapping the marker tape.

5

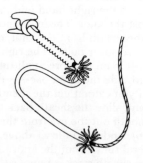

(6) Tape the core firmly to the wire about 150mm (6in) from the wire marker, and carefully unlay the strands back to this tape.

6

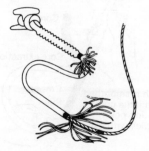

(7) Neatly divide the loose strands into three, and bind each group together.

7

(8) Pass the Swedish fid under two wire strands and tuck the first rope strand, making sure the strands lay flat and neat.

8

(9) Follow round the wire taking the next two wire strands, and make the next tuck and the third the same.

9

(10), (11), (12), (13) Continue until three full tucks are completed, and then cut off the loose ends of rope.

10

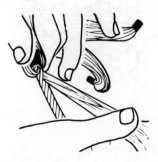

11

12

13

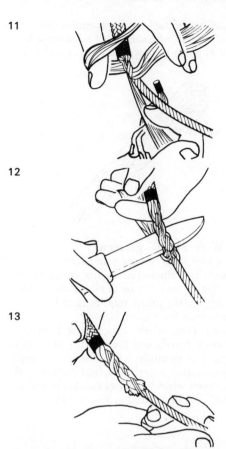

(14) Smooth the sheath back over the splice, taking care not to ruck the cover over the wire, and make sure that all the slack sheath is worked back from the knot.

14

(15) Tightly bind the sheath where the core splice finishes, and unlay the rope strands and divide into three. Proceed as for the core splice, but add a fourth tuck, cutting out half of the strands to form a taper before tucking.

15

(16) Binding the tucks is not essential but waterproof tape can be used with advantage for this purpose. Keep the rope tucks neat and flat.

16

11.4.15 Wire rope – general

Wire is used for both standing and running rigging, for which the requirements are different. Running rigging needs to be flexible, whereas for standing rigging the prime requirement is minimum stretch for a given size.

The construction of wire rope is described by the number of strands and the number of wires in each strand. For example, a 6 × 7 steel core rope has six strands over a steel core, and each strand consists of seven wires (six wires twisted round a central one) – as illustrated in Fig. 11(34).

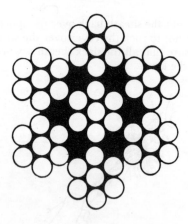

Fig. 11(34) 6×7 steel core.

11.4.16 Standing rigging – wire

The simplest, and most expensive type of standing rigging is steel rod, which may be either round or lenticular in section. It has very little stretch, but is easily damaged.

More usual is single strand, 1 × 19, made up of six wires twisted round a central core with an outer layer of twelve further wires, as shown in Fig. 11(35). Although more flexible than rod rigging, 1 × 19 cannot be bent round a thimble for splicing, so special end fittings are required, see 11.2.2. This form of construction gives a good smooth surface to reduce wind resistance, and to allow sails and sheets to pass smoothly with little

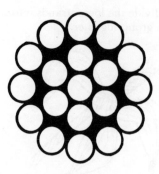

Fig. 11(35) 1×19 steel core.

chafing. 1 × 19 is made of stainless steel which lasts longer than galvanised wire, but is not so strong and a good deal more expensive. It needs to be handled carefully when stepping or unstepping the mast.

11.4.17 Running rigging – wire

Many types of ropes are used for running rigging. Wire rope is usually found in halyards because of its non-stretch properties, resistance to chafe, and small windage for a given strength. Its main disadvantages are that it can and does rust, and it does not like sharp bends. Obviously wire used for running rigging needs to be a lot more flexible than that used for standing rigging, but even so sheaves over which it passes should be not less than 26 times the diameter of fast moving rope, or 12 times the diameter of wire used for halyards.

A typical wire rope used for running rigging is the 6 × 19 with fibre core, as illustrated in Fig. 11(36). This may be made of galvanised or stainless steel wire, the former being slightly stronger.

All wire rope needs to be examined regularly for any signs of corrosion or broken strands. If it is lightly oiled from time to time its life will be prolonged. With galvanised wire surface rust can be removed with a wire brush. If the rusting is serious, try bending the wire; if a strand breaks it should be discarded.

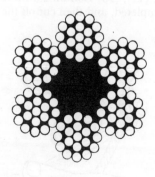

Fig. 11(36) 6×19 fibre core.

11.4.18 Wire ropes – minimum breaking loads (tonnes)

| Size | | Galvanised wire rope | | Stainless steel wire rope | | |
| | | Standing rigging | Running rigging | Standing rigging | | Running rigging |
dia. (mm)	approx circ. (in)	6 × 7 with steel core	6 × 19 with fibre core	1 × 19	6 × 7 with steel core	6 × 19 with fibre core
2	¼	0.28	–	–	0.24	–
3	⅜	0.63	0.50	0.72	0.55	0.43
4	½	1.12	0.88	1.28	0.97	0.77
5	⅝	1.75	1.38	2.00	1.51	1.20
6	¾	2.52	1.99	2.88	2.18	1.73
7	⅞	3.43	2.71	–	–	–
8	1	4.48	3.54	–	3.87	–
9	1⅛	5.04	4.48	–	–	–
10	1¼	7.00	–	–	–	–
12	1½	10.10	–	–	–	–

11.5 Sails

11.5.1 Sails – general

The correct shapes of sails, combined with their strength and reliability, are important matters for any sailing yacht. For one which races, the precise set of the sails and their proper interaction are major factors in success, and modern racing yachts aim to control the trim and camber of their sails very closely, depending on the relative speed and direction of the wind. The names of the more common sails, and the various parts of them, are shown in Fig. 11(37) and in Fig. 11(38).

The efficiency of modern sails (which make boats more close-winded than hitherto, and faster in a wider range of conditions) depends on the chemical processes which have produced the materials now in use; modern weaving techniques and heat treatment which provide tough and stable cloths; and on ever-increasing sophistication in the actual design of sails in terms of putting them together.

It should be understood at the outset that racing and cruising yachts have quite different requirements. The former can sacrifice almost everything to speed, but cruising yachts need sails which are more versatile (because fewer are carried) and which are easy and safe to handle, are not too expensive and have a long life.

11.5.2 Sailcloth and sailmaking

To understand sails, and how to make the best use of them, it is necessary to know something about their design and manufacture. Most fore-and-aft sails are now made from Terylene (Dacron), a product of the petro-chemical industry. Very fine filaments of polyester are formed by extruding a liquid at high pressure and temperature, and a number of these filaments make up the polyester fibre, which has several very desirable properties. It has good tensile strength, it resists abrasion, and it is not affected by moisture. The fact that the resulting cloth is hard can be a disadvantage, because stitches tend to stand proud of the surface and therefore wear more easily than if they bedded down into the material. Terylene is also subject to degradation by ultra-violet light, so it should not be exposed unnecessarily to bright sunlight.

Spinnakers are made from nylon, which has more stretch but is just as strong and resistant to rot as Terylene. More recently other synthetic materials such as Kevlar and Mylar have been used for sails, but mostly in specialist racing applications.

Terylene, like other woven materials, is woven from threads at right angles to each other – the warp running lengthwise, and the weft across the length. A certain weight of cloth may consist of heavier threads with rather an open weave or a larger number of thinner threads which are more compacted. The latter type of cloth, more closely woven, is more stable and durable: it also has less porosity, although this quality depends too on the dressing the cloth receives from fillers in the finishing stages.

While sailcloth will quite strongly resist any deformation if tension is applied uniformly along either the warp or the weft, it is a different matter if it is pulled on the bias – at an angle, say, of 45° to the warp and weft. What then happens can be demonstrated by pulling two opposite corners of a handkerchief along the diagonal, when folds can be seen to appear close to the line of tension. This fact can be utilised in sail-making, as one way of getting the required shape into a sail. But if the stretch cannot be limited the sail will pull out of shape, so it is necessary to use a certain

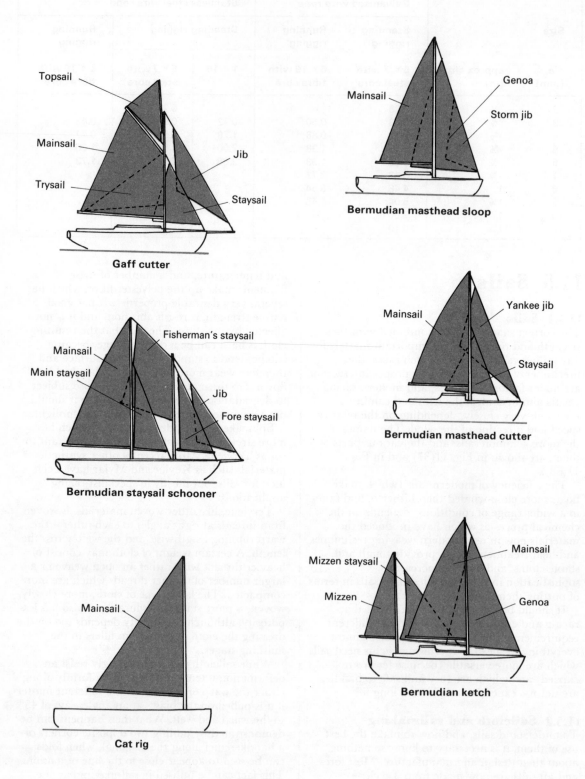

Fig. 11(37) Different rigs.

Topsail

Mainsail

Trysail

Jib

Staysail

Gaff cutter

Mainsail

Genoa

Storm jib

Bermudian masthead sloop

Fisherman's staysail

Mainsail

Main staysail

Jib

Fore staysail

Bermudian staysail schooner

Mainsail

Yankee jib

Staysail

Bermudian masthead cutter

Mainsail

Mizzen staysail

Mizzen

Genoa

Bermudian ketch

Mainsail

Cat rig

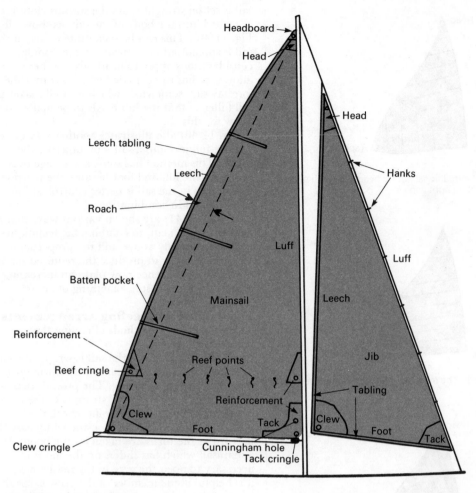

Fig. 11(38) The parts of a sail.

minimum weight (strength) of cloth for each application, and to control the stretch along the luff of a sail (and the foot of a mainsail) by attaching the cloth to a rope or a tape.

Sailcloth is specified according to its weight per unit area. In Britain this is measured in ounces per square yard, but the Americans use a different unit which is ounces per yard of a cloth which is only 28½in (72cm) wide. Comparative figures for cloths in British, American and metric weights are shown in Fig. 11(39).

Shape is also induced into a mainsail by rounding the luff and the foot, so that when the

British	American	Metric
(oz per sq yard)	(oz per yard, width 28½ in)	(gram per sq metre)
1	0.8	34
2	1.6	68
3	2.4	102
4	3.2	136
5	4.0	170
6	4.8	203
7	5.6	237
8	6.4	271
9	7.2	305
10	8.0	339
11	8.8	373
12	9.6	407
13	10.4	441
14	11.2	475
15	12.0	508

Fig. 11(39) Equivalent sailcloth weights in British, American and metric units.

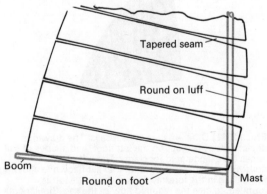

Fig. 11(40) Exaggerated sketch showing how fullness is worked into a mainsail (a) by tapering the seams, and (b) by the rounded shapes of luff and foot.

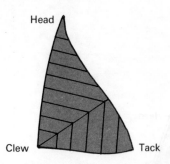

(a) Mitre cut. The traditional cut for headsails, with seams meeting the leech at right angles.

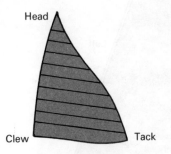

(b) Horizontal cut. The most common cut for mainsails.

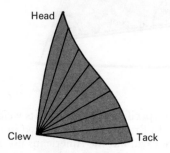

(c) Radial or sunray cut.

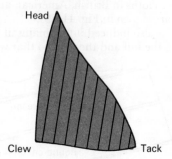

(d) Leech cut.

Fig. 11(41) Different cuts of headsails. The drawings depict sails as laid out on the loft floor, and shapes of sail edges are exaggerated for clarity. The luff of a jib is hollowed towards the head, for it to set flat while allowing for the sag in the forestay. Lower down the luff is rounded, to give the required flow to the sail. Similar cuts are also used for mainsails, but since there is no forestay to consider the mainsail luff has a slightly rounded convex curve.

sail is set on straight spars the surplus cloth is absorbed into the body of the sail, as shown in Fig. 11(40). This can be seen quite clearly if the sail is spread out on a clean surface. Similar considerations apply to headsails, but here allowance has to be made for the fact that the forestay sags somewhat, which in itself makes the sail fuller so that the luff needs to be hollowed to allow for this.

Fig. 11(40) also illustrates another way of putting fullness into a sail – by tapering the seams. This method has some advantage over rounding the luff and foot because the position of the fullness in the sail is better controlled, but the two are used in combination.

In Fig. 11(41) are shown various ways that a headsail can be cut, to combine the techniques mentioned briefly above and the properties of the sailcloth in order to produce the required shape of sail. Even if science now plays an increasing part, sailmaking is still something of an art.

11.5.3 Mainsail reefing arrangements

There are various methods of reefing the mainsail:

(1) Roller reefing, where the sail is wrapped round the boom by rotating the latter by worm gear at the main gooseneck fitting. The procedure is simple: remove the kicking strap; take the weight of the boom on the topping lift; check the mainsheet slightly if sailing on the wind; ease the halyard as the turns are taken on the boom. With a mainsail which has sliders on the luff it is necessary to open the gate in the mast track, and it is helpful if one member of the crew keeps the leech of the sail pulled well aft and is available to remove the lower batten should this be necessary. When the required reduction in sail area has been made, set up the halyard tight, ease the topping lift, and close the mast gate. For unreefing, follow the reverse procedure. Despite its simplicity, roller reefing does have some disadvantages. The kicking strap has to be removed, although there are ways of getting round this by using a clawfitting on the boom (but this is inclined to wear the sail), or by winding in a webbing strap as the rolls are taken in the sail: the reefing gear requires regular maintenance, and could fail: the reefed sail does not set very well: and roller reefing really requires a boom with a round section, which is not the best shape from other considerations.

(2) Through-mast roller reefing is a variation of (1), in which the reefing gear passes through the mast and is operated by a handle on the forward side. It can be quicker to use than the worm gear type, but suffers from the same disadvantages. Furthermore it requires a fixed gooseneck, so that tension of the mainsail luff is not so easy to control.

(3) Point reefing is the traditional method. It involves reeving reef pendants through special cringles on the luff and leech of the mainsail, and

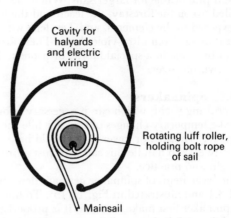

Fig. 11(43) Mast section for internal roller reefing/furling gear.

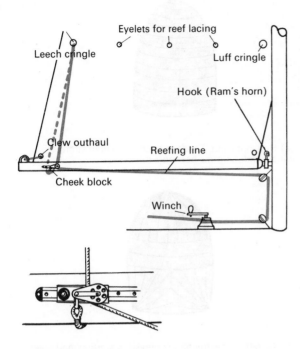

Fig. 11(42) Diagrammatic sketch of slab (or jiffy) reefing system. In practice the gear is often more complicated, with two or more reefs, adjustable cheek blocks mounted on tracks along the boom, and reefing lines led internally through the boom.

hauling them down to the level of the boom as the halyard is eased. Reef points in the sail are then tied (preferably passing between the sail and the boom, where possible) to bunch up the surplus sail; alternatively a reef lacing may be used. The kicking strap is not affected, and if the system is well laid out it is possible to get a better setting sail than with roller reefing, but the work involved is difficult when short-handed. Also, although there are usually two depths of reef, and sometimes three with mainsails of high aspect ratio, point reefing is not as flexible as roller reefing, where the reduction of sail can be adjusted roll by roll.

(4) Slab (or jiffy) reefing is a variation of (3), using modern materials and equipment. The gear is illustrated diagrammatically in Fig. 11(42). Only one reef is shown, but two or more can be provided. The procedure is to ease the kicking strap and set up the topping lift, then ease the main sheet. Heave in on the reefing line so that the boom is pulled up to the leech cringle, and make fast. Then slacken the main halyard until the luff cringle can be slipped over the hook at the gooseneck (it helps if the halyard is marked, so that it is slackened the right amount). Tighten the halyard again. Ease the topping lift, tighten the mainsheet, and set up the kicking strap. The spare folds of the bottom of the mainsail can be gathered by a lacing passed through the eyelets in the sail for that purpose. The gear needs to be

good and strong, and it is important that the cheek blocks on the boom are properly positioned so that the sail is pulled to the boom and also kept stretched along the foot.

(5) Roller furling for mainsails is a comparatively new system, where the luff of the sail is rolled up either inside the mast or on a jackstay which runs down the aft side of the mast. Operation can be manual or by an electric motor, and the sail can be partially rolled up for reefing or fully rolled for furling. An interior roller needs a special mast, see Fig. 11(43), but an exterior roller can be fitted to most masts provided they are not the bendy variety. The system is very easy to operate and is likely to become more popular. One disadvantage is that as the sail is reefed its centre of effort moves further and further forward, which can upset the balance of the helm.

Any reefing system depends on proper maintenance of the gear, and its availability in an emergency. Roller reefing gear must be lubricated and worked regularly; if a separate handle is used it must be stowed in a safe place, and a spare provided. With slab reefing the various pendants and sheaves must be kept in good condition, so that even a third reef (which is probably seldom, if ever, used) is readily available should it be required.

11.5.4 Headsail furling and reefing
Traditionally sail area in the foretriangle of a yacht has been reduced, as the wind speed increases, by changing to a smaller sail. This process was made easier in recent years by the advent of forestays with grooves to take the luff of the jib, which speeded things up by eliminating the need to hank and unhank sails on a pitching foredeck. Now the development of efficient roller furling/reefing gear means that a cruising yacht can conveniently set a large genoa, progressively reef it, or totally furl it, without the need for anybody to venture on the foredeck at all.

The idea is not new, but it has taken the development of modern rigs and sailcloths to make it practicable for larger sails. When the sail is rolled up on the forestay, the leech and the foot are exposed to the elements, and Terylene will suffer damage from ultra-violet light. These areas should be made in a special fabric, or protected by a sewn-on cover.

11.5.5. Spinnakers

In a cruising yacht, which can if necessary afford to make temporary changes of course while the spinnaker is hoisted or lowered, it should be perfectly easy to handle this sail with just a little foresight and practice.

The basic items of spinnaker gear are described in 11.3.1 and illustrated in Fig. 11(15). To hoist the spinnaker first make sure that it is properly flaked down in its bag with no twists. Attach the bag to the pulpit, or to the guardrails on the lee side, under the jib. Rig the spinnaker guy along the windward side, outboard of everything, through the pole end fitting, and clip it to the tack of the sail. Rig the sheet on the lee side, outboard of everything, and clip it to the spinnaker clew. Pass the halyard under the foot of the headsail, outboard and clear of everything, and clip it to the head of the sail, which has a swivel. Attach the heel of the pole to the mast and heave on the pole lift so that the pole is at right angles to the mast. Take down the slack on the pole downhaul. With the boat running roughly downwind it is easy to hoist the spinnaker quickly under the lee of the headsail and mainsail, then trim the guy and the sheet to set the sail. Then drop the headsail. The pole should be trimmed at right angles to the apparent wind, and its height on the mast adjusted so that the tack and clew of the sail are about the same height. Keep the spinnaker sheet eased out as far as possible without the luff of the sail falling in.

Gybing procedure depends on the gear fitted. With the main sheeted well in amidships and the boat's stern to the wind, the spinnaker guy is released from the pole end fitting and becomes the new sheet. By controlling the two sheets the spinnaker should be kept drawing while the pole is moved across and clipped onto the new guy (the previous sheet). The gybing of the mainsail can then be completed.

Lowering (handing) the spinnaker is simple if the boat is running downwind. First hoist the headsail. Then ease the guy so that the pole swings forward near the forestay. Release the tack of the sail from the pole end fitting. One crew member then gathers in all the foot of the sail somewhere aft of the shrouds on the lee side. When he is ready to gather in the rest of the sail, lower the halyard steadily. The sail is then pulled inboard and stowed down below. Clear away the spinnaker pole and secure all the gear.

Different cuts, and hence shapes, of spinnaker are available for best performance on different points of sailing. Originally the spinnaker was

(a) Horizontal cut. Tends to become fuller in stronger winds, and performs best on a run.

(b) Tri-radial construction minimises distortion, and gives a good all-round sail.

(c) Star cut. A flat, but broad-shouldered spinnaker which is best for use with the wind on or ahead of the beam.

(d) Radial head. A compromise sail, with a radial head and a flat, horizontally cut bottom, which combines good reaching and downwind performance.

Fig. 11(44) Different types of spinnakers.

essentially a running sail: now, using modern sailcloth and new cutting techniques, spinnakers can be carried effectively with the wind well forward of the beam. The more common types of spinnaker are shown in Fig. 11(44).

Since one of the requirements of a spinnaker is that it must support itself in the air, it is necessary to use a material which is as light as possible, consistent with strength and resistance to stretch. Normally nylon cloth is used, typically about 1–1½oz/sq yard, reinforced to discourage it from ripping. Reaching spinnakers are made of slightly heavier cloth because it is more important that they retain their shape. It is important not to carry a spinnaker in wind speeds greater than that for which it is designed. The suggested maximum wind speeds in Fig. 11(45), are rather lower than might have been expected.

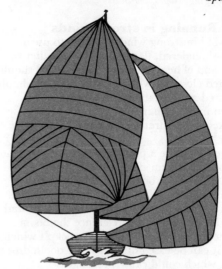

Fig. 11(46) A yacht, bows-on, running downwind with tri-radial spinnaker (left) and big boy or blooper (right).

Nylon weight	Boat size	Run	Broad reach	Beam reach	Close reach
0.5 oz	Under 30ft (9m)	6	6	5	–
	Over 30ft (9m)	5	5	4	–
0.75 oz	Under 30ft (9m)	22	17	14	12
	30–40ft (9–12m)	16	13	12	11
	Over 40ft (12m)	13	12	11	9
1.5 oz	Under 30ft (9m)	30	26	22	15
	Over 30ft (9m)	26	23	17	13

Fig. 11(45) Suggested maximum apparent wind speeds in knots for different weights of spinnaker cloth and on different points of sailing.

Fig. 11(47) Tallboy.

To improve their performance under spinnaker, racing yachts use supplementary sails such as the big boy, or blooper, see Fig. 11(46). This is a very light triangular sail, set on the same side as the mainsail. It has a very full skirt, near the water, and it collects wind which passes under the foot and round the leech of the mainsail. It can only set effectively when the wind is not more than about 30° out on the quarter. Mutual adjustment between sheet and halyard is necessary in order to get the sail as far out to leeward as possible. In light winds the blooper may set better by slightly over-trimming the mainsail or by taking down a reef in the main.

The tall boy, Fig. 11(47), is a long, narrow sail sometimes set forward of the mast in conjunction with a spinnaker (or during a headsail change). Its function is to smooth the airflow over the

Fig. 11(48) Spinnaker staysail.

leading edge of the mainsail. It is set flying (not hanked to a stay), and is normally tacked down to windward of the centreline of the boat, in similar fashion to the more traditional spinnaker staysail, as shown in Fig. 11(48).

11.5.6 **Running in strong winds**

Downwind in strong winds it is best to use a narrow-shouldered, flat spinnaker – smaller than normal and of heavier cloth. The halyard should be hoisted close up, with no drift, the pole should be lowered somewhat, and the sheet kept trimmed in more than usual – so that the spinnaker is well stretched out and made more stable.

There should be a preventer rigged to the end of the boom, and an efficient boom vang is needed to keep the boom from rising and to eliminate undue twist near the head of the sail, which can push the masthead to windward and help induce rolling. For preference the boom vang should be controlled from a cockpit winch, so that it can be eased quickly if the boom dips in the sea, which could cause breakage.

If the boat is surfing, gybing can be risky. It may be better to hand the spinnaker, and re-hoist it on the new gybe.

Broaching is usually caused by a combination of circumstances, but in bad conditions any one of them may result in the helmsman losing control of the yacht, which rounds up, beam on to wind and sea, and lies over on her side. The causes are: carrying too much sail, resulting in excessive heel, inbalance of the immersed shapes of the hull forward and aft, and producing a turning couple between the centre of lateral resistance and the centre of effort of the sail plan; the diminished effect of the rudder as the boat heels; the diminished effect of the rudder as the crest of a wave passes under the stern of the boat, thereby reducing the flow of water past the rudder; the turning effect on the boat when the bow ploughs into the trough of a wave and the stern is swung round by the following crest, which is moving faster.

Action to counter a broach should be to let the mainsheet run (if the boom is not already squared off), ease the boom vang to allow the mainboom to sky and thus spill some wind, and let go the spinnaker sheet. When the boat rights, get the boom vang and the spinnaker sheet in again, so that the boat can be brought under control.

In a cruising yacht it is more comfortable, safer, more sensible (and not a lot slower) to goosewing the genoa, or perhaps a smaller headsail, when running downwind in heavy weather, instead of having to cope with a spinnaker when probably short-handed. Rig the spinnaker pole on the mast, with lift and downhaul attached, and pass the genoa sheet through the pole end fitting. It may also be sensible to steady the pole and stop it swinging about by rigging the appropriate spinnaker guy to the pole end.

Yachts intended for long downwind passages are often fitted with twin running foresails – a rig which minimises chafe with the mainsail lowered. But it is important to remember that it takes time to hoist the mainsail and get back to windward in the event of somebody going over the side.

11.5.7 **Cruising spinnakers**

Many sailmakers now provide assymmetrical cruising spinnakers, which are easier to handle. With the wind well aft such sails are set on the opposite side to the mainsail, with or without a bearing out spar. Or with the wind on or somewhat abaft the beam they can be used as a reaching headsail, either set flying or hanked to the forestay.

There are also devices to facilitate handling a conventional spinnaker. A British invention is the Spee-Squeezer, marketed by Parbury Henty & Co Ltd, Kingswick House, Sunninghill, Berkshire, SL5 7BJ. It consists of a glassfibre bell mouth, on the end of a long nylon sleeve. When required, the sleeve with the spinnaker packed inside it is hoisted on the spinnaker halyard, like a long sausage. An uphaul, attached to the bell mouth at the bottom of the sleeve, is then pulled so that the sail is progressively unpeeled from the bottom up. While the spinnaker is set and drawing the bell mouth and the bunched up sleeve remain at the masthead. When the spinnaker is to be furled the uphaul is released and a downhaul is pulled, so that the bell mouth and sleeve progressively smother and house the sail as the sheet is eased. The sleeve can then be lowered, with the spinnaker inside it. If it is required to gybe, the sail can be temporarily furled inside the sleeve, while the mainsail and spinnaker pole etc are moved across, and then unfurled on the new gybe.

11.5.8 **Sail trim**

Good performance when sailing to windward depends not only on a jib and a mainsail which both set well, but on how they are trimmed in relation to each other. In combination the two sails act like an aerofoil with a slot through the middle. To optimise performance this slot must be exactly the right width from top to bottom – wide enough to give a sufficiently smooth flow of air (parallel to the mainsail and not backwinding it), but narrow enough to speed up the flow of air over the lee side of the mainsail, and thereby lower the pressure there in order to develop maximum power from the sailplan.

Starting with the jib, the correct trim can be easily assessed, with a little bit of practice, from three or four sets of telltales placed at equal intervals up the luff of the sail, and close to it. When the sail is correctly trimmed the windward and leeward telltales should all stream aft, and lie flat against the sail. If the sail is sheeted in too hard, or the boat is not high enough on the wind, the leeward telltales lift and flutter in the turbulent air flow which is created. If the sail is under-sheeted, or the boat is heading too high, the windward telltales flutter and dance. The correct fore-and-aft sheeting position can be judged by observing how the telltales react as the boat is luffed. Ideally all the windward telltales should lift together. Halyard and luff tension need to be adjusted in conjunction with sheeting arrangements in order to obtain the optimum shape of the headsail.

Mainsail shape is determined by halyard tension, clew outhaul, mainsheet setting, mainsheet traveller adjustment, and possibly by mast bend (backstay tension). Thus there are four or five variables to consider. In place of luff telltales as for a jib, the actual luff of the mainsail can be observed, the general aim being to keep it just not lifting. But telltales on the leech of the sail (usually at the end of each batten pocket) are very useful. If they all stream steadily aft it indicates that smooth, laminar flow prevails over both sides of the mainsail.

Any set of adjustments for jib and mainsail which may be established as the optimum (or near optimum) in, say, moderate winds will only be valid for those certain conditions of wind and sea. Major changes will be needed for light airs or for heavy weather.

In light winds it is important to have enough flow (fullness) in the mainsail, by easing the halyard and the clew outhaul. Similarly the jib should not be sheeted too hard, and if it has any adjustment in the luff this should be eased in order to put more flow into the sail. Then try moving the jib sheet lead forward one notch in order to tighten the leech slightly – or, if possible, move the sheet lead inboard a few inches in order to narrow the slot and thereby speed up the flow of air over the lee side of the mainsail – all the time watching the jib (luff) and the main (leech) telltales.

In strong winds it is necessary to keep the boat on her feet and balanced on the helm, first by flattening the sails and using any flattening reefs provided, and then by changing the headsail and/or reefing the mainsail (see 11.5.3). With a smaller headsail less air passes through the slot, so the mainsheet traveller can be moved to leeward which will reduce heel and weather helm. Halyard tension must be increased to keep the flow of the sails well forward. When trying to achieve the optimum trim it is important to make one change at a time, so that the effect can be established.

On a reach sail trimming becomes even more important in maintaining boat speed, since with the helmsman steering a fixed course any small variations in wind direction or speed must be met by the sail trimmers. When reaching, the genoa sheet can be moved further outboard, if the rules allow, and it should be played so that the luff of the sail is just not quivering, as should the mainsheet. With the apparent wind forward of the beam the slot effect between jib and mainsail is still important and, as when going to windward, the aim should be to keep the leech of the jib parallel to the lee side of the mainsail –

which becomes increasingly difficult as the sheets are eased. With the wind aft of the beam more fullness is needed in the sails: this happens automatically in the jib as the sheet is progressively eased, but with the mainsail the clew outhaul will need to be adjusted together with halyard tension.

When reaching or running it is necessary to control the twist in the mainsail. As the mainsheet is eased the boom end moves up as well as outboard, so that the upper part of the mainsail spills its wind while the lower part is still drawing. This effect can be minimised by an efficient kicking strap or boom vang (see 11.3.1). A small amount of twist is desirable because the wind speed is greater near the masthead (due to surface friction at sea level), and hence the apparent wind draws further aft towards the top of the mast.

11.5.9 Sail care

Examination of a new sail should convince its owner that much skilled workmanship has gone into it. The sailmaker having done his bit, it is up to the yachtsman to look after and make the best use of this new addition to the boat's wardrobe. A good sail can easily be spoiled by bad practices and careless handling.

A sail will only set as well as the mast and rigging allow, and notes on rigging adjustment are given in 11.2.4. In order to avoid creases and unfair strains, a mainsail must fit the mast and boom properly, with clew and tack cringles correctly positioned for the pins which are to hold them. The sailmaker should have taken detailed measurements of the gooseneck etc on board. Headsails are easier to fit, but it is important that the tack fitting is aligned with the forestay, and that the sail does not foul fittings such as the pulpit.

Even though a Terylene sail is reasonably robust, it should first be set and broken in for 2–3 hours in a wind not exceeding force 3–4, and it should not be reefed during this period. A sail should always be hoisted or lowered by pulling on the luff – never along the leech. When a mainsail is hoisted or lowered the weight of the boom should be taken on the topping lift (or by hand in a small boat), to avoid the leech stretching. The leech is not reinforced with roping or tape, or with a luff wire as in the case of a headsail, so it is particularly vulnerable to maltreatment. When sails are hung up to dry they should be hoisted by the head and the tack, not by the clew. Sails should not be allowed to flap unnecessarily, since this damages the structure of the cloth – particularly in the leech area where the flutter is greatest.

It is easy to put too much tension on halyards or outhauls. A mainsail should only be hoisted and pulled out along the foot enough to allow it to take its designed shape. In light to moderate winds only tension the halyard enough to remove any horizontal creases, and adjust the outhaul so that sufficient flow is given to the lower part of the sail. In stronger breezes they should both be tensioned more, so that little folds appear close to the luff and foot when the sail is hoisted. In strong winds maximum tension is needed to flatten the sail, and in order to keep the flow in the sail well forward extra luff tension may be applied by taking down on the Cunningham hole – a device near the tack of the sail which in effect shortens the luff.

Similar considerations apply with headsails. Before hoisting check that the halyard is clear aloft and that the sail is correctly hanked onto the forestay. It is also important to see that the sheeting positions are correct each side. Do not sheet the sail in before it is fully hoisted. Headsails which have a wire luff rope, or a wire on which the luff can slide, need to have the halyard set up tight, so that the luff is as straight as possible. Headsails which have a stretchy luff should have the halyard adjusted according to the wind strength – harder in heavy winds and less in lighter winds. If fitted, it is important not to overtighten the leech line of a sail.

While sailing, do not allow the running backstay or the topping lift to flap against the lee side of the mainsail, nor allow the sail to press unnecessarily against the lee rigging when running off the wind – this all causes damage to the cloth and to the stitching. Done properly, reefing should not damage a sail but if (for example when unreefing) the full weight is taken by reef points or the reef lacing, instead of by the reef pendants at luff and leech, the sail may be seriously distorted.

When a sail is lowered, bag it and stow it away below as soon as possible: sails left lying around on deck only get damaged by being walked on, or made damp from spray. Sail bags should be roomy, so that sails do not get unduly crushed or creased. Sails should be bagged so that they are ready for instant use – e.g. the tacks of headsails on top.

Any sail, but particularly a light nylon spinnaker, will rip on sharp objects such as split pins which are not taped over, so it pays to check all rigging, guardrails, spreader ends etc regularly.

On return to harbour, release the tension on the clew outhaul of the mainsail, remove the battens, flake the sail down over the boom and secure it with ties, and put on the sail cover (even if it is only overnight – it keeps the sail clean and dry, and protects it from the sun). If the mainsail is taken off the boom, flake it down carefully to the foot, roll it up from tack to clew, and put it in its bag. When flaking a sail avoid putting a crease across any window, and avoid flaking to the same creases on each occasion. See Fig. 11(49) and Fig. 11(50).

It is bad to dry sails by allowing them to flap in the wind – this causes chafe and damages the

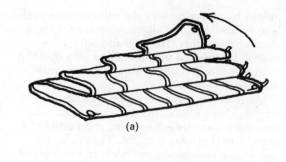

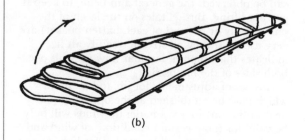

Fig. 11(49) Folding a mainsail. A mainsail should be flaked down either towards the foot (a), or towards the luff as in (b). If there is a window in the sail (a) is preferable, the first fold being taken over it so that it is not creased. Two people are needed, so that the fold is straight and even. Then roll neatly towards the clew (a), or towards the head (b), to fit in bag.

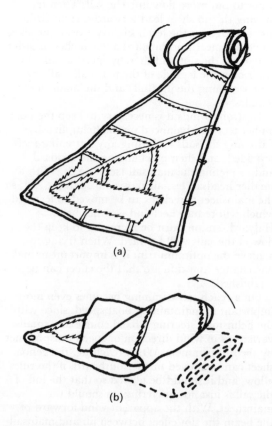

Fig. 11(50) Folding a jib. Headsails can either be flaked down towards the foot – as for a mainsail – or rolled down the luff from head to tack, as shown in (a), and then rolled as shown in (b).

structure of the cloth. If sails are wet it is better to leave them spread out in the boat, should it not be possible to dry them on deck. Do not leave wet nylon sails bagged up, since sometimes the colours will run.

Salt and dirt form an abrasive surface on sails, which damages the cloth and the stitching. This can be reduced by keeping the deck and rigging clean, as well as by washing the sails themselves regularly with fresh water.

At the end of the season, or if sails get really dirty, they should be washed properly in warm water (not more than about 120°F or 50°C) using ordinary soap or a mild liquid detergent, and scrubbing gently with a sponge or a soft brush. After washing, sails must be very well rinsed with fresh water, and dried carefully. Then they should be closely inspected for the smallest signs of damage before being stowed away – or sent to the sailmaker. Check both sides of each sail, panel by panel, seam by seam, for any small holes in the cloth, broken stitches, wear on the roping or tabling, loose hanks on headsails, worn or damaged cringles at the corners, and defective slides or batten pockets on mainsails.

It is not easy to wash and inspect sails properly on board, and the work is better done if they can be spread out on a clean surface ashore. If this is not available most sailmakers will undertake the service, and store your sails for the winter.

Certain stains on sails need speedy attention and special treatment. These notes refer to white sailcloth: coloured sails which need special cleaning are best treated professionally. Some of the solvents such as carbon tetrachloride are poisonous and others may involve a fire risk, so it is best if any cleaning is done in the open air and away from naked lights. After cleaning be sure to wash that area of the sail very thoroughly in order to remove all traces of whatever chemical has been used.

Oil or grease can usually be shifted by carbon tetrachloride or trichloroethylene in the form of proprietary stain removers like Thawpit – or by rubbing with Swarfega followed by washing in warm water with a mild detergent added.

Rust stains can be stubborn, but try a 5 per cent solution of oxalic acid or 2 per cent hydrochloric acid in warm water. Mix the solution in a plastic container, wear rubber gloves, and do not let the acid solution come into contact with metal fittings or the luff wire of a sail.

Tar or pitch stains can be treated with a solvent such as Polyclens, trichloroethylene, carbon tetrachloride or white spirit.

Paint or varnish should be removed as soon as possible using white spirit or turps substitute. If this fails try Swarfega with a liquid detergent and warm water. Polyurethane varnish can be softened with chloroform, and ordinary varnish with surgical or methylated spirit. Never use alkali-based paint strippers on Terylene cloth.

Blood stains should, if possible, be washed off immediately with plenty of cold water, and then with soap powder. Old stains should be soaked in cold water containing $\frac{1}{4}$pt (0.15lt) of ammonia to $\frac{1}{2}$gal (2.2lt) of water. Residual stains can be treated with a 1 per cent solution of pepsin in water, to which has been added a few drops of hydrochloric acid.

Mildew is caused by dirt, a damp atmosphere and poor ventilation. On synthetic sailcloth it is more unsightly than harmful, but it can be removed by scrubbing when dry with a stiff brush, and then soaking in a cold solution of 1 part household bleach to 15 parts of water.

11.5.10 Sail repairs

Any sailing yacht or motor sailer should carry sufficient repair gear in the form of needles, threads, spare material and a palm, so that even a moderately torn sail can be made serviceable once more. Small holes or splits, which if left unattended would soon extend, can often be given a temporary patch which will last until the chance occurs for a sailmaker to make a more finished and permanent repair. On occasions the safety of a boat may depend upon somebody being able to re-stitch a mainsail seam, or reconstruct the torn out clew of a headsail. In any case, sails are expensive items, and regular examination of them and prompt attention to minor defects will help to prolong their life.

Sail repair gear suitable for the average yacht should include the following items.

(1) Terylene thread, ranging from lightweight machine thread for spinnaker cloths to (say) 6lb thread suitable for cloths of 12oz/sq yd. The upper limit depends upon the size of boat. Roughly the weight of thread needed is half the weight of the cloth. So a 3lb thread is right for a cloth of 6oz/sq yd, and so on.

(2) Needles, similarly, must be selected for the weight of the cloth and the work to be done. They vary from domestic size (No. 19) to No. 13 for very heavy cloth. Two No. 18 and two No. 16 should suit a small yacht. Bigger boats need larger needles, as for example when sewing several thicknesses of cloth, but try not to use too large a needle for the job in hand, since it will make too large a hole in the cloth and thereby weaken it. When repairing highly stressed parts of a sail such as head, tack or clew, use a heavier thread and a larger needle than the weight of cloth would otherwise require. The thread should normally be doubled, or sometimes even quadrupled, to give strength with the minimum number of stitches.

(3) Beeswax is needed for treating the thread, partly for protection and partly to make it easier to work. The thread should be pulled through the beeswax three or four times. If no beeswax is available candlegrease makes an acceptable substitute.

(4) A palm is needed, with which to push the needle through the material.

(5) Repair material – off cuts of sailcloth in the form of strips of different sizes and weights – can usually be obtained from your sailmaker. They are used for patches which, as explained below, give a stronger repair than a simple darn.

(6) Special adhesive tape is useful for temporary repairs to sails in light weather, and also for holding a patch or a tear together while it is being stitched.

(7) A bench hook, with a line attached, is useful for tensioning the work while it is being stitched.

The sailmaker's darn is a form of herringbone stitch, as shown in Fig. 11(51), used for pulling together the edges of a rip in a sail. The thread should be doubled and waxed, and the end knotted. Then, working from the left, the needle is passed up through the cloth on the far side of the rip, and down through the cloth on the near side. It is then brought up through the gap, to the left of and over the top of the first stitch, and down under the cloth on the far side of the gap. It is then passed up again through the cloth on the far side of the gap, and the process is repeated. The stitches should be about 5mm ($\frac{1}{4}$in) from the edges of the cloth each side of the rip, and spaced about that far apart or slightly closer. As each stitch is formed it should be tightened just enough to pull the edges of the tear together. When the end of the tear is reached, the repair is finished off with a couple of half-hitches, stitched over.

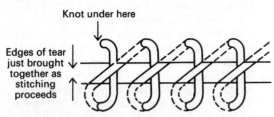

Fig. 11(51) Sailmaker's darn.

A patch will produce a stronger repair than a straight-forward darn, but it involves correspondingly more work. The material for the patch should ideally be the same as the sail – both in weight and texture – but in emergency a near equivalent will suffice. The patch should overlap the tear by 50mm (2in) each end and on each side, and should be positioned so that its weave (warp and weft) corresponds with the sail.

Unless the edges of the patch can be heat sealed to prevent them fraying (by using a hot knife, which is a specialist bit of sailmaking equipment), they will need to be turned under and secured with pins or tape for stitching.

A patch must be worked from one side of the sail, so an overhand stitch is used as shown in Fig. 11(52). Starting off with a knot in the end of

the thread, the needle is pushed down through the sail, and up through the sail and the patch opposite as indicated. Then take a rather longer diagonal stitch, down through the sail outside the edge of the patch, and repeat. Spacing should be similar to a sailmaker's darn. The stitching is continued right round the rectangular patch, working from left to right, until the starting point is reached.

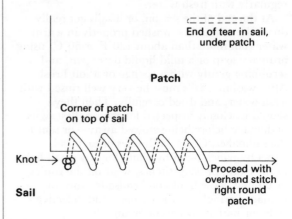

Fig. 11(52) Sewing a patch.

The sail is then turned over, and a rectangle is cut around the tear with its sides parallel to the edges of the patch which have been stitched, and at least 40mm(1$\frac{1}{2}$in) from them. See Fig. 11(53). At each corner of the rectangular hole thus formed, make a diagonal cut in the sail, about 20mm ($\frac{3}{4}$in) long towards the corner of the patch underneath. Turn the four edges under, so that they are between the sail and the patch, and then stitch round the rectangle (securing the turned in edges of the sail to the patch) in just the same way as the patch was originally stitched from the other side. Work from left to right as before, and take care to keep the tension of the stitches uniform.

If it is necessary to re-sew part of a bolt rope to a sail, first make sure that any twists are removed from the rope. If more than a very short length is to be re-stitched, it should be temporarily attached about every foot, so that it is sewn on

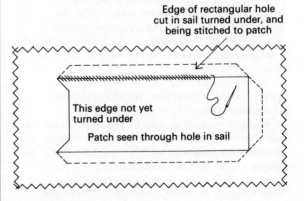

Fig. 11(53) Finishing a patch.

Fig. 11(54) How to re-sew a bolt rope to a sail.

evenly. The stitch used for hand roping is shown in Fig. 11(54), the needle being passed between the strands of the rope. To rope more than a short length properly takes experience if the correct tension is to be applied evenly.

11.6 Bibliography

Spars
Care of Alloy Spars and Rigging by David Potter (Adlard Coles Ltd)

Sails
Looking at Sails by Bruce Banks & Dick Kenny (Nautical Books)
Make Your Own Sails by R. M. Bowker & S. A. Budd (Nautical Books)
Sails By Jeremy Howard-Williams (Adlard Coles Ltd)
Spinnaker by Bunty King (Adlard Coles Ltd)
The Best of Sail Trim (Adlard Coles Ltd)
More Sail Trim (Adlard Coles Ltd)
This is Downwind Sailing by John Oakley (Nautical Books)

Ropes and knots
Ashley Book of Knots by Clifford Ashley (Doubleday)
Colour Book of Knots By F. Hin (Nautical Books)
Handbook of Seaman's Ropework By Sam Svensson (Adlard Coles Ltd)
Handling Ropes and Lines Afloat By Paul & Arthur Snyder (Nautical Books)
Knots and Splices By Cyrus L. Day (Adlard Coles Ltd)
Modern Rope Seamanship By Colin Jarman & Bill Beavis (Adlard Coles Ltd)
The Knot Book By Geoffrey Budworth (Elliot Right Way Books)

Chapter 12

Deck gear

Contents

12.1 Anchors and equipment

12.1.1 Anchors and cables

Anchors come in various shapes and each has its supporters but just as in the case of sterns, for instance, there is no 'best' shape. The traditional anchor is known these days as the fisherman (or stocked) type and though it needs to be rather heavier than modern types for equal holding power and is rather awkward to haul aboard it is still a versatile anchor worthy of consideration. It is essential that the key which holds the stock in place is securely fastened. The fisherman anchor will hold well in any reasonable bottom, and once aboard with the stock unshipped it stows neatly and without the projections of the more modern shapes. A disadvantage is that the upper fluke may be fouled by the cable when the yacht swings (e.g. at the turn of the tide), possibly causing the anchor to drag. Performance is improved if the flukes are sharpened somewhat with a file and the exposed bare metal given a couple of coats of epoxy paint for protection. Though one of the common zinc-rich paints (such as Galvafroid) will preserve it excellently on deck, they are rather soft and soon wear off if the anchor is used at all frequently. Fig. 12(1) shows the principal parts of a fisherman anchor, and the stock should weigh about 20 per cent of the total weight.

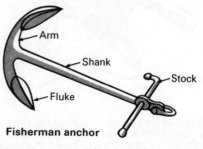

Fig. 12.(1) The various parts of a fisherman or stocked anchor.

353

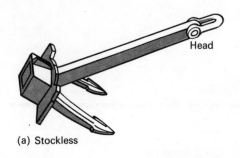

(a) Stockless

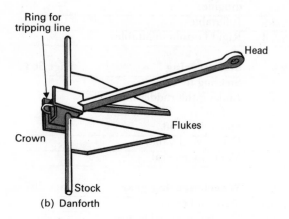

Ring for
tripping line

Head

Crown

Flukes

Stock

(b) Danforth

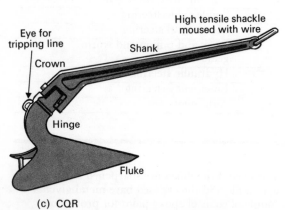

Eye for
tripping line

Crown

High tensile shackle
moused with wire

Shank

Hinge

Fluke

(c) CQR

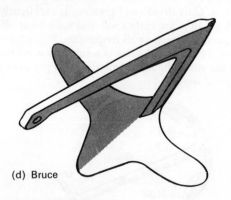

(d) Bruce

Fig. 12(2) Anchors in common use include: (a), the stockless type which is normally stowed in a hawse pipe; (b), the Danforth, sometimes also known as a spade anchor; (c), the CQR or plough anchor; and (d), the Bruce anchor.

Fig. 12(2) shows four other types of anchors: the stockless; Danforth; CQR and Bruce. The stockless variety is the one normally seen hanging from a hawse pipe where it stows easily. That is its greatest and almost only advantage, for its short shank and the absence of a stock to turn it so that the flukes are in their digging position means that it has to be heavier than any of its rivals for equal holding power. The Danforth can also be stowed in a hawse pipe but it is a good general purpose, deck-stowed type as well. Its only failing is that (like the CQR) it tends to skate over a weed-infested bottom rather than dig in. The CQR, which was developed for mooring flying boats, is another type of anchor designated as 'High holding power' by Lloyds and its weight should be about the same as the Danforth. A CQR anchor can be arranged to stow neatly in the bow roller fitting at the stemhead – see Fig. 12(3). The Bruce anchor originated as a mooring for oil rigs and can be lighter than any of the other types, but it is a somewhat awkward object on deck though special stowage chocks are made for it. There are imitations of both CQR and Danforth types

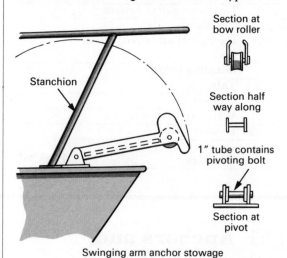

Section at
bow roller

Stanchion

Section half
way along

1″ tube contains
pivoting bolt

Section at
pivot

Swinging arm anchor stowage

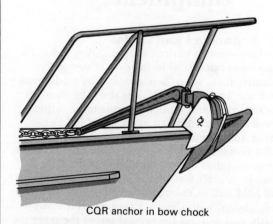

CQR anchor in bow chock

Fig. 12(3) Rather than stow an anchor on deck it may be pulled against a bow chock as with this CQR type. On the other hand if deck stowage is a requirement the work of getting the anchor aboard can be reduced by using a swinging arm arrangement.

available, the former coming under the general heading of 'plough' anchors, and though some are good others are not, and if there are any doubts it pays to buy the genuine article.

The following table shows suggested sizes of anchors and cables for various boat lengths but these, it should be noted, are minimum sizes and anything larger will be a bonus. A normal person can man-handle a 50lb (23kg) anchor without too much difficulty and some people can manage up to maybe, 75lb (34kg). Above that size things get difficult and the anchor will either have to be hauled aboard via an anchor davit of sufficient height for the anchor to clear the top rail or guard wire, or hawse pipes will have to be considered. Other than those two schemes it may be possible to arrange for the anchor to haul up flush with the deck, or to reach up to a swinging arm which is finally swung back on board complete with anchor. Fig. 12(3) shows those two methods. The fittings themselves can be fabricated from steel and subsequently galvanised or epoxy-painted. The swinging arm must have a very secure attachment through the deck.

Opinions vary about whether it is best to anchor to a long length of a springy rope like nylon or to a shorter scope (but still at least three times the depth of water) of comparatively heavy chain. If nylon is chosen, and it is important that the rope is just that and not an unreliable polypropylene, for instance, a couple of fathoms (3.3m) of chain should be shackled on between the rope and the anchor itself to lend a bit of weight and to take the chafe that might occur on the sea bottom. Nylon is susceptible to chafe and its lead over the deck edge should be as smooth as possible. Lloyds require 30 fathoms (55m) of chain or nylon for each anchor and actually require two anchors per boat. The second anchor, which might be considered to be the kedge anchor, may be 70 per cent of the weight of the main, or bower, anchor. The weight shown in the table are not necessarily those recommended by Lloyds, incidentally, and in many instances are probably lighter. To make use of Lloyds requirements it is necessary to know what is called the Equipment Numeral for the boat concerned, and that is something best left to the designer.

Should it be necessary to join two lengths of chain cable this is best done with what is called a chain joining link, this being a good deal stronger than using a shackle. The chain should be clearly marked (e.g. with coloured paint) at intervals of about 5 fathoms (9m). The inboard end of the chain, known as the bitter end, should be lashed, not shackled, to an eye or some other secure anchoring point. If the chain stows in an inaccessible chain locker it is sensible to have the lashing long enough for it to show through the chain pipe on deck. Then, if the chain and anchor have to be abandoned in a hurry, it can be quickly cut (preferably after attaching some kind of buoy and line to it).

Chain cable which is to be used with a windlass (see 12.1.4) must be calibrated chain which, when under tension, fits the indentations of the gypsy concerned. Since there is no universal standard, care is needed when matching chain to gypsy or vice versa.

12.1.2 Stemhead rollers and chain stoppers

On all but the smallest of boats a stemhead roller is a necessity. It keeps in place the chain or anchor warp when anchored, and allows it to be retrieved reasonably easily. The roller itself should be of good size and free-running on its spindle. The lips that bound it each side should

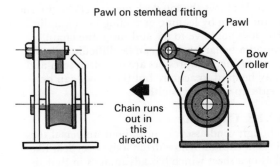

Fig. 12(4) A pawl at the bow roller will help when retrieving anchor, while a chain compressor allows the chain to be paid out under complete control.

Minimum sizes for anchors and cable

Overall boat length ft (m)	20 (6)	25 (7.3)	30 (9)	35 (11)	40 (12)	45 (14)
Bruce lb (kg)	11 (5)	16 (7.5)	22 (10)	33 (15)	33 (15)	44 (20)
CQR (plough) lb (kg)	20 (9)	25 (11)	35 (16)	45 (20)	60 (27)	75 (34)
Fisherman lb (kg)	26 (12)	31 (14)	40 (18)	51 (23)	71 (32)	90 (41)
Stockless lb (kg)	30 (13)	40 (18)	50 (22)	60 (27)	80 (36)	100 (45)
Chain in (mm) dia (short link)	$\frac{1}{4}$(6)	$\frac{5}{16}$(8)	$\frac{5}{16}$(8)	$\frac{5}{16}$(8)	$\frac{3}{8}$(10)	$\frac{7}{16}$(11)
Chain weight lb/fathom (kg/m)	$5\frac{1}{4}$(1.1)	$7\frac{1}{2}$(1.6)	$7\frac{1}{2}$(1.6)	$7\frac{1}{2}$(1.6)	10(2.2)	$11\frac{1}{2}$(2.8)
Nylon in (mm) dia	$\frac{1}{2}$(12)	$\frac{1}{2}$(12)	$\frac{5}{8}$(16)	$\frac{5}{8}$(16)	$\frac{3}{4}$(18)	$\frac{3}{4}$(20)

be canted in at the top to keep the cable down and prevent it jumping out when the lead is not exactly fore and aft. The whole fitting needs to be solidly bolted down.

Though rarely seen these days, a stemhead fitting incorporating a pawl can be a great advantage where chain cable is used. Fig. 12(4) shows one way of fitting the pawl. With it lifted the chain can run out freely. When it is dropped the chain can be hauled in but is prevented from running out. This is a useful attribute on a sailing craft with no windlass but even with one, it allows the operator to take a breather without having to make the cable fast with the risk of jamming his fingers. Stemhead rollers can be bought separately from the stemhead fitting, and an arrangement such as that shown can be made easily enough by any competent blacksmith. It can be galvanised after fabrication. The two points worth noting when designing it are that the pawl should drop into the chain at the point where it passes over the roller, and it must be possible to lift the chain out if required past the pawl pivoting point. The pawl itself must be robust and of a thickness that allows it to sit neatly into the chain. The bolt on which it pivots should also be stout.

A chain stopper or compressor, also shown on Fig. 12(4), is another useful, though rarely seen, item. It allows the foredeck man to check the run of the chain by leaning or pulling on a handle. He does not have to try and surge the chain round a bollard, which can be difficult. Like the pawl fitting, compressors are not often seen and may be hard to acquire but they, too, can be made up by a blacksmith.

12.1.3 Capstans

Though windlasses are just about universal these days, a capstan whose drum axis is vertical like that of a sheet winch has advantages in that the lead to it can be taken from any angle. This is useful, especially when warping a boat into a berth. The snag with capstans and presumably one reason why they are not more popular is that on the small sizes that would be used on yachts the handles, which operate on a horizontal axis, tend to be rather low. This means that the operator is usually reduced to kneeling on deck, in which position he cannot exert nearly as much force as he can standing up and working the to-and-fro motion of a windlass handle. Powered capstans are widely used in ships, and also for handling stern lines in large yachts.

12.1.4 Windlasses

Windlasses may be had with single or double action. That is, they may operate on only the pulling stroke or on both strokes. They may also be had with two speeds – one for when the work is easy and the chain can come home fast, and the other for when there is a real load on the chain. The gypsy (the drum at the side round

which the cable runs) can be designed to suit chain only or a combination of chain and rope, which is useful where rope is the main anchor cable but is joined to the anchor with a short length of chain. There is also normally a separate rope drum on the opposite side of the windlass from the chain gypsy.

Hand operated windlasses in the larger sizes can be used for loads up to 1000lb (450kg) or more and are capable of handling chain up to $\frac{1}{2}$in (12mm) diameter with a mechanical advantage of 40:1 in low gear, but once the requirement for such a powerful piece of equipment is reached, people tend to start thinking of electric or hydraulic windlasses. Normally, smallish boats use electric types but as craft get bigger with more elaborate engine arrangements, the tendency is to switch to the, perhaps, slightly more reliable and robust hydraulic types. The requirement then is for a hydraulic pump to be driven off the main engine or a generator (usually by belt) which transmits power through a hydraulic hose to another pump in the windlass itself. Clearly nothing will work unless the engine is running.

Typically, the battery drain using an electric windlass would be, on a 12-volt system, 34 amps for 100lb pull; 69 amps for 300lb pull: and 100 amps at 500lb. The corresponding figures for 24 volts would be 20 amps, 33 amps and 44 amps, while at 1000lb the drain would be 80 amps. These pull figures are a bit confusing but for smallish boats that use up to $\frac{5}{16}$in chain, the maximum likely pull would be 300lb, while for those with $\frac{3}{8}$in chain the figure rises to 400lb, and on those that have $\frac{1}{2}$in chain the maximum likely is 500lb. Most electric windlasses can be fitted with an overload protection unit which will trip if the windlass is overloaded other than briefly, and some are equipped with a gear change mechanism. To conserve battery power, an electric windlass should normally only be operated when the engine is running and the alternator is charging. Both hydraulic and electric types can normally be fitted with a lever for hand operation in an emergency. Some have an indicator which shows how much cable has been veered.

12.1.5 Chain lockers

Allowing anchor chain to collapse into the bottom corner of an undrained chain locker is asking for trouble and unpleasant smells. The locker should have a perforated tray in it on which the chain sits, and a good-sized drain plug at the bottom. A hose can occasionally be squirted into the locker to wash off the mud, which can then be collected from a suitable place in the bilges to where it has drained. If the locker is not directly under the chain pipe on deck, the chain should be led to the locker in a trough, not through a pipe in which it is bound to jam eventually.

12.2 Deck fittings

12.2.1 Pulpits and guardrails

A pulpit is fitted to allow people to work round the forestay in safety and with reasonable ease. This means that a man must be able to get forward of the stay and be sustained in that position. If the pulpit does not extend far enough forward things may be difficult, and if it is too wide he may be flung from side to side in bad weather. There is more to the design of a pulpit than simply running a railing round the bow. Remember, too, that it will probably be necessary to haul the anchor on to the foredeck and this may be difficult if the lower rail is fixed at an inconvenient height. A pulpit must be at least 24in (600mm) high and its bases should be designed to take transverse loads as well as fore and aft.

Stanchions were discussed in 10.5.5 but it is worth repeating here that they should be at least 24in (600mm) high (and are better if even more than that) and must be very securely through-bolted at their bases. Stanchions have a top wire (or rail in bigger craft) and, lower down, a second wire at just above mid-height. The lead of these wires should be checked to see that they do not chafe. The wires themselves are probably best made of a plastic-covered stainless steel. Somewhere along their length they should be arranged to clip to, rather than pass through, the stanchions to make a gateway for getting aboard. Stanchions may be of mild steel (epoxy painted after fabrication), stainless steel or aluminium alloy tube.

12.2.2 Mooring bitts and bollards

A bitt is usually taken as having one vertical post with a horizontal member of some form through it, while a bollard has two vertical posts. Either is much more acceptable on the foredeck than a cleat since there may be a multiplicity of lines attached (such as breastlines and springs) while at different times the anchor chain or warp will need securing other than to the windlass. A cleat can really only handle one line at a time without risk of everything jamming up. Of the bitts available, those which are made up of tubes are preferable to those which have a solid bar as the horizontal member, since a bar can cause nasty wounds round the ankle as life gets hectic on the foredeck. Fig. 12(5) shows the various types most often seen. Whatever is fitted should be as large as practical and very well bolted down. The RNLI constantly complain that if they have to tow a yacht there is often no adequate fixing point for their tow rope. Even the bottom of a deck-stepped mast is not always man enough for the job, and they often have to resort to wrapping the rope right round the superstructure. In the old days boats commonly had a sampson post forward which was a stout

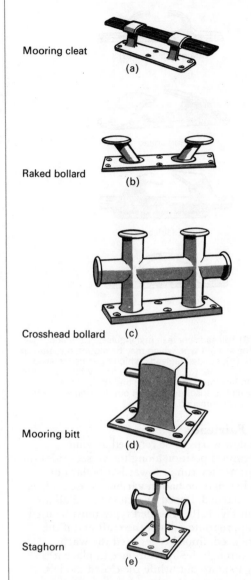

Fig. 12(5) Rope and chain require good attachment points, particularly on the foredeck. Typical of these are (a), a mooring cleat; (b), a raked bollard; (c), crosshead bollard; (d), a mooring bitt, though the horizontal bar can be dangerous; and (e), a better type of mooring bitt, or staghorn.

timber post (usually oak) which was stepped on the keel or stem and ran up through the foredeck. This could taken immense strains and though it might not be practical today on some small yachts, the need remains for a secure fixing point forward that is big enough to take a number of light warps or one really hefty one. Stout bollards or bitts on the foredeck should be complemented by a pair aft with two more, though perhaps of a lesser size, port and starboard somewhere near 'midships. These last are the principal securing points for the springs (warps that lead diagonally out from the boat and help to prevent her surging backwards and forwards when moored).

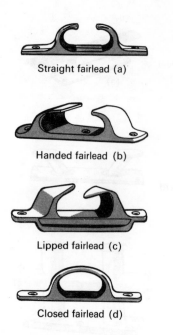

Straight fairlead (a)

Handed fairlead (b)

Lipped fairlead (c)

Closed fairlead (d)

Fig. 12(6) Fairleads come in many guises. Common ones are (a), the straight type which may be mounted to port or starboard; (b), handed fairleads which must be installed on the correct side; (c), a lipped type from which a rope is unlikely to be loosed accidentally; and (d) a closed fairlead which is absolutely secure but through which the warp has to be threaded.

12.2.3 Fairleads

These allow warps to be retained at some predetermined position along the vessel's sides (or transom) as they run in towards a bollard or cleat. They may be had in various types, such as straight, handed, lipped and closed, and all are shown in Fig. 12(6). Handed types must be used on the appropriate sides of the craft and if this done are good; lipped types need the warp slotting through the lips but once in place it is unlikely to jump out; while the closed models require the warp to be threaded through the fairlead, which is sometimes a nuisance though it can be guaranteed to stay in position. The larger and better made the fairlead is, the less it will chafe the rope.

12.2.4 Lifelines

Unless a yacht is very securely bounded by bulwarks and stanchions supporting guardrails, lifelines are a wise precaution. These generally take the form of a wire starting at the aft end of the cabin top running forward as far as practical towards the mast and anchored both ends. On bigger boats, or those with a centreline hatch, two lines may be necessary. These lines, which are probably best of plastic-covered stainless steel wire, may be used as handholds when going forward or to provide a securing point for safety harness. Obviously their anchoring plates fore and aft must be through-bolted and not merely screwed down.

12.2.5 Latchway Safety System

Though lifelines are a good aid to safety their limited scope is restrictive and running along the deck or cabin top as they do, they can trip the unwary. Better on nearly all counts is the Latchway Safety System. Here the normal lifeline is replaced with a wire which, with specially designed fastenings, can bound the deck and be fixed to stanchions, shroud plates, toe rails, standing rigging or other similar fittings. What is known as a 'Transfastener' is attached to the safety harness and can traverse these fastenings without needing to be undone. Since the wire can run from stern to bow, cross the deck, and then run back the other side there is no part of the yacht that is out of reach of the wearer of the safety harness. The Transfastener can only be removed from the wire at entry/exit terminals at each end of the span. Maintenance consists of washing off salt deposits with fresh water from time to time.

12.2.6 Ventilators

Very little attention is paid to natural ventilation on most small craft. It is hoped that the provision of an opening port or two, or sliding windows, plus a couple of hatches will do the trick. And so they would if they could be left open, but in bad weather or when the craft is deserted things are generally tight shut. This leads to an unpleasant atmosphere which induces condensation below decks and, in the case of a wooden boat, provides splendid conditions for the development of dry rot.

Properly there should be one air change every 20 minutes or so, and that is a reasonable figure on which to base calculations. If the cabin of a yacht were, say, 800 cu ft (23 cu m) in volume and an average 1-knot wind speed (100ft/min or 30m/min) was estimated while she was closed up, the ventilators must be able to cope with 800/20 = 40 cu ft of air for there to be a change every 20 minutes. If that 100ft/min figure is taken then the cross-section area of the vents must be 40/100 = 0.4 sq ft. That would be given by two 3in (75mm) diameter vents matched by a further two vents of the same size to get rid of the old air.

The figure of 100ft/min is a low one but the average yacht ventilator is so full of chokes and restrictions that it is probably realistic. In bad weather, though the wind may be blowing hard, some of the vents will probably be closed and what remains will have to cope with a wet and heavy-breathing crew below.

There are various types of special mushroom ventilators available, such as the Aeolian, that permit air to pass while keeping out all but solid water. Such types are claimed to be able to move approximately 8 cu ft (0.23 cu m) per minute in even a light wind. The Aeolian Solarvent is a solar powered extractor ventilator, in which a silicon cell generates sufficient electricity during normal daylight hours to drive a small motor and blade: this will remove 11 cu ft (0.3 cu m) per minute even in still air.

Normal mushroom ventilators have a central bolt projection downwards, so that they can be shut tight when required and at other times opened as far as seems reasonable. Cowl vents are more efficient, as might be expected, but have the drawback that their projection above deck makes them a prime target for errant sheets which tend to take a turn round them and then whisk them overboard. The classic type of nearly-watertight vent is the Dorade, Fig. 12(7), where a cowl vent is mounted on a box while some little distance from the cowl in the same box is a simple tube. Water getting in through the cowl will simply swill around the box, from which it can drain away, and will not find its way below unless so deep that it overflows the tube. Cowl vents should have some provision made so that the cowl can be removed from its spigot and a watertight cap snapped on in its place.

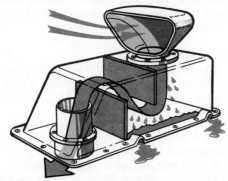

Fig. 12(7) A Dorade ventilator which is watertight in all but extreme conditions. Water getting down the cowl will normally drain through holes cut in the surrounding box.

12.2.7 **Davits and other boat lifting gear**

The usual modern yacht is too small to carry a davit-hoisted dinghy anywhere but over the stern, where it tends to be a nuisance (especially when mooring stern-to) and to put weight just where it is not wanted (at the end of the boat). However, unless the dinghy can be swung inboard from a single arm swivelling davit, it is probably even more of a nuisance hanging over the side than it is on the stern. Further, its height above deck when in side davits would probably preclude its use on most sailing craft. So if davits are required they will be of the fixed type and mounted at the stern, and all that can be asked of them is that they are light and strong. Certain types have extending arms which can be valuable when trying to accommodate different dinghies while, once the dinghy is lowered, davit arms can be shortened, with advantage. A davit can be used to sling an aft gangway, when its arms may be used as handrails.

Dinghies can often be lifted aboard via the main halyard though it is a two-man operation – one to push the boat away from the parent vessel's sides and the other winching or heaving

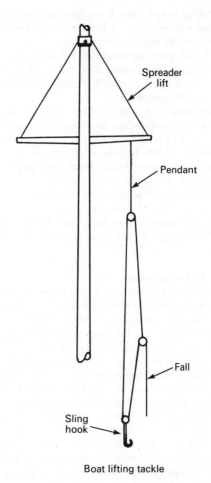

Boat lifting tackle

Fig. 12(8) American fishermen hoisted their dories aboard via a tackle mounted on a spreader.

down the halyard. Incidentally, if the dinghy is to be stowed upside down it is best to fix the falls or slings on to eye bolts on the outside of the stem and transom. It can then be turned over in the air with the slings still attached. American fishermen usually bring their dories aboard via a tackle on a spreader, Fig. 12(8), while yachts with a stout boom and a topping lift may be able to employ the boom as a lifting derrick.

12.2.8 **Boarding ladders**

Some form of rigid boarding ladder is an essential item on all but the very smallest of cruising boats. The ladder may be of plastic, aluminium alloy, stainless steel or teak (a rope ladder is not an easy thing to use without practice), or it may be built on to the yacht in the form of rungs up the transom. Whatever form it takes, it acts as the base for operations in getting a man aboard. Someone who has been in the water for some time is unlikely to be in his first flush of strength and vigour and will almost certainly be unable to pull himself over the deck edge. The crew leaning over the side cannot exert much useful lifting power, and there have been cases of people simply being swept away from the tired arms of their would-be rescuers. A ladder down the boat's side or transom, that can be unshipped when not required, will give the unwilling swimmer a chance to get himself aboard or, failing that, will provide a footing from which a crew member can act in a useful manner.

The bottom rung of the ladder should be at least 12in (300mm) below the water level at rest, as the craft may well be heeling away from the person in the water. In quieter times a boarding ladder makes getting aboard from a dinghy less of a scramble. It should be strong and demonstrably capable of taking the strains likely to be put on it. There may be two men on the same rung at times and at least one of them may have added weight in the form of waterlogged clothing.

12.2.9 **Tabernacles**
The traditional tabernacle, which allows the mast to pivot backwards or forwards on a bolt through the spar passing through the cheeks of the tabernacle, allows the pivoting point to be at any convenient height, within limits. This facility can be useful in that it may permit the mast to lie horizontally when lowered aft over a doghouse, for instance, or to have its truck no higher than the highest point of its parent yacht when lowered forward and sitting on the pulpit. This is worthwhile when the mast has been dropped so that the craft can pass under a low bridge where it is important to have the minimum overall air draught. As opposed to modern deck-stepping methods the tabernacle also gives some degree of control over the mast as it is being raised or lowered since the cheeks extend a little way above the pivoting point and the spar is confined within them.

In practice some of the load is taken off the bolt by driving a wedge under the heel of the

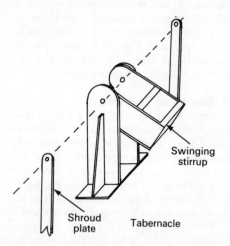

Fig. 12(9) A tabernacle allows a mast to be raised or lowered under reasonable control. Even greater control is assured if shrouds are set on the same plane as the mast with their attachment points to the shroud plates in line with the pivoting point on the tabernacle.

mast once it is raised but this wedge sometimes jams while the bolt hole in the mast gradually becomes worn and elongated. Both factors make handling the mast more difficult than it should be. Fig. 12(9) shows the set-up of a modern tabernacle where the mast sits in a stirrup which swings about studs in the main structure. When lowered it can simply be slipped out of the stirrup. To ship it again, the stirrup is angled correctly and the mast slipped back. There is no awkward lining-up of bolt holes needed.

Though it may not always be possible, if a pair of shrouds can be arranged such that they lie in the same plane as the mast, and if their connections at the chain plates are in line with the pivoting studs, these shrouds can be kept tight when lowering or raising the mast and will thus prevent it swinging from side to side. Achieving this set-up usually means extending the chain plates well above deck level.

Tabernacles of this type work best if the bottom of the mast is square. This implies a timber spar which can be made to change from a square to a round or oval section without problems.

12.2.10 **Gallows**
Rather like the tabernacle (12.2.9), boom gallows have fallen from favour despite their real utility. They can be made from timber and steel pipe and can often be sited at the aft end of the superstructure where they will provide a good handhold. A boom stowed in gallows is much more secure than if supported by a topping lift and restrained with the sheet. If the gallows incorporate three stowage positions the boom can be hauled over to one side when required so as to keep the cockpit clear. Fig. 12(10) shows a type built up from pipe frames (which drop through and into supports rather like deck stanchions) connected by a stout timber cross-piece. The gallows can thus be unshipped and the cross-piece unbolted when the time comes to stow it. The whole structure should be robust and securely fastened but there are endless variations on the theme.

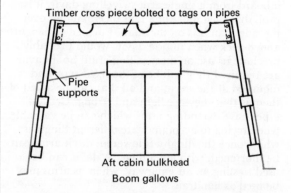

Fig. 12(10) Boom gallows will hold a boom and sail securely in place when stowed. The gallows themselves can be made to slot in place and to be taken apart for easy stowage.

12.2.11 Warps and hawsers

Any craft may have to be towed at some time, hence the need for a stout bollard or bitt forward. Equally, though, she may be called on to tow another vessel and should be equipped to do so. For both purposes a towing hawser is needed and this, on the average yacht, should consist of some 30 fathoms (55m) of ⅝in diameter (16mm) nylon rope, which has a breaking load of about 5 tons. This hawser could also be streamed astern in a bight when running downwind in bad weather. Towing procedure is discussed in 15.4.1.

Every yacht should also have two mooring warps of about one size down from the towing hawser and at least twice the length of the vessel, plus a further length of light line (about ¼in (6mm) diameter) as a heaving line. This should be about 50ft (15m) in length and be weighted at one end. The weight might consist of a big brass nut or something similar worked into a monkey's fist knot. Recommended sizes of warps (and other ropes) for yachts of different sizes are given in 11.4.4.

12.2.12 Fenders

All yachts need fenders to absorb any impact and spread the load. Hence the larger they are the better. The modern air-filled types are very good and the cylindrical models which can be hung vertically or horizontally are the most generally useful, supplemented by large spherical fenders for use at bow and stern. When mooring against piles a short plank is needed to suspend outboard of a couple of fenders and to bear against the piles. Fenders should always be brought inboard when under way. If left hanging they cause damage and spray, can be carried away in rough water, and look untidy swinging about with the boat's motion.

12.3 Tenders

Until comparatively recently very few yachts had berths from which the crew could step ashore dry-shod. Rather, at the end of a cruise they would pick up a mooring and then row to a boatyard in the dinghy. This had, more often than not, been towed astern for the duration of the trip since anchoring or, as a special treat, picking up a vacant mooring, was the order of the day at every port of call. Outboards were not much in use being considered noisy and smelly (which they still are, of course) and, above all unreliable (which is much less true these days). Consequently people had to row, and there is considerable pleasure to be had from drifting down through an anchorage studying and criticising the assembled craft. Such an occupation is much less attractive in an outboard-powered dinghy, which is much too fast and whose noise prohibits quiet conversation.

Though there have been inflatable boats in existence for a long time the sort of thing so widely used today was only properly developed after World War II. Today few cruising boats go to sea without an inflatable dinghy which despite its high cost and short life compared with the normal, rigid type can at least be stowed on board all but the smallest vessels. It is thus always available as a makeshift liferaft in emergencies and as a conveyance of sorts. There is no pleasure and little progress to be had from rowing an inflatable and it makes a poor vehicle for, say, laying out a kedge anchor, but it is vastly better than no dinghy at all.

12.3.1 Rigid dinghies

The main advantages a rigid dinghy has over an inflatable are that it is better suited to rowing and, having some worthwhile depth of hull below the floorboards, it is drier inside. Since it has more freeboard it can be used in worse weather without soaking the occupants and their baggage while propelled by oars, and it is a better vehicle for rowing out an anchor than is the inflatable. With added buoyancy in the form of buoyancy bags, slabs of foam or an inflatable collar round its gunwale it is nearly as good a makeshift liferaft. Few small cruisers, however, can stow a dinghy on deck with any ease and towing it may cause difficulties when manoeuvring in the confines of a marina. In any case a towed dinghy is always a potential source of trouble in that during bad weather it may fill with water and break away. A proper cover reduces this risk but does not completely eliminate it and such a thing is a nuisance to have to fit. Unless specially designed for the job a dinghy will not tow at all happily behind a motor cruiser which would normally be travelling too fast, causing the dinghy to sheer from side to side until it eventually started to tow broad-side on, when it would capsize.

Thus for most yachts (and especially those that are berthed in marinas) a rigid dinghy is not worth having unless it can be stowed on deck. Its occasional real advantages would be outweighed by its general drawbacks. If a dinghy is to stow on deck it will have to be quite small, with something like 6ft 6in to 7ft 6in overall (2m to 2.3m) being the maximum that could be accommodated aboard the average cruising yacht. Although at that length it will not be a good rowing boat it will be tolerable if the craft has been properly designed. A stem dinghy is not very sensible since a lot of useful space forward has been lost, and the boat either sheers away or capsizes if anyone is unwise enough to step aboard near the bow. A normal pram dinghy will be better – this has a transom at the bow as well as the stern – while a W-cross-section hull should be better still. With the last-named shape the buoyancy of the hull is out at the sides so that the boat will be more stable and with what amounts to twin hulls will tend to row and tow in a

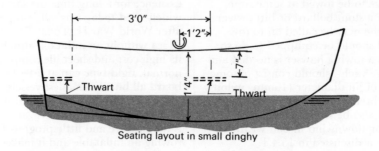

Seating layout in small dinghy

Fig. 12(11) Some minimum height and lengths for easy rowing in a small dinghy.

straighter line than will a more conventional type.

Fig. 12(11) shows the dimensions that should be adhered to, or nearly so, on a small dinghy and they demonstrate why the usual inflatable cannot ever be rowed with much success – it is simply too shallow. On most really small dinghies of the type under discussion feet will be braced against the transom while rowing. If this cannot happen there should be some type of alternative brace on the floorboards since rowing is done as much by the leg, stomach and back muscles as by the arms. When sitting on the rowing thwart legs should be slightly flexed with feet against the transom or brace. Beam of the dinghy would be about 4ft (1.2m) and the oars as long as will stow inside the dinghy. Thus 6ft 6in (2m) oars will fit neatly in a 7-footer. If thwarts and floorboards are easily lifted out this will make the dinghy lighter for slinging aboard and to that end there should be stout eyebolts fore and aft. It should be possible to fasten the rowing thwart down in alternative positions so that the balance of the boat is roughly right whether there is one person or two board, and whether a mountain of baggage is being carried forward or the boat is empty. This means two rowlock positions as well. There should be a sculling notch in the transom. Sculling is a useful art to acquire but the notch is also useful if the anchor, or its cable, is to be laid out while under way. If the dinghy is to be towed very often, the forward eyebolt should be supplemented on pram and W-type hulls with a further two eyebolts somewhere near the bottom, outside corners of the forward transom. On these can be fastened a bridle and the towing warp taken to the centre of this, or twin towing warps used. The dinghy will travel better under such an arrangement than if towed only from its centreline.

There is no best material for building a dinghy. Probably the lightest will be stitch and glue ply, and lightness is always a virtue in such craft.

12.3.2 **Collapsible and folding dinghies**

Carrying on from the conception of a small, rigid dinghy that can be lifted aboard, one way to increase its length and thus its usefulness, and to

better its rowing performance is to have a further, short length of hull that can be bolted on to the stern transom. Thus an easily-stowed dinghy 6ft 6in (2m) in length could be converted into a 10-footer with the addition of a 3ft 6in (1m) length of hull. That extra length of separate hull would not present too many problems in stowage on board and it might even be stowed inside the main hull.

Collapsible boats of various kinds appear on the market from time to time. Some have rigid sides that fold down flat on to the rigid bottom, so making a very shallow package; others fold up lengthways, concertina fashion. Some are made almost entirely of a flexible plastic, but whatever the building system the thwarts and transom are usually used to brace the sides apart. For some reason these craft never seem to find much favour with the public, though if robustly built of good materials there is much to recommend them. The hinging medium is usually canvas or, these days, heavy duty plastic. Buoyancy bags could be fitted after erection, and if the erecting can be done really quickly and does not require much space to lay out the individual parts the type is worth investigating. It should have a reassuringly solid feel about it when put together and in the water.

12.3.3 **Inflatables**

There is a wide range of inflatable dinghies on the market, most of which follow the same basic idea of multi-chamber inflatable tubes set on a fabric floor. There may also be an inflatable keel to reduce leeway while wooden floorboards are usually available. The transom is of timber so it can take an outboard. Rather basic rowlocks are provided to go with stumpy oars. At the expensive end of the market buoyancy tubes are normally a hand-glued Hypalon/nylon material, but a bit lower down the price scale there are craft available with welded Dynalon tubes. Welding is cheaper than hand-glueing. The craft may be pump-inflated but CO_2 inflation bottles are also available with most types; they speed up the operation enormously.

A good quality inflatable is expensive and is not to be confused with the toy boats that are blown off beaches complete with their young occupants. The materials used are of far better quality; there are separate buoyancy chambers so that springing a leak does not mean the collapse of the whole craft; and the whole dinghy is much more robustly built.

The British Standards specification for inflatables, MA16, covers both materials and manufacture and insists, for example, that any ply used in the craft – such as for transoms and floorboards – should be to the marine ply specification BS1088.

Inflatables for use as tenders come in sizes ranging upwards from about 8ft (2.4m) to a maximum of roughly 12ft (3.6m). Much bigger types are also made for commercial applications. All this excludes rigid bottom inflatables which are dealt with in 12.3.4. Some inflatables can be had with sailing gear. They make a very safe sailing dinghy which is unlikely to capsize under normal wind pressure alone. In fact one of the inflatable's advantages is that it is very stable. It requires deliberate action by the crew, or exceptional action by wind and waves, to turn one over. And, of course, the tubes that bound the edges ensure a soft landing against the parent yacht's sides when getting aboard.

Though an inflatable is not a liferaft some are offered with a canopy that can be lashed in place to give the occupants a measure of protection against the elements. For a craft set on a lengthy cruise where the expense of a liferaft would be the straw that broke the proverbial camel's back, a canopied inflatable complete with sailing gear might be worth considering.

All reputable inflatable manufacturers can supply a repair outfit with their craft and the instructions should be followed, but in an emergency a bicycle puncture repair kit will do a temporary job. The glue supplied with the manufacturer's outfits has a useable life of only about a year, so after that it should be replaced. Bostik No.3 is suitable and this is available from many ironmongers or yacht chandlers. If a big tear has occurred it is best to sew the edges together using a herringbone stitch and a thin fishing line as the thread before applying the patch.

Before an inflatable is stored for any length of time it should be washed down in fresh water. If it can be stored partially inflated so much the better, but if it has to be put back in its valise fold it carefully and in the same manner as it was originally packed.

12.3.4 Rigid bottom inflatables

The normal inflatable with its soft floor cannot make a very satisfactory motor boat because the bottom is all the wrong shape and changes what shape it has with every wave that passes under it. Thus the rigid bottom inflatable was developed, where the buoyancy tubes are mounted on a GRP hull that stops at cockpit sole level. This

level is above the waterline so that it can be made self-draining, and with the very buoyant tubes round the deck edge the result is a safe boat and one that can be driven as fast as any other high speed motor boat. On a parent vessel big enough to sling such a craft in davits, the rigid bottom inflatable is excellent for towing water skiers. It is widely used by the RNLI, the Royal Navy and many commerical companies as a patrol and rescue boat.

The fact that the bottom is rigid means that this type of craft loses the advantage the normal inflatable has of being capable of being folded into a small package where it can be stowed on even quite small yachts. Hence it is not a substitute for the inflatable nor, really, for the normal rigid dinghy. However, types are available that will sail and row quite reasonably.

12.4 Self-steering

12.4.1 Steering by sail

Anyone who has played around with model yachts will know that if the craft is reasonably well-balanced it can be made to steer quite an accurate course with the rudder free, downwind, upwind or reaching, simply by freeing or hardening the main and jib sheets. The mainsail tries to drive the boat's bows into the wind while the jib has the opposite effect, and these opposing forces have to be balanced. This is normally achieved by sheeting in the jib harder than would otherwise be desirable and freeing the main. What can be achieved on a model can usually be achieved on a full-size yacht, and this is one form of self-steering. Joshua Slocum must have done just this during his single-handed circumnavigation. Certainly he did not have any sophisticated vane gear (after all, he set out in 1895) but was still able to leave the helm untouched for days on end. Though a modern fin and skeg form would not respond to this basic treatment as well as did his traditional, long keel vessel, even so, experimenting with different main and headsail areas and sheeting ought to bring reasonable results.

12.4.2 Linking the rudder and sails

Using sails alone, their drive must be adjusted to the demands of self-steering rather than to maximum efficiency, and so a reasonable development is to link the main sheet to the tiller in an attempt to allow the sails to develop their full power. Fig. 12(12) shows one such scheme. Here the sheet leads through a block on the weather side of the boat and then back to the tiller. Under way the main tries to turn the yacht's head into the wind but is resisted by the rudder being pulled in the opposite direction. The harder the wind blows, the greater the pull on the sheet and thus on the rudder via the tiller.

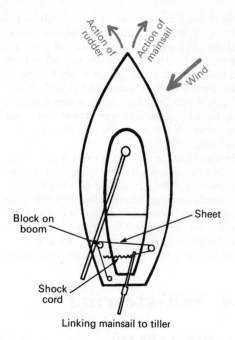

Fig. 12(12) The most basic form of positive self-steering is to link the main boom sheet to the tiller via a quarter block.

The point at which the sheet joins the tiller is adjustable so that the leverage can be altered, and there is normally a length of shock cord made fast on the opposite side, as shown, whose tension can also be adjusted and whose main function is to speed the return of the tiller to its correct angle. In practice two sheets are used with blocks on both quarters so that the system can be used on either tack. It works well enough on most small yachts when beating or close reaching and as the whole arrangement is finally adjusted with the headsails pulling hard there is

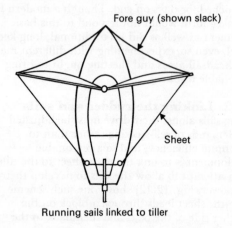

Fig. 12(13) Running sails may be linked to the tiller for downwind self-steering.

little loss in efficiency, but it does not act so satisfactorily on a run or with a quartering wind. Hence single or short-handed sailors may link their running sails (usually twin staysails or twin spinnakers) to the tiller as shown in Fig. 12(13). The way it works is clear. If the yacht veers off course the pressure on one of the sails is increased and on the other, reduced. These pressures are transmitted back via lines and quarter blocks to the tiller, which then automatically heads the boat back on to a course where the pressure in both sails is the same. Such running sails can be reefed through Wykeham-Martin furling gear (still available) which rolls them up on their stays. There are many variations on this basic theme.

12.4.3 Self-steering by vane and apparent wind

The French yachtsman and artist, Marin-Marie, who crossed the Atlantic under sail single-handed in 1933, made the return, west-east, run in 1936

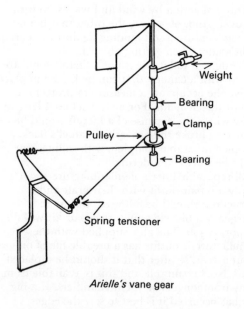

Arielle's vane gear

Fig. 12(14) The French painter and author, Marin-Marie, built what must have been the first practical wind vane steering and installed it on his motor boat *Arielle* for his 1936 west-east single-handed Atlantic crossing. It was entirely successful.

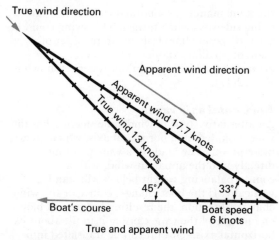

True wind direction

Apparent wind direction

Apparent wind 17.7 knots

True wind 13 knots

45° 33°

Boat's course

Boat speed
6 knots

True and apparent wind

Fig. 12(15) The difference between true and apparent wind with a yacht working to windward. The apparent wind is from further ahead and stronger than the true wind on this heading.

but this time in a motor boat, the 42ft (13m) *Arielle*. He was again single-handed. On board he had a hastily-installed and experimental auto-pilot plus vane steering of his own devising. This must have been the first vane steering ever used on a yacht, and even the auto-pilot was a considerable novelty though the system was even then in use on aircraft and big ships. Anyway, during an average 24 hours he used the vane for about 15 hours; the auto-pilot for four or five hours; and the rest of the time he took the wheel himself. The pilot was switched on when there was no wind, and Marin-Marie steered generally when there was not much wind but a big sea was running. In those conditions the mechanism of the auto-pilot tended to be overworked.

The wind vane is illustrated in Fig. 12(14) and its action is uncomplicated. First the vane, which was V-shaped, of ply and about 4ft(1.2m) high, was unclamped from the spindle and allowed to rotate until it faced the apparent wind. This is the wind felt on board and is neither the same strength nor (generally) from the same direction as the actual or true wind. If a boat was sailing directly downwind at, say, 6 knots in a 13-knot breeze, the apparent wind on deck would be 13 − 6 = 7 knots and would still appear to be coming from directly astern. However, if the boat was going to windward at 6 knots in a 13-knot breeze which was blowing at 45° to the boat's course, the apparent wind would be 17.7 knots at 33° to the yacht's heading. Fig. 12(15) shows this in diagrammatic form. When the vane on the *Arielle* was steady it was clamped on to the spindle. If the boat got off course the wind acted on the vane from one side or the other, and would turn the vane (and thus the tiller) until it once again faced the wind and equalled the pressure on both sides of the V. This wind vane acted on an auxiliary rudder hung on the transom, and while it was in operation the wheel steering was locked to keep the main rudder fore

and aft. There have been many systems since similar to Marin-Marie's.

12.4.4 Other wind vanes
These days vertical axis vanes are usually more complicated than their originator's and more directly linked to the rudder they steer. Perhaps the most common types has the vane set on a vertical, or nearly vertical, axis operating a trim tab which may be mounted on the main, transom-hung rudder or hung separately but still directly linked to the rudder. The trim tab system is illustrated in basic form in Fig. 12(16). What happens is the vane turns the trim tab. The rush of water past the tab causes the rudder to turn in the opposite direction and to steer the boat back on course.

Pendulum type
Another type of vertically-mounted vane steering is the pendulum gear developed by 'Blondie'

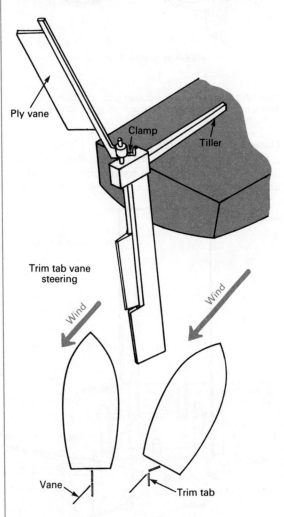

Ply vane

Clamp

Tiller

Trim tab vane steering

Wind

Wind

Vane

Trim tab

Fig. 12(16) A vertical wind vane operating a trim tab on the main rudder. Its action is fairly obvious but a commercial model would have a more refined method of setting the wind vane on the spindle than a clamp. In all probability it would be operable from the cockpit.

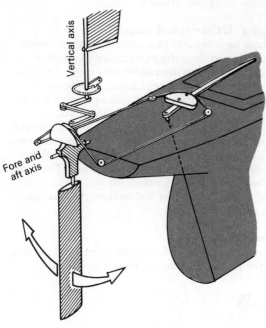

Hasler pendulum gear

Fig. 12(17) The Hasler Pendulum gear translates the swing of a rudder about a fore and aft axis into pull on tiller lines.

Hasler. It works on the principle that if an auxiliary rudder blade could pivot sideways on a fore and aft axis (like an athwartships pendulum) and could also be turned into the water stream in the same manner as a normal rudder, it would swing sideways when turned. This swing could be used to operate lines fastened to the tiller of a main or auxiliary rudder. The general arrangement of this pendulum system is shown in Fig. 12(17).

Horizontal axis vanes
An alternative type of wind vane steering has the vane mounted on a horizontal axis, which gives more power. The blade of a vane pointing directly into the apparent wind, with a counterbalancing weight below, will stand vertically. If the boat changes course or the wind changes direction, the resulting breeze will blow on one side of the vane causing it to tilt about its horizontal axis. This tilt can be translated into movement on tiller lines linked to the main or auxiliary rudder. Fig. 12(18) shows the scheme in sketch form.

12.4.5 Vanes in general
The better balanced and easier to steer a boat is, the more chance a vane has of working well. To that end it is usually worth experimenting with shifting ballast, altering the rake of the mast and even, perhaps, trying different proportions of sail area ahead and astern of the mast to improve balance if the yacht is hard on the helm and good vane steering is a major requirement. Shifting ballast aft, for instance, will move the CLR aft by putting the stern deeper in the water and should reduce weather helm. Raking the mast aft, on the other hand, will shift the CE astern and may increase weather helm. A larger headsail and smaller main (adding up to the same working sail area) will move the CE forward and reduce weather helm.

A wind vane can only produce a very limited amount of power unless it is so large that it is cumbersome and a nuisance on board. Hence a balanced rudder (that is, one with some blade area forward of the stock) which takes less power

Horizontal axis vane

Sheave

Sheave

Weight

Clamp

Sheave

Fig. 12(18) With a vane mounted on a horizontal axis, lines round a drum convert the tilt of the vane when it no longer faces directly into the wind into a pull of tiller lines. As with the vertical axis type, some form of remote control would be arranged to allow the vane to be set from the cockpit.

to turn than an unbalanced rudder will be a good thing and bearings should be examined to make sure they are as friction-free as possible. The power required from the vane can be reduced if it is connected to an auxiliary rudder (if the yacht's rudder is forward, at the aft end of the keel), or to a trim tab if the rudder is transom-hung.

Many people have made their own vane systems with complete success. The criteria must always be to produce a robust structure with low friction, though the vertical axis vanes seem to be able to cope with friction better than the horizontal axis types. The vane gear must incorporate some method of disengagement that can be operated very quickly so that a helmsman can take over. And however good the design, it will probably not be too effective in really light winds; nor in big seas where the vane may be blanketed from time to time; nor where a big slop left over from a dying wind knocks the boat about to the extent that the breeze on the vane cannot control her. A vane will not usually work as well downwind as upwind (remember that the apparent wind is less than the true wind when running but is greater when going to windward) but on long voyages the system is a great boon. It is not, however, a substitute for a man on deck keeping watch. It simply allows him to do that more efficiently since he does not have to bother about steering. The Amateur Yacht Research Society publish an excellent book on the whole subject, called *Self Steering*.

12.5 Wheel steering gear

12.5.1 Wire and cable

The simplest and (generally) the cheapest form of steering gear is that where flexible wire cables are led back from the wheel via sheaves along the hull side to a quadrant on the rudder stock. The quadrant may be replaced by a tiller with a sliding collar attachment for the cables on an even cheaper system. The mechanical advantage can be varied by altering the size of the quadrant (or length of tiller) and the diameter of the wheel.

In its simplest form the wires may be attached to a drum on the wheel but a more usual arrangement is to fit a chain sprocket on the wheel. The wire cable is made fast to the ends of the chain and a typical layout is shown on Fig. 12(19). A system like this is positive and if all the sheaves are carefully aligned and lubricated it is sensitive to pressures on the rudder. This is important on sailing vessels where 'feel' at the wheel makes for more responsive handling. It is important that the tension in the cables can be adjusted – even though everything is normally set

Fig. 12(19) The basic chain and wire wheel steering system shown on a Simpson-Lawrence gear.

up quite slack. To this end there are rigging screws or other tensioners at the quadrant or, alternatively, a similar device somewhere along the cable. Rudder stops should be fitted to prevent shock loads to the rudder (as in a broach) being transmitted directly to the cables. Though the basic components in this system are comparatively inexpensive and there is very little to go wrong (and if it does it is easy to repair), the chain and cable gear may not be very much cheaper than more sophisticated systems if installed professionally. This is simply because siting, aligning and bolting down the sheaves is quite a time-consuming business. Auto-pilots and dual steering positions can be arranged in the layout.

Many fishing boats and similar commercial craft used chain throughout. This was because nearly all the gear was on deck at the deck/bulwark edge and chain would last much longer than the wire then available.

12.5.2 Conduit wire cable gear

Basically similar to the normal wire and chain steering is the type where the wires are led to the quadrant in a conduit. At the quadrant there is a

special box designed to take the end of the
conduit, and this box moves with the quadrant,
transmitting the cable movement through
sheaves. Auto pilots and twin steering positions
can be incorporated into the steering gear which
is very quick to install since the conduit can lead
along any convenient path and needs no sheaves
to guide it. A typical layout is shown in Fig.
12(20). Rudder stops are vital.

12.5.3 Single cable steering

In essence this type of steering moves the tiller
through a single push-pull cable very similar to
that used for the operation of gears and throttle
on modern marine engines. The cable is
contained in a conduit fastened at both ends, and
is generally actuated by a rack and pinion at the
wheel. The system is positive in operation and
simple to install. Maintenance requirements are
low and consist of checking on the free-running of
the cable and on lubrication of exposed moving
parts, but there is virtually no 'feel' with such an
arrangement and it is thus most suited to motor
boats where it is widely used on craft up to about
50ft (15m) in length.

12.5.4 Mechanical steering

Mechanical steering may be achieved through a
gearbox and simple rod to the tiller as in Fig.
12(21), this being a very effective and
comparatively low-cost system where the wheel is

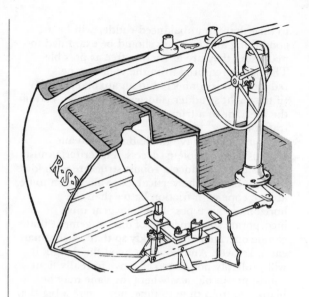

Fig. 12(21) The rotary motion of the wheel is converted
into a push-pull movement on a connecting rod in the
Whitlock Cobra gear.

sited close to the rudder stock. Where greater
distances are involved torque tube steering is
usually used. On this the rotary movement of the
wheel is converted to rotary movement in a series
of connected tubes, known as torque tubes. The
rotary motion is finally converted to a back and
forth movement on an arm linked to the tiller.
The torque tubes themselves require bearings to
support them if they are over about 8ft (2.4m)
long but can change direction between bearings
by the use of universal joints or, in more extreme
cases, through angled transfer boxes. Various
gear ratios are normally available in the bevel
boxes below the steering wheel and in the final,
aft end box, so that different mechanical
advantages can be obtained. In addition the
number of turns of the wheel to achieve a hard-
over helm can be selected.

Fig. 12(20) If the wire of a steering gear is enclosed in a conduit, installation will be simplified as accurately aligned
sheaves will no longer be required. This is the Whitlock Constellation arrangement.

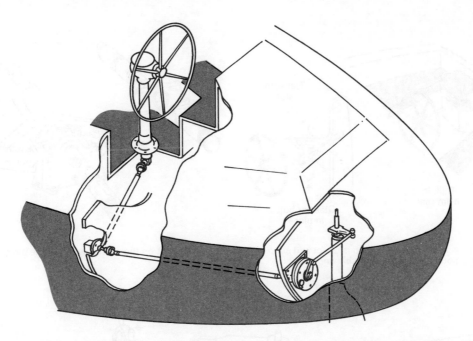

Fig. 12(22) A torque tube mechanical steering system. As shown the torque tube runs directly to the helm unit near the tiller. If this cannot be achieved the line of the torque tube can be changed by the use of universal joints or angled transfer boxes between bearings.

With a mechanical system, power assistance can be added as well as the gear for an auto pilot and, if necessary, dual station steering. It is a strong and reliable system, and in many cases the various gearboxes are sealed and lubricated for life. Some attention has to be paid to the universal joints, bearings and ball joints to keep them greased and clean but this is a straightforward process. Fig. 12(22) shows a layout and Fig. 12(23) two types of rudder stop.

12.5.5 **Rack and pinion and worm gears**
There are two other types of wheel steering gear in general use. The first is the rack and pinion type, where the pinion on the wheel drives the rack on a circular path pivoted about the line of

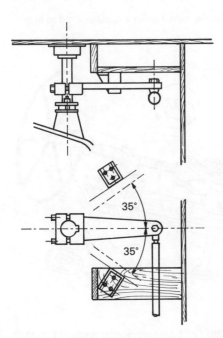

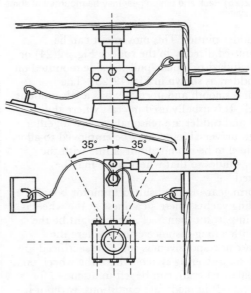

Use ¼″ wire. Do *not* use chain

Fig. 12(23) Rudder stops are essential on virtually all steering gears. Two possibilities are shown which prevent the gear from being damaged under the extreme circumstances of, for instance, a high-speed broach. Stops also prevent the rudder from assuming an extreme angle when going astern under power.

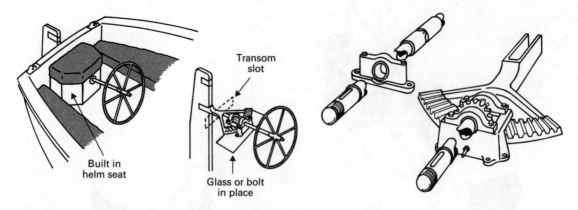

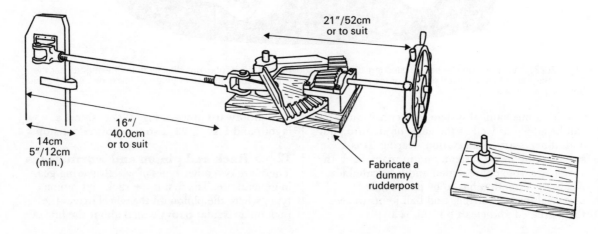

Fig. 12(24) Rack and pinion steering is direct and simple. With a universal joint on the shaft forward of the pinion, the wheel can be mounted at any reasonable angle.

Fig. 12(25) Rack and pinion gear may be mounted at some distance from the rudder using a push-pull rod as in this Edson system.

the rudder pintles. This movement can be transmitted directly to the rudder Fig. 12(24) or can be linked to a push-pull rod side mounted on the rudder, as shown in Fig. 12(25). The system is smooth and normally has a fair amount of 'feel'. It is usually used in craft where the wheel and rudder are reasonably close together, though universal joints may be employed to allow the wheel to be mounted out of line with the rudder pintles so that wheel angle may be adjusted.

Worm gears are best suited to motor boats or to sailing yachts where steadiness at the wheel is more important than 'feel'. Such might be the case with a long-distance cruiser where the ultimate in responsiveness could be sacrificed in return for a steering system where the wheel, on a well-balanced craft, can be left unattended for short periods in moderate conditions, without it being turned by the heaving of the boat. The gear tends to be heavy and very robust and usually requires more turns of the wheel from hard-over to hard-over than do other types. Fig. 12(26) shows a typical installation.

Fig. 12(26) The Edson worm gear is robust but offers little 'feel' at the wheel. It is thus most suited to motor boats and to sailing yachts where 'feel' is less important than the ability to hold course for an appreciable time without much attention at the wheel.

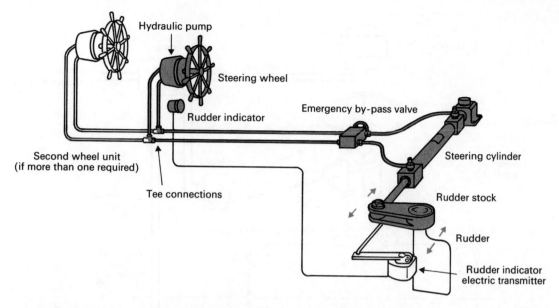

Fig. 12(27) Wills-Ridley hydraulic gear. The emergency by-pass valve allows hand steering on an emergency tiller to override the hydraulics. This can be important in the event of a malfunction.

12.5.6 **Hydraulic steering**

There are various types of hydraulic steering available which have different features, but basically they all consist of a hydraulic pump near and directly actuated by the wheel, leading via hydraulic hoses to a ram near the rudder stock. Fig. 12(27) shows the basic layout.

Powered versions can be had for bigger craft and such things as auto-pilots and dual station steering can easily be incorporated in the layout. Hydraulic steering is quick to install since the hoses can follow any reasonable path and need no lining-up. Maintenance requirements are low. For power craft this type of steering has the advantage that a locking valve prevents kick-back from the rudder, allowing it to be held in one position for considerable periods with little attention since it cannot drive the wheel. This feature is not wanted on sailing craft where some feed back from pressure on the rudder is desirable.

An emergency by-pass valve should be incorporated so that in the event of malfunction tiller steering can be used.

12.5.7 **Emergency steering**

However good and sound the basic wheel steering system, there should always be some way of hand steering by tiller. This is best done by extending the rudder stock up to just short of the deck or cockpit sole level. A hole is cut in the deck or sole sufficiently large for an emergency tiller to be shipped over the end of the stock. When the tiller is not required the hole is covered by a reasonably watertight plate held down with thumb screws or wing nuts. It is important that the helmsman using the emergency tiller has a reasonable view, and is not confined to an aft cabin or has to steer with his head in a locker.

12.5.8 **Auto-pilots**

There are two basic types of auto-pilot. One is known as a course follower and the other as a compass follower. With the former the boat is steered manually on to the desired course and the pilot then engaged. It will maintain that course until disengaged and a new course steered and set. With a compass follower, though, the desired course is set on the auto-pilot which will then keep to that course until it is changed, which can be done at any time. On some types it can be changed by remote control, which is useful in bad weather when someone is keeping a watch from on deck.

An auto-pilot is best selected and installed by an expert who can assess individual requirements. In action a properly adjusted model can steer a better course than the normal helmsman, and keep doing it for hours or days on end – provided the power supply can be sustained. However useful this facility is it does not reduce the need to have a man on deck, who can keep a better lookout if he does not have to steer. He should also make an occasional check on the pilot to confirm that it is doing its job properly. Fig. 12(28) shows the basic layout of an auto-pilot. In principle it functions as follows: the desired heading is set on the course selector (if it is of that type) or the boat is steered to the required course and the auto-pilot engaged. The true heading is sensed by the course or error sensor (which usually has its own compass). The difference between the steered course and the set course – the course error – is calculated. Should the course error become greater than some pre-set value the drive of the auto-pilot operates the rudder sufficiently to bring the boat back on course. The drive motor may be a fractional horsepower electric type with an electro-magnetic

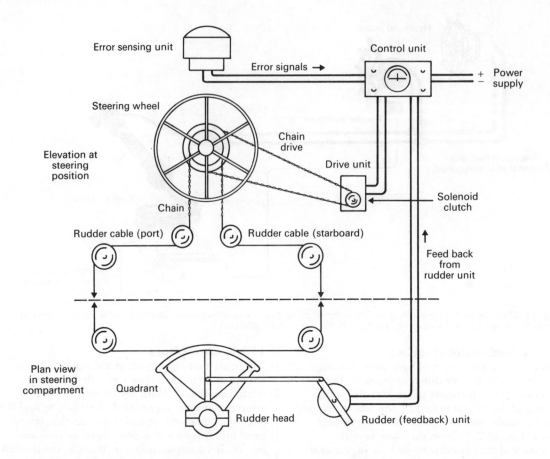

Fig. 12(28) The layout of a typical auto-pilot system. On some types various of the functions may be incorporated in one unit and items such as the rudder feedback unit may be dispensed with; the information it supplies being gained from other sources.

clutch or an electrically driven hydraulic pump type which can be coupled directly into the system of a boat with hydraulic steering.

On some models there is a rudder feedback unit which monitors the rudder angle and passes the information back to the control unit, but in other models this information comes from the output of the control unit itself or from the drive of the steering motor.

On modern auto-pilots there are various refinements and additions. Thus, for instance, the amount of deadband (the angle through which the craft is allowed to veer off course before the rudder starts to correct) can be selected to take into account sea state and the general qualities of the boat.

The rudder control can act rather like a human helmsman in that it can react to course error and correct accordingly before it builds up sufficiently to require major rudder movement, while the rate at which the rudder is applied can be selected and automatically controlled. Overswing may be automatically counteracted by applying counter rudder during course changing. The auto-pilot in some cases can be overridden in an emergency after which it will bring the craft back on to the original course. Navigational

systems (such as Loran) can be incorporated with the pilot so that the vessel will be steered from one position to another automatically rather than simply steering a selected course. Off-course alarms may be fitted as well as display units showing the rudder angle at any time (and so a judgement may be made on how hard it is having to work). The actual course, not just the selected one, may be shown as a further guide. Corrections for trim, weather helm and helm bias can be set to allow for the fact that most craft under sail or power have a tendency to pull to one side or the other. Some makes of auto-pilot also incorporate wind vane steering.

Pilots for tiller steering work on the same principles as those for wheel steering, but are modified so that the mechanism is linked to the tiller.

The maintenance requirements on an auto-pilot are low, being mainly concerned with keeping all working parts of the steering gear free and eliminating backlash as far as possible. A radio transmitter close to the auto-pilot can cause uncontrolled course changing, and it should go without saying that any magnetic object close to the boat's compass or auto-pilot's sensing unit can lead to major trouble.

Chapter 13

Engines and Electrics

Contents

13.1 Marine engines – construction

This chapter emphasises what a yachtsman can do to look after the engine of his boat, and to ensure that it gives long and reliable service. But to achieve this it is first necessary to have some understanding of how the engine works, and some knowledge of the various systems associated with it.

13.1.1 Petrol engines

Many readers will be familiar with the principle of the petrol engine. Air and petrol, mixed together in the carburettor in the correct proportions for efficient combustion (about 15 parts, by weight, of air to one of petrol), are drawn into the combustion chamber above each piston of the engine in turn. The upstroke of a piston compresses the mixture, which is ignited by a spark-plug when that piston is nearing the top of its stroke. The burning mixture expands and forces the piston down. The reciprocating movement of the pistons is transformed into rotation by connecting rods between the pistons and the crankshaft. Off the crankshaft is driven a camshaft, which runs at half the speed of the crankshaft, and controls the opening and closing of the inlet and exhaust valves for each cylinder.

Most petrol engines work on the 4-stroke cycle. On the downward (induction) stroke the inlet valve is open, allowing the air/petrol mixture to be drawn into the cylinder from the carburettor. During the (upward) compression stroke both valves are closed, so that compression heats and vaporises the mixture in the combustion chamber. After the mixture has been ignited by the spark-plug both valves remain closed for the (downward) power stroke. When the piston is near the bottom of the power stroke, the exhaust valve opens so that on the (upward) exhaust stroke the burnt gases are expelled. The cycle is then repeated. With the 4-stroke cycle each cylinder produces power every fourth stroke, or every two revolutions of the crankshaft. Hence with a four-cylinder engine there are two power strokes per revolution, a typical firing order being 1,2,4,3.

The great majority of outboard engines (see 13.4) and a few other marine units work on the 2-stroke cycle, where the various operations described above are arranged to occur within one complete revolution of the crankshaft. The sequence of events is described in 13.4.2.

For a given power, a 2-stroke engine is compact and light in weight; but it consumes more fuel than a 4-stroke, mainly because the scavenging of the exhaust gases is inefficient, a proportion of the incoming charge being lost with the exhaust.

The power output from an engine depends on the weight of air/fuel mixture that can be drawn into each cylinder, and how much it can be compressed. A typical compression ratio when using ordinary petrol is 9:1. Too high a compression ratio results in uneven burning of the fuel (detonation), which is inefficient and can result in damage. An additional weight of air/fuel mixture can be pushed into the cylinder by a supercharger, either driven off the engine or from a turbine operated by exhaust gases.

13.1.2 Diesel engines

Outwardly a diesel engine looks very similar to a petrol one, but there are essential differences in its operation. Nearly all diesel engines work on the 4-stroke cycle, but on the induction stroke only air is drawn into the cylinder, see Fig. 13(1). On the compression stroke this air is heated to a temperature which will ignite a very fine spray of diesel fuel, injected into the combustion chamber just before the piston reaches the top of the stroke. The fuel then burns and performs useful work on the power stroke, after which the exhaust gases are expelled on the next upstroke. In order to achieve the necessary temperature for ignition of the fuel, very high compression ratios are needed in diesel engines – roughly double those for petrol engines: this means that their construction must be more robust, and consequently they are heavier for a given power output.

Instead of the carburettor, ignition system and spark-plugs of the petrol engine, a diesel unit has a fuel injection pump which supplies very accurately metered quantities of fuel at very high pressure and at precisely the right time to fuel injectors which are situated at the top of each cylinder – see 13.2.3.

13.1.3 Choice of engine

The choice of a petrol or diesel engine depends on the application. In general terms petrol engines are cheaper and lighter for a given power, and are more easily maintained; but they involve a greater risk of fire, and the electrical ignition system does not react kindly to salt water. Diesels are safer, potentially more reliable, and cheaper to run; but they are more expensive, heavier, noisier and smellier, and maintenance of fuel injection equipment needs proper workshop facilities.

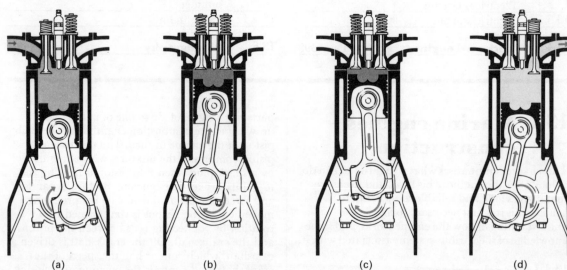

(a) (b) (c) (d)

Fig. 13(1) Diesel engine, 4-stroke cycle. (a) On the inlet stroke air is drawn into the cylinder, through the inlet valve. (b) On the compression stroke both valves are shut, and the air is compressed and heated. Near the top of the compression stroke, fuel is sprayed into the combustion chamber by the injector. (c) The fuel ignites in the hot air: the burning gases, expanding, force the piston down on the power stroke. (d) Near the bottom of the power stroke, the exhaust valve opens, and on the exhaust stroke the burnt gases are evacuated.

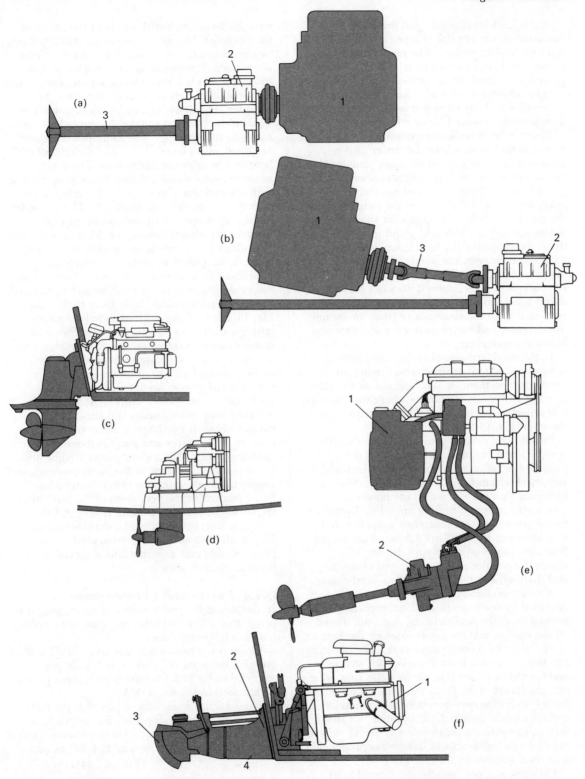

Fig. 13(2) Types of engine installation found in yachts.
(a) Conventional gearbox and shaft layout. 1 — engine, 2 — gearbox, with drop centre transmission, 3 — propeller shafting.
(b) V-drive installation. 1 — engine, 2 — separately mounted V-drive gearbox, 3 — articulated shaft connecting engine and gearbox.
(c) Outdrive power unit. Engine and transmission are installed as a single unit.
(d) Sail drive unit, with (non-steerable) folding propeller.
(e) Hydrostatic drive. 1 — hydraulic pump coupled to the engine, 2 — hydraulic motor connected to the pump by flexible pipes, and driving propeller shaft.
(f) Water jet propulsion. 1 — engine, 2 — pump, 3 — jet, 4 — water intake.

If it is used intelligently and properly maintained, the fire risk of a petrol engine should not be over-emphasised. The merits listed above make petrol engines very suitable for auxiliary propulsion, certainly for smaller yachts, while weight considerations make their choice essential for smaller high-speed motor boats. Larger craft are normally powered by diesel engines.

Most yachts have a conventional inboard engine installation, where the power unit is mounted in the bottom of the boat (usually about two-thirds of the way aft) and is connected to a gearbox which provides ahead/neutral/astern operation – Fig. 13(2) (a). To the output side of the gearbox is bolted the propeller shaft which passes through a watertight gland in the hull to drive the propeller. Such an installation has several advantages: the weight of the engine is low, and roughly amidships, and if situated under the cockpit or wheelhouse it does not occupy useful space within the hull; the engine is well protected from the elements, or from unwanted interference; and the propeller is well immersed below the waterline.

If, for considerations of weight distribution, it is necessary to mount the engine further aft, it can be turned through 180° and the drive taken forward to a V-drive gearbox where the direction is reversed to a conventional propeller shaft, as shown in Fig. 13(2) (b).

Instead of a normal gearbox, hydraulic drive may be fitted between the engine and the propeller, which allows the engine to be fitted anywhere within the hull. The engine drives a hydraulic pump, from which the power is transmitted through flexible pipes to a hydraulic motor connected to a shortened propeller shaft, as is shown in Fig. 13(2) (e). Apart from giving flexibility in the layout, hydraulic drive eliminates problems with alignment of engine and shafting, but there is some loss in efficiency.

Another version of inboard installation is provided by water jet propulsion, replacing the normal propeller and shafting. A pump, driven off the engine, takes in water through the bottom of the boat and forces it out astern. The resulting reaction drives the boat. Provision for steering and for astern power is made by deflectors, which aim the thrust of the jet in the required direction. Such installations are normally only found in specialist craft, designed, for example, for shoal waters, or for rescue work or water skiing, where the lack of a vulnerable or dangerous propeller is a distinct advantage, see Fig. 13(2) (f).

Outdrive engines (sometimes referred to as sterndrives) consist of a power unit mounted on the forward side of a boat's transom, through which a short horizontal shaft transmits the drive to an external lifting leg similar to that of an outboard, with bevel gears at top and bottom Fig. 13(2) (c). The gears incorporate ahead/neutral/astern operation, and whatever reduction ratio is required. In order to steer the boat, the leg

swivels like an outboard, to direct the thrust of the propeller. Outdrives are commonly fitted in smaller transom hulled boats, and have several attractions. The engine is mounted inside the boat, where it is protected and secure. Installation is simple, and there is no shaft alignment to consider. The drive leg can be raised out of the water if the boat has to take the ground, or for access to the propeller, and more powerful units are fitted with power tilt, so that the trim of the boat can be adjusted under way. There are, however, some disadvantages. Some power is lost with the two sets of gearing, each changing the direction of the drive through 90°. The propeller is not very deeply immersed, which can be dangerous with a following sea. Handling is more difficult at lower speeds, since when the propeller is not driving there is no directional effect.

Sailboat drives are a more recent innovation, rather similar in concept to an outdrive, but with the engine mounted in the bottom of the boat – Fig. 13(2) (d). Originally intended for smaller sailing yachts, they are also suitable for small motor cruisers. Like an outdrive, they are easy to install, and can be located where most convenient on the fore and aft line of the boat.

Outboard motors are familiar to many yachtsmen as the power units for tenders, whether solid or inflatable. But they are also extensively used for the propulsion of small cruisers, both power and sail. Outboards are self-contained units with a good power/weight ratio, easily portable (at least in the lower powers), and simple to install or to move from boat to boat. Being secured to the very stern of the boat, the engine does not occupy useful space, and the complete unit can be tilted in shallow water. Nearly all outboards are 2-strokes, which are heavy on fuel and also consume a special lubricant mixed with it.

13.1.4 Power and performance

In discussing the performance of an engine, or in comparing different makes or types, the word power is frequently used.

Power is the rate of doing work. The SI unit of power is the watt (W), which is 1 joule per second, but for practical use with engines power is expressed in kilowatts (kW).

The basic imperial unit of power is the foot-poundal per second (ft pdl/s). But in practical engineering the technical term horsepower (hp) is used, and equals 550ft lb/s, or 17 695ft pdl/s.

1hp = 0.7457kW   1kW = 1.3410hp

The technical unit of metric horsepower is a cheval-vapeur (CV) in France, a Pferdestarke (PS) in Germany, and a hastkraft (HK) in Scandinavia, and it equals 75kgf m/s, or 0.7355kW.

1hp (Imp) = 1.014hp (metric)
1hp PS, CV or HK = 0.986hp (Imp)

The actual power developed is measured with

the engine on a test bed, using a brake or dynamometer. In practice the torque produced is measured, and the brake horsepower is calculated from the formula:

$$bhp = \frac{Torque \ (lbf \ ft) \ \times \ rpm}{5252}$$

If all the various ancillary equipment such as alternator, water pump, gearbox and exhaust system are fitted to the engine, an indication is given of what power will be transmitted to the propeller in service, and this is termed the shaft horsepower (shp). But engine tests are usually conducted without all the above impedimenta, and the resulting figures for brake horsepower (bhp) as taken at the engine flywheel can be 15–20 per cent greater than shp.

The power an engine develops may be quoted, for example, as 'continuous' or 'intermittent'. The former is the power that the engine will develop hour after hour. The intermittent rating is a higher output that can be used for a short period, usually one hour in 12, without mechanical damage or overheating.

Technical information about an engine should include power curves – intermittent and continuous outputs plotted against rpm. The torque curve may also be plotted on the same graph, and also a typical propeller law curve, showing the power the propeller absorbs at different rpm. Where the propeller law curve meets the power curve represents the conditions

at which the engine will develop maximum continuous power. At lower rpm the engine is only under partial load, the vertical distance between the power curve and the propeller curve showing the reserve of power available at that speed.

Factors that are of interest when comparing two engines of similar power include (apart from the price!) the power/weight ratios, piston speeds, and specific fuel consumptions. Engine weight can be important in a high performance boat, but one way of getting extra power from an engine is to run it faster, and piston speed is a useful measure of the likely life of an engine.

$$Piston \ speed \ (ft/min) = \frac{Stroke \ (ins) \ \times \ rpm}{6}$$

Long lasting marine diesels usually have piston speeds of about 1500ft/min. Faster running diesels (almost certainly with better power/weight ratios) have figures of 2000–2500ft/min. Petrol engines may have figures of 3000ft/min or higher.

Specific fuel consumption, the quantity of fuel used per horsepower per hour, is obviously a measure of an engine's economy – or otherwise. There are striking differences between types of engine, with medium-speed diesels returning figures that are nearly twice as good as some 2-stroke outboards. Sadly the internal combustion engine is not a remarkably efficient machine, and only about one-third of the available energy in the fuel is transferred into useful thrust from the propeller of a boat.

13.1.5 Basic engine construction

All 4-stroke engines, whether petrol or diesel, have similar structural and internal parts. The internal details of 2-stroke engines differ somewhat – see 13.4.2.

The main structural items are the cylinder block and the cylinder head, shown in Fig. 13(4). The former contains the bores of the cylinders, usually arranged in line, together with passages for cooling water and oilways for the lubrication system. The block also normally incorporates the crankcase, housing the crankshaft which rotates in the main bearings, and to the cranks of which the connecting rods deliver the thrust of the pistons.

The piston has to transmit the force of the burning and expanding gases in the cylinder to the connecting rod, form a good seal within the cylinder, take away the heat to which its crown is subjected, be strong enough to carry the bearing for the small (upper) end of the connecting rod, and be able to suffer continual reversals of movement – about 80 or 90 times a second. Pistons are therefore made of a light alloy which combines strength at high temperatures with a low coefficient of expansion, to permit small clearances to be used. Typically two compression (or gas) rings are fitted, and below them an oil

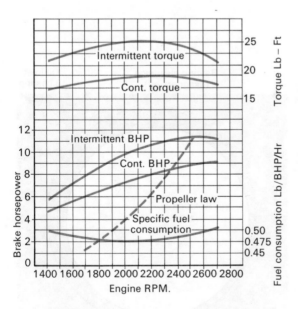

Fig. 13(3) Curves of torque, power and specific fuel consumption, plotted against engine rpm, for a small twin-cylinder diesel. Also shown (dotted) is a propeller law curve — for a propeller which is matched to the engine at 2500rpm, when it will absorb the full 11bhp that the engine can deliver. At lower (cruising) speeds (say 2000rpm, where the specific fuel consumption is least) the propeller can only absorb about half the power that the engine could theoretically deliver.

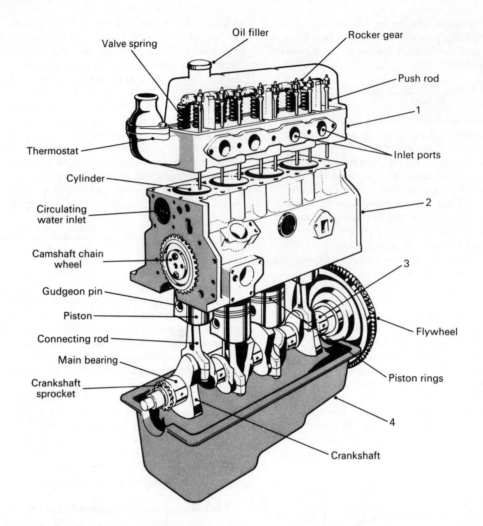

Valve spring
Oil filler
Rocker gear
Push rod
1
Thermostat
Inlet ports
Cylinder
2
Circulating water inlet
Camshaft chain wheel
3
Gudgeon pin
Piston
Flywheel
Connecting rod
Main bearing
Piston rings
Crankshaft sprocket
4
Crankshaft

Fig. 13(4) The main components of an internal combustion engine. 1 — cylinder head, with inlet and exhaust valves and the rocker gear to operate them, inlet and exhaust ports, and combustion chambers. 2 — cylinder block, with bores for the pistons, cooling passages for water, and oilways for the lubrication system. 3 — crankshaft assembly, with pistons linked to the crankshaft by connecting rods, and engine flywheel. 4 — sump, enclosing the bottom of the engine, and forming a reservoir for lubricating oil.

control (or scraper) ring which removes excess oil from the cylinder walls. Some pistons are oil-cooled, to prevent the piston rings sticking, or gumming up.

The bottom of the connecting rod (usually a steel forging) is split, and is bolted round the crankpin of the crankshaft. This bearing is known as the crank head bearing or big end bearing, and it is lubricated through holes drilled in the crankshaft, pressure fed from the main bearings.

The function of a bearing is to reduce friction where one part rotates within another. Main and big end bearings have steel shells lined with a suitable bearing metal – an alloy such as copper-lead or tin-aluminium. White metal may be used for lightly loaded bearings. Apart from the correct design and precise manufacture of

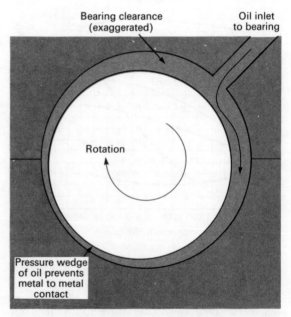

Bearing clearance (exaggerated)
Oil inlet to bearing
Rotation
Pressure wedge of oil prevents metal to metal contact

Fig. 13(5) As the journal (shaft) rotates inside the bearing, oil is carried round with it, and builds up into a wedge at the point of maximum loading, preventing metal to metal contact.

bearings (and the journals, or shafts, which rotate within them), it is essential that they are given adequate quantities of clean, cool oil. This enters the bearing under pressure at a point of low bearing load – where there is maximum clearance between the journal and the bearing. As the journal (shaft) rotates inside the bearing it builds up a wedge of oil which is thinnest along the line of maximum bearing load, but which builds up sufficient internal pressure to prevent metal to metal contact. The oil also removes heat from the bearing.

Oil from the main bearings passes through holes drilled in the crankshaft to feed the big end bearings of the connecting rods, which may also be drilled to supply oil for the gudgeon pins (which hold the top end of the connecting rods in the pistons) and for piston cooling. Often however the gudgeon pins are lubricated, like the cylinder walls, by the oil escaping from the bearings of the rotating crankshaft, surplus oil being removed by the oil scraper rings on the pistons. Details of the general lubrication system of an engine are discussed in 13.2.6.

Above the cylinder block, and bolted to it with a joint called a gasket in between (to prevent the escape of cylinder gases or cooling water) is the cylinder head. This contains on the underside the combustion chambers of the cylinders, at the sides the inlet and exhaust ports which connect with the inlet and exhaust manifolds respectively, and on top the valve operating mechanism (rocker gear) for the inlet and exhaust valves of each cylinder. Through the cylinder head run cooling water passages, particularly round the combustion chambers and the exhaust ports where very high temperatures are reached.

The valves are held on their seats by valve springs, and are opened at the correct moment by rocker arms: these may be operated directly by a camshaft running along the top of the cylinder head (overhead camshaft engines), or via push rods from a camshaft along the side of the cylinders, as in Fig. 13(6). In either case there is a cam for each inlet valve and for each exhaust valve, and the camshaft is driven at half engine speed by chain, belt or gears. At the correct moment in the engine timing cycle, the cam for

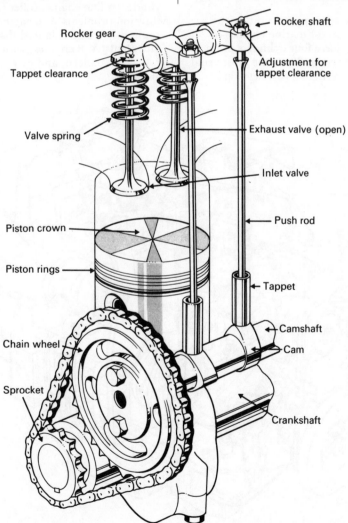

Fig. 13(6) Valve gear for push-rod engine. For a 4-stroke engine the camshaft rotates at half engine speed.

an individual valve depresses the valve stem, opening the valve against the pressure of the spring. Further movement of the cam releases the pressure on the valve stem at the right moment, and the spring closes the valve. A gap is provided between the top of the valve stem and the rocker arm to allow for expansion, and this tappet clearance must be kept correctly adjusted according to the maintenance instructions for the particular engine.

13.1.6 Engine configurations
The simplest 4-stroke engine consists of a single cylinder, mounted vertically over a crankshaft with a single throw (crank), and there are a few low-powered boat engines of this type which are available for small boats. They are fitted with a relatively heavy flywheel to help improve the uneven torque which results from one power stroke for every two revolutions, but the out-of-balance revolving and reciprocating forces within the engine inevitably cause vibration. Even the addition of a second cylinder greatly improves the balance of the moving parts, and reduces vibration.

Although there are a few power units with three cylinders in line, most marine engines of between 30 and 80hp have four cylinders in line. Above 80hp, six cylinders in line is the most usual arrangement, and such engines can develop powers of 200hp or more, with the emphasis on turbo-charged diesels at the top end of the range.

A four-cylinder in-line engine, with two power strokes for each revolution, gives smoother running and better mechanical balance than one, two or three cylinders. A six-cylinder in-line engine is even better in these respects, and also allows more main bearings for better support of the crankshaft. Fig. 13(7) shows a cut-away drawing of a six-cylinder Perkins diesel engine.

There are however other possible layouts, and one which is found in boat engines is with the pistons horizontally opposed. This arrangement gives a shorter crankshaft for the same number of cylinders, and also better balance of the moving parts than with an in-line engine, since the movement of a piston in one direction is offset by the movement of its opposite number in the other direction.

Engines with the cylinders arranged in V formation are not common afloat, except in powerful V-6 and V-8 petrol engines, as are fitted to larger outdrive units. V-4 engines, although compact and with torque as even as a four-cylinder in-line engine, suffer from inherent vibration problems. V-6 engines (with a V of 60°) are slightly worse balanced than their in-line equivalents. V-8 engines (with a V of 90°) are very well balanced, and extremely smooth running.

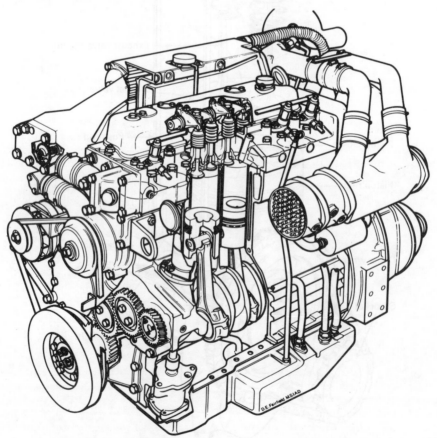

Fig. 13(7) Cut-away drawing of Perkins T6.3544 marine diesel engine.

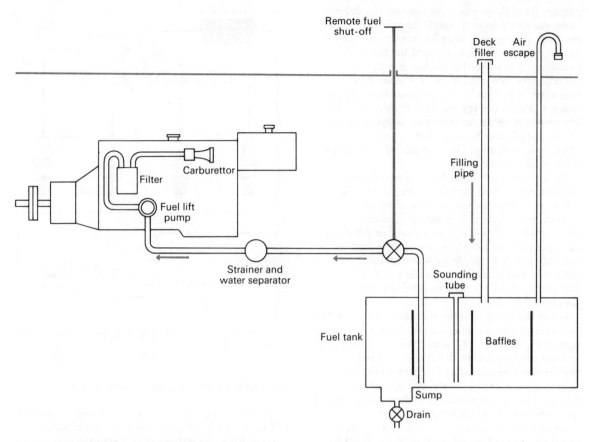

Fig. 13(8) Fuel system — petrol engine.

13.2 Marine engine systems

13.2.1 Fuel system (petrol engine)

To save space and to keep weight low, fuel tanks are usually sited in the bottom of the boat, and need to be firmly secured. Petrol tanks should be made of galvanised steel, lead-coated steel, brass, or copper (tinned on the inside).

The filling position should be on deck, so that any overflow does not get inside the boat, Fig. 13(8). With a car the vapour from a petrol leak is easily dispersed, but with a boat any leak in the fuel system can cause a dangerous concentration of petrol vapour in the bilges. Filling positions for fuel and fresh water must be clearly tallied, so that no confusion can result. If a flexible hose is used for the filling pipe, the deck connection and the tank must be electrically bonded, in order to avoid the possibility of any build up of static electricity causing an explosion.

The tank needs an air escape, leading to a position on deck which is sheltered and fitted with a gauze, or spark arrestor. Unless it is very small, the tank should have internal baffles. There must be a fuel gauge or dipstick. Ideally there should be a sump at the bottom of the tank, with a drain cock to remove any sediment or water, but with tanks in bilges this is obviously difficult to arrange. There must be a shut-off cock where the fuel pipe leaves the tank, and this must be operable from a remote position – on deck or in the cockpit.

Fuel pipes should be made of seamless copper, copper-nickel or stainless steel tube with the minimum of joins, and properly clipped at regular intervals. The final length before the engine should be of an approved type of flexible tubing. Somewhere, in a convenient place for examination and cleaning, there must be an efficient fuel filter. In most marine petrol engines the pump which draws petrol from the tank to the carburettor is driven off the engine, and often fitted with a hand priming lever.

A petrol engine relies on the carburettor to provide the correct mixture of air and petrol for efficient combustion, and in the right quantity for the power to be developed. All carburettors work on the principle that air which is being drawn into the cylinder by the induction (down) stroke of the piston passes through a venturi, or choke tube, where the speed of the airstream increases and its pressure drops. The low air pressure sucks petrol from the float chamber, where it is maintained at a certain level by a float controlled needle valve working on the same principle as a lavatory cistern. A throttle valve controls the quantity of air flowing through the venturi to the engine. At high speeds, with the throttle valve open, more air flows through the venturi, resulting in a greater drop in pressure and hence more petrol being sucked out of the float chamber. When the throttle valve is partly closed, to reduce engine speed, less air flows – so that there is not such a big pressure drop in the venturi, and hence less petrol is drawn into the airstream. A choke, or strangler, is fitted so that the air supply can be restricted to give a richer mixture for starting. There should also be an air filter, with a flame trap.

Because air and petrol have different flow characteristics, and because an engine needs different mixture strengths depending on operating conditions (e.g. starting, idling, cruising and full power), a carburettor needs to incorporate various refinements in the form of variable jets or multiple jets for maximum efficiency and economy to be obtained. Naturally, these jets need to be clean and properly adjusted.

Good design of the inlet manifold (between the carburettor and the inlet valves) is necessary to ensure vaporisation of the air/petrol mixture and its even distribution to the cylinders. High performance engines may be fitted with more than one carburettor, in which case correct tuning is needed to ensure that they deliver equal quantities of fuel at all throttle settings.

In any petrol engine it is important to use the specified grade of petrol, technically defined by the octane number but more commonly identified in Britain by the star rating. Two-star petrol corresponds to a minimum octane number of 90; three-star to 94, four-star to 97 and five-star to 100 octane. In a 4-stroke engine there is no objection to using a higher-grade (more expensive) petrol than is specified, but neither is there any advantage in doing so. Use of a lower grade than specified, or overheating of the engine, will cause uncontrolled burning of the fuel in the combustion chamber. This is called detonation, and is accompanied by a noticeable knocking sound: it will soon cause damage to pistons if allowed to continue.

Petrol tanks should be kept as full as possible to reduce the amount of moisture from the atmosphere condensing on internal surfaces and entering the fuel, but at the same time petrol does not improve if stored for long periods.

13.2.2 Ignition system (petrol engine)

A petrol engine is dependent on the spark from very high voltage at the spark-plug to ignite the air/fuel mixture in the combustion chamber of each cylinder in turn, at precisely the right moment. The spark may be provided by a magneto or a high-tension coil. The latter is more common, and gives a better spark at (low) starting speeds, but the former has the advantage that an engine can be started by hand even with a flat battery.

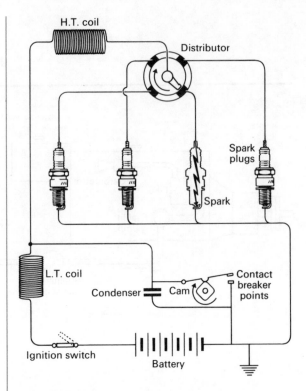

Fig. 13(9) Coil ignition system — petrol engine.

In the conventional coil ignition system, as shown in Fig. 13(9), a primary coil is energised with current from the battery, and generates a magnetic field in the iron core. The secondary winding consists of very many more turns of wire, and is connected via the distributor to the spark-plugs. When the primary circuit is broken by the contact breaker, the magnetic field around the secondary coil collapses, and this generates a very high voltage in the secondary coil which creates the spark across the gap of the appropriate spark-plug. The ignition switch, in the primary circuit, supplies current from the battery to the primary coil when it is turned on; when it is turned off the supply ceases and the engine stops. The contact breaker and the distributor are combined into one unit, gear driven off the engine. The 'gap' of the contact breaker is opened by a number of cams, depending on the number of cylinders, and it is important that this gap (or maximum opening) is kept to the right dimension (usually about 0.015in) to avoid alteration of ignition timing. To give a quick break in the primary circuit and to prevent sparking across the contact breaker, a condenser is fitted across the contacts. The distributor consists of a rotating arm, which engages in turn with segments which are connected to the plug leads for each of the cylinders.

On many engines the distributor incorporates an automatic timing device, which optimises the timing of the ignition depending on the engine speed. This may be a centrifugal advance, which depends on the speed of the engine, or a vacuum advance operated from the inlet manifold to the carburettor.

A magneto works on much the same principle as coil ignition, except that it generates its own primary current internally so that no battery is needed for ignition purposes. This is obviously an advantage for small petrol engines which can be started by hand, and so this system is particularly applied to outboards, where the magneto is housed in the flywheel on top of the engine.

An increasing number of petrol engines, particularly outboards, are now fitted with capacitor discharge (CD) ignition systems, which eliminate contact breakers, distributors and other moving parts and give greater reliability. Each spark-plug has a separate coil; rotating magnets in the flywheel generate a voltage stored in the capacitor; at the correct moment a sensor magnet in the flywheel triggers the discharge of this voltage to the appropriate coil, where it is stepped up to give a very high voltage at the spark-plug. The higher voltages achieved by CD ignition give better spark, and allow the use of surface-gap spark-plugs where the spark can jump radially from a central electrode in any direction; this reduces plug fouling and routine maintenance.

Spark-plugs are vital components of the ignition system, but can be maintained by any competent boat owner who knows how they function. A plug consists of a metal body, with a hexagon portion whereby it is screwed into the cylinder head, with a copper sealing ring between. Inside the body is a ceramic insulator, down the centre of which passes the central electrode, connected at the top to the plug lead from the distributor or magneto. Since the body of the plug is earthed in the cylinder head, a high voltage spark will pass across the gap between the bottom of the electrode and the plug body.

Different engines require different types of plugs, and it is most important to use the specified type. A boat should carry a complete spare set. Apart from physical dimensions which alter the reach of the plug into the combustion chamber, the length of the insulator inside the plug can vary so that heat from the plug is dissipated into the cylinder head at a controlled rate – keeping it hot enough to burn off deposits which would prevent a spark, but cool enough to avoid pre-ignition (of the air/fuel mixture before the spark occurs).

The gap between the central electrode and the plug body must be kept clean, and the right dimension – usually about 0.030in. When adjusting the gap never try to move the central electrode. For further notes on spark-plug maintenance see 13.5.13.

13.2.3 Fuel system (diesel engine)

So far as tanks and filling arrangements are concerned, diesel engines need similar

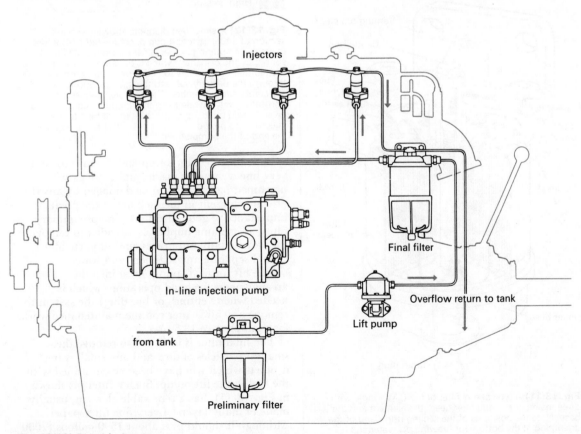

Fig. 13(10) Diesel fuel system.

arrangements to petrol engines (see 13.2.1) but, due to the chemical composition of diesel fuel, tanks must not be copper or galvanised steel. Plain steel or lead-coated steel are the preferred materials, but glassfibre tanks built into the boat are satisfactory if proper provision is made for access for cleaning purposes: such tanks should not be adjacent to fresh water tanks.

For diesel fuel mild steel piping is acceptable, apart from the materials already suggested for petrol engines. There is also the possibility of using nylon tubing (but only of an approved, flameproof specification) which facilitates tracing any air which may get into the system (see 13.5.6).

In other respects the fuel system of a diesel engine is totally different from that of a petrol engine, and deserves detailed explanation. A typical diesel fuel system is illustrated in Fig. 13(10). Fuel is sucked from the tank by a lift pump mounted on the engine, via a preliminary filter which should include means of separating any sediment or water in the fuel. The lift pump then passes the fuel through a very fine, final filter to the fuel injection pump, which delivers it at extremely high pressure to the injectors (or atomisers) mounted near the top of each cylinder. Fuel which is surplus to the requirements of the engine is returned to the tank through a separate pipe.

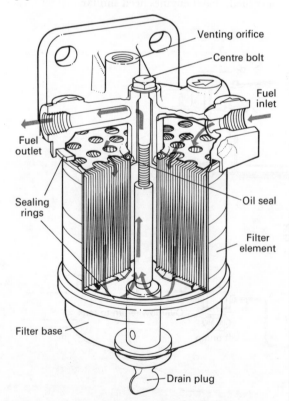

Fig. 13(11) A typical fuel filter of the CAV range, with three main parts — the filter head, the element and the base. Note the positions of the sealing rings, and of the drain plug at the bottom for drawing off water and sediment.

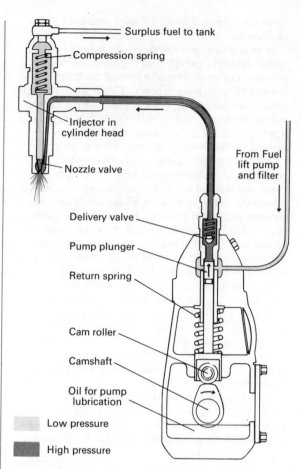

Fig. 13(12) A simplified diagram, showing a cross-section of a fuel injection pump, connected to one fuel injector. The pump plunger is cam operated, against a spring, by the camshaft which is driven off the engine. As the plunger rises, fuel is forced at very high pressure through the delivery valve to the injector, and thence to the combustion chamber. The delivery valve acts as a non-return valve while the pump plunger is descending, gives a rapid build-up of pressure in the pipe to the injector, and provides a quick cut-off of fuel injection at the end of the pump stroke.

Both the injection pump and the injectors have very fine clearances inside, and these closely machined parts can soon be damaged by any dirt or water present in the fuel: hence the great importance of good filtration. The preliminary filter, as its name implies, is intended to remove the worst of any impurities, and in particular it should separate any sediment and water.

The lift (or feed) pump must include arrangements for hand operation, which is needed when venting (or bleeding) the system to remove any air – after routine maintenance work, for example (see 13.5.6).

The final filter is intended to remove the smallest particles of dirt, and any small water droplets which will have become emulsified with the fuel in the lift pump. Such a filter, as shown in Fig. 13(11), has a renewable element, usually made of many layers of very fine filter paper. Although it should pass about 1500 gallons (7000 litres) of fuel before choking, it is a sensible precaution to change the filter in a boat engine at the start of every season. The procedure is explained in 13.5.5. If the filter bowl is fitted with a drain plug, this should be removed every month or so, to draw off any water or sediment that may have collected.

The fuel injection pump is the most important unit in a diesel fuel system: it has to deliver very small, accurately metered quantities of fuel, at extremely high pressure, to each cylinder in turn, and at exactly the correct moment. Fig. 13(12) is a simplified cross-section of an in-line fuel pump connected to one injector. Each cylinder has its individual pumping element, consisting of a plunger in a barrel. A camshaft driven off the engine operates the plungers of each pumping element, which are mounted in a line. The length of stroke of each plunger is constant, but the working part of the stroke, during which pressure is applied, can be varied by rotating the plunger so that a helical groove cut in it uncovers a spill port, and releases the pressure in the barrel – see Fig. 13(13). The rotation of the plungers, and hence the amount of fuel delivered to the injectors, is done by the throttle control and the engine governor, via a rack which is incorporated within the fuel pump.

Some engines are fitted with a distributor type of pump, which operates on a different principle. It has only one pumping element, from which fuel is fed through a distributor to each injector in turn.

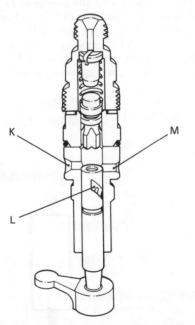

Fig. 13(13) Diesel fuel injection pump — details of one pumping element. K — inlet port; M — spill port; L — helical spill groove in plunger. The plunger is shown at the bottom of its stroke. When it rises, and covers the inlet port, pumping starts. Pumping continues until the upper edge of the spill groove uncovers the spill port, allowing high pressure oil above the plunger to pass down the central hole in the plunger and out through the spill port. The effective stroke of the plunger is determined by rotating the plunger in the barrel.

Maintenance or repair of fuel injection pumps must not be attempted except by authorised service agents, who have the necessary equipment and data. But the yachtsman owner can play his part by keeping the pump clean and free from leaks. With in-line pumps the lubricating oil for the internal camshaft should be drained off and replenished at intervals of 100 running hours. Above all, make sure that the injection pump is always supplied with good, clean fuel – free of any water and impurities.

The fuel injectors (or atomisers) provide the fuel to each cylinder in a form most suitable for good combustion – in a very fine spray. Injector nozzles come in different types, specially designed for individual engines, and it is essential to use the right one. An injector is a spring-loaded valve, operated by the pressure of fuel from the injection pump. When the pressure rises suddenly to a peak, the nozzle opens, and when the fuel pressure suddenly drops it closes.

Injectors need professional servicing. The maintenance period varies, from as little as 100 running hours in some high powered engines to nearly 1000 hours in lower rated engines. It is however within the capacity of the average owner to replace a defective injector with a spare one. Loss of power, overheating, black smoke from the exhaust, difficult starting, cylinder knock and increased fuel consumption are all possible signs of injector faults.

A defective injector can be identified by running the engine at a fast idling speed, and slacking back on the union of the pressure pipe to each injector in turn. Little or no change in engine revolutions indicates a faulty injector. Disconnect both ends of the pressure pipe (do not bend it), and remove the defective injector by slacking back the two securing nuts each side. Store the faulty injector carefully until it can be sent away for reconditioning.

It is important to fit the replacement injector properly in the cylinder head: it must be seated squarely, with the clamp or securing nuts tightened evenly, and with the correct washer or insert in place. Do not overtighten the fuel pipe unions.

13.2.4 Air supply

For every pound of fuel supplied to it an engine needs about 15 pounds of air in order to achieve proper combustion. There should be an air filter to remove harmful impurities, and this will require servicing at the intervals given in the engine handbook. Some air is also required to help keep the space round the engine reasonably cool, and a forced draught fan may be used for this purpose. Petrol engined boats should have an exhaust fan, sucking from the bottom of the engine compartment; this fan should be run for five minutes before the engine is started, to remove any dangerous petrol vapour which might be present.

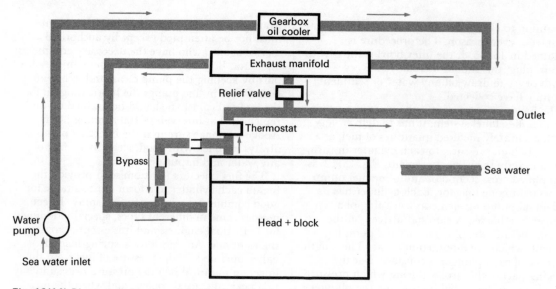

Fig. 13(14) Direct cooling system — Perkins 4.108(M) Lowline diesel.

13.2.5 **Cooling system**

Any engine must have some form of cooling system to remove surplus heat, which represents about one-third of the total energy available from the fuel. The cooling system of a marine engine is quite different from that of an automotive unit of similar power. Instead of an air cooled radiator, boat engines mostly use the water in which the boat is floating as the cooling medium, although a small number of low-powered boat engines are air cooled.

A typical, simple cooling system is shown in Fig. 13 (14). Raw (e.g. sea or river) water is sucked in through a seacock and a strainer by a pump, driven off the engine. The water passes through an oil cooler (for the engine lubricating oil) and then round the cylinder block and exhaust manifold before it is discharged overboard. Engine temperature is controlled by a thermostat, as in a car.

Direct (raw water) cooling does however have some disadvantages. First, corrosive seawater is circulating round inside the engine. Second, unless the engine is run at an unduly low temperature (which is inefficient), salt deposits can and will build up on internal surfaces. So a better arrangement is for the engine to be cooled by fresh water, pumped round it in a closed circuit, and the fresh water then to be cooled by sea (raw) water. An illustration of a fresh water (or indirect) cooled engine is shown in Fig. 13(15). It should be noted that raw water is used for the

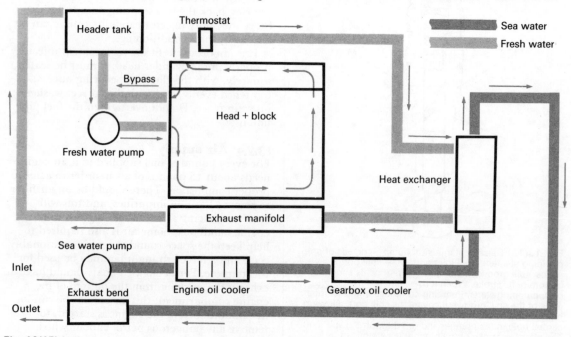

Fig. 13(15) Indirect cooling system — Perkins 4.108(M) Lowline diesel.

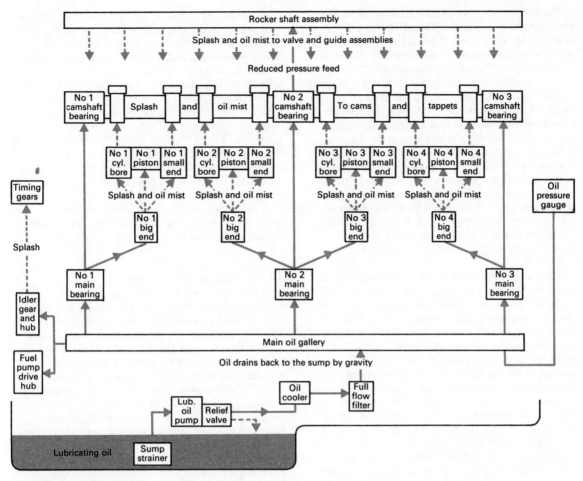

Fig. 13(16) Lubrication system diagram — Perkins four-cylinder diesel engine.

gearbox oil cooler and engine oil cooler before it is pumped through the heat exchanger, and then overboard via the exhaust pipe.

A variation of fresh water cooling is keel cooling. Here the engine coolant (fresh water) is passed through external pipes which run along the bottom of the boat and are thus cooled by the surrounding water.

Maintenance of the cooling system involves making sure that inlet strainers are kept clean, that there are no leaks in the system (hoses and hose clips being kept in good order), and that in fresh water (indirect) cooled engines the fresh water header tank is kept topped up, just like a car's radiator. Pump impellers are liable to wear if operated in sandy or muddy water, or if run dry. A spare should always be carried. Thermostats can also give trouble: in emergency the thermostat can be removed, if a spare is not available. Whenever the engine is started, check that cooling water is flowing correctly, and while the engine is running keep a watch on the temperature gauge.

13.2.6 Lubricating system

Mention of bearings and their lubrication has been made in 13.1.5. The lubricating systems of all 4-stroke engines, whether petrol or diesel, are basically similar. Most 2-stroke petrol engines have a different method of lubrication, described in 13.4.3.

Fig. 13(16) shows a typical system for a 4-stroke engine. The sump forms a reservoir for the oil, which is pumped through a cooler and a filter to the various working parts. A relief valve controls the pressure, indicated by a gauge or warning light. The oil drains back to the sump under gravity.

Modern oil filters have a renewable element made of impregnated paper which should be changed every season, and whenever the oil is changed. Filters can be either full flow, where all the oil passes through the filter as it circulates, or of the by-pass type where only a proportion of the oil goes through the filter each time.

From the filter the oil passes to the main oil gallery, running the length of the engine and feeding the main crankshaft bearings, and thence to other moving parts, as already described in 13.1.5.

In some marine units the gearbox is lubricated from the engine system, but a modern hydraulic gearbox has its own lubricating system complete with oil cooler.

Looking after engine lubrication presents few problems if some simple rules are followed. Always check the level of oil in the sump (and in the gearbox, where applicable) before starting the engine: with some engines and gearboxes a specific method of checking oil level may be given in the handbook. Only top up the system with clean oil of the recommended grade (see below). Cleanliness is essential, and oil must never be stored in opened cans which can easily become contaminated with dirt or moisture. While the engine is running keep a careful watch on the oil pressure, and investigate any low reading which could be due to a blocked filter, overheating, insufficient oil in the sump, the wrong grade of oil, or (more ominously) worn bearings. Finally, change the engine oil and renew oil filter elements as recommended in the engine handbook.

The correct type and grade of oil must be used, since modern oils are complex substances which include various oil-soluble chemicals to improve their performance and to increase their life. Viscosity is an indication of how an oil flows: a thin oil has a low (numerical) viscosity, and a thick oil has a high viscosity. Viscosity is measured by the time a certain quantity of oil flows through a standard orifice at the specified temperature (because viscosity drops with increase of temperature). The viscosity of an oil affects the oil film thickness, and the load which a bearing can carry; its correct choice is a compromise to give good starting from cold, rapid oil film formation on starting, satisfactory load carrying at high temperatures, and low oil consumption. Additives reduce the amount the viscosity drops with rise of temperature and also lower the temperature at which the oil remains fluid.

The Society of Automotive Engineers (SAE) system is used for classifying lubricating oils for engines and gearboxes, the lower the SAE number the thinner the oil. SAE 5W, SAE 10W, SAE 15W and SAE 20W are oils with viscosities falling within certain limits at 0°F (−18°C), the W signifying that they are suitable for winter use. Viscosity ranges of SAE 20, 30, 40 or 50 however indicate that the oil falls within certain limits at 210°F (99°C) which is a typical engine operating temperature. Multigrade oils are designated (for example) as SAE 20W-50, indicating that the oil has the viscosity of a 20W oil at 0°F, and of a SAE 50 oil at 210°F. Multigrade oils give easier starting in cold conditions but retain their lubricating properties at high temperatures.

Other additives are put into oils to improve detergency, oxidation resistance and dispersancy. Detergent qualities are needed to keep internal surfaces clean – particularly pistons and rings. Oxidation inhibitors reduce the chemical reaction between oil and air at high temperatures in the crankcase, and the tendency to form lacquer and gummy substances. Dispersant additives keep combustion products of the fuel and lubricant in suspension in the oil, so that they do not form harmful sludge which might otherwise block filters or oilways: instead such products are held in the oil, and drained away from the engine when the oil is changed. Darkening of the oil in service shows that it is doing its job. But the additives in an oil gradually get used up, and cannot continue to fulfil their important functions. Diesel engines are particularly dependent on lubricating oils which have the necessary additives included, and this applies especially to turbocharged engines which operate at higher temperatures.

A great deal can be learned about the mechanical condition of an engine from regular chemical analysis of samples of the lubricating oil.

13.2.7 Exhaust systems

Any internal combustion engine needs an efficient exhaust system to remove the hot, waste gases as freely as possible while at the same time keeping exhaust noise to the minimum. Carbon monoxide in exhaust gases is very poisonous, so that very great care is necessary where exhaust systems pass through living spaces or cabins.

Most boat engines have wet (water injected) exhausts, which do not need bulky or expensive jacketing. The (raw) cooling water from the engine is injected into the silencer, where it quietens and cools the exhaust gases. It is important that the layout ensures that water cannot get back into the engine through the exhaust system; where the engine is fitted on or below the waterline a swan neck should be fitted high enough for all possible sea conditions, angles of heel, or boat loading. In some installations which do no provide much of a gradient or fall in the exhaust pipe, it is sensible to fit a shut-off valve which can be closed when the engine is not in use.

Exhaust pipes may be iron or galvanised steel: copper or brass are acceptable for petrol engines, but not diesels. Suitable synthetic hose can be used for the wet part of the system, from the point where water is injected. A flexible length of pipe is needed between the engine and the silencer if the engine is flexibly mounted.

13.2.8 Gearbox

All but the very simplest type of boat engine needs a gearbox, or some equivalent means of controlling its operation, whereby ahead/neutral/astern can be selected. Usually the gearbox also incorporates reduction gearing, so that the propeller revolves at about half engine speed which gives more efficient propulsion. Some small sailing cruisers fitted with auxiliary engines have a sailing clutch, which automatically engages by centrifugal force when the engine speed is raised above idling. An alternative to the conventional marine gearbox is a controllable pitch propeller, which provides ahead/neutral/astern power by

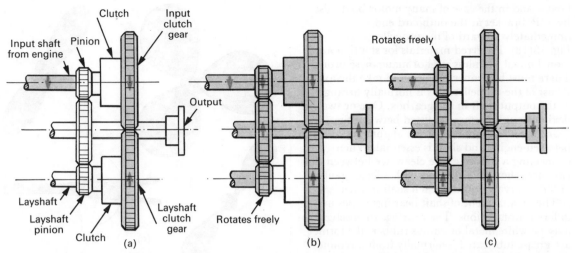

Fig. 13(17) How a layshaft gearbox works. The arrows up and down the page indicate the directions of rotation of the revolving parts, viewed from above. (a) Neutral — both clutches disengaged. Power from the input shaft only revolves the input clutch gear — nothing else revolves. (b) Ahead — input clutch gear engaged, so that power returns through that clutch and its pinion to drive the output shaft. (c) Astern — layshaft clutch gear engaged, so that power passes through the layshaft, to rotate the output shaft astern.

altering the angle of the propeller blades, with the engine rotating steadily in one direction.

There are two main types of marine gearbox – layshaft and epicyclic. Layshaft gearboxes have two sets of clutch plates, one being engaged for ahead and the other for astern. In neutral both are disengaged. The principle of operation is shown in Fig. 13(17). The clutches may be engaged mechanically in small gearboxes, but with larger units this is done hydraulically, the oil pressure also being used to lubricate the bearings and the gear teeth.

With epicyclic gearing, astern operation is obtained by a brake band which locks the gear assembly, making the intermediate (planetary) gears rotate in the opposite direction and drive the output shaft astern. Most such gearboxes are hydraulically operated.

It is most important that the correct lubricant is used in a gearbox, and this is usually different from the engine oil. Hydraulic gearboxes often use automatic transmission fluid. Oil level should normally be checked at the same time as the

engine oil level – before the engine is started. But with some gearboxes the correct level is taken after the engine has been stopped. Certain marine gearboxes cannot be trailed in neutral for any length of time without risk of damage from lack of lubrication. If applicable, this should be stated in the engine handbook. Hydraulic gearboxes have an oil cooler, which must be supplied with cooling water from the engine cooling system, and may be fitted with temperature and pressure gauges. In some cases the gearbox can be locked in 'ahead' operation, to permit the boat to get back to harbour in the event of any hydraulic failure.

Never shift the gearbox control from ahead to astern, or vice versa, with the engine turning at more than a fast idling speed, or damage may result.

13.2.9 **Propeller shafting**
The drive from the gearbox to the propeller is transmitted by the propeller shaft, which is supported by bearings in the stern tube of the

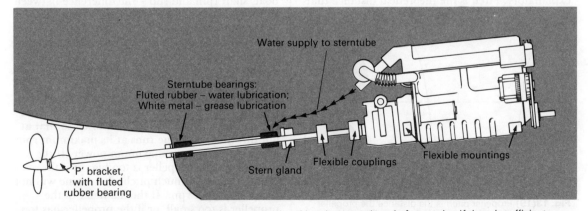

Fig. 13(18) Sterngear arrangement, with rigid stern gland and bearing at each end of sterntube. If there is sufficient length of shaft between the gearbox and the sterntube, a single flexible coupling may be fitted.

boat – and in the case of many motor boats also by a 'P' bracket at the outboard end, immediately forward of the propeller – see Fig. 13(18). Preferred materials for shafting are monel metal, stainless steel or manganese bronze. There must be proper provision to take the axial thrust of the propeller: this is normally arranged at the output shaft in the gearbox. One or two flexible couplings may be fitted between the gearbox and the shaft. Correct alignment between engine and shaft is essential. When connecting a coupling, the clearance between the two faces should be checked with a feeler gauge at 90° intervals, rotating each shaft in turn.

The arrangement of shaft bearings varies in different installations. The bearings themselves may be white metal or cutless rubber: the former are grease lubricated – normally from a remote greaser which should be replenished as required and given a turn before using the engine, and about every four hours while the engine is running. Cutless (fluted rubber) bearings rely on water lubrication, and if fitted at the forward end of the stern tube such a bearing will be supplied from the engine cooling water system.

The stern gland, at the forward end of the stern tube, prevents water getting into the boat, and may need tightening occasionally to prevent undue leakage. This should be done very carefully: a small drip of water is perfectly acceptable, and helps keep the gland cool.

13.2.10 Propeller

However efficient or powerful an engine may be, it is the thrust from the propeller which drives the boat through the water. It is most important that the correct propeller is fitted to match the characteristics of the hull concerned, and the power/rpm available from the engine and its gearbox.

The main factors which determine the shape of a propeller are its diameter, pitch, blade area, number of blades, and direction of rotation: other details such as the precise shape and sections of the blades need not concern us here. Diameter, blade area and number of blades are self-explanatory. Pitch is the theoretical distance that

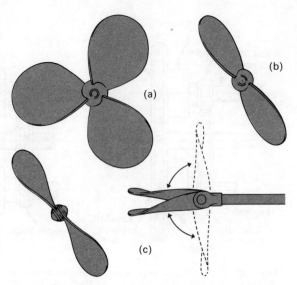

Fig. 13(20) Types of propeller. (a) High-speed. (b) Two-bladed propeller for auxiliary powered yacht. (c) Folding propeller.

the propeller would move ahead through the water in one complete revolution, if there was no slip – as, for example, when a screw is driven into wood – see Fig. 13(19). Direction of rotation is defined as right-hand for a propeller which, when driving ahead, turns clockwise when viewed from astern.

The function of the propeller is to convert the torque in the propeller shaft into thrust which will drive the boat. This is achieved by changing the momentum of the water which passes through the propeller, which is done more efficiently when the quantity of water is large and the change of velocity is relatively small. This implies that, for maximum efficiency, a propeller should be as large as possible – which obviously presents problems in trying to fit it into the available space under the stern of a boat.

So propeller design is a compromise. Diameter obviously governs the total blade area that can be achieved, and is related to the shaft horsepower and shaft rpm. The choice of pitch is governed by the designed (required) speed of the boat, shaft rpm and slip – the difference between the actual speed of the propeller through the water and what would be calculated from propeller pitch multiplied by rpm. Different types of propeller are illustrated in Fig. 13(20).

The correct choice of gearbox reduction ratio is important. As a rough rule, preliminary calculations of reduction ratio can be based on a propeller speed of 100rpm for each knot of boat speed. Diameter and pitch are chosen so that at full throttle the engine runs at its maximum rpm and is developing its maximum power. If the diameter of the propeller is too big, or if the propeller has too much pitch, the engine will not reach its proper rpm. If the diameter of the propeller is too small, or if the propeller has too little pitch, the engine will tend to overspeed

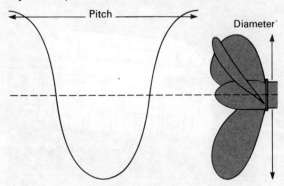

Fig. 13(19) Propeller pitch is the distance the propeller would move ahead in one revolution, if it did not slip in the water.

without producing the required power. In practice there is a certain amount of trial and error in selecting the correct design of propeller for a new boat.

Propellers are accurately machined and balanced. Any damage, such as may occur to the tip of a blade, will not only detract from performance but cause unbalance and consequent vibration and wear of bearings. Propellers are also liable to corrosion from galvanic action unless the proper precautions are taken (see 10.5.7), and also to erosion which can be aggravated by cavitation. Cavitation is not normally a problem in low-powered craft, but is common in more powerful motor boats. It occurs when the water flow breaks down, and cavities are formed on the forward sides of the blades where there are low pressure areas; when these cavities collapse the water impinges suddenly on the blade surface, causing pitting.

13.2.11 Controls and instruments
The controls for engine throttle and for the gearbox must be positioned where they can be easily reached from the steering position; for simplicity their movements should be in the correct sense – that is the gearbox lever should be pushed forward for ahead, and the opposite way for astern. Similarly it is helpful if the throttle is pushed forward to increase the rpm. If 'single-lever' control is fitted (operating both throttle and gearbox) it is important that both are correctly adjusted, so that the moment of engaging ahead or astern can be felt, and so that it is quite evident when neutral has been selected. Most engine controls are of the cable type, and need very little maintenance other than an occasional smear of grease over the end connections.

The minimum instrumentation for any boat engine should consist at least of oil pressure gauge, thermometer for circulating water, tachometer for rpm, ammeter, and a contents gauge for the fuel tank. More complex installations need a greater variety of instruments – for boost pressure and gearbox oil pressure, for example. Some form of instrument lighting is needed for use at night.

13.3 Electrics

13.3.1 Electrical systems – general
Most boat engines rely on electric starting (see 13.3.5), although smaller units can often be started by hand. With the proliferation of navigational aids, radiotelephones, auto-pilots, electric winches, water pumps, refrigerators etc. that are now available, electrical systems have become more and more complex, and the total requirement for electric current more and more demanding.

Luckily the modern alternator can generate a high current even when driven at modest rpm, as discussed in 13.3.3. Apart from an engine-driven alternator, other methods of power generation are also available. Batteries may be charged by a wind driven generator, a water driven generator, a shaft driven generator, or even by solar cells. Larger yachts have self-contained generator sets, usually diesel driven, which can be run independently of the main machinery.

In harbour increasing use is made of shore power to keep batteries topped up while the boat is idle, or to run essential services when lying alongside. For continuous operation it is important to use a proper marine charger, such as a Constavolt or Lucas Marinapower, which will convert AC shore power to DC for battery charging, while at the same time float any DC load on board. Such chargers will automatically shut down when batteries reach gassing level, at about 80% of full charge.

Whenever possible a yacht should have a separate battery which is reserved purely for engine starting, a second one being used for domestic and other services.

13.3.2 Batteries
Lead/acid batteries are most commonly fitted in boats, and systems in small yachts are usually 12 volt – although there are advantages in using 24 volts, as commonly fitted in larger craft. The capacity of a battery is measured in ampere-hours, and it is important that a battery with adequate capacity is fitted to allow for reduced performance with age, plus the probable addition of new electrical equipment to the boat. The charge to discharge ratio of most batteries is about 1.4, which means that for every 100 ampere-hours of discharge, 140 ampere-hours of charging are needed to restore full capacity.

The capacity of a battery is normally expressed in terms of a 10-hour rating, when for example a 150 ampere-hour battery will give 15 amperes for 10 hours. At higher rates of discharge the capacity is reduced quite considerably.

A battery should normally be charged at the 10-hour rate, but a higher rate of charge may be used if the battery is in good condition, provided that its temperature is kept below 110°F (43°C). The charging rate is automatically controlled in a properly fitted marine installation, allowing a higher rate of initial charge, then falling off as the battery voltage rises. It is possible to damage a battery if it is left connected to an ordinary car battery charger for too long.

Lead/acid batteries must be charged regularly to keep them in good condition and available for use, particularly in warm weather, and must not be left standing idle for more than a month or two. The state of charge of a lead/acid battery is determined from the specific gravity of the electrolyte, as measured by a hydrometer. Typical readings at 60°F (16°C) are: 1,280 – fully charged; 1.200 – half discharged; 1.115 – fully discharged.

The level of the electrolyte should be checked weekly, and distilled water added as necessary to keep the tops of the plates just covered. Some modern batteries are sealed, and do not need this attention.

Alkaline (nickel-cadmium) batteries are more expensive but have the advantage of retaining their charge for long periods, and therefore do not require special attention during winter lay-ups. They come in two basic types: one is high-performance, for heavy discharge currents and hence particularly suited for engine starting; the other is more for general service purposes. Discharge capacities of the former (high-performance) batteries are quoted at a 2-hour rate, while those of the latter (normal resistance cells, for general use) are given at a 5-hour rate. The specific gravity of the electrolyte in an alkaline battery does not vary with the state of charge, and is usually 1.200 at 68°F (20°C). This figure falls as the electrolyte deteriorates, indicating that it should be renewed.

Whatever type of battery is fitted, it must be securely mounted in a tray which will collect any possible spillage. The compartment must be well ventilated, to remove explosive gases generated during charging and discharging, and the battery must be readily accessible for maintenance. There must be a main isolating switch which will disconnect both poles of the battery when it is not in use. This switch must never be opened when the alternator is running, or damage will be caused to the rectifying diodes (see 13.3.3).

When two batteries are fitted, blocking diodes are used to allow both to be charged from one alternator, and to prevent mutual discharge between them.

13.3.3 Generating equipment

Alternators are fitted to the engines of most modern boats. The alternating current (AC) generated is converted into direct current (DC) for battery charging by silicon diodes which function like non-return valves – allowing a free flow of current in one direction, but giving a high resistance in the other. A regulator is fitted to control voltage, and also to control current if the alternator is not self-limiting in this respect. Great care is needed in handling and testing these items, since they contain semi-conductors which can be damaged by excess voltages or by reverse polarity.

On smaller or older engines, dynamos or dynastarts (combined dynamos and starters) may be found. Whatever type of generating equipment is used, it must have sufficient capacity to recharge the battery and to sustain the total electrical load, during its expected running time. Here an alternator is an advantage, because it can generate a high current even when driven at modest speed. The correct pulley ratio must however be selected for a particular application, care being taken that the alternator does not exceed its designed speed at full engine rpm.

Apart from ensuring that the drive belt is kept at the right tension, a modern alternator needs little maintenance. When depressed by moderate finger pressure in the middle of its longest run, the belt should only give about $\frac{1}{4}$in. It is advisable to carry a spare belt.

13.3.4 Electrical circuits

The electrical installation of a boat must be carefully designed to avoid long cable runs, and to site components such as switchgear in convenient places. Stranded copper cable, with an insulation of approved marine specification, must be used, and all items such as switches, fuses and junction boxes must be non-corroding and waterproof. Special arrangements may be necessary where electrical equipment is subject to high ambient temperatures.

Cables should be installed so that they are accessible for subsequent inspection and maintenance, high up in the boat and clipped at regular intervals. Insulated return (two wire) systems should always be used for boat electrics: any insulation failure on earth return circuits (as used in cars) can cause dangerous electrolytic action. Different circuits (such as navigation lights, radio, or general lighting) should be individually fused or fitted with their own circuit breakers.

In order to avoid unwanted interference on radio circuits, it is important that the whole electrical system is properly suppressed. The most likely causes of interference are engine-driven generators and their control systems, but other sources can be fluorescent lighting, electric motors (as in water pumps, bilge pumps or windscreen wipers), or ignition systems in petrol engines. Although local reduction of unwanted radio energy can be achieved by the proper use of capacitors and inductors, serious problems of radio interference need professional advice.

Of even more importance can be the corrosion of underwater fittings due to leakage currents from faulty insulation or badly installed electrical components. Even if the boat is fitted with cathodic protection (see 10.5.7) this can be overcome by leakage currents, which render former cathodic areas anodic and thereby cause serious damage. Apart from ensuring that electrical circuits are properly wired (particularly where extra equipment is added) and well maintained, make certain that the main battery switch is always broken when the boat is not in use, and that water is excluded from all sockets, switches, junction boxes etc.

For technical details of boat electrics reference is suggested to the booklet *Marine Electrical Systems* published by Lucas Marine.

13.3.5 **Electric starting**

Apart from those small engines which can be started by hand, the great majority of boat engines rely on electric starting. The function of the starter motor is to turn the engine at sufficient speed for ignition of the fuel to be achieved, and then be sustained so that the engine will continue to run.

Usually the pinion of the starter motor shaft engages with teeth on the engine flywheel through a Bendix drive, which connects the starter to the flywheel when the starter begins to rotate, and disengages it once the engine fires. A possible fault is for the pinion not to disengage properly from the flywheel, in which case the starter can be freed by applying a spanner to a square on the other end of the armature shaft, and turning it clockwise. This trouble is usually caused by dirt on the Bendix drive. First disconnect the battery leads to the starter, and then remove the starter motor. Carefully clean the drive (only) with WD40 or petrol, until it operates freely by hand.

A lot of current is needed from the battery to get the engine turning over quickly enough, particularly in cold weather if the engine oil is thick (see 13.2.6). If the engine fails to start, continual cranking will soon discharge the battery or damage the starter. Attempting to start an engine with a partly discharged battery, where the terminal voltage is low, only gives too low a cranking speed and the likelihood of putting too high a current through the starter motor. Hence the importance of reserving one battery for engine starting, and ensuring that it is kept well charged at all times.

To avoid an unacceptable voltage drop, the cables which carry the high current from the battery to the starter motor must be heavy, and they must be kept as short as possible. Consequently the switch in this circuit is remotely controlled by a solenoid, which is operated by a smaller switch at the helmsman's position. It is important that all cable connections, such as battery terminals, are kept clean so that they ensure a good electrical contact.

Diesel engines, with their high compression ratios, make a very heavy demand on their starter motors. Many diesel engines are fitted with starting aids for use in cold weather. Usually these consist of heater plugs, fitted in the cylinder head, which are actuated for a short period before using the starter motor. A decompressor may also be fitted, whereby a higher cranking speed can be achieved before the mechanism is released – so that normal compression is restored to enable the engine to start.

13.4 **Outboard engines**

13.4.1 **Outboard engines – general**

Outboards are the natural choice for propelling small tenders and dinghies, and for auxiliary propulsion in small sailing craft; they are also extensively used in small motor cruisers up to about 25ft (6m) in length. Very powerful outboards are available for high-speed powerboats.

Outboards are ideal for dinghies of all types. They are light and easily portable; they come as a complete installation, with no need for propeller shafting or steering gear; they do not take up useful space within the boat; and the engine and propeller can be tilted up in shallow water – as for example when coming to a beach.

But outboards also have some disadvantages. Most of them work on a petrol/oil mixture and are expensive on fuel; being outside the boat they are exposed to the elements and to theft; since steering is done by swivelling the entire engine, and thus altering the direction of the propeller thrust, there is no steering effect when the propeller is not rotating; installation is not easy on a boat which does not have a flat transom of suitable height; and spares tend to be rather expensive.

In choosing an outboard it is important to buy one of suitable power for the particular

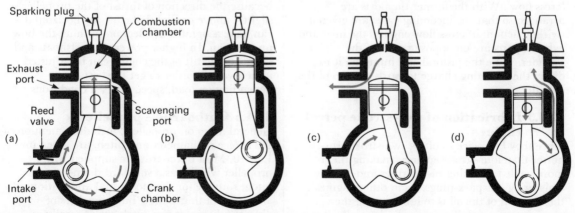

Fig. 13(21) Combustion cycle — two stroke engine. (a) Up stroke, drawing fresh charge into crankcase, and compressing charge already in cylinder. (b) Down (working) stroke. (c) Near end of down stroke the exhaust port is opened. (d) New charge being transferred from crankcase into cylinder.

application. If in doubt, get advice, because too small an engine will not give the required performance, while too large a one will incur penalties not only of cost but also of weight and portability.

Powers of outboard engines are rated according to tests that are specified by the American Boating Industry Association (BIA). These give the power at the crankshaft, and are a 'sprint' rating, so they tend to exaggerate the power available at the propeller.

13.4.2 Two-stroke outboards

Nearly all outboards have two-stroke engines, and run on a petrol/oil mixture (typically 30:1 or 50:1). Fig. 13(21) shows a two-stroke engine with a reed valve controlling the air/fuel mixture entering the crankcase from the carburettor. In (a) of Fig. 13(21) the piston is moving up the cylinder, drawing in behind it a fresh charge of air/fuel into the crankcase: above the piston the previous charge is being compressed, and will be ignited by the spark-plug when the piston nears the top of its stroke. In (b) the piston is on its working (power) stroke: the reed valve is shut, and the next charge in the crankcase is being compressed as the piston descends. In (c) the piston is more than half-way down its working stroke, and has started to open the exhaust port, through which the burnt gases are starting to flow: the transfer port is about to open, to allow the next charge of air/fuel mixture to be transferred from the crankcase to the cylinder. In (d) the piston is at the bottom of its stroke, the transfer of fuel is almost complete, and the cycle recommences.

Remembering that the engine may be running at 5000rpm, it will be appreciated that the expulsion of the exhaust gases and their replacement by a fresh charge of air/fuel mixture has to be achieved very quickly. Efficiency suffers if exhaust gases are not properly scavenged, or if part of the incoming charge is lost through the exhaust port. This problem is tackled in two ways – some engines are 'loop charged', and other are 'cross flow'. With the former the ports are arranged so that the incoming gases are given a swirling action: in cross flow engines the inlet and exhaust ports are on opposite sides of the cylinder, while the piston has a hump on it to direct the incoming charge towards the top of the cylinder.

13.4.3 Lubrication of two-stroke petrol engines

Since they fire twice as often, two-strokes run hotter than four-stroke engines, making them more liable to sticking piston rings and whiskering on spark-plugs. As in other engines, the function of the oil is to lubricate all the moving parts, including the cylinder walls. But instead of being pumped around, the oil is added to the fuel in a certain ratio as dictated by the maker. The amount of oil entering the engine therefore depends upon the throttle opening. Having done its job, the oil is burnt with the fuel, and it must not leave excessive deposits of carbon at exhaust ports or in the combustion chamber.

For these reasons it is most important that the correct oil is used, and that it is mixed in the proper proportions. Some manufacturers specify slightly more oil during the running-in period. Never use ordinary multi-grade engine oil in a two-stroke. Outboards even need slightly different oil from that used in two-strokes ashore, because they are water cooled and operate at somewhat lower temperatures. They also tend to run for longer periods at fixed throttle settings.

Two-stroke engines consume a great deal more lubricating oil than four-strokes, which is one reason that their operating costs are considerably higher.

13.4.4 Outboards – installations

The transoms of most boats intended for outboard propulsion have a height of 15–20in (380–500mm) above the bottom of the boat. A 20in transom needs a long shaft engine, and a 15in transom needs a short (standard length) shaft. The exact measurements differ from make to make, and some models are available with extra-long shafts for special applications.

When the engine is fitted to the boat the cavitation plate above the propeller should be about level with the boat's bottom, or slightly below it. Make sure that the circulating water inlet is well immersed. The tilt of the engine should be adjusted so that it is vertical when the boat is running. Small engines are secured by two clamps, which should be well tightened, and checked periodically. An anti-theft device of some kind is essential, and the engine should also have a strop which should be secured to some fixed point in order to prevent accidental loss overboard. Larger engines are bolted in place.

It may be found that the tilt of the engine needs to be altered slightly so that the trim of the boat is correct when she is under way; this is because the direction of thrust of the propeller – slightly above or slightly below the horizontal – can have a significant effect on pushing the bow up or down. In higher powered sportsboats and ski-boats the tilt of the engine can be adjusted under way, in order to get the best trim depending on load, speed and sea conditions.

13.4.5 Outboards – propellers

General notes on propellers, including mention of the choice of diameter and pitch, are given in 13.2.10. Most outboards are supplied with a propeller which has a standard diameter and pitch, suitable for the most usual applications of an engine of that power. But propellers of different diameter and pitch are generally available, if required for special purposes. This can be very useful, because it is such a simple matter to swap the propeller of an outboard. For example, it is quite feasible to operate one engine on two boats with quite different hull characteristics – having widely varying speeds and weights. In such cases it may well prove that different propellers for the two jobs will greatly increase performance or economy.

13.5 Maintenance

13.5.1 Maintenance – inboard engines

If an engine is supplied with clean fuel and lubricating oil, air for combustion, and plentiful quantities of cooling water (or air in the case of air cooled engines), very little should ever go wrong. There are other details which require periodical attention, as should be stated in the engine handbook, but if all these matters are attended to methodically (preferably with the aid of some kind of check list), any yachtsman should be able to ensure reliable service from his engine, and not have to incur heavy repair bills. Keep a careful check on engine running hours, so that maintenance is undertaken at the correct intervals: the easiest way to do this is to fit an hour meter, if not already provided.

Proper maintenance of an engine cannot be undertaken without the relevant handbook or workshop manual, nor without a good set of tools and appropriate items of spare gear.

13.5.2 Tools

Sufficient tools must be carried not only for routine maintenance, but for coping with any breakdowns at sea. Most engine manufacturers will give advice on the outfit needed for any particular engine – for example, whether any special socket spanners are required – but a basic tool kit should include: sets of open ended and ring spanners; screwdrivers, including Phillips; a pair of mole grips; pliers; hammer; mallet; files, rough and smooth; Allen keys; small hacksaw; plug spanner (petrol engine); hydrometer (for battery). The competent mechanic will know how this list should be extended.

13.5.3 Spares

The quantity of spares carried depends partly on the usage of the boat. Obviously more items are needed in a boat which makes extended cruises than in one which seldom moves far from her home port. A suggested list should include: a set of drive belts (alternator, circulating pump etc as appropriate); a set of hoses and spare hose clips; a set of gaskets; fuel and lubricating oil filter elements; circulating water pump impeller and gasket; thermostat; spark-plugs (petrol engine) or injectors (diesel engine); points and plug leads (petrol engine); lubricating oil for a complete refill of engine and gearbox; general purpose grease; penetrating oil; distilled water for battery;

fuses of all capacities on board; spare bulbs for navigation lights etc.

13.5.4 Fuel system – general

Be sure to have enough fuel on board for any intended passage, and preferably a reserve supply: if this is petrol it must be stowed in a proper metal can on deck – never down below. You should have either a calibrated dipstick or an accurate fuel gauge.

Use the correct grade of fuel, and keep it clean. Fuel can easily be contaminated by dirty containers or filling funnels, or by water entering deck filling connections – always replace the cap tightly as soon as fuelling is complete. Filters must be serviced at the stipulated intervals.

If there is a drain cock on the bottom of the fuel tank, this should be opened periodically to drain off any sediment or water which may have collected.

13.5.5 Diesel fuel system

Cleanliness is half the battle. The injection pump and the injectors must be professionally serviced at the stated intervals. Keep the pump clean, and connections tight. With some injection pumps the cambox should be drained and replenished every 100 running hours. It is perfectly within the capacity of the average owner to change a faulty injector, as described in 13.2.3, but care is needed when working on diesel fuel systems. It is easy to damage fuel pipe nipples by overtightening, or to bend pipes by faulty assembly. Injectors must be correctly installed, on clean seatings, squarely mounted, and with any seating washer or insert properly in place.

Fuel filters must be cleaned and serviced at the interval given in the handbook. In the average yacht it is appropriate to do this at the start of the season. Cleanliness is essential, and it is first necessary to clean off all external dirt around the filter assembly. It is good practice to keep all parts of an engine clean, since this reduces corrosion and permits any leakage to be identified at an early stage. If there is a drain plug on the filter bowl, open it and drain out the contents into a suitable can. Dispose of all dirty oil ashore – not over the side. Hold the base of the filter and unscrew the central bolt at the top Fig.13(22a). Twist and pull the base downwards. At this point observe exactly how the element and sealing rings are positioned, so that the filter is reassembled correctly Fig.13(22b). Discard the used element, but keep the sealing rings if they are in good condition – otherwise renew them. Clean out the base and rinse with diesel fuel. Clean, refit and replace the drain plug, if present. Using a clean cloth (not a fluffy one) or a brush, wipe out the underside of the filter head including the groove for the sealing ring Fig.13(22c). Reassemble the filter with a new element, carefully rotating it slightly so that it slides easily over the small 'O' ring at the top. Do not overtighten the bolt.

13.5.6 **Diesel fuel system – venting**

Running out of fuel, or any work on the fuel system such as servicing filters, will allow air to get into the system and will prevent proper

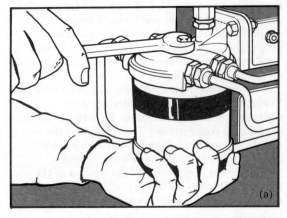

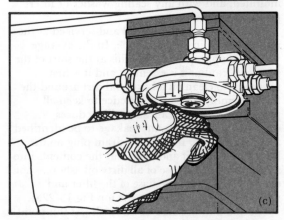

Fig. 13(22) (a) Servicing a diesel fuel filter. First remove all external dirt, turn off the fuel supply if by gravity, and drain the base if the filter has a drain plug. Unscrew the centre bolt, while holding the filter base to prevent rotation. (b) Release the element and base by pulling downwards with a twisting action, to free from the internal 'O' ring. Discard the element, but retain lower sealing ring. Clean filter base, and rinse with clean fuel oil. Renew sealing ring, if necessary. Refit and tighten drain plug (where fitted). (c) Clean the filter head with a clean brush or a non-fluffy cloth, particularly the groove housing the sealing ring. Fit new sealing ring and 'O' ring where necessary. When replacing new element, turn it slightly so that it slides over the 'O' ring. Do not overtighten the central bolt. Turn on the fuel system, and vent it in accordance with the engine handbook.

operation of the fuel injection pump. It is then necessary to vent or bleed the system before the engine will start. The exact procedure varies slightly from engine to engine, and should be described in the engine handbook. It is important to know the correct drill, since it may have to be done at sea or in the dark. Basically the procedure is to slacken vents on the final fuel filter and on the injection pump in turn, while operating the hand priming lever of the fuel lift pump until all the air has been expelled. Finally the connections at the injector end of two high pressure fuel pipes are slacked back, and the engine tuned over on the starter until fuel free from air emerges. Then re-tighten the connections.

Before venting the system, make certain that vent screws and connections which are to be slackened are completely clean externally, in order to prevent any dirt entering the system. It is a good idea for such vent screws to be painted a distinctive colour to assist identification. With some installations, during the final stages of venting, the governor may not function correctly, so be prepared to stop the engine in the event of any overspeed.

13.5.7 **Lubrication system**

Be careful to use an approved type and grade of oil, both for the engine and for the gearbox. Always check the levels in the engine and gearbox before starting up. On a long passage under power, oil levels should be checked at intervals of 4–6 hours. Oil must be clean, which means that is must only be stowed in a closed container, which should be clearly marked as to the contents.

Do not overfill. Investigate any departure from the correct level, whether it is too low or too high. The latter may be caused by fuel or water getting into the sump, and both are serious matters.

13.5.8 **Cooling system**

In the case of air cooled engines, there is little to attend to provided that air intakes and exhausts are kept clear and are not obstructed.

With water cooling the most likely cause of trouble is blockage of the circulating water inlet strainer. If the engine temperature rises, check the water discharge overboard if this is readily visible: steam from it will indicate that the strainer is probably blocked, but this can soon be rectified by shutting the inlet seacock and examining the strainer. If this proves to be clean, the trouble may lie with the pump or thermostat. If the engine is fresh water cooled, then the fresh water system may need replenishing – rather like a car radiator.

Before starting the engine make certain that the circulating water inlet seacock is open. If the engine is fresh water cooled, check the level in the header tank.

13.5.9 Electrical system

As already described in 13.3.2, it is most important that lead/acid batteries are kept charged, and not left idle for more than a month or so. The level of the electrolyte should be checked weekly. The tension of the alternator drive belt should also be checked regularly.

On starting the engine, the alternator will initially charge at quite a high rate, gradually reducing as the battery becomes fully charged.

When the boat is left unattended, the main battery switch should be broken.

13.5.10 Engine checks

Before getting under way, check:

    FUEL TANK CONTENTS AND FUEL
        RESERVE
    ENGINE AND GEARBOX OIL LEVELS
    SPARE LUBRICATING OIL ON BOARD
    HEADER TANK LEVEL (Fresh water
        cooling)
    CIRCULATING WATER SEACOCK
        OPEN
    BATTERY SWITCHES ON
    ENGINE COMPARTMENT FAN (Run for 5
        minutes, if fitted)
    ENGINE BILGES CLEAR
    FUEL FILTER BOWL CLEAR
    BATTERY ELECTROLYTE LEVEL
        CORRECT
    ENGINE IN NEUTRAL
    NO ROPES NEAR SCREW

After starting engine, check:

    LUBRICATING OIL PRESSURE
    CIRCULATING WATER FLOW
    GENERATOR CHARGING
    AHEAD/NEUTRAL/ASTERN
        OPERATION OF GEARBOX
    ENGINE IDLING RPM

While engine running, check:

    ENGINE RPM
    LUBRICATING OIL PRESSURE
    GEARBOX OIL PRESSURE (if separate
        system)
    COOLANT TEMPERATURE
    TURBOCHARGER OIL PRESSURE (if
        fitted)
    TURBOCHARGER BOOST PRESSURE (if
        fitted)
    AMMETER, OR CHARGING LIGHT
    FUEL TANK CONTENTS

On return to harbour, check:

    ENGINE COMPARTMENT FOR LEAKS
        ETC
    PETROL COCKS SHUT (leave diesel
        systems open)
    CIRCULATING WATER INLET
        SEACOCKS SHUT
    MAIN BATTERY SWITCHES OPEN
    FUEL REMAINING
    LUBRICATING OIL LEVELS
    ENGINE RUNNING HOURS (enter in log)
    BILGE CLEAR

13.5.11 Laying up – care of engine

Any engine which is left idle for more than two or three weeks at a time will start to deteriorate. So during the winter months it is most important that machinery is either run regularly or is properly inhibited; much more damage can be caused by one winter of neglect than by many summers of normal use.

The protection needed during the winter falls into two categories. First all the internal working surfaces such as crankshaft journals, cylinder walls (and particularly, with a diesel engine, the insides of fuel injection pump and fuel injectors) must be suitably treated to prevent corrosion. Second, with a water cooled engine, the cooling system must be treated not only to eliminate corrosion but also the possibility of frost damage. So attention is needed to the lubricating system, the fuel system, and the cooling system. In addition the battery must be removed from the boat, and stored where it is safe from frost and can be charged about once a month.

In order to achieve the desired result, it is necessary that the various jobs are undertaken in the correct sequence, and in some cases concurrently, briefly as follows. First run the engine to warm it up. Stop it and pump out all the lubricating oil into a suitable drum for disposal ashore: also drain the gearbox. Fit a new oil filter element. If an oil bath air filter is fitted, this should be cleaned and filled with fresh oil. Replenish the engine with a rust-proofing oil such as Duckhams Adfilm 730, and the gearbox with its normal transmission oil. Run the engine for about 15 minutes at a fast idling speed, with the gearbox in neutral.

Next, the fuel system. With a diesel engine, drain the fuel filter, disconnect the suction pipe from the fuel lift pump and insert it in a can with a mixture of 2/3 diesel fuel and 1/3 rust-proofing oil. Bleed the system, start the engine, and run it at idling speed for five or ten minutes so that the preserving oil reaches the injection pump and the injectors. With a petrol engine, drain out and clean the carburettor, fuel pump and fuel filter. Preferably empty and clean the petrol tank. During this work remember the danger when working on petrol systems in a confined area – no smoking and no naked lights.

Concurrently with the above, tackle the cooling system. If the boat is to be left afloat during the winter, treat the fresh water system with anti-freeze. Shut (and lash) the circulating water inlet seacock, and drain down the salt (raw) water side of the system through whatever drain plugs are provided. Remove the cover from the circulating pump, take out the impeller and store it carefully. However, if the boat is out of the water or if circumstances permit (perhaps alongside, with fresh water readily available) the following additional flushing procedure is recommended. Drain all the raw water from the cooling system, including the gearbox oil cooler, through the drain plugs, and then close these again. Shut the inlet seacock, disconnect the pipe from it, and insert the end in a bucket which can be kept topped up with a supply of fresh water. Run the engine at a fast idling speed for ten minutes to flush through the system with fresh water. (It is not advisable to connect the mains water supply direct to the engine, since the pressure may be too high). Then flush through with water to which some soluble rust-proofing oil has been added. During these operations do not allow the pump to run dry, or damage may be caused to the impeller. Finally, drain out all the water from the system as before, and reassemble the pump suction to the inlet seacock.

Remove the injectors (or spark-plugs) and pour a little preserving oil into each cylinder, rotating the engine with the starter so that the oil is distributed on the cylinder walls. Fit old injectors/spark-plugs (or suitable blanks) to the engine for the winter. Injectors should be sent away for servicing.

Using polythene and sticky tape, seal off all the openings to the engine (e.g. air filter, exhaust). Wash off the exterior of the engine, and touch up any damaged paintwork. Any bare metal parts should be sprayed with WD-40 or equivalent. Grease all control mechanisms or similar fittings.

If the boat has an outdrive, rather than conventional shafting and propeller, drain off some oil from the gear case through the drain plug at the bottom of the leg to make sure that it is clean and with no sign of water. Then fill the drive fully with oil for the winter, and remember to restore it to the normal working level in the spring.

13.5.12 Engine – preparation for summer

Preparing the engine for the coming season involves putting into reverse the preservation that should have been done in the autumn. It is necessary to pump or drain out inhibiting oil, and replace it with oil of the correct type and grade. Blanks that have been fitted must be removed, and hoses reconnected; at the same time check the condition of all hoses and their clips. Replace the water pump impeller, having made sure it is in good condition, and shut all drain cocks on the water system. Renew filter elements, if this was not done before the winter.

Check that the battery is fully charged, and that the level of the electrolyte is correct, and fit it in the boat. Remove temporary blanks fitted in place of injectors or spark-plugs, and turn the engine over on the starter to remove most of the oil that was put into the cylinders, but place some rags over the holes to avoid oil splashing about. With a diesel engine, replace the injectors, which should have been serviced during the winter. Before starting the engine it will be necessary to bleed the fuel system. With a petrol engine it is wise to fit new spark-plugs at the start of the

season. Check drive belts for wear, and make sure they are correctly tensioned.

When the boat is afloat, run the engine and check all control and instruments. Look around all systems for leaks. Remember to replace all spares that may have been used since the previous season, and make sure that any tools or gear that may have been taken ashore are brought back on board.

13.5.13 Maintenance – outboard engines

The general arrangement and features of outboards have already been discussed in 13.4. Where applicable the previous comments about the maintenance of inboard engines apply equally to outboards, but these engines have certain characteristics which demand special attention.

Outboard engines are particularly exposed to the elements so it is important to keep them in good condition externally, to inspect them regularly for damage which can lead to corrosion, and to grease the various lubrication points indicated in the engine handbook at the intervals stated.

Internal lubrication has been discussed in 13.4.3, but it is worth repeating the importance of using the correct outboard motor oil, and of mixing it with petrol of the correct grade and in the proper proportions. Before filling the tank give the can a good shake to make sure that the petrol and oil are well mixed.

The lower unit (the bottom part of the leg, near the propeller) requires special attention. Most engines have a zinc anode here to give protection against galvanic action. This must not be painted and should be inspected periodically, and replaced when it is about half wasted.

Check the oil level in the lower unit regularly by means of the plug(s) fitted in the gear housing, and change the oil as recommended in the engine handbook. A special gear oil must be used. Drain a little oil off from time to time to check for any sign of water, since there is always the possibility of leakage at the seal between the the propeller shaft and the housing. This danger can be minimised if the engine is always tilted up after use, so as to raise the propeller and gear housing out of the water.

All outboards have some means of protecting the gearing, should the propeller hit anything solid. In small engines this takes the form of a shear pin, passing through the propeller boss and the shaft, which breaks if too large a force is suddenly applied. A new shear pin must then be fitted by removing the fairing cone at the aft end of the boss. Larger engines have a slipping clutch on the final drive to the propeller. Do not run the engine at high speed if a propeller blade is damaged.

As already explained, most outboards have two-stroke engines, which are sensitive to spark-plug fouling at low rpm. So particular attention should be given to plug maintenance. Always keep a spare set of plugs on board. Ideally a plug removed from the engine should be fairly clean, with only slight deposits light brown or light grey in colour. The electrodes should be intact, and there should be no deposits of oil or carbon. Before removing a spark-plug make sure that the surrounding area is clean, so that no dirt will enter the cylinder. Use a proper plug spanner, and take care not to damage the insulator. The spark can be tested by placing the plug body against the cylinder head and turning the engine over so that the spark can be observed visually. Plugs can be cleaned with a stiff brush in a bath of petrol or white spirit. Re-set the gap only by bending the earthed (outer) electrode: do not exert any pressure on the central electrode, or the insulation will be damaged.

Before using a new engine read the instruction book carefully and make yourself familiar with the controls and with the various parts of the motor. Open the fuel cock (usually on the side of the engine) and the air vent on the filler cap. If the engine has a separate, remote, tank see that there are no kinks in the fuel line, and prime the system with the hand bulb.

If the engine does not start, first ensure that there is enough fuel in the tank and that it is getting to the carburettor. Then check the spark-plug(s), which should be clean and dry: if they are wet with unburnt fuel, pull the engine over several times to expel the excess, before cleaning and replacing the plug(s). If the engine still will not start, check the spark as described above. Care is needed, since modern engines generate a high voltage in the secondary circuit of the ignition system. Possible causes of ignition failure with a magneto system could be breaker points pitted or wrongly set, cam follower worn or cracked, defective condenser, or faulty plug lead. With multi-cylinder engines check that the plug leads have not been crossed. Capacitor discharge systems are in general more reliable, since they do not have so many moving parts. If the engine is still obstinate, even if the spark is satisfactory, it is necessary to turn again to the fuel system, and check for dirt in the filter or in the carburettor. Also check the float and needle valve assembly, so that it gives the correct level in the float chamber.

After any trip, shut off the fuel cock and close the air vent. Tilt the engine to raise the lower unit out of the water. When carrying an outboard, or laying it down on the jetty, do not allow the propeller end to rise above the engine, or water may possibly run into the engine and cause serious damage.

13.5.14 Rescuing a drowned outboard
If the engine should ever get immersed, it should be given professional attention as quickly as possible. But in the meantime, speedy action will help to minimise any internal damage. Flush the whole engine liberally with fresh water, to remove as much salt and dirt as possible. Flush out the interior by removing the spark-plug(s), turning the engine upside down, and turning it over by hand. If the motor does not rotate easily, do not use excessive force because it may have suffered internal damage (e.g. a bent connecting rod) if it was running when it entered the water. Repeat the process using methylated spirit or any other suitable fluid available, and then several times with lubricating oil – pouring it in through the plug hole(s) and the carburettor in turn, and turning the engine end for end so that the oil is thoroughly distributed inside. Replace the plug(s) and get the engine to the nearest dealer or workshop as quickly as possible.

13.5.15 Laying up an outboard
Before the winter an outboard engine needs similar inhibiting to that required by an inboard unit. First carefully clean the whole exterior. Flush out the cooling system with fresh water: this can be done most conveniently by running the boat in fresh water, but if this is not possible the engine should be mounted so that the lower unit is well immersed in fresh water in a suitable container such as a dustbin. Empty and refill the container, this time adding a corrosion inhibitor such as Esso Kutwell 40 – an emulsifying oil to preserve the internal parts of the cooling system – and run the engine for about five minutes. Towards the end of this period, before cutting off the fuel supply and stopping the engine, inject a suitable preservative such as Duckhams Adfilm 730 or Esso Rust-Ban 623 into the air inlet, to protect the moving parts during the winter. It should be noted that this is a different type of oil from that used in the cooling system. Remove the spark-plug(s) and insert a teaspoonful of oil into the cylinder(s), turning the engine by hand so that it is well distributed. Replace the plug(s).

The carburettor should now be empty, but check this, and give it a good clean out. Clean the fuel filter. Empty the fuel tank, or gummy deposits may form during the time the engine is left idle. Examine the contact breaker points (where fitted), clean them up as necessary and adjust the gap; if the points are pitted a new set should be fitted before the engine is re-commissioned. Check all wiring and connections.

Drain the lower unit, examining the oil for any signs of water, which would require replacement of the propeller shaft seal. Refill the lower unit with an inhibiting oil for the winter (remembering to replace it with gear oil in the spring). Remove the propeller, clean off the propeller shaft and grease it. If necessary, get the propeller faired up during the winter, or order a replacement if it is badly damaged.

Check that all fastenings are secure to the correct torque, as in the engine handbook, using a torque wrench. Clean and grease all cables, linkages, mounting brackets, swivel and tilt mechanism etc. Blank off the air inlet and the exhaust. Touch up any damaged paintwork, and store the engine in a dry place, hanging on its normal support and not standing on the skeg.

13.5.16 Preparing an outboard for the summer

Assuming that the motor was properly inhibited (as described in 13.5.15) for the winter, getting it ready for the following season is mostly a matter of reversing the process. Clean off the exterior from any winter grime. Drain and refill the lower unit with the approved type of gear oil. Remove and clean the spark-plugs, and turn the engine over to expel the worst of the lubricant inserted into the cylinders in the autumn. Replace the plugs and connect the ignition leads. Fill and prime the fuel system. Choke the engine and start it. As the inhibiting oil is burnt away there will be quantities of blue smoke, and the spark-plugs may become so fouled that they will require cleaning. Check the cooling water system – most engines have a visible discharge. All this should be done with the engine either installed on the boat, or mounted in the same tank as was used to inhibit it in the autumn. Never run the engine dry. When the engine is running satisfactorily, fit new spark plugs for the coming season.

13.5.17 Fault finding

When a fault develops in an engine there are certain logical steps that should be taken to find the reason, depending on the particular circumstances. Usually the cause is fairly obvious: the most likely reason for an engine to stop while it is running is that it has run out of fuel. Modern engines are very reliable in the mechanical sense, but they cannot (yet) replenish their own fuel or lubricating oil, or clean their own circulating water strainer. It is in these respects (human failure) that nearly all trouble originates.

Try to use all your senses when looking for the trouble. Is there a hot smell somewhere, if so locate it; did you notice any unusual noise or vibration before the engine stopped; are any parts of the engine unduly warm? In the list which follows only the more common reasons for failure appear, but they are ones where the remedies are obvious and are within the capability of the average yachtsman to rectify – even at sea, given the engine handbook, proper tools and a sensible outfit of spares. Other more sinister defects, usually including mechanical failure of some part of the engine, are less likely and have not been included because in general it would be impossible to rectify them without outside help.

(1) *Starter will not turn engine.* Battery discharged. Main battery switch off. Fuse blown. Faulty battery connections. Starter pinion jammed. Faulty starter or switch.

(2) *Starter only turns engine slowly.* Battery low. Faulty or dirty battery connections. Wrong grade of oil.

(3) *Engine turns satisfactorily, but does not start.* *Petrol:* Choke not operated. No fuel reaching carburettor – tank empty or fuel cock closed: defective fuel pump: dirt or water in petrol: filter choked: air vent on tank closed. Ignition failure – check for spark at plug: dirty plugs: damp plug leads: contact breaker points need cleaning or adjusting: defective rotor arm: loose or broken ignition lead. Air filter choked. Restriction in exhaust pipe (e.g. valve shut). *Diesel:* No fuel reaching injectors – tank empty or fuel cock closed: filter choked: engine stop control needs re-setting: fuel lift pump defective: fuel system requires venting: incorrect throttle setting. Wrong operation of cold starting aid. Choked air filter. Poor compression (e.g. worn bores, rings, valves/seats). Restriction in exhaust pipe (e.g. valve shut).

(4) *Engine stops while running.* Fuel tank empty. Dirt or water in fuel. Fuel filter choked. Defective fuel pump. Air vent on tank closed. Rope round screw. Ignition system failure (petrol engine).

(5) *Engine does not deliver full power.* Restriction in fuel system. Faulty fuel pump. Dirty fuel. Blocked fuel tank vent. Wrong fuel. Defective throttle mechanism. Propeller fouled or damaged. Boat overloaded. Dirty bottom. Defective revolution counter. *Petrol:* Faulty spark-plugs. Dirty carburettor. Ignition timing wrong. *Diesel:* Faulty or dirty injectors. Incorrect fuel pump timing.

(6) *Engine overheats.* Lack of cooling water – strainer blocked: seacock shut: circulating water pump worn/defective. Defective thermostat. Lack of coolant in heat exchanger (fresh water cooling). Blocked air channel (air cooled engine).

(7) *Low oil pressure.* Low oil level in sump. Wrong grade of oil. Oil filter choked. Defective oil pump. Relief valve sticking. Worn bearings. Defective pressure gauge.

13.6 Bibliography

Trouble Shooting and Maintenance in Boat Engines by Peter Bowyer (Nautical Books)

Practical Points on Boat Engines by Hans Donat (Nautical Books).

The Care and Repair of Marine Petrol Engines by Loris Goring (Adlard Coles Ltd).

The Care and Repair of Small Marine Diesels by Chris Thompson (Adlard Coles Ltd).

Marine Conversions by Nigel Warren (Adlard Coles Ltd).

Electrics and Electronics for Small Craft by John French (Adlard Coles Ltd).

Outboard Motor Handbook by Nigel Warren (Stanford Maritime)

Power for Yachts by Tom Cox (Stanford Maritime).

Boat Electrics by John Watney (David and Charles).

Motor Boat and Yachting Manual by Dick Hewitt (Stanford Maritime).

Chapter 14

Below Decks

Contents

14.1 Accommodation layout

14.1.1 Human dimensions

Though human beings come in all shapes and sizes the sketches of Fig.14(1) represent the space occupied by the average male, who is assumed to be about 6ft (1.8m) tall. From these, various deductions can be made as, for instance, to the proper height of a table or working surface; how much space needs to be left between obstructing items for a reasonable passage between; the amount of foot room needed in front of a toilet and so on. They may also demonstrate why a settee wide enough to form a berth is much too wide for comfortable sitting unless special provision is made to reduce the width when required.

14.1.2 Cabin entry

The majority of small and medium size sailing craft use hatch boards rather than doors to close the entry between the cabin and the cockpit. These boards, which drop individually down channels each side of the entrance, are complemented by a sliding hatch to give headroom where it is required. The argument for hatch boards rather than doors is that in bad weather only the lower boards need be dropped in place, leaving a gap at the top for ventilation and through which there is some line of communication between the helmsman and those below. If the entrance is above a bridge deck at the same height as the cockpit seats, or the entrance is cut at this height, it means that the cockpit can be flooded to that depth before water starts to find its way below. Hatch boards are not in themselves watertight, of course, though they will prevent anything more than a minor stream getting past them. After the 1979 Fastnet Race, in which several yachts foundered, the RORC recommended that hatch boards be permanently fastened to the parent vessel (with simple lanyards being the easiest method of achieving this) and that the hatch over the entrance should

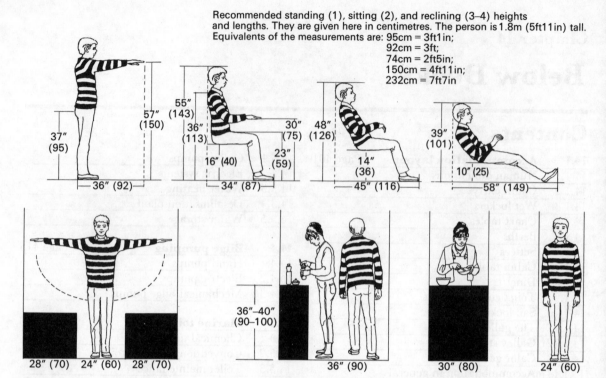

Recommended standing (1), sitting (2), and reclining (3–4) heights and lengths. They are given here in centimetres. The person is 1.8m (5ft 11in) tall. Equivalents of the measurements are: 95cm = 3ft 1 in; 92cm = 3ft; 74cm = 2ft 5in; 150cm = 4ft 11 in; 232cm = 7ft 7in

Fig. 14(1) Man needs a certain minimum space to move about comfortably on board. These are some typical limiting dimensions.

be lockable from both sides. In other words, the hatch should be arranged such that it is impossible to lock from one side without it equally being possible to unlock it from the other side.

The argument against hatch boards is that they are not very quick to operate. That is, it takes time to take out or drop in the individual boards, and though it is normally possible simply to slide back the hatch and climb over the boards in an emergency, this may not be a sensible course in bad weather. An open hatch is an invitation to disaster. A door can be opened and shut in a trice, and if properly and stoutly made is just as waterproof as hatch boards. If a stable door arrangement is employed, with the door opening in two halves, the bottom half can be left closed in bad weather to give ventilation and communication through the open top half. On some sailing vessels the angle through which the door swings as it hinges back may get in the way.

Motor boats are generally not planned with bad weather in mind. Their cockpits are not intended to be watertight, and large doors for easy access are the order of the day.

14.1.3 Wet lockers
Fig. 14(2) shows the layout of a 28ft (8.5m) centreboard cutter. The boat is a 'one off' but will serve as a discussion vehicle for the various aspects of a below-decks layout.

Few production yachts have proper wet lockers in which to house soaking oilskins or even wet clothing when going below, but such a locker is essential if the interior is to be kept reasonably

dry in bad weather. It should be tall enough to stow a full-length oilskin coat and should have a grating at the bottom draining into the bilges. Clothing will dry more quickly if draped over a plastic clothes hanger than if merely suspended from a hook, and so there should be a short rail in the locker. The door should have a louvred section to admit air. Alternatively hit or miss ventilators, Fig. 14(3) should be fitted top and bottom. The locker should be immediately inside the cabin door for best results.

14.1.4 Chart tables
Somewhere reasonably close to the cabin door should be the chart table. The navigator may need to talk to the helmsman while, if the skipper and the navigator are the same person, quick access to the charts is important. On sailing craft the table should be sited for the navigator to sit fore and aft, but on motor boats the table can be arranged in any way to suit the layout. In both cases, though, the minimum size of the table is 2ft 6in by 1ft 9in (0.76m × 0.55m) which will take a folded Admiralty chart. Spread out, the chart occupies a space about 3ft 6in by 2ft 6in (1m × 0.76m). The table should have a full-size but quite shallow drawer to hold spare charts, but if this is not possible for some reason a large net on a bulkhead is a reasonable substitute. Spare charts are often also stowed under bunk mattresses where at least they stay flat.

Convenient to the navigator should be a bookshelf and a rack where he can stow the pencils, rubbers, pencil sharpeners, parallel rules

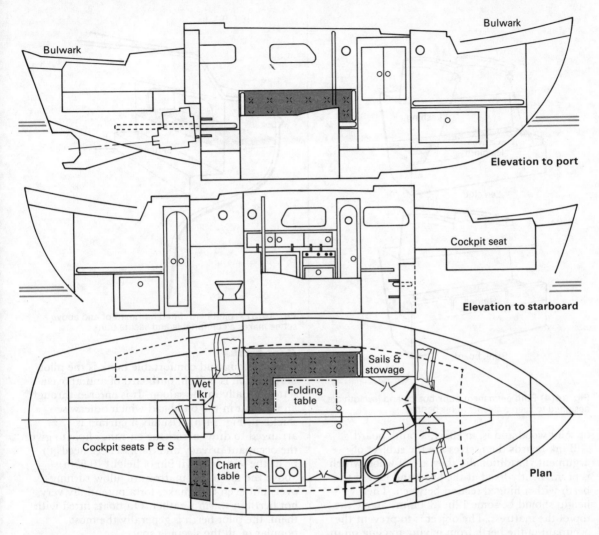

Fig. 14(2) The layout of a 28ft (8.5m) centreboard cutter. Stable doors give entrance from the cockpit above a bridge deck formed by the engine box. A wet locker is sited close by the cabin steps and the back of the settee is removable to make it wide enough to double up as a berth when required.

etc. Ideally there should be a red light for night work and a spot light for more detailed work when the rest of the crew are asleep. This can have a dimmer with advantage. Additionally, good natural lighting through a port or window is always helpful. To the basic chart table set-up can be added as many instruments or their repeaters as the owner wants or can afford. Whatever is fitted should be visible and controllable by the navigator without his having to stretch or twist about too much.

Fig. 14(3) Hit or miss ventilators fitted to lockers in the accommodation allow a circulation of air.

14.1.5 Berths

Yacht berths should be at least 6ft 3in (1.9m) and preferably 6ft 6in (2m) in length. They should not be too wide, 2ft 6in (0.8m) being a reasonable figure, but berths as narrow as 2ft (0.6m) are still perfectly useable. From that width at the shoulders they can taper down to about 1ft 6in (0.5m) at the foot if required. Bunk cushions or mattresses ought to be at least 4in (100mm) thick and preferably, if of a foam material, covered in cotton or some other fabric that does not sweat. Vinyl, for instance, is not very satisfactory. The bunk base on which the mattress lies should have holes drilled in it to allow air to get at the underside of the mattress or it will become damp.

Double bunks, which were once derided as being hopelessly non-seagoing, are increasingly used on yachts. They are perfectly satisfactory provided there are two mattresses and it is possible to erect a division between them for use in rough weather. The division may be of canvas

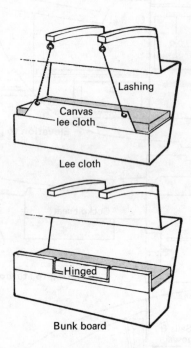

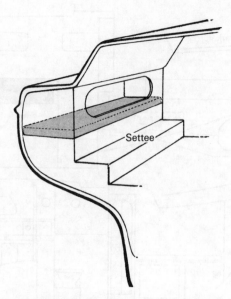

Fig. 14(4) Both permanent bunk boards and leecloth are designed to keep a sleeper in his berth.

Fig. 14(5) A pilot berth fitted outboard of and above a settee makes a comfortable and secure bunk.

or solid wood and is, in effect, a bunk board.

Bunk boards themselves are the subject of argument. Traditionally they are of wood which is permanently fixed at the head and foot of the berth with a hinged section between. Their height should be some 12in (300mm) above the top of the mattress. The object is to prevent the occupant of the berth from having to cling on in order to stay in and, in the last extremity, to prevent him being pitched on to the cabin sole. A typical bunk board is shown in Fig. 14(4), as is a leecloth. The latter has the same objective, that is to contain the berth occupant, but here it is done by stretching a cloth, which is held down under the mattress, up towards the deckhead with lanyards. A leecloth is lighter and cheaper. It also is more comfortable to lean against than a bunk board (though the latter can be upholstered), but it tends to create rather a hot berth in warm weather. If used, a leecloth ought to extend at least 12in (300mm) above the top of the mattress and the lanyards should be capable of being tightened or slacked off by the man in the bunk.

Quarter berths
When a bunk extends under some permanent part of the boat's structure, usually the cockpit seats, it is called a quarter berth. Such a berth is shown on the port side, aft on Fig. 14(2). These berths are usually snug and comfortable since it is impossible to roll out, but they demand the use of sleeping bags since there is no way the bunk can be made up in the normal manner.

Pilot berths
Another snug and comfortable bunk is the pilot berth which is built in outboard of and above a settee, usually in the saloon. It is entered through an oval cut in the bulkhead which otherwise shields it, Fig. 14(5). Usually a curtain is arranged to draw across the entrance hole to give the occupant privacy and dark. There needs to be at the very least 1ft 9in of height (0.55m) above the top of the mattress to allow turning-over, but even that makes for a potentially very hot berth in warm weather. On boats fitted with them, the pilot berth is generally the most popular of all the sleeping spaces.

Fo'c'sle berths
Up in the bows of the boat V-berths are usually found. These join at their feet and can be seen on

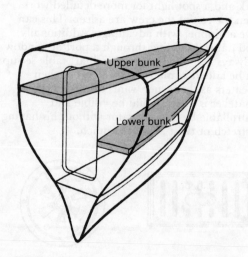

Fig. 14(6) In some craft it may be possible to install fo'c'sle berths one above the other with the feet crossing towards the bow.

Fig. 14(2). An alternative, where there is plenty of height, is to use two berths one above the other on different sides of the boat, Fig. 14(6). Their feet cross and the two berths at this point should have about 12in (300mm) difference in height. This is a practical solution in many cases and is preferred where strangers may be called on to share the fo'c'sle. It is difficult to be dogmatic about the height between sole and deckhead required to achieve this arrangement, since the shape of the boat will govern how low the lower bunk may be sited, but as a guide it is worth considering where headroom is 5ft 6in (1.7m) or more.

Pullman berths

This type of bunk forms the backrest of a settee during the day but is hinged up to form a berth at night. It is important that the angle to the horizontal the berth makes when up can be adjusted, especially on sailing craft. The space behind the berth when it is lowered forms an excellent stowage for bedding.

Pipe cots

These are made up with tubular steel or aluminium alloy surrounds with tightly stretched Terylene or similar material between forming the base of the berth. Normally their outboard edges sit in U-shaped brackets fastened to the vessel's sides, while the inboard faces have lanyards lashed to them which make fast to eyes on deck beams. Therefore their angle can be adjusted. Pipe cots are most often found in fo'c'sles. They are perfectly satisfactory and light in weight but need some sort of mattress to make them comfortable. The one trouble with berths like the pipe cot and pullman berth mentioned earlier is

that on sailing craft it is usually necessary to adjust their angle on each tack. This is a confounded nuisance for the occupant. Leecloths can be fitted but cannot be set up tight without the whole weight of the berth coming on their lashings which may be more than they can stand.

14.1.6 Settees

Whereas it is possible to sit for quite a few hours on a seat in an airliner without too much discomfort, the same cannot be said for the average yacht settee. The trouble is that the settee, being used at different times for sitting, lounging and sleeping, cannot be designed to be really satisfactory in any of these roles. If simple sitting comfort can be catered for, Fig. 14(7) shows the cross section through a suitable shape. The cushions should be about 3in (75mm) thick and of firm foam. The 4in (100mm) thickness recommended for bunks is too much for seats.

14.1.7 Cabin tables

At one time cabin tables were quite often gimballed so that they remained level whatever the heel of the yacht. On a narrow table this is still a good idea, though the table needs to be ballasted with weights in a box well below the table top and its pivoting point. In addition it may be necessary to dampen the swing of the table. On high-class work this used to be done with a brake on the pivot but shock cord can be substituted. With a wide table gimballing is not recommended since the table top will be up around the ears of the occupant on one side and hitting the ankles of the person on the other side, Fig. 14(8).

Most yachts these days make do with a fixed table bounded by fiddles. The shape of a proper fiddle is shown on Fig. 14(9). It should stop short of the corners of the table or work-top or wherever it is fitted so that crumbs and other debris can be swept clear. Alternatively it can be removable. This is achieved with pegs in the

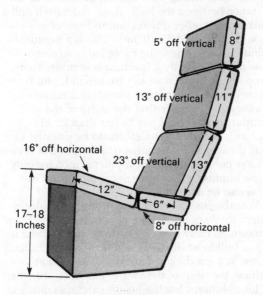

Fig. 14(7) If room is available for a comfortable seat that does not have to double up as a berth, this gives a suitable shape and is akin to airline seating.

Fig. 14(8) A wide gimballed table is not much use at big angles of heel.

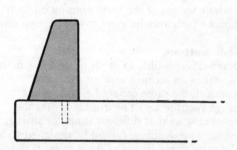

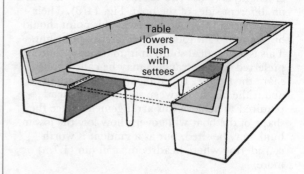

Fig. 14(11) A dinette is most often found in motor boats. With the table lowered a berth is formed.

Fig. 14(9) A fiddle should have a vertical inner face and be some 2½–3in (65–75mm) high. If pegs in its bottom drop into holes in the surface it bounds, the fiddle can be made removable.

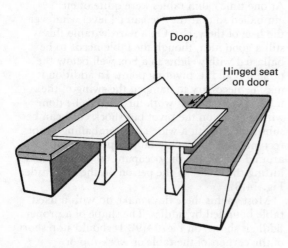

Fig. 14(10) Sometimes it may be possible to arrange a passageway through a table with a hinged flap filling the gap as required.

bottom of the fiddle dropping into holes in the surface it is bounding.

Someone plying a knife and fork occupies a space at least 2ft (0.6m) wide and preferably could do with a little more than that. This dimension governs how many people can sit round a table. If there are problems in arranging enough seating it is sometimes possible to have a passageway through a pair of tables which is closed with a hinged section at mealtimes, Fig. 14(10). The table on the cutter of Fig. 14(2) is hinged on the centreboard case so that it can be dropped out of the way as required. A permanently wide table is always a nuisance on board a small yacht.

14.1.8 Dinettes
On motor boats in particular, use is often made of dinettes where a table set between

athwartships seats can be lowered to be flush with those seats. The overall length of the structure is then sufficient for it to form a berth, Fig. 14(11). The result may be a single or double berth but the arrangement is not really suitable for sailing craft, where seating should run fore and aft to cater for the fact that under sail a craft may be well heeled over.

Dinettes are space-savers since they combine the functions of eating, sitting and sleeping. The backs of the settees are normally removed to fit over the table when it is used as part of a berth. This multiplicity of rather inadequate berth cushions means that a dinette is not really very comfortable as a bunk. Nor is it ideal as a spot for lounging, since seats narrow enough to allow comfortable eating are too narrow for sprawling on.

14.1.9 Toilet compartments
Fig.14(1) showed the space needed for comfortable sitting with the implication that the distance between the back of the toilet itself and a bulkhead or other obstruction in front of it should be around 3ft (0.9m). This is a practical minimum and one to be exceeded wherever possible but equally important is shoulder room. People have to be able to turn around, pull their trousers up and generally stretch in a minor manner. This means that the width of the compartment should not be less than 2ft 6in (0.76m). Ideally the toilet should be situated so that the user is sitting athwartships but this is not always possible and since a toilet is used for only a few minutes a day some departures from the ideal can be accepted.

Washbasins are too often set under side decks where they are impossible to use effectively. Even if mounted clear of such obstructions but close to, say, a bulkhead or cabin side they can be difficult unless at a good height above the sole. That reduces the need of the user to lean forward when at his ablutions. Such a height can be as much as 3ft 4in (1m) with advantage and even at that quite short people would have no problems. Otherwise 3ft (0.8m) is normally right.

There should be a fiddle at the basin surround and somewhere to stow the paraphernalia of washing: preferably each crew member should have an individual space. Since there may be a fair amount of water splashing around, the sole should have a non-slippery surface and by the same token the door sill should be reasonably high, especially if there is a shower installed in the compartment. A 6in (150mm) sill is not excessive.

14.1.10   Sail lockers

Small cruising yachts commonly store sails in the cockpit lockers but there is a good case for having them in the accommodation. Here they will stay drier and can be sorted out under more favourable conditions. If fitted, the sail locker should be convenient to the forehatch. It may take the form of a simple bin, but if a proper full-height locker is used the top half may be employed for general stowage. There is generally a shortage of good stowage on board and one more will not come amiss.

14.1.11   The galley area

Though most small yachts have the galley arranged at the aft end of the accommodation there is really no best place for it, and each position has its advantages. The motion is generally worse forward than somewhere nearer midships, but the cook is less bothered by the passage of people wanting to get by and go on deck or into the cockpit if the galley is forward. The draught through a boat is generally from aft forward, so that with the forehatch open a crack the somethimes hideous smells from the galley have less far to travel before they escape overboard. The odour of cooking will not appeal to potentially seasick members of the crew. On the other hand, the draught close by the companionway (but to one side of it) will be less fierce than that forward so that there is less danger of the gas blowing out with an aft galley. In the end the galley will be found where it is convenient for the designer to put it, and very good reasons will then be concocted for its position.

In any case since only one person at a time is usually occupying the galley, the floor space can be small and, indeed, it is an advantage if the cook has everything within easy reach. Since, especially on sailing boats, the motion may be wild and the vessel well heeled it is useful if the galley is so shaped that the cook can wedge his or herself in position aided by a strap to lean back against and a bar to reduce the risk of falling forward into the stove. This means that the most practical galley configuration is either an L or a U. In Fig.14(2) the galley is U-shaped and there is only 2ft (0.6m) between the arms.

Cooking at sea is not quite like doing the job at home and the layout needs to be rather different. Sandwiches of one sort or another are frequently the principal source of sustenance in bad weather, and there should be an adequate working surface to prepare them. On the other hand a draining board is not a requirement since everything would fall off it. Its place can be taken either by a rack above the sink or by a second sink in which dirty dishes and pots and pans can be deposited until they can be attended to. If space is really tight, the sink (which should be at least 8in (200mm) deep) can be closed off with a portable cover which is used as an additional working surface.

Within these limitations the galley has to be arranged to suit its equipment. A gimballed stove needs to have its axis fore and aft so that it can swing as the boat rolls. Since gas piping (if gas is used) should be as short as possible, the stove will be sited as close to the gas cylinder and locker as can be arranged. Refrigerator doors must open into the centre of the vessel if they are to take advantage of the fact that many can accept quite fierce rolling without harm. The outlet pipe from the sink should be as short as possible so that its downward path is steep to get rid of the water quickly.

Working surfaces must be bounded by non-continuous fiddle rails to allow the mess to be swept off without difficulty and all potentially harmful corners should be rounded. All locker shelves, even those behind doors, should have fiddles or some form of retaining bar to prevent the contents from raining out. If gas is used the tap to turn off the supply (which should be used every time the stove is not wanted and is quite separate from the main supply shut-off which is on the gas bottle itself) must be visible and easy to reach. Good natural lighting through a port or window is a desirable feature, as is the provision of proper artificial lighting. The cook does not want to operate constantly in his own shadow. A ventilator in the galley is a good thing but it should be able to be closed. There can be quite fierce draughts through a vent which may blow out the gas. That is inconvenient at best and dangerous at worst.

The galleys of motor boats are not often arranged with seagoing cooking as a priority. The implication is that food will be prepared beforehand if a passage is to be made and proper cooking only undertaken in a sheltered berth. If that is the intention, then the normal motor boat galley will suffice but otherwise the same rules apply as to sailing craft. It is, though, worth mentioning that pre-cooking some sort of meal and storing it in a large vacuum flask is a sensible way of going about things even under sail if only a short passage is to be made. The same thing applies to hot drinks or soup but there must be a good stowage for the flasks.

Stowage

It is sensible to use unbreakable crockery and glasses on a boat but even so their stowage should be secure. They should not simply be piled up in a locker from which they can avalanche if the door is opened on the wrong tack. There are many ways of achieving neat stowages, the most basic being to drop the plates, for instance, between vertical dowels. These hold them in position but allow them to be extricated without difficulty. Cutlery is probably best stowed in a box with an open top.

In the absence of a refrigerator or other cooling unit it should be remembered that the hull will be cooler below the waterline than some way up the topsides, so that vegetables and other perishables are best stowed low down and even in a suitable container in the bilges if this is feasible. If these perishables have to be kept in lockers around the galley the doors should be louvered or have some similar way of ensuring a flow of air in the locker itself. Airtight containers should be used for items like salt, sugar, flour and biscuits. There must be some form of rubbish or gash bucket convenient to the cook but preferably stowed out of sight. There are household containers made which hold disposable plastic bags and can be fastened to a locker door. These are handy and, with a bag clipped at the top, taking the rubbish ashore is not the messy task it might otherwise be.

A dustpan and brush and damp cloth will find frequent employment in the galley area and should be stowed somewhere handy. On this score it is worth mentioning that cutting bread on board seems to spread the crumbs over unimaginable distances. Sliced bread, despite its rather poor image, is preferable.

14.1.12 Galley stoves
Cooking may be done by solid fuel, electricity, paraffin, alcohol (methylated spirits) or bottled gas. On large yachts the Aga, Esse or Rayburn type of solid fuel burning stove is appropriate, especially where the constant heat given off is appreciated. However such stoves really need to be backed up by something more speedy, such as a couple of gas rings, for times when nearly instant meals are called for. Electric cooking where micro-wave ovens can be used to back up the main cooker for really speedy work is popular in bigger craft, too, but having to run the generator even to boil a kettle is a nuisance for those on board as well as to other boats nearby. If for any reason the electric supply fails then the crew will go hungry unless some form of emergency cooking has been catered for.

Paraffin pressure stoves in the form of the much-revered Primuses were once just about the sole form of cooking aboard smallish cruising boats and there is still much to recommend the method. Paraffin is relatively easy to procure in any part of the world, though it has recently become rather expensive. Though paraffin burns of course, it does not present the explosion hazard of gas and the stove is quick in operation. Its

main drawback is that it is not quite as clean, or as swift to start as a gas stove. The paraffin has to be pre-heated either by using methylated spirits in a cup below the burner or, on the latest models, pumping up the pressure and lighting an auxiliary jet directed towards the main burner. In the fullness of time, (something like one minute) either pre-heating method will allow the main burner to light properly. Failure to pre-heat properly can lead to spectacular jets of burning paraffin climbing towards the deckhead. Although, if the stove is turned off immediately, this is more alarming than dangerous it does tend to deposit oily soot about the place. It is not easy to get a really satisfactory oven for a paraffin pressure stove nor to turn the heat down sufficiently for gentle simmering (although an asbestos mat can be used), but it adds a properly nautical air to the galley.

Overseas, methylated spirit stoves are popular but they, too, need pre-heating and the smell of the meths is not pleasant for those with squeamish stomachs. The fuel in this country is expensive and not easily procurable in any but small quantities. Alcohol is safe and a fire can be put out with water, but the great majority of boat-owners here choose bottled gas for cooking since it is convenient, readily available, clean and quick. It is also dangerous if leaks occur. As mentioned further in 14.2.2 the piping should be as short as possible and it should be professionally installed. Gas cookers should have a flame-failure shut-off device.

Cookers on sailing yachts need to be gimballed and on all types of craft should have adjustable fiddle rails such that individual pots and pans can be clamped in position. Two burners and a grill are about the minimum requirements; an oven will be much appreciated at times.

14.1.13 Calor Gas
Calor Gas Ltd (Calor) is the leading UK supplier of butane and propane, in a variety of cylinder sizes which are hired to the user. Strictly speaking, these cylinders may only be refilled by Calor dealers, but Calor recognise that cruising yachtsmen will, where possible, get them refilled abroad. Liquefied petroleum gas (LPG) used in the UK, and in France and Mediterranean countries, is predominantly butane, whereas in Scandinavia it is propane. Generally there is no inter-changeability of cylinders in different countries.

All Calor cylinders, whether marketed as butane or propane, are designed to the higher propane specification, and in practice Calor cylinders can often be refilled in foreign ports because the cylinder threads and connections used by Calor are commonly used by other LPG suppliers. All Calor propane cylinder valves have a female POL connection with a $\frac{5}{8}$in BSP female left hand thread. 4.5kg Calor butane cylinder valves have a $\frac{5}{8}$in BSP male left hand thread, on to which a hexagonal union nut screws. 7kg and 15kg Calor butane cylinders are quite different, and are designed to take the 21mm 'Kosantechnova Compact' system of connectors, available from Calor dealers.

For safety reasons an LPG cylinder must never be filled to 100 per cent capacity. In tropical or semi-tropical regions 70 per cent capacity should not be exceeded, and in temperate regions 80 per cent. The weight of the empty cylinder (tare weight) is stamped on the shroud.

Check each appliance in the boat, to see if it is designed for butane or propane. This can be determined from data on the appliance, from handbooks etc, from Calor dealers, or from the manufacturer. Ideally gas appliances should be approved for both butane and propane operation. Most boats built in the UK are fitted originally with a butane installation, but since propane is more universally available it is wise to convert to propane before an extended cruise.

As noted above, butane and propane cylinders have different connections, and the regulators are not interchangeable. However, the gases may be interchanged with safety if certain precautions are taken. For appliances approved for butane use only, the butane regulator (28m bar) may be exchanged for a propane regulator (35m bar), as described below. The resulting performance may not be perfect, but it will be satisfactory and safe. Similarly, if butane appliances and a butane regulator are supplied with propane, they will work safely but the performance will be reduced, since the calorific content of propane by volume is less than of butane.

To overcome the problem of different connections, the regulator should be fitted to a bulkhead with a 'wall-block manifold', and not direct to the cylinder. The regulator can then be connected via high pressure LPG tubing to a suitable male connector to propane cylinders (or female connector for butane cylinders), and secured by a stainless steel hose clip at each end. It is essential that Calor 'approved' tubing is used, since rubber and other materials are attacked by butane or propane.

As Camping Gaz International market their range of small butane cylinders in over 100 countries, it may be good sense to take their largest cylinder (2.5kg) and a Camping Gaz/ Calor adaptor (available from Calor dealers), thus allowing a Camping Gaz cylinder to be connected to a Calor butane installation. It should be noted however that the amount of gas contained in a Camping Gaz cylinder is fairly limited.

Camping Gaz is universally obtainable in Spain, where it is also possible to get Calor cylinders recharged with butane at certain major ports – Alicante, Barcelona, Bilbao, Cadiz, Giron, Huelva, Ibiza, Alcudia (Mallorca), Ciudadela (Menorca), La Coruna, Malaga, Pontevedra, San Sebastian, Santander, Tarragona, Valencia. Be warned, however, that the Butano factory is often well outside the town.

In the Republic of Ireland LPG is provided by Kosan, a sister company of Calor Gas Ltd, in both butane and propane form. Calor cylinders can be exchanged for Kosan, but the latter are bigger and may not fit in a boat's gas locker.

In Norway, Calor cylinders can be refilled by Progas Co at Oslo, Kristiansand, Stavanger and Bergen. This can also be done at a few places in Denmark, and at Holtenau at the E end of the Kiel Canal.

Mention should also be made of BP Caravangas, which comes in a 7kg aluminium cylinder, and is fairly generally available in Europe except in France and Italy. The cylinder does however have rather a large shroud, and as the name implies it is intended primarily for caravans.

For a lengthy cruise to foreign countries it is advisable to take about three metres of Calor LPG tubing and half-a-dozen hose clips, for connecting local butane or propane cylinders to the boat's system. The ends of the tubing so used must be kept in good condition, and cut back as necessary, while it is important to tighten hose clips by just the right amount. Always check for possible gas leaks after installation with a little soapy water, and turn the gas off at the cylinder after use.

Any gas appliance must have adequate ventilation in order to avoid the generation of carbon monoxide – invisible, tasteless and deadly poisonous.

Further information on LPG can be obtained from Calor Gas Limited, Appleton Park, Riding Court Road, Datchet, Slough, SL3 9LG so far as the United Kingdom is concerned, and from the European Liquefied Petroleum Gas Association (AEGPL), 4 Avenue Hosche, 75008, Paris in respect of European countries.

For further notes on LPG, see 14.2.2.

14.1.14 Accommodation in general

Though it is tempting to take into account the fact that going up a few inches from the cabin sole probably increases the available sole width quite dramatically, and some builders succumb to that temptation by elevating dinettes or making the floor height in a sleeping cabin higher than elsewhere, all the accommodation should lie on the same level. Steps up or down are dangerous at sea and it is all too easy to trip over them in bad weather. Keeping one's feet below is aided by handholds. These may take the form of handrails under the deckhead or vertical pillars at strategic points. There are for instance, a pair of pillars bounding the forward end of the centreboard case in Fig.14(2). These double up as supports for the deck-stepped mast. All corners should be rounded as in the case of the two ends of the galley on the 28ft cutter.

There are many neat catches on the market

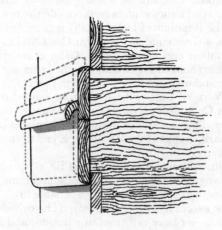

Fig. 14(12) If a drawer is arranged such that it has to be lifted to slide out, it will remain secure under almost any angle of heel.

which can be used on lockers and doors but the old-fashioned barrel bolts and cabin hooks should not be forgotten. They may not look quite as smart, but they are completely reliable and their operation is obvious to any newcomer on board. Drawers should be of the lift-out type, Fig.14(12), and not rely on catches. Hinging locker fronts should hinge along their bottom edges as a general rule.

The sole should have inspection hatches in it and not be a single sheet of material. There may be an urgent need to have a look at the inside of the hull bottom at some time. The sole itself can be of timber in some form but it might be considered a luxury for a family cruising boat to have carpet. As long as a wet locker is provided, and used, this is not as impractical as it may sound. The actual area of the sole to be covered will probably be quite small and a meagre offcut from the carpet shop will often suffice and leave enough over for a spare. So when the original becomes too stained, chuck it out and, after using it as a pattern, replace it with the spare. Provided the carpet was a good fit to begin with it will probably not need fastening down, but the edges will need binding.

14.1.15 Condensation

In the days when wooden boats were the norm, condensation was not a serious problem though the generally damp conditions on board might have led people to believe otherwise. The comparatively thin skins of modern craft, built of materials such as GRP and steel with far poorer insulating properties than timber, have led to the need to take active steps to reduce condensation. This is achieved in some cases by the use of an inner skin in the cabin area of GRP craft and, though the object of that skin is as much to give a smooth surface to the inside of the accommodation as it is to cut down condensation, it is quite effective.

The first defence against damp is good ventilation. A flow of air works wonders. After this some form of insulating layer against the skin is valuable. On steel craft, for example, the plating between frames can be sprayed with a polyurethane foam up to the level of the frames, and then lined. This is excellent but rather expensive. A cheaper method is to use slabs of foam tailored to fit between those frames. The latter have timber battens fastened to them into which can be screwed the ply lining. Not quite as effective but good enough for most purposes is to stick a foam-backed vinyl direct to the steel, alloy or GRP shell. The thicker the foam, the better. Overheads can have battens glued, bonded or in some other way fastened in position; slabs of thin foam wedged between; and then tongue and groove planking screwed up to cover everything. This looks nice, and the combination of timber and foam has good insulating properties. This sort of approach is difficult on cabin sides where there are probably window or port cut-outs to contend with.

In areas where a lining might be inappropriate, such as in wheelhouses, forepeaks and the like, a paint containing cork chippings, such as Korkon, made by International Paints, is surprisingly good.

14.2 Cabin heating

14.2.1 Solid fuel

Though infrequently seen these days, except on such rather specialised craft as canal boats, a solid fuel or bogie stove is a very good and quite convenient source of cabin heat. It circulates and dries air better than any other type and, on models where the fire can be seen through the doors, gives a cheerful glow guaranteed to lift the spirits after a cold watch on deck. It is quiet, undemanding and not in the least technical. It takes no power to operate and the amount of heat given off is simply controlled.

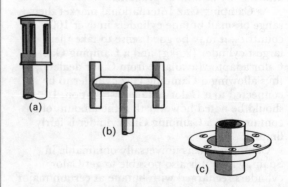

Fig. 14(13) The chimney of a solid fuel stove may have a Liverpool head (a) or a twin head (b). If the stove pipe passes through the deckhead without any form of outer casing, a water well (c) should be fitted.

There are several stoves made for yachts but it is important when choosing one to ensure that there are draught controls both at the firebox and flue. It must be capable of being bolted down, and if it is fed through opening doors these must have a secure fastening. The flue pipe will get very hot on occasions. Thus it should either have an expanded metal or some other form of guard round it; or the flue should be a double one, with inner and outer pipes. With the latter arrangement the outer pipe is continued up through the level of the deckhead to obviate the danger of burning the structure. Where a guard only is used a water well should be fitted, Fig.14(13). This projects down through the deckhead and is filled with water to keep the surrounding area cool. The flue pipe fits over the lower projection of the water well and the chimney, or smoke head, over the upper.

The Liverpool head type of chimney is normally quite effective under yacht conditions and is unobtrusive. If space is not at a premium in the deck area around the smoke head, the twin head type is excellent especially if it can be swivelled to suit wind direction. Both are shown in Fig.14(13). Fuel for a solid fuel stove can be anything from the gleanings of a beach to coal packed in standard 22lb (10kg) plastic bags. Using the latter a stove should be able to burn for at least eight hours without attention.

A typical stove is the Tor-Gem which is 21in high by 13½in deep by 11in wide (550mm × 340mm × 280mm). The flue has a diameter of 4in (100mm). Bulkheads and similar structures in way of a stove should be lined with a heat resistant and fire-proof material while the cabin sole in the immediate vicinity should be similarly treated.

14.2.2 Gas heating

The liquefied petroleum gas (LPG) used on board yachts may be either butane or propane. Both are heavier than air and thus an escape will collect in the bilges where it is a potential source of explosion. Good installation and care in use minimises the risk, but pipes should be as few in number and as short as possible, which is a reason why a gas fire is not often seen on board. The appliance itself, though, is generally safe enough since modern types are fitted with flame failure cut-offs and atmospheric sensors. This means that if the flame is extinguished for any reason the gas supply is automatically cut off. The same thing happens if the CO_2 in the atmosphere rises above a certain limit. The latter device is not quite as important if the appliance has a flue. There must always be some permanently-open ventilator in any area heated by gas.

Butane ceases to vapourise at about freezing point while propane can withstand temperatures of $-44°F$ ($-42°C$) before this happens, so that on a boat used all the year round propane may be preferable. On the other hand butane has a higher calorific value and is less highly pressurised in its container. Propane is at about 100lb/sqin (7kg/sqcm) and butane at 30lb/sqin (2.1kg/sqcm) so the latter is slightly safer should a fire break out. If the intention is to use butane in the summer and propane in the winter then the 32lb (14.5kg) and 10lb (4.5kg) butane cylinders are the same size as the 29lb (13kg) and 8½lb (3.9kg) propane cylinders, and will thus stow in the same size locker.

Gas bottles should preferably be stored in a locker on deck with an overside drain at the bottom. Failing this, the locker must be gas tight but again with an overboard drain. Bottles may be coupled together so that when one is empty the other can be turned on to operate through the same regulator and supply pipe. If this means too big a locker it is hardly much trouble to bring in a spare and link up after taking away the empty. Gas should always be turned off at the cylinder when it is not required, and this means after every cooking or heating session – not just at the end of the day.

14.2.3 Hot air heating

Most hot air heating sets work in the same way. They comprise a glow plug which lights an atomised paraffin or diesel supply, the latter being generally drawn from the engine fuel tank. In the case of a boat without an engine or one with a petrol motor, a separate jerry-can type of container may be installed with a suitable connection. The heat from this burning warms outside air passing through a heat exchanger which is then blown into the cabin, or is trunked to different parts of the boat. Normally safety devices are fitted such that if the heater does not ignite or goes out unintentionally it is switched off. Similarly, if it becomes overheated it will switch off, and most models have a thermostat control fitted to allow the cabin temperature to be selected. When this has been reached the unit will cut out. It will start again automatically once the temperature has dropped below the desired level.

Some models require the main body to be installed in or around the cockpit where there is plenty of fresh air; others can be installed below decks where fresh air is trunked to them. There are various sizes available from about 1.5 to 3 kilowatts and fuel consumption is modest, from about 0.05 to 0.09 gallons (0.2 to 0.4 litres) per hour. Models of 12 and 24V are available. The 3000W Volvo Penta Ardic Minimax, for example, on 12V operation has a current consumption of about 3 amps during combustion but, due to thermostat control, the average consumption is about 1 amp.

14.2.4 Heating by hot water

A development of the Ardic heater mentioned in 14.2.3 uses the unit to heat up water by trunking

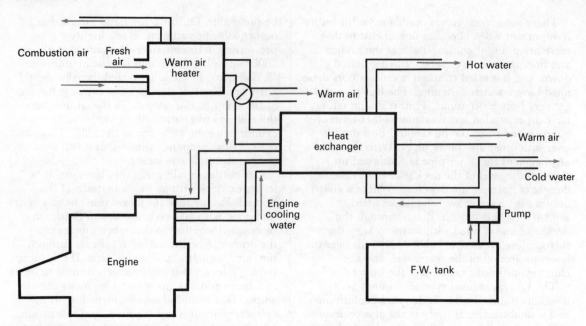

Fig. 14(14) A hot air blower can be used to heat water in a heat exchanger, and also used as a calorifier to extract waste heat from the engine cooling system.

the hot air through a calorifier or heat exchanger. Alternatively the water may be heated by using the cooling water from an indirectly-cooled engine (see also 14.3.3). A third method is to plug into the mains and employ the immersion heater built into the heat exchanger. The hot water so produced can heat radiators in various parts of the boat and, of course, be used for washing as well. If required, the hot air heater could be used on its own – diverted from the calorifier – or part of its output could heat the water and the other part still be employed in producing hot air. Fig.14(14) shows the whole layout in diagrammatic form.

A more conventional approach and one suitable for bigger vessels is to fit what amounts to a miniature central heating boiler, such as the types made by Perkins Boilers. Models may be selected producing 60,000, 100,000, or 150,000 BTUs/hr and operate off the engine diesel fuel. Hot water circulates through small bore piping to radiators or panel heaters. It may also be used, in a heat exchanger, to heat air. Heat exchangers also allow this circulating water to be used for domestic hot water supply. A 60,000 BTU type would weigh about 212lb (96kg) and would be about 28in (720mm) high; 22in (560mm) deep; and 14in (360mm) wide.

In such a system it is important to bear in mind the need for protection against frost while the boat is lying unattended during the winter months. If the boat is lying alongside, the simplest solution is to install one or more electric heaters of the simple tubular type, run off shore power. These will protect the entire contents of the boat against both damp and frost. If this is not possible, all water systems must be drained down, but it is difficult to avoid small pockets of

water remaining. A small bore central heating system can be protected by adding anti-freeze (ethylene glycol). A 25 per cent solution by volume will give protection down to $+10°F$ ($-12°C$). Anti-freeze must not of course be added to water systems which form part of the domestic supply.

14.3 Fresh water systems

14.3.1 Galley pumps
There is a wide range of manual and foot-operated galley pumps available, ranging from those where the actual pump is mounted at sole level and is worked by the foot (useful if the galley slave has his or her hands fully occupied); to those where the pump is a little lever that is flipped backwards and forwards and mounted integrally with the tap; and others where the pump is a more conventional up-and-down affair. There are also pedal operated diaphragm pumps on the market. All these have quite a modest output of somewhere between about 1 and 2gpm (4.5 to 9 litres per minute). This is quite adequate for galley use and serves also to keep water consumption down. It is astonishing how dramatically the demand for water increases once it is freely available through an electric pump, and how inadequate once-ample water tanks then become. However sophisticated a water pumping system is fitted, there should always be a hand pump at the galley sink for emergency use.

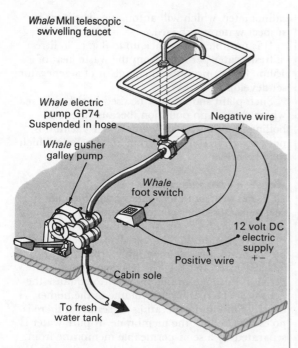

On craft intended for long cruises a pump drawing on sea water is also useful. Washing up can be done in salt water, potatoes can be washed in sea water, and a dash of salt water in the fresh is suitable when cooking many vegetables.

14.3.2 Electric systems

The simplest form of electric water pumping is to install a pump in an existing hand-operated system. Whale make such a suitable model and it is light enough ($\frac{1}{2}$lb or 220g) to be suspended from the water hoses, which eliminates mechanical vibration. This particular pump is not self-priming and in the absence of a gravity fed system has to be primed through the manual pump. Fig. 14(15) shows a typical layout. In the event of it failing the hand pump will still operate, which is a considerable advantage. As will be seen the electric pump has to be switched on each time it is needed.

This is in contrast to the more sophisticated pressure sets where the whole system is kept under pressure by a pump with automatic operation. When a tap is turned to allow water to flow out, the pressure is reduced and the pump cuts in to keep the water flowing, and to keep the

Fig. 14(15) The simplest type of electric water pump is incorporated into an existing system with a foot-operated pump.

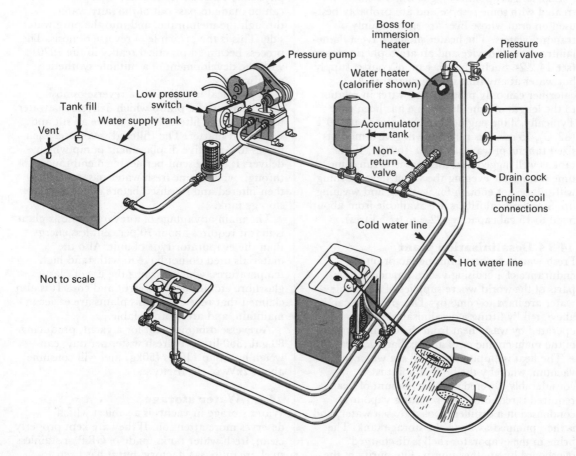

Fig. 14(16) A pressurised water system. Some form of manual water pump should be added.

pressure up to the required level. An accumulator tank in the system is an advantage since it holds a pressure reservoir of trapped air. This makes for a smooth flow of water and also means that the pump does not have to start every time an outlet is opened. This lengthens its life and reduces battery drain. These electric systems tend to be rather noisy but they do mean that showers and running hot water are available. Fig. 14(16) shows a typical layout which includes a calorifier to produce the hot water.

14.3.3 **Water heating**

The three principal methods of heating water on board (apart from putting a kettle on the stove) are to use an electric immersion heater in a tank; put a gas heater (like a geyser) in the system; or employ the engine cooling water from an indirectly-cooled engine to give up its heat in a calorifier or heat exchanger. The first and last of these methods are usually combined in that an immersion heater is sited in the calorifier. Since operating an immersion heater would lead to an impossible load on the battery it is normally only linked to a main voltage connection. On bigger yachts with ample generating capacity an immersion heater can be run without relying on shore facilities.

Like all gas appliances, gas water heaters are treated with some reserve and are probably best used on craft whose lives are spent mainly on tranquil waters. The heater should have a flame-failure shut-off device and an atmospheric sensor (see 14.2.2). Such a heater can, of course, supply hot water at any time in any quantity. A calorifier can only produce hot water in relation to the length of time the engine has been run. Typically, if the engine cooling water is at 180°F (82°C), 15 minutes running will give a modest-sized tankful of water at 140°F (60°C). If the tank is well lagged and the engine is run some time during the evening the water next morning will still be hot enough for washing and washing up. Standard calorifiers are available from about 5 gal to 15 gal capacity (22.5 to 67.5 litres).

14.3.4 **Desalinisation plant**

Fresh water can be a limiting factor on the endurance of a cruising yacht, particularly in parts of the world where supplies of drinkable water are hard to come by. This problem can be alleviated by fitting a desalinisation plant, operated by waste heat from the cooling system of the main engine or of an auxiliary generator.

The heat is employed to boil sea water in a vacuum, whereby the boiling point is considerably lowered and the amount of heat required is reduced. The resulting vapour is condensed in a distiller, cooled by sea water, and is then pumped away to the storage tank. The brine in the evaporator shell is discharged overboard by another pump. The purity of the made water is continually monitored by a

salinometer, which will automatically divert any suspect water overboard.

It is possible to produce up to 8 gal (36 litres) of fresh water per hour from the waste heat of a 15hp (11kW) propulsion engine or of a generator set developing 7.5kW.

Such plant should only be used in the open sea where there is no pollution, because the low boiling point of the sea water under vacuum is not enough to sterilise it from any bacteria which may be present.

Reverse osmosis plants

In recent years a new desalinisation method, by reverse osmosis, has come into prominence. The normal process of osmosis is defined as the property of a fluid of a given density, separated by a semi-permeable membrane from a fluid of lower density, to draw the less dense fluid through this membrane, in order to equalise the densities – increasing the volume of the higher density fluid and generating a pressure if there is no escape behind the membrane. If pure water is separated by a semi-permeable membrane from salty water, then pure water will pass through the membrane into the salty side.

If however sufficient pressure is exerted on the salty water, and if a suitable membrane can physically resist such pressure, then pure water can be made to pass out of the salty water, through the membrane, and into the pure water side. This is the principle of reverse osmosis. The process became a practical reality in the 1970s with the development of a suitable synthetic membrane.

In practical installations a reverse osmosis plant consists of a pump which delivers sea water to one or more filters which remove all silt and suspended matter. The (filtered) sea water then passes to a positive displacement pump which delivers it to the semi-permeable membrane, through which some fresh water passes. This is then filtered and sterilised before going to the storage tank.

The main advantage of a reverse osmosis plant is that it requires about 70 per cent less energy than the evaporator type of unit. Also the materials used do not have to withstand high temperatures, which permits the use of plastics, glassfibre etc. to reduce weight and cost. It is also claimed that reverse osmosis plants are easier to maintain, and are more reliable.

A reverse osmosis plant for a yacht, producing 80 gal (360 litres) of fresh water per day, can weigh less than 110lbs (50kg) and will consume about 2kW of electricity.

14.3.5 **Water storage**

Water storage in yachts is a subject which deserves more attention. If they are kept properly clean, fresh water tanks made of GRP or stainless steel are quite satisfactory, but it has been established that even short lengths of some types of clear plastic tubing, as commonly used in boats, can produce an unpleasant taste in the water. This is probably due to the chemical reaction of added chlorine in the water with the material of the tubing, producing excessive levels of phenol. Black polythene tubing does not have this effect, and there are also advantages in using an opaque material which discourages the internal growth of mould and algae.

As a palliative, it is possible to fit one of the types of water filter, such as the Fresh-Ness, which are charged with activated carbon. These will eliminate unpleasant tastes, but they will not completely remove bacteria, for which purpose water purification tablets are available.

14.4 Bilge pumping

14.4.1 Hand pumps

It is not so long ago that semi-rotary pumps were the standard bilge pump. In their way these were good because the back and forth motion of the handle was not tiring and a big type could pass 40gpm (180lpm) at 52 double strokes per minute. However such a model was big and heavy – weighing some 90lb (40kg) – and once semi-rotaries became a bit worn they were no longer self-priming. In other words, water had to be introduced to the top of the pump before it would suck. The innumerable bolts holding the face plate to the main body of the pump made it impractical to pour water in there before starting since it would all drain away before the plate

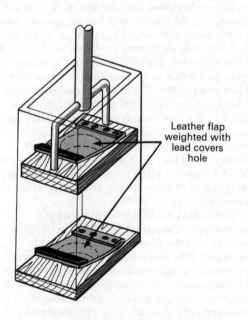

Leather flap weighted with lead covers hole

Fig. 14(17) This is the traditional wooden deck pump made up, basically, from four planks. It is effective and usually has a standard and lever mounted on deck to ease the pumping process.

could be re-assembled. Thus a special priming spigot, with a shut-off valve and water container, was often threaded into the face. This worked well but since the pumps also did not really like passing even the smallest bits of rubbish their popularity diminished. Other pumps such as the traditional wooden deck pump, Fig. 14(17), which could be home-made and worked moderately well even when quite badly worn have also passed from the scene, though deck pumps made of modern materials are still available. These days diaphragm types dominate the market. They are robust, reliable and easily taken apart to clear blockages though, in fact, they will pass surprisingly large bits of debris. They range in capacity from about 5gpm (22.5lpm) to about 25gpm (112lpm) but at the top end of the scale these are capacities at maximum pumping rates which cannot be sustained for very long.

Diaphragm pumps are made easier to work if over-length handles are used, and all pumps must be sited where the user is reasonably sheltered and comfortable at his work. Strum boxes or strainers should be fitted at the inlets, and the whole of the boat should be capable of being pumped dry. Thus, if the yacht has a watertight bulkhead in its length there should be a diverter valve close to the pump itself such that either length can be pumped. Equally, if a sailing vessel has a wide, shallow bilge it may very well be that when she is heeled, an inlet on the centreline will not pick up bilge water. That means there should be two suctions; again with a diverter valve. A combination of a shallow bilge and watertight bulkheads may very well mean that two pumps are required. If so, so be it, for every boat, regardless of whether she also has electric or mechanical bilge pumps, should be capable of being cleared by hand. On some form of marine toilets, such as the Lavac (14.5.2), the toilet pump, again with the aid of a diverter or change-over valve, can be used as a bilge pump. It can suitably be employed for the accommodation space bilges. The most likely area of leaks is around an engine where there are usually several holes in the hull to take such things as the propeller shaft, sea water cooling inlet, exhaust outlet and so forth.

Bilge pumps outlets should run directly overboard and not pump into a self-draining cockpit, for instance, for bilge water is often oily and a smear of oil left on the cockpit sole will make the going hazardous. There should be a sea cock fitted at the outlet, unless it is well above the waterline and a swan neck curve can be made in the pipe before it reaches the outlet. This curve will have its highest point well above the skin fitting and so will reduce the chance of water flooding inboard, as could happen if the craft were heeled over and the outlet submerged. All curves in the piping should be gentle and smooth or there will be back pressure which will reduce the pump's capacity, and the inlet suction hose, in particular, should be of the reinforced type.

14.4.2 Electric pumps

Electric bilge pumps can be had in a wide range of capacities and can either be mounted high up, clear of likely bilge water, or be of a submersible type which will operate under-water if required. The pumps may be switched on manually or may be fitted with a switch which automatically operates when the bilge water reaches a certain height. There are two types of automatic operation available. One has a float mounted in the pump casing which is then installed at the required height. With the other, the pump is mounted remotely with a hose and air bell reaching into the bilge. The air bell transmits air pressure through a tube to a diaphragm switch, turning the motor on or off. Clearly, as the bilge water rises in the air bell, air pressure will increase.

Generally speaking, belt driven electric pumps are to be recommended on non-submersible types since this form of drive allows the motor to turn more slowly than a direct drive type and the pump will be quieter and have a longer life. As a guide, the current draw on a small bilge pump with a capacity of around 4.5gpm (21lpm) will be about 7 amps on 12V operation and 5 amps on 24V while at 19gpm(41lpm) on a bigger pump the draw will be 9.5 amps on 12V and 7 amps on 24V. An electrical bilge pump is a valuable tool on board but just to emphasize the need for hand pumps as well, it will only function when the electrics are working and the battery has not been flooded.

14.4.3 Mechanical bilge pumps

These are the giants of the bilge pumping brigade, and big versions will shift tremendous volumes of water. The dual pump is an interesting variation on the theme of bilge pumps since it combines the operations of the engine cooling water impeller with that of a bilge pump. It is shaft driven off the engine and continuously pumps the bilges. When they are dry the bilge pump impeller is automatically lubricated by a bleed from the cooling pump chamber. A typical Jabsco dual pump, for example, can handle a flow rate of 46gpm (208lpm) on the cooling side with a bilge pumping rate of 20gpm (92lpm). Smaller versions are available.

More conventionally, mechanical bilge pumps are belt-driven off the main engine or generator, and incorporate either a remotely controlled electro-magnetic clutch or a manual clutch. At 1500rpm and absorbing 1½hp such a pump will discharge about 43gpm (195lpm) which will cope with most leaks. By use of change-over cocks and a sea water inlet, pumps like this can double up as deck wash and fire pumps. They will continue to pump down to about 100rpm. Types capable of discharging nearly 70gpm (315lpm) can be had.

14.5 Marine toilets

14.5.1 Chemical toilets

Though much derided, chemical toilets are really not at all bad, especially if they can be installed in a compartment where their rather odd smell can be isolated. Most models come in two parts. The top section holds the flushing water, while the bottom half is the waste holder: a chemical is added to one or the other, depending on make. The two separate once a sliding clamp arrangement has been operated, and the bottom can then be carried away for emptying. The jointing clamp is secure and a very basic, though quite effective, hooked catch keeps the whole toilet in place on board. In civilised surroundings the waste is emptied ashore. At sea it can be dumped overboard. These chemical affairs are much preferable to the traditional bucket since they can be carried without fear of spillage and need not be emptied after every use. A full upper tank will give about 40 flushes, but the waste container in practice only lasts two people two or three days with normal use. A chemical toilet is cheap and needs no pipework or through-hull inlets and outlets. There are superior types available where the chemically treated flushing water is stored in a separate tank, and electrically recirculated. These models can usually also be had as a permanent installation with pump-out connections.

14.5.2 Conventional marine toilets

These come in a bewildering array of types and arrangements. All have inlets and outlets leading to the sea but after that the situation changes. Some, like the SL 400 and Lavac, require a single pump operation only. There are no levers to throw or wheels to turn or valves to open (apart from seacocks). Others have a single pump with a lever to operate or a valve to open, and yet others have two pumps, one inlet and one discharge. Many can be converted to electric operation (that is, the pumping is done electrically rather than manually). All toilets from reputable manufacturers are reliable and if serviced according to their instructions will have a long life. Choice will ultimately depend on cost, size, weight and comfort. Some are really rather small for easy sitting.

These days as the authorities become increasingly concerned over the discharge of raw sewage into the oceans of the world and especially into confined harbours and rivers, pumping out directly is often forbidden. Thus holding tanks have to be incorporated into the toilet systems. Such tanks can be bought commercially in small sizes with something like 5 or 10 gal capacity (22.5–45 litres) but most are fabricated by the boatbuilder. Fig. 14(18) shows a typical arrangement allowing the toilet to discharge direct into the sea or into the holding

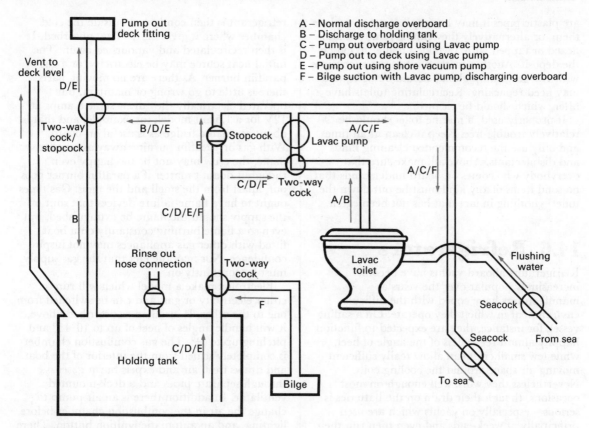

A – Normal discharge overboard
B – Discharge to holding tank
C – Pump out overboard using Lavac pump
D – Pump out to deck using Lavac pump
E – Pump out using shore vacuum pump
F – Bilge suction with Lavac pump, discharging overboard

Fig. 14(18) A Lavac toilet pump can be used to pump the toilet to an overboard discharge or to a pump-out connection on deck. It is also used to flush the toilet, and can be arranged to pump the bilge in emergency. This diagram shows a versatile layout.

tank from which it can be pumped either by the boat's own toilet pump or by an onshore facility. The system illustrated is based on the Lavac toilet since that has a separate pump which is normally sited above the toilet bowl, but something similar can often be arranged with other types.

The holding tank may also be used to collect the waste from basins, sinks and showers. If so its size will have to reflect this use. A shower, for instance, will need about three gallons of water (13.5l) for each operation. If the tank is connected to the toilet only, a guide to its minimum size is given by multiplying the number of berths by the number of days anticipated between pump-outs and then multiplying this figure by 1½. That gives the answer in gallons capacity. Thus a five-berth yacht with an anticipated 14 days between pump-outs would ideally need a holding tank of $5 \times 14 \times 1.5$ = 105 gallons (473l) capacity. This is a hefty affair which, when full, would weigh 1000lb (450kg) excluding the weight of the tank itself. Clearly on many small five-berthers this is simply not on, and pump-outs would have to be undertaken much more frequently.

The tank itself is usually of GRP but aluminium alloy and stainless steel are very satisfactory, if more expensive. A large inspection hatch must be arranged in the top surface.

14.5.3 Toilet maintenance
Marine toilets require and deserve routine maintenance since this is the best way to avoid possible trouble, which can be inconvenient in the middle of a family cruise. Most of them have some perishable parts such as rubber seals, glands, washers etc. which, together with items like hose clips, need checking periodically and probably require renewal about every five years. Most manufacturers provide kits of these parts, and it is advisable to carry these on board.

When the time comes to lay up, make sure that the whole system is well washed through, rinsed with disinfectant, and then drained out. If any water is liable to be lingering somewhere, add a little anti-freeze. Chemical toilets must be emptied out and cleaned. Some of these units are sensitive to chemicals, so that use of the wrong materials can cause damage; it is best to stick to the maker's instructions.

At the start of the season, or whenever the boat is out of the water, check the strainer on the sea water inlet and make sure that the seacocks are free and in good condition. The tapered plug type of seacock is best, but make certain that the plug is seating correctly, and that the gland is tight but not so tight as to make the seacock hard to operate. It is a good rule to turn off all seacocks when the boat is unattended. Soil pipes can become restricted with a hard deposit. If they are plastic pipes it may be simplest just to replace them, or alternatively they can be removed and flexed or tapped with a wooden mallet to loosen the deposit. Another method is to treat such pipes with vinegar. Pump glands should be tight, and may need repacking. Recirculating toilets have a filter, which should be cleaned.

If properly used, a marine toilet should be relatively trouble-free. Keep it clean at all times, and only use the recommended cleaning fluids and disinfectants. Above all, make sure that everybody who comes on board understands that no solid items of any kind must be put down the toilet – nothing in fact that has not been eaten.

14.6 Refrigerators

Refrigerators aboard yachts have become increasingly popular over the years as manufacturers have coped with the difficult environment in which they operate. On a sailing vessel, for instance, they are expected to function happily almost regardless of the angle of heel, while few small craft can allow really sufficient moving air space around the cooling coils. Nevertheless they work well enough on most occasions, though their drain on the batteries is serious – especially on yachts which are used principally at week-ends and even then run their engines only occasionally. In these cases a well-insulated ice box or even a cooling cabinet is probably preferable. The latter have been in existence for many years and have a porous lining which is kept moist by pouring water on it. The water evaporates and in doing so cools the interior of the cabinet. This is not a refrigerator and will not freeze or cool anything put in it, but if milk, for example, is taken from a proper fridge and placed in the cabinet it will be kept cold far longer than if stowed in a locker. These coolers come in sizes up to about 1cuft (0.028cu m) and Easicool is one make. They should be installed such that air can circulate round, and so that water can be tipped into the recess at the top. This is a complete, insulated unit but an ice box is generally fabricated especially for the boat.

Going back to refrigerators, since cold air is heavier than warm air it tends to fall out of the usual front opening door. Naturally this happens in the home too but there the fact that the refrigerator has to work hard to cool the new warm air passes un-noticed. Hence a top opening is the better bet though it may not be easy to site where this can be accomplished. On absorption refrigerators (see 14.6.1) which have a front-opening door, the door should face the centreline of the boat and not be installed fore and aft.

14.6.1 Absorption refrigerators
These operate by causing a liquid, usually ammonia, to vapourise in a coil inside the unit. In vapourising it absorbs heat. The vapourised refrigerant is then condensed outside the cold chamber where it gives off the heat absorbed. It is then recirculated and vapourised again. The initial heat source may be electricity, or a gas or paraffin burner. As there are no moving parts there is little to go wrong or maintain, but operated electrically they draw some 5 amps at 12V for a 1.5cuft model, for example, and that is about as small a fridge as is useful on board. With gas or paraffin burning away as a naked flame, the crew may not be too happy even though it doesn't matter if a paraffin burner goes out, apart from the smell and the mess. Gas types ought to have flame-failure devices that shut off the supply should the flame be extinguished, but even so a flame burning constantly on a boat fitted with other gas appliances may not inspire confidence. Nor may the fact that the gas supply must be constantly on.

Electrolux make a model which will run on either electricity or gas, and can be switched from one to the other. If installed as described above, it will handle angles of heel of up to 10–15° and pitching up to $7\frac{1}{2}°$. The gas combustion chamber is completely sealed from the interior of the boat, and draws fresh air and expels burnt gases through separate pipes and a deck-mounted ventilator. In addition there is an air pump to change the air in the combustion chamber before lighting, and an automatic ignition button. There is the usual flame failure device. These features appear to answer most of the safety queries that are posed by absorbant refrigerators.

14.6.2 Thermo-electric refrigerators
In the early 1800s the Frenchman, Jean Peltier, noted that when a voltage is applied across the junction between two dissimilar metals, heat is removed from one of the metals and transferred to the other. This Peltier effect is the basis of thermo-electric refrigeration. In practice aluminium alloy fins inside a cold chest absorb heat and transfer it through thermo-electric modules to heat-dissipating fins outside. A fan helps disperse the heat into the surrounding air. The fan, and a shroud on the cold fins, circulate the air in the cabinet. This fan is the only moving part and these units are quite efficient in operation, though really good insulation is required if the demand for electricity is to be kept down. On the other hand they are unaffected by heel or pitching and are quiet in operation. This type of refrigerator, the Coolaspace being an example, is normally sold as a module which can be fitted very easily to an insulated cabinet. The unit draws about 4 amps at 12V when running, but only comes into operation when needed and is controlled by a thermostat. Thus its normal current drain is around 3 amps when operating with a well-insulated 3cuft (0.08cu m) cabinet. If a yacht has a shore supply, an automatic 10-amp or higher battery charger could be fitted connected to the mains to keep the unit running.

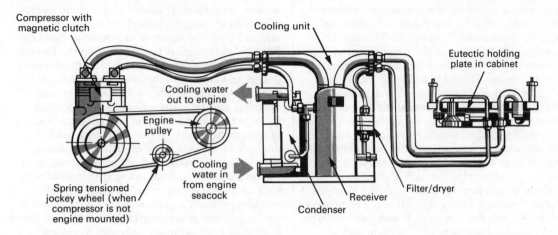

Fig. 14(19) An engine-driven refrigerator unit for larger yachts.

14.6.3 **Electro-mechanical refrigerators**

These are electrical-driven compressor types. An electric motor compresses a refrigerant such as Freon which then expands in coils inside the cooling cabinet, extracting heat as it does so. This heat is released when the gas is cooled in an outside condenser, whether by air or sea water. The latter is necessary if the refrigerator is to work in a high ambient temperature.

The compressor normally used is a rotary type but better results are obtained with a 'swing motor' or linear compressor which has the compressor piston connected to a vibrating mechanism which, apart from eliminating surge currents, is quieter. It can be arranged to function on either AC or DC. Electrolux and Engel make refrigerators of this type and, typically, current consumption is about 2.5 amps when the unit is running on a 2.1cuft (60l) model. Being able to switch from 12V DC to mains voltage AC means that for yachts berthed convenient to a mains supply the refrigerator can be allowed to operate without draining the batteries. The swing compressor unit will work up to 45° of heel, and is available in modules that can be installed in well-insulated cabinets.

The length of time a refrigerator needs to run to maintain the selected temperature can be considerably reduced by the use of holdover plates in the cabinet. These plates contain a eutectic solution which freezes at a low temperature and by virtue of its latent heat stores coldness within the cabinet for several hours. Using such eutectic plates the refrigerator's cooling unit need only run for an hour or so, twice a day. This is a considerable advantage. The plates themselves need to be installed vertically or horizontally near the top of the cabinet but with at least ¾in (15mm) clearance from the body of the cabinet to allow for proper air circulation.

On bigger yachts a deep freeze compartment is quite common in addition to the normal refrigerator. Fig. 14(19) shows the Simpson Marine Refrigeration system. A twin-cylinder compressor is driven via a magnetic clutch from a vee belt from the main engine. The sea water supply to the condenser is incorporated with the engine cooling system; the cooling water passing through the condenser on its way to the engine. Holdover plates are designed to maintain the desired temperature for up to 12 hours. Standard kits provide for refrigerators/deep freezers from 4–16cuft (110–450l). With this system the cooling unit and main engine should be reasonably close together to reduce the length of cooling water and refrigerant pipes.

14.6.4 **Ice boxes and cooling cabinets**

Such things are quite easily built as a DIY job. Fig. 14(20) shows the professional approach

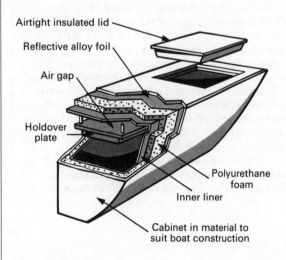

Fig. 14(20) Ice box or refrigerator construction using the hull side as one face of the box.

utilising the hull side as one part of the structure, but it may be easier for the amateur to achieve well fitting joints if he first makes a rectangular box to fit into the available space. This can be of $\frac{1}{4}$in (6mm) ply and to it is glued the required thickness of polyurethane foam. For a cabinet of 2cuft (0.06cu m) at least 2in (50mm) thick foam should be used and as cabinet capacity rises, so must the thickness of the foam at the rate of $\frac{1}{2}$in (12mm) per cuft (0.03cu m) capacity. Thus a 6cuft (0.17cu m) box would need at least 4in (100mm) of foam insulation. The foam panels installed must be a tight fit on the ply shell. Next Formica (or something similar) is glued to more $\frac{1}{4}$in ply to form a bottom panel with the Formica forming the inner face of the cabinet. The process is repeated with the fore and aft and athwartships panels, glueing each panel to the foam and making sure it is a tight fit. A drain should be provided at the bottom, and finally all joints can be sealed with a silicone bath sealer. A close fitting lid is made the same way. The object of having the ply behind the Formica is to give something to screw into if shelves or racks are to be installed. A refinement that improves insulation is to place a sheet of reflective aluminium foil inside the outer casing of ply, as shown in Fig. 14(20).

If a cooling unit such as the Coolaspace (14.6.2) is to be installed it should face into the cabin or some other reasonably large area to allow adequate movement of air. To this end, if a locker is to enclose the unit (and the locker must have a volume of at least three to four times that of the ice box and should not be too full of gear) there must be louvres or vents top and bottom.

14.6.5 Air conditioning

The need for air conditioning is seldom felt aboard yachts in British waters, where more commonly there is a need for warmth, as already described in 14.2. But in some yachting areas conditions can considerably exceed those in which human beings are reasonably comfortable – temperatures of around 65–70°F (18–21°C) and relative humidities of 40–65 per cent.

Air conditioning is theoretically quite possible even in a small boat, but there there are practical difficulties with the space occupied by the unit and, more notably, with the large amount of electric power consumed. The latter disadvantage can of course be overcome if the yacht is alongside and shore power is available.

Full air conditioning implies the delivery of air which can be cooled or warmed, and have its humidity either lowered or raised, to maintain a desirable internal atmosphere regardless of outside conditions. It should also include means of removing dust, smells and bacteria from the air, and even the injection of beneficial elements. Enough oxygen must be provided, in the form of fresh air, for the crew to breathe. So the detailed design and control of the amounts of fresh and recirculated air, together with the positioning of air inlets and exhausts, are all very important factors. The design involves a detailed calculation of heat gained from outside the yacht (which depends on the efficiency of such insulation as may be fitted), from the fresh air admitted, from the occupants, and from internal sources of heat such as the galley, electrical appliances and machinery. Such a plant would only be found in the largest and most luxurious yachts. Units fitted in smaller craft normally only aim to reduce temperature and humidity to more acceptable levels, combined with some form of air circulation and perhaps a dust filter.

Air conditioning sets found in yachts are of the compressor type. In larger yachts a central refrigeration unit, probably sited in the engine room, distributes chilled water to air treatment units situated in the various spaces. Smaller yachts normally have individual air conditioning units in each cabin or space to be cooled, but since each unit has its own compressor and fan they are more noisy.

An approximation to the cooling capacity per hour required is 14 BTU per cu ft for cabins and spaces below deck level, and 17 BTU per cu ft above. Hence a cabin of 450 cu ft (13 cu m) might require a unit of about 6500 BTU/hr. Such a unit would take about 1kW to run, but on first starting up the compressor might take a surge load of 3kW. These sorts of loads obviously require an auxiliary generator, unless the yacht is connected to shore power.

Good heat insulation of superstructure, deck and topsides reduces the demands on air conditioning units (and makes any yacht not air conditioned more comfortable in hot or cold weather). Teak decks have good insulating properties, but even a wooden-hulled boat can be improved with an insulated lining. As already stated in 14.1.15, foam plastic is widely employed, although it should be noted that such materials are flammable and may give off toxic fumes in the event of fire. Large windows in the superstructure can make the interior very hot, and in warm climates it is sensible to have external screens which can be rigged in harbour, plus awnings to keep the decks cool.

Chapter 15

Boat handling

Contents

15.1 Boat handling – general

15.1.1 Handling under sail

Many yachts habitually start their engines and lower their sails before the simplest manoeuvre – even just anchoring – and thereby miss the satisfaction of doing such evolutions under sail. What is more, their owners are foregoing experience in handling their boats under sail against the day when they may need to do so.

It may be unwise to enter a marina or a crowded anchorage under sail, but a good skipper should be able to cope if the situation requires. There are few problems that cannot be resolved under sail – albeit perhaps with the help of a warp or two, or even the anchor or the dinghy.

For manoeuvring under sail it is essential to have an understanding of hull and sail balance, as described in Chapter 10 (10.1.14). Plan ahead against every eventuality. Navigational details and tidal problems should be sorted out well in advance. Explain to the crew exactly what has to be done, and have all gear likely to be needed ready at hand. If it is in the nature of a training exercise, by all means have the engine ticking over in neutral in case it should be needed.

Never be in a hurry – proceed as slowly as possible (while still retaining full control) so that there is time to make any manoeuvre within the limited space that may be available. It takes as much skill to sail a boat as slowly as possible as it does to achieve maximum speed on a spinnaker reach, maybe more, but there are plenty of opportunities to experiment with this in open water and to allow each member of the crew to share the experience. Find out how the boat handles under different combinations of sail, and in different wind strengths. Obviously more sail is needed in light airs, and at the other end of the scale it is necessary to know how the boat behaves under bare poles.

Apart from making the best use of tidal streams for coastal passages, they can be a great help when manoeuvring in confined waters. For example, with wind against tide, careful sail trimming should allow progress over the ground to be reduced to a fraction of a knot, greatly facilitating evolutions such as coming alongside or picking up a mooring. In other circumstances, when approaching a berth roughly against wind and tide, the latter may be used to ease the boat almost sideways into a small space. In these situations it is important to be able to lower whatever sail is set at a moment's notice, and also to observe any local eddies in the tidal stream that can be used to advantage.

15.1.2 Handling under power

When handling any type of boat under power it is necessary to recognise certain factors:

(1) A conventional rudder has no steering effect unless water is flowing past it in one direction or the other; similarly, for an outboard or outdrive installation, there is no steering effect unless the propeller is driving either ahead or astern.

(2) When a boat is under helm she swings around her pivoting point, the position of which varies. When she is at rest the pivoting point is amidships, but when she is going ahead it moves forward – so that as she turns the stern describes a bigger circle than the bow. Conversely, when going astern the pivoting point moves well aft, so that when the boat is under helm the bow describes a larger circle. When running astern in any weight of wind the boat will tend to 'weather cock', with the stern 'seeking the wind'. Steering may be very difficult in such conditions with a single-screw boat.

(3) A rotating propeller generates sideways thrust, as well as propelling the boat ahead or astern. Most single-screw boats have right-handed propellers – revolving clockwise when viewed from aft, with the engine going ahead. When starting from rest, a right-handed propeller kicks the stern to starboard. When starting off astern, or going from ahead to astern, it kicks the stern to port, and the effect can be very significant see Fig.15(1). With a left-handed propeller the effect is opposite. Provided its action is understood and anticipated, propeller effect (or paddlewheel effect, as it is sometimes called) can be put to good use when handling a single-screw boat.

Before manoeuvring any boat at close quarters, it is wise to test her reaction to helm and to engine movements in open water. See how she lies to the wind, and how she steers at different speeds, and when going astern.

Special factors apply in restricted waters. Keep speed as low as will provide good steerage. Most boats will steer provided that the propeller is creating some slipstream for the rudder so, when coming to a berth or an obstruction, reduce engine rpm well beforehand so that the engine can be kept ticking over ahead as long as possible, and hence retain steerage way.

Shallow water greatly modifies the normal flow pattern round the hull of a boat. Larger waves build up at bow and stern, increasing resistance. If excessive speed is maintained the boat becomes directionally unstable. It is also more difficult to turn a boat in shallow water.

In channels that are both shallow and narrow, such as a canal, steering can be made difficult by what is known as canal effect. Due to the restricted flow of water past the hull, waves build up ahead and astern of the boat. In between these two areas of higher pressure is a trough of low pressure amidships. A stream of water flows down each side of the boat, and in at each quarter: if this stream is disturbed, due to the boat getting close to the bank, the boat may take a sudden, violent sheer. The moral is to keep speed low.

15.1.3 Twin-screw boats

With practice a twin-screw boat is easier to handle because with one shaft going ahead and the other astern she can be turned at rest in her own length. For manoeuvrability a twin-screw boat should have out-turning propellers – right-handed on the starboard side, and left-handed on the port side. Then their propeller effect cancels out when both are running ahead or astern, and when turning at rest the joint effect of both propellers assists the swing.

Fast motor boats have very small rudders, in order to reduce drag at high speeds. But at low speeds such rudders are ineffective for manoeuvring, and it is best to put the helm amidships and steer only on the engines.

15.1.4 Fouling a propeller

A real danger, particularly to motor boats, is the possibility of fouling a propeller on moorings, or on lobster pots or other fishing marks. Even in daylight fishing marks are sometimes very difficult to see, possibly with the floats almost submerged in a strong tidal stream.

Several turns of rope are likely to be bound tightly round the shaft before it is brought to rest, and it may be necessary to cut them strand by strand. But if it is possible to get hold of the end of the rope, and if the shaft can be rotated *by hand* in the astern direction, the worst of the tangle may be unwrapped. Make certain, however, that the engine cannot possibly start while attempting this.

A face mask is better than nothing for this sort of work, but some motor yachtsmen very sensibly carry sub-aqua gear for this purpose, and for other underwater work and examinations.

15.1.5 Running aground

Depending on the boat, the state of the sea and the type of bottom, running aground can be a serious matter or a trivial occurrence. The deep

Going ahead   Going astern

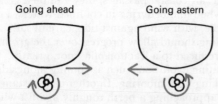

Fig. 15(1) Propeller (or paddlewheel) effect for a right-handed propeller, viewed from aft, pushing the stern of the boat in the direction indicated by the arrows. The effect is opposite for a left-handed propeller.

keel of a sailing boat is the first thing to make contact, whereas with a motor boat the sterngear and rudder may be very vulnerable to damage. Therefore in a motor boat the first action should be to put the engine into neutral and take stock of the situation. On a rising tide, perhaps uncertain of the boat's true position, it is wise to anchor while the boat floats off and her position is established. On a falling tide more urgent action is needed, particularly on a lee shore.

It is seldom wrong to turn the boat through 180°, if possible, and steer a reciprocal course until deeper water is regained. The draught of a keel boat can be reduced by heeling her over, by any available means, and the spinnaker pole can be used to swing her round or propel her. A shallow-draught boat can be manhandled into deeper water, but it is important to be able to get people in the water back on board again and the engine must not be used if anybody is near the stern of the boat. A more seamanlike, but slower, operation is to lay out a kedge from the dinghy, using the longest warp that is available. Alternatively, it may be possible to tow the boat off, either with her own tender or with the help of some other craft with less draught, when the dinghy may be useful to pass a line across.

If a yacht is truly stranded on a falling tide, all that can be done is to safeguard her as far as possible. If she is on the edge of a bank it is most important to ensure that she heels over in an 'uphill' direction, not towards deep water. This can be done by transferring weights to the 'uphill' side, and by taking a masthead line inshore to pull her over in that direction.

Should the hull be going to settle on rocks or stones, it must be padded with whatever is to hand – bunk cushions, sail bags etc.

15.1.6 Picking up a mooring buoy
Picking up a buoy is a good way to start boat handling, since it teaches the skipper to take charge of the boat, and if the buoy is small and in reasonably open water there is no risk of any damage – apart from the possibility of getting the buoy rope round the propeller.

Under sail the aim must be to bring the boat to rest with the buoy nicely positioned close under one bow or the other. First check the directions and strengths of wind and tide, and in particular their relative effects on other moored boats nearby: how they are lying will determine the proper approach. If there is little or no tide it is usually best to lower the headsail early, and steer for a point to leeward of the buoy on a close reach; then come into the wind when to leeward of the buoy, so that the boat stops at the buoy. This is a matter of judgement, depending on the characteristics and displacement of the boat as well as the prevailing conditions. Do not lower the mainsail until the buoy is inboard, and if it becomes obvious that the manoeuvre has been misjudged do not hesitate to abandon that

approach – bear away while still retaining steerage way, and go round again for another attempt.

The same tactics are employed if the tide is running strongly with the wind, except that of course the boat will not travel so far over the ground once she is brought head to wind.

When there is significant strength of tide, and it is against the wind, a different approach is needed – downwind, against the tide. Then it is best to come to the buoy under headsail only, so trimmed that the boat is just stemming the tide. Just before the boat reaches the buoy, spill the wind completely from the headsail, and be ready to lower it as soon as the buoy rope has been secured.

When the wind is across the tide, which is often the case, the above tactics must be modified according to the conditions. It may be possible to approach under headsail, stemming the tide – as for the downwind approach just described above. Or it may be best to come to rest head to wind just uptide of the buoy, allowing her to drift down to it.

Care is needed when coming to a large mooring buoy, contact with which could damage the boat. Particularly if short-handed, one of the patent boathooks which snaps a picking up rope to the eye of a buoy can be most useful.

Some of the considerations above apply equally when coming to a buoy under power. In a single-screw boat remember that if it is necessary to go astern at the last moment to check the boat's way, propeller effect (see 15.1.2) will throw the bow to starboard with a right-handed screw. In this case keep the buoy fine on the starboard bow during the final approach. On all occasions it is helpful if the person on the foredeck continually points in the direction of the buoy, because the helmsman inevitably loses sight of it at the critical moment. Other signs, such as 'come ahead' or 'go astern' can be mutually arranged.

When leaving a buoy under power it is best to drop astern initially, until the buoy is well clear ahead, so that there is no danger of fouling the mooring with the propeller. Tactics under sail depend on the relative directions of wind and tide. If the wind is against tide, and the boat is riding to the tide, it is preferable to slip from the buoy under headsail – rounding up in open water to hoist the mainsail. If the boat is lying head to wind, hoist the mainsail and throw the boat off on the required tack by walking the buoy (or the buoy line) aft down whichever will be the windward side.

15.2 Anchor work

15.2.1 Anchor gear
For safe anchoring it is first necessary to have the right gear, which is discussed in Chapter 12 (12.1.1–12.1.4).

For a cruising yacht there is no substitute for chain cable: its weight helps to keep the pull on the anchor horizontal and the catenary which it forms absorbs the jerks on the cable as the yacht pitches; cable also resists chafe, on the bottom and at the stemhead. The minimum amount of cable to be veered should be not less than three times the depth of water at high water.

Boats up to about 33ft (10m) in length may often be able to use a nylon anchor warp – in moderate conditions, or where the boat is not to be left unattended for any length of time. There should be about 3 fathoms (5m) of cable between the anchor and the warp. This gives a little bit of weight where it is most needed, and takes the chafe on the bottom. Where an anchor warp is used, veer a minimum of five times the depth at high water. Particular care is needed to prevent chafe where the warp passes over the stemhead roller; a piece of canvas, stout rag, or split polythene hose firmly seized to the warp at this point should do the trick.

Whatever the cable or anchor warp is secured to on the foredeck – bitts, bollards or anchor windlass – must be extremely strong, and well connected to the vessel's structure. Many modern boats have inadequate cleats for this purpose. The inboard end of the chain or warp should be secured in the chain locker, but in a way so that it can be slipped quickly if necessary. The cable or warp should be marked at intervals, so that it is easy to tell how much has been veered.

15.2.2 Choosing an anchor berth
When approaching an anchorage study the chart carefully and decide where best to anchor – considering the depth (at high and low water), the holding ground, the present and forecast direction of the wind, any obstructions in the area, and the position of any landing place. Any boat which anchors must keep clear of craft already at anchor or on moorings nearby, so it is important to visualise how the boat will swing and where she will lie if the wind shifts or at the turn of the tide. Never anchor amongst, or too close to, moorings because there is every likelihood of your anchor becoming foul of the ground chains. It is also necessary to anchor clear of channels or fairways.

Unless the sea is rough, it is wise to fake out on deck sufficient cable for three times the depth of water – ranged so that it will run out clearly when the anchor is let go.

See which way any boats already at anchor are lying, because this will indicate the direction of your final approach to the chosen position for dropping the hook. Don't forget that after the anchor has been let go the yacht will drop back several lengths before she is riding to the cable – depending of course on such factors as the depth of water and how much cable is veered, and how quickly the anchor gets a hold.

It is important to know the range of the tide at the place that day, and the times of high and low water – so that the present height of tide can be calculated. Then it is possible to work out the depth in which the yacht can be safely anchored, and still remain afloat at low water: also what the depth will be at high water, which will govern the amount of cable to be veered.

15.2.3 Anchoring
Normal practice is to come up head to wind (or head to tide, if this is stronger), let go the anchor as the boat comes to rest at the chosen spot, and then allow her to drop astern as the cable is veered. Initially don't let go much more cable than is needed to allow the anchor to reach the bottom – or there is a danger that it will pile up on top of the anchor and foul it. As the boat falls astern the cable (or warp) can be snubbed to help set the anchor; this effect can be increased by running the engine astern for a short burst.

In a sailing yacht it is easiest to come up head to wind, dropping any headsail previously and lowering the mainsail when the anchor is let go. But there may be times, in a very strong tide for example, when it is necessary to anchor downwind. In such cases lower the mainsail first, to windward of the chosen position, and blow down to it under jib alone. The speed of approach can be adjusted with the jib sheet, or by partly lowering the sail if necessary. The jib should be fully lowered when the anchor is let go as the chosen position is reached.

If no engine is available, it is important to be able to set sail again quickly – should the anchor drag, or should there be danger of fouling another vessel.

When the boat has 'got her cable', that is to say is riding to her anchor, take anchor bearings of three prominent objects and write them in the log, so that later it is possible to tell if the anchor has dragged. Also note the depth of water shown by the echo sounder, or lead line.

If the bottom is foul it may be wise to buoy the anchor by securing a tripping line (longer than the depth at high water) to the crown of the anchor and the other end of a small buoy. If the anchor becomes foul, hauling on the tripping line may help to clear it.

15.2.4 Mooring with two anchors
A boat lying to a single anchor swings through quite a big circle as wind or tide changes, and in restricted waters it may be helpful to moor with two anchors. Two anchors also give greater security, if properly laid, in the event of bad weather.

In a tideway two anchors would normally be laid in line with the tidal stream, so that the boat lies to one on the flood and the other on the ebb, the heavier anchor being arranged to take the heavier load. This is best done by dropping the first anchor as normal – the upstream one on the ebb, or the downstream one on the flood. The

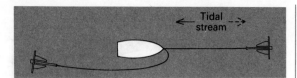

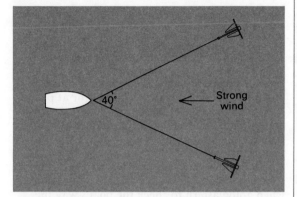

Fig. 15(2) Lying to two anchors in a tideway.

Fig. 15(3) Boat lying to two anchors, open hawse.

boat is then allowed to drop back by veering twice as much cable as normal, when the second anchor is let go. The boat is then middled between the two as in Fig. 15(2). Alternatively the second anchor can be laid by taking it away in the dinghy.

In the event of bad or threatening weather it is always best to lie to two anchors if possible – both set ahead of the boat, one on either bow, with their cables or warps making an angle of not more than 40°, as in Fig. 15(3). If the anchors are properly set, and their cables or warps adjusted correctly, they will share much of the load – although there will be times when all the weight is on one. However two anchors do reduce the amount that the boat sheers about. In a boat with an engine mooring with open hawse, as this is called, can be conveniently done when first anchoring, if conditions are not too bad. Or in favourable weather the second anchor can be laid out later from the dinghy. When doing this it is important to decide on which bow to set the second anchor, and this, in the event of impending bad weather, will depend upon the forecast wind direction.

When laying out a second anchor or the kedge with the dinghy, put the anchor in the bottom of the boat with the warp coiled down neatly on top. Then row away from the yacht, paying out the warp. If the anchor is to be buoyed it can be lowered to the bottom, when the full extent of the warp has been reached, by the tripping line attached to the crown – thus still keeping the warp well extended.

When lying to two anchors in a tideway, to avoid the likelihood of the chain and warp getting foul at the stemhead and damage to paintwork on the topsides, it is a good idea to lash the warp securely to the cable at deck level,

and then veer them both well below the waterline. The warp should be parcelled (wrapped) where it is in contact with the chain, to prevent chafe.

In some harbours, more particularly abroad, it is usual for boats to moor stern to the quay with an anchor out ahead. In this case it is important to drop the anchor in the right place – opposite the berth, and the right distance from the quay. Just a little weight on the cable helps keep the boat straight when going astern into the berth, but good communication between the helmsman and the foredeck is necessary.

It is sometimes useful to drop an anchor when coming alongside in a tideway under bad conditions – both to control the approach to the berth (in the case of a strong onshore wind, for example) and to help haul the boat off when leaving.

The anchor can also be used when turning the boat in a narrow channel with the tide under her, by dropping the anchor under the forefoot and allowing the boat to swing on it.

15.2.5 **Weighing anchor**

Before weighing anchor it is essential to have made all necessary preparations for getting under way and leaving harbour. If leaving under sail it is important to decide which tack to be on, once the anchor is aweigh. Before setting sail much of the cable can be hauled in until the anchor is at short stay; it helps to go slow ahead on the engine while heaving in. When unmooring with two anchors, first weigh the one which has less weight on it. This may have to be done from the dinghy, in which case it is useful to have rigged a tripping line.

If a tripping line has been used for the main anchor, recover the anchor buoy and bring it inboard. Once the cable is up and down (when the boat is directly over the anchor) it should be possible to break the anchor out, using the tripping line if necessary, and heave it in as quickly as possible. If the boat is reluctant to pay off on the required tack, back the headsail, and remember to reverse the helm if the boat gathers sternway. If necessary be prepared to re-anchor. Be ready to clean the anchor of mud etc as soon as it is brought inboard, and preferably beforehand.

15.2.6 **Foul anchor**

By misfortune the anchor may get foul on the bottom, usually on an old cable or a mooring chain. Or another boat may have dropped her anchor across your cable. This is where a tripping line may help. Otherwise try pulling on the cable from different directions, using the engine, to free it from the obstruction.

If the anchor is foul of a chain or cable it may be possible to bring it near enough to the surface to pass a warp under the obstruction, and the anchor then dropped clear. Otherwise try lowering a loop of chain on a warp down the cable, in the hope that it can be manoeuvred near the crown of the anchor, and then pulled from the opposite direction to free it.

15.3 Mooring alongside

15.3.1 Coming alongside

When arriving in a strange harbour always check the depth of water alongside any quay or jetty, the rise and fall of the tide, and the state of the tide at the time. Also check from the chart or sailing directions whether there are likely to be any underwater obstructions. If it is intended to dry out alongside it is important to know the kind of bottom, and also what the wall is like to rest against. Should there be piles along the face of the wall it will be necessary to have a couple of short planks, each placed across two fenders next to the hull and to bear against convenient piles. It will also be necessary to find somewhere to lead a mast line to hold the boat against the wall.

When coming alongside a quay where there are mooring bollards, it may be useful to put bowlines, in the ends of the mooring warps in advance, particularly if short handed.

If there are already one or more warps looped over a bollard, the eye of a fresh warp should be passed up through the eye(s) of existing warp(s) before slipping it over the bollard. In this way any individual warp can be let go without interfering with the others, as is shown in Fig. 15(4).

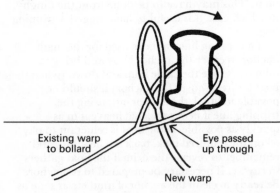

Fig. 15(4) Passing the loop of a warp up through the loop of a warp already on a bollard.

When coming alongside, always approach at as slow speed as possible consistent with maintaining steerage way, and heading into wind or tide – whichever is the stronger. Have warps led ready for taking ashore, and fenders in position.

Four ropes are normally necessary to secure a boat alongside a jetty, quay or pontoon – a head rope led well forward and a stern rope led well aft, and springs led from bow aft (fore spring) and from stern forward (after spring). These are shown in Fig. 15(5). In non-tidal waters, or when lying alongside another vessel, breast ropes can

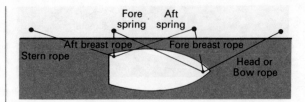

Fig. 15(5) Boat moored alongside, port side to, with head and stern ropes, springs, and breast ropes fore and aft. The latter should be dispensed with if there is any rise or fall of tide since they will need continual adjustment, but they are useful when mooring alongside another vessel.

be added at right angles to the jetty. When lying on another vessel, whether alongside or at piles or buoys, always take out your own lines forward and aft, and secure them to shore/piles/buoys as appropriate, and adjust them so that they are taking their share of the weight.

Under power in a boat with a right-handed screw, it is easier to berth port side to, because when going astern to check the boat's way the stern swings to port and helps to bring the boat parallel to the quay.

15.3.2 The use of warps and springs

Apart from securing a yacht alongside, warps can also be used to manoeuvre a boat – as for example by the proper use of a spring when entering or leaving a difficult berth.

The effect of a warp secured to a boat depends upon its point of attachment and the direction of pull. For a simple example, as in Fig. 15(6), if it is desired to haul a boat ahead along a quay, or a canal bank, a warp secured at the chainplates (at the deck edge, abreast the mast) will pull the boat ahead, clear of the wall, with little or no rudder needed. Should the warp be secured right forward, it continually pulls the bow towards the wall.

Fig. 15(6) Hauling a boat with warp attached to the chainplates.

By motoring ahead against a fore spring, with a suitably placed fender, the stern of the boat will swing out when the other lines are let go. Similarly, going astern against an aft spring will swing the bow out – see Fig. 15(7) and Fig. 15(8).

A spring can be most useful when a boat has to turn a significant corner, perhaps when leaving a difficult berth. For example in Fig. 15(9) the boat at A has to proceed in the direction E, involving a turn through 180° in a confined space. A spring is rove from the port quarter round a bollard at the end of the jetty, and brought back inboard.

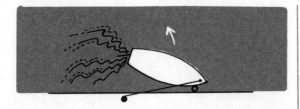

Fig. 15(7) Swinging the stern out by going ahead against fore spring.

Fig. 15(8) Swinging the bow out by going astern against aft spring.

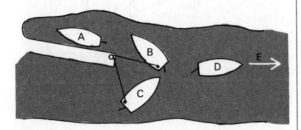

Fig. 15(9) Use of spring for leaving a difficult berth.

The boat then proceeds slow astern out of the berth. At B the spring is snubbed, and the boat starts to swing as shown, still going slow astern, until she reaches C – when the spring can be recovered, and the boat can go ahead with starboard helm as in D. During the evolution the boat is in complete control.

15.3.3 **Leaving an alongside berth**
Before getting under way from an alongside berth, consider carefully the effects of wind and tide, and decide in which order the various warps should be let go.

If the boat is heading into the stream, or a strong wind in still water, let go the lines in turn until the boat is lying just on the after spring, which should have been arranged previously as a slip rope (taken round a convenient object ashore, and the end brought back inboard). Push the bow out, or go slow astern on the engine, and tide or wind will then complete the process so that the spring can be recovered and the boat allowed to proceed ahead out of the berth. Watch the stern against the quay or other craft and make sure the stern rope is kept clear of the screw. Once clear, get the fenders inboard and coil down all the warps.

When wind or tide is from astern, or if there is a wind blowing the boat onto the jetty, it is best to proceed astern out of the berth. In this case the fore spring is rigged as a slip rope and is the last to be let go. One of the crew is stationed with a fender near the bow, and the engine is put slow ahead to swing the stern out from the jetty. When the boat has reached the required angle, let go the spring and go astern – but not before being sure that no other craft is approaching.

15.3.4 **Drying out alongside**
Apart from the occasional need to dry out alongside for a scrub, there are many attractive harbours which can only be visited by yachts prepared to take the ground.

The operation depends on several factors – the details of the wall or jetty, the nature of the bottom alongside it, the hull form of the boat, and the rise and fall of tide.

Not all harbour walls are smooth or vertical: there may be protrusions below the water. The bottom may be uneven, perhaps rocky, or it may slope downwards from the foot of the wall at a dangerous angle. So seek advice in a strange harbour, and whenever possible survey the site beforehand.

Some boats take the ground better than others. Catamarans or boats with twin bilge keels present no problem, unless the ground slopes significantly away from the quay. Cruising yachts with long, straight keels should dry out comfortably, but steps must be taken to ensure that they lean towards the wall. Boats with shorter keels, and particularly the extreme fin and skeg type of hull, can give difficulty.

Much depends on what part of the keel touches first, and starts to take the weight. This in turn depends upon the shape of the keel and the slope of the bottom (not outwards from the wall, but along the length of the boat). If one end of the keel takes the ground first, the boat can pivot laterally about this point as the water falls, so that either the bow or the stern may tend to swing towards the wall. Consequently the boat must be firmly secured, with warps taken well out ahead and astern if there is any appreciable rise and fall: and she needs to be very well fendered at points about one-third and two-thirds along her length, where she will rest against the wall. To avoid continual adjustment of the headrope and sternline, heavy weights can be attached to the bight of each.

Weights, such as chain cable, should be transferred to the inboard side of the yacht so that she has a slight list towards the wall. If the boat is going to be alongside for just one tide a masthead rope can be rigged to some object ashore, possibly backed up by a preventer round the mast to a convenient bollard on the quay as in Fig. 15(10). But this type of masthead rope needs constant adjustment, and for a longer stay it is more convenient to rig a mastline to a block running on a halyard close to the mast, as in Fig. 15(11).

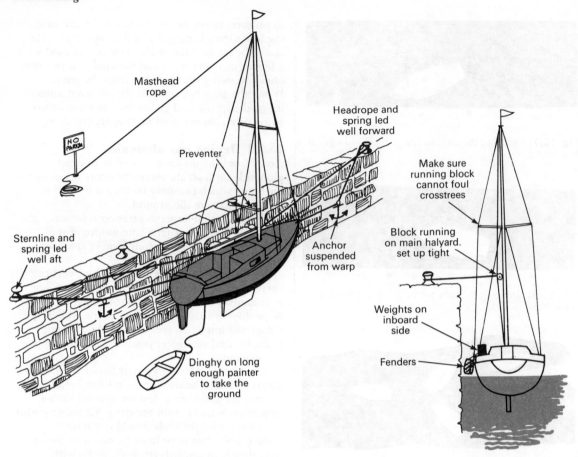

Masthead rope

Headrope and spring led well forward

Preventer

Make sure running block cannot foul crosstrees

NO PARKING

Block running on main halyard. set up tight

Sternline and spring led well aft

Anchor suspended from warp

Weights on inboard side

Fenders

Dinghy on long enough painter to take the ground

Fig. 15(10) Drying out alongside. In conjunction with Fig. 15(11), this diagram shows the basic precautions to be taken.

Fig. 15(11) As an alternative to a masthead rope, a running block can be attached to a halyard, set up tight down the mast.

Some of the above points apply to motor boats, but their main consideration is often the protection of sterngear and rudders. Many fast motor cruisers are not suited to taking the ground without risk of damage to these items.

15.4 Towing

15.4.1 Towing – procedure

Every seagoing yacht should have at least one really long warp – say 50m or 30 fathoms in length, and perhaps 16mm nylon or 18mm polyester of three-strand construction. Such a rope can be useful for kedging, or when an extra long mooring warp is needed – or for towing, at sea. In smooth water a boat can be towed at short stay, or alongside in a congested harbour.

Even in good weather, towing requires co-operation between the two boats concerned and amongst the crew of each. In calm water the towing craft can usually manoeuvre with her stern close to the other's bows, so that the tow can be passed. In any wind or sea it may be necessary to establish contact by heaving line, by which the tow rope can then be hauled across. In

severe conditions a line can be floated down to the other craft. In all these cases it is usually more sensible for the towing craft to supply the tow line, since she will probably be to windward of the other, but see 15.4.4 in respect of salvage situations. It is essential for both boats to be almost stationary, or moving at the same speed through the water, while the tow is being passed.

Only tugs are designed for towing, and the average yacht is poorly equipped in this respect, since it is impossible to get the point of tow far enough forward. Normally the tow rope has to be made fast to a cleat near the stern, and this prevents the towing boat manoeuvering freely. In a tug the tow hook is almost amidships, and certainly well forward of the propeller, but in a yacht things like backstays and guardrails normally prevent any such arrangement. If possible however, avoid having to tow from one quarter because this will make steering even more difficult; some form of bridle between bollards or cleats on each quarter should overcome this difficulty.

When a boat is stopped in the water it takes quite a weight on the towline to get her moving, so the tow must be taken up very gently or it will part. The towing craft must not go ahead until the other signifies that she is ready. If a tow parts, anybody standing near is likely to be injured.

While lying stopped, waiting for the tow to be connected, the yacht is likely to be lying beam-on to any swell or sea. When the tow is taken up, the towing vessel should start towing across the swell before gradually entering course into it, if this is necessary.

The tow should be secured so that it can be released under load, which may be necessary if the tow has to be slipped in an emergency. In a large boat it is advisable to have an axe handy. When towing a small boat like a dinghy or runabout, the line should be turned up on a cleat and tended by hand – so that it can be slipped immediately, if the boat being towed takes a sudden sheer or is about to collide with something for example.

It is a great help if the boat being towed can steer, so that she does not yaw from side to side. This may not always be possible, but in any event the boat being towed should be trimmed somewhat by the stern, and not by the bow.

When towing, avoid any sudden alterations of course, particularly if the tow is unable to steer; and try to give advance warning of your intentions. When reducing speed, do so gradually – most important when towing a heavy vessel which carries a lot of way. Always be careful not to tow too fast – a common fault when yachts are taken in tow by larger ships. When towing a small boat which has been swamped proceed very slowly, or either the boat will be damaged or the tow will part.

In calm water it is easier to tow alongside if any manoeuvering is involved. The tow boat should be positioned well aft, on the other's quarter. The choice of side may be dictated by the job in hand – where the other boat is to be berthed for example. When going ahead the weight is taken by a spring led aft from the bow of the towing boat: similarly when going astern the pull is by a spring led forward to the boat being towed. Proper positioning of the towing craft and correct adjustment of the warps give surprising freedom of manoeuvre. Good fendering is of course necessary.

If towing more than one boat the biggest should be next astern, and the lightest at the end of the tow. If towing a large number of dinghies it is better to form two lines, one from each quarter.

Towing at sea can put tremendous strains not only on the tow rope but on the samson post, bollard, bitts or cleat to which it is secured. In many boats the bottom of the mast, at deck level, may be the strongest point of attachment – although it will be necessary to constrain the towline at the stemhead in order to avoid damage to the forestay. Special precautions must be taken about chafe at this point. One method of towing at sea is to attach the towing vessel's

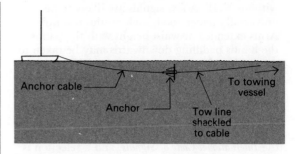

Fig. 15(12) Towing at sea, using the boat's anchor cable.

hawser to the anchor of the casualty, who then veers her cable as shown in Fig. 15(12). The weight of the anchor and cable gives some spring to the tow, apart from being stronger than the average warp.

In many modern yachts there is no fitting on the foredeck sufficiently strong for towing in a seaway, and even the foot of a mast stepped on deck may not be designed for this. In such cases it may be possible to rig some kind of towing bridle from strong warps taken round the superstructure and cockpit at deck level, and attached to strong points such as sheet winches. Depending on the details of the boat, this is not likely to be easy, and will certainly take time if a proper job is to be made of it – anything hastily contrived will soon come adrift once the tow is taken up.

Most tows are taken or given as a matter of convenience, and on an informal basis between the parties concerned. If commercial bargaining is necessary it is advisable to agree on a reasonable sum for a pluck into harbour. But what may start as a simple towing operation can develop into salvage, if for example the weather deteriorates or the tow gets into danger through no fault of the towing boat.

15.4.2 Signals when towing

Under the *International Regulations for Preventing Collisions at Sea*, vessels towing or being towed are required to show certain signals, and these are given in section 2.1. Yachts or other craft not normally used for towing are excused from showing the special towing signals required by Rule 24(a) and (c), but are required to take measures to indicate the relationship between the towing vessel and the vessel being towed, as for example by illuminating the towline.

A vessel being towed should show sidelights and sternlight, but not a masthead light. In poor visibility a vessel towing sounds one long blast followed by two short blasts ('D'), at intervals of not more than two minutes. The vessel being towed sounds one long blast followed by three short blasts ('B'), when practicable immediately after the signal sounded by the towing vessel.

15.4.3 Communication between vessels

Communication between the two vessels is important, and often difficult in bad weather without VHF. A few signals are likely to be universally understood, such as 'thumbs up'. Arms extended at waist height with the palms of the hands paddling downwards may be taken to mean 'slow down'. Arms extended slightly higher with palms upwards conveys 'increase speed'. Arms waved criss-cross in front of and above the head should be interpreted as 'no good' (the opposite of 'thumbs up') or 'stop'.

There are a number of appropriate groups in the *International Code of Signals*, and a selection is given below:

Z	I require a tug
KK	Towing is impossible under present weather conditions
KL	I am obliged to stop towing temporarily
KM	I can take you in tow
KN	I cannot take you in tow
KP	You should tow me to nearest port or anchorage
KQ	Prepare to be taken in tow
KR	All is ready for towing
KS	You should send a line over
KT	You should send me a towing hawser
KU	I cannot send towing hawser
KV	I intend to use my towing hawser/cable
KW	You should have towing hawser/cable ready
KX	You should be ready to receive the towing hawser
KY	Length of tow is … (numbered) fathoms
KZ	You should shorten in the towing hawser
LA	Towing hawser/cable has parted
LB	You should make towing hawser fast to your chain cable
LD	You should veer your hawser/cable
LE	I am about to veer my hawser/cable
LF	You should stop veering your hawser/cable
LG	You should prepare to cast off towing hawser
QD	I am going ahead
QE	I have headway
QF	I cannot go ahead
QG	You should go ahead
QH	You should not go ahead any more
QI	I am going astern
QJ	I have sternway
QK	I cannot go astern
QL	You should go astern
QM	You should not go astern any more
RL	You should stop your engines immediately
RM	My engines are stopped
LI	I am increasing speed
LJ	I am reducing speed

15.4.4 Salvage

A successful claim for salvage may be made if the person concerned can show that he voluntarily saved, or helped save, a vessel and perhaps her crew, which was in danger on tidal waters, while he was not performing any legal or official duty. Danger must have existed, and another basic principle of salvage is 'no cure, no pay'.

Some acts of salvage are self-evident – where a boat is towed off a lee shore or off rocks in a rising wind, for example – but other instances may not be so obvious. A claim might be upheld because a vessel answered a distress signal, even if that had been made hastily and prematurely (and hence also illegally). The moral here is that if you require assistance, but are not actually in distress, you should use the appropriate signal such as 'V' (Victor) in the *International Code of Signals*, meaning 'I require assistance'. Again, a vessel might claim salvage just because she stood by and gave advice; or if she assisted in pilotage to avoid a local danger; or if she provided equipment such as pumps, fire extinguishers, or even a towing warp to a boat in danger. For the last reason it is better (when possible) for a boat to use her own warp when being taken in tow in emergency, or at least to show that she has a suitable rope for the purpose.

Other factors which might support a claim for salvage could be the physical condition, ignorance or lack of skill of the crew of a boat in danger. Even their unguarded remarks might be construed as evidence that the boat was in real trouble.

Unless the boat is really in danger, do not accept help from a stranger without politely making it quite clear that you have the situation well in hand, and that you are only availing yourself of his kind offer of assistance as a matter of convenience.

The normal yacht insurance policy covers salvage, but not a convenient tow if the boat is becalmed or the engine has broken down. In such cases it is always important to agree beforehand a price for a pluck into harbour. Although yachtsmen can be expected to provide such a service free to their fellows, the same cannot be said of commercial craft to whom time is money.

If the situation is such that a claim for salvage may arise, there are two suggested courses of action. First, it may be possible to agree a reasonable sum in advance – either verbally or better (if feasible in the circumstances) by a written agreement in the form shown. In emergency this could be torn out of the Handbook and used for the purpose. If a verbal agreement is made, be sure that your crew witness what is discussed and the price quoted, and write down the conversation promptly. In practice it may be impossible to agree a figure, or even to establish proper communication, and then it is necessary to adopt the second course of action – to turn the whole business over to your insurers as soon as possible on reaching harbour, for them to negotiate a settlement. They will need to know the full facts, including the degree of risk to your own vessel and also to the salvor. In this connection it is important to be able to produce the boat's log, the chart with previous course and position correctly plotted, and relevant

SIMPLE FORM OF SALVAGE AGREEMENT
NO CURE NO PAY

On board the yacht ....

Date...

IT IS HEREBY AGREED BETWEEN ....

....

(afterwards called 'The Master') and ....

....

(afterwards called the 'Contractor') as follows:-

1.   The Contractor agrees to use his best endeavours to salve the yacht
...............................and take her into...or
other place to be hereafter agreed with the Master providing at his own
risk all proper assistance and labour. The services shall be rendered and
accepted as salvage services upon the principle of 'no cure no pay'
and the Contractor's remuneration in the event of success shall be
£   – or if no sum be herein named such sum as may be decided
by subsequent arbitration in accordance with the terms of Clause 3
herein.

2.   The Contractor may make reasonable use of the vessel's gear
anchors chains and other appurtenances during and for the purpose of
the operations but shall not unnecessarily damage abandon or sacrifice
the same or any other of the property.

3.   Any question or difference at any time arising out of this agreement
whether as to construction or otherwise or the operations thereunder
shall be referred to arbitration by a sole arbitrator to be nominated by
agreement between the parties hereto or in default of agreement by an
arbitrator to be appointed by the secretary of Lloyd's.

Any award by arbitration shall be final and binding on the parties
hereto and the arbitrator shall have power to obtain call for receive and
act upon any such oral or documentary evidence or information
(whether the same is strictly admissible as evidence or not) as he shall
think fit. Save as aforesaid the statutory provisions as to arbitration for
the time being in force in England shall apply.

4.   All costs of and incidental to any arbitration shall be paid by such of
the parties hereto as the arbitration shall direct.

Signatures of Master and Contractor

....

....

Fig. 15(13) Simple form of salvage agreement.

information on the present and forecast weather.

Do not disclose the value of your boat to the claimant. Also be warned that although your policy includes salvage claims it might not cover the full sum if the boat is under-insured.

It should be noted that the RNLI never claims salvage or makes any charge for rescuing persons or property. Yachtsmen who benefit accordingly should at least make a healthy contribution to RNLI funds, while some personal appreciation to the crew would not be amiss. Very occasionally a lifeboat crew may claim salvage, but if they do they have to bear the cost of the rescue and of any damage to the lifeboat, regardless of the outcome of the claim.

15.5 Practical passage making

15.5.1 Navigational records
Any seagoing yacht should keep a form of log. Some owners like to write up a fair record of their various cruises: while this is a nice idea and often useful for subsequent reference, it is not essential. What is essential however is a ruled notebook of some kind in which the following information can be recorded periodically and on specific occasions, such as when course is altered or when a fix is obtained.
(1) Course ordered
(2) Course actually steered
(3) Log reading
(4) Distance run
(5) Wind speed and direction
(6) Barometer reading

There should also be a wide column for general remarks such as the bearings of shore objects (and time taken), and the times at which lights appear or disappear etc.

When under power engine readings should be taken and recorded regularly, so that it is possible to detect any change in cooling water temperature or oil pressure. Details will depend on the installation, but other readings which should be noted include engine rpm, ammeter, fuel gauge, and turbocharger boost pressure (where applicable). It is sensible to make provision for these to be recorded in the log too, perhaps on the opposite page to navigational entries.

While all the above figures are often only of passing interest, they can be invaluable when something goes wrong. If for example the visibility starts to deteriorate it can become vital to know what the log reading was when passing a buoy an hour or so previously, and what course has been maintained meanwhile.

If the cooling water temperature appears to be higher than normal it is useful to be able to check what it was half-an-hour ago, and whether the

rate of increase is significant. At least if the skipper insists that the necessary readings are entered in the log regularly it is more likely that any problem will be detected before it becomes really serious.

Times of starting/stopping the engine(s) should be noted, so that a record can be kept of engine running hours. In motor yachts it may be preferred to keep a separate record of engine maintenance, but otherwise it is useful to record in the log the dates (and engine hours) at which routine maintenance is carried out. This should include such items as cleaning fuel filters and injectors, renewing oil filter elements and changing lubricating oil, checking drive belts and flexible hoses, and other similar routines in the engine handbook. The log may also be a convenient place to keep a record of such things as fuel and oil consumption, and when batteries are topped up.

15.5.2 Passage planning
Before embarking on any seagoing passage in a boat it is necessary to do some preliminary planning. The amount of work involved depends upon the scope of the passage, and to some extent upon the experience of the skipper and crew, but there are some matters which should always be examined beforehand. They include the seaworthiness of the boat and the strength of the crew, in relation to the waters concerned and the likely weather conditions; preliminary chart work to establish the best route in the light of principal dangers, tidal streams, reliable navigational landmarks and other pilotage details – together with the distances involved and hence the likely time required; and an examination of possible harbours of refuge which will give good or acceptable shelter in the event of bad weather, with a study of any restrictions on entering them due to tidal or gale conditions.

For motor yachts it is also necessary to relate the cruising range of the boat with the distance to be covered, and to investigate the fuelling facilities at the port of arrival or along the way.

All this can mean quite a lot of reading when planning a passage or cruise to a strange place or coast, but it is work which will be amply repaid, particularly if events don't go entirely as planned.

For a start it is essential to have the necessary charts and other publications for the area concerned: make sure that charts are also held of adjacent areas, in case of any diversion due to bad weather. Charts must be corrected, up to date. Large scale charts are needed of ports and harbour approaches.

Where it is necessary to navigate through an area of sandbanks or narrow channels – such as the Thames estuary – select the preferred route taking account of the lack of obstructions, the available navigational marks, depth of water and tidal streams, but be prepared to accept other routes in the event (for example) of a head wind. It is obviously preferable to choose channels which are wide enough to permit some margin of error should the visibility be bad, even if they add to the distance to be sailed. Often it is possible to plan alternative routes, leaving the final decision until the time comes.

In selecting a route take account of the height of tide at the time you expect to be there. It may be possible to plan on taking a short cut with perfect safety if the tide permits, but always have a fall-back plan if things don't go as expected.

Particularly in a sailing yacht the time for starting a passage is likely to be dictated by the time the tide turns in your favour – not necessarily at your moorings, but out in the main channel. It is often worthwhile plugging for a while against the last of a foul tide in order to be in the best position to take full advantage of the next six hours of favourable stream.

Special consideration may have to be given to rounding certain headlands, or passing through narrow channels where the tide runs strongly. Information on these points is contained in the various sailing directions and should not be disregarded.

Sort out all your charts, put them in the order in which they are going to be used, and rub out all previous pencil markings. Most skippers like to mark up the tidal atlas with the time of each tidal stream for ease of reference. Times and heights of HW and LW can also be extracted from the tide tables for the ports of departure and arrival, and for any other Standard Port along the route. All this information can be written in a navigator's notebook, which should be small enough to go into an oilskin pocket so that it can be referred to in the cockpit if necessary. The characteristics of the principal lights, the frequencies and call signs of appropriate radio-beacons, and the times of various weather forecasts can also be included.

The more such work that can be done beforehand, the less worry there will be when the boat is at sea. Preliminary chart work is particularly important in fast planing motor cruisers. In these boats it is often impossible to write or draw a line on the chart when under way, so all courses and distances should be worked out and listed in advance. In such craft it is also necessary to keep an accurate record of the fuel state, and it is important to know the likely speed through the water and fuel consumption at various engine r.p.m. Here allowance must be made for factors such as a strong head wind, dirty bottom, or an exceptional load on board.

Other matters which need planning are food (including fresh provisions), water and galley fuel. Warn the crew what gear to bring and when to be on board.

If the boat is bound foreign, passports will be required, and should any of the crew be of another nationality it is necessary to conform to the immigration rules. Part 1 of Form C1328 must be completed and delivered or posted to the local Customs office. The Certificate of Registry (or, where acceptable, the international Certificate for Pleasure Navigation) should be on board, and in any case it is important to make sure that the insurance policy covers the intended cruising area.

If the boat participates in the HM Coastguard Yacht and Boat Safety Scheme (Form CG66) make sure that your shore contact is kept informed of the boat's movements and knows what to do should you fail to report.

15.5.3 **Sailing directions**
When cruising in strange waters it is important to be able to refer to sailing directions which supplement the navigational details shown on even the largest scale chart. In some areas where pilotage is particularly difficult such information is almost indispensable – unless many attractive places and secure anchorages are not visited.

Like any other navigational information, sailing directions and pilot guides become dated, unless they can be corrected periodically, so older copies of these books should be used with caution. Some of the publications listed are out of print but have been included because they may be available from clubs, libraries and other yachtsmen.

Inclusion of any publication in the list which follows is not necessarily a recommendation. Pilot guides for yachtsmen vary considerably in their accuracy and usefulness. The information they give should be regarded as additional to, and not a replacement for, a good up-to-date chart of the area concerned.

General
Cruising Association Handbook (Cruising Association) – British Isles and Europe, Elbe to Gibraltar.
The Atlantic Crossing Guide edited by Philip Allen (Adlard Coles Ltd).
Ocean Passages for the World (NP 136), (Hydrographer of the Navy).

England – South Coast
Channel Harbours and Anchorages – by K. Adlard Coles (Nautical).
Creeks and Harbours of the Solent by K. Adlard Coles (Nautical).
South England Pilot Vols. I–V by Robin Brandon (Imray).
The Shell Pilot to South Coast Harbours by K. Adlard Coles, revised by J. O. Coote (Faber).
Stanford's Harbour Guide, North Foreland to the Needles by Campbell (Stanford Maritime).
Stanford's Harbour Guide, Christchurch to Mousehole by Campbell (Stanford Maritime).
The Channel Handbook, Vols. I–III by Bowker (Bowker and Bertram).
Sail West by Shaw (West of England Press).
A Yachtsman's Guide to Scilly (Ennor Publications).

England – East Coast

East Coast Rivers by Jack Coote (Yachting Monthly).

Stanford's Harbour Guide, River Medway to the Swale by Campbell (Stanford Maritime).

Tidal Havens of the Wash and Humber by Henry Irving (Imray).

Sailing Directions, Humber Estuary to Rattray Head (Royal Northumberland Yacht Club).

North Foreland to the Wash by Derek Bowskill (Imray).

Scotland

North and North East Coasts of Scotland Sailing Directions and Anchorages (Clyde Cruising Club).

Forth Yacht Clubs' Association Pilot Handbook (Forth Yacht Clubs' Association).

Orkney Sailing Directions and Anchorages (Clyde Cruising Club).

Stanford's Harbour Guide, West Coast of Scotland by Campbell (Stanford Maritime).

Clyde Cruising Club Handbook (W. Coast) (Clyde Cruising Club).

Outer Hebrides Sailing Directions and Anchorages (Clyde Cruising Club).

Scottish West Coast Pilot by Mark Brackenbury (Stanford Maritime).

Shetland Sailing Directions (Clyde Cruising Club).

Solway Sailing Directions and Anchorages (South West Scotland Sailing Association).

Kintyre to Ardnamurchan (Clyde Cruising Club).

Ardnamurchan to Cape Wrath (Clyde Cruising Club).

Firth of Clyde, including Solway Firth (Clyde Cruising Club).

Ireland/Irish Sea

Irish Sea and Bristol Channel Pilot by Robert Kemp (Adlard Coles Ltd).

Cruising Guide to Anglesey and Menai Strait by Dr. Kemp (J. Laver Printing).

Cruising Guide to the Isle of Man by Robert Kemp (J. Laver Printing).

Ireland, East and North Coasts (Irish Cruising Club).

South and West Coasts of Ireland (Irish Cruising Club).

Bristol Channel Yachting Conference Handbook (Bristol Channel Yachting Conference).

Rivers and Inland Waterways

Port of London Authority Guide for Pleasure Craft Users (Port of London Authority).

London's Waterway Guide by Chris Cove-Smith (Imray).

Visiting Yachtman's Guide to the London River by E. Evans, revised by A. A. Robinson (Cruising Association).

Inland Waterways of Great Britain by Lewis Edwards (Imray).

Nicholson's Guide to the Waterways (Five regional volumes – British Waterways Board).

Inland Waterways Guide (Haymarket Publishing).

The Thames Book, The Broads Book and *The Canals Book* (Link House).

Inland Cruising Map of England (Stanford Maritime).

North West Europe – General

Cruising Association Handbook (Cruising Association).

Planning for Going Foreign (Vol. 1) (Royal Yachting Association).

European Harbour Pilot (Hans Gades).

Waterways in Europe by Roger Pilkington (John Murray).

The Guinness Guide to Waterways of Western Europe by Hugh McKnight (Guinness Superlatives).

France and Channel Islands

Channel Harbours and Anchorages by K. Adlard Coles (Nautical).

North Brittany Pilot by RCC Pilotage Foundation (Adlard Coles Ltd).

Channel Islands Pilot by Malcolm Robson (Nautical).

French Pilots – Volumes 1–4 by Malcolm Robson (Nautical).

Normandy Harbours and Channel Islands Pilot Mark Brackenbury (Adlard Coles Ltd).

Brittany and Channel Islands Cruising Guide by David Jefferson (Stanford Maritime).

Through the French Canals by Philip Bristow (Nautical).

Inland Waterways of France by David Edwards-May (Imray).

France the Quiet Way by John Liley (Stanford Maritime).

The Shell Pilot to the English Channel by J. O. Coote (Faber).

North Biscay Pilot by K. Adlard Coles and A. N. Black, revised by RCC Pilotage Foundation (Adlard Coles Ltd).

South Biscay Pilot (Gironde to La Coruna) by Robin Brandon (Adlard Coles Ltd).

Yachting in French Waters (French Government Tourist Office).

A Cruising Guide to the Lower Seine by E. L. Howells (Imray).

Cruising Guide to the Channel Islands (Capra Press).

Cruising French Waterways by Hugh McKnight (Stanford Maritime).

Belgium

The Yachtsman's Pilot, Antwerp to Boulogne by W. T. Wilson (Imray).

North Sea Harbours and Pilotage, Calais to Den Helder by E. Delmar-Morgan and Jack Coote (Adlard Coles Ltd).

Through the Belgian Canals by Philip Bristow (Nautical).

Netherlands

North Sea Harbours and Pilotage, Calais to Den Helder by E. Delmar-Morgan and Jack Coote (Adlard Coles Ltd).

Inland Waterways of the Netherlands by E. E. Benest (Imray).
Through the Dutch Canals by Philip Bristow (Nautical).
Almanak Voor Watertoerisme (Vols. I and II, in Dutch) from Royal Netherlands Touring Club.
Small Boat Through Holland by Roger Pilkington (Macmillan).
On Lowland Waterways by John Liley (Stanford Maritime).

West Germany
Frisian Pilot – Den Helder to Brunsbuttel and the Kiel Canal by Mark Brackenbury (Stanford Maritime).

Scandinavia
Baltic Southwest Pilot by Mark Brackenbury (Stanford Maritime).
British Kiel Yacht Club Guide (British Kiel YC).
Norwegian Cruising Guide by Mark Brackenbury (Stanford Maritime).

Admiralty Sailing Directions
In all these consist of 74 volumes, covering the entire world. They are corrected by supplements which are usually issued every two years, and by periodical new editions. Those which cover the British Isles and North-West Europe are listed below:
NP 22 *Bay of Biscay Pilot.*
NP 27 *Channel Pilot* (South coast of England west of Selsey Bill, and north coast of France west of Cap d'Antifer, Scilly and Channel Islands).
NP 28 *Dover Strait Pilot.* (South coast of England from Selsey Bill to Orford Ness, and coast of Europe from Cap d'Antifer to Scheveningen).
NP 37 *West Coast of England Pilot* (Lands End to Mull of Galloway, including Isle of Man).
NP 40 *Irish Coast Pilot* (Coast of Ireland).
NP 52 *North Coast of Scotland Pilot* (Faeroes, Shetlands, and Orkneys).
NP 54 *North Sea (West) Pilot.*
NP 55 *North Sea (East) Pilot.*
NP 66 *West Coast of Scotland Pilot* (Mull of Galloway to Cape Wrath, including Hebrides).

Spain, Portugal, Mediterranean
The Atlantic Coasts of Spain and Portugal Pilot by D. M. & A. A. Sloma and C. G. Grainger (Imray).
East Spain Pilot (Chapters I–VII) by Robin Brandon (Imray).
Down the Spanish Coast by Philip Bristow (Nautical).
South France Pilot by Robin Brandon (Chapters I–VI) (Imray).
Tyrrhenian Sea by H. M. Denham (John Murray).
Italian Waters Pilot by Rod Heikell (Imray).
Greek Waters Pilot by Rod Heikell (Imray).
The Adriatic by H. M. Denham (John Murray).

The Aegean by H. M. Denham (John Murray).
The Ionian Islands to the Anatolian Coast by H. M. Denham (John Murray).

15.5.4 Preparations for sea
Before any trip to sea, and particularly before a lengthy passage, it is necessary to make a thorough examination of the boat's material state and to check a number of things. The details depend a good deal on the size and complexity of the boat, but here are summarised the more common items which need attention. For convenience they are given under different headings.

On deck
— All deck gear, dinghy etc stowed and secured for sea
— All hatches and openings closed
— Anchor secured, but available for letting go if required
— Standing rigging checked. All bottlescrews and shackles moused
— Sails to be used bent on, sheets led correctly, battens in
— Ensign and burgee hoisted
— Radar reflector in place

Engine
— Check battery state indicator (if fitted)
— Fuel tank contents
— Lubricating oil in engine and gearbox
— Header tank contents
— Battery level correct
— Grease for stern tube etc
— Circulating water seacock open
— Circulating water strainer clear
— Spares, tools, engine handbook on board
— Spare lubricating oil, grease, distilled water on board
— Visual inspection of drive belts and hoses
— Bilges vented and clear of water
— Check no ropes over side, propeller clear
— Check gearbox in neutral
— After starting check oil pressure, circulating water flow and charging rate
— Check ahead/astern operation of controls
— Read engine hour meter

Navigation
— All required charts and publications on board
— Tidal details extracted from tide table
— Functional checks of echo sounder, radio, radio-telephone (as fitted)
— Compare ship's head by steering compass and handbearer
— Navigation and compass lights
— Horn
— Log reading
— Barometer reading
— Clock checked and wound
— Obtain and record weather forecast
— Determine pilotage details and course to be steered on leaving harbour

Safety equipment
— Gas detector – switch on and check
— Lifejackets
— Safety harnesses
— Flares
— Fire extinguishers
— Liferaft
— Bilge pump – test operation
— Emergency steering arrangements
— First aid box
(All crew should know the positions of the above, and how to use.)

Other items
— Fuel for outboard and galley
— Steering gear examined and tested
— Provisions, water and fresh food embarked
— All moveable gear down below secured for sea.

15.5.5 Night passages
There is often much to be gained by making a night passage. Apart from increasing cruising range within a given period, it may also allow full advantage to be taken of favourable wind or tide.

There is nothing difficult about being at sea by night, and sometimes navigation is easier because lights can be positively identified by their characteristics. Experienced cruising yachtsmen often arrange to make their landfall just before dawn, when lights are still available, and then make the final approach into a strange harbour in daylight.

At sea by night it is important to retain one's night vision, by using the minimum amount of illumination possible for the compass, engine instruments, chart table etc. In a sailing yacht the crew should be able to perform all normal sail drill in the dark, knowing the position of ropes and cleats by feel. Bright spreader lights may help on the foredeck but they leave the helmsman and navigator almost blind for the next few minutes.

It is of course essential to carry the correct navigation lights, and to be able to recognise the lights of other craft. These are described in section 2.1.

A good radar reflector, combined with powerful navigation lights, is the best safeguard against being run down. A powerful torch and white flares to attract attention should be stowed close at hand.

With nothing else to steer by (no distant point of land, or cloud on the horizon) the compass is even more important by night than it is by day. Proper illumination, with a dimmer so that it can be adjusted to the minimum level depending on the conditions, is essential. Preferably there should be stand-by compass lighting for emergency use.

D/F bearings taken at night of beacons more than 25 miles (40km) away may prove unreliable, particularly near sunset and sunrise, so they should be used with caution.

Sufficiently warm clothing and oilskins should be worn by those on watch: even summer nights can be cold. Personal safety requires even greater attention on deck in the dark: when conditions warrant the crew should wear safety harnesses and be clipped on.

Before it gets dark make a complete check of the boat. See that everything is secured on deck, and that any items which may be required during the night are to hand; check the navigation lights and compass light; pump the bilges; inspect the engine compartment; read the barometer; if bad weather threatens, consider the advisability of reefing or shortening sail before darkness falls. The cook may well prepare some snacks or sandwiches which can be eaten at the change of the watch.

The skipper must leave clear, written instructions to the man on watch so that there is no doubt about navigation or other matters.

A book which covers the subject in more detail is *Night Sailing* by J. F. Whitaker (Stanford Maritime).

15.5.6 At sea in bad visibility
Many of the remarks under 'Night passages' (15.5.5) apply equally to bad visibility, but the fundamental requirements when at sea in fog are to sound the required fog signal, to slow down (or even stop if necessary), and to double the efforts of lookouts in detecting other shipping by eyes or ears.

The main danger is the risk of being run down by a larger ship, but this can often be avoided by keeping in relatively shallow water – just out of the main channel for example, rather than in it. A really efficient radar reflector is another safeguard. There remain however the possibilities of collision with small craft, or of going aground due to the inability to locate buoys or shore objects.

Fog is the time when radar in a small boat is a real bonus – both for collision avoidance and for navigation. But it will only be an advantage if the set is working efficiently and adjusted correctly, and if the operator has sufficient experience in interpreting what is on the screen.

It is usually possible to see that visibility is deteriorating, and the following action should be taken:
(1) Slow down.
(2) If possible get a fix, and note the time, log reading, speed. Review the course to steer in the changed circumstances.
(3) Hoist radar reflector (if not permanently fitted).
(4) Sound the prescribed fog signal. A sailing vessel sounds one long followed by two short blasts ('D') at intervals of not more than two minutes. A power-driven vessel making way through the water sounds one long blast (and if stopped two long blasts) at least every two minutes.

(5) Switch on navigation lights.

(6) If near land, or where soundings may help navigation, switch on the echo sounder and record depths at regular intervals.

(7) Keep a very good look-out. If possible post one person in the bow. If he should see or hear anything, tell him to point in the direction concerned.

(8) Lifejackets to be worn and inflated if conditions and traffic warrant.

(9) Check liferaft or dinghy ready for launching.

(10) In inshore waters prepare the anchor for letting go.

(11) At night have flares and a powerful torch or signalling lamp ready.

(12) In a sailing yacht run the engine, or have it available for instant starting.

In fog a small yacht without radar must rely on accurate plotting to determine her estimated position, although this can be supplemented by soundings and by bearings of radio beacons. It is therefore important that the helmsman maintains the course ordered, and that changes in course are properly recorded with times and log readings.

Tactics depend on the situation. If offshore the only danger is from other shipping. If a large ship is seen directly approaching, only a radical alteration of course (preferably to starboard) plus the use of the engine may take the boat clear. In a fast motor boat the best initial action may be to turn sharply through 180° and increase speed, while deciding which way to avoid her without crossing her bows.

Always try to keep clear of shipping lanes. If possible get into shallow water inshore, where no larger craft can be, and anchor until the visibility improves.

If coasting it may be possible to make slow progress in comparative safety well inshore, by maintaining a certain depth on the echo sounder, but this depends on the coastline.

The best advice in respect of fog is to try to avoid it. If the forecast hints that visibility will be poor, stay in harbour – particularly if your passage involves crossing shipping lanes.

15.5.7 Preparing for bad weather

With modern radio forecasts available a yacht should never have to face heavy weather without some warning. Even if her radio is out of action, or a vital forecast has been missed, the tell-tale signs of the sky and a falling barometer should give sufficient notice of bad weather in the offing (see Chapter 7).

The onset of what may be called bad weather varies from boat to boat and from crew to crew, but for our purposes we can define it as the point where the conditions of wind and sea dictate the handling of the boat rather than the skipper's original passage plan. For a small sailing cruiser with a family crew this will probably be less than real gale force winds – perhaps even force 6 or the top end of force 5 in some cases. Most modern yachts, properly handled, are perfectly seaworthy and it is often the ability and the physical strength of the crew which are the limiting factors in rough weather.

Given due notice that strong winds are on the way, certain action should be taken in advance of their arrival. First the general strategy must be decided. If there is a suitable port or other shelter within a convenient distance, then it is sensible to head for it – always provided that it can be reached before conditions in the approaches could be dangerous, and without hazarding the boat on a lee shore. If possible aim for a harbour to windward, so that you will be sailing into sheltered water.

There are comparatively few harbours round the coasts of Britain which can be entered in safety in bad weather and at any state of tide. Seas get shorter and steeper, and are more likely to break in shallow water. Wind against tide can greatly aggravate sea conditions, and this is more commonly experienced off headlands and in the approaches to harbours. Such factors as the tidal state at the likely time of arrival, and whether the harbour marks or buoys will be visible all need to be carefully considered.

Larger commercial ports, even if they lack the normal facilities sought by yachtsmen, are usually safer to enter in bad weather. They are deeper and wider, with better marks and buoyage, and with lights which are more likely to be seen in poor visibility.

Motor boats which have a limited fuel endurance should consider seeking shelter at an earlier stage than sailing boats, but having taken that decision they are better equipped to get into harbour without undue delay.

If no suitable shelter is available within a safe distance the only alternative is to stay at sea, and then the prime consideration is to ensure that the boat has plenty of sea room. Having once decided not to close the land, the main aim should be to keep as far away from it as possible, but also choosing a course which will keep you clear of tide races, shipping routes and shallow water.

If however the direction of the approaching storm is reasonably certain it may be possible to progress slowly towards a lee – provided by a stretch of coast for example – but only if an unexpected shift of wind is not going to put the boat on a lee shore.

In a sailing boat it is important to take early action to shorten sail, before conditions get too bad. The skipper should insist that safety harnesses are put on at an early stage, and that they are always secured to a suitable strongpoint on deck. All the crew should be dressed in warm clothing, with lifebelts worn, even if uninflated.

Since poor visibility will prevent any fix being obtained once the bad weather arrives, every effort must be made to determine the boat's position, and then to keep an accurate plot of DR and EP. Remember that in strong winds leeway will be more pronounced.

Check that all gear on deck such as the tails of halyards and the ends of sheets are well secured. Any rope which may be swept over the side may foul the propeller if the engine has to be started. All hatches, ventilators and other openings must be closed; if necessary ventilators should be blanked off by stuffing in towels or tea cloths. The bilge should be pumped dry and then examined at regular intervals. All moveable gear down below should be stowed away so that the decks are cleared for action. Shut all seacocks, and have buckets available in case pumps get clogged. If washboards are available for the companionway leading from the cockpit, they should be fitted. Cockpit drains should be checked clear.

Items such as storm canvas, foghorn, torches, flares, reefing gear, warps and sea anchor (if carried) must be readily accessible – not buried under other gear.

Take every opportunity to get weather forecasts, from whatever radio stations are available, so as to build up the best possible picture of the developing weather situation. The barometer should be read and recorded every half-hour. A record of the estimated wind speed and direction, sea state, and type of cloud cover should be made at similar intervals. In fact keeping a check on the weather situation is almost a full time job in bad weather, but few small yachts have the resources for this.

Meanwhile it is advisable for the cook to take the opportunity to prepare some sandwiches or similar food, and to put some soup or coffee into a thermos flask for consumption later on, when it may not be possible to use the stove.

15.5.8 Handling in bad weather

As wind and sea increase, and sail area is progressively reduced, there will come a time when it is imprudent to try to make any real progress in a particular direction and it is necessary to heave-to. This is something which can and should be practised under less demanding conditions. When cruising, and time is no object, it is often sensible to heave-to for an hour or so in order to eat in comfort.

Most yachts will heave-to satisfactorily under reefed main and storm jib but it all depends on balance, and boats with longer keels behave best in this respect, so it pays to experiment. The jib should be backed, that is the weather sheet should be hauled in, and the reefed main sheeted

well in, with the helm lashed down. A boat may also be hove-to under trysail, or well reefed main, with no headsail, either being steered or with the helm lashed up – but this will depend upon the type and can be determined by trial and error.

In even more severe conditions it will be necessary to lie a-hull – with all sail lowered, allowing the boat to drift as she pleases. This is probably the best tactic to adopt in a multi-hull in really bad weather. It may help prevent the boat gathering way if the helm is lashed down, and this also reduces leeway. Seas will break on board (so the crew should keep below) and they may knock the boat on her beam ends or even capsize her completely in extreme conditions. Then her survival will depend largely upon how well she was designed and built.

Most authorities, but not all, consider that a sea anchor is of doubtful benefit in a modern yacht, although it may be useful in a yawl or a ketch with the mizzen set to keep the boat head to wind. But very large strains are put upon the gear, and there is also danger to the rudder when the yacht gathers sternway.

Under survival conditions, but only if there is ample sea room to leeward, an alternative is to run before the wind and sea, streaming long warps over the stern to hold the boat steady and reduce her speed.

Motor boats are usually best able to cope with heavy seas by being kept almost bow on to them, speed being adjusted to give little more than steerage way. Under less severe conditions it may be possible to make progress to windward by careful manipulation of the throttle(s) to help the boat over the waves, the techniques being to accelerate when the bow begins to fall and to ease back as the bow lifts to a wave. If it is necessary to run off before the sea, warps or a drogue towed astern will help to keep the boat running straight but care is obviously needed to prevent them fouling the propeller(s).

Bad weather can be very frightening for those who have not previously experienced it, but if the boat is well equipped and maintained, and if the correct preparations are made in advance, it can be faced with confidence provided the right decisions are taken in sufficient time. Remember that everything will take much longer to do, and that you can't afford to make mistakes.

For those who sensibly would like to study the subject in greater detail, the following books are recommended: *This is Rough Weather Cruising* by Erroll Bruce (Nautical), *Heavy Weather Sailing* by K. Adlard Coles, and *Power Boats in Rough Seas* by Dag Pike (Adlard Coles Ltd).

Chapter 16

Running a boat

Contents

16.1   Where to keep a boat

16.1.1 Moorings – general

Moorings are a problem in most popular yachting centres, and if it is desired to keep a boat in one of these the only counsel that can be given is to explore every possible source (harbour master, boatyards, marinas, clubs) and to get your name on any waiting list(s) that may be open. Contrary to common opinion, moorings do become available from time to time, but to hunt them down often requires both patience and perseverance. Every season a number of yachtsmen give up the sport for some reason or other – age, finance, change of family circumstances, or even moving house to a different area – so there is in fact a steady turnover. However it must be admitted that in a number of harbours the waiting time for a berth is unduly long, in which case it is best to look elsewhere in the short term.

Deep water moorings are somewhat naturally more difficult to come by than those in shallower water, but the latter are perfectly acceptable for some boats which are able to take the ground for an hour or two near low water. Multihulls, bilge keelers and motor boats which have outdrive units can all use such moorings if the minor inconvenience of drying out is accepted. In fact this is not always a great disadvantage because it gives a good opportunity to scrub or antifoul the hull, if the harbour bottom is hard enough to walk on.

Details of individual moorings vary, depending on the weight of boat they are intended to take, but basically a mooring consists of a heavy sinker of some kind, a heavy chain called the riser, plus a buoy rope and a buoy to take the weight of the mooring when it is unoccupied. Sometimes a number (or trot) of moorings are all secured to a ground chain lying along the sea bed with an anchor or a sinker at each end of it. Heavier moorings often have a separate picking-up buoy: where the rope for this is attached to the top of the riser, there is usually a strong rope strop which can be taken inboard and secured to the boat's mooring bollard or bitts, with the large mooring buoy remaining in the water.

16.1.2 Laying a mooring

In some more remote places it is possible to lay your own mooring. While this is a cheap approach to the problem, it also involves a lot of work – not just in originally laying the mooring, but in lifting it each year for examination which requires special gear.

Ideally a permanent mooring should have two special mooring anchors (or two heavy sinkers) which are laid in line with the tidal stream, and are connected together by a heavy ground chain, which should be about three times the length of the boat. A swivel is shackled to the centre of the ground chain, and above this is shackled the riser. Except in very shallow water, the riser should be divided into two lengths of chain,

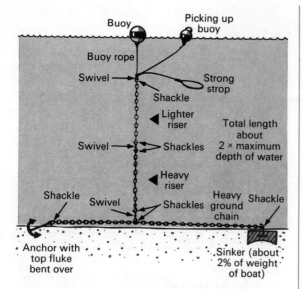

Fig. 16(1) A typical yacht mooring. The riser chain, some of which is going to drag around on the bottom, should be considerably heavier than the yacht's anchor cable.

separated by another swivel. The lower riser is made up from heavier chain, because the bottom end of it will be in regular contact with the bottom. The upper riser can be one size larger than the yacht's normal anchor chain. A sketch of the general arrangement is shown in Fig. 16(1). The total length of the two risers should be about twice the depth of water at HW springs.

16.1.3 Marinas

Although some yachtsmen positively dislike marinas, preferring a quiet berth up some secluded creek, it must be said that the majority of people who have savoured the convenience of a marina would not willingly return to a swinging mooring. It depends what you like, and what you can afford, and also on the way that you use the boat.

Most marinas operate under the terms of business agreed by the National Yacht Harbours Association, and it is as well to read the small print of the agreement, which is likely to include various restrictions that might not have been expected. Outside contractors or workmen can only be brought in to work on your boat with permission, which should not be withheld for warranty repairs or for work which the marina cannot undertake from its own resources. Except by written permission, a boat in a marina cannot be used for commercial purposes of any kind. When the boat is sold, the marina will require a small commission on the sale price – usually one per cent.

16.1.4 Security

Wherever a boat is moored, it is necessary to think about security. Although most yachtsmen are familiar with the Police slogan 'Watch out! There's a thief about', many boat owners take no

serious precautions regarding the security of their craft. In creeks and harbours all round the coast there are rich pickings for sneak thieves – items such as outboard motors and liferafts worth several hundred pounds apiece, and sometimes even entire boats.

An elementary precaution is to record the serial numbers of all items of equipment that are remotely portable – radios and other navigational instruments, portable generators, outboards, binoculars and the like. This at least may help recover any stolen property, but it is better to stop it disappearing in the first place.

If the boat is being left for any length of time, even items such as the liferaft should be taken below. It is important that the cabin door should be fitted with a really stout lock – something of a rarity in the average boat. Hatches must be firmly secured from inside, with some form of strongback if necessary. Windows in yachts are seldom large enough to gain access, but they must be securely fastened too.

It is useful to have one really good stowage down below – a strong locker which can be fastened securely, and in which all valuables can be placed.

If an outboard engine cannot be locked away, it must be locked in place so that it cannot be unshipped, even by a determined thief with spanners and screwdrivers.

The smaller the boat, the more difficult it is to guard against her removal. Unless they can be stored in a locked shed (or firmly chained to some solid object) tenders, dinghies and runabouts are all very simple to remove. Any boat which is kept on a trailer is simply asking to be stolen, unless the trailer is immobilised in some way.

Larger boats can be fitted with anti-burglar devices, which safeguard equipment as well as the boat herself. As another form of deterrent, consideration should be given to ways of immobilising the engine. A lock on the stop control of a diesel engine is one suggestion, and there are various simple ways of rendering a petrol engine inactive.

Advice about the security of your boat can be obtained from the local Crime Prevention Officer.

16.2 Trailers and trailing

16.2.1 Advantages of trailing

Small cruising boats, whether sail or power, can be conveniently moved from place to place on a road trailer. Apart from saving mooring fees, trailing allows the boat to be kept at home where it is conveniently placed for maintenance work, and of course it greatly extends the possible range of operation. It is, for example, perfectly feasible to trail a boat from Britain to the Mediterranean for a summer holiday.

There are however practical difficulties in trailing a boat which is over about 20ft (6.1m) in length, notably the problem of getting the boat into the water and back onto the trailer, which depends very much on the type of boat and the configuration of her keel. Fairly obviously, a heavy boat with a deep keel is much more difficult to handle than one with a centreboard or retracting keel – or a motor cruiser with a relatively flat bottom and outdrive engines which tilt out of the way.

The other main problem is that the laws which govern road trailers are very complicated and for ever changing. What follows is a digest of the regulations applying in 1984, but if intending to purchase a boat with a trailer it is advisable to consult the latest regulations on the subject – available from HM Stationery Office or from motoring organisations. Much useful advice is given in the Indespension Trailer Manual, obtainable for a small fee from Mechanical Services Ltd, Belmont Road, Bolton, BL1 7AQ.

The law differentiates between trailers with and without brakes, and in some respects it varies with the date of manufacture of a trailer.

16.2.2 Trailers without brakes
A trailer does not need to be fitted with brakes if its weight plus the weight of the load carried is less than 1650lb (750kg). Such a trailer must be marked with the maximum gross weight, the capacity of a given trailer depending on its suspension, wheels and tyres. It is an offence to exceed the stated gross weight. It is illegal to tow a new, unbraked trailer unless the towing vehicle is at least twice the weight of the trailer and its load. From 1 October 1986 this law will apply to all unbraked trailers, whatever their date of manufacture.

16.2.3 Trailers with brakes
Braking systems on trailers manufactured since 1 October 1982 must comply with EEC directive 71/320, which requires hydraulically damped overrun couplings (instead of the old spring operated type), with correctly matched brakes and linkage, giving a minimum braking efficiency of 45%g, as tested on a special instrument.

16.2.4 General regulations – all trailers
(1) Two triangular red reflectors must be fitted at the rear of the trailer.
(2) Two red rear lights and two red brake lights (operated with the brakes of the towing vehicle) must be fitted.
(3) Trailers manufactured since 1 October 1979, and first used since 1 April 1980, must have one or two rear fog lights.
(4) Amber direction indicators, flashing in unison with those of the towing vehicle, must be fitted.

(5) The trailer's number plate must correspond with that of the towing vehicle, and must be illuminated.
(6) The normal speed limit for a vehicle towing a trailer on unrestricted roads is 40mph, but if the following conditions are complied with this may be increased to 50mph. (a) A 50mph plate must be fitted. (b) The kerbside weight of the towing vehicle must be marked on its front, nearside. (c) The laden weight of an unbraked trailer must not exceed 60 per cent of the kerbside weight of the towing vehicle. (d) The laden weight of a braked trailer must not exceed the kerbside weight of the towing vehicle. (e) If the requirements of (c) and (d) are not met, speed is limited to 40mph.
(7) Larger trailers must be fitted with front marker lights, if over 7ft 6in (2.3m) in length excluding drawbar; and with side reflectors, if over 16ft (5m) in length.
(8) There must be no dangerous projections. Hence items such as outboard motors should be well covered and padded.
(9) Tyres and tyre pressures must conform to legal requirements.
(10) Mudguards must be fitted.
(11) The length of a trailer and its load must not exceed 23ft (7m), unless special conditions are fulfilled. The width of the trailer must not exceed 7ft 6in (2.3m), and the width of the load must not exceed 9ft 6in (2.9m)

16.2.5 Trailing – general
Most vehicle insurance policies cover the towing of a trailer, but this should be confirmed – if necessary with the insurance company. It should be noted however that such insurance only covers the trailer, not the boat loaded on it.

It is important to have a trailer which is suitable for the shape and weight of the boat concerned. It should support the weight of the boat, along the length of the keel, on rollers which also run the boat on and off the trailer. Side rollers support the boat athwartships, and should be adjusted to hold her steady with the minimum of transverse movement. When loaded, the trailer weight at the coupling should be about 50lbs (23kg), and the boat must be securely fastened.

Break-back trailers, which have a hinged backbone, can be used to facilitate loading and unloading. They may also eliminate the need to immerse the trailer's vulnerable wheel bearings in water. Where this is necessary, consideration should be given to fitting Bearing Buddy seals. These replace the dust caps in the wheel hubs, and a spring-loaded piston maintains a slight pressure inside the hub, which is filled with grease, and keeps the water out. Otherwise it is necessary to clean and repack the bearings after every launching, or risk inconvenient and expensive failures. Against this possibility it is a wise precaution to carry a spare bearing kit in the car. Hub bearings should in any case be greased annually, and oil seals checked. The tow hitch should be greased every three months, when other moving parts such as brake linkages (but not brake assemblies) should be oiled.

When trailing a boat abroad it is important to ensure that both boat and trailer are included in insurance documents, or on the 'Green Card' required in most European countries.

16.3 Organisation

16.3.1 Boat management

Back in Chapter 1, we briefly mentioned the importance of an organised approach to running a boat. In the intervening chapters we have discussed some of the detailed considerations involved – not just in handling and navigating a boat, but also details of her equipment with some indication of the care and maintenance which it deserves. So by now readers may have a better idea of the many points which need regular attention if skipper and crew are to enjoy safe and trouble-free cruising.

Do not underestimate the number of items which need systematic attention in a boat of any size. Only a small proportion require any degree of technical skill, but the important thing is that they should all be looked at. This implies some kind of documentation, even if this only comprises simple check lists, in order to be sure than nothing vital is overlooked.

The more that an owner can do himself, the more he will learn about his boat, and the less will be the cost. But it is appreciated that many owners are busy people, and if it is not possible to carry out routine inspections in person, then some system is needed to ensure that the work is satisfactorily completed by somebody else. In either case it is a matter of organisation. The question of maintenance has been mentioned in several places throughout this book, when dealing with specific parts of the boat or different items of equipment. Some of this work can be progressed on a week to week basis, but there comes a time when proper provision must be made for the more major items to be undertaken. This involves making the boat available for whatever period is needed for the work to be done, making arrangements for somebody to do it, and making financial provision to pay for it! In other words, the more significant items of the maintenance bill do not just happen, they have to be planned and arranged, or important things will get overlooked, probably affecting the boat's safety.

Traditionally yacht maintenance has been conditioned by the fact that nearly all yachts had wooden hulls which needed extensive re-painting at the start of each season (both to preserve them and make them presentable), and this period was a convenient time to undertake the other essential work. Also in those days the sailing season was short for most yachts, probably only from May to September, when they were hauled out of the water or put in a mud berth for the winter.

Now things have changed. For many owners the sailing season relates more closely to the duration of British Summer Time. The great majority of yachts are constructed in GRP, requiring only to be hauled out for a coat of antifouling, and otherwise they are kept in the water throughout the year. It makes good sense to visit and live in the boat during the winter, because items such as engines and electrical equipment which are used regularly are not so likely to deteriorate, and do not need the same degree of preparation to withstand the rigours of the winter.

So work can now be spread more conveniently over the year, rather than concentrated into what were well defined periods for fitting out and laying up. It is however necessary to evolve a sensible plan. Jobs undertaken in the spring should include all those important checks, without which the season might come to an early end. Similarly work that is done in the late autumn must include whatever is necessary to safeguard the boat during the winter. Otherwise, within reason, maintenance work can be undertaken whenever it is convenient – or perhaps least inconvenient – but always remembering that certain jobs go hand in hand. For example, while the boat is out of the water for antifouling is the logical time to do all other underwater work; if the mast has to be unstepped for any reason, there is an opportunity to survey all the rigging and the mast fittings; if the engine should have to be removed, seize the chance to clean and examine everything in that area and do any repainting.

16.3.2 Dealing with boatyards

Many owners rely on a yard for doing at least part (and some most) of the annual maintenance work on their boats. This means facing up to a fairly hefty bill, but may be necessary because the owner does not have the necessary time, skill, or inclination to tackle the work himself. In order to get the right result it is essential to give the yard precise instructions about what is to be done, which means compiling a defects list. This is best divided into two parts, one of the items affecting seaworthiness and safety, and one of those which are no more than desirable for reasons of comfort or appearance.

Some of the items on the list will be routine ones which need to be done every year – things like antifouling, examining underwater fittings, changing oil filters and lubricating oil, overhauling winches and checking all rigging fittings. Other important items may be defects which have arisen during the past season but which have not received immediate attention.

Then there are a number of items which do not need annual attention but which should be examined, say, every three or four years. These might include withdrawing the propeller shaft(s), examination of keel bolts and other important fastenings, looking at rudder bearings, and more major items of engine maintenance. It is best to plan these ahead, and to budget accordingly for the work involved and for the probable replacement of expensive items such as batteries.

Items of lower priority include cabin furnishings, interior paintwork or varnishing, joinery, and other matters of a more domestic nature which do not affect the boat's seagoing capability.

Having produced the list of work, inspect each job with the yard manager, and request an estimate for each one (not the total bill). The quotations should be broken down into costs for labour and material, which enables individual items to be queried if the estimate seems to be unduly high. It is then also possible to assess the priority of work in order to keep within a budgeted figure, and perhaps make other arrangements for certain items. Some you may decide to tackle yourself, or to defer to a later date.

Then it is necessary to decide a programme for the work to be done. The earlier that agreement can be reached on all these matters, the more likelihood there is of the boat being ready when required. Remember that boat yards are always very busy in the spring, when all their customers want to have their boats refitted and put back into the water.

It often happens that, when the yard are carrying out work on some item of equipment or some part of the boat, it is discovered that certain additional work, not originally foreseen, should be undertaken. It is advisable to get a quotation for this, just as for the bulk of the work, even if this involves a little delay. This is another reason for making an early start. Boat yards are notoriously bad at meeting dates, but you at least can help by trying to anticipate your requirements and by allowing a reasonable time for the work to be completed.

In order to keep a proper record of the general state of the boat, it is important to get full details of what has been done by the yard at the end of a refit. For example, if the anchor windlass has been overhauled and put in working order, the owner really wants to know exactly what was wrong with it in the first instance and what has been done to rectify matters. If spare parts have been used, have these been replaced? Has a proper trial been carried out to ensure that the windlass is now working to its proper specification – if there is an overload trip does it function at the right loading? What caused the original problem, and what has been done to avoid a repetition? As the person paying the bill, you have a right to know the answers to all these

questions, and often it is advisable to record them in some form of notebook for future reference – in case something similar occurs at a later date.

And, talking about bills, it is not a bad idea to file receipted invoices because these can be a help when budgeting for future refits.

16.3.3 Budgeting

It used to be said of yachting that if you were worried about what it cost you could not afford it. If that was true in an era when a young man could often afford to run a ten-tonner and have a paid hand to look after her, it is certainly true today. Sadly, the costs of owning any kind of boat have soared in recent years, and it is therefore essential to have some kind of financial plan to meet recurring expenses. If the thought depresses you, it is best to skip the next paragraph, but no attempt has been made to insert actual figures because these can vary so greatly, depending on the type and size of boat, where she is kept, and how she is run and used.

Marine mortgage payments, insurance premium, mooring fee, hauling out and antifouling, fuel, sail repairs and replacement, club subscription, charts and publications, and travelling to and from the boat are likely to be the main items of expenditure. Most of these can be anticipated on certain dates. It is also sensible to make some provision for contingencies – miscellaneous costs for maintenance and repair, chandlery etc.

16.4 Clubs and associations

16.4.1 Clubs

Most owners find it of benefit to belong to one or more clubs or associations. Quite apart from the social contacts derived, clubs provide a wonderful opportunity for the interchange of information between members. A very good example is the Cruising Association, which was founded in 1908. At its headquarters in Ivory House, St Katharine's Dock (close by Tower Bridge on the River Thames), the Cruise Planning Section comprises material which has been collected by members for members. Here is a wealth of information for anybody planning a cruise to North West Europe, the Baltic, the Mediterranean, or the eastern seaboard of North America. Apart from all the necessary publications (such as pilots and light lists) there are files which are compiled from information sent in by members who have cruised the different areas. There is also an excellent library, containing more than 10,000 books on subjects related to ships and the sea, with antique volumes on navigation, seamanship and early voyages. For further information contact The Cruising

Association, Ivory House, St Katharine's Dock, London, E1 9AT. Tel: 01-481 0881.

The Little Ship Club, slightly upstream, has a rather different emphasis and runs a whole series of courses on navigation, seamanship and related subjects during the winter months. These are followed up by practical training afloat during the summer, organised from the club's centre at Yarmouth, Isle of Wight. The address is The Little Ship Club, Bell Wharf Lane, Upper Thames Street, London, EC4R 3TB. Tel: 01-236 7729.

The Royal Cruising Club has its headquarters at 42 Half Moon Street, London, W1, and is the elite of the cruising organisations. For over a century it has encouraged good seamanship, and its membership of genuine cruising yachtsmen is respected world-wide. It too provides port information, largely compiled by members, and in recent years the club has been active in producing pilot guides for yachtsmen.

In the context of clubs which have a national interest, mention should be made of the Royal Ocean Racing Club, founded in 1925 when ocean racing on this side of the Atlantic was in its infancy. It is no exaggeration to say that the RORC has greatly influenced the sport in Europe as a whole, while it still continues to administer British ocean racing activities from its pleasant clubhouse at 20 St James's Place, London, SW1A 1NN. Tel: 01-493 5252.

Yachting affairs in Britain are co-ordinated by the Royal Yachting Association (RYA), notes on which appear in 2.8.1. The names and addresses of affiliated organisations are published each year in an RYA booklet, G25. This indicates which clubs operate in the different regions.

16.4.2 Visiting clubs

Many yacht clubs are preoccupied by racing, or by domestic matters, but there are a few who do encourage cruising in an active way and who welcome visiting yachtsmen to their premises. Some can even offer useful facilities such as moorings or a club launch, and in other parts of the world major clubs often have attached to them a small boat yard where yachts can be repaired or hauled out – the like of which is sadly lacking in Britain.

The fact that a club welcomes visitors does not mean that a yachtsman can just arrive and make himself at home without further ado. The owner or skipper should call on the secretary, or in his absence see the club steward or boatman. Most probably an invitation will be extended to use the club's facilities, and it is tactful to enquire about temporary membership (which in any case is likely to be needed to comply with licensing regulations), at the same time indicating the probable length of stay.

Visitors should be punctilious about observing club rules – in the matter of dress for example – and also about the appearance of the yacht,

particularly if she is lying on a club mooring. Flag etiquette should be followed (see section 6.7), and this is very important in foreign harbours in the matter of flying the correct courtesy flag (6.7.3).

Club servants should never be tipped, but contributions to the club and staff funds are appropriate ways of expressing appreciation for services received. Hospitality ashore can sensibly be repaid by entertaining a few of the club's officers or members on board. Another way, which can be pursued separately, is to ensure that visitors get the same sort of treatment at your own club.

16.5 Crews

16.5.1 Advice to crews

Much of this book contains information or advice which is equally applicable to skippers and their crews, but it seems appropriate to direct just a few words to crews – particularly the less experienced ones or those who are embarking in a strange boat for the first time. Some well organised skippers have available a check list which covers the points mentioned below, even with spaces in which can be inserted the time and place to join the yacht. But for any cruise or passage a crew member needs to have certain information, and it is the responsibility of the skipper to provide it.

(1) What sort of clothing, shoes, equipment etc should be brought? Will there, for example, be shoregoing functions to attend which may require a certain standard of dress?

(2) Are lifejackets and safety harnesses provided on board? If not, take your own.

(3) Take and use your own brand of anti-seasick pills, which suit you and do not have undesirable side effects.

(4) Take your own waterproof torch, and a yachtmans's knife on a lanyard.

(5) Take off shoregoing shoes before stepping on board.

(6) As soon as convenient after arrival on board, find out the stowages (and where necessary the method of operation) for all safety and emergency equipment. This includes fire extinguishers, lifejackets and safety harnesses (if provided on board), liferaft, man overboard gear, flares, first aid kit, bilge pump and distress radio.

(7) Remember that many yachting accidents occur in dinghies or tenders.

(8) Be able to tie, and use correctly, the following basic knots: reef knot, clove hitch, bowline, and round turn and two half-hitches.

(9) Find out how the heads work.

(10) Always return any items of equipment to their correct stowage – winch handles, for example.

(11) Do whatever the skipper tells you. Should you have queries, ask tactfully afterwards.

(12) Dress sensibly and warmly. In rough weather, or when so directed, wear a safety harness and keep clipped on.

(13) Alcohol is splendid for a party in harbour, but should be taken in strict moderation when at sea.

(14) Keep the immediate area of your allocated bunk clean and tidy at all times. Do not leave gear lying around.

(15) Do your fair share of domestic chores.

(16) If in doubt – ask.

16.5.2 Consider the crew

Most owners (and certainly those of racing yachts) rely on crews to help them sail their boats. Crews, whether they are friends or family, are presumably on holiday too, and they deserve full consideration when individual passages are being planned or when other arrangements are being made. In this context let us discount the contrived discomforts of modern ocean racing, and just consider the average cruising yacht.

For enjoyment, as well as ultimately for safety, it must be possible to break down the crew into two watches, either of which can handle the boat under normal conditions without continual supervision by the skipper. There are obvious occasions, as for example when in soundings or making a landfall, that the skipper will want to be around. There may also be times, such as when shortening sail, which require all hands on deck. But otherwise the watch on deck should be able to cope, and those below should be allowed to feed and rest in peace. On any passage which lasts more than about 12 hours this is essential, or the entire crew will become exhausted. Offshore sailing makes big demands on stamina, and people who come straight from an office desk at the end of a tiring week can soon succumb to the effect of hard work and lack of sleep – to say nothing of being cold and wet, and possibly seasick.

A proper watchkeeping system should be put into effect soon after leaving harbour, and the skipper ought to ensure that those off watch go below and get some rest. The watchkeeping system is a matter of personal choice, but the traditional four hours on and four hours off has withstood the test of time.

Sadly it must be said that very few family cruising yachts match the requirements above. Many are very under-manned, with the skipper having to do the lion's share of all the work. While this may be reasonably satisfactory on a short passage in fair weather, it allows no margin for contingencies such as deteriorating weather or trouble with the boat – nor of course for anything untoward happening to the skipper.

If it is necessary to go to sea short-handed, the skipper should arrange the passage very carefully – making optimum use of tidal stream, for

Fig. 16(2) In a family crew the watchkeeping routine must be planned to make the best use of the available persons. In this example the son is assumed to be capable of standing watch by day, but the daughter is learning the ropes and does not keep watch alone.

example. The watch bill should be made out so that the skipper is most likely to be on watch at 'key' times, but he should be careful not to over-work himself. The less-experienced members should do the bulk of the watchkeeping, and if the skipper can do a short spell with each of these in turn he can give them guidance and confidence in the prevailing conditions, see Fig. 16(2).

By the same token, the overall plan for a family cruise needs to be most carefully considered – how far to go, adequate rest days in harbour, and a flexible programme which allows ample time for the passage home in the event of bad weather.

16.5.3 Ship husbandry

Cleanliness on board is good not only for health and aesthetic reasons, but because dirt harbours moisture and encourages deterioration. There is truth in the old saying that if the corners are kept clean, the rest will look after itself, and the crew have a part to play in this.

Cleaning has become something of a science both in the home and in industrial applications, but once afloat these principles tend to get overlooked. Always use the right materials, not only to get the best results, but to avoid damage to the surfaces being cleaned. Use clean materials, cloths, brushes etc, and change the water frequently. When washing down, do not use more water than necessary.

Proper care of a boat reduces the amount of cleaning that is needed, and minimises the number of minor repairs that have to be carried out. Remember that guests may not be familiar with practices afloat, so tactful instruction about not blocking the heads or the galley sink may not come amiss. Some owners may seem obsessed with tidiness, but in a small yacht gear which is left lying about soon collects damp and dirt, or gets damaged. Galley spillages are not only dirty but dangerous, by causing slippery conditions on the cabin sole.

Crew members can make a more positive contribution to the cleanliness of a boat if their efforts are properly directed. Painted surfaces or Formica should be wiped down with warm water, to which a small quantity of soap or detergent has been added, and then be lightly rinsed off. Glass (such as doghouse windows) should be washed with soap and warm fresh water, and then be polished with newspaper – unless a proprietary window-cleaning fluid is available. Perspex needs care to avoid scratches, and should be cleaned with a soft cloth. Dirty leather cloth should be washed with soap and warm water, although normally it is sufficient to wipe it over daily with a damp cloth, not using too much water. Shower curtains need to be washed down with liquid soap and water, with the addition of a mild antiseptic to prevent mould or mildew and the possibility of permanent staining.

16.6 Bibliography

Trouble Shooting and Maintenance in Boat Engines by Peter Bowyer (Nautical Books).

Ready for Sea by Basil Mosenthal and Dick Hewitt (Adlard Coles Ltd).

Care and Repair Below Decks by Percy Blandford (Adlard Coles Ltd).

Care and Repair of Marine Petrol Engines by Loris Goring (Adlard Coles Ltd).

Care and Repair of Alloy Spars and Rigging by David Potter (Adlard Coles Ltd).

Care and Repair of Hulls by Michael Verney (Adlard Coles Ltd).

Care and Repair of Small Diesels by Chris Thompson (Adlard Coles Ltd).

Fitting Out by J D Sleightholme (Adlard Coles Ltd).

The Boat Owner's Fitting Out Manual by Jeff Toghill (Stanford Maritime).

Motor Boat and Yachting Manual by Dick Hewitt (Stanford Maritime).

Index